12/25

95

A History of Cornell

Ezra Cornell

A HISTORY OF
CORNELL

By Morris Bishop

DRAWINGS BY

Alison Mason Kingsbury

CORNELL UNIVERSITY PRESS

Ithaca and London

First published 1962 by Cornell University Press

International Standard Book Number 0-8014-0036-8

Library of Congress Catalog Card Number 62-17815

PRINTED IN THE UNITED STATES OF AMERICA

Cornell University Press strives to use environmentally responsible suppliers and materials to the fullest extent possible in the publishing of its books. Such materials include vegetable-based, low-VOC inks and acid-free papers that are recycled, totally chlorine-free, or partly composed of nonwood fibers.

Cloth printing   10   9

To Cornell

Contents

Contents

Contents

Illustrations

Illustrations

MAP

A History of Cornell

I

Prelude

A CONTEMPLATIVE traveler, journeying to Ithaca a century ago by the road along Fall Creek, might well pause at the hilltop above the valley. He might even feel a quake of destiny underfoot.

Northwestward he looks to Cayuga Lake, disappearing to the horizon, taking its color for the day, gray to flashing green-blue. The level wall of West Hill is backed to the southwest by far steps rising to Connecticut Hill, twelve miles away. Stump-fenced, weed-bordered roads of dribbling brown, heedless of topography, divide the landscape into squares. There is little woodland, for most of the accessible first-growth forests have been mercilessly lumbered over. Here and there stands an inviting white-pillared farmhouse, but many country structures are mere unpainted boxes in unkempt farmyards.

The valley below, "the Flats," is occupied mostly by the Black Ash Swamp, a pestilent region of sluggish waters, quivering mud, snakes, mosquitoes, jungle flowers, and water birds. At the foot of Fall Creek, hidden from the traveler's view, lies a cluster of mills and houses.

He looks southwest to the village of Ithaca, a thriving settlement of some six thousand people. From its nucleus in the business district it spreads north to Cascadilla Creek and west halfway to the railroad station, and it sends several filaments up South Hill. A tattered green cover of tree tops half hides it in summer. (Proud of its shade trees, Ithaca sought even to impose on itself the cognomen "the Forest City.") Ithaca is red brick at the heart; the homes round about are mostly of white frame. The bulk of the Cornell Public Library, just completed, dwarfs the Town Hall at its side. About the "gospel and school lot," later DeWitt Park, certain of the grander houses are destined to last a century. The chief landmark, visible from afar, is the Clinton House, Ithaca's special pride, surmounted by its cupola (pronounced "cupalo").

The traveler descends to the city streets, and in spirit we accompany him.

The houses are low-lying and spacious, each with its "yard" for vegetables and chickens, fenced against marauding dogs. No apartment houses exist, for two excellent reasons. Every household needs a cellar, cool in summer, warm in winter, for food storage; and every household needs level access to the back-yard privy. Only a few of the fine houses have running water; bathrooms and flush toilets are rare luxuries. There was no general water system in Ithaca until the seventies, and no sewers until the nineties.

The unpaved streets turn to moats of mud when the rains descend. (Today, in our black-topped world, we have forgotten mud, the foot scraper on every doorstep, the sodden brown-caked boots, the footprints on the carpet, the squelch, the clutch of mud at the plunging foot.) If the sun shines, the streets become Saharas of blowing dust, browning the lace curtains, depositing a gritty layer on the hair and in the nose and ears.

Horses enliven the streets, pulling buggies or democrats, or tossing their nose bags at hitching posts. Scavenging pigs are no longer allowed to run free; in the 1850's a city ordinance declared that they are not "free commoners." But a pig grunts in many a backyard, where he serves as the household garbage-disposal plant. Rats are taken as a matter of course; their favorite home is under the wooden sidewalks. In summer, clouds of flies follow the animals, and, sated, enter screenless windows to circle dark rooms in droning endurance flights. At evening, endless squadrons of mosquitoes come to the attack from Black Ash Swamp. And fleas and bedbugs are accepted as one of man's necessary afflictions.

Pausing to pat the cast-iron greyhound on the lawn, we enter one of the more imposing houses. The parlor is heavily carpeted, save for a rectangle in which the grated register indicates a hot-air furnace below stairs. A marble-topped table supports a giant family Bible, flanked by a velvet photograph album with brass clasps and a Friendship's Garland bound in repoussé leather, incorporating bits of ivory and glass. The room is crowded with plush chairs, a patent rocker, a horsehair sofa, a needlework tabby on a red and gold cushion. It is swathed in portieres, lambrequins, and Berlin woolwork. The whatnot contains family treasures: gilded sheaves of wheat, a bottle of water dipped from the River Jordan by the Presbyterian minister, a portrait of a dear departed, contrived of his own hair. Proud on a pedestal stand Cupid and Psyche in alabaster; on the walls are steel engravings, implicating Washington and Columbus. In the window hangs a transparency of Niagara Falls.

We sniff the smell of other days, which still returns in memory to certain ancients. It is compounded mustily of volatilized mutton fat caught in wool draperies, of choking gusts of coal gas from the banked hot-air furnace with the damper down, of old extinct cigars, of illuminating gas and coal oil, or even the sour organic smell of sperm oil.

We inspect the spacious kitchen, peer into pots. The diet of 1865 is impressive by its abundance, its meat-and-potato-and-pie monotony, and its threat to health. The nature of infectious disease, its control and cure, are hardly recognized. The chances are that in one of the bedrooms upstairs lies a fat man with something vaguely known as liver trouble, or a thin man with tuberculosis gained from infected, but unsuspected, milk, or a petulant woman suffering from female complaint. (The ill health of American women was notorious, and was attributed by European writers to lack of exercise, overheated homes, stays, or tea.)

The men who pass the front-parlor window show a marked class distinction in their dress. Manual workers, teamsters, laborers, farmers, wear overalls, or overhauls. Countrymen are still clad in the wool of their own sheep, home-spun and home-loomed and dyed with butternut or goldenrod. Those with any claim to gentility, clerks or storekeepers, wear a black frock coat and a high silk hat. The frock coat is a status symbol, not necessarily very clean, for the world is dirty and dry cleaning is not yet invented.[1] We are struck by the universal bagginess of the mud-edged trousers; the trouser crease is frowned upon, as the mark of a hand-me-down, stacked in piles on cheap clothiers'

[1] Surgeons even operated in frock coats. See Thomas Eakins's painting, "Clinic of Dr. Gross," 1875. "The surgeon operated in a slaughterhouse-suggesting frock coat of black cloth. It was stiff with the blood and filth of years. The more sodden it was the more forcibly did it bear evidence of the surgeon's prowess" (Sir Frederick Treves, *The Elephant Man and Other Reminiscences* [New York, 1923], p. 57).

counters. Women's costumes are enormous in bulk and weight. Their trailing skirts, or "street-sweepers," catch refuse, papers, cigar butts in their wake, to be discharged inopportunely. (And note that half the male population chews tobacco, and spits with the periodicity of geysers.) It is a dangerous ordeal for a woman to cross a busy street, and dangerous to descend the steep stairs of the home, with perhaps a baby on one arm and the gathered burden of the skirt's train in the other. No wonder dress reform, blending with political reform, was bruited by such high-minded upstaters as Susan B. Anthony and Amelia Bloomer.

Life in Ithaca was, on the whole, grim. There were few diversions, no theatre, no organized sports. Baseball, developed by Civil War soldiers in their camps, was just making its own rules. An occasional circus, horse race, agricultural fair, or religious revival released the confined spirits. The men could in season fish, hunt, and swim; in every season they could drink in taverns. The women could gossip in interminable sewing bees.

Diversion was frowned upon, as a needless distraction from man's duty, which was to labor in this world and to strive for the privilege of resting in the next. This rule of life, this ethic, was a product of mid-century needs and environment. There was so much work to be done, in the transformation of wilderness into civilization! All honor was paid to the pioneer virtues of strength, endurance, frugality, and to the builder, the maker, the doer. Men felt their kinship to the Romans of the Republic, conquering the world by their energy, hard practical sense, and pure political faith; they cultivated Old Roman virtues, as they did Old Roman given names and place names, as they read Plutarch, as they built pillared farmhouses to indicate that Cincinnatus and Cato had found a new home on York-state hills.

They were Old Testament men, as well as Old Roman. They were fierce patriarchs, thumbing the Old Testament rather than the New, with its gentle, womanish counsels. They too were farm folk, like Abraham and Jacob. When they read of sheep and cattle on a thousand hills, of corn and wine and oil, of day-long labor in the vineyard, the Book seemed their own—as it hardly can to modern city dwellers.

Culture, selfish culture serving no materially useful end, had little place in men's lives. The curricula of the schools, primary and secondary, were far more restricted than a century later. And if one asserts that a restricted curriculum makes for intensiveness, that people learned less but better in 1865 than they do today, a faithful reader of old letters and manuscripts may be permitted his doubts. Even in the matter of spelling, a sacred fetish then as now, one notices that the spelling of educated men, scholars and secretaries of the faculty, was likely to be of a capriciousness not permitted to modern stenographers.

Ithaca had no public library until Ezra Cornell made his gift of the Cornell Library, in this year 1865. In some few households, those of ministers, lawyers, bankers, books were bought and read. And Ithaca had its publisher, Mack and Andrus, who did a thriving business in elementary school books and popular lives of heroes like Lafayette and Washington. Nevertheless, serious, reflective readers were rare and lonely. Appreciation of elevated art and music did not exist. The cultural level was woefully low, according to any modern standards.

This "chromo civilization" was marked by contradictions which now seem paradoxes. Comprehension of these paradoxes may help us to understanding of our early heroes.

The adoration of honest toil, as the first of human virtues, was balanced by a general delight in gambling and speculation. The beloved Biblical hero, Joseph, had himself cornered wheat in his time. The common mind was animated by a sense of opportunity, of sharing in America's mighty destiny. The country had just erased the stain of slavery from its banner; it might now march, with God's particular favor, toward heavenly cities soon to rise, toward new Jerusalems in America's green and pleasant land. This confident sense of opportunity had its consequence, that even the most prudent would believe any promise, and, assured of reaping tenfold in a few years, would make a down payment on mining or railroad ventures or on western lands. The close of the Civil War was followed by an outburst of financial adventures, sagacious, deluded, or cynical. Even in local affairs, private letters reveal that the average citizen, paying lip service to honest industry, was involved in dozens of fantastic schemes and projects, often ending in lawsuits and bankruptcies. Those who succeeded, by luck or astuteness, became the great men of their towns; the unlucky regarded the great men with outward respect and covert jealousy, recalling delightedly in private the great man's youthful mistakes and misdeeds. European visitors frequently remarked on the envy and rancor that colored American life.

Another paradox was the blending, or the incomplete emulsion, of eighteenth-century rationalism with a revival of pietist fundamentalism. Orators proclaimed on occasion the Jeffersonian phrases of the Enlightenment, unconcerned with bringing them into harmony with man's innate depravity, his single duty of seeking God's grace. Here and there the village atheist lingered, often a wandering printer, or a cobbler with time for meditation at his solitary bench. However, the new questions aroused by Darwin's *Origin of Species* were as yet hardly diffused in the countryside. The average Ithacan accepted a dolorous Calvinism. He sang on Sundays of his weariness of life, his conviction of sin, his terrors, his hopes of heaven; and on weekdays, with no apparent difficulty, he displayed the boastful optimism of a young and confident land.

Some few, the reflective men who demanded a sort of coherence in their thoughts, tried to resolve these oppositions. Such reflective men were Ezra Cornell and Andrew D. White. With others, scholars, New England Unitarians, philosophic men of affairs, they agreed on what Carl Becker calls the nineteenth-century liberal-democratic creed. They believed that man tends to virtue, not depravity; that his history is one of progress, material and spiritual, not one of retrogression; that his progress is proof that a benevolent deity exists, promoting man's happy destiny; that the universe is far more wonderful than ancient prophets realized, and that science is the new tool God has given us for the understanding and ordering of his universe; that man's highest duty is to labor for the service of his fellows, and that in working honorably for his own advantage he advantages his fellow men; that enlightenment is steadily conquering error, superstition, and material distress; and that if only mankind will have a little good sense and patience, it can, it will, attain to the earthly Paradise.

A final paradox was the contrast between the aesthetic barrenness of ordinary life and an ecstatic appreciation of natural beauty. The pioneers feared the aesthetic, as a weakening influence, distracting man from his dutiful labors. They were supported by their religion, still battling against the allurements of Catholic ritual. The Presbyterians, like the Quakers, permitted no instrumental music in their churches and no decorations on their walls. Beauty was clearly an agency of the devil. Nevertheless, the love of flowers and of natural scenery was widespread. Several Ithacans wrote descriptions of their gorges, with lyrical outbursts approaching frenzy. A few fumbling painters tried to capture the loveliness of lake and glen. Little by little, the grim-faced men began to yield to the seductions of art. They attended, though disapproving, the opera in New York. They hired architects to build their houses, and bought faked old masters to adorn them. Innocents Abroad, they visited Europe, and their facetious vulgarity was sometimes stilled in awe.

All of these paradoxes appear in the character of Ezra Cornell.

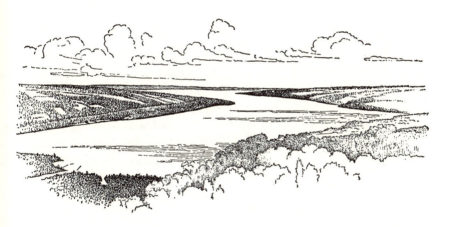

II

Ezra Cornell

EZRA CORNELL was born at Westchester Landing, New York, on 11 January 1807. The exact spot has been identified as the southwest corner of Williamsbridge Road and Silver Street, Borough of the Bronx, in New York City.[1] His father, Elijah Cornell, and his mother, born Eunice Barnard, traced their ancestry to seventeenth-century Puritan Massachusetts. Both came of that laborious yeomanry to which America owes so much of its greatness; none of their stock had gained any worldly distinction. Both were birthright Quakers; when and why their forebears espoused the rebel doctrine they did not know. Both were devout in the faith, wearing the garb, using the plain language. Both had something of the traditional Quaker character, earnest, dour, enduring, scornful of imposed orthodoxies, desirous of spiritual release through a roughcast mysticism. They believed and taught devoutly, in the face of much evidence to the contrary, that industry plus virtue would bring material success.

Elijah Cornell was a potter. He set up his kilns and fired his ware in various settlements near New York City. Ezra, the eldest child (he was to have five brothers and five sisters), helped the father at his trade and obtained, on occasion, a little desultory schooling.

Elijah had bought, in 1807, an uncleared hilltop farm in De Ruyter, 43 miles northeast of Ithaca. The hard times of 1818 persuaded him to

[1] Edith M. Fox, "A Search for Founder's Birthplace," *Cornell Alumni News,* 1 March 1956.

8

exploit his farm in earnest. With his wife, six children, and his scanty household goods in a single covered wagon, he made the toilsome three-week journey in November and December 1818. Ezra was nearly twelve.

De Ruyter is not one of New York State's garden spots. While the valley farms thrive, the hills are stony and forlorn, marginal land at best. Elijah Cornell had chosen his 150 acres on Crum Hill, three miles east of the village. He was determined in his choice by a Quaker enclave in the region; it is still known as Quaker Basin.

A log house was quickly built, with young Ezra giving valiant aid. Then followed years which he later recalled as filled with hard work and happiness. He attended school for three-month winter sessions. "It generally required the first month of each winter," he says, "to regain the knowledge lost during the summer vacation." The curriculum was simple: reading, writing, spelling, arithmetic through decimals, and a single lesson in geography, in which New York State was bounded on the west by "the unknown regions." The scholars' final achievement was about equal to that of a fifth-grade student today.

The adolescent Ezra Cornell was powerfully built, lean and long. Everyone who describes him in later years mentions his tallness. It is surprising, therefore, to find on his passport, issued in 1863, the notation that his height was 5 feet 10½ inches. He would not seem very tall today. But his gauntness, his erect bearing, and his upstanding crest of hair accentuated his height. And the stature of Americans has apparently risen.

Ezra's hair was brown, his eyes were blue. He had high cheekbones and a prominent forehead. The mouth was wide and thin-lipped, compressed with the habit of determined reticence. His voice tended to "shrillness and harshness, but in its more quiet modulations was not unpleasant. His utterance was slow and precise, as if every word was carefully if not painfully thought out." [2] His smile was rare, but suddenly illuminating. He possessed an ironic humor, sometimes whimsical, sometimes wounding. He uttered his pleasantries with a straight Yankee face, *pince-sans-rire*, pinch-without-laughing. He had even in youth a stern and rugged look. His brother-in-law later remembered: "He was a tall, slender, gaunt boy—not altogether an attractive lad, and yet he had a rather forcible manner after all." [3]

[2] *Cornell Era*, 8 Jan. 1875.
[3] Recollections of Ezra Cornell by Otis E. Wood, reproduced in Carl Becker, *Cornell University; Founders and the Founding* (Ithaca, 1943), p. 183.

His character gleams in certain memories of his youth. At seventeen he helped a group of carpenters build a shop for his father. He noticed an error in the laying out of the frame, and pointed it out to the boss, Mr. Hugaboom, with, one suspects, some complacency. After some discussion,

Hugaboom foamed with rage, and father reprimanded me for my presumption and impudence. I, however, was not to be put down by angry words, for I knew I was right, and I insisted upon it and at last secured an examination of the subject by some other carpenters who worked on the frame. They saw the error and took sides with me, and the "boss" had finally to give it up and correct his mistake.[4]

In the following summer Ezra proposed to build a frame house for the family, to replace their log cabin. (Both house and cabin have long since moldered away.) The guild of carpenters, offended at his presumption, misplaced certain timbers and tried to catch him out—vainly, of course. "The frame was pronounced by all hands the best one that had ever been raised in the neighborhood. My triumph was so complete on this occasion that my friends mounted me on their shoulders and marched me around the frame in the highest glee of enthusiasm."

Here is competence in dealing with the material world, its tools and devices. Here too is the builder's purpose, with intelligence to guide it. Here also is a self-conscious superiority, a sense of apartness which readily expressed itself in scorn of weakness and incompetence. He knew he was right, though the world be wrong; and if the world was wrong, he had no pity for it, but rather contempt. One may well suppose that many in De Ruyter took his rightness somewhat ill.

He was essentially a man who stands alone, a nonconformist. He belonged to that great line of men who take their stand on a belief, defiant of men and gods, never conceiving that their belief may be in error, or that all beliefs may ultimately be called in question.

His Quaker background certainly enforced his nonconformity. It imposed also his seriousness of purpose, which implied contempt of ease, of diversion, even the simple pleasures of the new-cleared wilderness. There is a revealing letter from his cousin, Henry Macy, in nearby Homer, written in June 1828:

My Dearest Cousin I pitty your situation—Ezra if you all ways let work keep you home you never will se the world I am afrade, for the work is never don in Deruyter, that I know by expearinces, but for my part I ant

[4] *The Autobiography of Mary Emily Cornell* (Ithaca, 1929), p. 24.

agoin to worke all my days and take no comfort. I beleave I shall se the time that I shall se the Niagagra falls before I dy. . . .[5]

At nineteen Ezra Cornell was a man, a competent farmer, carpenter, and potter. It was time for him to seek his fortune.

In 1826 he bade farewell to the farm. With nine dollars in pocket and with his possessions over his shoulder in a checked handkerchief made by his mother, he walked to Syracuse, thirty-three miles away. He stood all day on the hiring bridge over the Erie Canal, and found employment as a carpenter. (According to Goldwin Smith, he was cheated by his employer, and thus conceived a lifelong hatred for Syracuse, and would hear none of Andrew D. White's plea to establish his university in that Gomorrah.) [6] Within three months he began taking jobs by contract. He built two sawmills, made money and lost it. He removed to Homer, worked in a shop making wool-carding machinery, learned to make drawings of machines, and studied mechanics' handbooks.

In April 1828 he journeyed on foot from De Ruyter to Ithaca, which was momentarily a boom town. He took the road through Dryden, past Free Hollow (originally, says legend, Flea Hollow, and today Forest Home), and along the swamp which has become Beebe Lake. When the gorge-side road opened on the valley view, he paused to gaze. He stood on the site of his University.

In Ithaca, Cornell immediately obtained work as a carpenter. And in July he engaged himself to serve Otis Eddy as mechanic in his cotton mill for one year, at the wage of eight dollars per month and board. The mill stood approximately on the site of Cascadilla Hall. At the year's end he became the mechanic, and later the manager, of the more imposing plaster and flour mills of Colonel Jeremiah S. Beebe, at the foot of Ithaca Falls, on Fall Creek.

Land plaster or gypsum, regarded by farmers as a sovereign fertilizer, was one of Ithaca's major products. It was brought by barge from the foot of the lake, ground in the mills, and shipped far by wagon. It gave Ezra Cornell his local name—"Plaster Cornell."

The water power for the mills was channeled from the summit of the falls by a rickety sluiceway hung from the top of the cliff. This was often destroyed by ice and flood waters. To replace it, Cornell

[5] This letter, as in general others of unspecified provenience, is in the Cornell University Archives.

[6] Goldwin Smith, *Reminiscences* (New York, 1911), p. 371.

built a dam above the falls and blasted a tunnel, 200 feet long and 15 feet high, through the solid rock. When the shafts from the two ends met, they were only an inch or two out of line. The feat was a remarkable one, for Cornell had had no experience with tunneling or with blasting powder. The tunnel, still in use, is the first of Ezra Cornell's permanent works. Ten years later he built a dam above Triphammer Falls, impounding Beebe Lake, to make a storage reservoir for dry seasons.[7]

In March 1831 Ezra Cornell married Mary Ann Wood, daughter of a substantial farmer whose acres lay near the village of Etna, a few miles from Ithaca. Her letters reveal an intelligent person, constant, brave, enduring through many difficult years. In later times she had the affectionate respect of the makers of Cornell University. As she was an Episcopalian, Cornell married "out of meeting." The De Ruyter Society of Friends formally excommunicated him, though suggesting that he might be reinstated if he should express proper regret for his misalliance. Regret, said Cornell, for the best action I have ever done? He rejected the suggestion with scorn. Henceforth he was to be a solitary in religion, seeking and making his own faith.

He built for his wife a cottage in a dark glen two hundred yards north of Fall Creek. It was a crude and simple home, woefully ugly, if a certain early sketch is authentic. It began with a common kitchen-living-bedroom, with an attic for prospective children. Much built over, it stood until 1961, directly below the Cornell Mausoleum in Lake View Cemetery. In "The Nook" his nine children were born, and from it four of them were buried.

Through the thirties Ezra Cornell led the life of the industrious small-town artisan. He built a fine new flouring mill for Colonel Beebe. He took part in local politics in the Whig interest, but running behind his ticket, he failed of election to the post of village trustee. And, like everyone else in booming Ithaca, he speculated in real estate. He wrote some significant words to his father in March 1834: "I had got out of debt and a little to spare, but not being able to injoy sound sleep while I remained in that situation (a situation that some would call happy) I have removed the evil by running in debt for the large

---

[7] The original Beebe Lake was about ten feet lower than it is today. People ask about the name of Triphammer. A gun-barrel factory was established there about 1820 on the site of the present Hydraulic Laboratory. A sluiceway operated an actual triphammer.

house and lot." (The large house and lot stood near the foot of Ithaca Falls.)

1837 was Panic Year. Ithaca, which had built fantastic hopes on a ship canal to connect Cayuga Lake with Lake Ontario, was hard hit. Colonel Beebe was forced to sell his mills, and on 1 January 1839 Ezra Cornell was out of a job.

He turned his hand to various enterprises. He was a partner in a small grocery store at Ithaca Falls, which did not thrive. He returned to farming, renting Colonel Beebe's property, apparently the present Cornell Heights. He was a progressive farmer—too progressive for his profit. He bought a prize-winning pure-blooded Shorthorn bull; but Ithaca farmers would not pay the fees required to make the bull a paying investment. He revived the Tompkins County Agricultural Society, and was named marshal of the 1841 fair. In the same year he was appointed to the viewing committee on swine for the State Fair in Syracuse. He had also time for self-improvement. It is interesting to compare the clumsy, hard-fisted script of his letters of 1831 with the easy-flowing hand he developed some six years later. But all his life he wrote with a dictionary ready to hand.

He was too venturesome to prosper. He was respected in Ithaca; evidently he was not much liked. He was too independent, too much the outsider, refusing membership in any church, scornful of the good fellows wasting their time in taverns and social jollities. Perfectly self-confident, even self-righteous, he looked to the future for his rewards. "He had a peculiarity in his early life in the way of entire forgetfulness of his own needs and those of his family," remembers his brother-in-law, Otis Wood.

He did not even attend to their education. And he was forgetful of himself. There was no selfishness in the man; he was unreasonably generous—it would have been better for himself and for his family if he had been more selfish. He had no credit at home or abroad. He couldn't even buy a sack of flour for credit; and he was always forgetful in money matters—small accounts against him ran at the mill here for years.[8]

In December 1846 Colonel Beebe, venting the spleen of a failure, wrote to his father-in-law:

Cornell is a hickory Quaker—close, selfish, Pharisaical, destitute of gratitude and the kindlier feelings of poor human nature. I hired him in 1830. . . . I

[8] Reproduced in Becker, *Founders*, p. 184.

found him steady and ingenious, and capable for a very ignorant uncouth man. . . . He was constantly experimenting in mechanicks, which probably cost me much money. . . . He was always a coarse impudent man, so much so that many complaints was made to me about him when he was in my service.

These are angry rancorous words; but they have their value if, as the existentialists say, we exist only by reflection from the minds of others.

By 1842 Cornell concluded that there was no issue in his precarious way of life. A way of escape appeared. Two neighbors had patented Barnaby and Mooers' Double Mold-board Plow, adjustable either for level lands or side hills. Cornell obtained the rights for its sale in Maine and Georgia. He spent the summer in Maine, demonstrating the plow to skeptical farmers. Though he made few sales, he made a fateful acquaintance, with F. O. J. Smith, editor of the *Maine Farmer*, Member of Congress, and a dabbler in many enterprises.

At the end of January 1843 Cornell set off from Ithaca to try his luck in Georgia. His letters give a vivid account of the hardships of travel. He journeyed by stage and in an open farm wagon, in bitter weather, to the railroad head at Goshen, and thence to New York and southward. The second-class railroad car was a heatless "pig pen upon wheels, or a hyena cage, with rough naked boards for seats and slides for windows. . . . I have had to pinch clost. I am here [in Plymouth, N.C.] and have got 57 cents left. . . . I shall have to let you pay the postage on letters untill I can rase the wind." He did most of his traveling on foot, a procedure which any sales manager would condemn. He sold few plows, in a country where Negroes were cheaper investments than improved machinery. He saw a slave auction, and was inspired with a lifelong destestation of the peculiar institution.

In July 1843 he returned to Maine, to meet and grasp his fate. He paid a business call on the Honorable F. O. J. Smith.

I found Smith on his knees in the middle of his office floor with a piece of chalk in his hand, the mold-board of a plow lying by his side, and with various chalk-marks on the floor before him. He was earnestly engaged in trying to explain some plan or idea of his own to a plow manufacturer, who stood looking on with his good-natured face enveloped in a broad grin that denoted his skepticism in reference to Smith's plans. On my entrance, Mr. Smith arose, and grasping me cordially by the hand, said: "Cornell, you are the very man I wanted to see. I have been trying to explain to neighbor Robertson a machine that I want made, but I cannot make him understand it," and proceeding, he explained that he wanted "a kind of scraper, or machine for digging a ditch, that will leave the earth deposited on each side, convenient to be used for filling the ditch by means of another machine. It is for laying our telegraph pipe underground. The ditch must be two feet deep, and wide enough to enable us to lay the pipe in the bottom, and then cover it with the earth. Congress has appropriated $30,000 to enable Professor Morse to test the practicability of his telegraph on a line between Washington and Baltimore. I have taken the contract to lay the pipe at $100 per mile, and I must have some kind of a machine to enable me to do the work at any such price."

An examination of a specimen of the pipe to be laid, which Mr. Smith showed us, and a little reflection, convinced me that he did not want two machines, as he said, one to excavate, and the other to fill the trench after the pipe was deposited. I therefore with my pencil sketched a rough diagram of a machine that seemed to me adapted to his necessities. It provided that the pipe, with the wires enclosed therein, was to be coiled around a drum or reel, from whence it was to pass down through a hollow standard, protected by shives, directly in rear of a colter or cutter, which was so arranged as to cut a furrow two and a half feet deep and one-fourth inch wide. Arranged something like a plow, it was to be drawn by a powerful team, and to deposit the pipe in the bottom of the furrow as it moved along. The furrow being so narrow would soon close itself and conceal the pipe from view.[9]

Though Smith was hardly convinced that the machine would work, he consented to pay for its construction. Cornell wrote excitedly to his wife, on 6 August:

If [the machine] succeeds it is worth thousands, and my faith is strong, as it usually is in favour of projects of my own origin. . . . You wont get excited I trust my Dear if you should see some flourishes in the "dailies" about the success of a rum "pipe layer" dont think because "dad" is "Esquire" that we are all Esquires. Keep cool and be ready when the bad comes round, don't leap too soon.

On his own part he kept cool, not losing his touch with realities. Only a fortnight later he wrote Mary Ann:

I have spent part of the day in setting a patch on the seat of my pants, and I can assure you that I have improved in that branch of mechanics since I commenced in Georgia. I have discovered and fully understand the art of making large stitches look small, so you may be assured the job is done decent. I am sorry that I have to sit on such sharp pointed bones, for it is unpleasant to have a hole punched through your pants every now and then.

[9] Alonzo B. Cornell, *Biography of Ezra Cornell* (New York, 1884), pp. 472–473.

The pants were patched in time for a visit from Professor S. F. B. Morse. The machine worked perfectly. Ezra Cornell was put in charge of the pipe-laying between Washington and Baltimore.

The work began in October, and Cornell succeeded in laying half a mile of pipe per day. His private tests convinced him, however, that the insulation of the wires was defective. His efforts to warn Morse were ill received. But one day Morse drew him aside and said: "Mr. Cornell, can't you contrive some plausible excuse for stopping this work for a few days? I want to make some experiments before any more pipe is laid, and I don't want the papers to know that the work is purposely stopped." As Cornell recalled, "I stepped back to the machine and said: 'Hurrah, boys, whip up the mules (we were using a team of eight mules to draw the machine), we must lay another length of pipe before we quit for the night.' The teamsters cracked their whips over the mules and away they started at a lively pace. I grasped the handles of the machine, and watching an opportunity, I canted it so as to catch the point of a rock, and broke it to pieces." [10]

Cornell promptly devised a machine for withdrawing the wires from the pipes and reinsulating them. He spent the winter in Washington at this task, and in reading everything he could find on electricity in the Library of Congress. His reading convinced him that underground wiring was impracticable and that the wires should be strung on glass-insulated poles. Although Cornell claimed the invention, certainly with justice, the same idea occurred to others. Indeed it had already been put in practice in England.

In the spring of 1844 Cornell built the overhead line from Washington to Baltimore. On 24 May, Morse tapped out the historic message: "What hath God wrought!" from the Supreme Court chamber in Washington. (The receiving instrument is lodged in the mechanical museum in Kimball Hall at Cornell University.)

Cornell spent the following winter demonstrating the telegraph in New York and Boston, trying vainly to enlist capital for development. In the spring he built the line from Philadelphia to New York for Morse and his associates.

Morse and Cornell were instinctively hostile. Morse, who was not in fact a very competent mechanic, resented Cornell's proposals for improvements and no doubt the tactlessness with which they were presented. On his part, Cornell took ill the superciliousness of "the

[10] EC to S. I. Prime, 28 April 1873.

16

Professor" and accused Morse of appropriating his own ideas for a recording register and a magnet.[11]

If Cornell had no great opinion of Morse, he saw well the future of the telegraph. His imagination was stirred to almost poetic heights. After the first public trial of the telegraph he wrote his wife (31 May 1844): "Is not space annihilated? . . . The critter electricity has been brought down from heaven and tamed, as mild as a dove and as gentle as a lamb, yielding obedient submission to man."

The story of Ezra Cornell during the next dozen years is the story of the telegraph in America. The tale is immensely tangled and embroiled, and far too long for any telling here.[12] Feeble enterprises were born, breathed briefly, and died; more vigorous growths passed from hand to hand, in a welter of lawsuits, stockjobbing, rascality, and deception.

Ezra Cornell was first of all a builder of telegraph systems, for others at the outset and then for himself. He took willingly a large part of his pay in stock; he began in 1844 by subscribing $500 toward the pioneer New York–Philadelphia line, the sum to be taken out of his salary of $1,000 a year. He asserted in July 1849 that he had built one third of the telegraph lines in America. He was, secondly, a manager, director, president of telegraph companies—a businessman. In this role his constant policy was to build more lines, on credit or without, trusting to the future to pay the construction costs; and sometimes the future was far too slow in arriving. As a businessman he has been sharply

[11] S. F. B. Morse wrote Alfred Vail on 12 Jan. 1846: "Let us get along as quietly as we can with the plague [Cornell] until we can cut loose from him." And a month later: "Cornell has so bewitched and befouled everything he has touched about them [the instruments] that I have hard work to restrain my indignation." And somewhat later, when his indignation had cooled: "Ezra Cornell is ingenious and shrewd; he is thought to be rather close and narrow-minded" (S. F. B. Morse, *Letters and Journals* [New York, 1914], II, 443). Cornell summed up his own views in a letter of 15 Oct. 1852 to Jeptha H. Wade: "Professor Morse, although not possessing an original and inventive mind, caught the happy idea of applying the galvanic current to the production of the electro-magnet as the most likely to be successful for telegraphing. . . . The professor adopted and marshalled [the inventions of others], sometimes paying the inventor a trifle and at other times appropriating them without pay or credit. The Professor however is entitled to great credit for the enthusiasm and perseverance with which he adhered to his project through poverty and derision."

[12] See Robert Luther Thompson, *Wiring a Continent* (Princeton, 1947), and Philip Dorf, *The Builder* (New York, 1952).

criticized. While evidently he lacked some of the orderly virtues of the perfect administrator, his imagination, determination, and dominating force are business qualities, and very important ones too. He succeeded in veining the east and middle west with telegraphs, he kept his control and his stock through black years of discouragement, privation, and the treacherous defections of his closest friends and even his relatives. While most of his early associates failed and were forgotten in the savage, unscrupulous war, he emerged triumphant and with his conscience clean. This fact creates at least a presumption of business competence.[13]

But they were hard years. "His way of doing business was to starve others out—and he didn't mind starving himself out at the same operation," said Otis Wood. An Ithacan told of meeting Cornell in New York in the early fifties. He asked how the telegraph magnate was getting on. Cornell took a quarter dollar from his pocket and said: "There, that will buy my dinner, but where the next is coming from I don't know." When, years later, the story was told to Mrs. Cornell she capped it by saying: "I've known when he was worse off than that. One morning he had nothing in his pocket, but as he was going down Broadway he found ten cents on the sidewalk and bought himself some breakfast." [14] In 1852 President Ezra Cornell of the New York and Erie Telegraph was summoned to an important discussion with the directors of the Erie Railroad. Ashamed of his patched clothing, the President borrowed $3.50 from a friend for a new pair of pants. He did not dare ask enough to buy a coat.

He was seldom home in Ithaca, and when he did return he was likely to bring no provisions, but a "trunkful of gilt-edged books." Mary Ann and the children lived precariously on grudged credit and on

[13] Carl Becker (*Founders*, pp. 57-59) roundly calls Cornell a bad businessman. He quotes hostile allegations, which Cornell specifically denied. He says also that Cornell, defeated, was forced against his will into the Western Union merger in 1855. He does not say that consolidation was Cornell's dream. Cornell claimed to be the initiator of the policy (EC to C. Livingston, 17 May 1854); he proposed an "American Telegraph Union," which should have, with other features, public reading rooms in the great cities (EC to Speed, Wade, and Theodore Faxton, 19 December 1850). He wanted consolidation, but on his own terms. The final agreement gave his interests 150,000 shares, more than half of them in his own name, to 350,000 shares for the Hiram Sibley interests, which held a much greater telegraph mileage. These seem like excellent terms.

[14] Becker, *Founders*, p. 186.

18

farm produce contributed by her father. Her letters are filled with doleful complaints of hardship, of abandonment.

Privation, worry, and the infections lurking in American air, food, and water seriously affected Cornell's health. He had a delicate stomach and a recurrent liver trouble. In Montreal in 1847 he contracted ship fever, surely typhoid in our terminology. Half delirious, he left his bed and took train to Burlington, Vermont, where there was a hotel with a proprietress he trusted. Defying the doctors, he wrapped himself in a cold, wet sheet, drank ice water, took no food, and got well, of course ascribing his recovery to his self-treatment, in accordance with the precepts of hydropathy. In April 1855, at an acute moment in his affairs, he fell ill with smallpox in Indianapolis. Smallpox had to yield to business; he appeared in Michigan City "with a face so marked that I feared it would lead to my arrest." (We may see here a little of the recklessness that hid in his character.) Two months later he suffered a frightful accident. Sitting in an oversized passenger coach with his left elbow out the window, he was struck on the arm by a loose board of a bridge structure. The arm was fractured in four places and there were numerous breaks in the hand and fingers. He carried on his business from the sickbed. "Sickness," he wrote, "is the only obsticle that I bow to, and I bow moderately even when the old tyrant is in possession." [15]

He bowed moderately, admitting that he had neither the strength nor the desire to fight for domination within the new-formed Western Union Telegraph Company. Though he was a director and the largest single stockholder, owning nearly a sixth of the stock, he took no active part in the company's affairs. He was sick of the telegraph and its broils and battles. He had long dreamed of retiring and devoting himself to scientific farming. He thought briefly of settling at Forestville, near Dunkirk, New York, or in the vicinity of Cleveland. But Ithaca claimed him.

He had left Ithaca in 1842, poor, visionary Ezry Corn'll, Plaster Corn'll, off to seek his fortune. When he returned thirteen years later, with the aura of fortune about his head, he was Ezra Cornell, Esq. Close companions, even his family, persisted in the old pronunciation. His brother Elijah said the name was "*Corn*'ll until some of us got to be high-toned, and now it is pronounced Cor-*nell*." [16]

[15] EC to J. J. Speed, 8 Dec. 1849.
[16] Anna B. Comstock, *The Comstocks of Cornell* (Ithaca, 1953), p. 38.

In Ithaca there was one tract of land which had for him a special meaning. This was the DeWitt farm, on the hill crown and slope between the Cascadilla and Fall Creek gorges. In April 1828 he had trudged along the road at its northern edge, and had paused at the summit to look for the first time at the lake and village below, on the home of his manhood. Twenty years later, in a moment of prosperity, he bought a half share in the farm land, and the following year he was forced to yield his interest to a brother-in-law, Orrin Wood. In 1857 he became again its owner.

Those of us who have a sentimental feeling for the soil on which our lives are lived must be interested in its history. "Clay of the pit whence we were wrought yearns to its fellow-clay," says Kipling. This farm land was early cleared. In 1812 it was grown to wheat.[17] A second growth of timber gradually repossessed it, and the lower slope, known as the seminary grounds in memory of a collegiate dream of 1822, became a pasture. The original purchaser, Simeon DeWitt, passed it on to his son Linn in 1837. A comfortable farmhouse was built in 1839, at what is now the junction of Stewart Avenue and Campus Road. Transformed by many rebuildings, it forms the core of what is at this writing the Triangle fraternity. Wheat fields, orchards, and pasture land rippled up and over the hilltop. A tenant house and large basement barn stood beside Fall Creek, between the old Sibley College, now occupied by the College of Architecture, and the gorge. The DeWitt farm, entwined in the history of Ezra Cornell, was to become Cornell University.

"The farm," Cornell wrote his wife (13 February 1857), "is the only place that I have seen between the Hudson and the Mississippi that seemed in the least to possess the attractions requisite to compensate for the old homestead. Here I can transplant my affections and cultivate a garden of Eden for my bird of Paradise."

If not a Garden of Eden, his Forest Park, as he named it, quickly became a model farm. He decided to specialize in purebred cattle, especially Shorthorns. "I shall have the finest herd in the country," he said characteristically; and characteristically, he turned out to be right, or nearly right. He bought the best of stock, including a prize-winning bull at the unheard-of price of $1,500. Soon his cattle were winning their own prizes at local fairs and at the State Fair. He experimented with potatoes, wheat, grass, and fruit, doing the farm "choars" with

[17] "Reminiscences of W. T. Eddy," in Mulks Scrapbooks, XIX, C.U. Library.

much satisfaction. He wrote letters to the press, especially the Ithaca *Journal,* on agricultural subjects. He organized a farmers' club and provided, free of rent, an agricultural reading room in Ithaca. Naturally he was elected president of the Tompkins County Fair, and naturally he made acquaintances among the important stock raisers and agricultural leaders of the state.

At the same time he came to realize the general lack of exact knowledge about agriculture. Rule of thumb was well enough; it needed supplementing by rule of brain. He physicked a sick heifer desperately, and the heifer died. "Ignorant of the disease I did not know what remedy to apply," he confessed. But why, he pondered, need a farmer be ignorant of cattle diseases? Is ignorance a necessary doom? We may well recognize Ezra Cornell's answer, and his remedy. He began to take an interest in agricultural education.

The Civil War came. Cornell was in Washington for the inauguration of President Lincoln, and he shook hands with the object of his adoration. He witnessed the rout of Bull Run, and, refusing to retreat as fast as the Federal soldiers, he found himself for a time between the two armies. In Ithaca he headed a committee for the relief of soldiers' dependents and served in many ways, public and hidden.

As the town's leading citizen, he inevitably entered politics, though without his own solicitation. In November 1861 he was elected to the Assembly of the New York State legislature as a Republican. He was made chairman of the Committee on Agriculture. Shortly after, he was chosen president of the New York State Agricultural Society, an honorable post, and as such he was an ex officio trustee of the Ovid Agricultural College, twenty-five miles from Ithaca.

In the summer of 1862 he made a trip to Europe, with his wife, as official delegate of the Agricultural Society. He attended the International Exposition in London and various agricultural shows, bought Southdown sheep for his farm, visited the Royal Agricultural College at Cirencester, and closely observed farm practice in England and France.

Early in 1863 he disclosed the theme of long meditation. He proposed to build, and to endow, a great public library for Ithaca and Tompkins County.

It was a noble purpose, welcomed with clamorous enthusiasm. The idea that a rich man should give his surplus for the general good was still a novel one. American philanthropy was not yet an organized

industry. The list of private benefactors of the public was short—
Benjamin Franklin, Stephen Girard, George Peabody, Peter Cooper,
James Smithson—there were not many others.

Ezra Cornell was moved less by emulation of others than by the
logic of his character. He had fought to make and build worthily, and
he had dreamed of wealth as reward. But when he had won, and ceased
to make and build, the wealth that flowed in seemed to him dispropor-
tionate, undeserved. His lifetime of frugality, his faith in the homely
virtues, made wealth look even menacing. He set arbitrarily the sum
of $100,000 as the portion he might leave to each of his children, to
their benefit. A greater bequest would cause them only moral harm.
What should he do with the surplus? He must buy with his money
the greatest general good. And how? He must ponder the matter
soberly.

The Cornell Library was only a provisional solution to his problem,
a trial essay. He bought the lot at the southeast corner of Tioga and
Seneca Streets. (He was living across the way, in his son Alonzo's
fine house, on the site of the Ithaca Savings Bank. He had turned over
Forest Park, with the management of the farm, to his son Franklin.)
He drew plans for a large, imposing building, in which the post office,
a bank, offices, and an auditorium seating 800 would serve as an income-
producing endowment. He was his own building superintendent and
clerk of the works, inspecting every stone and brick, driving hard
bargains with great enjoyment. The building, massive, though not to
modern eyes beautiful, richly fulfilled its purpose for nearly a century,
and then was torn down to make a parking lot.

He was learning the delights of philanthropy. "Old man useful," a
correspondent termed him. In usefulness, in the practice of the golden
rule, he found his joy.

In November 1863 he was elected to the State Senate. When he took
his seat in January, he had in pocket the draft of a bill incorporating
the Cornell Library. The Board of Trustees was to be composed of
nineteen members: three local officials ex officio, the pastors of the
seven existing churches and the principals of the Academy and the
public school, Mr. Cornell or his eldest male lineal descendant, and six
citizens to be elected by the Board. Thus the representation of religion
was assured and the dominance of any one sect precluded. Here in
embryo is the structure of the Board of Trustees of Cornell University.

The bill was referred to the Chairman of the Committee on Literature, Senator Andrew Dickson White, and in his pocket we shall for

the moment leave it, big with consequence though the meeting of Cornell and White was to be.

Before proceeding with the story we may pause to look at the Founder, at the age of fifty-seven.

He was still spare of body, and he had developed a slight stoop. His face was gaunt and tense, with marked vertical lines between the brows, which gave him a suspicious, even forbidding, expression. His ragged beard, which it was his fancy to leave unkempt, and his shaven upper lip suggest the style of a farmer. As he would smile at no man's order, his photographs lack the "illumination, the shrewd, genial smile which occasionally played round the firm mouth." He seemed to many to be of the Lincoln type. "With a little more gentleness and kindness of expression he would have been a perfect model to sit for the mythical 'Uncle Sam.' " [18]

He wore invariably a full-skirted black broadcloth frock coat and a large black satin stock with a stiff collar. His hat was by no means the crumpled slouch which his bronze figure on the campus carries, but a tall silk hat, "which served as a portable office, for he always kept it filled with important papers stuffed in the hat-band." [19] He wore made-to-order boots, with square toes and soft leather tops. He drove, perhaps with affectation, a sturdy but not showy horse, hitched to an old buggy. (Goldwin Smith was delighted with the buggy, a typical American invention with a risible name. He used to say: "Your founder must have a statue, but he must be seated in his buggy and not on horseback.") [20]

His manner was likely to be sharp, even harsh; he could "deal out rebuke with savage force." He had no patience with sloth, incompetence, intemperance, or duplicity. Naturally his ready reproofs made him enemies. Ithacans whom he had bested or outdistanced loved to tell anecdotes of his former poverty, of his unwillingness to pay old overdue debts, of his new overweening pride.[21] The rancorous felt that in abasing the great they were elevating themselves.

[18] James Morgan Hart, *Founder's Day Address*, 25 March 1913 (pamphlet); Burt G. Wilder, in *Era*, May 1907, p. 414; William Horace Corbin '70, in *Ezra Cornell Centennial* (Ithaca, 1907), p. 31.

[19] Charles Ezra Cornell, *Personal Recollections of Ezra Cornell, Founder's Day Address*, Ithaca, 1922 (pamphlet). Let us not blame the sculptor, who no doubt foresaw student indignities to a stovepipe.

[20] Note in Andrew D. White's hand, in *Massachusetts Historical Society Proceedings*, Dec. 1915, in C.U. Library.

[21] F. M. Finch, *Life and Services of Ezra Cornell* (Ithaca, 1887), p. 11; "V. D.'s

Earnestness, steadiness, perseverance carried to the point of obstinacy, and power and strength held in reserve—such were the qualities that marked him.[22] Life was real, it was earnest, and only a fool would waste his time in play. William H. Corbin '70 recalled that the students of the new-fledged university wanted to play baseball. A committee sought subscriptions for equipment. The Founder, when interviewed, said only: "When I was a boy and wanted to play ball, my mother took an old stocking and unraveled it, and wound the yarn into a ball, and I found an old boot-top and cut out the leather, and covered my ball. That was a good enough ball for me; I think it ought to be good enough for you." The students were of course outraged, but Corbin, on reflection, recognized the moral: "He had a serious view of things. The importance of economy in the Cornell boys, the dread of allowing them to acquire extravagant and wasteful notions in their new surroundings, the relative unimportance of mere play contrasted with the paramount significance of the work of education—these things stood uppermost in his mind." [23]

His seriousness, his grimness, was in part due to his Quaker background and to the Old Roman ideal, but chiefly it was the product of his own rugged life, totally given to work. It did not exclude a sardonic, whimsical humor, or even, on occasion, gayety. Amusement, though usually a waste of time, was not a sin. Cornell enjoyed circuses, and for university celebrations of his birthday provided music for dancing. But his taste in music was elementary. On a visit to New York in 1860 he noted in his diary: "Fooled the day away by going to the opera [the Barber of Seville]." Once he was taken to a concert by Mme Sontag. He wrote home (5 January 1854): "The pieces were Italian and French excepting 'Home, Sweet Home,' which was so distorted by artistic skill that it made me nervous."

Though he loved and tried to describe with struggling words the beauty of Nature, he was unaware, until his last few years, of the world of art, of man-made beauty. Andrew D. White was in constant terror lest Cornell should make of his university "a great staring work-

---

Stories," anecdotes of Virgil D. Morse (typed copies in C.U. Archives and DeWitt Historical Society). Also Samuel J. Parker, "An Ithaca Boyhood" (MS, C.U. Library).

[22] T . F. Crane, in *Proceedings and Addresses at the Semi-Centennial of Cornell University* (Ithaca, 1919).

[23] *Ezra Cornell Centennial*, p. 32.

shop." White's adjutant, W. C. Russel, wrote him: "I dread Mr. Cornell's wall paper [for McGraw Hall] more than you do. I expect horrors in every figure." White replied: "I fear regarding the wall paper. Ezra Cornell may be canonized some day, but not beatified for such qualities as ennobled Fra Angelico among the blessed. The aesthetic was quite left out of him." [24]

On the other hand he had a perhaps instinctive sense of the form and cadence of English prose. His letters are full of sharp phrasings, cogent in thought and pleasing to the ear. White recognized the fact, with a hint of condescension: "My wife insists sincerely that you are a masterly writer, and indeed I begin to think one of your 'best holts,' as Artemus Ward says, is Literature." [25]

Good writing must be the product of good thinking. Ezra Cornell was a most excellent thinker. He kept to the end, with all his convictions, an open mind. The devoutest of Republicans, he worked harmoniously with Democrats. He could yield to the views of others; though his first thought was to establish a technical university, he was persuaded by White that the humanities, the classics, should stand equal with mechanics and agriculture.

He tried to guide his life by moral conviction, by principle. He wrote to his son Alonzo (23 September 1840): "There is no other safe rule than to establish character upon a fixed principle; do right because it is right, for the sake of right and nothing else. Every act should be measured by that rule—'is it right?' Let a pure heart prompt an honest conscience to answer the question and all will be well."

He did his best to live by this inner light, a Quaker inheritance. To give one example from a thousand, when he became State Senator he received as a matter of course free passes from the important railroads. He returned them. Only one other Senator was as scrupulous.

He did right by giving abundantly of his surplus to those in need. He was generous not only with his money, but with his time and comfort. His grandson recalled that when a boy he had accompanied his grandfather on the night boat from New York to Albany. The two were annoyed by a woman pacing the deck with a crying, obstreperous baby. The boy discovered in the morning that his grandfather's bed had not been slept in. Mr. Cornell had gained the woman's confidence,

[24] ADW to EC, 3 July 1868; Russell to ADW, 15 July 1870; ADW to Russel, 19 Aug. 1870.
[25] ADW to EC, 31 July 1869.

had sent her to bed, and had spent the night on deck, shielding and comforting the child.[26]

He did not pretend to love all mankind indiscriminately. He despised idlers, weaklings, and "gentlemen loafers." He had a strong sense of class, pride in the sturdy workers of America. His great benefaction was designed to give poor ambitious boys like himself the opportunities which would have been precious to himself.

He was justified, we hope, by good works. But in the view of nineteenth-century Protestantism works done without faith have the nature of sin. What was the faith of Ezra Cornell?

He was roundly accused of atheism. Read out of the Community of Friends, he never joined another church. His wife and children were faithful Episcopalians. But he wrote to Mary Ann: "I had scruples to attending an orthodox church." He disliked the evangelical orders, blaming the Methodists for the hysterical state of his sister Jane:

Her mind is acted upon too vehemently in those exciting meetings for her reason, and produces partial insanity, that is what the Methodist calls experiencing religion. . . . Reason should be the basis of religion, but unfortunately it too frequently occurs that the reason has to be chased from the mind to make room for the spurious coin that is palmed off as religion.[27]

The religion that Ezra Cornell made for himself was an uncritical deism, which dispensed with sin, the atonement, all formal Christian theology. He believed that God was directing the affairs of this world toward a good end and that science was the newest means of God's revelation. Herein he reflected, perhaps, the influence of popular positivism. He urged his wife to describe him as one who

most sincerely believes in the divine goodness of the being who created us, and as sincerely disbelieves that he ever entertained other than feelings of love toward the works of his own hand. I have no doubt that God's first and unalterable design was good will to man. The happiness of man is the completion and perfection of his works. Anything short of the full and complete happiness of man would mar the grand design of the architect of the heavens.

The truth of religion, he wrote again, can be tested by its effects.

[Religion] should be so expounded that the hearer could embrace it as a practical reality, and put it to an everyday use, make it his rule of action in

---

[26] A. J. Lamoureaux '74, in *Era*, May 1907, p. 394.

[27] EC to his wife, 12 March 1854 and 23 Feb. 1851. Also 19 Dec. 1871: "The greatest fault [of cousin Monroe] is that he is a Baptist, but that fault he inherited."

the daily business occurrences of life. . . . But the gospel as it is preached . . . falls more like a mildew upon a benighted world, and tries to shield the deformities of the dead and putrid carcass of "the Church" from the penetrating eye of advancing science and enlightened humanity. . . . The steam engine, the railroad and the electric telegraph are the great engines of reformation, and by the time we enter upon the twentieth century the present will be looked back to as we now look back to the dark ages. . . . A new era in religion and humanity will have arrived.[28]

With such convictions, he could hardly be comfortable in any church but the Unitarian. The First Unitarian Society of Ithaca was established in 1865, and Cornell was a regular attendant until his death.

In sum, Ezra Cornell was, in Carl Becker's words, a "tough-minded idealist." He was a visionary builder, too optimistic to be the perfect businessman, too ready to hazard everything on his confidence in the future. Such men are often undone by their faith, and indeed Cornell's own life ended in something near financial disaster. But he was not building for the brief term. The foundations that he laid were intended to endure, and will endure, for centuries.

He wrote a kind of *apologia pro vita sua* in 1865, in answer to vicious attacks on his character and purpose. He remarked that all his wealth was the product of his own labor, which had given him a share in a business which had grown with the growth of the country. All his forebears and relatives were mechanics or farmers.

All have procured an honest and competent support for their families by *productive labor;* none but myself have acquired anything like a fortune, and mine is placed at the disposal of the industrial classes. . . .

I never in any instance exacted or accepted in any form more than 7% for money loaned [a low rate of interest at the time], and the only loans which I have made to individuals have been to persons who were unable to furnish such securities as capitalists or bankers exact, and who required the money to protect their business and property from the grasp of the usurer, or from some misfortune in business—to young men to purchase farms or to engage in business—to widows of soldiers to purchase a small house, and for like objects. I have $100,000 thus invested, on what bankers call doubtful securities, but the loans are such as humanity demanded, and the security such as the parties could give. . . .

My ruling passion is to dispose of so much of my property as is not re-

---

[28] EC to his wife, 20 Aug. 1843, 2 April 1854. See also his letter to Mrs. Alonzo B. Cornell, 24 Sept. 1854, quoted in Albert W. Smith, *Ezra Cornell* (Ithaca, 1934), p. 209.

quired for the reasonable wants of my family in a manner that shall do the greatest good to the greatest number of the industrial classes of my native state.

Such was the Founder of Cornell University. Looking back at him with the perspective of a century, we may rejoice that the University bears the name of such a man. He appears to us still as he appeared in the flesh to the English historian James Anthony Froude: "Mr. Cornell would be a sublime figure anywhere; he seems to me the most surprising and venerable object I have seen in America." [29]

[29] Quoted in *Proceedings and Addresses at the Twenty-fifth Anniversary of the Opening of Cornell University* (Ithaca, 1893), p. 46. Froude visited the University for a lecture series in 1872.

III

Andrew D. White

IT is a sobering thought to your historian, had he need of one, that he has personally known every President of Cornell University except Charles Kendall Adams, and every Acting President except William Channing Russel. In the college year 1912–13 he was one of the editors of the *Cornell Era*. The editors had two obsessing aims: to obtain tolerable matter, free of cost, to fill their pages, and to survive long enough to bequeath the accumulated deficit to a new board of editors. In pursuance of the first purpose a committee, including your historian, waited twice upon former President White. He received us cordially in his study, walled with books, furnished with ponderous oak and weighty mementos, a perfect setting for the serene scholar. Mr. White was all courtly grace. He sat in his easy chair, his square white beard bobbing, his pince-nez flashing; he inquired eagerly of our problems, talked of *Cornell Era*'s and editors of the past. He wrote for us, indeed, an article on the lessons of his long life. At eighty he was still eager to give good advice. Unhappily, your historian is unable to remember what it was.

Andrew Dickson White was born on 7 November 1832 in Homer, New York, twenty-five miles distant from Ithaca and twenty-five from Ezra Cornell's boyhood home in De Ruyter. If there is anything in the theory of the *genius loci*, the character of the two men must have been subject to the same influences of climate, soil, food, and environing ideas and ideals. But there was a difference. Ezra Cornell's folk were farmers and artisans, barely literate; Andrew D. White's people were well-to-do, dealers in money, well served in spacious houses. His grandfather, Andrew Dickson, had been the richest man in the township and a member of the State legislature; his father, Horace White, became one of the leading bankers of Syracuse. In the old Anglo-Saxon distinction, the Whites were thanes, the Cornells ceorls, churls.

When Andrew was seven the family moved to Syracuse. The boy was fortunate in finding there some excellent schoolmasters, to whom he ever rendered his gratitude. If not a prodigy, he was an eager student, insatiably curious. He is said to have built a working printing press at ten, a steam engine pulling a miniature train at twelve. He certainly performed electrical experiments in the basement of the Syracuse home. His family foresaw great things, coddled his poor health, gave him a sense of destiny.

There was a closet drama, barely hinted in his *Autobiography*, and due to have its sequel in the great drama of Cornell University. His father was senior warden of the Episcopal Church; his mother's devotion was ardent and unquestioning. Their beloved clergyman was "a medieval saint," a militant High-Churchman, who taught that without the Protestant Episcopal Church there was no salvation—*extra ecclesiam Anglicanam nulla salus*. At about the age of twelve, Andrew's confusions grew to be doubts, his doubts rebellions on the ground of conscience. He ceased to recite certain phrases of the Creed. And he refused to be confirmed.[1] Thus he betrays the character of his maturity: insistence on the satisfaction of reason as a preliminary to action, and obstinate refusal to yield to any pressures of expediency or emotion when a principle is at stake.

He dreamed of Yale or Harvard; his father, in the hope of reclaiming the lost sheep, decreed attendance at the church college, Geneva, later to become Hobart. He entered Geneva College in 1849, at sixteen, and owing to his evident superiority was immediately put in the sophomore class.

"The college was at its lowest ebb," he says in his *Autobiography* (a book which every Cornellian—and not Cornellians only—should read).

Of discipline there was none; there were about forty students [in actual fact, thirty-seven], the majority of them, sons of wealthy churchmen, showing

---

[1] His mother, the twenty-first of an unstated month, 1870, pleads with him to be confirmed, to save his soul from damnation (letter, C.U. Archives).

ANDREW DICKSON WHITE, President 1866–1885

no inclination to work and much tendency to dissipation. The authorities of the college could not afford to expel or even offend a student, for its endowment was so small that it must have all the instruction fees possible, and must keep on good terms with the wealthy fathers of its scapegrace students. The scapegraces soon found this out, and the result was a little pandemonium. Only about a dozen of our number studied at all; the rest, by translations, promptings, and evasions escaped without labor. I have had to do since, as student, professor, or lecturer, with some half-dozen large universities at home and abroad, and in all of these together have not seen so much carousing and wild dissipation as I then saw in this little "Church college" of which the especial boast was that, owing to the small number of its students, it was "able to exercise a direct Christian influence upon every young man committed to its care." . . . It was my privilege to behold a professor, an excellent clergyman, seeking to quell a hideous riot in a student's room, buried under a heap of carpets, mattresses, counterpanes, and blankets; to see another clerical professor forced to retire through the panel of a door under a shower of lexicons, boots, and brushes, and to see even the president himself, on one occasion, obliged to leave his lecture-room by a ladder from a window, and, on another, kept at bay by a shower of beer-bottles.

Among his other memories is that of a stuffed wolf, dressed in a surplice, adorning the chapel roof.

It was a lonely year for young Andrew. True, he was elected a member of the Sigma Phi fraternity and he made a few lasting friends. True, there were two or three of the professors whom he respected and admired. But on the whole, college life—which, to be sure, he saw at its nadir in America—was a bitter disappointment to the budding intellectual. His year at Geneva left with him a lifelong distrust of clerical control of higher education.

The best of his hours were spent in the library of the Hermean Society, which numbered all of four thousand volumes. Here he had an experience momentous for the future Cornell University. He happened, he says in his *Autobiography*, upon a fine volume depicting the English universities.

As I read in this new-found book of the colleges at Oxford and Cambridge, and pored over the engraved views of quadrangles, halls, libraries, chapels,— of all the noble and dignified belongings of a great seat of learning,—my heart sank within me. Every feature of the little American college seemed all the more sordid. But gradually I began consoling myself by building air-castles. These took the form of structures suited to a great university:—with distinguished professors in every field, with libraries as rich as the Bodleian, halls as lordly as that of Christ Church or of Trinity, chapels as inspiring as that of King's, towers as dignified as those of Magdalen or Merton, quadrangles as beautiful as those of Jesus and St. John's. In the midst of all other occupations I was constantly rearing these structures on that queenly site above the finest of the New York lakes, and dreaming of a university worthy of the commonwealth and of the nation. This dream became a sort of obsession. It came upon me during my working hours, in the class-rooms, in rambles along the lake shore, in the evenings, when I paced up and down the walks in front of the college buildings, and saw rising in their place and extending to the pretty knoll behind them, the worthy home of a great university. But this university, though beautiful and dignified, like those at Oxford and Cambridge, was in two important respects very unlike them. First, I made provision for other studies beside classics and mathematics. There should be professors in the great modern literatures—above all, in our own; there should also be a professor of modern history and a lecturer on architecture. And next, my university should be under control of no single religious organization; it should be free from all sectarian or party trammels; in electing its trustees and professors no questions should be asked as to their belief or their attachment to this or that sect or party.

How happy is the man who in youth discovers his dream, who in maturity fulfills it, who in his decline sees other men take it up and carry it even beyond the scope of his young imagination!

After his year in Geneva College, Andrew was determined not to return there. His father was equally determined that he should. Here was a head-on collision of wills. Andrew D. White revealed the qualities of the future diplomat, inflexibly set upon his end, but willing to yield on the form. He duly presented himself at Geneva for enrollment, and then doubled back to the village of Moravia, taking refuge with one of his former masters in the Syracuse Academy. He informed his parents that his intention was to prepare for admission to Yale. Horace White was furious, averring that he would rather have received news of his son's death than of such a disgrace. After a few months, of course, the matter was compounded, through the intercession of Andrew's mother. Meanwhile he read steadily for the Yale entrance examination.

Early in January 1851 his father conducted him to New Haven, making a desperate diversion to tempt him into Trinity, the Episcopalian college in Hartford. As a bribe, he offered to give his son the best private library in the United States. But Andrew would not waver. The overcoming of his awesome father was, he asserts, probably the greatest diplomatic triumph of his career.

Naturally he passed the examination brilliantly, and, though he had missed the fall term, was entered as a member of the sophomore class.

The years at Yale were on the whole happy and rewarding. The undergraduate body contained a number of exceptional young men, marked for future eminence. Andrew was evidently popular. He was elected to Skull and Bones, joined a rowing club,[2] and was familiarly known as "Toots." He won most of the essay and declamation prizes, displaying already a mature power of analysis, a cultivated prose style, and a certain intellectual arrogance. And he suffered from the eye trouble, headaches, and fits of depression which were to afflict him throughout his life.[3]

But for the "Yale system" of education, as he was subjected to it, he has little good to say. "Instruction at Yale in those years was at the lowest point, so far as I know, that it has touched in any modern nation." [4] And again, in his *Autobiography:* "Never was a man more disappointed at first. . . . There was too much reciting by rote and too little real intercourse between teacher and taught. The instructor sat in a box, heard students' translations without indicating anything better, and their answers to questions with very few suggestions or remarks." The work in classics dealt with grammatical construction alone. In a course in science, or Natural Philosophy, the textbook was merely recited, in the Chinese manner. "Almost as bad was the historical instruction given by Professor James Hadley. It consisted simply in hearing the student repeat from memory the dates from 'Pütz's Ancient History.' " Alone, Professor Noah Porter and President Theodore Dwight Woolsey succeeded sometimes in breaking through the paralyzing system. "Strange to say, there was not, during my whole course at Yale, a lecture upon any period, subject, or person in literature, ancient or modern." The celebrated Benjamin Silliman climbed, by ladder, out of the dungeon he used for a laboratory to lecture on science; White followed the Yale fashion of paying no attention.

After his graduation in July 1853, White lingered for a few months, undecided, in New Haven. In December he and his friend Daniel Coit Gilman, Yale '52, destined to be the first president of Johns Hopkins University, sailed for Europe. White's passport tells us that his height

---

[2] It has been often written that White was a member of the Yale crew. There was in fact no Yale crew; there were only boating clubs. White rowed occasionally in the eight-oared shell; he was certainly too short in stature and light in weight to have been chosen for serious contests.

[3] Letters to his mother, 13 July and 15 Oct. 1852, 13 July 1853.

[4] *Yale Literary Magazine*, Feb. 1886.

was 5 feet 5 inches, his eyes blue, his hair and complexion light, his nose and forehead ordinary. The passport omits mention of his quick, nervous energy, of his earnest, even priggish manner, of his ready outbursts of impassioned eloquence.

After a thrilling visit to Oxford he went to Paris. He lodged with a French schoolteacher, who became a lifelong friend. He studied French, saw the proper sights, attended the correct theatres, followed courses in history at the Sorbonne and the Collège de France, and read widely, especially in French history. He learned also the delights of buying books. Throughout his life the collection, care, and reading of books was his dearest occupation and solace. In Paris, at twenty-one, he began assembling that precious store which is now the Andrew D. White Library of Cornell University.

In the autumn of 1854 young Mr. White was appointed attaché—in fact, French interpreter—to former Governor Thomas Hart Seymour of Connecticut, Minister to Russia. The experience was valuable in many ways, chiefly as an introduction to diplomatic routine and manners, with useful lessons in human behavior. White met the ministers who were shaping Russian destiny. "This gave me some chance also to make my historical studies more real by close observation of a certain sort of men who have had the making of far too much history."

In the summer of 1855 he returned from St. Petersburg to Paris. In the autumn he went to Berlin, matriculated at the University, and followed the lectures of the galaxy of German professors who were remaking the concept of historical study. And of course he developed his taste for music, and of course he made the ritual journey to Italy.

He found in Germany a kind of culture unknown in Syracuse, Geneva, and New Haven. It was composed of intellectual vigor directing material advance, of profound respect for abstract thought and thinkers, of broad freedom of speculation, of state generosity toward universities, professors, musicians, artists.

More than sixty years later the United States declared war on Germany. The heartbroken old man looked down on the thronging campus, and wrote (17 April 1917) to a German-American friend, Christian Sihler of Cleveland:

I have ever since my boyhood loved Germany. . . . The two nations once seemed predestined each to give the other what it needed and each to stir in the children of the other the noblest thoughts. . . . Germany a second mother country. . . . What a blessed dream then was my life in Germany. . . . I look out on the students in training. . . . Anguish. . . .

White returned to the United States in July 1856, with such a scholarly equipment as few Americans could match. He was probably one of the hundred best-educated men in the country. How should he use his privileged quality? The Episcopal ministry, for which he felt aesthetic yearnings, was closed to him by his rationalist convictions. But he later alleged that if such men as Phillips Brooks and Bishop Henry C. Potter had then been in the church he would undoubtedly have taken orders.[5] He thought of authorship. (His mother proposed to have his letters from Europe published, and he was not averse.) He discussed buying a farm, the kind of Horatian farm on which he could sit and meditate and write. He was much tempted to study law at Harvard. His father urged him to go into politics, to help elect Fremont. In later life he regretted that he had not chosen journalism or architecture. He ended by spending a year in New Haven, reading, arranging his already remarkable library, writing magazine articles, and taking an M.A. in the offhand way of the time. The Yale authorities hinted at the professorship of history, but President Woolsey took fright at reports of young Mr. White's broad religious views. History at Yale must needs be regarded from a sound Congregational viewpoint.[6]

The suggestion of his next step was, he tells us, an overheard remark of President Francis Wayland of Brown University: "The best field of work for graduates is now in the west." The suggestion fitted with his mood of bafflement and resentment in New Haven. He wrote to influential friends, and in 1857 received the offer of a professorship of history at the University of Michigan, the new, free, unconventional university.

But before accompanying White to the distant west, we may well contemplate the state of higher education in the mid-century.

It was, said White, "as stagnant as a Spanish convent, and as self-satisfied as a Bourbon duchy."[7] The concept of a college and its organization descended from seventeenth-century Oxford and Cambridge. The curriculum consisted of Latin, Greek, and mathematics,

[5] ADW to W. T. Hewett, 1894.

[6] ADW to his mother, 23 July 1857; *Autobiography of Andrew Dickson White* (New York, 1905), II, 557. Carl Becker (*Cornell University: Founders and the Founding* [Ithaca: Cornell University Press, 1943], p. 229) cites the first draft of the *Autobiography*, to the effect that President Woolsey consulted a college tutor as to White's fitness. The tutor was adverse, because of White's lack of interest in revivals and prayer meetings.

[7] *Autobiography*, I, 272.

moral philosophy and Christian Evidences, and timid excursions into very elementary science. The chief purpose of higher education was taken to be the disciplining of the mind, with some regard for the professional training of the clergy.

The free spirits of the eighteenth century had done their best to break the crust of educational tradition. Benjamin Franklin, Thomas Jefferson, President Samuel Johnson of King's College (our Columbia), Provost William Smith of the University of Pennsylvania, advocated a practical education adjusted to the needs of American life. At King's College in 1754 even "Agriculture" and "Merchandise" were proposed for the freshman year. The College of William and Mary and the University of Virginia were in their time homes of educational dissent.[8]

By about 1820 the revolutionary impulse had spent itself, in education as in ordinary life. Only in the University of Virginia did the spirit of Jeffersonian liberalism linger. Some few of the eighteenth-century innovations, as in the teaching of geology, meteorology, and political economy, were incorporated in the curricula of Harvard, Yale, and Brown, but they were regarded less as useful furniture for the mind than as variant means of discipline. The colleges in general settled back to what Sydney Smith called "the safe and elegant imbecility of classical learning." A Harvard professor, about 1845, introduced a revolting German to his class with the words:

This is Professor Blank. He has read Cicero through every year for fifty years for the sake of settling some important questions. He has discovered that while *necese est* may be used either with the accusative and infinitive or with *ut* and the subjunctive, *necesse erat* can be used only before *ut* with the subjunctive. I should think it well worth living for to have made that discovery.[9]

Here and there certain dissatisfactions manifested themselves. Union College established in the 1820's an alternative course, concentrating on science and modern literature, and in 1845 it offered the first engineering course connected with a regular college. Amherst in 1827 complained of the neglect of modern languages and proposed a Department of the Science of Education. President Wayland of Brown in 1850 called, though vainly, for freedom of choice among studies and the adaptation of education to the country's needs. He said: "Our

[8] Becker, *Founders*, ch. i, "Life and Learning in the United States"; Ernest Earnest, *Academic Procession* (Indianapolis, 1953); Louis F. Snow, *The College Curriculum in the United States* (New York, 1907).

[9] George F. Hoar, *Autobiography of Seventy Years* (New York, 1903), I, 98.

colleges are not filled because we do not furnish the education desired by the people."

Against the radical suggestion that the colleges should be service institutions, the conservatives quoted—and indeed they still quote—the famous Yale Report of 1828. It was "a charter, a bill of rights in collegiate history." [10] The cause it represented, says Carl Becker, was

the traditional conception . . . of the purpose of learning and the function of colleges in the community. According to that conception, the function of such institutions was to preserve and transmit rather than to increase knowledge; and more especially to prepare a select group of young men, taken for the most part from the educated and governing classes, for the learned professions by giving them a limited command of the classical tongues, and transmitting to them the factual knowledge and ideas about man and the world in which he lived that would lend support to the political institutions, the moral habits, and the religious convictions acceptable to the best progressive-conservative thought of the time. The end desired, as the Yale Report said, was the disciplined and informed mind; but a mind disciplined to conformity and informed with nothing that a patriotic, Christian, and clubable gentleman had better not know.[11]

Discipline the teachers may have enforced; intellectual curiosity they could not communicate, since most of them, chosen for their innocuous orthodoxy, and often because they were deserving clergymen in failing health, were entirely incurious themselves. The famous Mark Hopkins, president and professor of philosophy at Williams, admitted readily that he had never got beyond the first paragraph of the *Critique of Pure Reason,* and he could not understand that paragraph. It might have done Mark Hopkins good to sit on one end of a log with Immanuel Kant at the other. Louis Agassiz, professor at Harvard in the 1850's, called that institution "a respectable high school where they taught the dregs of learning." Henry Cabot Lodge, who was in Harvard from 1867 to 1871, said that, except in Henry Adams's course in medieval history, "I never really studied anything, never had my mind roused to any exertion or to anything resembling active thought." [12]

Since the colleges refused all composition with the educational needs of the public, the public regarded the colleges with distrust, if not

[10] Snow, *College Curriculum,* p. 142.   [11] *Founders,* p. 19.

[12] G. Stanley Hall, *Life and Confessions of a Psychologist* (New York, 1923), p. 169; Edward D. Eddy, *Colleges for Our Land and Time* (New York, 1957), p. 3; Allan Nevins, *Emergence of Modern America* (New York, 1927), p. 265.

contempt. From this period dates the concept of the college man as a weakling dude, a pedant, incompetent in the struggle for life—a concept which endured even into the twentieth century. Some statistics gathered by President F. A. P. Barnard of Columbia in 1870 indicate the steady dwindling of college enrollments, in relation to population. His figures show among the white population the proportion of one college student to 1,549 people in 1840; of one to 2,012 in 1860; and one to 2,546 in 1869.[13] (The proportion of college students to the white population in 1960 was one to 41.)

The rebellion against the aristocratic colleges came naturally from the people, and naturally it was strongest in the democratic west. The idea of a "manual-labor" college, where poor students could work for their education, took shape in the 1830's. Oberlin, combining manual labor, coeducation, free admission of Negroes, evangelical religion, the Graham-cracker diet, and abstention from alcohol, tobacco, tea, coffee, and pepper, opened its doors in 1833. Twenty years later Horace Mann established Antioch College, with a liberal, even radical spirit. He emphasized scientific and historical studies, and conducted class-room discussions on such subjects as soil fertilization and the economics of public charities. There were other free-minded colleges in the midwest. Of these the greatest was certainly the University of Michigan.

It was opened officially in 1841. Ten years later Henry Philip Tappan was called to the presidency. Tappan, professor of philosophy at New York University, knew Europe well and admired the organization of the German universities. He abolished the dormitory system and there-with the principle of faculty parentalism, the supervision of student behavior. He established departments of physics and civil engineering, and the first graduate program in the United States. He taught a course in English literature, with readings from contemporary poets. He in-vited eminent professors and lecturers from the east and from abroad.

Evidently Andrew D. White was just the man Tappan needed. He appointed the twenty-four-year-old scholar professor of history, at a salary of $1,000 for the first year, to be raised thereafter to $1,500.

White celebrated his establishment in the world by marrying, on 24 September 1857, Miss Mary Outwater of Syracuse. Tributes to her beauty, social grace, and character abound; her letters are those of a rarely intelligent, high-minded woman. The couple arrived in Ann Arbor in October, bringing Andrew's extraordinary library and the

[13] Earnest, *Academic Procession,* p. 125.

first grand piano in town. (The piano is now in the Heller House on Eddy Street, Ithaca.)

White's coming to Michigan has been likened to that of Chrysoloras in Florence five centuries before, bringing the Renaissance to the west.[14]

He recalls his unhappy first impression in his *Autobiography*. The university "was a flat, square inclosure of forty acres, unkempt and wretched. Throughout its whole space there were not more than a score of trees outside the building sites allotted to professors; unsightly plank walks connected the buildings, and in every direction were meandering paths, which in dry weather were dusty and in wet weather muddy." The students were as uncouth as their surroundings. Uncouth, in comparison to Yale men, and ill prepared for college. But they were serious, hungry for knowledge. "It may be granted," he says, "that there was, in many of them, a lack of elegance, but there was neither languor nor cynicism. One seemed, among them, to breathe a purer, stronger air."

White flung himself into his work, lecturing with impassioned earnestness, devising new schemes of instruction, displaying precious documents from his library to bring the past in strange Europe to life, encouraging investigation and independent judgment, trying to inculcate a sense of the philosophy of history, inviting his classes every fortnight to an evening in his home. His students, who were mostly close to his own age, adored him. One of the best of them, Charles Kendall Adams, was to succeed White as President of Cornell University.

Revolted at the barren ugliness about him, he began setting out avenues of elms and evergreens on the campus. The astounded authorities made him Superintendent of the Grounds, with a salary of seventy-five dollars per year. He persuaded the students to help him, each planter having his tree named and recorded.

A half century later, on a spring day of 1912, the Dean of the Medical School observed an elderly man on the campus, consulting a sheet of paper and patting each tree in turn. The Dean recognized him. Mr. White explained that he had reflected that just fifty-one years before, the Class of 1861 had set out these trees, under his direction. Half of the graduates had enlisted in the Union armies. Mr. White

[14] Herbert B. Adams, *The Study of History in American Colleges* (Bureau of Education Circular of Information 2; Washington, 1887), p. 97.

brought his old planting plan to Ann Arbor for his memorial rite. He said sadly: "There are more trees alive than boys." [15]

All the boys are long since dead, but many of their trees still cast a grateful shade on the lawns of the Michigan campus. White learned a great deal in Michigan. He learned how to teach, discovering that good teaching is mostly the communication of enthusiasm, that it requires an impulse of passion in the teacher. He lost his conventional eastern prejudices among his frontier students. He saw a nonsectarian college in successful operation. He found unusual freedom granted to the students and thought that it was seldom abused. He observed the wise devices of a great president, Henry Philip Tappan. "To no man is any success I may have afterward had in the administration of Cornell University so greatly due as to him." [16] He accepted Tappan's conception of a university, with medicine, law, engineering on a parity with arts and letters, and with integration in the public-school system of the state. He was impressed by the system of visiting university lecturers. These included such men as Ralph Waldo Emerson, Wendell Phillips, Carl Schurz, and George William Curtis.

Curtis, eminent man of letters, spent an evening in White's home. The host, disarmed by the guest's geniality, was moved to reveal his secret preoccupation.

There, in the warmth and confidence of his friendship, [White] unfolded to me his idea of the great work that should be done in the great State of New York. Surely, he said, in the greatest state there should be the greatest of universities; in central New York there should arise a university which by the amplitude of its endowment and by the whole scope of its intended sphere, by the character of the studies in the whole scope of the curriculum, should satisfy the wants of the hour. More than that, said he, it should begin at the beginning. It should take hold of the chief interest of this country, which is agriculture; then it should rise—step by step, grade by grade—until it fulfilled the highest ideal of what a university should be. It was also his intention that there should be no man, wherever he might be—on the other side of the ocean or on this side—who might be a fitting teacher of men, who should not be drawn within the sphere of the university. Until the hour was late this young scholar dreamed aloud to me these dreams; and at the close, our parting, our consolation was that we lived in a country that was open to

---

[15] Walter F. Willcox, "White's Trees," *The Cornell Plantations*, Winter 1956–1957, p. 19. The date of the incident has been corrected by consultation of White's diary.

[16] *Autobiography*, I, 281.

every generous idea, and that it was still a possibility that his dream one day might be realized.

Ten years later, at the Inauguration of Cornell University on 7 October 1868, Curtis spoke these words.

Horace White died in September 1860, leaving his widow and two sons. Andrew's share of the estate amounted to about $300,000, a very handsome sum indeed. The troubles of settling a large property, the outbreak of the Civil War, and ill health determined him to take a long leave of absence from Michigan, beginning in the summer of 1862. He says that he attempted to enlist in the Union forces, but was rejected for physical reasons. (However, he did not want to be drafted; Judge Cooley wrote him from Ann Arbor, 12 August 1862: "If you chance to be drafted I will see that a substitute is provided as you request.") He returned to Syracuse and threw himself into war work.

The old obsession haunted him still. In August 1862 he wrote, after making repeated drafts, a proposal to Gerrit Smith, wealthy reformer and abolitionist of Peterboro, New York, near Syracuse.[17] He proposed nothing less than "a new university, worthy of our land and time." To help in founding and building such a university had long been his aim. Now, having inherited a substantial fortune, he was anxious to devote the greater part of it to his purpose.

"There is needed," he wrote, "a truly great university."

First, to secure a place where the most highly prized instruction may be afforded to *all*—regardless of sex or color.

Secondly, to turn the current of mercantile morality which has so long swept through this land.

Thirdly, to temper and restrain the current of military passion which is to sweep through the land hereafter.

Fourthly, to afford an asylum for Science—where truth shall be sought for truth's sake, where it shall not be the main purpose of the Faculty to stretch or cut science exactly to fit "Revealed Religion."

Fifthly, to afford a center and a school for a new Literature—not graceful and indifferent to wrong but earnest—nerved and armed to battle for the right.

Sixthly, to give a chance for instruction in moral philosophy, history and political economy unwarped to suit present abuses in politics and religion.

Seventhly, to secure the rudiments, at least, of a legal training in which Legality shall not crush Humanity.

[17] The entire letter is reproduced in Becker's *Founders,* pp. 154–158.

Eighthly, to modify the existing plan of education in matters of detail where it is in vain to hope improvement from the existing universities.

Ninthly, to afford a nucleus around which liberally-minded men of learning—men scattered throughout the land, comparatively purposeless and powerless,—could cluster, making this institution a center from which ideas and men shall go forth to bless the nation during ages.

Such an institution must be splendidly endowed, to force respect from the public and its inevitable enemies. "To admit women and colored persons into a *petty* college would do good to the individuals concerned; but to admit them to a great university would be a blessing to the whole colored race and the whole female sex—for the weaker colleges would be finally compelled to adopt the system." He adjures, promises, and seeks to inspire. He concludes: "I write in one of the darkest periods of our national history; but I remember that the great University of Leyden was founded when Holland was lying in ruins."

Here, in its essentials, is the plan of Cornell University. Here also is the mind of Andrew D. White—his fervor, his broad humanitarianism (with special notice of Negroes and women), his hostility to organized dogmatic churches, his concept of literature and history as moral and social forces. But—and this is a little curious—he seems not to have thought of the opportunities for technical and agricultural education offered by the Morrill Land Grant Act, passed only a month before the writing of his letter.

Gerrit Smith replied that his health was very poor and he really could not think about establishing a university. Thus it happens that these words are written in Ithaca and not from a Gerrit Smith University of Peterboro, New York.

White continued to work on his dream university. He revised the curriculum, calculated costs, sketched buildings. He had a friend inspect Holworthy Hall at Harvard, considered America's model dormitory. And no doubt he looked in vain for a patron.

In the late autumn of 1862, troubled by a severe dyspepsia, he went abroad, with the quixotic idea of rallying British opinion to the Union cause. He wrote public letters and pamphlets, without much effect. He spent the spring and summer on the Continent, taking health cures and buying books.

Shortly after his return to America, he was nominated, to his amazement, Republican candidate from the Syracuse district for the New York State Senate. The only reason for his selection, he says, was a deadlock between two rival candidates. There was certainly another reason. He was uncommitted, inoffensive; he was also fairly well known as a young man of brilliant promise, a compelling speaker, politically orthodox, and the well-to-do son of the mighty Syracuse banker.

He was elected, and took his seat in Albany on 2 January 1864. For obvious reasons he was appointed chairman of the Committee on Literature, which dealt with education. The youngest Senator (he was thirty-one), he found himself immediately in conflict with the august Ezra Cornell, chairman of the Committee on Agriculture.

And now, as Cornell University is about to be born, we may look for a moment at the man who most determined its form, its character, its ideal.

In 1871 someone who obviously knew White well described him as a small man, very slight, weighing not over 120 pounds, all energy and endurance, but stooped under mental labor and thought. His mouth was large, his blue eyes mild and intelligent. His hair was light auburn, his complexion fair almost to boyishness.[18] (He was sensitive about his short stature; I am told, on good authority, that he wore elevator shoes.) At this period he displayed a coquettish fringe of whisker under each jaw for about four inches from the ear lobes, leaving the cheeks, the mobile mouth and chin, free. Those of us who remembered him in old age see his white moustache and square white beard, brushed sideways from the middle, still coquettishly. We see in memory the invariable formality of his dress, the square-topped derby already outmoded in our youth. We remember also his air of kindly dignity as he took his way from his house to the Library. "The President's Walk," the tree-lined avenue was termed. His progress was constantly interrupted. To each interlocutor, man, woman, or adoring campus child, he would ceremoniously doff his derby.

His health was always bad. From childhood on he complained of eye trouble, sick headaches, dyspepsia. Nervous indigestion, we might say, perhaps even a gastric ulcer. At any rate, he was intensely emotional, even excitable, and his emotions operated on his physical being. When at work on some task of importance, he would push himself to the edge of collapse. His friend Dr. Stebbins of the Unitarian Church called him "a Leyden jar ready to discharge." White once wrote to Ezra Cornell: "Within the past few days the physicians have ordered me to stop

[18] A Vicksburg, Miss., newspaper clipping, 21 Feb. 1871, in ADW Papers. The ADW Papers, as in general others of unspecified provenience, are in the Cornell University Archives.

work. I shall not. It is not *work* that wears me out—it is waiting." [19] Surely he was right; it was waiting, agitation, worry, that made the evil deposits in his stomach.

He could work endlessly, but only if the purpose was passionately sought. The routine of administration bored him; most of his later troubles at Cornell arose from his eagerness to abandon the tiresome tasks and to escape for months or years.

His queasy stomach imposed moderation upon him. He wrote in 1870: "I never smoke and never take a glass of wine save three or four times a year when wine is set before friends." [20] Later, however, he began to take pride in his well-chosen cellar, and he would yield to a good cigar.

Born to wealth, he never knew insecurity. He was early imbued with a respect for property and was always an excellent manager of material possessions. On 1 January 1875 he reckoned his wealth at $595,459.78, and it remained at approximately that figure.

"In the intellectual, no less than in the financial sense, Mr. White always lived, as one may say, in easy circumstances," says Carl Becker.[21]

There is no evidence that he ever experienced, even in the mildest form, any intellectual or spiritual crisis, or even that he was ever seriously troubled by doubt or disillusionment.[22] He exercised in the happiest, most unconscious way the will to believe. Never given to the critical examination of fundamentals, all of his thinking was in the nature of a facile manipulation of wide knowledge and varied experience in the support of certain general ideas which he, like so many men of his generation, appropriated from the main current of thought, and cherished with the emotional conviction that commonly sustains a religious faith.

The general ideas of enlightened liberals of the period have already been summarized. They were inspired by an optimistic faith in progress, in the eventual triumph of the good, the true, the beautiful, under the urge of resistless evolutionary forces. The general ideas pointed the duty of the intelligent man—to aid and hasten human progress, by seeking understanding of history's lessons, by espousing worthy causes, by battling the obscurantism that lingers in the dogmatic churches, venal politics, unjust social structures, and by enlightening the unen-

[19] 5 Dec. 1872, EC Papers.   [20] ADW to W. C. Russel, 27 Dec. 1870.
[21] *Founders*, p. 77.
[22] I disagree, in that I posit a spiritual crisis at about the age of twelve and a period of disillusionment at Yale.

lightened. For if only men are instructed of the truth they will choose the path of virtue.

Of his own enlightenment White had not a moment's question. Fortified by his knowledge of history and of foreign lands, he knew his judgments to be superior to those of the uninstructed. Never, or almost never, in all his voluminous writings, does he suggest that he may have been mistaken. This serene confidence arose in part from his family background and conditioning. He could not help it if he belonged to the small minority, the gentlemen of wealth and breeding. Not for worlds would he have revealed the condescension, but the condescension was there. Some part of his loneliness in the early years of his presidency at Cornell was caused by his secret conviction that only three companions—Goldwin Smith, Willard Fiske, and William Channing Russel—were his social equals.

His intellectual merit was genuine. He was a mighty reader, always in the midst of a large, sober volume in German, French, or Italian. His interest was mostly in the history of the centuries immediately preceding our own, in which the embryonic forms of our day can be discerned. He had little concern with archaeology or folklore, little time for fiction, and none for poetry. The historical knowledge he sought was useful knowledge.

He had young a sense of destiny, encouraged by his family and friends. His gifts and his advantages laid upon him a cruel burden of obligation. How should he employ his gifts and advantages? The answer was never clear. He was pulled in contrary directions. Loving scholarly ease, loving the enormous parade of the past which we call history, he felt his destiny to be the interpretation, by spoken and written words, of man's upward struggle. Much of his intellectual life was devoted to one insistent theme: the history of the warfare of science with theology in Christendom.[23] He was a brilliant, an impassioned

[23] His book, with that title, was first inspired by the warfare of free inquiry with Protestantism attending the opening of Cornell University. The title, he says, was forced upon him by circumstances (ADW to Willard Fiske, 28 May 1889), but he called it in jest his "Histoire de la bêtise humaine." The book appeared, in its final form, in two fat volumes in 1896. It is still in print at this writing. An anonymous reviewer of a new edition says in the London *Times Literary Supplement* (14 Oct. 1955): "White's thesis is simple. In the conflict between science and religion, the theologians have always been in the wrong; and the sooner theological control of the universities is ended, the better it will be both for science and for religion. . . . It is sustained with amazing learning. The book would be a marvel even if White had composed it wholly in his library at Cornell . . . and when

lecturer. "Such words of fire I have not known in any other lecture-room," said his disciple, George Lincoln Burr '81. The syllabi of his historical courses at Cornell, leading the students to a common search for a philosophy of history, must inspire in any teacher the profoundest respect.

But after a period of immersion in the scholarly life, White would become restless. Was he not destined for the larger stage? Should be not make history instead of recording it? We have seen him as State Senator; he was to serve the public in many other posts, as Commissioner to Santo Domingo, as Minister and Ambassador to Germany, as Minister to Russia, as president of the American delegation at the Hague Peace Conference in 1899. When a summons to public service came, he would always groan at being torn from his beloved studies. But he nearly always yielded.

How high did his ambition vault? He was talked of for the governorship of New York many times between 1872 and 1900, but he refused to advance his candidacy. He had no desire to compete in the state's politics. His name was frequently mentioned as a possibility for Secretary of State, and doubtless he would have welcomed such an appointment. At the Republican Convention of 1884 he was regarded as a dark horse for the presidential nomination. But James G. Blaine was chosen —and defeated in the election. Again, White was boomed for the Republican vice-presidential nomination in 1900. He was sixty-eight years old, and tired; he discouraged his partisans. But if he had been picked in place of Theodore Roosevelt, he would have been our twenty-sixth President.

However, he suffered one serious drawback as a competitor for an elective post. It was whispered that he was unsound on religion.

What, in fact, was his religion? A letter to his mother reveals that he had passed through a stage of actual infidelity. He once called himself outright a theist. But in later life he insisted always that he was a Christian. He told Moses Coit Tyler that he prayed to God daily. He sometimes spoke of himself as a "member" of the Protestant Episcopal Church, but he was never confirmed and never took communion. He refused to accept any theological system, preferring to make his own, a

---

we consider that it was brought to completion in the intervals of diplomatic missions we can only query whether the human species has degenerated." (A good share of the research, though not of the writing, was done by George Lincoln Burr, who refused to have his name on the title page as collaborator.)

kind of evolutionary deism.[24] Herein he found himself in harmony with Ezra Cornell, and at odds with most of the population of Ithaca and of America. Hence arose many of the troubles of the young university.

White's awareness of his gifts and his advantages enforced his greatness. His awareness inspired in him also a sharp sense of the respect due him. This sense of his due is called, in lesser men, vanity.[25] He could absorb the most hyperbolic flattery; and criticism, troubling his secret image of himself, could cast him down for days. He did not like to be outshone. It was whispered in Ithaca, in 1885, that he opposed the proposal that James Russell Lowell should succeed him as President, only from fear of being overshadowed.

A hostile New York *Tribune* reporter described him, in Santo Domingo in 1871, as "an inoffensive, quiet, gentlemanly man, slightly dogmatic, dictatorial, and self-opinionated." [26] Well, he could have seemed so, and did seem so. All our qualities have good and bad names, and our judges are always prejudiced, comparing us with eidola they hide within themselves. There were some who found Mr. White a young prig, altogether too high-minded for this world. Moses Coit Tyler addressed him playfully as "Your Majesty." One of his wife's friends wrote her: "Remember me to Saint Andrew."

Not all the early undergraduates adored their President. He had no patience with student pranks and misbehavior. He could not forgive a prank because he could not understand why anyone should commit one. In June 1871 some undergraduates printed a program for a "mock scheme," entitled "Old Ezra's Foundling Hospital." It is scurrilous, offensive, and of most lamentable wit. But it is instructive to the historian. Andrew D. White is referred to therein as "Andy Deity White." We are told that "this lump of abnormal life passes the greater part of his time in rolling his eyes at an imaginary halo which he supposes to hang round his head."

The anonymous authors displayed a good deal of penetration. Your

[24] ADW to his mother, 23 July 1857; E. P. Evans Papers, 31 Jan. 1877, C.U. Archives; Tyler's Diary, 11 July 1890, C.U. Library. T. F. Crane, one of his closest friends, dwelt at length on his religious spirit, in *Alumni News*, 14 Nov. 1918. And see especially his own long (and fascinating) discussion of his religious development in the *Autobiography*, II, 513–573.

[25] True, T. F. Crane said at Mr. White's death (*Alumni News*, 14 Nov. 1918): "I never in the 52 years of our friendship saw the faintest sign of vanity or self-appreciation." But plenty of others did. What mysteries we are!

[26] Quoted in *Cornell Era*, 3 March 1871.

historian remembers Andrew D. White as a great man, looking with forbearant understanding on the world he has created. And as the historian reflects, he has a sort of underimpression—of a great man playing the part of a great man.[27]

He took himself seriously; he took life seriously. He had few of the failings of common humanity, and he seems often out of touch with it. In his addresses to students, as in his *Autobiography*, he drums forever on the words *noble, manly,* and *earnest.* The word *noble,* especially, soothed him like a syrupy drug. His diversions were few, and noble, manly, and elevating: solid reading, good music (though he detested Wagner), and contemplative walks. He seems somehow a little alien in our coarse and noisy world. He saw his first variety show in 1899, at the age of sixty-seven. He found it "amazingly interesting."

For a college president, he revealed strange areas of aloofness from the collegiate world. The first ball he attended in Ithaca was in 1910, at the age of seventy-seven—but he stayed till 2:00 A.M. Although he fostered physical training and although he was proud of his oarsmanship at Yale, he never saw a Cornell crew race until 1890, after his retirement from the presidency. He boasted to alumni gatherings that he had never seen a game of football, baseball, or basketball. Football he regarded as a vestige of barbarity. Since the matches were played beneath his windows until 1893, he was frequently obliged to draw the blinds. The well-loved story is authentic that in 1873, when he was asked to authorize a game with the University of Michigan in Cleveland, he decreed: "I refuse to let forty of our boys travel four hundred miles merely to agitate a bag of wind."

But for the human predicament, for the distresses of students who were serious, manly, and noble, he had every sympathy. There are innumerable recollections of his aid, material and moral, to poor, sick, or suffering students. He was a very kind man, readily moved by any

[27] Many of his faculty judged him harshly. Moses Coit Tyler, who was one of his chief intimates, wrote in his diary (19 March 1882): "He is not a man to lean on—for when the time comes, he will let you fall. He promises and forgets." And on 5 April: "He does not meet my expectations. He seems in many ways a very weak man. . . . He is constantly spoken of contemptuously and distrustfully. They even scoff at his historical scholarship, and deride his lectures as mere dilettante displays of cheap, second-hand biographical gossip. The worst charge is that affecting his truthfulness and directness of character; they say his word is not to be believed, and that he is very tricky in conduct. He certainly has misrepresented the state of the Library to me." Anyone who has lived on a campus will make a proper discount for campus spite.

spectacle of misfortune. A campus child of the early 1900's remembers a certain trip up the hill in an Ithaca streetcar. At one stop a woman struggled to board the car, maneuvering an enormous basket of laundry. The passengers gazed incuriously. But President Andrew D. White stepped from the car, swept off his square-topped derby with courtly deference, and carried the laundry basket aboard.[28]

And he loved small animals. In the early 1880's he expelled a student for killing a chipmunk with his cane. Squirrels entered his library freely; though they chewed his precious books, White would not allow them to be poisoned, nor would he permit a cat in the house. George Lincoln Burr, the faithful secretary, persuaded a squirrel to nest in his pocket, to the President's delight.[29]

He was a kindly man, and a great man, earnest, noble, and manly. His spirit, more than that of any other, irradiated the young university.

"I can bear to die," he once wrote, "but not to be forgotten." [30] Surely he will not be forgotten. Not alone his works and deeds, but the admirable bronze statue in front of Goldwin Smith Hall will preserve his memory through mortality's measurable time.

Nevertheless, your historian, pausing to salute the familiar seated figure, sometimes reflects that there never was a man more at ease on a pedestal than Andrew D. White.

[28] Oral communication from Miss Edith Emerson.
[29] For a lovely description of Mr. White in his library by Ellen Coit Brown Elliott, see Excursus I.
[30] ADW to Clarence Esty, 24 Aug. 1886.

IV

The Conception of a University

WE have seen that Ezra Cornell looked to science, embodied in the steam engine and the telegraph, as the maker of the coming religion of humanity. Andrew D. White, in his 1862 proposal to Gerrit Smith, conceived of his university as an asylum for science in its highest aspects. The two men expressed the hunger for scientific knowledge prevailing among thoughtful Americans.

Until the mid-century and after there was little opportunity for sating this hunger. News came from Europe of great advances in pure science —of Justus Liebig's research laboratory for organic chemistry in Giessen, of Sir Charles Lyell's sensational demonstrations of the antiquity of the earth, of Faraday's discoveries about electricity. Americans learned with amazement—and shame—that (about 1840) the Sorbonne's Faculty of Science numbered twenty-three professors and instructors, while nine leaders in pure science lectured at the Collège de France. By contrast, the science courses in our colleges were mostly elementary, ill equipped, and discountenanced.

Scientific missionaries came to us from abroad. Sir Charles Lyell gave the Lowell Institute Lectures in Boston in 1841. He was amazed to confront 4,500 auditors "of every station in society, from the most affluent and eminent in the various learned professions to the humblest mechanics, all well dressed and observing the utmost decorum." [1] Louis Agassiz, Swiss zoologist, came in 1846 to give the Lowell Lec-

[1] Charles Lyell, *Travels in North America* (London, 1855), I, 108.

tures on "The Plan of Creation, especially in the Animal Kingdom." In America Agassiz remained, to found Harvard's Museum for Comparative Zoology, and to be a constant inspiration to American scientists, students, and general public.

Native efforts to advance pure science were made, though with little official or academic encouragement. James D. Dana, at Yale, did important work in mineralogy. Joseph Henry, in the basement of the Albany Boys' Academy, discovered electrical self-induction. Asa Gray, at Harvard, performed a mighty task in botanical classification. Nor were these the only exemplars.

The federal government and many states undertook surveys of their physical composition and resources. The professional scientific journal appeared, with the *American Journal of Mineralogy* in 1810; it turned into the influential *American Journal of Science,* long edited by Benjamin Silliman of Yale. Scientists formed their professional societies; the first was the Association of American Geologists, in 1840. The American Association for the Advancement of Science began in 1848. (The railroads were now making it possible for scholars to meet in convention.) The Smithsonian Institution was established in 1846; its director, Joseph Henry, turned its activity toward original research, especially in physics, archaeology, and ethnology. The Astronomical Observatory at Yale was founded in 1830, that of Harvard in 1839.

The general public became aware of the existence of fundamental science. The lyceum system took form in the late twenties, and scientific lecturers began to travel the roads, with boxfuls of elementary physical and chemical apparatus. In 1834 nearly three thousand lyceums were numbered in the United States. As to the lecturers' competence we may judge from the example of Samuel Colt. He left school at ten to work in a textile factory. With the chemistry he learned in bleaching and dyeing he became a lyceum lecturer, under the name of Dr. Coult. I suspect he was a very good lecturer, for he did sensational tricks with "laughing gas." He also invented the Colt revolver, which has killed probably a million men.

Despite these manifestations, for most of the citizens science was understood and valued only for its evident applications. The coming of the railroads demonstrated the need for trained civil engineers, as did all the crowding inventions of the time. Howe's sewing machine (1846) proved the usefulness of mechanics, Goodyear's vulcanization of rubber (patented in 1844), that of chemistry.

In Ezra Cornell's case, the distinction between pure and applied science was blurred. Firmly implanted in his mind was the conviction that poor, intelligent boys should have access to instruction in the mechanic arts and in agriculture. He remembered his struggles to inform himself of the elements of electricity by puzzling out the difficult technical works in the Library of Congress. His efforts to establish a model farm in Tompkins County, to improve agriculture in the state, had revealed to him how haphazard, how fumbling, was the farmer's knowledge of soils, crops, insect pests, animal diseases. With Ezra Cornell, the awareness of a need turned promptly to the search for its satisfaction.

In December 1846, when he was thirty-nine, he wrote his son Alonzo not to waste his time on the study of Latin. "You had better pay very clost attention to Mathematics, Algebra, Trigonometry, Civil ingineering &c &c, with that you want to larn thurorly the English language, History, Composition, Writing, Geography, Phylosophy, Chimistry &c &c." In short, all the things that he longed to know himself.

Where, indeed, could the eager youth learn the theoretical background of the mechanic trades? In the face of the new complexity of industrial processes, the apprenticeship system was proving incompetent and was on the wane. Most of America's trained engineers came from West Point. The first school of nonmilitary, or civil, engineering in the English-speaking world, Rensselaer Polytechnic Institute, was founded in 1824. Harvard, Yale, and Lehigh had their scientific schools, but all these were beyond the reach of a poor boy.[2] Here and there mechanics' institutes existed, like Cooper Union in New York. On the whole, however, the advances in industrial technology were not accompanied by any satisfactory provision for technological education.

Scientific education in agriculture was in even worse case. While England, France, Germany and even Russia fostered flourishing agricultural schools and experiment stations, America had nothing at all.

The first suggestion of a real agricultural college (overlooked in most histories of American education) has a particular interest for Ithacans and Cornellians, as it certainly had for Ezra Cornell.

Simeon DeWitt, Surveyor-General of New York State, first saw our hills and valley in the closing years of the eighteenth century. Enchanted with the prospect, he did not content himself with making a

---

[2] A. D. White insisted that the first American engineering school was the Gardiner Lyceum in Hallowell, Maine, founded by Benjamin Hale in 1823 (*Sibley Journal of Engineering*, June 1915). It did not last long.

survey. He bought most of the present site of Ithaca, and presumably gave to the tiny settlement its name. He built a home on East Hill (on the present DeWitt Place), and spent there what time he could spare from his duties in Albany, and by his homestead he was buried.

In 1819 DeWitt published in Albany a pamphlet thus entitled: "Considerations on the Necessity of Establishing an Agricultural College, and having More of the Children of Wealthy Citizens Educated for the Profession of Farming." He praises the country life and deplores the drift of young gentlemen into the law. But how, he inquires, can the sons of gentry be trained for the supervision of agriculture, in the manner of English squires? At present, only by apprenticing themselves to farmers. We need, he says, an institution which will make agricultural pursuits not only profitable but fashionable. To this end he proposes the establishment of "The Agricultural College of the State of New York," to teach the theory and practice of agriculture, with such branches of other sciences as may be serviceable to them, and to make improvements in agriculture. (Thus he propounds the principle of experimental research.) He discusses the qualifications of the professors and the regime of the college farm, which shall be used primarily for demonstration and experiment, but which should prove that a good farm can make a profit. "The food will be . . . as far as possible the sole produce of the farm." No tea, coffee, or spirits will be served. This first public enunciation of the agricultural-college idea, made by Ithaca's godfather, must have lodged in Ezra Cornell's mind, to bear fruit many years later.

The idea was well lodged, at least, in the minds of Albany legislators. Lieutenant-Governor James Tallmadge made a report in 1826, recommending a school of "Agricultural Mechanics and Useful Arts." "The school should be organized . . . with the expectation that the manufacturer, the journeyman, apprentice and laborer will become the pupils, and there learn the principles upon which successful practice in their several occupations depend." Thereafter similar proposals were made to the legislature (e.g., in 1834, 1847, 1849, 1850, and 1852) and invariably broke against the members' distrust of book learning and their reluctance to spend the taxpayers' money. Said one committee regarding the proposers: "They have allowed their imaginations to form a kind of kaleidoscope, into which, as bits of colored glass are thrown, they place short-horned Durhams, Rohan potatoes, *Morus multicaulis*, Liebig's Agricultural Chemistry, an agricultural college and experimental farm, and lastly a rose, to give the whole a suitable coloring." [3]

Baffled of state action, the high-minded citizens of the Finger Lakes made their own plans.

Some Fate, some brooding Genius, marked this region as propitious to education. (Was not Odysseus' clear-seen Ithaca a rugged land, but a good nurse of young men, ἀγαθὴ κουροτρόφος?) In 1822 the Methodists of the Genesee Conference proposed to build "Ithaca College" between Cascadilla and Fall Creeks (about where Cornell University's men's dormitories now stand). The sponsors were unable to raise the $50,000 the State Regents demanded as a preliminary to chartering.

The idea of higher training in agriculture and mechanics was much bruited in the countryside. In 1822 Geneva College (now Hobart) proposed a two-year course "in direct reference to the practical business of life, by which the Agriculturist, the Merchant, and the Mechanic may receive a practical knowledge of what genius and experience have discovered, without passing through a tedious course of classical studies." [4] The proposal was not, however, put into effect.

At the end of the forties a People's College was conceived by an organization of mechanics. Horace Greeley's interest was aroused. He wrote an editorial in his New York *Tribune*, promised a gift of $1,000, and was immediately elected to the Board of Trustees. Charles Cook of Havana, New York, now Montour Falls, just south of Watkins Glen, made dazzling offers on condition that the institution stand in his village. The People's College was incorporated in 1853. Its purpose was stated to be "the dissemination of practical science, including chemistry, geology, mineralogy, and those sciences most immediately and vitally essential to agriculture and the useful arts, and to make ample provision for instruction in the classics." Every pupil and teacher would be required to do from ten to twenty hours of manual labor a week, for pay. An accompanying prospectus pointed out that the first educational institution was a manual-labor school in the Garden of Eden, with Adam and Eve as undergraduates. In accord with this coeducational precedent the Founders proposed to train females in such branches as Housewifery, Dressmaking, and fine Needlework, to

[3] Report of Minority Committee on an Agricultural College and Experimental Farm, N.Y. State Assembly, No. 116, 20 March 1851.

[4] F. D. Hough, *New York State University; Historical and Statistical Record* (Albany, 1885), p. 260.

qualify them for Independence and Usefulness in Life. Here is an early exemplar of a college of home economics.

At length the cornerstone of a large building was laid in 1858, with speeches by Horace Greeley, Mark Hopkins, and other notables. The grandiose structure cost $60,000, mostly contributed by Charles Cook. (It survives as St. John's Atonement Seminary.) But Cook's generous impulses were constantly submerged by succeeding waves of prudence. He would build, he would not endow. When the college opened in 1860 it had only four professors, no equipment, and no students of college grade. Here we shall leave the People's College, to see it soon again as the dragon in the path of the young Cornell University.[5]

Twenty-five miles east of Ithaca, in the village of McGraw, near Cortland, stood the New York Central College. This interesting institution deserves a larger place in the history of higher education than it has received. Sponsored by the Anti-slavery, or Free, Baptists and by such eminent liberals as William Lloyd Garrison, Wendell Phillips, Henry Ward Beecher, Horace Greeley, and Gerrit Smith, it opened its doors in 1849. About half the students were colored, as were at least two of the professors. These were the first colored professors in the United States. (One of them did the college no good by eloping with the daughter of a prominent white family.) Though, to be sure, a Negro had graduated from Bowdoin in 1827, and though Oberlin admitted Negroes in the late thirties, nowhere was the principle of racial integration carried so far as at the New York Central College.

Political and social opposition, a smallpox epidemic, and financial difficulties finished it off in 1860. Today all that remains of it is the cupola of the main building, transported to the barn of a whimsical McGraw farmer.[6]

Meanwhile the friends of agricultural education obtained a charter (15 April 1853) for the New York State Agricultural College, to be erected in Ovid, twenty-five miles northwest of Ithaca. This was the first chartered agricultural college in America. The great-hearted citizens of Ovid raised $40,000 by subscription (an enormous sum for a country village) and obtained a state loan of $40,000. A noble farm of 720 fat acres on the shore of Seneca Lake was bought, and a college building erected on a commanding site, looking afar to five counties. It still stands, and still serves, as a unit of Willard State Hospital for the

[5] See Albert H. Wright, *The New York People's College* (Ithaca, 1958).
[6] See Albert H. Wright, *The New York Central College* (Ithaca, 1960).

Insane. After many vicissitudes, the college was inaugurated on 5 December 1860, with a faculty of four and a student body of twenty-seven. One of the students was Ezra Cornell's son Perry, and another was his nephew Benjamin Cornell.

Perry wrote doleful letters home. He called the college a drunken hole and said "the institution has got the worst kind of a name from one end of the county to the other." [7] Not a decent lesson was recited during the term. But the college was hardly to blame. The Civil War began in April. The President, Major M. R. Patrick, was summoned to Albany to organize the raising of volunteers, and many of the students enlisted. The college closed its doors in November.

Here Ezra Cornell had his first direct contact with higher education. In 1862 he was a State Assemblyman and chairman of the Committee on Agriculture. In the same year he was elected president of the New York State Agricultural Society. As such he became an ex officio trustee of the college at Ovid. And as such, characteristically, he pondered earnestly on the nature and needs of agricultural education.

When Cornell University was a-building, he was interviewed by a correspondent for a New York newspaper.

We asked Mr. Cornell if he had revolved in his mind for many years the project of founding a great University, or if the plan had been presented to him by some fortuitous concurrence of circumstances. He replied that very much was due to the fact of his election as one of the Trustees of the State Agricultural College at Ovid, and the discovery made at two meetings of the Trustees of that institution of the great want of a suitable provision in our country for the education of young men in agriculture and the mechanic arts.[8]

On two other subjects Cornell's ideas were hardening. The first was the importance of manual labor in higher education, the second the provision of higher education for women.

The manual-labor plan, by which students were obliged to work a fixed number of hours, educating their hands and reducing their college expenses, seems to have originated at Josiah Holbrook's Derby (Connecticut) Academy in 1824–1825. In the thirties and forties it flourished amain. Ezra Cornell wrote his son Alonzo, on 15 February

---

[7] 2 June 1861, EC Papers. Other letters harp on the same theme. For the college's history see Albert H. Wright, *The New York State Agricultural College* (Ithaca, 1958).

[8] New York *Evening Post*, 2 Oct. 1868.

1846: "Enclosed . . . I send you an article on the subject of Manual Labour Schools. I have always been in favour of combining labour and Studdy. I think schollars would improve more rappidly with their Studdies were they engaged four hours a day in some profitable manual labour."

By the fifties the manual-labor system, as a system, faded away, leaving behind a plethora of unsalable brooms and cane-bottomed chairs. But the new establishment of agricultural colleges revived the idea, in a more rational form. The Michigan Agricultural College, chartered in 1855, and the first such college with sufficient vitality to survive to our own day, required three hours' daily work of the students on the farms and gardens. The People's College propounded the scheme anew. Its prospectus reads: "Productive Labor shall be practically honored and inflexibly required of all." A note in Ezra Cornell's hand brackets "and inflexibly required," with the marginal note: "O. K. Except the compulsory clause. Labor to be successful must be subject to freedom of choice, and fair compensation. E. C." [9]

The second subject of Cornell's concern was the education of women. The first noteworthy effort in this direction was Emma Willard's Troy Female Seminary, established in 1821. Elmira College, chartered in 1852, claims to be the first real women's college. Oberlin was the pioneer in coeducation, and the State University of Iowa admitted women from its opening in 1855. Ezra Cornell warmly supported a bill for the chartering of Vassar College in 1862; [10] he sent his daughter Mary there in 1866. It is evident that his approval of women's higher education, and of coeducation, was well fixed in his mind before his own university opened.

The event which crystallized Ezra Cornell's convictions into intentions was the passage of the Morrill Land Grant Act in 1862. This act has been authoritatively called "the most important piece of agricultural legislation in American history." [11] Its principles transformed the concept of higher education in America; its material aid resulted in the creation of some two dozen universities and state colleges. On how many a campus stands a Morrill Hall, a gray patriarch among its glittering glass-faced companions!

[9] In Cornell University Pamphlets, No. 3, C.U. Library.

[10] William Kelly to EC, 8 March 1862. Vassar was in fact chartered in 1861. The bill in question must have been supplementary.

[11] S. E. Morison and H. S. Commager, *The Growth of the American Republic* (New York, 1942), II, 196.

Justin Smith Morrill, erstwhile country storekeeper, introduced in the U.S. Senate in 1857 a bill appropriating public lands for aid to state agricultural and mechanical colleges. The bill passed the two houses by a narrow vote, and was vetoed by President Buchanan. On 8 December 1861, in the darkest days of the Civil War, Senator Morrill presented a second bill, which was passed and signed by President Lincoln, to become law on 2 July 1862.

The act donated public lands to the several states, to provide colleges for the benefit of agriculture and the mechanic arts. The amount of land is specified: 30,000 acres for each Senator and Representative in Congress. If federal public lands existed within a state's own borders, the state might claim them. But since in many states, such as New York, there were no public lands at all, the Secretary of the Interior was instructed to issue to such states land scrip representing the number of acres to which they were entitled. Here arose a difficulty. If an eastern state, scrip in hand, should locate a great block of land in a western state, it would create an *imperium in imperio;* it would establish a colony within another's sovereignty. The act therefore required that the land scrip be sold and that the proceeds be applied to the uses prescribed in the act. These proceeds should be invested in safe stocks, yielding not less than five per centum per annum, and the interest should be devoted to "at least one college where the leading object shall be, without excluding other scientific and classical studies, and including military tactics, to teach such branches of learning as are related to agriculture and the mechanic arts, in such manner as the legislatures of the States may respectively prescribe, in order to promote the liberal and practical education of the industrial classes in the several pursuits and professions of life." It was further specified that the proceeds might be used for the purchase of land, but not for the erection or maintenance of buildings, and that each state must provide one such college, or allocate its funds to an adequate existing institution, within five years, or its grant would lapse.

New York, the most populous state, with thirty-three Senators and Representatives, would be the chief beneficiary of the act. It was due to receive about one-tenth of the total grant—exactly 989,920 acres. (I do not know why New York was eighty acres short.) There was joy in Albany, and joy in Ovid, in Havana, and in the presidential studies of a score of hungry colleges within the state. A share in the land grant would come as a blessed blood transfusion in their wartime anemia.

Most aggressive in the battle for the land-grant bounty was the People's College. Its president, the Reverend Amos Brown, having nothing much to do in the empty college, had gone to Washington and lobbied vigorously for the passage of the Morrill Act. The sponsor of the People's College, Charles Cook, secured election to the State Senate in the campaign of 1862. In the legislative session which began on 2 January 1863, Mr. Cook argued that the entire benefits of the grant should go to his college. On 4 March, New York State formally accepted the congressional land-grant offer; on 5 May, the Comptroller was authorized to receive and sell the land scrip; and on 14 May the legislature directed that returns from the sale of the scrip should be appropriated to the People's College. *Provided, however,* that within three years the said college should have ten competent professors in agriculture and the mechanic arts, that it should have accommodations for 250 students, proper equipment, a farm of 200 acres, and workshops for technical education.

Ezra Cornell had joined with others in circulating petitions asking that the land-grant benefits go to the Ovid Agricultural College. There is no indication, however, that as yet he felt very strongly about the matter. He was chiefly concerned with his plan to build and endow a public library for the citizens of Tompkins County.

In November 1863 Ezra Cornell was elected State Senator. And Andrew D. White was chosen from the Onondaga district.

The Senate convened on 2 January 1864. On that auspicious date the two men met. "Though his chair was near mine," says White in his *Autobiography,* "there was at first little intercourse between us, and there seemed small chance of more. He was steadily occupied, and seemed to have no desire for new acquaintances."

Cornell was appointed chairman of the Committee on Agriculture, and White chairman of the Committee on Literature, which by tradition dealt with education. To White's desk came a bill proposing the incorporation of Mr. Cornell's public library. Mr. White remembered:

On reading this bill I was struck, not merely by his gift of one hundred thousand dollars to his townsmen, but even more by a certain breadth and largeness in his way of making it. The most striking sign of this was his mode of forming a board of trustees; for, instead of the usual effort to tie up the organization forever in some sect, party, or clique, he had named the best men of his town—his political opponents as well as his friends; and had added to them the pastors of all the principal churches, Catholic and Protestant. This breadth of mind, even more than his munificence, drew me to him.

A second charter promoted by Cornell presumably came to White's committee. A group of Ithacans, headed by Cornell, proposed to establish Cascadilla Place, a water-cure sanitarium and school for the education of women doctors. The mother of this scheme, Dr. Samantha Nivison of Dryden, a graduate of the Female Medical College of Philadelphia in 1855 (only six years after America's first diploma'd woman physician's graduation) and a person of great force of character, deserves a tiny meed of remembrance.[12] Ezra Cornell was being drawn, by various pulls of circumstance, to think about higher education, and particularly about the higher education of women.

Cornell and others were by this time concerned about the land grant, and the action of the previous legislature in turning it over entirely to the People's College. That unhappy institution's benefactor, Charles Cook, suffered a paralytic stroke and could make no move to fulfill the requirements laid upon the college by the legislature. The friends of the Ovid Agricultural College rallied, and on 12 January 1864 Judge C. J. Folger of Geneva introduced a bill cutting the People's College's share of the land grant to a half. On 18 February, Ezra Cornell presented his own bill, calling for an equal division of the land-grant benefits between the People's College and the Ovid school. The bill was referred to the Committee on Literature. And Chairman White there buried it, refusing to report it out.

His reason for obstruction was, he says, that he recognized the paramount importance of keeping the land-grant money together, not allowing it to be dissipated. Surely he associated the opportunities promised by the land grant with his lifelong dream of a great university for New York State. He did not see clearly how such a university could come to being, but he was certain that it could rise neither in Havana nor in Ovid. He bided his time. And Cornell bided his.

The seed was sown, to be slowly warmed and ripened.

At some time in these months Cornell revealed a scheme destined to bring his university much weal and himself much woe. The land grant threw on the market ten million acres of public land. According to the act, the beneficiary states could not locate the land; they were obliged to sell scrip to individuals, entitling them to choose lands as yet unlocated. The nominal price of the land was $1.25 per acre. But with the war still raging, buyers were few and timid. In the glutted market

---

[12] The bill was passed on 25 April 1864. Cornell had proposed, even in 1851, a hydropathic establishment to face Ithaca Falls, presumably on the site of the present Zeta Beta Tau house.

the price of the scrip dropped as low as forty-one cents per acre. At this price, even New York's million acres would yield only about $400,-000. Cornell found the logical answer: that men of good will should purchase the scrip, locate the better lands while they were still available, and hold them in trust for their colleges. He proposed to the trustees of the Havana and Ovid schools that they should "make up a fund sufficient to purchase all the scrip of the State and locate it for the benefit of both colleges, entering into an agreement for an equal division of the profits to arise from the transaction between the two colleges." He offered to supply a tenth of the funds necessary, but he found no other trustees of equal good will, wealth, and foresight.[13]

In Ezra Cornell's mind dwelt a gathering concern about the obligations of wealth. The fat dividends from the war-prosperous Western Union Telegraph brought him worry as well as satisfaction. In January 1864 his close friend, the brilliant young lawyer, Francis Miles Finch, urged him to make his will. He replied:

I don't know what to do with my property in framing the provisions of a will. My wife owns the house we live in and 75 acres of the farm, and owns stock enough to give her an income of $3000 besides the farm, hence she don't want my property. I have five children. It would not benefit them to give them more than $100,000 each, thus less than half is disposed of. . . . What shall I do with the balance? I hope to do much good with it, but I really don't know how to dispose of it in a will so as to do the good with it that I should desire to do. . . . If you have any suggestions to make, you may shell them out, for they will not have a particle of influence upon me unless they seem rational, and if they exhibit absurdity on your part, I will in turn assume them to be *confidential*.

In August he picked up the "Cyphering Book" in which, as a boy, he had fairly inscribed his sums, ending with many problems in Loss and Gain. He wrote in the book (which is now in the Cornell Archives): "The yearly income which I realize this year will exceed One Hundred Thousand dollars. . . . My greatest care now is how to spend this large income, to do the most good to those who are properly dependent on me, to the poor and to posterity."

By summer's end he had come to a conclusion. A meeting of the trustees of the Ovid Agricultural College was called, for the twenty-fifth of September, in Rochester. It was presumed that the trustees could merely pronounce their college officially dead and that they could

[13] Samuel D. Halliday; *History of the Federal Land Grant* (Ithaca, 1905), p. 14.

61

attribute the deathblow to Senator Andrew D. White, who had buried in committee the bill giving half the land-grant money to Ovid. Cornell wrote to White, with whom his relations were naturally strained, and invited him in urgent terms to attend the meeting.

The ceremonies were obituary. Several speakers pronounced informal funeral orations, to voice their burial of hope. White wondered why he had been asked to attend, in the role of the deceased's assassin. Then Cornell fished a slip of paper from his pocket. He read:

I have listened patiently to the discussion . . . until I have come to the conclusion that the Trustees would be justifiable in changing the location of the college. . . . Therefore I submit for your consideration the following proposition. If you will locate the college at Ithaca, I will give you for that object a farm of three hundred acres of first quality of land desirably located, overlooking the village of Ithaca and Cayuga Lake and within ten minutes walk of the post office, the Cornell Library, the churches, the railroad station and steamboat landing. I will also erect on the farm suitable buildings for the use of the college, and give an additional sum of money to make up an aggregate of three hundred thousand dollars, on condition that the Legislature will endow the college with thirty thousand dollars per annum from the Congressional Agricultural College fund, and thus place the college upon a firm and substantial basis.

Andrew D. White remembers:

The entire audience applauded, as well they might; it was a noble proposal. But, much to the disgust of the meeting, I persisted in my refusal to sanction any bill dividing the fund, declared myself now more opposed to such a division than ever; but promised that if Mr. Cornell and his friends would ask for the *whole* grant—keeping it together, and adding his three hundred thousand dollars, as proposed—I would support such a bill with all my might.

Thus the cooperation of Cornell and White, in furtherance of their great purpose, began.

Cornell's sensational proposal was well publicized. It brought him, amid showers of begging letters, much well-intentioned advice. His friend George Geddes wrote: "Do let us have in this State the best University in the world—teaching all useful knowledge." The Reverend Amos Brown, President of the People's College, hinted that he would be available for the presidency and made the first recorded proposal (on 31 December 1864) that the institution be named the Cornell University.

When the legislature met in January 1865, the principals had had time for reflection. Cornell one day accosted White on the Capitol steps, and the two walked together down icy State Street. Cornell remarked in his most casual manner: "I have about half a million dollars more than my family will need; what is the best thing I can do with it for the State?"

For such a question White had a ready answer.

Mr. Cornell, the two things most worthy of aid in any country are charity and education; but in our country the charities appeal to everybody. Anyone can understand the importance of them, and the worthy poor or unfortunate are sure to be taken care of. As to education, the lower grades will always be cared for in the public schools by the State; but the institutions of the highest grade, without which the lower can never be thoroughly good, can be appreciated by only a few. The policy of our State is to leave this part of the system to individuals; it seems to me, then, that if you have half a million to give, the best thing you can do with it is to establish or strengthen some institution for higher instruction.

Touching shrewdly Cornell's desires, he said that scientific and technical education must be provided; and, associating his own dreams to those of Cornell, he insisted "that education in history and literature should be the bloom of the whole growth."

The two met often to bring their vaulting visions into accord and to translate them into reality. White offered to give half his own fortune to the enterprise, on condition that it should stand in Syracuse. But Cornell would have none of Syracuse. "I will do better than that myself," he said.

It was evident to both these practical legislators that even a great philanthropy would meet enemies. Essential to their plans was the securing of the whole of the state's share in the Morrill Land Grant. This had been lightly bestowed on the People's College; and in politics—and not only in politics—you cannot revoke a gift without bitter outcries from the deprived. All the twenty existing colleges in the state were waiting hungrily for the forfeiture of the grant to the People's College; and each of the twenty colleges stood ready to demand, through its representatives in the legislature, its share in the heavenly manna of Senator Morrill.

The first step of Cornell and White was to win over, if possible, the trustees of the People's College. A combined meeting of the People's College and Ovid Agricultural College trustees was called for 12 January 1865. No representative of the People's College accepted the invitation. But at this meeting Cornell increased his already magnificent offer. He proposed to donate $500,000, if the legislature would transfer the entire land-grant returns to the projected institution. A second meeting was likewise boycotted by the People's College trustees, all but Horace Greeley, who was won over by Cornell and White.

Meanwhile Cornell converted his scheme for an association to purchase land-grant scrip for the benefit of the two small colleges into a personal project. If no one would join him in a sound and worthy effort, he would go it alone, for the eventual profit of the Cornell University. He began hunting for agents who might locate for him good western timberlands.[14]

The idea of a university grew and grew in Cornell's mind. On 27 January he wrote to Francis Miles Finch: "The enterprise expands from an Agricultural College to a university of the first magnitude—such as we have to go to Europe to find. . . . If we secure this congressional college fund, I am confident that we can make Ithaca the seat of learning in America." And five days later, to his son Alonzo: "The college matter looks more hopeful. . . . Ithaca will become the seat of learning of New York if not of America." The prophecies sound like an echo of Andrew D. White, of common midnight visions in some gaslit bedroom of the old Delavan House in Albany.

On 7 February 1865 the die was cast. White introduced into the State Senate a bill "to establish the Cornell University, and to appropriate to it the income of the sale of public lands granted to this State." (Cornell had demurred a little to giving his name to the proposed university, but White had alleged the excellent precedents of Yale, Harvard, and Merton College, Oxford.) [15] The object of the corporation was stated to be "the cultivation of the arts and sciences and of literature, and the instruction in agriculture, the mechanic arts and military tactics, and in all knowledge." Ten incorporators were named, including Ezra Cornell, Horace Greeley, John McGraw of Ithaca, and Hiram

[14] E. Goddard of East Saginaw, Mich., to Douglass Boardman, 28 Jan. 1865, gives the terms on which he would locate lands. "One year from now it will be very difficult to get desirable government land here, and Mr. Cornell ought to hurry the thing at once." On 22 March Cornell wrote I. Miller, asking the cost of locating lands. On the same date W. A. Woodward proposes himself as land-locator. Woodward was employed; his services ended in a long and bitter lawsuit.

[15] A little later, Willard Fiske urged *Academia Cornelia*. He wrote White (26 May 1868): "Academia Cornelia will be a happy hit. It will make a good cry for the students, a good chorus for their songs, and will enable anybody bursting with eloquence to compare the institution to the mother of the Gracchi."

Sibley of Rochester, but not, notably, Andrew D. White. A Board of Trustees of twenty-five persons was stipulated, some ex officio, as the Governor of the state and the librarian of the Cornell Library, some elective. Cornell inserted in the draft of the bill "the eldest male lineal descendant of Ezra Cornell," thus adding the hereditary principle. It was provided that "the said Board of Trustees shall be so constituted . . . that at no time shall a majority thereof be of any one religious sect, or of no religious sect." [16] To this corporation would be appropriated the income produced by the sale of the Morrill Act lands, on condition that within six months Ezra Cornell's endowment of $500,000 should be attested and that lands, buildings, and equipment should be provided within a fixed period. Further, the corporation might not hold real and personal property exceeding three million dollars in the aggregate. And note: "Persons of every or no religious denomination shall be equally eligible to all offices and appointments." And finally: "The corporation . . . shall receive annually one student from each Assembly district of this state . . . and shall give them instruction in any or all the prescribed branches of study . . . free of any tuition fee." (White, who proposed this magnanimous provision, thought he was offering 128 free scholarships annually, one for each Assembly district. The catch was in the word "annually." The state's Attorney-General interpreted it as providing a four-year course for each annual appointee. Thus the University might have 512 scholarship holders at one time.)

The introduction of the bill, says White in his *Autobiography*, was a signal for war. The friends of the People's College saw the Morrill bonanza torn from their grasp. The twenty colleges of New York State, sitting in a slavering ring around the dying People's College, saw the guarded booty suddenly jerked out of reach. They sent their agents to Albany, worked on the representatives of their districts, made the usual deals and bargains. The bold nonsectarianism of the bill gave them their opportunity; they stirred the religious press to attack— already!—the "godless university."

Andrew D. White was no mean warrior himself. He labored mightily to convince his colleagues, and when conviction failed he resorted to bargains, though, of course, noble ones. In one case fate did him an

---

[16] Cornellians often claim primacy for this broad statement of nonsectarian control. But it was probably prompted by a remembrance of the charter of Union College in 1795, which provided that the majority of the trustees must never be from the same religious sect (Dixon Ryan Fox, *Union College: An Unfinished History* [Schenectady, 1945], p. 11).

almost indecent favor. Senator J. C. Folger of Geneva warmly approved the Cornell bill, had, indeed, helped to draft it, but he could not vote for it, for in his district stood the Ovid Agricultural College. No Senator can vote to destroy his constituents' hopes. As it happened, an eminent alienist, Dr. Sylvester D. Willard, had been struggling for years to establish a state hospital for the chronic insane. Making an impassioned plea before a legislative committee in April 1865, Dr. Willard fell dead. The legislators were moved by his dramatic self-immolation as they had never been by his arguments. White immediately proposed to Judge Folger that the state turn the Ovid Agricultural College into the Willard State Asylum, thus bringing prosperity to Ovid, assuaging the senatorial sense of guilt, and freeing Judge Folger to vote for his convictions. (To be sure, the later success of Cornell University inspired some angry second thoughts in Ovid. Said an embittered Ovidian to the celebrated historian, J. Franklin Jameson: "A university would have been worth three insane asylums!") [17]

Ezra Cornell seems to have played only a minor role in the battle. "I shall not go into fits to induce the State to accept $500,000 of my money," he wrote to his son. On 12 February, five days after the introduction of the University bill, he even proposed to establish an orphan asylum in Ithaca. A little later, a Washington paper reported that he planned to build a $400,000 asylum for Civil War orphans. One may imagine Andrew D. White's fury.

The stirring events of the battle to create Cornell University have been often and excellently told, notably in White's *Autobiography* and in Carl Becker's *Founders and the Founding*. Let a summary here suffice. White introduced a resolution, on 4 February, that a committee of the Regents should visit the People's College to determine if it could fulfill the conditions imposed for its reception of the land-grant money. The committee immediately descended on Havana and found the college's position quite hopeless. The Senate, on 16 March, courteously granted the People's College a stay of three months to comply with the terms of the grant, failing which the grant would be withdrawn.

The enemies of the proposed Cornell University fought an unclean war. Unable to find cogent arguments, they and their local newspapers resorted to vilification of Mr. Cornell's character and to the traducing of his purposes. The words "land grant" were readily transformed into "land grab." The average man, whose own speculations had mostly

[17] Carl Becker, *Cornell University: Founders and the Founding* (Ithaca, 1943), p. 100.

come to grief, willingly assumed that a rich man's operations must have succeeded only through his superior villainy. Mr. Cornell was unquestionably a rich man. It could therefore be assumed that his university design cloaked some sinister purpose. What purpose exactly was far from clear, but it was all the more sinister for that reason. The rich are much too smart to show their hand to simple legislators.

Typical was a public hearing before a combined legislative committee. As White recalls the dramatic scene, the presentation by Cornell's lawyer was cold and labored; the speech by Charles Cook's lawyer was "thin and demagogical, but the speaker knew well the best tricks for catching the average man":

He indulged in eloquent tirades against the Cornell bill as a "monopoly," a "wild project," a "selfish scheme," a "job," a "grab," and the like; denounced Mr. Cornell as "seeking to erect a monument to himself," hinted that he was "planning to rob the State"; and, before he had finished, had pictured Mr. Cornell as a swindler and the rest of us as dupes or knaves.[18]

I can never forget the quiet dignity with which Mr. Cornell took this abuse. Mrs. Cornell sat at his right, I at his left. In one of the worst tirades against him, he turned to me and said quietly, and without the slightest anger or excitement: "If I could think of any other way in which half a million of dollars would do as much good to the State, I would give the legislators no more trouble." Shortly afterward, when the invective was again especially bitter, he turned to me and said: "I am not sure but that it would be a good thing for me to give the half a million to old Harvard College in Massachusetts, to educate the descendants of the men who hanged my forefathers." [19]

White, with the somewhat reluctant Cornell, fought indomitably for the bill, against what seemed to them the leagued forces of envy and evil. "We have never had a more corrupt Assembly than this," Cornell wrote his son in April. He accused Cook's agent of spending $6,000 to buy votes. No doubt; but White had devices of his own. He refused to report out bills for raising the rates of the New York Central Railroad and for building a new State Capitol until the Cornell bill should be disposed of.

[18] Cook's lawyer was David B. Hill, later a prominent politician of Elmira, Governor of the state, and U.S. Senator. He appeared again as the nemesis of Cornell in the great Fiske-McGraw Will Case.

[19] So White remembers in his *Autobiography*. But I can find no reference to such a public meeting during the legislative session of 1865 in any newspaper or official record. I suspect that the memorable scene was enacted on some different occasion.

To one unpleasant bargain White and Cornell were forced to submit. Genesee College, a frail Methodist institution at Lima, demanded 100,000 acres of the land scrip. It would, however, withdraw its demand if Cornell would endow it with $25,000. The political power of Genesee College was so great that Cornell thought best to yield, insisting however that the condition be inserted in the bill, for he would do nothing underhand. Thus it happens that the Charter of Cornell University contains the provision that no endowment from the Morrill Land Grant shall take place until Ezra Cornell, of Ithaca, shall pay to the trustees of Genesee College the sum of $25,000, for the purpose of establishing in said Genesee College a professorship of agricultural chemistry. This very barefaced deal aroused much indignation. The Ithaca *Journal* proposed that the professorship be termed the Blackmail Professorship, the Captain Kidd Professorship, or the Professorship of the Christian Footpads. Cornell himself bitterly resented the deal and his own humiliation in accepting it. He wrote in his "Cyphering Book" in November of this year: "I have just endowed the Cornell University with the sum of $500,000, and paid to the Genesee College $25,000 for the privilege of endowing the University as above. Such is the influence of corrupt legislation." But in justice to the legislators it should be recorded that shortly afterwards they added $25,000 to Cornell University's endowment, as amends for an unworthy action.

With White acting as the whip, or scourge, of marplots and faint-hearts, the bill was forced out of committee.

The bill is the Charter of Cornell University. It had undergone a number of revisions, including the specification of the payment to Genesee College and a grace of three months given to the People's College to provide the equipment of a university or to deposit a sufficient sum to pay for such a transformation. And a noteworthy revision rephrases the language of the Morrill Act to state the concept of Cornell University. "The leading object . . . shall be to teach such branches of learning as are related to agriculture and the mechanic arts, including military tactics, in order to promote the liberal and practical education of the industrial classes in the several pursuits and professions of life. But such other branches of science and knowledge may be embraced in the plan of instruction and investigation pertaining to the university as the trustees may deem useful and proper."

The bill was approved in the Assembly and in the Senate, and was signed by Governor Reuben E. Fenton on 27 April 1865.

Cornell University was born.

V

The Making of a University

THE first meeting of the Board of Trustees of the Cornell University was held in Albany on 28 April 1865, the day after the University was created. Present were Governor Reuben E. Fenton, Horace Greeley, Ezra Cornell, Francis Miles Finch, and six others. The grant of powers and of the land scrip was accepted. Seven new trustees, including Andrew D. White, Charles J. Folger, and Erastus Brooks, editor of the New York *Express*, were elected, and the meeting adjourned.

The trustees did not define their own powers or their relation to the future University. Such a procedure did not suggest itself. The trustees assumed that they were the absolute masters of the institution, like the Board of Governors of a hospital. It probably occurred to no one present that the trustee system of university government is an American invention. In Oxford and Cambridge the faculty is the governing body; on the Continent the university is an organ of church or state.

For the moment the trustees could do nothing but wait. The three-month stay granted the People's College ruled out any action; the unpredictable Mr. Cook might at the last moment deposit the $185,000 which the Regents had specified as a guarantee.

In the meantime Ezra Cornell busied himself with the completion of the Cornell Library and with plans for locating the land-grant scrip. And Andrew D. White, expressing a desire to see "what sort of a place Ithaca really is," inspected, on 24 May, his future home. It was not his first sight of the town; he had been brought here at the age of seven on his way to visit an uncle near Geneva. He remembered his childhood delight with the view from East Hill; Cayuga Lake had thrilled him, since he had never seen any water larger than a millpond. In 1865 he thought the city still attractive from a distance, but ugly to the near observer. "It had sprouted, bloomed, borne fruit and gone to seed." [1]

Ezra and Alonzo Cornell, White, and Finch were eager to fix the University's location. They drove to the hilltop, the present site of Morrill Hall. Ezra Cornell's three companions agreed that the shelf below them, where stand today the men's dormitories, would be the ideal situation. "Young gentlemen," said Cornell, "you appear to be considering the location of half a dozen buildings, whereas some of you will live to see our campus occupied by fifty buildings and swarming with thousands of students."

"Well, where would you build?"

Cornell turned to the east, swung his arms north and south, and said: "Here, on this line extending from Cascadilla to Fall Creek. We shall need every acre for the future necessary purposes of the university."

The three demurred and argued—Mr. Cornell's solution was not practical. The site, beautiful indeed, was inaccessible, far from the village, rough, gullied, roadless. But Cornell bore them down, and at his direction they drove stakes to mark Building No. 1.

Thus Ezra Cornell, so often qualified as a merely practical man, opposed his dreams and visions to the practicality of others. He chose one of the most beautiful college sites in America, and he has stimulated the dreams and visions of many a young man and young woman.

On the first of June he drilled to find the depth of rock, and carried home the first shovelful of earth.

On 27 July, the stay granted the People's College expired, with no word from Havana. Cornell deposited with the State Comptroller his bond for $500,000, and wrote (his pen dipped in gall) a cheque for $25,000 to the Genesee College.

The second meeting of the Board of Trustees was held in the damply plastered rooms of the new Cornell Library, on 5 September 1865. The proceedings were mostly formal. A Building Committee was empowered to select a site. Mr. White was appointed a committee to draft bylaws. Mr. Cornell's endowment, by his note for $500,000 bear-

---

[1] EC Papers, 18 May 1865; ADW, Diary, 24 and 25 May 1865; *Alumni News,* 8 Feb. 1905.

ing interest at 7 per cent, protected by $700,000 worth of Western Union stock as collateral, was gratefully accepted.

Immediately after the meeting, Cornell visited Harvard University, in quest of useful suggestions. Conducted about the Yard by President Thomas Hill, he was impressed by Holworthy Hall, with its student suites. He planned to buy the largest telescope in the world. He was forced, however, to recognize that the most gigantic telescope would avail nothing without astronomers, learned and learning.

During the winter nothing much was done. Cornell was willing to let time pass, to let funds accumulate, to avoid spending capital. The income from the endowment and from land-scrip sales was about $40,000 annually, enough for the first building costs.

The third meeting of the Board was held in Albany on 14 March 1866. The Building Committee reported, favoring separate buildings, because of the fire hazard; stone construction, free of extravagance; and within the buildings separate units with separate entrances, as at Yale. (Hence for a century, in Morrill, McGraw, and White Halls, students have been running downstairs, outdoors, in at the next door, and upstairs again.)

Bids for Building No. 1 were called for, and the contract awarded, for $58,000. The stone was quarried from the base of the Library slope. Ezra Cornell kept an officious eye on all the work.

It is evident that, as is so often the case, the trustees were thankfully leaving the burdens of management to those willing to bear them. These two were Ezra Cornell and Andrew D. White. Between them there was an informal division of duties. Cornell undertook the financial management and the buildings; White made the educational plans.

Cornell was conscious that the fair promises of the Morrill Act were more than delusive. Few honest settlers would buy land scrip; most of them could qualify for the free land offered by the Homestead Act. But in the future America good farm land and timberland would surely be precious. Since the state was forbidden to locate the lands, the only solution was for friends of the University to buy the scrip, locate the holdings, and turn over the eventual profits to the University. And since no other friend of the University would risk actual cash, Ezra Cornell would have to do it himself. He bought scrip for 100,000 acres, at fifty cents an acre, even before an act of the legislature (10 April 1866) defined the terms. This act provided that the trustees of the University, or an individual acting in their interest, were entitled to buy the scrip for the future benefit of the institution.

The Comptroller sold, then and later, scrip representing over 500,000 acres to the Hon. Ezra Cornell, for a down payment of thirty cents an acre, or approximately half the market price. Cornell agreed that as the lands should be resold he would pay into the State Treasury a further thirty cents an acre. On such sales Mr. Cornell would be reimbursed by the University at the rate of sixty cents per acre, plus locating and management costs, taxes, and so forth. All surplus would be paid to the Cornell University Endowment Fund.

Thus the University's endowment, in the early years, was in three parts. There was, in the first place, Cornell's outright gift of $500,000, long known as the Founder's Fund. Second, there was the state's College Land Scrip Fund, the sum realized by the sale of the land scrip by the state to Mr. Cornell. This sum, retained in the hands of the state, is now $688,576.12, and annual interest at 5 per cent, or $34,429, is still faithfully set down in the state's budget as a payment to Cornell University. And third, there was the Cornell Endowment Fund, to be drawn from eventual profits on land sales.

Cornell flung himself into the delightful task of locating a half-million-acre principality, nearly as large as Luxemburg. On the advice of his lumberman friend, Henry W. Sage, he concentrated on the pine lands of Wisconsin.

The expenses of locating and holding these lands soon proved to be enormous. The costs were great enough if the work was honestly done. Intelligent timber cruisers had to walk the length and breadth of each section, estimating the value, present and future, of the timber and reckoning the means of transport to a river or railroad. It cost as much to inspect a worthless section as an area of rich growth. And the land business was notorious for its crookedness. A land merchant was automatically termed a land shark, and usually only the sharks survived among the innocent and upright. Ezra Cornell, a fat food fish among the sharks, was soon plentifully lacerated.

He discovered that he could not comfortably sit back and wait for his land to increase in value. The western settlers burned with hatred for the eastern speculators who intended to profit by the settlers' energy and privations. Often they had good reason. As soon as a promising hamlet took shape, outsiders would buy all the surrounding land, hold it unimproved, and thus deprive the town of its hinterland, even of its existence.

Cornell fondly hoped that he could persuade the state of Wisconsin to remit taxes on his lands, destined for educational service. Quite the contrary; the resentful Wisconsonians built useless roads, scholarless schools, and pillared courthouses out of taxes, which fell entirely on the absentee owners.[2]

In the summer of 1866 Cornell went to Wisconsin to inspect the pine lands. By night he heard the howling of wolves around his forest camps; by day he dealt with others in log land offices. In spite of all, he located his land well and wisely. He was inspired by the sight of Nature's endless wealth. His "grand idea" was to hold this wealth in confidence and patience, till time, Nature, and the needs of a growing country should unite, to provide a great endowment for his university. He wrote to his wife (on 4 August 1866, immediately after the signing of the contract with the New York State Comptroller):

I now feel for the first time that the destiny of the Cornell University was fixed, and that its ultimate endowment would be ample for the vast field of labor it embraces, and if properly organized for the development of truth, industry, and frugality it will become a power in the land which will controll and mold the future of this great state, and carry it onward and upward in its industrial development and support of religious liberty and its guaranty of equal rights and equal laws to all men.

Of Cornell's trials and pains in the fulfillment of his grand idea we are to hear more.

Meanwhile White was busy with his assignment, the preparation of bylaws. His fluent thought, his ready pen, responded with a Plan of Organization, presented to the Board of Trustees on 21 October 1866.[3] It is a memorable document, the manifesto of a radical, enlightened scholar, rebelling against the smug obscurantism of the established colleges.

He pointed out that there were few or no precedents for the kind of institution he envisaged. The educational problem was double; it was necessary to give instruction in special departments, such as agriculture and industrial mechanics, which should be regarded as the peers of all other subjects; and it was necessary to give a general education to those young men whose purposes were not yet defined. For the latter class the usual curriculum, a rigid classical-mathematical course, was unsatisfactory. "Higher general education has lost its hold upon the majority of the trusted leaders of society, it has therefore become

[2] See especially Paul W. Gates, *The Wisconsin Pine Lands of Cornell University* (Ithaca, 1943).

[3] *Report of the Committee on Organization* (Albany, 1867).

underestimated and distrusted by a majority of the people at large, and therefore it is neglected by a majority of our young men of energy and ability."

We must then, he says, make a college of wider scope, remembering the oft-repeated declaration of our founder that he "wishes to make such provision that every person can find opportunity here to pursue any study he desires."

(Here is the first appearance of the motto which stands upon Cornell University's Great Seal: "I would found an institution where any person can find instruction in any study." The lapidary form is that of Andrew D. White. George S. Batchellor, an intimate, testified: "His pen traced the present motto as the language of Ezra Cornell." White liked to improve, for publication, the utterances of his rude companions. Possibly Cornell actually said something like: "I'd like to start a school where anybody can study anything he's a mind to.") [4]

We shall divide our structure, continues Mr. White, into two parts: one, for the students who have chosen their career, a Division of Special Sciences and Arts, as Agriculture and Engineering, with special emphasis on Jurisprudence, Political Science, and History; and a second part for those seeking a broad preparation for life, that is, a General Course, or Division of Science, Literature, and the Arts in General.

The objection will immediately be made, he recognizes, that "the function of colleges is to give discipline, that knowledge is subordinate. We answer that they should give both, and that as a rule the attempt

[4] Carl Becker, *Cornell University: Founders and the Founding* (Ithaca, 1943), p. 188. Cornell at least approved the present wording (EC to ADW, 23 Feb. 1868). Unwittingly, he paraphrased Dr. Samuel Johnson, who said to Boswell: "I would have the world to be thus told, 'Here is a school where everything may be learnt.'" One is reminded of President Wayland's *Report to the Corporation of Brown University on Changes in the System of Collegiate Education* (Providence, 1850). He proposed a system in which "every student might study what he chose, all that he chose, and nothing but what he chose." John Humphrey Noyes, the extraordinary founder of the Oneida Community, saw a Cornell *Register* in 1872, and on reading the Founder's motto remarked: "I would like to found an institution where a person can get systematic instruction on the way to find God, in the art of walking in the Spirit, in the art of love, general and special, in the theory and practice of social life, in the art of conversation, in the art of sexual intercourse, in scientific propagation as applied to human beings, in the art of managing infants, in the art of rearing boys and girls, and to sum up all, in the art of making a happy home" (Robert A. Parker, *A Yankee Saint* [New York, 1935], p. 239). Mr. Noyes would have found some of his ideals realized in the College of Home Economics.

to give mental discipline by studies which the mind does not desire is as unwise as to attempt to give physical nourishment by food which the body does not desire. Discipline comes not by studies which are 'droned over.' " (Modern educational psychology thoroughly bears out White's conviction.)

He proposes then a Department of Commerce and Trade, of which there was as yet no example in America.

The General Course would present various alternatives, with or without Classics, and with ample opportunity for work in the sciences. Those who should find the several alternatives too restricting might take an Optional Course, choosing any three subjects from the University's offerings.

(Thus the "elective system" is formally proposed. At Cornell it was established in effective and lasting form, for the first time in America. Charles W. Eliot is often credited with propounding it, at his inauguration at Harvard in 1869. But the idea goes back to Benjamin Franklin and Thomas Jefferson. Vain efforts to broaden the curriculum were made at Amherst and the University of Vermont in 1826, at New York University in 1831. White had seen free election [*Lernfreiheit*] in successful operation in Paris and Berlin and a marked loosening of the curriculum at Michigan. White always resented the acclaim which Eliot, a late-comer, received for publicizing a Cornell innovation.)

White defends warmly the principle of liberty in the student's choice of studies. "The usual imposition of a single fixed course is fatal to any true university spirit in this country; it cramps colleges and men; it has much to do with that strange anomaly under the existing system— scholars stepping out of the highest scholastic positions in college classes into nonentity in active life; it has been the main agent in bringing about that relaxation of the hold which colleges once had upon the nation, which all thoughtful men deplore." Most students, if well advised, are entirely competent to choose the work they desire and need.

But discipline, discipline! Well, there is no discipline in the unwilling pursuit of distasteful subjects. "Vigorous, energetic study, prompted by enthusiasm or a high sense of the value of a subject, is the only kind of study not positively hurtful to mental power."

White then offers his dearest proposal: that the faculty consist of a group of young, ardent, ambitious resident professors, supplemented by nonresident professors, or visiting lecturers, who should be the world's most eminent scholars, original thinkers, inspirers. Their presence on a campus would happily stimulate both the students and the resident faculty.

What manner of men shall the professors be? They are the discoverers and diffusers of truth. And "the power of discovering truth and the power of imparting it are almost invariably found together." We expect that with breadth of mind will be associated elevation of character.

This University must not only make scholars; it has a higher duty; it must make *men*—men manly, earnest, and of good general culture. We must not make the mistake so common in older colleges—in selecting to govern and guide bright, high-spirited young men tutors who do not and cannot know anything of the world and of what the world is thinking—instructors who lead students to associate learning with boorishness or clownishness.

These manly teachers must be the friends and companions of the students. "It is recommended that the duty of acquaintance and social intercourse with students be impressed upon the faculty, and that additions be made to professors' salaries expressly as an indemnity or provision for such social privileges to students." (This admirable proposal has never yet been put into practice.)

White recommends that a President of the University be elected at an early day. Contrary to the usual practice, the President shall not be responsible for student discipline. This shall be a duty of the faculty. The faculty shall be organized in departmental legislative units, presided over by the President or a Dean. The combined faculty shall meet regularly "for the purpose of conducting the general administration of the institution and memorializing the Trustees, discussing general questions of educational policy, and presenting papers upon special subjects in literature, science, and the arts." This body shall be known as the Academic Senate.

The everlasting problem of tenure and efficiency is touched upon, with the question how the administration may rid the institution of incompetent and superannuated scholars. No clear conclusion was reached, nor is the problem yet disposed of.[5]

[5] In the following year, 1867, White thought he had found a way. In a report to the Committee on Faculty he wrote: "At the end of each college year there shall be held a scrutiny of the work done in the University during the year by every person employed by the Trustees in the Administration or Instruction of the University. . . . The work of each professor as an instructor and participant in University authority shall be scrutinized repeatedly and a ballot shall be held

As for professors' salaries, it was noted that the usual scale ran from about a thousand dollars a year to four or five thousand, in the exceptional case of Columbia University. White recommends a rate of $1,750 to $2,250 for full professors.

For the trustees a six-year term was proposed. In addition to the yearly elections of new trustees by the Board, the graduate alumni, when they should reach sufficient numbers, should annually choose a representative.

The report now discusses physical equipment, an experimental farm for agriculture, workshops for engineering, museums for the various departments. White, himself an impassioned collector, had great faith in museums. And the library, the culmination of all. "A large library is absolutely necessary to the efficiency of the various departments. Without it, our men of the highest ability will be frequently plodding in old circles and stumbling into old errors."

As for the code and conduct of the University, White rejects a military government and a system of college policing. The students should be free.

Much is trusted to the manliness of the students. The attempt is to teach the students to govern themselves, and to cultivate acquaintance and confidence between Faculty and students. This the Committee believe is possible. They believe that by rigid execution of a few disciplinary laws, by promotion of pleasant, extra-official intercourse between teachers and taught, by placing professors over students, not as police, but as a body of friends, this government may be made to work better than any other.

On the vexed question of manual labor, it is recognized that the experiment, often tried, has usually failed. Nevertheless, Cornell University might properly encourage, without requiring, student labor.

Further, "it is one of the strange things in the history of education that American votaries of classical scholarship have been so neglectful of that bodily culture which, in the ancient civilization they justly honor, was the main culture." The University must require knowledge of the body's behavior and inculcate health through exercise. All students must attend lectures on anatomy, physiology, and hygiene. A gymnasium must be erected, grounds be set apart for the national

---

to determine the estimation in which the year's work of each is held by the Board. There shall be prepared three sets of ballots inscribed severally: 'approved,' 'fair,' 'unsatisfactory.' . . . The inscription upon a plurality of ballots shall pass as the judgment of the Board" (quoted by Walter P. Rogers, *Andrew D. White and the Modern University* [Ithaca, 1942], pp. 161-162).

game of baseball, and boating clubs on Lake Cayuga be encouraged. "Deterioration in physical culture will be held in the same category with want of progress in mental culture. Either will subject the delinquent to deprivation of university privileges."

Tuition will be set at twenty dollars per year. It is hoped that lodging and board will be provided by the citizens of Ithaca. The dormitory system is thoroughly undesirable.

Large bodies of students collected in dormitories often arrive at a degree of turbulence which small parties, gathered in the houses of citizens, seldom if ever reach. No private citizen who lets rooms in his own house to four or six students would tolerate for an hour the anarchy which most tutors in charge of college dormitories are compelled to overlook.

The professors should not have to play the part of spies and policemen.

The University must have a vital connection with the school system of the state. The provision in the Charter that one student from each Assembly district shall receive free tuition is itself a recognition of the University's role. Cornell is intended to serve the people. "We must never lose sight of that great body of men to whose mental needs the Act makes special reference, and of whom it speaks as 'the industrial classes.' "

And finally, a resounding chord to ring in the hearers' ears:

A general principle, fundamental and formative, a principle to serve as a test and guide—it is the principle so admirably enunciated by Wilhelm von Humboldt and elaborated by John Stuart Mill: "The great and leading principle is the absolute and essential importance of human development in its richest diversity."

In this ample Plan of Organization there are two noteworthy zones of silence. White does not mention coeducation, in which he devoutly believed. The time was not yet ripe. And he says nothing of his cherished nonsectarianism; indeed, he says not a word about religious education. No doubt there were tender susceptibilities on the Board of Trustees.

I have quoted this document at such length because it seems to me one of the most important in the history of Cornell University, nay, in the history of American higher education. White had often dreamed of a shrine of learning, an American Oxford, complete with ready-made ivy and miraculously springing lawns. Now he was forced to fit his dreams within a frame of reality. He had to think seriously about the demands of teachers and students, about equipment, about money. The dream was not dissipated; it is accorded with the requirements of cruel facts. The great ideas remain, the ideas which set Cornell University apart in its time, which still set it apart. Here is Cornell in embryo; and even today, I think, the character of Cornell preserves the essential forms foreseen in the Plan of Organization.

The genesis of White's ideas might be discussed at any length. Some of them came from his experience in Paris, Berlin, and Michigan. For instance, the "optional, or partial course" was established by President Tappan of Michigan in 1851. There were other predecessors. White had the highest admiration for Francis Wayland, who, at Brown in the forties, attempted vainly to inaugurate practical courses and free electives. White called him the strongest man who has ever stood in an American college presidency. But, he recalled, poor Wayland admitted that he had been "nibbled to death by ducks." [6] Some of White's proposals were in the air. He quotes with approval John Stuart Mill's demand for diversity rather than uniformity in education. He might also have quoted Edward L. Youmans, whose views were expressed in his *Popular Science Monthly*.[7] But whatever the origin of White's ideas, he made them his own and cast them in a coherent, practicable program.

With most of this program Ezra Cornell had no quarrel. But the body of his own convictions and purposes was somewhat different. Each ideal man portrayed by most philosophers, college presidents, and professors on curriculum committees strangely resembles the speaker. The needs which Ezra Cornell sought to satisfy were the needs

[6] Andrew D. White, *Scientific and Industrial Education*, address to New York State Agricultural Society, 10 Feb. 1869 (New York, 1874), p. 4. For the whole subject, see Rogers, *White and the Modern University*.

[7] Youmans says (*The Culture Demanded of Modern Life* [New York, 1867], p. vi) that the chief fault of education is the lack of study of nature. "In place of the excess of verbal acquisition, we need more thinking about things; in place of passive acceptance of mere book and tutorial authority, more cultivation of independent judgment; in place of the arbitrary presentation of unrelated subjects, the branches of knowledge require to be dealt with in a more rational and connected order; and in place of much that is irrelevant, antiquated, and unpractical in our systems of study, there is needed a larger infusion of the living and available truth which belongs to the present time." And on page 51: "The first thing to be done by the teacher is to awaken the pupil's interest, to engage his sympathies and kindle his enthusiasm, for these are the motors of intellectual progress; it is then easy to enchain his attention, to store his mind with knowledge, and carry mental cultivation to the point of discipline." White was a good friend of Youmans, and read his book on the Albany train, with frequent marginal ejaculations of approval.

79

of his own young remembered self. He had small concern with the General Course; what interested him was the practical training of "the industrial classes" in agriculture and the mechanic arts. And he was far more taken with applied technology than with scientific theory. (Remember that he had been wont to apply the contemptuous term "professor" to S. F. B. Morse.) On the virtues of manual labor, which had made his own strong body, he was inflexible. But physical education, he thought, was just monkey tricks, serving no practical end. Cornell students would have to get out and sweat with axe and shovel. Do 'em good.

After his death a writer who obviously knew him well said that Ezra Cornell's concept of a university was "a sort of school of refuge, with the penal features left out." [8] It was destined for poor boys in need of practical instruction. He had little understanding of the highest scholarship. "He looked upon scholars as men who were generally harmless, and might occasionally even become useful."

Ezra Cornell's insistence on practicality was important in making the Cornell idea. The test of utility has remained a settled constant in the University's behavior. Cornell restrained White, kept him in touch with earthy reality. In his turn, White frequently had to restrain Cornell. For Cornell was a dreamer too.

At the meeting of the Board of Trustees on 21 November 1866 the Plan of Organization was read by Mr. White and loudly applauded. The Board proceeded to the election of a President of the University. The Honorable Andrew D. White of Syracuse was unanimously chosen.

White insists that he was taken totally by surprise. "Nothing was further from my expectations or wishes." He expostulated, insisting that the University needed an older man, in stouter health, of wider reputation. But he was borne down, and he accepted finally "as a temporary matter. I had no idea of remaining in [the presidency] for more than a few months. My purpose was in the meantime to get the new enterprise started, to aid in selecting a man who should carry it on." [9]

Such is his remembrance, rearranged by deferential memory. However, several people had suggested openly that he was the inevitable

---

[8] *Cornell Era*, 8 Jan. 1875, p. 108.

[9] *Autobiography of Andrew Dickson White* (New York, 1905), I, 307; "Notes on History," ADW Papers.

president. Cornell himself had given the strongest of hints. In July 1866 Yale University offered White the post of professor and director of the proposed School of Art and Architecture; and White seems to have refrained from giving a definite answer before the Cornell trustees' meeting. His alleged surprise at the proposal of the presidency, his reluctance to accept, was surely a little game he played with himself. Who would not rather yield, protesting, to duty than to ambition? [10] At any rate, he accepted, with becoming words. "May Heaven strengthen me!" he wrote that night in his diary.

During the winter of 1866–1867 not much was done. Both White and Cornell were serving their last terms in the State Senate. Cornell was occupied with the opening of the Cornell Library (on 20 December 1866) and with far-reaching plans for Wisconsin land purchases. In the spring he was able to devote himself to the university building. The skeleton of Building No. 1 (Morrill Hall) stood already, solitary on the hilltop. Cornell harried the architect and the contractor, who replied with bitter complaints that the benefactor was months behind with his payments. For all his wealth, Cornell was chronically short of cash, and further he had a lifelong reluctance to pay bills until legal action was threatened.

A rare opportunity for campus planning was explored and lost. Frederick Law Olmsted, celebrated designer of Central Park in New York City, was called in by White as landscape consultant. Olmsted's principle was to develop the natural features of the site, with use of native bushes and wild flowers, to make a harmonious irregularity. He wished to arrange the Cornell buildings in an interesting echelon. His views proved to be too novel; Andrew D. White had been dreaming since boyhood of Quadrangles.[11]

Plans were drawn for a second building, the present White Hall, to be in "a massive Florentine style of architecture." And Cascadilla Place was completed and reordered as a residence for teachers and students. Despite bitter outcries from Dr. Samantha Nivison, the investors in the water cure renounced their purpose and accepted fifty cents on the dollar for their contributions.

Since it was evident that Ithaca householders could not or would not

[10] T. M. Cooley to ADW, 20 Sept. 1865; George F. Comfort to ADW, 16 March 1866; EC to ADW, 15 Aug. 1866; George Geddes to EC, 29 Nov. 1866; Becker, *Founders*, pp. 121–122.

[11] 13 June 1867 *et passim*, ADW Papers; Kermit C. Parsons, "History of Campus Planning at Cornell" (typescript, 1952, C.U. Archives).

lodge the expected students, the projected buildings were designed to be part dormitory, part classroom.

Ezra Cornell, captured by the delights of building, now proposed to erect a fitting residence for himself. The house, the present Llenroc, home of the Delta Phi fraternity, and one of the best existing examples of mid-century construction and decoration, was destined to absorb a large measure of Cornell's time and money.

"The University needs buildings much, a fine faculty more," said White in his annual report for 1867. "Buildings never yet made a great university. . . . Better a splendid and complete faculty in a barn than an insufficient faculty in a palace."

The discovery of a splendid and complete faculty was no easy task. There was as yet no professional corps of college teachers in America, no system for their advanced training, no real graduate school. (The first American Ph.D. was granted by Yale in 1861.) The teachers were likely to be well-connected failures in the law or the ministry, content with a professor's pittance. The economic level of the faculties was that of the clergy, but without the clergy's security. Few were specialists in any modern sense. Most of the early applicants for posts at Cornell professed themselves perfectly ready to teach anything.

White proposed to the trustees in February 1867 the first two Cornell professors: Evan W. Evans of Marietta College, Ohio, who would organize the Department of Mathematics, and William Channing Russel, to be professor of modern languages and associate professor of history. (This is apparently the first use of the term "associate professor" in American higher education.)

Russel played a great part in the early history of the University. He was a Columbia graduate, who had practiced law in New York for thirty years, had lived abroad and evidently spoke French. He was already in his mid-fifties. Though he was a man of scholarly tastes who had read widely and who wrote uncommonly well, his only professional qualification was a year or two in the Department of Metaphysical, Moral, and Political Science in Antioch College. One wonders a little that White should have chosen such an obviously unprofessional historian to aid him in his darling Department of History. Perhaps the fact is that he recognized in Russel a gentleman of his own class, a nephew of the famous William Ellery Channing and a connection by marriage of James Russell Lowell. And Russel was recommended (by no less a person than Edward Everett Hale) as a man who was "long on discipline," who would be generally useful in a college.

During the summer of 1867 White visited various universities, in quest of ideas for the technical departments and particularly in quest of brilliant young men. At the trustees' meeting in September he made four nominations. Two of these, George C. Caldwell, professor of agricultural chemistry, and Burt Green Wilder, professor of comparative anatomy and natural history, were to serve out their active lives at Cornell, and Wilder was to become a legendary figure.

More candidates were presented to the trustees at their meeting in February 1868. Important among them were the resident professor of military science, Major J. H. Whittlesey, and the professor of north European languages, Daniel Willard Fiske, who would play both hero and villain in the Cornell drama. And an astounding slate of nonresident professors: Louis Agassiz in natural history; James Hall, State Geologist and famous paleontologist; James Russell Lowell in English literature; George William Curtis in recent literature; Governor Fred Holbrook of Vermont in agriculture; Theodore W. Dwight of Columbia in constitutional law.

As the reports of the new university and its sensational faculty appeared in the press, they were greeted with wonderment, approbation, and animosity.

The animosity was inevitable. The Cornell idea itself, with its proclaimed need for an overturn in educational theory and practice, insulted every established college. Cornell's capture of the land grant left burning jealousies in many a starveling institution. Ezra Cornell's own road to success was littered with bested, impoverished rivals. His very wealth was an offense. It was much magnified, its origins called into question, and his benevolent purposes aspersed. It is always very hard to make the poor love the rich.

In fact, the wealth of the university was more *in posse* than *in esse*. The first costs of building, which were to come out of income, strained the budget. Ezra Cornell was putting all his own available funds into land purchase. In January 1868 Western Union passed its dividend, and he found himself actually out of cash. He tried to borrow $40,000 from Hiram Sibley, at 7 per cent. The university administration was rich in possessions but poor in pocket, and in this situation it was to continue for many a year.

The enemies of Cornell University made a last desperate effort to recapture the land-grant money. They were joined by the Protestant denominations and their powerful press. These were alarmed by the proclaimed nonsectarianism of Cornell, by the election of a layman as president, and by the absence of any reference to religious instruction in the Plan of Organization.

Nonsectarianism was not indeed an invention of Andrew D. White's. In the liberal eighteenth century the University of Pennsylvania, Brown, the University of Georgia, and, later, New York University refused any religious tests. The charter of Union College, in 1795, provided that the majority of the trustees should never be of one denomination. Matthew Vassar laid down for his college, in 1861, the rule that all sectarian influences should be carefully excluded. Cornell was not unique, but it was, in the 1860's, the most conspicuous, and, in the opinion of many honest Christians, the most threatening to moral and spiritual welfare.

In March 1868 White went abroad, to visit model institutions, to buy books and equipment, to collect professors.[12] In France, Germany, and England, White spent his days in a happy flurry, like a mother given carte blanche to purchase a trousseau. A stream of packing cases flowed to Ithaca, containing chemicals, laboratory apparatus, anatomical, architectural, and engineering models, a collection of miniature plows of all ages and nations, pictures and statues of the nobler sort, and of course books, whole libraries of books.

He found the horse doctor Ezra Cornell demanded—James Law, educated in British and French institutions, professor in the Veterinary College of Edinburgh, a true scientist, a man of force and vigor. Dr. Law was to be one of the great pioneers of American veterinary science, and the efficient first cause of Cornell's Veterinary College.

White found another prize. Goldwin Smith was an eminent historian and publicist, recently Regius Professor of History at Oxford. He was a friend of the United States and had effectively upheld the Union cause in England during the Civil War. He was apparently going through a period of self-questioning and reorientation; he had resigned his Oxford professorship and was casting about for a more worthy employment of his life. White's suggestion that he should join the brave new venture in Ithaca appealed to his troubled mood. White's eloquent idealism and educational radicalism corresponded to his own.

---

[12] According to an oft-repeated anecdote, told in White's *Autobiography*, Ezra Cornell saw White off in New York, and as the ship drew away from the pier he cupped his hands and shouted across the gap: "Don't forget the horse-doctor!" But it seems certain that Cornell was not in New York for the leave-taking. Probably White's memory transposed the circumstance from the Ithaca station to the ship's pier (Max Farrand to G. L. Burr, 27 Oct. 1913, in Burr Papers).

He was lured by the thought of a bold new beginning in a high-minded rustic Utopia, with possibly just enough hardship and abnegation for his soul's good. "White has sent me some photographs," he wrote to Charles Eliot Norton. "There seem to be a great number of waterfalls, which I abhor. . . . My soul is heavy within me when I think of the Yankee bread." [13]

Meanwhile, in Ithaca, Cornell was superintending construction and purchasing all the equipment for a new university. Classroom seats, desks, blackboards, erasers, chalk; furnaces, stoves, coal scuttles; beds, mattresses, chiffoniers, slop jars; kitchen equipment, china, napkins, carpets, paint, coal. . . . There was everything to be thought of, everything to be haggled over.

White returned to Ithaca on 28 July and on the following day reported at the eighth meeting of the Board of Trustees. To the confusion of historians, the record of this meeting was somehow overlooked. It is omitted in the printed *Proceedings of the Board of Trustees;* therefore all succeeding meetings have been misnumbered, and a puzzling gap has existed in the formal record.[14]

[13] 8 Oct. 1868, in *Massachusetts Historical Society Proceedings*, Dec. 1915, p. 140.

[14] The manuscript minutes are in the first box labeled "Trustees' Meetings," in the C.U. Archives. For the record: Major Whittlesey explained his views and purposes as Military Professor. There was a valuable discussion of modes of college government, in which Professors Russel, Blake, Dwight, Evans, Caldwell and Whittlesey, and Trustees White, Brooks, Kelly, Andrus, and Williams participated. Ezra Cornell reported on organization and finances. President White reported on his investigations and acquisitions in Europe. The purchase of the Anthon classical library was authorized. The question of rules for the government of the University was referred to the President of the Board (Mr. Cornell), the President of the University, and members of the Faculty. A memorial was read from the New York State Teachers' Association, requesting that the privileges of the institution be made free to all without regard to sex. Referred to a special committee. The following professors were elected: William D. Wilson, professor of moral and intellectual philosophy; William Charles Cleveland, professor of civil engineering; James Law, professor of veterinary surgery; and Goldwin Smith, nonresident professor of English history. Ezra Cornell was requested to sit for his portrait, at University expense. A communication from Professor James Peck advocating instruction in music was referred to the Executive Committee. The opening of the University was postponed to 7 October, to avoid conflict with the State Fair. The Executive Committee was authorized to appoint professors to vacancies. Reported that Cascadilla Place could be leased for a rental of $9,000. Mr. Cornell reported a delay on Building No. 2, owing to the difficulty in obtaining white stone. The erection of a temporary wooden laboratory building was authorized.

One enormous uncertainly hovered over every decision. How many students would appear on the opening day? Too many? Or too few? Fearing, perhaps, that there would be too few, Cornell wrote a letter to the New York *Tribune*, on 10 August, pointing out that students could work their way through the new university. He listed the opportunities, in farm labor, landscaping, machine operation, carpentry. Some early comers were already earning two dollars a day, haying and harvesting. "I will assure the boys that if they will perform a quarter as much labor as I did at their ages, or as I do now at 60 years of age, they will find no difficulty in paying their expenses while prosecuting their studies at Ithaca."

President White was aghast. Some two thousand letters poured in, mostly from totally unqualified young men or from their impecunious parents, who recognized that to obtain a college education while working a quarter as hard as the Founder was a rare bargain.

As the summer waned, the professors arrived, seeking quarters for themselves and their families, and finding them only within the new but already repulsive walls of Cascadilla Place. Among the appointments was a remarkable young man, Charles Fred Hartt, professor of geology, who was frankly termed a genius; and Albert N. Prentiss, professor of botany, superintendent of grounds, and director of manual labor.

On 22 September the Faculty of Cornell University met for the first time. A communication from the Executive Committee was read, requiring each professor to make a monthly report. The Faculty was informed that the engagement of all professors by the trustees was terminable at the pleasure of either party on the giving of three months' notice. No professor should be removed except by majority vote of the whole Board. To the trustees, accustomed to firing employees with no notice at all, this statement of tenure seemed uncommonly generous.[15]

On 6 October all candidates for entrance were ordered to report at the cellar door of the Cornell Library building for examinations. The examinations in spelling and grammar were held in one corner of the cellar room, arithmetic in another, geography in between, wherever there was sufficient light to read by.

(One may be a little startled by the subjects of the entrance examinations. Of the forty students who entered the classical course a sufficient preparation in Latin and Greek was required. The others were admitted on demonstrating only a knowledge of the common-school

[15] ADW Papers, 21–30 Sept. 1868; Faculty Minutes, in hands of Dean of the Faculty.

subjects, plus algebra through quadratics. Most of the early land-grant colleges asked nothing more; some of them dispensed entirely with entrance requirements.)

The following day, 7 October 1868, was Inauguration Day. Happily, it was bright and warm, though a brisk wind blew. This was fortunate, for the autumn had been marked by torrential rains. Faculty and students that year gained an impression of Ithaca weather which still persists.

At sunrise on Inauguration Day, said the New York *Times* envoy, "from all the hills poured forth delightful music, and every few minutes the thunder of artillery from the eastern hills responded to the booming of cannon from a lofty eminence on the west side of town." Students and citizens thronged to Library Hall, which was tastefully decorated with marble vases of flowers and a large cross covered with moss, entwined with myrtle. On the side wall the motto of the new university was blazoned in evergreen letters, and behind the speakers the illustrious names of CORNELL and WHITE appeared in large white letters against artistically draped red flannel, on which stars cut out of silver paper were pinned at pleasing intervals. Thus, entirely unintentionally, the Cornell colors were established for all time, on the first Cornell banner.[16]

Cornell and White had both been ill, but they roused from their beds for the ceremony. It was expected that Governor Fenton would address the meeting; he had been in Ithaca the previous day to review the National Guard. But—evidently sensing that Cornell University was politically dangerous—he had fled on the evening train. The Lieutenant-Governor, Stewart L. Woodford, ever the University's faithful friend, substituted.

At ten o'clock Whitlock's Band played "Hail to the Chief," and the Founder, the President, the trustees, and the distinguished guests took their places.

Mr. Cornell, seated, read his brief address. He admitted that his university was unfinished; but no matter, it is a commencement we now have in hand. "I hope," he said, "we have laid the foundation of

---

[16] All the red flannel in Ithaca was borrowed from the ardent storekeepers. The names "Cornell" and "White" were formed by twisting each letter of wire, then dipping them in a bath of dilute alum. As the water evaporated, the alum formed on the wire in beautiful crystals. See the recollections of the artificer, William G. Johnson, in the Ithaca *Journal* for 8 Oct. 1893. A copy is in the Van Cleef Scrapbook, C.U. Archives.

an institution which shall combine practical with liberal education, which shall fit the youth of our country for the professions, the farms, the mines, the manufactories, for the investigations of science, and for mastering all the practical questions of life with success and honor. I believe that we have made the beginning of an institution which will prove highly beneficial to the poor young men and the poor young women of our country." Thus he put on record his intention to admit women. He pointed out the services to agriculture of the trained chemist, veterinarian, and technologist. "I desire that this shall prove to be the beginning of an institution which shall furnish better means for the culture of all men of every calling, of every aim; which shall make men more truthful, more honest, more virtuous, more noble, more manly; which shall give them higher purposes and more lofty aims, qualifying them to serve their fellow men better, preparing them to serve society better, training them to be more useful in their relations to the state, and to better comprehend their higher and holier relations to their families and their God. It shall be our aim and our constant effort to make true Christian men, without dwarfing or paring them down to fit the narrow gauge of any sect." [17]

They are good words, needing no revision today. On the whole, Cornell University has subscribed, and still subscribes, to the stated ideal of the Founder.

Lieutenant-Governor Woodford then administered the oath of office to President White and put in his hands the keys of the University and the Great Seal. The President, gathering strength as he spoke, delivered his Inaugural Address. He dealt at length with the ideas incorporated in the University. First the Foundation Ideas: the close union of liberal and practical education, unsectarianism (with many examples—perhaps too many examples for prudence—of the ravages of intolerance in contemporary colleges), the union of the University with the school system of the state, and the concentration of revenues for higher education. He passed then to the Formative Ideas: equality in prestige between the courses of study, variety of courses to suit different tastes and purposes and freedom of choice among them, the combination of study and physical labor, the magnification of scientific study. In short, the University would adapt itself to current needs of the nation. He quoted the advice of Goldwin Smith, to act independently of European educational experience "and to remain uninfluenced, either in the way

[17] *Account of the Proceedings at the Inauguration* (Ithaca, 1869; reprinted 1921).

88

of imitation or antagonism, by other educational institutions or ideas."
Then the Governmental Ideas: the constant renewal of the Board of
Trustees and the election of alumni trustees; student self-government
within a kindly military organization, the refusal of any distinction of
race or sex. (But unfortunately, he avowed, the University was not
yet physically equipped to admit women.) Next the Permeating or
Crowning Ideas: the need of labor and sacrifice in developing the
individual man in all his nature, in all his powers (thus English literature, music, and art appreciation would become curricular subjects),
and the application of the powers of man to the needs of society.
Finally the Eliminated Ideas: those of pedants ("out upon the whole
race of these owls!") and those of Philistines, who would make all
education serve mean advantage.

It was a thrilling speech, a splendid declaration of educational independence, wildly applauded by all the liberal-minded listeners. It remains a fundamental statement of the Cornell Idea. President Edmund
Ezra Day in his Inaugural Address in 1937 restated and reaffirmed the
Inaugural Address of President White. The influence of White's educational manifesto was long-lasting. If one reviews his specific proposals,
one observes that all of them, except perhaps the manual-labor plan
and the military organization, have prevailed, and have been incorporated into the structure of nearly every American university.
White proved his own greatness by enunciating the ideas of the future.
But that future is now past, and the battle is won; and one must admit
that White's ideas are not of much service to us in forecasting our
own future. On the other hand, Ezra Cornell's more general purpose,
to train aspiring youth to social usefulness, is still valid and can still
remain our guide.

In White's program, the modern teacher may well remark the absence of any reference to research, which has become a university's
second aim, sometimes its first. The fact is that the concept of research
was as yet hardly formulated in America.[18]

[18] In Germany, of course, the university had already become a research center.
Henry P. Tappan, at Michigan, inspired by the German example, made research
central in his scheme for an ideal university. And agricultural research was in
progress at the University of Maryland, Michigan Agricultural College, and elsewhere. President Evan Pugh of Pennsylvania State College regarded investigation
as a faculty's duty, even in 1864. White had himself touched on investigation in his
Plan of Organization (Edward D. Eddy, *Colleges for Our Land and Time* [New
York, 1957], p. 76).

After President White, Professor W. C. Russel spoke for the faculty, very well too. Chancellor John V. L. Pruyn of the University of the State of New York concluded the morning's ceremonies.

The audience lunched briefly; and afterwards an immense throng climbed to the University, which consisted only of South University Building (which we shall henceforth term Morrill Hall) and the shell of North University, now White Hall. The doors of Morrill Hall stood wide open in welcome; in fact, they had to, as the hinges had not yet arrived.

The visitors gathered about a rough wooden structure, on the site of the present undergraduate library, wherein hung a chime of nine bells, the gift of Miss Jennie McGraw of Ithaca. Francis Miles Finch presented the chime, in resonant words which battled with a high west wind. The bells rendered "Old Hundred" and "Hail Columbia." Six other speakers vented wind-blown eloquence. Louis Agassiz of Harvard said: "I hope I shall live to see the time when all the old colleges will draw fresh life from this young university, when they will remodel their obsolete methods and come up to the mark." George William Curtis recalled young Professor White's utopian dream of a university ten years before in Michigan; he called upon God to bless the ship, the builder, the captain, faculty crew, and undergraduate passengers.

The next day, 8 October, the students were assembled before the steps of the Cornell Library. (The faculty had done an arduous and unrecognized service in correcting all the entrance exams in two nights.) The names of the successful applicants for entrance were read forth—332 in the freshman class, 80 with advanced credit in the higher classes. They were ordered to report immediately to Cascadilla Place. They panted up Buffalo Street and were met at Cascadilla by Major Whittlesey. As Professor John L. Morris remembered, "he lined them up two abreast down the entire length of the long south corridor, and then went down the line, counted off a certain number of men, and said: 'You are Company A.' Next he picked out an intelligent-looking boy from among their number and said: 'You are Captain,' and to a second: 'You are Lieutenant.' In all he formed thus six companies. Companies A, B, and C were sent off to their new quarters in Morrill Hall. The officers were given the best quarters downstairs, and the privates were in the dormitories above." [19]

Cornell University was in operation.

[19] *Cornell Magazine*, Nov. 1895, p. 51.

VI

The Early Years:
A Perambulation of the Campus

THE valiant Cornellians of the early days had the beauty of lake, hill, and valley before their eyes, the beauty of cliffs and plunging streams at hand, and to this beauty most of them responded. Goldwin Smith remembered forever the un-English splendor of the sunsets, seen from his Cascadilla window, and he recalled looking down, with emotion, upon a soaring eagle.

But in the man-made structures where the students spent their days there was little to satisfy even an unexacting aesthetic sense. Andrew D. White exhorted Ezra Cornell to achieve beauty: "The place where we are must be made beautiful and attractive. Nothing should be allowed to injure its symmetry or mar its beauty." [1] However, the word "beauty" was obscure to Quaker Cornell, as to many of his contemporaries. Some few thought the original buildings, Cascadilla, Morrill, McGraw, White, Sibley, beautiful. A visitor in 1873 called them "a fair specimen of the palaces in which Education holds perpetual levee in this land of thought." [2] But Goldwin Smith said frankly: "Nothing can redeem them but dynamite." At best, they embody the character of Ezra Cornell, grim, gray, sturdy, and economical. (And the following group, the President's House, Sage Chapel, Sage College,

[1] ADW to EC, 3 July 1868.
[2] Journal of James Hungerford Rawlins, C.U. Archives.

Franklin—romantic upstate gothic, quaintly pinnacled and bedizened
—portray the taste and the soul of Andrew D. White. It would be
perhaps dangerous to push the fancy farther, to assert that Goldwin
Smith Hall, a business structure with a Greek front, represents the
character of Jacob Gould Schurman. Or farther yet. . . .)

Cascadilla Place was the center of student life, though some undergraduates dwelt in Morrill and White and some found quarters downtown, typically in the attic rooms of Greek revival houses, sloping down
to low windows protected by the cast-iron grilles which have now
become collectors' items. The "townies" climbed to the campus by a
path known as the Bone-Yard Cut, through the cemetery (*aliter* "the
Bone Orchard") and a series of cow pastures. By 1876 an omnibus
service was available, leaving the Clinton House six times daily and
arriving at the University in a half hour.

Cascadilla, which White called "an ill-ventilated, ill-smelling, uncomfortable, ill-looking alms-house," [3] had at least the merit of housing
under one roof students and professors, with their families, and thus
enforcing an intimacy which the students appreciated more than did
the faculty.

The structure was of stone drawn from the adjacent glen. The
ground floor contained the college offices (until their transfer to Morrill
Hall), the dining halls, and a large parlor (with a piano and an ingrain
carpet!) filling nearly the whole west front. To lighten the parlor's
gloom, President White stood bronze statues in the corners and hung
on the walls noble engravings and an actual oil painting, "The Corn-
Husking," by Eastman Johnson. (It is now in the Syracuse Museum of
Art.) When the parlor was not too bitterly cold, the Cascadillans
would assemble there after supper for an hour of singing and dancing.

The students had their large dining room, lit by a skylight, and
the faculty had their own, a dark inner room with blue glass windows
opening on an airshaft. The food was said to be of an incredible bad-
ness, though a menu, apparently of 1871, offers Bean Soup; Boiled
Corn Beef; Boiled Ham; Roast Beef; Lamb; Pork and Beans; Beans,
Tomatoes, Lettuce; and Rhubarb Pie and Tapioca Pudding. Hardly a
gourmet meal, but at least there was nourishment there.

The second and third floors were divided into boxlike rooms for
the faculty and their families, while the students were lodged mostly
in dismal cells on the fourth floor, where they could occasion the
utmost disturbance for the faculty below them. The provident lived in

[3] ADW to W. C. Russel, 7 Dec. 1871.

constant terror of fire; White and others equipped themselves with coiled rope ladders. The halls, seldom washed and never aired, smelt perpetually of past dinners. As for heat, one may judge by the experience of a Russian student in January 1869. He put his high Russian boots outside his door, apparently in the expectation that they would be polished. A whimsical student filled them with water; and in the morning they were frozen solid. The Cornell *Register* boasted of running water, which was forced into Cascadilla by a hydraulic ram in adjacent Willow Pond, but the machinery was so commonly out of order that outdoor privies were provided. (In 1877 the trustees offered a reward of $100 "for the apprehension of the miscreants who set fire to the privy at Cascadilla Place.") The prospectus proudly proclaimed that the building was lit by gas. The students immediately discovered that by blowing down a gas jet they could extinguish the gas in their neighbors' rooms—and perhaps produce asphyxiation and a universal fire. A student was expelled in November 1868 for such an exploit.

Although Cascadilla stands at the brink of a lovely glen, the surroundings were for some time as distressing as the interior. A reporter noted: "An agglomeration of unpainted sheds and fences surrounding the place, a dismantled steam engine keeled up near the door, and the rough platform of unplaned boards, give one anything but a favorable preliminary impression." [4] Part of Otis Eddy's cotton mill was left standing at hand, until some aesthetically minded students set fire to it and nearly burned down Cascadilla itself. As late as 1878 the manager of the dining room kept a pigsty beside the walk to Cascadilla Bridge.

The early campus guidebooks urge the visitor to begin his inspection by taking "the Stroll," a series of charming walks laid out on the banks of the romantic stream. The stroller took, as he still may, Goldwin Smith Walk up the glen's southern side to Agassiz Rock and Eddy's Dam, now in ruins. Here one crossed the stream and returned by the Lowell Walk to the waterfall below the bridge—"an exquisite bit of scenery scarcely excelled even in the mountain valleys of Piedmont. Nor is the winter view less striking, when the rocky sides of the gorge are filled with huge icicles and the overhanging pines heavy with their weight of snow." [5]

---

[4] Unidentified Boston newspaper, 1 Feb. 1869, in EC Papers.
[5] Moses Coit Tyler tells in his diary (11 Jan. 1882) Mr. White's recollections of designing the walks and having the entrances marked with cast-iron signposts: "Agassiz Walk," etc. At his urging, Mrs. John McGraw and her daughter Jennie went to inspect them. Their report revealed a horrified displeasure. Mr. White

Emerging from the Stroll, one took the new road up the steep slope north of Cascadilla Bridge. At the top of the slope one found (on the site of Myron Taylor Hall) a rude wooden gymnasium. To the right, (in the midst of the present Engineering Quadrangle) stood the rickety terminal of Ezra Cornell's rickety railroad, the Ithaca and Cortland, commonly known (I do not know why) as "the Shoo-Fly Road." Near the station was the engine shed, housing the locomotive "Cornell University," with a view of the campus painted on her tender. The railroad, opened in 1871, followed what is now Campus Road to cross Cascadilla Creek at Dwyer's Dam, whence it climbed to the present right of way of the Lehigh Valley's Cortland branch.

Proceeding north from the railroad station, one came to a deep gully, at the junction of the present Central Avenue and Campus Road. Until this was bridged it presented a major hazard. Professor George C. Caldwell remembered: "When snow, slush, and mud alternated with each other in November, even a professor sometimes forgot his dignity and slid down the bank, and by inadvertence not always all the way down on his feet either; the hearty sympathy bestowed upon such an unfortunate by student spectators can be imagined, if not believed in." [6] No wonder it was the fashion for students and faculty alike to wear heavy cavalry boots.

One continued then on a plank walk (replaced by flagstone in 1875), past some new-made professors' houses, with, to the right, dainty Sage Chapel, the mere core of the present building. The stained-glass windows were to be admired. Thus one came to the University proper, where the three sisters, Morrill, McGraw, and White, faced the west.

The present quadrangle was a bare, undulating, gullied pasture, rather hay than greensward, bisected by an uncertain rail fence and inhabited by occasional cows and baseball players. But for botanists and entomologists the campus had a primitive charm. The shy trailing arbutus could be found there, and many another timid creature. A dozen apple trees, Tompkins County Kings, remnants of Mr. Cornell's orchard, lingered long, and the succulence of their fruit longer in old memories.[7]

---

was taken aback; he inspected and found that during the night some malefactors had pulled up the signposts and replanted them on the way to the Cascadilla privy. Privies were a perpetual source of gross comedy, which has been flushed away by modern plumbing.

[6] Quoted in W. T. Hewett, *Cornell University: A History* (New York, 1905), I, 174.

[7] Jared Van Wagenen '91, in *Cornell Countryman*, March 1959.

Morrill and White, the first two buildings, were part classroom, part dormitory. In the living sections, two students occupied a fair-sized study, with a fireplace or stove, and two small bedrooms. (This luxury of space and privacy is seldom to be found in our modern dormitories.) Elevators for coal were provided, and every suite had its own ash chute. The most grievous lack was water, which had to be fetched by bucket from a campus well. The toilets were of the dirt-and-chemical type. There were no baths.

White Hall included quarters for the Christian Association and other student clubs, and also a faculty room. The faculty complained that they had to sit through endless meetings on benches, or bring their own chairs.[8]

Between Morrill and White rose McGraw Hall, the gift of John McGraw of Ithaca in 1869. To its high western tower were transported the famous chimes, apparently the first to peal over an American campus.[9] To the students' delight, they played everything from "Home, Sweet Home" to "Captain Jinks of the Horse-Marines." By order of President White, they began the day, as they still do, with the "Cornell Changes," adapted from a carillon tune which White had heard and loved one Christmas Eve in London. The "Changes" were soon rechristened "The Jennie McGraw Rag," though Jennie herself knew nothing of them. The tune she always commanded was "Robin Adair."

The central part of McGraw was a large, but dark, three-story Museum of Natural History. Of some of the displayed marvels—the plesiosaurus, the megatherium, the bottled brains of scholars and murderers, the two-headed calves—the administration was very proud. Of some, such as the Silliman Collection in Mineralogy and the Newcomb Collection of Mollusks, it still has reason to be proud.

McGraw Hall housed the library, uncomfortably from the first. In the basement were the janitor's quarters, "Uncle Josh's Parlor," described as an odorous, flea-haunted Avernus. Here Uncle Josh kept

[8] On 8 March 1872 the Faculty petitioned the trustees for sand and paper for the privies (Faculty Records).

[9] The Chimes are not properly chimes at all, but a carillon, or a set of fixed bells which are hit by hammers operated by wires attached to a playing stand. A chime is a set of swinging bells operated by a man or men pulling ropes, to make usually a tuneless clamor. Andrew D. White studied the Belgian carillons with attention, and suggested to Jennie McGraw that she give the bells to Cornell. The bells were increased in number to eighteen by 1939; they can play even "The Star-Spangled Banner." See, *inter alia*, Robert V. Morse '11 in the *Alumni News*, 27 Sept. 1928.

open house, no doubt with snacks for the breakfastless. For years his parlor was the only refuge for students between classes, when the few library chairs were all occupied. The basement also held the dens of Professor Wilder's snarling cats, awaiting their doom in the service of Comparative Anatomy. Their fleas were so ferocious that Uncle Josh took to wearing anklets of flypaper, with the sticky side outside. Professor Wilder, sensitive to the criticism of humanitarians, placarded the door of the cats' quarters with the following poem, of his own composition:

> Snugly housed,
> Fully fed,
> Happy living,
> Useful dead.

The three buildings, with their precious contents, were the reverse of fireproof. A south wind was likely to blow ashes down the chimneys and out onto the floors. President White was haunted by fear of fire. In his report for February 1869 he points out that in Morrill Hall thirty-two dormitory stoves are under the care of students, and four stoves and four furnaces are tended by assistants. The students, he pursues, have in their rooms about fifty kerosene lamps, one of which has already exploded. And there was no water available. Not until 1875 was a reservoir constructed, on Observatory Hill above the President's House. The water was pumped from Fall Creek above Triphammer Falls and was passed through a filter bed. "Denizens of the hill will no longer use a hooked pole in drawing water from an ever failing cistern," said the *Era* with satisfaction.

At the north end of the campus stood Sibley College of Mechanic Arts, given by Hiram Sibley of Rochester in 1870. The original building was only the west section of the present Sibley. It contained the print shop of the University Press and the educational machine shops, powered both by steam and by water power derived from a turbine wheel far below in Fall Creek Gorge and conveyed to Sibley by a running wire cable.

In the shops hung this large lettered message from Hiram Sibley: "There are two most valuable possessions which no search-warrant can get at, which no execution can take away, and which no reverse of fortune can destroy; and they are what a man puts into his brain—knowledge, and into his hands—skill." (The plaque now hangs in Kimball Hall. The 1870's loved sonorous admonitions, and so in fact does your historian. He was distressed to be told by Dean Dexter Kimball that Sibley's actual words to Andrew D. White were: "One thing is damn sure—you can't take away from a fellow what he puts into his head and into his hands." And White chuckled: "I trimmed it up a little; I trimmed it up a little.")

Behind Sibley College, on the gorge's edge, stood an ungainly wooden structure, housing twenty working students, and an old tenant farmhouse, occupied by Professor Isaac P. Roberts.

At this point of his inspection, the visitor was urged to undertake the "University Walk," for a charge of ten cents. The walk began at approximately the south end of the present Triphammer Bridge. One walked eastward above the chasm, crossed the stream on a rustic bridge below Beebe's Dam, at about mid-height of Triphammer Falls. Then one descended a stairway boxed in a wooden frame to the gorge's floor, continued downstream past Rocky Fall, Foaming Fall, and Forest Fall (names now forgotten), recrossing the stream to the summit of Ithaca Falls, where an inscription indicated the site of Johnson's Tumble. One then walked through Ezra Cornell's tunnel, on a plank above rushing waters, and so to the valley road, where one's carriage was bidden to attend.

If one chose not to attempt the University Walk, one turned back southward from Sibley. On the approximate location of Goldwin Smith Hall stood a large wooden building, housing the chemical, agricultural and photographic laboratories. The more knowing visitors were impressed by the arrangements and equipment of the laboratories for student work. (Instruction by the laboratory method was still a rarity in America; as late as 1872 only six colleges had adopted it.) [10]

On its hillock, crowning all, stood the President's House, described as Swiss Gothic. Andrew D. White was taken by the lines of a rough office building in Ithaca; he found that the architect was a Cornell student, William H. Miller. He entrusted the design of his home to Miller, who later gained considerable fame in these parts, but who never afterward had time to finish his college course. The President's House, which can only be called a Mansion, still pleases the contemplative eye. The detail, the interior finish, betray White's liking for fine workmanship and for uplifting symbolism. The visitor should notice particularly the stonework, intricately carved by Robert Richardson, a local master, whom White dubbed *Magister de vivis lapidibus*.

[10] Edward D. Eddy, *Colleges for Our Land and Time* (New York, 1957), p. 74. But this seems hard to believe.

The corbels of the entrance porch illustrate the theme: "By their fruits ye shall know them." To the left are evil fruits, toadstools, poison ivy, deadly nightshade, with imps, newts, and lizards; to the right beneficent fruits, flowers, birds, and butterflies.

In a grove behind the President's House stood at least one flimsy structure built by energetic students for their own lodging. Here lived David Starr Jordan '72 (the first president of Stanford University) and a jolly band of penniless squatters. He kept an elaborate journal of their trials by cold and hunger, and of the intellectual delights of their *soirées littéraires.*[11]

Heading south, we come to Sage College, the young university's architectural pride. Completed in 1875, it was noteworthy for its two-stage tower, which has since been sadly truncated, for its elaborately carved stonework and for the spaciousness of its interior arrangements, its grand richly carpeted parlor, its music rooms, reception rooms, reading rooms, bathrooms and gymnasium.

The burrowing researcher, while admiring the lavishness of Sage College's construction and provisions for the gracious life, is nevertheless struck by one underground fact. The sewer from the building was carried to the edge of Cascadilla Creek, and the effluvium was dumped in the setting of so many poetic rhapsodies.[12]

We have now seen the Cornell campus as it existed in the mid-seventies. Much had been achieved in a half-dozen years. The rough upland farm had been smoothed and somewhat ordered. Especially around Sage College, planting of trees and serious landscaping were under way. Buildings and equipment were provided, inadequate, of course, as university equipment nearly always is, but passable, and in some cases superior. Cornell University had its home, in which to test the Cornell Idea, to discover whether or not the Cornell Idea was true, potent, and fruitful.

[11] In the C.U. Archives.
[12] *Proceedings of the Board of Trustees* (Ithaca, 1940), 29 Nov. 1876. The Ithaca health officer complained of it (W. C. Russel to ADW, 25 March 1877).

VII

The Early Years: The Men

"GOD bless the ship!" George William Curtis had cried on Inauguration Day, into a high hostile wind. The ship was indeed barely sea-
worthy when it left harbor, and it ran immediately into storms.

"God bless the builder!" The builder, serene and craggy, had no
doubts of God's blessing on his work. He had written to Andrew D.
White (on 9 July 1866): "It is my practice to do what my judgment
convinces me to be right, and to let the consequences take care of themselves." But what he regarded as judgment was likely to be an apoca-
lyptic vision. He frequently told his associates that some of them would
live to see five thousand students in their institution.[1] His hearers
sneered covertly. Goldwin Smith remembered the overweening prophecy, and later commented:

I answered that if the day did come, instead of being a great benefactor
he might be thought to be rather the reverse; that there would not be a
market for the 5000 graduates; and that the balance would be unprovided
for, and perhaps dangerous to society; too much money's being given to
universities, and men are being tempted away from the humbler and for
them happier callings to which they were born and for which they are
fit.[2]

---

[1] Cornell wrote to John D. Caton on 25 Oct. 1869 (in his "Letter Book"): "My
plans contemplate an Institution that will furnish adequate room and the best
attainable facilities for 5000 students."

[2] To Lord Mountstephen, 4 March 1902.

Cornell's prediction was at length fulfilled in 1913; and the professional historian's prediction not yet.

Ezra Cornell had his hand in everything, checking on every detail of the building and of other business, usually with some sharp admonishments. He liked to sit on a high stool in the machine shop and watch the boys at work. He would address them gruffly with the words: "What are you wasting your time at now?" But the boys understood. One of them remembered: "He stood among us like a fond and anxious father." [3]

His peremptory manner grated, however, on the faculty. Goldwin Smith recognized his virtues, but described him as a taciturn, resolute, self-willed man, "whose ignorance of [education] quenches the lightnings of the gods. . . . He has been praised highly and with the greatest justice for his munificence; and he not unpardonably takes the praise as extending to his wisdom in the management of his foundation." [4]

In George William Curtis's elaborate image, the Builder accompanied the vessel on her cruise, and he could be at times a great nuisance to the Captain. Curtis's phrase: "God bless the chosen captain!" may have returned to White with special significance.

In the beginning, the President ruled his small domain from his rooms in Cascadilla Place. His wife did not at first join him. (She detested Ithaca and urged her husband to try for a professorship at Yale.) [5] White therefore spent most of his weekends with his family in Syracuse. In the mild seasons the trip was pleasant enough, by steamer to Cayuga Bridge and train to Syracuse. But in winter until the Ithaca and Cortland Railroad was opened in 1871 he had to drive twenty miles overland to the train at Cortland. On one such journey, lasting twelve hours, he was three times upset in snowdrifts. To his exposures he attributed the throat trouble which for years hampered his eloquence.

He threw himself into his work with characteristic nervous energy. One of his colleagues said to him: "I always think of you as carrying a load that would break down a dozen common men." [6] There was everything to be done, in furtherance of his lofty programs. As Wal-

[3] Joseph C. Hendrix '73, in *Proceedings and Addresses at the Twenty-fifth Anniversary of the Opening of Cornell University* (Ithaca, 1893), p. 67.

[4] To Charles Eliot Norton, 17 July 1870, in *Massachusetts Historical Society Proceedings*, Dec. 1915, 155-157.

[5] Letter to ADW, 5 Oct. 1870.   [6] Homer B. Sprague to ADW, 21 Aug. 1869.

ter P. Rogers points out, there is hardly another example of a man's formulating plans for a new university, establishing it, and guiding it through its formative years.[7] He put upon the institution the seal of his own character, idealistic, impetuous, earnest. "My whole soul is wrapped up in this enterprise," he wrote, "because I regard it as the most hopeful of recent times. I am willing to sacrifice comfort, property, ambition, and to shorten my life for it, to give this country one institution most suited to the wants of these times—and which is fettered by no sectarian tests." [8]

He did the work of administration faithfully and valiantly. But in fact he hated the crowding duties—attention to leaky roofs, freezing pipes, student misbehavior, the wounded sensibilities of professors and their wives. "My repugnance to office work, to travelling in cars, to discussing educational subjects, to hearing statements made and passing upon them, to selecting professors, etc., is rapidly becoming invincible," he wrote Daniel Coit Gilman on 22 September 1873. He concluded by offering Gilman the presidency (but it is not clear if the letter was actually dispatched).

He eased his distress somewhat by appointing a Vice-President in 1870—William C. Russel, already professor of modern languages and history. For a stipend of $250 yearly the Vice-President hired and dismissed junior members of the faculty, ran the University during White's frequent absences, addressed catalogues, answered all routine letters in his own hand. He also gave his master occasionally unpalatable advice, for the Vice-President was proud of his forthrightness. When White proposed to raise the salary of his friend Willard Fiske and not that of poor sick Cleveland of Civil Engineering, with his large family, Russel wrote sharply (on 30 December 1870): "Business is business. Friendship has no place beside it. Friendship thrives by favor, business depends on justice."

What White liked was the construction of grandiose schemes from his fervid imagination, leaving lesser men to deal with the practical details. What he liked, further, was teaching, or rather lecturing; and as a lecturer he was superb. "Whatever else one might or might not elect, no student missed 'Prexy's lectures,' " remembers George Lincoln

[7] *Andrew D. White and the Modern University* (Ithaca, 1942), p. 142. One might, however, cite G. Stanley Hall and Clark University, and even Bob Jones and Bob Jones University.
[8] To W. C. Russel, 22 July 1870.

Burr. His classroom technique had only one fault: he found it almost impossible to stop at the end of his allotted hour.[9]

He was admired by all, or almost all. His generosity was great and constant. He gave his salary (of $2,500) for the support of poor students and for prizes. He bought the first piece of equipment for mechanical engineering, a power lathe. By the close of the first college year he brought his gifts up to the sum of $10,000.

His relations with Ezra Cornell mingled affection and fury. He loved the Founder for his nobility of purpose, his greatness of spirit. But Mr. Cornell could endanger the whole university by some crotchety proposal, like that of building a shoe factory on the campus to provide employment for students. Such projects could be fought and overcome; but, ominously, Cornell became fascinated by railroad building, in the hope of making Ithaca a metropolis. White watched the fortune awaited by the University being poured into little, doomed railroad lines. In a mood of angry frustration—fortunately a passing one—White wrote his wife, on 11 January 1873, about an endless meeting of the Executive Committee. "It was another of the agonizing times which come periodically in the history of this institution. Mr. Cornell pursued by the demon of unreason, the rest of us struggling vainly against it. . . . I think that of all the difficult men to get along with in this world Mr. Cornell must be the most so. Nothing but my desire to keep the institution from wreck in his hands prevents me from throwing up the whole thing—and to think that he has not one grateful word or even thought toward one of us for all we have done—but rather the contrary of that. . . . Only the annoyance of Mr. Cornell's manner of procrastination—incurring debts—and general crookedness makes a life that would otherwise be delightful into a purgatory." ("Crookedness," perhaps, has taken on a harsher connotation than it then possessed.)

Frustration, overwork, ill health brought White many hours of black discouragement. "I am breaking down physically and mentally," he wrote Russel on the day after Christmas of 1873. "I do not average four hours sleep at Ithaca—indeed many nights I cannot properly be said to have any sleep at all." On 12 November 1871 he wrote in his diary: "A gloomy day. How much longer can I live separated from wife—children—old friends—home—attacked in newspapers, denounced in pulpits—suspected by Professors and students. Few com-

[9] G. L. Burr in *Alumni News,* 19 Sept. 1902; Rogers, *White and the Modern University,* p. 173; *Cornell Era,* 30 Sept. 1870.

forts and thousands of annoyances." Again on 20 April 1874 he cried to his diary: "How long, O Lord, how long!"

He was, after all, free. He was bound to his task by no economic necessity, only by an inner obligation and by honor. He could wash his hands at any time of Cornell University and its troubles. But to do what? To rest, to travel abroad, to return to a comfortable professorship of history? The idea allured him; on the other hand he was haunted by his sense of destiny. Everyone agreed that he was a great man, and he did too. Should he then retire from his presidency to do something less or something more? He wrote to Ezra Cornell, on 2 April 1872: "I shall next year be forty years old. In all probability the next ten years—if I live—will be the best of my life. I feel a conviction that I can do higher and better things than any I have done hitherto." And, he continued, he had no ambition to nurse along one more inadequate college.

In such moods, he proposed to resign. He stated his purpose to the trustees, or presented his resignation in form, every year from 1870 to 1873. He was dissuaded, and mollified, by the trustees' protests and expressions of admiration.

He was mollified also by evidences of esteem from the great. In 1870 or 1871, he recalls, he was offered the post of Minister to Greece, and was thinking of accepting it when Henry W. Sage proposed to endow the Sage College for Women. "This led me to decline the diplomatic post and to devote myself to the new structure and its purposes." [10] At about the same time he accepted a mission to Santo Domingo, to determine whether it would be a good idea for the United States to annex that island as a refuge for our colored people. On this mission he spent a happy springtime (1871) in a romantic tropical journey, with the uplifting sense that he was making, not merely recording, history.

Despite all his dubieties, White resolved, in 1871, to bring his family to Ithaca and to build a mansion from which Presidents, through all future time, should look down on the busy campus. The President's House was occupied by the family in 1874; it remained White's home until his death. President Farrand and President Day lived there in their turn. It is now, appropriately, the Andrew D. White Museum of Art.

[10] E. P. Evans Papers, 2 March 1911. But perhaps White's memory betrayed him as to the date. John M. Francis inquired, on 20 Sept. 1873, if he would be interested in the Greek Ministry (ADW Papers). I do not find that the post was actually offered him.

In the early days Cornell life was centered upon Cascadilla Place. Here President, faculty, and students, captain, crew, and passengers, lived together in crowded discomfort. They complained, of course, and bitterly. But afterwards memory hallowed their early experience, and the survivors looked with kindly scorn on those who had not known the woes, and joys, of Cascadilla.

Commonly a nonresident professor occupied the guest suite. The first was the great naturalist, Louis Agassiz, who delighted all with his knowledge, enthusiasm, simple, winning ways, and ability to draw on the blackboard with both hands at once. There were other nonresident professors, and lecturers, whose fame is still bright: James Russell Lowell, George William Curtis, Bayard Taylor, Theodore W. Dwight, John Fiske, the English historians Edward A. Freeman and James Anthony Froude. George Washington Greene gave several extended courses in American history, from 1872 to 1874. Cornell University is proud of establishing the first chair of American history in 1881; but even Cornell seems to have forgotten the precedent of Greene, who, though nonresident, was the first titular professor of the subject. His lectures, incidentally, were said to be uncommonly dull.

The most brilliant of the nonresident professors was Goldwin Smith. Tall, slim, well-groomed, he reminded one girl of a silk umbrella.[11] His lectures were models of acumen, wit, and pungent phrasing. To his rough-hewn colleagues, some of them graduates of forlorn colleges set in campuses of mud and tree stumps, he stood as an exemplar of ripe Eton-Oxford classical culture. He who had hobnobbed with England's rulers now hobnobbed as readily, and evidently as happily, with self-made scholars reared on frontier farms. Goldwin Smith was a singularly genuine person, devoid of affectation; he recognized the merits of his companions, admired and liked them. He wrote to Charles Eliot Norton: "My high opinion of our staff of Professors is confirmed. It does the highest credit to White's judgment in selecting it. I do not think I ever had to do with a set of men whose character and ability I esteemed more highly. The only question is whether they can be held together." [12]

Goldwin Smith was fond of the students, joined in their sports, contributed to their enterprises. The students responded, denominating him publicly their most esteemed and most beloved professor.

Though officially a nonresident, he spent most of the first two years

[11] Alfreda Withington '81, *Mine Eyes Have Seen* (New York, 1941), p. 23.
[12] 17 July 1870, also 10 March 1869, in *Mass. Hist. Soc. Proc.*, Dec. 1915.

at Cornell, and thereafter he returned from his new home in Toronto to give frequent series of lectures. Throughout his life he kept his affection for Cornell, which no doubt represented to him his own period of psychological refreshment, his recapture of self-understanding and purpose. "Cornell did more for me than I can ever do for Cornell," he told Andrew D. White in 1910. He did a great deal for Cornell, giving it his splendid historical library and making it the residuary legatee of his ample fortune. "When I am cremated, as I hope to be," he wrote in his old age, "I shall be obliged to the wind if it will waft a grain or two of the ashes to the campus at Cornell." [13]

The nonresident professorship system was very dear to Andrew D. White. Almost his only cause for self-reproach, in later years, was that he had yielded to pressures to diminish its importance. The great visitors indeed brought light and inspiration to the isolated little country college. They provided ardent undergraduates with experiences never forgotten. Young David Starr Jordan, botanizing in the country, happened on two shirt-sleeved men lying under a tree. He stopped to chat, and realized that they were George William Curtis and James Russell Lowell. He hurried home and wrote:

> Once in his shirt sleeves lying in the grass
> Under the shadow of a chestnut tree,
> I saw James Russell Lowell face to face,
> And the great poet rose and spoke to me!

Not quite Browning, he admits.

However, the resident professors had many criticisms to make of the nonresident system. Many of the touted lectures were frankly bad. George Washington Greene did nothing but read aloud from his printed book on the American Revolution. Edward A. Freeman, fa-

---

[13] GS to ADW, 10 Jan. 1910 (in Goldwin Smith Papers); Goldwin Smith, *Reminiscences* (New York, 1911), p. 378. During Goldwin Smith's stay he had a stone seat carved, with the inscription: "Above all nations is humanity." It stands fittingly in front of Goldwin Smith Hall. The maxim has had a surprising success, as the motto of the Cosmopolitan Clubs of America and otherwise. Scholars have fruitlessly sought its origin in the classics. Goldwin Smith certainly made it up. In his opening lecture in 1868 he said he would try to be impartial, "for while I love England much, I love humanity more." Some hold that "Above all nations is humanity" is a distressingly obvious remark, hardly worth all the fuss.

Goldwin Smith made another remark, not obvious at all. He said in a lecture in 1878: "Ultimately one of two nations will control the world: either the English-speaking nations or the Russians" (*Alumni News*, 1 Sept. 1944).

mous Oxford historian, appeared for a formal evening lecture in a very rough shooting coat, and spoke sitting, with his gouty foot on a settee, enlivening his discourse with screams of pain. A crowded fortnight of lectures by a nonresident professor was likely to upset all the routine of required studies. The Registrar was nonplussed how to award credit for such special courses, given without reading requirements, examinations, or attendance records. And of course the great grievance was that the University's precious funds for instruction were spent in high fees to visiting stars, who might turn out to shine none too brilliantly after all. Goldwin Smith wrote to Norton: "I try to keep [White] from spending more money on flashy public lectures (of which we have far too many already) and other unsubstantial things, and to get him to turn all his resources, limited as they are, to the provision of means for hard work. I plead however for a little beauty, if it can be had cheap, in the buildings, which are in danger of being very hideous. . . . Curtis and Lowell come to lecture next term. . . . They will both be most brilliant I have no doubt, and the more brilliant they are the less inclined our boys will be after hearing them to go back to their hard work." [14]

The resident professors were an exceptional group, by any standards. They were mostly young, not much older than the students, and with the students they enjoyed a ready, even affectionate, companionship. Forty years later one of the original teachers, James Morgan Hart, summed them up as keen, enterprising, opinionative, informal—bumptious, in short. Three, perhaps four, he boldly termed geniuses. The individual counted for more than nowadays, he continued; and the teacher knew the students better.[15]

It would be pleasant to pass this first faculty in review, to record their merits and their little failings. Since obviously this may not be, we can choose only a few, destined to loom large in Cornell history and folklore.

First, hierarchically, stands William Channing Russel, Vice-President and professor of modern languages and history. Fifty-four years old at the opening, he seemed a patriarch to the young faculty and assumed among them an air of authority. They called him privately "the Old Roman." He was an able, conscientious teacher, one of the first in America, perhaps the first, to conduct classes on the German seminar

[14] 10 March 1869, in *Mass. Hist. Soc. Proc.*, Dec. 1915, p. 148. Also *Era*, 9 April and 14 May 1875, and Russel to ADW, 26 Dec. 1879.
[15] *Era* (1907), pp. 381–383.

plan. He had a gift for supercilious humor, which caused him many misfortunes but which makes his correspondence a delight. In his thirty years as a practicing lawyer he had markedly developed the art of questioning and cross-examination. The better students appreciated his searching methods; the poorer were made to feel like defendants accused of crime. His lack of tact was notorious and eventually disastrous to him.[16]

Daniel Willard Fiske was professor of north European languages, librarian, and director of the University Press. Reared in Syracuse, he was a boyhood friend of White, and was the only Ithacan privileged to greet the President as "Andrew." (In his letters to Fiske, White indulges in a special playful humor, unwonted in his other correspondence. He addresses Fiske with comic names, "lieber Fixius, liebstes Fixlein, Fix Pasha, Mithter Fix.") Fiske entered Hamilton College in 1847, and was suspended in his sophomore year, for breaking into the chapel and carrying off firewood. Somehow he conceived a romantic interest in Icelandic and Norse literature. He went abroad after graduation and studied at Copenhagen, supporting himself by writing letters to the American press. He wintered at the University of Upsala in Sweden, and delivered a series of lectures, in Swedish, on American writers. He returned to America, and spent seven years as assistant librarian in the Astor Library in New York, a year as Secretary of the American Geographical Society, and another as secretary to John Lothrop Motley, Minister to Austria. At the same time his passionate devotion to chess led him to found the *Chess Monthly*, to organize the first American chess congress (with Paul Morphy as star), and to collect the largest chess library in the country. He returned from Vienna to Syracuse, where he was an editor of the Syracuse *Journal* and was partner in a bookstore. There he renewed his friendship with Andrew D. White. He then joined the Hartford *Courant*, edited by his college roommate, Charles Dudley Warner. While reporting for the *Courant* the opening of the Suez Canal in 1868 he received news of his appointment to Cornell.

His character appears in this bald vita. A rolling stone who had gathered considerable moss, he was readily captured by diverse intellectual enthusiasms. His European experience gave him social polish

---

[16] "Russel made some unfortunate remarks to the students which were repeated with an unfriendly gloss, and have been handed down from class to class, and this has engendered a sort of chronic dislike of him" (John Stanton Gould to ADW, 5 April 1874).

and a kind of malleability which made him at home, and warmly welcome, from Iceland to Egypt. An excellent linguist, he was fitted for his professorship of north European languages. Well trained in the best American scholarly library, and a true bibliolater, he was equally well equipped to establish Cornell's Library. A practiced journalist, he could supervise Cornell's publications and serve as an unofficial Director of Public Information.

As professor, he gave instruction in German, Swedish, and Icelandic, and even offered a course in Persian. (I find no record that anyone accepted the offer.) He reported the campus news for the metropolitan press and contributed amply to the college papers. His most important service, however, was the direction he gave the Library. In those days a college library was likely to be a sorry accumulation, open an hour or two a week for the withdrawal and return of wholesome reading matter. (The first president of the University of North Carolina kept the University Library in an upstairs bedroom of his house for twenty years. The librarian of Columbia resolutely fought every effort of the faculty to add a book, in order to turn back half his appropriation unused.) Fiske's conception was wholly different. He held that Cornell's collection should be a reference library, like the Astor or the Bodleian, expanding the studies of the faculty and stimulating the students' curiosities. His effort was to obtain, by gift or purchase, fine scholarly collections entire. The historical libraries of Goldwin Smith and Jared Sparks, the classical library of Charles Anthon, the philological library of Franz Bopp were thus secured, to Cornell's great and increasing benefit. From the first, the Library was open nine hours a day—longer hours, boasted Fiske, than in any other American university. (And today Cornell's Library, open fifteen hours and forty minutes daily, makes the same boast.)

Fiske, a bachelor, was a kindly friend to young men, particularly the young men of the Psi Upsilon fraternity. White had to intervene to prevent him from giving an inordinate proportion of his small salary to the new chapter and to needy brothers. Again, White was obliged to reprimand him for offering a glass of ale to a student. Fiske retorted that his hand was forced; he was enjoying his ale with a friend, as he did once a fortnight, when the student entered, and he felt bound by the laws of hospitality. Further, he was not going to change his personal habits for any Board of Trustees.[17] *Tempora mutantur, nos et mutamur in illis.*

---

[17] Fiske to ADW, 4 Sept. 1869.

Early Years: The Men

Fiske was a nervous, volatile, irascible man. Abounding in generosity, he could never forget or forgive a slight or insult. Since Vice-President Russel's gift of mockery matched his own, he detested Russel, and Russel thoroughly mistrusted Fiske. Especially when spurred by passion, Fiske could write brilliantly, with a verbal felicity that Andrew D. White himself could not equal. (Yet his only two actual books bear the strange titles of *Chess in Iceland* and *An Egyptian Alphabet for the Egyptian People.*)

Thomas Frederick Crane, renowned in song and story as "Teefy," was a Princeton graduate of 1866, established as an Ithaca lawyer. He filled the hours of waiting for clients by the private study of foreign languages. Since Fiske had not returned from Egypt at the opening in 1868, Crane was pressed into service as librarian and instructor in German (at a salary of $800). He enjoyed the experience so much that on Fiske's arrival he went abroad to learn the languages. When he returned, James Morgan Hart, assistant professor of south European languages, suggested to Crane, in the casual manner of those times, that they swap chairs. This they did, two weeks before the registration day of 1870, and Crane taught French, Spanish, and Italian ever after.[18]

The phenomenon of Teefy Crane, revelatory of the state of higher education, deserves a moment's attention. The idea of professional preparation for a professorship was still only vague. A good teacher was a good teacher, no matter what he taught. And in the particular case, a language teacher was hardly expected to speak like a native. Your historian can personally testify that in the matter of pronunciation Teefy made few concessions to foreign idiosyncrasies.[19] But he had the true character of a scholar. He did valuable work in several fields, notably folklore and the study of popular tales. His case would seem to support the contention that a classically disciplined mind can be readily productive in whatever field it chooses.

Another ornament of the early campus was F. L. O. Roehrig. Born and educated in Germany, he held a minor diplomatic post in Constantinople, so improving his time that he published a Turkish grammar.

[18] Walter H. French, in *Alumni News*, 15 Nov. 1950. Crane had already declared his special devotion to the Romance languages. George Ticknor, the great Hispanicist, described him, on 14 Dec. 1868, as "a passionate admirer of Spanish literature, of which he has read a good deal" (*Letters to Pascual de Gayangos* [New York, 1927], p. 362).

[19] He said to me once: "You should read my book on Boy-lo." This pronunciation might bust him in a modern elementary course in French.

He was thereafter a student in Athens, a teacher of languages in Paris, an oculist, an army surgeon in the American Northwest, where he learned several Indian languages, and a teacher in Philadelphia schools. He came to Cornell as assistant professor of French. Thenceforth the *Register* contained hopeful announcements of courses in Chinese, Japanese, Malayan, Arabic, Mantchoo, Turkish, the Tartar languages, and Turanian philology. His Chinese course was indeed a surprising success, attracting at one time forty or fifty students. In his idle hours he composed popular music. But this phenomenal linguist, this abyss of learning, remained for fifteen years an assistant professor of French. It appears that his strong German accent in English inspired doubts in the administration.

Burt Green Wilder, appointed professor of natural history in 1867, gave his long life to Cornell, to the students' great profit and unending delight. He was recommended by Louis Agassiz as his outstanding pupil. A graduate of Lawrence Scientific School and the Harvard Medical College, he had served as a surgeon in the Civil War. Fortunately his preparation and his interests were broad; his province included the realms of anatomy, physiology, zoology, entomology, and hygiene. His method was the still novel laboratory system; even beginners found themselves implicated in the research which Wilder pursued with unflagging passion. The great Theobald Smith '81 said to him on the twenty-fifth anniversary of his labors at Cornell: "It was a fortunate thing for us that your laboratories were so small and crowded, because all of your work was done in the presence of your pupils, and we could not very well escape the infection of your enthusiasm." [20]

The procedures of biological research are likely to startle the merely humane. Wilder's famous collection of brains of the great in wisdom and in wickedness provoked many a jest. Goldwin Smith told him he was as welcome to his old brain as to his old hat. Wilder was forever searching for strange specimens. He tried to get an elephant which died in a circus in Ontario, but the customs guards at the border were adamant. A series of letters to President White describe his efforts to obtain a whale stranded off Nantucket. He could have it first for a hundred dollars, then for twenty-five dollars, then for nothing; and finally it baffled even his doughty stomach.

In his "Anatomical Uses of the Cat" [21] he proclaims the merits of that creature as a vile body for dissection by students of anatomy. The

[20] W. T. Hewett, *Cornell University: A History* (New York, 1905), II, 219.
[21] *New York Medical Journal*, Oct. 1879.

human subject, he says, is inconveniently large, expensive, and offensive, and inspires the student to *smoke*, thus rendering him, as a future physician, unwelcome in gentlemen's houses. And further, the disposal of the remnants of the human subject is difficult, "and its character would hardly justify resort to the expedient practised with bodies of dogs used at the laboratory in one of our large cities, viz., tieing them to the rear of outgoing freight trains." Since the admirable cat has none of these drawbacks, Wilder used great numbers for dissection, and he and his juvenile agents were the ogres of Ithaca's cat-lovers.

For a time he kept a wire pen in front of McGraw, with deer and other fauna. His daughter, Mrs. Robert Reed, remembers that the family had an armadillo, a Gila monster, a lynx, or Texas wildcat, in their back yard. Andrew D. White poked the lynx, Bob, at its dinner, with a silk umbrella, which Bob tore to shreds.

Wilder's vigorous, ingenious mind and his impassioned purpose made him a superb lecturer. Andrew D. White, in his *Autobiography*, speaks of his platform style as the best possible lesson in public speaking. White imposed on him the duty of giving annually an obligatory course of lectures in physiology and hygiene to the freshman class. In later times the course dwindled to a single lecture in sex hygiene, in which his dramatic demonstrations caused many an auditor to faint.

He was a man in a perpetual fury. He hated idleness, prudery, smoking, secret societies, class spirit, stamping in classrooms, and intercollegiate sports. In June 1891 the Athletic Association came begging for contributions to pay its debts. Wilder subscribed fifty dollars, on condition that before 15 October the faculty would forbid students to take part in any rowing, baseball, or football contest with persons other than members of this university. Your historian remembers the folding blackboard which he would set out in front of McGraw, inscribed with his comments and castigations of the day. On football Saturdays his message was, in brief, death to football, its savage players, and its imbecile spectators.

After the redecoration of Sage Chapel in 1903 Wilder would enter it only by necessity, so outraged was he by the impossible musculature of angels with both wings and arms.

The first professor of chemistry was young James Mason Crafts, fresh from four years working with Wurtz in Paris. He imposed the laboratory method of instruction here, and wrote a textbook on qualitative analysis. But he left us after only two years. During a long residence in Paris he discovered the famous Friedel-Crafts reaction. He became a professor and eventually president of the Massachusetts Institute of Technology.

William A. Anthony was the creator of Cornell's famous department of physics. When professor of physics at Iowa State, he had planned to go east for study during a summer vacation, but the Iowa trustees required him to remain and supervise the plumbing of a new building. He did most of the installation with his own hands. This experience persuaded him to accept a call to Cornell. A man of great initiative and inventiveness, he built in 1872–1875, with the aid of a student, George S. Moler, the first American Gramme dynamo for direct current. It was constructed from a brief magazine description of Gramme's machine and was powered by a five-horsepower gas engine, itself an amazing novelty. Electricity was delivered through underground wrought-iron pipes to two campus arc lights, the wonder of the countryside and indeed of the engineering world. This was the first underground distributing system for electrical energy, and the first outdoor electric-lighting system in the country. The dynamo, shown at several world's fairs, was in active service at Rockefeller Hall at least till 1930, but has now become emeritus, performing only at high engineering festivals.[22]

Anthony also invented and built a tangent galvanometer, the first apparatus for the electrolytic generation of limelight, and other devices. In the true spirit of the investigator, he never bothered with patents and seldom with publication. His brilliant lectures and his dominant personality turned many bright students to the lifelong study of physics and to the illustration of Cornell's department. Many today will remember the names of his pupils, among them George S. Moler, Edward L. Nichols, and Ernest Merritt.

[22] Professor Edward L. Nichols '75 describes the underground cables (*Alumni News*, 22 May 1930). They "were constructed of gas piping through which copper wires were drawn. These wires were so thoroughly insulated by means of a composition of tallow pumped into the pipes that when tested after having been buried more than twenty years they were found to be still in excellent condition." Professor Charles H. Hull '86, who grew up in Ithaca, adds: "The tower then attached to Sage Chapel, an inept structure which suggested to Hiram Corson 'a four-legged woman holding up her skirts,' used to give quadrupedal shelter to the buzzing and spluttering electric lamp animated by Anthony and Moler's first dynamo. . . . It was an open arc lamp; and its carbons were not copper-cased pencils but flat plates, so that the arc, instead of travelling continuously around and around to fit irregularities in the wear, jumped back and forwards along their edges, from one point to another of approximate contact. Polychromatic flames resulted, startling to behold" (*Alumni News*, 22 Oct. 1931).

The first professor of civil engineering was William C. Cleveland, evidently a very remarkable man, one of James M. Hart's "geniuses." He died in 1873, and was succeeded by Estevan Antonio Fuertes, known for thirty years as "the Mogue" (because he looked and acted like the Great Mogul, and smoked Mogul cigarettes). Born in Puerto Rico, educated in Spain and at the Rensselaer Polytechnic Institute, imprisoned in Puerto Rico for political subversion, he was a civil engineer of high standing when called to Cornell. Overflowing with ire and tenderness, he brought an exotic note to the campus, while teaching his subject with Roman rigor. His emotional outbursts, his love of music and letters, his engaging and lovable character, caused many affectionate anecdotes to cluster about him.[23] And, of course, he established an eminent Cornell dynasty.

Grievous early troubles of the Department of Agriculture were resolved by the appointment of Isaac P. Roberts in 1874. He has been called "the Father of Agricultural Science in America," and the characterization is not misplaced. Liberty Hyde Bailey termed him "the wisest farmer I have ever known." He was born at East Varick, on the shore of Cayuga Lake, in 1833. His *Autobiography of a Farm Boy*, not only a Cornell classic but an American classic, gives a vivid account of country life in the early nineteenth century. He attended the Seneca Falls Academy, farmed and carpentered in Indiana and Iowa, and read in his brief leisure moments. In 1869 he was put in charge of the Iowa State College farm. He did so well with the farm that he was appointed professor of agriculture. In that post he learned, by trial and error directed by clear-seen purpose, how to teach:

I began to tell the students what I knew about farming. It did not take me long to run short of material, and then I began to consult the library. I might as well have looked for cranberries on the Rocky Mountains as for material for teaching agriculture in that library. Thus, fortunately, I was driven to take the class to the field and farm, there to study plants, animals, and tillage at first hand. So again I was shunted onto the right track by sheer necessity, and ever since I have kept the rails hot on that particular spur. Much of the illustrative material necessary for agricultural teaching cannot be assembled in the classroom, and so I fell into the habit of taking the students to view good and poor farms, to see fine herds and scrub herds in the country roundabout, even though they sometimes had to travel on freight cars. I suppose I was the first teacher

---

[23] See Romeyn Berry's recollections of the Mogue in *Behind the Ivy* (Ithaca, 1950).

A History of Cornell

of agriculture to make use, in a large way, of the fields and the stables of the countryside as laboratories. . . .

One day, being short of lecture material, I went to the fields and gathered a great armful of the common weed pests. Handing them round to the class, I asked for the common and the botanical names, and the methods of eradication. I received only two answers and those quite inadequate, although these twenty-five young men had spent most of their waking hours since childhood in fields where there are more weeds than useful plants. This experiment provided material for a week's classroom talk and led me to place still more emphasis on field laboratory work— "walks and talks" we called them. . . .

It appeared to me that farmers should know how to tell the age of a horse with a reasonable degree of certainty; and hearing that many rather young horses had recently died of an epidemic in the immediate neighborhood, I had two farm hands dig them up, and preserved the heads and some special parts and such limbs as had been malformed by disease. By careful inquiry I was able to fix accurately the ages of most of these animals. Arranging my material on a workbench in the open, I placed the class on the windward side and taught them the fundamental principles of horse dentition.[24]

Even in this page Roberts's character appears: his energy, his clear view of aims and methods, his practicality, his novel and effective teaching methods, his lucid, racy style.

In 1873 Iowa State College was torn by a factional struggle, and Roberts resigned. William A. Anthony, already a transfuge to Cornell, recommended Roberts for the agricultural professorship, and the future of the Cornell department was assured.

His initiation here was very far from happy. He found only three senior students in agriculture; the farms and equipment were in a dreadful state. He and his wife were lodged in Cascadilla Place, "the Bastille." Plain people, they were suddenly sensitive about their plainness, their rustic speech, among the dons and scholars. "We suffered a sort of social neglect and felt ourselves in an alien atmosphere. The contempt for such practical subjects and their teachers was shared . . . by many of the professors of the technical subjects, who were not highly cultivated outside their own fields." Perhaps Roberts was unduly thinskinned. Willard Fiske liked him immediately. "He looks rough, but I think he is also ready." [25]

[24] *Autobiography of a Farm Boy* (Ithaca: Cornell University Press, 1946), pp. 96–98.
[25] To ADW, 31 Jan. 1873.

114

Of all the heroic early figures, Hiram Corson shone brightest in student memories. About his name a corpus of legend gathered, and even today it has not dissipated. Such is the living power of a great personality.

In person he was tall and imposing, with a handsome, well-shaped head, fine, positive features, a long, divided, Michelangelesque beard, which, when it turned white, suggested to everyone the look of a Hebrew prophet. He moved majestically. A dandy withal, he affected a flowing tie or a bright scarf and an embroidered velvet vest. He wore a large Roman ring on the first finger of his left hand. Most impressive was his voice, rich, sonorous, perfectly modulated to every occasion. "An old-time Shakespearean actor!" one may exclaim. That indeed he was; but he was a scholar and a teacher too.

Born in Philadelphia in 1828, he was considered in his youth a mathematician of great promise. But he renounced mathematics to become a stenographic reporter in the United States Senate. In recording the speeches of Daniel Webster and others he learned the love of noble oratory. Sated, perhaps, and craving silence, he turned to librarianship in the Smithsonian and congressional libraries, and improved his leisure by studying English, French, and German literature. He then became a popular lecturer on literary subjects; and thus, in the sidelong manner of those days, he entered the professorate, serving at Girard College and at St. John's College, in Annapolis. He seemed to be just the sort of inspired, inspiring teacher President White was seeking. Little White cared that Corson had never been enrolled as a student in any college.

Moses Coit Tyler crossed the Atlantic with him in 1882, and recorded in his diary:

I have never travelled with a more delightful companion. He is an inexhaustible source of entertainment. His mind is a magazine of anecdotes and literary quotations; his wit is brilliant; he has been in gay spirits most of the time; and I have had some of the finest talks with him I ever had with anybody. He quotes Shakespeare or Tennyson by the hour; you mention a word and he has a passage of poetry to quote in which the word occurs; and in critical and speculative thought his conversation is as rich as it is in literary reminiscence. Occasionally he gets out of patience with somebody or something on the ship; but his spurts of anger are also brilliant and amusing.[26]

He came to Cornell in 1870. In the following spring he played an impromptu role in a seriocomic drama. With Professor Albert S.

[26] Jessica Tyler Austen, *Moses Coit Tyler* (New York, 1911), p. 133.

Wheeler of Latin he got drunk in the Clinton House before lunch and made some sort of a public scene of which the details have been successfully buried in oblivion. In an abject letter of resignation he explained that he had been working very hard rehearsing the Commencement speakers, that he had gone breakfastless, that he was troubled by dyspepsia and was unaccustomed to strong drink. He had taken two or three beers, with surprising effect. His resignation was accepted by the trustees; a later action substituted a year's leave of absence. Wheeler, who would apologize for nothing, received no such consideration. A veritable Lucifer, he was animated by a stout moral, or immoral, courage. He eventually obtained a post as instructor in German at Sheffield Scientific School, and seems to have led there an exemplary life.

The episode did no injury to Corson's popularity. For forty years he moved the imagination of students and townspeople. He believed devoutly that the best way to interpret literature, especially poetry, is to read it aloud, to transfer the poet's thought and emotion directly to the mind of the hearer. Andrew D. White heartily agreed. (White was inclined to scorn pure literary scholarship. "It seemed to me more and more absurd that a man with an alleged immortal soul, at such a time as the middle of the nineteenth century, should devote himself, as I then thought, to amusing weakish young men and women by the balancing of phrases or the jingling of verses." [27])

Corson gave his meed to literary scholarship by producing a series of books on Anglo-Saxon, Chaucer, and the modern poets. Highly regarded in their time, they may still be read with profit. But his chief concern was with the teaching of literature. He wrote:

How is the best response to the essential life of a poem to be secured by the teacher from the pupil? I answer, by the fullest interpretative vocal rendering of it. On the part of the teacher, two things are indispensable, first, that he sympathetically assimilate what constitutes the real life of the poem; second, that he have that vocal cultivation demanded for an effective rendering of what he has assimilated. Lecturing about poetry does not, of itself, avail any more for poetical cultivation than lecturing about music avails, of itself, for musical cultivation. Both may be valuable in the way of giving shape to, or organizing, what has previously been felt to some extent; but they cannot take the place of inward experience.[28]

[27] *Autobiography of Andrew Dickson White* (New York, 1905), II, 488.
[28] Quoted by Hewett, *Cornell University*, II, 45.

There are many testimonies to the success of his method. I may cite only one: that of Woodford Patterson '96, for many years the beloved Secretary of the University. Patterson was a less than indifferent student, with small interest in any studies. But one day in Corson's class he felt a kind of rapture, almost a mystical experience. He was no longer the sullen undutiful scholar; he was the poet and the poem, he was rapt in beauty, he was plunged in an emotion never suspected. This was the capital experience of his life. Ever after, poetry was his companion, his solace, his hidden joy.

One may wonder just what this elocutionary style was which could release such power. Corson kept an immovable face; he never made a gesture. All was done with the voice, of extraordinary range, and with a cultivated modulation. He had "a musician's instinct for movement, pause, and variation of tempo." [29] His style might seem today overblown, actorish. In reading Shakespeare, he used a falsetto for the female parts. The thick, husky tones of his Falstaff were famous. A reporter for the *Era* (23 April 1875) applauded the subdued, tender notes of his *Lady of Shalott*. "Universal, almost painful stillness pervaded the audience." Corson topped off with Bayard Taylor's "The Pennsylvania Farmer," in the cracked, squeaky voice of a very old man.

Encouraged by the President, Corson let himself go, thundering Shakespeare to his classes and giving public readings every Saturday morning. Occasionally he arranged in Sage Chapel poetry readings accompanied by organ music. These recitals White found among the most uplifting and ennobling in his experience.

This was all very well, but one can easily understand that some of the colleagues regarded his popular performances with a jaundiced eye. W. C. Russel thought him superficial, and complained to White (4 April 1871) that Corson was unwilling to enforce the teaching of writing. "Our farm and our English Department are about on a level." We must have systematic hard work. "Corson will never do this. No man who loves to read aloud as much as he does can do such work." Russel reprimanded him, to his horror. Russel told White (1 May 1871): "He seemed to me half crazy." Three years later (3 April 1874) he informed White that the students were complaining. Corson's classes were out of control; the students were disrespectful, read newspapers in class, and so on. Indeed, a student, William H. French '72, wrote in his diary for 12 April 1871: "Prof. Corson spouted today and as

[29] *Alumni News,* 17 March 1927, Sept. 1933, 15 Sept. 1944.

117

usual he was not appreciated, and a shoe was thrown over the banister from below and came up near the desk." [30]

Of the Corson stories that clamor for admission to these pages, one must suffice.[31] Like any actor, Corson hated latecomers to his performance. One student, identified as Ralph Hemstreet '00, habitually arrived three minutes after the bell. One day Corson began the hour with a reading from *King John*. Three minutes after, the latecomer opened the door and made his way down the aisle to his seat. Corson stopped reading and fastened his piercing eyes on the student. The entire class watched the unfortunate in tense silence. Corson returned to his text, deftly flipped a couple of pages, and resumed: "Enter the Bastard. . . ."

As he grew older his eccentricities increased. He was invaded by an increasing melancholy. Leland O. Howard overheard a colloquy between Corson and Albert W. Prentiss of Botany at a party. Said Prentiss: "What would life be without coffee?" Corson returned in his sepulchral tones: "What is life with coffee?" He attended the funerals of his colleagues, chuckling: "Old So-and-so is gone. *He* always was careful of his diet; *he* always took plenty of exercise; *he* always kept his windows open!" For himself, he was satisfied with walking barefoot in the early morning dew, to obtain the magnetic contact of the earth. He became a convinced spiritualist, and held séances with a chair set for Tennyson or Browning, solemnly recording their poetic messages from the other world.

Eccentricity seems to loom large in the records of the early days. But what is eccentricity, after all, if not a conviction so resolute that it disregards convention's prudent dictates?

Let us remember George W. Jones, who taught mathematics from 1877 to 1907. He was invariably called Piute Jones, from his fancied resemblance to a Piute Indian. He was at least a striking figure. Dr. W. Forrest Lee '06 recalls that in his later years, his abdomen being an almost perfect hemisphere, he made use of it in class, with a blackboard pointer, to demonstrate spherical trigonometry. He had been a political radical in Iowa and chairman of a local Greenback party, and he had publicly defended some strikers. Some of our trustees regarded him with alarm, but W. C. Russel asserted: "It only shows that a good mathematician may be an ass in politics." In Ithaca he organized a Society for the Prevention of Crime, which devoted itself chiefly to the promotion of total abstinence from alcohol. He caused a mighty

[30] In C.U. Archives.   [31] Romeyn Berry tells others in *Behind the Ivy*.

118

sensation at a temperance meeting in the Methodist Church, concluding his address with the words:

The advocates of drinking base their great argument on the fact that Christ in his first miracle at the wedding feast changed water into wine, and they claim that if wine was not wholesome, good and a healthy drink, Christ never would have changed that water into wine. Now I have given that first miracle deep thought, great study, I have looked at it from every angle, I have given it the most profound consideration; and I have come to the conclusion that when Christ turned that water into wine, HE DID WRONG!

This was Piute's last public appearance in any Ithaca church.[32]

Piute Jones, Lucien A. Wait, and James E. Oliver collaborated on a calculus textbook famous in its day. Wait was a jolly, likable man, an admirable teacher. He found time to organize and direct the Cascadilla School on the side. Oliver was a remarkable, perhaps even extraordinary, mathematician. He gave a lecture proving mathematically the existence of God, but no hearer understood more than the first sentence. He had the gift of total concentration on the problem in hand, which we unfairly term absent-mindedness. We might better call the quality present-mindedness. But every campus must have its absent-minded professor, and Oliver was ours, from his coming in 1871 to his death in 1895. Numberless exemplary tales are told of his absorptions; unfortunately, the collegiate folklorist finds the same tales current in other colleges, with different protagonists. It seems nonetheless established that once on his way up the hill he paused to look at a fountain on which a ball danced and spun. Mentally working out the formula, he missed three classes. Again, he invited a young lady to the theatre. A mathematical question intervening, he presented himself after midnight at the door of her irate father. And once he walked along the lake shore, skipping stones as an aid to thought. He also skipped his gold watch. A friend asked him if the story were true. "Well," he said, "I was certainly taking a walk by the shore, and I was certainly skipping stones. And somehow or other, I've lost my watch."

They are all gone long since, these professors of the first Cornell; they have become part of our mythology. Aware of time's distortions, its enlargement of the exceptional, its suppression of the dull commonplace, may we venture any generalizations?

[32] Harlan Brown, *I Recall Cornell* (Mineola, N.Y., 1952), p. 36.

Andrew D. White assembled for his new university a faculty noteworthy in its own day and in any day, and proved himself a wise judge of the human quality. The professional training of his appointees was often scanty by modern standards. Some of them, not mentioned here, turned out to be frank incompetents. But by and large, the faculty was a group of original minds, positive characters, fitted to stir and excite the young. White inevitably chose men he liked, and the men he liked reflected his own character—his idealism, his faith in social emancipation by education, his dislike of dogmatism, confinement, and inherited orthodoxy.

May we venture farther? What of today? Is Cornell's faculty better or worse than that of a century ago?

We are certainly more competent. We are better trained, better equipped, better organized. Some of the abuses of which early administrators complained would be totally impossible now. We are professional, whereas many of the first faculty seem to us mere fumbling amateurs.

Nevertheless, they might well deem us distressingly conformist, too content with doing the same thing over and over. They might well say: "You are excellent fellows, no doubt. But you all look alike, with few exuberant beards to express your fancies as to your own characters. And you are inclined all to act alike, to carry your hearty, efficient good-fellowship a little too far. Where are your rebels? And your eccentrics? Why are your faculty meetings so dull? In our time, they used to resound with fervid oratory. As you have gained understanding and tolerance, you have lost excitement. In fact, if you will pardon us, it was a lot more fun in our time."

Probably it was more fun in those times. The raw campus was imbued with a mood of hope, with a sense of destiny. Many of the early faculty came to Ithaca, and many remained through difficult, uncomfortable years, because they were encouraged to do new things elsewhere forbidden, to shed conformity in their teaching and behavior, in short, to be themselves. They had the proud conviction that they were shaping great things to come. In this, of course, they were quite right.

VIII

The Early Years: The Boys

"GOD bless the passengers!" George William Curtis had cried in his inaugural benedicite.

The passengers made a diverse group, ranging in age from fifteen to thirty. They came mostly from New York State villages, though some were registered from California, Dakota, Florida, Nova Scotia, England, and Russia. One bold Brazilian appeared; he brought in subsequent years an entire colony. Few of the collegians displayed much elegance. Some army veterans wore their military coats dyed black, with plain buttons replacing brass. Most of them, having poverty in common, were attracted by Cornell's promise that an education could be had for $272.40 per year, plus washing, and that manual labor could effect a generous deduction from that sum.

The early students were rugged but rewarding. Goldwin Smith wrote:

We have excellent material to work on. Our students, young farmers and mechanics for the most part, are rough outside and inside, but they have the root of the matter in them. They are, as a body, very industrious and self-denying, and remarkably well-behaved. We hardly ever hear a complaint of them in the town. Their manners also, though not polished, are essentially good. My intercourse with them is very pleasant to me, and increasingly so the more I see of them.[1]

[1] To Charles Eliot Norton, 17 July 1870, in *Massachusetts Historical Society Proceedings*, Dec. 1915.

A natural selection determined the Cornell type. Sons of Harvard, Yale, Union men turned naturally to their fathers' schools. Pastors advised their dutiful charges to enter a denominational college where true doctrines were taught. Academy masters urged their best pupils toward their own Alma Maters. But those who chose the new radical college were likely to be the self-willed, the adventurous, who took with ill grace the advice of their elders. John A. Rea, a junior at Ohio Wesleyan, read the first announcement of the university, exclaimed: "I am going to Cornell!" and became one of the eight members of the class of '69. Joseph B. Foraker '69 chose Cornell because it was open to all races and colors. John Henry Comstock '74 recalled that both he and Simon H. Gage '77 first heard of Cornell in prayer meetings, when a clergyman declaimed against the godless institution. Their aroused curiosity led to fixed purpose, and both served Cornell through their long and useful lives.[2]

The first Cornellians were a serious lot. Thomas Hughes, Member of Parliament, a friend of Goldwin Smith and the then renowned author of *Tom Brown's School-Days,* visited Cornell in 1870. He said: "They know how to work at Cornell. Indeed everybody in the place is almost painfully in earnest; but I am not sure that they are, as yet, properly alive to the claims and needfulness of play." Others found our earnestness excessive, ruinous to the concept of the carefree student basking in bright college years, to the tune of his light guitar. A newspaper called Cornell "a school where hayseeds and greasy mechanics are taught to hoe potatoes, pitch manure and be dry nurses to steam engines."[3]

The spirit of the young university was happily remembered by all who shared in its courageous forthsetting. "The early years of my Alma Mater," wrote David Starr Jordan '72, "though relatively crude and cramped, were enriched by an enthusiasm hard to maintain in days of prosperity. And the pioneer impulse far outweighed, to our minds, any deficiency in coordination, equipment, or tradition. At that time we were all young together, freshman students, freshman professors, freshman president, without experience or tradition to guide or hinder."[4]

[2] Foraker to ADW, 17 Feb. 1885; *Gage Memorial Fellowship Exercises* (Ithaca, 1916), p. 8.
[3] Thomas Hughes, in *Every Saturday,* 20 May 1871; I. P. Roberts, *Autobiography of a Farm Boy* (Ithaca, 1946), p. 136.
[4] D. S. Jordan, *Days of a Man* (Yonkers, 1922), I, 79.

Early Years: The Boys

Let us single out a few of these pioneer students. There was David Starr Jordan himself, who entered with seventy-five dollars in pocket, who received not a penny from his parents, and who graduated with seventy-five dollars still in pocket. He earned his way both by menial labors and by botanical work. His genial group, including two English boys (who had brought guns for the buffalo-shooting) built their own house and carried on an eating club called "The Struggle for Existence." Jordan later became famous as an ichthyologist, president of Indiana and Stanford universities, and recipient of one of the two honorary degrees granted by Cornell. (The other was conferred on Andrew D. White.) [5]

Joseph B. Foraker '69, born in a log cabin in Ohio, fought for four years in the Civil War and rose to a captaincy before entering Cornell as a senior. He became twice Governor of Ohio, and served two distinguished terms in the United States Senate.

The beloved John Henry Comstock '74 established, while still an undergraduate, the first Department of Entomology in America. After a term as United States entomologist he returned to Cornell, making the University a world center for entomological study.

Julius Chambers '70 became a New York journalist, simulated madness for literary ends, spent a term in an asylum, and wrote a sensational but reform-compelling book about the treatment of the insane. He also located the headwaters of the Mississippi, founded the Paris *New York Herald*, and wrote many popular books and plays.

And Chester Loomis '72 became a well-known painter, member of the National Academy. John D. Warner '72 was a congressman from New York, Melville Best Anderson '72 a man of letters and a Dante scholar of note, Garrett P. Serviss '72 an acclaimed writer on astronomy. Joseph C. Hendrix '73 was president of the American Bankers' Association. John C. Branner '74 was a famous geologist and succeeded David Starr Jordan as President of Stanford University. Frank Cushing, a brief sojourner in 1875–1876, had an unusual career as an Indian ethnologist. William Oscar Bates '75 was playwright, dramatic critic, and producer. Edward L. Nichols '75 directed Cornell's Physics Department for many years. Julia J. Thomas '75 became President of Wellesley College. Riokichi Yatabe '76, eminent botanist, founded the first normal school in Japan. James B. Grant '77 was Governor of Colorado, and Charles S. Francis '77 Ambassador to Austria-Hungary,

[5] For a very harsh judgment of Jordan, see Willard Beahan to Walter C. Kerr, 23 Jan. 1904, in College of Engineering Papers, C.U. Archives.

123

and Leland O. Howard '77, as Chief of the U.S. Bureau of Entomology, was one of the country's foremost scientists. Martha Carey Thomas '77, first president of Bryn Mawr College, was chiefly responsible for its greatness. Ruth Putnam '78 was a respected writer on history. And let us add John Dobroluboff '74, whose career in engineering was cut short by his execution for nihilism in 1880.

The heady promises of the Cornell program attracted the inevitable originals and extravagants. A Russian, unable to speak English, arrived by the stowaway route and was admitted. A western teamster tried to enter in order to learn to read; he was refused. Those rejected appealed to Ezra Cornell, quoting his motto: "I would found an institution . . ." and Mr. Cornell took up their cause. Professor H. H. Boyesen listened to this conversation between Mr. Cornell and the professor in charge of admissions:

Mr. Cornell: These young fellows tell me you won't pass them, Professor.

Professor: No, Mr. Cornell, I have found it impossible to pass them.

Mr. Cornell: I should like to know why.

Professor: They don't know enough.

Mr. Cornell: If they don't know enough, why then don't you teach them?

Professor: I can't teach them the A B C.

Mr. Cornell: Do you mean to say they can't read?

Professor: That I don't know; but they can't spell.

Mr. Cornell: Well, if it comes to that, there aren't so very many persons who spell the English language correctly. I have known some people who simply never could learn to spell, but for all that were good and able men.

Professor: If you want us to teach spelling, Mr. Cornell, you ought to have founded a primary school and not a university.

In the end, the professor was obliged to give the candidates another examination, which concluded as one may suspect.[6]

One might suppose the University's welcome to all, without discrimination of race, would have brought us some Negro candidates. However, none were reported in the early days. White wrote to an inquirer on 5 September 1874 that no colored students were then enrolled. "If even one offered himself and passed the examinations, we should receive him even if all our five hundred students were to ask for dismissal on that account."

[6] *The Cosmopolitan*, Nov. 1889, p. 63.

124

The chosen found themselves, to their surprise, subject to military organization. We too may feel some surprise; but after all, the Morrill Land Grant Act required military instruction on the part of its beneficiaries, though it did not make clear if such instruction was to be compulsory. Andrew D. White, for all his outcries against educational discipline, could not escape the prevailing assumption that college students needed strict guidance of their private lives. He thought that military leveling and a common uniform would serve to break down the bulwarks of caste. He was distressed by the "rustic slouchiness" of many students, and he found them in need of military smartness. He also favored military training for a social purpose. While, he thought, civil and foreign wars were probably ended, the country was in constant danger from demagogic uprisings, and "of all things fatal for a Republic, the most fatal is to have its educated men in various professions so educated that in any civil commotion they must cower in corners, and relinquish the control of armed forces to communists and demagogues." [7]

At any rate, Cornell was at its beginning organized as a military school, with Major Joseph H. Whittlesey in charge. Reveille sounded in the dormitories at 5:00 A.M. from April to September, at 5:30 in March and October, and at 6:00 during the winter. The students then rose, dressed, made their beds, and swept their rooms. Half an hour after reveille, the cadets stood at attention, with broom or feather duster at Shoulder Arms, while the student officers made their inspection. The companies in Morrill and White were then marched to Cascadilla for breakfast.

At 1:15 Dinner Call sounded on the chimes, at 4:15 Drill Call, at 5:15 Supper Call, at 9:30 Tattoo, and at 10:00 Taps and lights out. To go downtown, dormitory cadets had to get a pass from the Commandant.

This rudimentary West Point lacked much of resembling the original. The state, of course, delayed in delivering the promised armaments, and the boys drilled with canes and umbrellas instead of guns. The dark gray cadet uniforms were late in appearing, and when they arrived they turned out to be very expensive, costing forty dollars. They were passed on from year to year, increasingly shabby and venerable, until the faculty, defeated in its hopes of smartness, stipulated that only the dark blue kepi with the University emblem need be worn. The

[7] ADW to John H. Barr, 10 Jan. 1916; "Scientific and Industrial Education in the U.S.," *Popular Science Monthly*, June 1874, p. 18.

student officers, to be sure, displayed their taste for military elegance, wearing red-lined cloaks, with one corner tossed romantically over the shoulder.

Even at the end of the first year, White reported to the trustees that he was in two minds about the success of the system, but recommended that it be continued. Ere long only freshmen were required to drill. In 1875, as a result of student protests, the trustees voted that other subjects might be substituted for military science. Passive resistance had conquered military force.

In the general view, a particular mark and distinction of the new university was its encouragement of self-help by manual labor. This idea was very dear to Ezra Cornell, who had an almost religious faith in the sanctity of work, and who recognized his own young self in poor, ambitious youths, familiar with toil. Said one who knew him:

He had a notion that the mind rested while the body was at work, and that, accordingly, it was feasible to work body and mind alternately, without detriment to one or the other. That students who had spent a couple of hours in plowing or digging usually went to sleep when invited to apply their minds to philosophy and higher mathematics, or seemed too stupid to grasp the simplest proposition, appeared to him a mysterious circumstance, and altogether at variance with his own experience. The boy of biography and fiction who, after a day of physical toil, burns the midnight oil in the pursuit of abstract knowledge was to Mr. Cornell a perfectly normal creature.[8]

In his conception, the University partook of the nature of a trade school. He liked to think that every graduate would possess a mechanic means of livelihood. He was by no means discouraged by the failure of the manual-labor system in other institutions. Cornell would be different, and Cornellians would be different. Mr. Cornell happily drew plans for a chair factory, and for a shoe factory with a capacity of a thousand pairs of boots daily. He conceived that this industrial campus, with its student factory hands, would go far toward the support of the University. (How he would have applauded the new Industrial Research Park!)

White accepted the Founder's program, though with reluctance. He had himself no great taste for manual labor. Agreeing that the future engineer or agriculturist should possess the mechanical skills of his

[8] H. H. Boyesen in *Cosmopolitan*, Nov. 1889. Cornell's theory is also stated by W. Brewer, letter to W. T. Hewett, in People's College MSS, C.U. Archives.

trade, he thought that shop and farm work should be educational and illustrative, not directed toward repetitious production. He feared that the necessary routine duties of the University, if done by students, would be badly done. However, on this matter Ezra Cornell was firm. His firmness was that of the nether millstone.

Cornell's incautious letter to the New York *Tribune,* promising that any industrious young man could work his way through college, raised many unreasonable hopes. White recalled one candidate who inquired if he could support himself and his family and lay up something for a rainy day, while obtaining his degree.

As it turned out, those who already possessed some useful skills, as carpenters, masons, printers, accountants, shorthand writers, were immediately and profitably employed. A student carpenter earned forty-five dollars a month making wardrobes, cabinets, and bookcases. A painter and a photographer did well. In 1869 the first university press in America was established, through the gift of a steam Hoe Press by the makers. Twenty students were there employed in their spare hours.

The unskilled workers were organized in a Voluntary Labor Corps. Some were given jobs as janitors and waiters. Some found congenial tasks on the farm. Others were set to grading for the new approach to the campus, north of the Cascadilla Bridge. Ezra Cornell watched with delight, and with kindly scorn for the clumsy and soft-handed. He liked to take a pickax in hand and demonstrate his own prowess. He was determined that his convictions concerning holy labor should prove successful. "It was almost pathetic," remembers H. H. Boyesen, "to see the anxiety with which he watched the behavior and standing in scholarship of the first students employed on the farm."

Of course the scheme did not work. Student labor was inefficient, of uncertain supply, and available only for a few afternoon hours. At the end of the first year, the manager of the Cascadilla dining hall reported that the system was a failure and that half of his crockery had been destroyed. Most of the working students found themselves by evening too sleepy to study. The *Era* stated, on 5 June 1869: "Only a small portion of the students now work."

Some few, however, the heroes like David Starr Jordan, worked their way through college, as the heroes have never ceased to do. A reporter for the New York *Times* interviewed an agricultural student. The boy was caught studying Sanskrit, certainly not a part of the agricultural curriculum. He told the reporter that he worked all summer and three hours daily in college with six hours on Saturdays. His yearly average earnings were four dollars per week, his expenses three dollars plus clothing. The correspondent was deeply impressed.[9]

Year by year, the *Register*'s announcements of the opportunities for self-help became more cautious. The death of Ezra Cornell in 1874 freed the administration from pressure to preserve the system. In the *Register* for 1876–77 the self-help rubric has dwindled to a brief monitory paragraph.

What with military discipline and the glorification of labor, life in these first days was dull indeed. As the town could offer little in the way of diversion, the students were driven to amuse themselves. Much jocosity was provoked by the autumnal "cider raids" to Free Hollow (or Forest Home). But the cider was benign and the cider miller, recompensed in advance, willingly played the part of victim. The Burial of Trigonometry, borrowed from other colleges, occurred just before Christmas. The ceremony of 1869 was typical. The crowd gathered at dusk at the Cornell Library building, and to the sound of drums and with the accompaniment of skyrockets two men in white emerged, one with a huge black horn. Others followed in various disguises, and then succeeded a coffin on a sledge. Behind the coffin marched the High Priest in a black gown and wearing a plug hat. The coffin was dragged up the hill, where a burlesque sermon was pronounced, and Trigonometry was joyously burned and buried.[10]

One of the few available pleasures was the dance, the after-dinner recreation in Cascadilla Place. Rather strangely, Ezra Cornell approved. (In his country rearing, the old peasant dances afforded almost the only means of social congregation.) In fact, his broad-mindedness caused the University some trouble. To celebrate his birthday, 11 January 1869, Mr. Cornell gave a grand party in Cascadilla. All the elite of Ithaca, as well as the University community, were invited. Despite a blizzard, Cascadilla was jammed with guests. Andrew D. White rewarded the successful contestants for prizes in physiology. Professor Burt Wilder presented to Mr. Cornell a giant birthday cake with sixty-two candles. J. H. Selkreg of the Ithaca *Journal* offered an Ithaca Calendar Clock. Dr. James Law read an original poem. The doors of the dining room were thrown open, and a frightful crush ensued. The refreshments, featuring numberless roast turkeys, were in the

[9] New York *Times,* 6 Nov. 1871. I would guess that the young man was William R. Lazenby '74, for many years professor of agriculture at Ohio State University.

[10] Henry L. Stewart MSS, C.U. Archives.

tradition of a New England Thanksgiving, hearty though inelegant. When most of the elders, sated, had left, the young people danced, under Mr. Cornell's benevolent eye.

Thereupon a group of Ithaca clergymen submitted a protest to the Faculty. They had assumed, they said, that their consciences and feelings would not be wounded, but to their horror the ceremony had ended with the dance, which is opposed to vital godliness and inconsistent with Christian obligations. They therefore summoned the authorities of the University to ban such diversions, and to take their stand on the side of pure and undefiled religion.

The implications were clear. The local clergy regarded themselves as empowered, by their responsibility for souls, to interfere in the conduct of the University's affairs. A principle of authority was clearly involved. It was the old ecclesiastical claim that spiritual power overrules temporal power. The Faculty laid the protest on the table, where it still remains. The following year, Ezra Cornell engaged an orchestra to provide dance music for his birthday reception.

Thus officially countenanced, the dance became formal, genteel, and expensive. The first Navy Hop was held in 1873, with an entrance charge of four dollars. It was "a most fashionable affair, full dress, and, in fact, recherché in every particular." [11] In the same year the first Senior Ball occurred. Cornellians were gaining in urbanity.

The tone of general undergraduate manners was commended by most observers. "The intolerable nuisances of horn-blowing, window-breaking, barring-out and the like, which trouble the peace of so many other colleges, are altogether unknown at Ithaca," said James Morgan Hart.[12] "Altogether unknown" is pretty strong; the custodian of Cascadilla could have told him a thing or two. But relatively to other collegians, the first Cornellians were well behaved. The violence, even the savagery, of college life in the mid-century was notorious. Arson was a commonplace, and student ebullience passed readily into grand larceny, assault and battery, and even homicide.[13] Andrew D. White had seen his share of disorder in his college years, and nothing shocked his idealism more than such misuse of precious opportunities. In his Report on Organization he wrote: "The University authorities will enter into no

---

[11] *Cornell Era,* 31 Jan. 1873.   [12] *Scribner's Monthly,* June 1873, p. 204.
[13] Yale holds the record, with four murders in twenty years. The history of the University of Virginia has a sanguinary charm. After some students shot and killed the Dean of the Faculty, a professor shot a student in his classroom, alleging that he feared for his life.

inquisitorial process to discover the authors of disorder, but if the tenants are not able to maintain good order, they must give place *en masse* to those who can." And in his Inaugural Address he adjured the students: "In Heaven's name be men. Is it not time that some poor student traditions be supplanted by better? You are not here to be made; you are here to make yourselves. . . . This is no place for children's tricks and toys, for exploits which only excite the wonderment of boarding-school misses."

White's idealism was soon put to cruel tests. On a snowy December night in 1868 the chimes clanged in frenzy. The citizens of Ithaca looked out and saw what they took to be Morrill Hall in flames. Mr. White, running from Cascadilla Place to the scene, collapsed, crying "Save the apparatus! Save the apparatus!" The volunteer fire department struggled up the hill, to find that an enormous bonfire had been built just below the building. Around it capered the students, jeering and crying "Sold!" The feelings of the firemen, of Mr. Cornell and of Mr. White need no description. Apparently the essential of a hoax (or a "sell," in the earlier idiom) is that it shall arouse intense but unjustified emotion.

At the end of the first year of operation the Business Manager, Erastus G. Putnam, included in his report the following items under the head of Malicious Mischief:

Damages to College Furniture by wanton breakage and cutting, besides ordinary wear and tear	$500
Damage to buildings (not including accidental damage)	500
Tools, lumber, and combustibles consumed in the Christmas bonfire	200
Outhouse destroyed at the July vacation	255
Loss by burning of Eddy's factory near Cascadilla House	1,000
Settees and beds stored therein, all new	890
Other property known to have been burned	300
Steam engine destroyed	500
Damage to Cascadilla House	100
	$4,245

This reckoning is clearly much inflated. It is nevertheless noteworthy, at a time when the operating budget of the University was about $100,000.

No doubt it was a good thing that in subsequent years the student urge toward destruction and violence was channeled into the celebration of Gate Eve, or Halloween, and into class rushes. Gate Eve, marked by the appropriation of wooden gates, signboards, and other combustibles, brought the students into conflict with the village police. White was scandalized; in 1871 he suspended the arrested students for a year. And a citizens' delegation, headed by the Chief of Police, came to protest the severity of the punishment. In a four-hour Faculty meeting the presidential judgment was reaffirmed.

For the Gate Eve of 1872 a wonderful opportunity presented itself. Professor Wilder had bought a bear from a passing menagerie for fifteen dollars. The bear was lodged in the basement of McGraw, and John Henry Comstock '74 was appointed his keeper. Comstock and the bear loved each other, and put on exhibition wrestling matches on the campus. But on Gate Eve some celebrants broke into the bear's home, led him to the chapel, on the third floor of Morrill Hall, and chained him to the preacher's desk. They then established one of Mr. Cornell's cows in the bear's quarters.

The fate of the bear? He was chloroformed and dissected in the spring.[14]

The class rushes began as soon as the numbers of the classes were somewhat equalized. The appearance of arrogant freshmen in stove-pipe hats was a signal for sophomore aggression. In October 1871 Vice-President Russel wrote to President White that he had valiantly intervened; "I was pushed and hissed and groaned at, and something was thrown over me." But, he alleges, he broke up the riot singlehanded.

There were other student misdemeanors, on the intellectual rather than the physical plane. It was the custom in many colleges to print a scurrilous "mock scheme" on the occasion of the Junior Exhibition. The mock scheme of 1871 has come down to us. It bears the title of "Old Ezra's Foundling Hospital." The faculty parade under deformed names: Andy Deity White, Chief Supe; Billy Christ Russel, Supernumerary and Handler of Diapers; Ardent Spirit Wheeler and Highly Drunk Corson, Committee on Drinks, and so forth. At one point

> Wheeler now gives Corson the wink,
> And both go out to get a drink.

And:

To close the Exhibition, Andy will now say a little piece, in which he will endeavor strenuously to prove that old Ezra didn't lie in his famous *Tribune* article. He will intersperse all this twaddle with his usual howls about *earnest* young men, and will boast of the University Reading Room

[14] Burt G. Wilder, "The Cornell Bear," *Cornell Review*, Nov. 1883.

(one daily and two weeklies), of the Machine Shops, &c. The impression upon the minds of the hearers after listening to these idiotic ravings is a general inability to decide which is the biggest liar of the two, old Ezra or Prex himself.

This was inexcusable, this was outrageous. And yet, perhaps it is a significant gloss on the official pronouncements.

On one familiar manifestation of college life the faculty were un-wontedly severe. Hazing was to have no place in Cornell life. To be sure, hazing was an ancient and dear college tradition. It was pointed out that hazing infested the universities of Athens, Berytus, and Carthage, and that Saint Augustine himself belonged to a society called the *Eversores,* or Overturners, or Destroyers.[15] Even such precedents did not weigh with Andrew D. White.

A tragic occurrence put a check to hazing at Cornell for many years. In October 1873 Mortimer N. Leggett '77, son of General M. D. Leggett, U.S. Commissioner of Internal Revenue, was pledged to the Kappa Alpha Society. Young Leggett was transported, blindfolded, into the country, and told to find his way home. After he had blundered about sufficiently, he was met by two of the brothers, who removed his blindfold. But all three were lost and were unfamiliar with the topography. They went down an open slope to a cliff edge above Six Mile Creek (near Giles Street). It was dark; all three plunged over; and Leggett was killed.

Sensational newspapers told of ghastly, hellish orgies on the cliff, and drew appropriate morals. But the inquiry exonerated, on the whole, the fraternity members. General Leggett made his own careful exam-ination. He wrote to his sons in Cleveland: "The miserable hocus-pocus heathenish custom of such a night ramble is the sin and disgrace of the society, but this mummery was invented and inaugurated long before any of these young men were born." [16] He showed his magnanimity by accepting initiation into the fraternity.

Despite all the examples here reported, student behavior was re-garded as generally good. In White's Annual Report for 1874 he says that the good conduct of the past two years is almost without parallel in the history of American institutions of higher education. In the following years he remarks that the presence of lady students exerts an elevating influence on undergraduate mores.

[15] F. Hedge, "University Reform," *Atlantic Monthly,* Sept. 1866.
[16] Reported in Ithaca *Journal,* 24 Jan. 1957.

Student turbulence was reduced by the new influence of athletics and sport in American colleges. It seems to us unnatural, inhuman, that the collegians of the early nineteenth century had no outdoor games, except a little gentle ball playing and, here and there, rowing. By the mid-century the physical condition of city-bred Americans was beginning to cause concern. The American thought of himself, as he still does, as a muscular outdoor man, whereas the sedentary worker or student often had no exercise except walking, while he subsisted on the farmer's traditional hearty diet.

The first formal work in physical education under faculty direction was undertaken at Amherst in 1860. The idea rapidly spread. But at Cornell it had to wait until more urgent matters were attended to. The boys and girls got most of their exercise by climbing up hill and running down, by tobogganing on Buffalo Street, by skating on the Inlet and on Cayuga Lake in favorable winters.

White warmly favored physical education, as an aid to health. Indeed, Ithaca's reputation for health was not good. The fever and ague, or malaria, abounded. "Ithacans may thrive on their dank, muggy air, but it is poison to other people," wrote a disgruntled student.[17]

Baseball was played from the first, in a rudimentary form. The participants were barehanded; the catcher, maskless, was in constant peril of a broken nose, or worse. One put out a runner by hitting him with a thrown ball. Fortunately the ball was a soft one, whereas "now a ball is selected harder than Nero's heart, so that if it hits a man it will knock his brains out." [18] The games were played mostly on the campus, which served also as the Cornell family cow pasture, and thus presented its particular hazards. Before an important game the Cornell cows had to be driven off the diamond and locked up in Forest Park. Robert H. Treman '78, who pitched for Cornell for seven years (two years while in the Ithaca High School, four years in Cornell, and one year in the hardware business) loved to recall a game of which the Ithaca *Journal* reported: "The main feature of the game occurred in the seventh inning, when the visitors' captain slid into what he thought was third base."

As there was no gate, there could be no gate receipts. But through

---

[17] *Niagara Journal*, Lockport, N.Y., 6 Sept. 1871, in EC Papers. Also T. B. Comstock in *Cornell Magazine*, Feb., 1892; and Goldwin Smith to C. E. Norton, 17 July 1870, in *Mass. Hist. Soc. Proc.*, Dec. 1915: "We had a severe epidemic in the winter, and a panic in consequence. . . . Malaria sent me to Philadelphia."
[18] C. V. P. Young, in *Era*, Feb. 1913.

subscriptions uniforms were bought, a shirt of white flannel with carnelian trimmings, pants of light gray flannel, and a cap with a carnelian star.

The first varsity game was with the Cascadilla Club of Ithaca, in May 1869. Five innings were played in three hours. Cornell won, 42 to 26. The first intercollegiate game was with Hobart in Geneva in 1874. Hobart beat us, 43 to 16. The Cornellians complained, however, that Hobart had an undue advantage in familiarity with its own field, which was on a slope, with the third base ten feet above the level of first base and with trees and other obstacles scattered about the diamond. One of our happiest contests was with the Actives of Owego in October 1871. Cornell won, 63 to 10, with 12 home runs, 50 one-base hits, and 108 two-base hits. Perhaps our unhappiest was in 1876, when the Ithaca Nine beat us 58 to 0.

Football, something between soccer and a civil war, began with an intramural contest in 1869, with forty men on a side. In the following year the first interclass game occurred. Eighty sophomores fought eighty freshmen all afternoon until dark, with occasional rests while the referee blew up the football.

In October 1870 a football game was organized in honor of our distinguished sportsman visitor, Thomas Hughes, M.P. Apparently any player was welcome; even Vice-President Russel joined in for a time. Hughes's own account of the match is memorable:

It having been settled after a good deal of confused talking that the class of '72 should play those of '73 and '74, all who cared to play collected into two irregular crowds, unorganized and leaderless, and stood facing one another. Most, but not all, of the players took their coats off. Then a big, oddly-shaped ball arrived, somebody started it with a kick-off, and away went both sides in chase, wildly jostling one another, kicking, catching, throwing, or hitting the ball, according to fancy, all thoughts more bent, seemingly, upon the pure delight of the struggle than upon any particular goal. "Are there any goals, and if so, where?" we asked, toiling after the ball, which appeared to be visiting all sides of the field with strict impartiality and equal satisfaction to the players. "Oh yes, any-where between those trees,"—two great elms, standing perhaps thirty feet apart. Occasionally the ball got wedged in a dense "scrummage" of the contending parties, and while some went in boldly to extricate it, many more would stand round looking on and naïvely clap their hands for joy.[19]

[19] *Every Saturday*, 20 May 1871.

It was in 1873 that Andrew D. White refused to allow a team of forty men to travel to Cleveland to "agitate a bag of wind" with a Michigan team. In 1875 and 1876 Harvard and Yale organized the rules into something resembling the modern sport, but Cornell insisted on its own game, combining the features of soccer, rugby, and a general free-for-all. Since no one else would play this "Cornell football," interest in the game waned, not to be revivified until 1886.

In those days rowing was the college sport par excellence. Cayuga Lake was already famous as the home waters of the champion professional sculler, Charles E. Courtney of Union Springs. In 1871 two Cornell boating clubs were formed, and in the following spring a regatta was held which would have seemed shocking to a visiting Oxonian. Three craft competed: a four-oared whaleboat named "Biz," a six-oared ark, and a six-oared structure named "Striped Pig." Robert H. Treman '78 (not yet in college) rowed in "Biz." He pulled so mightily that he broke his oar, and with great presence of mind leaped into the lake. But "Biz" went nonetheless on the rocks.

In 1873 Andrew D. White presented the students with a cedar shell, a little heavy, it seems. A professional coach, Harry Coulter, was engaged. His theory was that every man must be reduced twenty-five pounds in weight. He used heroic measures, terrific exercise with only sufficient water to support life. (In fact, one tumbler of water for breakfast, two for dinner, one for supper.) The crew, gasping and sullen and afflicted with boils, finished fifth in the intercollegiate regatta at Springfield, Massachusetts, both in 1873 and 1874.

In the fall of 1874, a senior, John Ostrom, took charge of the crew. Believing in the importance of morale, he let the boys eat and drink at their pleasure. He applied the principles of engineering to the boat's fittings. He concluded that weight in an oarsman was more of a detriment than an advantage; his 1875 crewmen had a maximum weight of 165 pounds, with two men of about 150 pounds. He evolved the first Cornell stroke, "with its characteristic vigor, strong toss of the head, the full swing of the body, with a shortening of the slide." [20]

In July 1875 Cornell astounded the world, or a fair part of it, by winning both the varsity and the freshman races in the intercollegiate regatta at Saratoga. Reporters dubbed its technique the "git-thar" stroke. Even in these days of overemphasis it is difficult to picture the excitement that was generated. According to a beloved story, when

[20] Albert W. Smith, in the *Cornell Daily Sun*'s *A Half-Century at Cornell* (Ithaca, 1930), p. 21.

the telegram of victory arrived, President White rushed to the McGraw tower, broke open the lock on the chime levers, and rang the chimes himself. He later insisted that he ran to the tower only to make sure that no amateur would ruin the mechanism. He was relieved to find there John Henry Comstock '74, the chimesmaster.[21]

It is, however, an indubitable fact that the crews were returned to Ithaca by a special train. On arrival they were placed on a platform on a hook-and-ladder truck. Speeches of welcome resounded. President White said that the victories had done more to tell the world about Cornell than the trustees could have done by spending $100,000. After the speeches, several hundred citizens attached themselves to the truck and dragged it up the hill, to the continuous explosion of rockets, roman candles, and cannon. At the entrance to the campus Professor John E. Sweet had constructed in a day a wooden arch fifty feet high, covered with evergreen boughs, surmounted by a rowing shell and crossed oars, and bearing the inscription GOOD BOYS.

White had hardly exaggerated in estimating the publicity value of the great victory. Every newspaper acclaimed the triumph with double-page spreads, imaginative illustrations, and editorials of congratulation. The conquest of the eastern rowing colleges by the self-trained out-landers touched the popular imagination to the quick. And memories of Saratoga still persist in Cornell song and story.

The great day of 1875 is noteworthy also as the birthday of the Cornell Yell. The originator was Charles W. Raymond '76, leader of a college quintet. The group had a song, imitated from Yale's "Eli-Eli-Eli-U," of which the refrain ran "Cornell-i-ell-i-ell-i-ell, Fol-de-rol-de-rol-rol-rol." In the fervor of victory Raymond and his friends screamed "Cornell-i-ell-i-ell-i-ell," and the crowd took it up in the form thence-forth consecrated.[22]

Cornell had already its colors, carnelian, or cornelian, and white, inspired by an inevitable paronomasia. (The exact shade of carnelian, its place in a color chart, was, and is, a matter of bitter dispute.) We have noted the appearance of the colors in the Inaugural decorations. A few dandies, at the beginning, wore a university cap of white flannel bound with a red cord. The *Era* suggested (30 January 1869) the formal

---

[21] *Autobiography of Andrew Dickson White* (New York, 1905), I, 352; Edwin Emerson, "Groves of Academe" (MS, C.U. Archives), p. 430. Albert W. Smith '78 quotes George S. Moler '75 as attesting that White did indeed ring the bells with his own hands (*Alumni News*, 13 May 1926).

[22] *Era*, May 1915.

adoption of carnelian and white. However, the early crews carried their club, not the college, colors.[23]

An interesting effort to establish something like intellectual Olympic games, in rivalry with athletics, was made in 1874. An association of a dozen colleges held in New York City public competitions in oratory and written examinations in the chief academic subjects, for handsome prizes. In the first competition Cornell did very well, and in the second it swept the examination hall, gaining the first prize in essays, mathematics, and Greek and the second prize in oratory. (Miss Julia J. Thomas '75, destined to be President of Wellesley College, was the winner in Greek.) In following years Cornell continued to shine, especially in Greek and mathematics. Our success in Greek provided President White with a telling rejoinder to those who accused Cornell of depreciating the classics.

While athletics were gradually finding their organization, fraternities and clubs were well established.

The fraternity, the chief originality and one of the chief determinants of American undergraduate life, has been the subject of endless dispute. Fraternities are natural products of the human instinct to associate with one's congenial fellows. Their secrecy, ritual, and coming-of-age rites appeal to the adolescent taste for romantic mystery. They breed group loyalty, the old Anglo-Saxon team spirit. They inculcate high ideals and give social polish to the uncouth. And if a university fails to provide proper housing, amenities, dining facilities, the fraternities will fulfill this physical need.

On the other hand, fraternities segregate students into small groups, from which they may hardly emerge for four years. They propose minority loyalties above college loyalties. They are often extremely snobbish, pursuing social ideals already archaic in the elder world. The false barriers they erect establish prejudices which one may have to unlearn with pain. They may discourage scholarship—their average scholastic standings at Cornell are regularly lower than those of non-fraternity men—and they may encourage drinking and gambling and especially time wasting. And they have caused innumerable heartbreaks, even suicides, among seventeen-year-olds who are informed that they are goats and not sheep.

This is no place to argue the matter. At least a university is, clearly, a world in miniature. It has its rewards and punishments, its selections

[23] Albert H. Wright, "Cornell's Colors," in his *Studies in History*, No. 17 (Ithaca, 1953).

and exclusions, its mercies and cruelties, like the great world it imitates. It gives a young man some knowledge of himself, and of the regard others have for him; and it gives him an opportunity to change that regard by his own efforts. Many a youth has been better served by failing to make a fraternity than he would ever have been by acceptance.

At any rate, Cornell from the first welcomed the fraternity. Andrew D. White had joined Sigma Phi at Hobart, Psi Upsilon and Alpha Sigma Phi at Yale, a cumulation which would now be frowned upon. His broad experience convinced him that the advantages of the fraternity far outweighed its drawbacks. Encouraged by administrative benevolence, seven societies established themselves in Cornell's first year, in this order: Zeta Psi, Chi Phi, Kappa Alpha, Alpha Delta Phi, Phi Kappa Psi, Chi Psi, and Delta Upsilon. They had their meeting rooms in the business blocks downtown (and at this writing some initials of the first members of Kappa Alpha may still be discerned, carved beside a door on Tioga Street, immediately north of State Street). Not until 1878 was the first chapter house built, with lodgings for the members. This was Alpha Delta Phi, on Buffalo Street at Schuyler Place. The house is today, or was yesterday, an Ithaca College dormitory.

Against the fraternities the Independents organized, as early as December 1868, with the declaration that fraternities are "the foulest blots upon college life."

Many another sort of club was formed. The "literary club," with its rooms, library, contests, and debates, had long been a feature of American college life. At Cornell the Irving Literary Association was founded only thirteen days after the University's opening, and the Philaletheian Society shortly after. The Curtis Literary Society, signal for its inclusion of men and women, appeared in 1872. These three published the *Cornell Review*. Their common clubroom was in White Hall. As gradually the dormitories were turned into classrooms and as the students moved downtown, only the hardiest enthusiasts would trudge up the hill for an evening of literature. In the eighties the clubs disappeared, or turned into debating societies.

In 1870 a distinguished trustee, Stewart L. Woodford, former Lieutenant-Governor of the state, established the Woodford Prize in Oratory, of $100 annually. This considerable reward, and the paucity of entertainment, made the Woodford Stage one of the great events of the college year. Most of the students and a throng of visitors crowded the largest hall available and sat, presumably enthralled, through an evening of exalted rhetoric. The winner was regarded as a college hero, marked for future eminence. The Woodford continues today, but a classroom suffices to contain the devotees of oratory. There is matter here for the *laudator temporis acti.*

Departmental clubs naturally took shape. The first, and one of the most noteworthy, was the Natural History Society, which stimulated a long series of undergraduates to become professional scientists.[24]

The drama had its devotees. In 1870 a troupe composed mainly of students put on a play. The Cornelian Minstrels, formed in 1872, produced a show in aid of the Cornell Navy. Other groups, part faculty, part student, assembled to play unpretentious farces and even attempted Sheridan's *The Critic* in 1878. But not until 1880 was a serious dramatic club established.

Musical organizations also came into being. The Orpheus Glee Club congregated in the first months of the University's existence, and the Harmonia and the Cornell Glee Club in the spring of 1869. A Philharmonic Society, a Mozart Club, a Cornell Musical Association appeared. Timid excursions to perform out of town were undertaken, including one in 1876, by railroad cattle car to Cortland. Most of these associations endured but for a season. With the formation of the Glee Club of 1880 Cornell musical history really began.

The offerings at the early concerts were the College Songs now embalmed in many a tattered piano-top collection. (Some day a musicologist will earnestly study these old fol-de-rols and co-ca-che-lunks, and will create such a vogue as now aureoles the folk song.) The ditties, delivered with more good will than art, were interspersed with gymnastics and tumbling.

Some original songs were contributed by Willard Fiske and Francis Miles Finch, including the long-popular "Smoking Song." Others were contrived by the students themselves. The origin of the "Alma Mater" was picturesque. Archibald C. Weeks '72 and his room-mate, Wilmot M. Smith '74, took great pleasure in singing together a lugubrious ballad of the period, "Annie Lisle," recounting the gradual decline and death of the tuberculous heroine. ("Wave, willows; murmur, waters; Golden sunbeams, smile; Earthly music cannot waken Lovely Annie Lisle.") As Weeks remembered: "I proposed that we adapt a College

---

[24] The records of the Natural History Society, full of curious information about early Cornellians, have been published by Albert H. Wright '04 in his precious series, *Pre-Cornell and Early Cornell* (Ithaca, 1954).

Song to the music, and suggested the first two lines of the first verse; [Smith] responded with the third and fourth, I with the fifth and sixth and he with the seventh and eighth. The chorus was the result of mutual suggestion. . . . The next two verses were shortly afterward composed by me." [25] This rare antiphonal method of poetic composition many excuse the outrageous rhyme of "waters" with "Alma Mater." It can hardly explain the anthem's phenomenal success on a large number of college and high-school campuses, where it is chorused with a volume almost sufficient to awaken lovely Annie Lisle.

The "Evening Song" was first sung by an ephemeral Glee Club in April 1876, to the tune of "Lauriger Horatius." The text, in five stanzas, appears in the *Era* for 6 April 1877, signed merely "T." The initial and the date cast doubt on the common ascription of the words to Henry Pyrell '90.

"The soldier loves his gen'ral's fame," a rather debatable proposition in modern military life, has been sung by a hundred Cornell Glee Clubs to the tune of "Dearest Mae." It is credited to George K. Birge '72.

A student Brass Band was organized in 1870, and was succeeded by the Cadet Band in 1872. Of the Cadet Band's efforts at a public function the Ithaca *Journal* caustically reported: "At this time the Cadet Band played a few strains, but the principal strain was on the audience." Its marching evolutions were likely to be surprising. At a review of the troops the band was supposed to march, playing, before the battalion at attention, and then reverse direction and countermarch. The maneuver was too difficult; the band simply marched off home.[26]

The long and honorable record of undergraduate publications begins with the *Cornell Era*, established by the secret societies. The name was chosen to indicate that with the founding of Cornell a new era, like the Elizabethan Era, had begun. Its early issues consisted largely of news of the campus, announcements, and editorials, with fillers in the form of learned articles by faculty members, and the poetry which undergraduates produced in much greater volume than they do today.

---

[25] A. C. Weeks to George William Harris, 18 Jan. 1887. Many stories were current about the song's origin, including one that it was a translation by Theodore Zinck of a German original (*Alumni News*, 8, 15, and 22 Feb. 1917, and *Era*, March 1917).

[26] Samuel D. Halliday '70, in Ithaca *Journal*, 5 June 1901.

When copy was short, the printers sometimes helped out with contributions of their own. One entire issue is said to have consisted of the printers' more than indelicate facetiae. No copy of this curiosity is known to exist.

A rival, the *Cornell Times*, briefly flourished. The *Cornelian* (*sic*) first appeared in 1869, published by a group of fraternities. A pretentious, and worthy, literary magazine, the *Cornell Review*, lived from 1873 to 1886, when it became the *Cornell Magazine*. The Brazilian students even bravely published the *Aurora Brasileira* during a winter.

The first humorous magazine was *Cocagne*, which existed only from April to June 1878. This publication is perhaps less remarkable for its contents than for the printing of some of the cuts, done by a photo-stereotype process invented by the University's photographic technician, Frederick E. Ives. This self-educated countryman refused an instructorship, migrated to the Great City, and invented the three-color printing process, the modern form of the binocular microscope, and, it is claimed, the half-tone screen.[27]

Most vigorous of the undergraduate societies was the C.U. Christian Association, which met on Sundays and for midweek Bible classes and prayer meetings. Doggedly pious students attended the daily eight o'clock services in the Morrill Hall chapel, conducted by the Registrar, William D. Wilson, who was an Episcopalian clergyman. The services were rigorously nonsectarian.

Andrew D. White always insisted that he had established the first unsectarian and voluntary college chapel in the country. (He overlooked the University of Virginia, which had voluntary chapel from its opening in 1825.) The word "voluntary" perhaps needs definition. The first *Register* states: "Simple religious services are held daily in the University Chapel, which all students, except those specially excused for due cause shown to the Faculty, are expected to attend." In 1872–73 the subordinate clause is abridged to "which students are expected to attend." In a Second Edition for 1872–73 the sentence becomes: "Simple religious services are held daily in the University Chapel." In 1874–75 we read: "There are also daily chapel services, to which students are invited, although none are compelled to attend."

However one may regard a "voluntary" system which requires a faculty excuse for absence, the services were certainly voluntary in

[27] See Ives's fascinating *Autobiography of an Amateur Inventor* (privately published, 1928), p. 23. Also *Alumni News*, 20 Feb. 1936.

fact, if only because the tiny chapel could accommodate a mere handful of the five hundred undergraduates. A student alleged that the average attendance was twelve, and it occasionally dropped to one.

With the opening of Sage Chapel in 1875, the students and townspeople were given the opportunity to hear the most eminent preachers of every denomination. At the same time large numbers of students, who after all lived in the village, preferred to attend the local churches.

What with the Christian Association on the hill, the chapel services, and the church organizations downtown, the religious needs of the students were amply provided for.

Thus by the mid-seventies, with the social clubs, the burgeoning "activities," and primitive athletic sports, the students had most of the appurtenances of college life which they might have found in the older established colleges.

IX

The Early Years: The Girls

COEDUCATION was not absolutely a new idea in 1868. Pioneer conditions, companionship in country labor of boys and girls, scarcity of students in the sparsely settled land, had naturally imposed coeducation in elementary schools, academies, and normal schools. On the college level, Oberlin received girls with boys from 1837, and Antioch followed its example. The state universities of Iowa, Utah, and Washington admitted women in the fifties and sixties. The Michigan Legislature in 1867 urged the Regents to open their university to women, but none were actually matriculated until 1870. In the east, no college yet dared to make the bold experiment. In general, parents of young women preferred the security of a Female College. Of these the first in date was Elmira College, opened in 1855, and the first that enforced high collegiate standards was Vassar, opened in 1865.[1]

The idea, at least, of coeducation was already abroad, to find a welcome in the minds of Ezra Cornell and Andrew D. White.

[1] Maria Mitchell, celebrated astronomer and professor at Vassar, wrote to Ezra Cornell (10 March 1868): "I consider Vassar College the best institution in the world *of the kind;* it is not of the right kind. When I was last in Boston I asked Dr. [Thomas] Hill, President of Harvard College: 'How soon will girls enter Harvard College?' and he replied: 'The most conservative member of the Faculty says: "in twenty years."' I also asked Prof. Peirce, the Mathematics Professor: 'If a girl knocks at your classroom door and asks for admission to your class, what will you do?' He replied: 'I couldn't turn her away and I wouldn't.'" She then urges Cornell to admit women students (EC Papers).

Ezra Cornell had always exhibited a special tenderness for girls, and a respect for women's abilities, which may perhaps be related to the equality accorded women in Quaker religious practice. From the first he proposed that his university should be open to women. He wrote his small granddaughter Eunice Cornell, on 17 February 1867: "I want to have girls educated in the university, as well as boys, so that they may have the same opportunity to become wise and useful to society that boys have." He even asked her to keep the letter, to show, in time, to the President and faculty. He conceived that his wife should be the patroness of a system by which impecunious girl students would work three or four hours a day at productive tasks. In his Inaugural Address he made his intention clear.

White was no less convinced. As early as 1857, his dear friend and mentor, the Reverend Samuel J. May, Unitarian minister of Syracuse, had adjured him to devote himself to the great cause of coeducation. It will be recalled (I hope) that in White's proposal of 1862 for a dream university he had specified that it should be open to women. And in his Inaugural Address he had reiterated his purpose, regretting only that it could not be put immediately into effect.

Such public declarations provoked much interest. After the ceremonies of the Inauguration, Henry W. Sage (who was soon to loom large in Cornell history), said with emotion to White: "When you are ready to carry out the idea of educating young women as thoroughly as young men, I will provide the endowment to enable you to do so." Sweeter words never fell on a college president's ear.

Even before the Inauguration, the New York State Teachers' Association submitted a memorial praying for coeducation at Cornell. White approved, and called for a committee to investigate the subject.[2] Miss Catharine E. Beecher, sister of the great Henry Ward Beecher, came to give advice. On 27 March 1869 the famous woman's rights advocate, Susan B. Anthony, made a sensational speech in Library Hall, in which she declared that the day Cornell University would admit women on the same basis as men would be celebrated by posterity as sacredly as the Fourth of July or the birth of Christ.

That holy day was postponed, despite the good will of Founder and President. Cornell wrote to a female applicant, Lucy Washburn, on 26 February 1869, explaining the difficulties in the way of accommodation, classwork, and self-help. He pointed out that if she should win a state scholarship the University would be required to admit her. He

[2] Annual report, Aug. 1868.

concluded: "I hope to see 1000 young women educated in this University, with as many or more of their brothers, and all working smoothly and in harmony for their best good—but I don't want the young women forced upon us before we are prepared to make a success of it."

Perhaps it was Miss Washburn who carried the Amazonian assault to the very President's office. White persuaded her, with "a suave request clothed in the richest morocco of his tones," to postpone her entrance.[3]

The problem was complicated by a request (19 October 1869) for admission from Miss Malvina Higgins of Maysville, East Tennessee. Miss Higgins was colored. Cornell had apparently written that colored people were not excluded. Miss Higgins, for whatever reason, did not present herself.

The male undergraduates, or at least the social elite of the fraternities, were from the beginning hostile to the admission of women. The first *Cornelian*, published by the secret societies in 1869, editorialized:

The Woman's Rights monomaniacs are attempting to mislead the public into the belief that female students are to be admitted here. The foundation of the rumor probably exists only in the imagination of some enthusiast, who, thinking that the thing ought to be so, unhesitatingly sets up the cry that it is so. . . . We sincerely trust that Cornell University will never come to be ranked and classed among the Oberlins of America.

The *Cornelian*'s forebodings were soon realized. In September 1870 Miss Jennie Spencer of Cortland presented herself, with a certificate for a state scholarship in hand. Perforce admitted, she faithfully attended classes. But as no lodging was available on the hill, she was obliged to climb the *gradus ad Parnassum* two or three times a day. When winter came she surrendered and bade farewell to Cornell with regret. Her stay, says White in his *Autobiography*, made a mere temporary ripple on the surface of our affairs. Miss Spencer's vain and valiant struggle touched Henry W. Sage and brought him nearer to the point of offering a women's dormitory.

The question of coeducation could no longer be evaded. At the trustees' meeting in June 1871 a Committee of Five, including White and Sage, was appointed to deal with the subject of Female Education.

In the autumn three bold girls, Emma S. Eastman, Sophy P. Fleming, and Mary Jordan, sister of David Starr Jordan, attended classes and

[3] F. M. Finch, *Life and Services of Ezra Cornell* (Ithaca, 1887), p. 6.

worked in the laboratories with the understanding that their work be counted toward a degree. And White busied himself with inquiries to institutions where coeducation had been tried. The replies were mostly enthusiastic in favor.

In the winter White and Sage made a journey of inspection to coeducational institutions: Oberlin, Antioch, Michigan, Northwestern, and the State Industrial University, now the University of Illinois. They interviewed administrators, teachers, students, and even janitors. The result was a remarkable printed report, couched in White's most ardent and trenchant style.[4] This Report deserves republication, as a capital document in the history of women's higher education.

White begins by casting savory scorn on the theorists about woman's nature, destiny, and proper place in society. He points to the success of coeducation in the academies and normal schools.

The disputants on this question, on either side, appear to have been straining their eyes in looking deep down into the human consciousness or afar off into the universe at large, to solve a problem which their fathers or mothers and sons and daughters had done so much already to work out, nay, in whose solution they themselves had taken part.

He tells of his observations at the colleges visited, of the good effects observed. He concludes that coeducation has tended to refine the young men, at no cost to their manliness, and that the men's desire to appear to good advantage before the young women, together with the conscientiousness of women in study, has elevated the general tone of scholarship. As for the effects on the young women, their health has not suffered, contrary to many dolorous predictions. No evil effects on character and manners were observed, and no loss of distinctive womanly qualities.

Under the head of "Effects common to both sexes" he takes up the question, so fearful to parents, of "the possible formation of acquaintances likely to ripen into matrimonial engagements." He admits this possibility. But, he inquires, how are such engagements now formed?

Choice is determined by mere casual meeting, by an acquaintance of a few weeks, by winning manners at a ball, by a pleasing costume in the street, and at the best by a very imperfect revelation of those mental and moral qualities which are to make or mar the happiness of all concerned. Should such engagements be formed in a university where both

[4] Albany, 1872; reprinted with *Proceedings at the Laying of the Corner Stone of the Sage College* (Ithaca, 1873).

146

sexes are educated together, they would be based upon a far more thorough and extended knowledge, upon an admiration of a much higher range of qualities, and upon a similarity in taste and temper, which could not be gained elsewhere.

As to the effects upon the university, all testimony pointed to an improvement in its scholarly tone. True, plenty of traditionalists feared that coeducation would bring to Cornell a loss of prestige; but such an argument should not weigh.

Even if there be opposition, all the winds of public opinion which the University has encountered thus far have not been so favorable as to leave us without experience in buffeting opposing blasts, or, to state the matter more plainly, while no institution has ever had more noble friends or a more kindly public instinct in its favor, none has ever had to encounter a more bitter storm of misrepresentation, sneers, and old-world arguments and pedantic missiles, and it is therefore of very little consequence whether there be or be not added one more cause of futile opposition.

After his examination of the specific problem, White develops his general view of woman's place in society. The common theory is that

woman is the helpmeet of man, that she gives him aid in difficulty, counsel in perplexity, solace in sorrow; that his is the vigorous thinking, hers the passive reception of such portions of thought as may be best for her; that his mind must be trained to grapple with difficult subjects, that hers needs no development but such as will make her directly useful and agreeable; . . . that man needs to be trained in all his powers to search, to assert, to decide; that woman needs but little training beyond that which enables her gracefully to assent; that man needs the university and the great subjects of study it presents, while woman needs the "finishing schools" and the "acomplishments"; and that, to sum up, the character, work, training and position of woman are as good as they ever can be.

As a result of this pervasive theory:

Strong men, in adversity and perplexity, have often found that the "partners of their joys and sorrows" give no more real strength than would Nuremberg dolls. Under this theory, as thus worked out, the aid and counsel and solace fail just when they are most needed. In their stead the man is likely to find some scraps of philosophy begun in boarding-schools and developed in kitchens or drawing-rooms.

White then utters an eloquent but not very pertinent diatribe against conventional extravagance and the tyranny of Parisian fashions, points to women's want of appreciation of art in its nobler phases, to their fear of new truths, to their bolstering of fetishisms and superstitions, to their direful, though indirect, influence on politics. Such faults, he maintains, would be corrected by higher education.

And now comes the big sensation: the announcement of an offer by Henry W. Sage of $250,000, on the condition that "instruction shall be offered to young women by the Cornell University, as broad and as thorough as that now afforded to young men."

White examines various ways of responding to this proposal, and concludes that a large college building should be erected adjacent to the University grounds. This building should be complete in all respects, with lecture room, recitation rooms, infirmary, gymnasium, bathing rooms and lodging rooms for from one hundred and fifty to two hundred lady students. The lecture and recitation rooms would serve for such delicate subjects as physiology. The Department of Botany and Horticulture, so suitable for young ladies and affording such opportunities for healthful exercise, should likewise be housed in this building. (The transfer of this department to obtain sustenance from the new foundation seems a brilliant example of presidential finesse. I can hear the "rich, morocco tones" of Mr. White: "Oh, Mr. Sage, how noble it would be if we could attach to your College Botany and Horticulture, so elevating, so suitable for young ladies!")

This establishment, concludes White, would be known as the Sage College of Cornell University.

At the trustees' meeting on 13 February 1872 Sage's offer was formally accepted.

The sensational news, well publicized, brought a swarm of feminine applications. Sixteen women were admitted to the University in the fall of 1872. In June 1873 Cornell's first woman graduate, Emma Sheffield Eastman, received the degree of Bachelor of Philosophy. Substantiating the theory that coeducation might lead to the formation of acquaintances likely to ripen into matrimonial engagements, she married Leroy A. Foster '72, and later gained some fame as a suffrage lecturer.

The cornerstone of Sage College was laid on 15 May 1873, with impressive ceremonies. Henry W. Sage asserted that "this is the first university in this country, if not in the world, which has at the same time boldly recognized the rights of woman as well as man to all the education she will ask, and pledged itself to the policy and duty of maintaining equal facilities for both." (To be sure, some of the western universities might cavil at these words.) Sage then stated his faith in education for the development of Christian culture and character; more, higher education would serve for the professional training of women for tasks now reserved to men. "The doors of opportunity must be opened wide. All women should have the liberty to learn what they can, and to do what they have the power to do." He foresaw women at work "in the arts and professions, as teachers, editors, and authors, as clerks and saleswomen, accountants and telegraphers, in all the higher mechanical employments, in architectural drawing, and in thousands of the less masculine pursuits which men now monopolize. . . . In short, the efficient force of the human race will be multiplied in proportion as woman, by culture and education, is fitted for new and broader spheres of education."

Mrs. Henry W. Sage then laid the cornerstone, with poetic words which perhaps belied her inward conviction. She is said to have told her husband: "You have meant to do women a great good, but you have ignorantly done them an incalculable injury." [5]

Ezra Cornell then spoke briefly, revealing that he had placed in the cornerstone a letter, of which he had kept no copy, addressed "To the Coming Man and Woman." In the letter he had indicated "to future generations the cause of the failure of this experiment, if it ever does fail, as I trust in God it never will."

When at length the day of Sage College is done, may some historian remember these words and rescue the tin box from the demolishers!

Although Sage College was not ready for occupancy in the fall of 1874, thirty-seven women enrolled in the University, versus 484 men. (I assume that Arasca and Sula Eddy were females.) The long debate as to the status of coeds was vigorously engaged.

For the *Era*, the question was an unfailing source of copy. A warmly favorable editorial appeared on 20 October 1871, perhaps from the pen of David Starr Jordan. But on 23 February 1872 the paper admitted that the majority of students were probably opposed. And on 3 October 1873 the editors were alarmed lest familiarity should breed contempt—and not one-sided contempt either.

The beings whom [the male student] was to worship beyond the shade of college towers, who were to make him forget for a brief time the struggles of the classroom—these fair creatures whom he had set apart as something not to be profaned by association with prosaic toil he finds

[5] Martha Carey Thomas '77, in *Memorial Exercises in Honor of Henry W. Sage* (Ithaca, 1898), p. 54.

with him in the classroom, their faces flushed with emulation, the spirit of rivalry gleaming from their eyes.

The senior class in 1872 voted on coeducation; fifteen (of whom three were women) were in favor, thirty-seven opposed. But the seniors of 1876 voted twenty-nine to twenty-nine.

The cold-shouldering of the females by the males existed from the first. As early as 1874 young Anna Botsford, on a Cattaraugus County farm, was told by a Cornellian: "You won't have a gay time, for the boys won't pay any attention to the college girls." She concluded: "Cornell must be a good place for a girl to get an education; it has all the advantages of a university and a convent combined." [6]

Anna Botsford's experience is significant. She was a very intelligent person, original, decided, and humorous, and beautiful even in her old age. In college she had no awareness of ostracism; indeed, she had to discourage men callers. She accepted the rule that women did not bow to their male acquaintances on the campus, not for fear of rebuffs but because there were just too many male acquaintances. She dwelt in Sage College in her sophomore year. Dances were held every Saturday evening; on one occasion the entire Kappa Alpha Society attended. She became engaged and unengaged; and shortly after her graduation she married her instructor, John Henry Comstock '74. The Comstock partnership, in science and life, vindicated Andrew D. White's judgment of college attachments and their results.

Sage College opened in 1875, with about thirty girl occupants. Since there was great need of dining facilities on the hill and at the same time a surplus of room in the Sage dining room, men students and instructors were admitted to it. The manager reported (8 February 1876) that he had fifty men boarders. The men refused segregation and insisted on sitting at "the coed tables." The Psi Upsilons were particularly troublesome; they demanded their breakfasts from the best end of the sirloin steak. The manager proposed restricting the men to two-thirds of the accommodations.

The internal control of the dormitory required definition. The first coeds were revolted by the idea of chaperonage. Farm girls like Anna Botsford had hardly heard the word; they were perfectly able to take care of themselves. Young rebels like mannish, short-haired Julia Thomas '75 found the very suggestion insulting. The girls formed their own organization, with rules for guidance and with proper penalties for social misbehavior. This was the ancestor of the Women's Self-

[6] Anna Botsford Comstock, *The Comstocks of Cornell* (Ithaca, 1953), p. 74.

Government Association. White approved of this democratic system. He had faith in the essential virtue of human nature, and especially of female nature, and he did not like to have his ideals disturbed. But Sage, perhaps counseled by his wife, thought Mr. White was too ready to grant complete freedom to the young women. He pointed to lurking moral dangers.[7] White and his girl allies seem to have won, for no chaperone, except the manager's wife, is discernible in the first years.

The early coeds were clearly an exceptional group. On the average, they were a few years older than the male students. They were courageous pioneers, ready to risk criticism in order to get the best education available to them. They did well in their classes, averaging about 10 per cent better than the boys.[8] Among them, of course, were certain unhappy misfits, certain angry self-conscious martyrs, who provoked the mockery of the young men, self-conscious enough themselves. However, it is clear that in the early days an attractive, intelligent woman suffered from no lack of male homage.

How then did the Cornell tradition of anticoedism (the ugliest of Cornell traditions) take form and persist? Partly, one supposes, as a reflection of current social concepts. In urban society women's isolation from the men's worlds was taken as a matter of course. But more, I think, because the first Cornellians were themselves extremely sensitive to mockery on the part of their school friends who had gone to the old eastern colleges. They wanted Cornell to rival Harvard, Yale, and Princeton socially. The sharpest shafts in the older colleges' quiver was the sneer that Cornell was a ladies' seminary. Add to this the fact that the average eighteen-year-old aspires to hearty maleness; he does not want any of the refining influence of womanhood on which the educators set such store. Especially he does not like being put to shame by women's superiority in class exercises and honors. And recognizing the allurement of the female and his own timidity, he castigates himself by punishing the female. It is a matter of preserving his masculine integrity.

However that be, the tradition of women's isolation in college grew, and continued until about the time of the First War.

"With all her mistakes and eccentricities, the pioneer woman of the sixties and early seventies remains a noble figure," said Dr. Mary M. Crawford '04, a distinguished graduate and a trustee of the University:

[7] H. W. Sage to ADW, 17 Dec. 1875.
[8] W. C. Russel to ADW, 30 Jan. 1874.

She was aggressive because she had to be. She went to institutions of higher learning because she desperately needed tools to hew her way. She dared masculine disapproval and defied the conventions of her day. . . .

The second generation proved what the pioneers had believed, namely that women could absorb education as well as men. They were in deadly earnest; their outlook was necessarily narrow, and their way was hard. They made the natural mistake of overemphasizing high marks and the passing of examinations, because in that accomplishment there was objective proof of mental ability. But there was a practical side to this viewpoint too. The great majority of Cornell women of this time were poor; they had to make sacrifices to get to college at all, and they were obliged to prepare for their life work while there. Thus evolved the popular legend of the feminine "grind."

There was no early Cornell type of woman, but the very qualities which made a young woman in the late seventies and eighties go to Cornell insured her fitness and stamped her as exceptional. Cornell women of today may look back with pride at the roster of their earlier sisters. In every Cornell women's club today these older women of an earlier Cornell stand out—valiant, strong, able, and devoted daughters of their chosen Alma Mater. . . .

It was the third generation . . . who took up the challenge [of technical education]. . . . The Cornell woman of this era reasserted her right to feminine charm. Her social life expanded and her interests widened. . . . She began generally to participate in the life of the University. . . . Gradually her sense of isolation from affairs Cornellian disappeared. . . . It is demonstrated again that all knowledge is sought by both men and women. There is no sex limitation in the quest for truth.[9]

[9] In the *Cornell Daily Sun*'s *A Half-Century at Cornell* (Ithaca, 1930), p. 40. For an excellent review of the early history of Cornell coeds, see Daniel Sachs '55, "The Origin and Early Years of Coeducation at Cornell" (MS, C.U. Archives).

X

The Early Years:
Instruction and Education

ESSENTIALLY, the early Cornell was the representation in fact of the ideas in the mind of Andrew D. White, tempered by the ideas of Ezra Cornell.

White's educational ideas were expressed and expounded in many utterances, of which the chief were the Plan of Organization and the Inaugural Address. These educational ideas proceeded from certain deep convictions, which represented the character of a libertarian aristocrat. Libertarian, in that White craved and forever celebrated freedom; for, he thought, man, if free, will inevitably choose the better way. But to know the better way he must be instructed by those who have already discerned it. Socially, the better way is that which has by resistless forces created an aristocracy of wealth, breeding, and intellect. Higher education will reinforce this natural aristocracy by leading superior youths to enlightenment. Enlightenment will develop our society in a constant evolutionary progress, and will protect it against the revolutionary efforts of uneducated, conscienceless demagogues.[1]

Ezra Cornell's thought did not concern itself with the nature of society. He accepted the American democracy and the economic sys-

[1] For an excellent exposé of White's thought, see Walter P. Rogers, *Andrew D. White and the Modern University* (Ithaca, 1942), pp. 211–217.

tem which had so well rewarded his own labor and ingenuity. His aim was to improve the system by improving the methods of agricultural and industrial production. The way to do this was, in his view, to train young men of sterling character by putting in their hands the means to advance the country's—and their own—material welfare.

The exemplification of these various ideas in the mechanism of a university brought many a vexing problem.

Who should be admitted to the privileges of Cornell University? The founders proposed to make entrance easy, in order to capture those poor, ambitious boys whose purpose transcended their opportunities.

At the outset, almost any fifteen-year-old male of good moral character could get into Cornell. The first General Announcement called only for "a good common English education," including orthography, geography, and arithmetic, the studies of ordinary grade schools. Entrants to the technical departments were examined also in plane geometry. For the Classical Course, Caesar, Cicero, and Virgil in Latin, three books of Xenophon and one of Homer in Greek, were demanded. And allowances were to be made for students imperfectly prepared. Even these hospitable specifications were too severe for many aspirants; sixty failed the first entrance exams.

Though in the following years requirements were rapidly stiffened, entrance to Cornell was still easy, by modern standards. Even in 1872 a critic wrote: "One can get into Cornell about as readily as into the Chicago High School. The examination papers are much the same." [2] But by 1876 plane geometry, physiology, physical geography, American history, and a modern language were required for most courses, and solid geometry and trigonometry for Architecture and Civil Engineering.

Once admitted, the Cornellian had to work. As to the quality of the courses, we have some means of valuation in the examination papers. They are on the whole sound and searching. In first-year French, translate such sentences as: "The German general likes to see his army every day, but does he wear your sword or his? He wore this one yesterday, he will wear that one tomorrow, but he prefers his son's." Twelve idiomatic pitfalls are concealed in this apparently straightforward statement. The examination for the President's Prizes in Modern History contains some real thought-provokers: "Give an argument on the comparative fertility of republics and monarchies in

[2] Truman H. Stafford in *The Illinois Teacher*, June 1872, p. 187.

great men. . . . How may the French revolutionary ferocity be accounted for on general principles? Name any agencies in training the French to it."

Recitations and lectures began at 8:15 and continued to 1:15. At first, the crowding was intolerable. Dissections and demonstrations were conducted in the furnace room. The first library was permeated with chemical smells from the basement laboratory. Although the completion of new buildings somewhat relieved the congestion, there were constant complaints of overcrowding, of bad lighting and seating, and especially of bitter cold. The classroom temperature sometimes fell to 40 degrees.

The ratio of faculty to students was excellent: 21 professors and assistant professors to 412 undergraduates in 1868–69. (At Harvard in the same year 23 faculty members taught 529 students.) The normal teaching load was fifteen hours, and in the ever-recurring emergencies the teachers were frequently called on for twenty hours or more a week.[3] They were busy also with perpetual committee meetings and incessant revision of the curriculum.

This was one of extraordinary liberality for its time. The first *Register* proposed five courses: the Course in Science, leading to the degree of Bachelor of Science; the Course in Philosophy, or Combined Course, which required Latin, modern languages, and a good deal of mathematics and science, and which was crowned by the degree of Bachelor of Philosophy; the Course in Arts, or Classical Course, which required Latin and Greek, and which brought the degree of Bachelor of Arts; the Elective or Optional Courses, which gave "the student full and entire freedom in the selection of studies—a freedom every way equal to that which prevails in the universities of continental Europe," and which would entitle him to an unspecified baccalaureate degree; and the Special Courses, which permitted students to elect particular subjects according to their desires and without expectation of a degree. But all were obliged to attend lectures in physiology, and, for a time, lectures in agriculture. And all were held to military drill, unless excused for physical reasons or for work in the Labor Corps.

At first the students, bewildered by their freedom, shifted capriciously from one course to another. But gradually the faculty brought order into the system. The number of optional and special students dwindled;

[3] Such a teaching load was normal in America. Professor Marshall Elliott of Johns Hopkins said in 1883 that college professors of modern languages commonly taught 22 hours a week (William R. Parker in *PMLA*, Sept. 1953, p. 20).

the Course in Science and new Courses in Engineering and Mechanic Arts flourished.

In 1873 the studies in Science, Literature, and Arts were grouped under the head of General Courses, and under the caption of Special Courses were listed the Courses in Agriculture, Architecture, Chemistry and Physics, Civil Engineering, Mechanic Arts, and Natural History. The distinction is stated to be "that while the General Courses have chiefly in view the culture of the mind, the Special Courses aim rather to fit students more immediately for some one of the departments of productive industry." Or, we would say, the cultural purpose is distinguished from the vocational aim. All of these Special Courses, save Physics and Natural History, have since developed into separate colleges or schools.

The Faculty legislated endlessly about degrees. The doctorate of philosophy was offered from the first, although the requirements were left vague. The Bachelor of Veterinary Science and the Doctor of Veterinary Medicine were provided for on 19 May 1871. The Bachelor of Agriculture and the Bachelor of Mechanical Engineering came on 22 November 1872. A Master's degree was decreed on 18 October 1872. On 18 April 1873 the requirements for the Ph.D. were recorded. On 31 October 1873 legislation provided for the degrees of Civil Engineer and Topographical Engineer. On 4 October 1876 came the Master of Science for graduates in science and philosophy, the Master of Literature for others. And on 20 October 1876 the Doctor of Science.

In the early *Registers* the various departmental faculties are denominated colleges. By 1873 they become schools, or departments, as (mostly) they are today. They are arranged in alphabetical order, to avoid any appearance of hierarchy among studies and to wound no sensibilities. In that order we may here consider them.

First, and perhaps in worst state, was Agriculture. Not only did the Morrill Act require the teaching of agriculture, this was the subject dearest to Ezra Cornell's heart. President White's task was to rationalize Mr. Cornell's purpose. He proclaimed his views in an address to the New York State Agricultural Society, on 10 February 1869.[4] The place for elementary instruction, he said, is the farm, as that for the mechanic trades is the workshop. The duty of the colleges is to in-

[4] *Scientific and Industrial Education* (New York, 1874).

vestigate new processes, to distinguish facts from fallacies, to examine the theory and practice of plows and plowing, of the enrichment of soils, of the drainage of lands, of the construction of buildings, of the breeding of animals, and so forth. Naturally a knowledge of practical agriculture must also be implanted. Thus White regarded the proper work of an agricultural school as primarily research and experiment, secondarily the training of agricultural leaders.

The trouble was that no one could be found to put in practice this admirable program. In all of America hardly a single scientifically trained professor of agriculture existed. White tried in vain to tempt eminent successful gentleman farmers to become resident professors. One of them accepted, but he appeared only once, to demand his salary. He was succeeded by a gentleman in delicate health, who spent most of his time at a watering place. The professorship remained vacant for a year, while the farm was leased to an apparently incompetent farmer. Then Henry H. McCandless was appointed, on the strength of his training in an Irish agricultural school. Totally unfamiliar with American farming, he imported some expensive machinery, unfitted to American needs, and built a gigantic barn, the grandiose monstrosity of the campus until it burned in 1890.[5] Professor McCandless, a dapper gentleman who always wore gloves, was regarded as something of a monstrosity himself. White recalls, in his *Autobiography*, the visit of a foreboding farmer, who said of the new professor: "Yew kin depend on't, he ain't a-goin' to do nothin'; he don't know nothin' about corn, and he don't want to know nothin' about corn; *and he don't believe in punkins!*"

The Faculty fiddled with the curriculum, establishing and rescinding courses of one, two, three, and four years. Professors Caldwell of Agricultural Chemistry, Prentiss of Botany and Horticulture, and Law of Veterinary Science carried on as best they could. But Agriculture slipped steadily downhill. By 1873–74 only seven students were registered in the department. Enemies of Cornell noted the fact and asked rhetorically if the University was contravening the provisions of the Morrill Act.

The condition of the farm was simply terrible. Visiting farmers observed its bedraggled state, scared away the rats from dead chickens,

[5] A piquant item for the sanitary history of the University: Liberty Hyde Bailey estimated that two million bedbugs perished in the fire, for Sage College was so infested that all its bedticks were condemned and stored in the barn.

spat, and wrote to the papers. But we need not depend on our enemies for a description. Vice-President Russel wrote to White, on 28 July 1870:

This afternoon I rode over the farm in every direction; saw some good oats and corn and potatoes; thousands of Canada thistles with seed vessels just bursting and ready to send the seed of future thistles into our neighbors' and our own fields far and near; fields mown in a slovenly manner, the hay filling all the fence corners, fields which have been cleared of their crops of weeds because no grain had been planted on them; pastures without fences; in fine a farm without manure, without fences, without proper culture—a sample of unthrift, improvidence, and waste. . . . Two milch cows running dry and none coming in; no manure because no animals; last year's hay wasting because there have been no cattle to eat it; no proper hay barn; no pretense of a vegetable garden; no carrots or turnips for stock—nothing except waste. . . . For Heaven's sake let us do something.

The solution eventually found was the appointment of Isaac P. Roberts as professor of agriculture. Roberts, of whom we have already spoken, was a thoroughly practical farmer who had acquired, at Iowa State, reasoned enthusiasm for scientific agriculture.

Roberts arrived in January 1874. Downcast by his dark rooms in Cascadilla and by what he took to be the condescension of his fellow professors, he passed from gloom to despair on his inspection of the farm. He says:

There were ten milch cows that had among them only twenty-two milkable teats, and the Veterinarian did not have to be called in to know that the herd was infected with tuberculosis. One of the work oxen was sound and strong, but it took most of his strength to hold up his mate. There was a stallion of noted Arabian lineage which had been donated to the University and which was said to be worth $15,000. He had not been out of his box stall for two years. Although he was the sire of a few colts he was withdrawn from service, perhaps because his colts did not have legs enough on which to place the curbs, ring-bones, spavins and deformities which he was capable of transmitting. When we took the Arab of the Desert out of his stall and rode him, he fell dead.[6]

It was small consolation to Roberts that the University possessed 187 models of plows from Egyptian times to the present, bought in Germany by Mr. White, at considerable cost.

[6] *Autobiography of a Farm Boy* (Ithaca: Cornell University Press, 1946), p. 114.

Roberts turned in a scathing, and picturesque, report (21 April 1874). He would resign unless money should be immediately provided to rehabilitate the farm. In fact, he did not want to resign. In the midst of desolation, he recognized the possibilities in agricultural education. He says: "I determined to lay the foundations of a College of Agriculture such as had never before been conceived."

The money was found; and under Roberts's energetic and inspiring leadership the state of the department began to improve. The enrollment steadily increased: 17 in 1874–75, 29 in 1876–77, 42 in 1877–78. Roberts renovated the farm, brought in new crops, such as alfalfa, and new methods, being well aware that the Cornell farm must serve primarily as a laboratory. He introduced the Holstein-Friesian cattle (to the anger of Trustee Alonzo B. Cornell, who saw his herd of prize Shorthorns threatened). He built the second permanent silo in America, and established the work in poultry husbandry. Not the least of his achievements was the recruitment of Liberty Hyde Bailey as professor of agriculture.

Isaac P. Roberts was one of the great creators of the Cornell of today. A second was his associate, Professor James Law of Veterinary Science.

At the beginning the work in veterinary medicine was comprised under Agriculture. The subject was particularly dear to Ezra Cornell. As a breeder of prize cattle he had been baffled by mysterious ailments in his herd, and he had found no veterinarian nearer than Poughkeepsie. As a legislator, he had advocated a system of veterinary sanitary police and had introduced a bill requiring the destruction of diseased cattle. (This act did not in fact work, for it spread disease by encouraging owners to sell their cattle at the first sign of infection.)

Law labored heroically in the face of the usual wants and shortages. His only laboratory, he remembers, was the open fields and nearby barns.[7] He had, however, the distinction of possessing one of the four microscopes in Ithaca, regarded with veneration by the students. (The others were the private property of Professors Wilder, Caldwell, and Prentiss. The first university-owned microscope was given by the trustee and nonresident professor of agriculture, John Stanton Gould, to the new Department of Entomology, to aid John Henry Comstock.)

[7] "A Half Century of Veterinary Medicine in the U.S.," in *Report of the Conference at the N.Y. State Veterinary College* (Ithaca, 1919), p. 6.

In spite of all, Dr. Law succeeded in awarding the first degree of Bachelor of Veterinary Science in 1871, and in 1876 the first degree of Doctor of Veterinary Medicine conferred in America, to Daniel E. Salmon, B.V.S. '72. His graduates must have been well prepared, for Salmon organized and captained for many years the U.S. Bureau of Animal Industry, identified the infectious pathogen *Salmonella*, and gave his name to the human disease salmonellosis; Arthur M. Farrington '79 became director of the U.S. Meat Inspection Service; and Fred L. Kilborne '81, with Theobald Smith '81, demonstrated that the southern cattle tick was the carrier of the microbian cause of Texas cattle fever—and thus prepared for the discovery that the anopheles mosquito carries the microbe of malaria, the stegomyia that of yellow fever, and the culex blood parasites.

For the first time in university history, veterinary science was taught on a parity with the other sciences. Nevertheless, Dr. Law was forced to spend what he terms twenty-eight years of laborious waiting before his science came of age, with a college of its own. In the meantime he was busy enough, as investigator and author, as State Veterinarian, and as director of campaigns against lung plague, tuberculosis, and other evils. His studies were important in the development of the theory and practice of antitoxins.

The Department of Architecture was one in which Andrew D. White took special interest. He liked nothing better than sketching pompous buildings; he sometimes said sadly, "I really should have been an architect." Even before the opening of Cornell he had collected abroad what was said to be the largest and most complete architectural library in America. In his Plan of Organization of 1866 he called for a chair of Architecture as one of those that first needed filling. This was a novel view, for in this country architects were generally trained as apprentices, if they were trained at all. Other more pressing demands made the President postpone momentarily his proposal. In his report to the trustees of June 1871 he asked the fulfillment of his purpose. As a result, a School of Architecture was established as a branch of the College of Civil Engineering, and the Reverend Charles Babcock was appointed professor on 18 September 1871. For five years Babcock carried on singlehanded, finding time to design and erect Sage Chapel, Sage College, and the Old Armory, and to conduct Episcopalian chapel services.

The claim is often made that the College of Architecture is a Cornell First. To sustain the claim, a little careful wording is necessary.

The only collegiate instruction then given in architecture was at the Massachusetts Institute of Technology, which in 1868 offered a two-year program in design, construction, and professional practice. It is apparently true that Cornell's was the first four-year course and that Cornell's Department of Architecture was the first proclaimed department in any American university, for the professor of architecture at M.I.T. did not call himself a department, whereas our professor did. And anyway, M.I.T. is not a university in the strict sense. Loyal sons of M.I.T. may regard this distinction as a quibbling one, and in fact honest Cornellians may too.

At the beginning, the Courses in Chemistry and Physics were linked together, and so they continued until 1880. The prospectus for the opening year indicates that specialists in chemistry would have laboratory practice in qualitative and quantitative analysis, in the use of the blowpipe for the determination of minerals and ores, in the special analysis of soils, ores, minerals, and technical products, in assaying and organic analysis. They would also do some work in mineralogy, geology, chemical physics, crystallography, and advanced inorganic and even organic chemistry, which was still in its embryonic stage.

In the following year the *Register* notes that the Course in Chemistry is designed to prepare not only teachers and analytical chemists but also technical chemists in manufactories and mines. Chester Wing was appointed in 1870 Professor of Chemistry Applied to Manufactures. Thus the concept of industrial chemistry, to have its later great development in chemical engineering, is already stated. The organizers of the early department showed a rare prevision, for as yet there were few industrial chemists in the country.

At first, Physics was overshadowed by Chemistry. The laboratory for chemistry was unusually well equipped for its time; that in physics consisted of little more than some miscellaneous apparatus, mostly in optics. In 1874 a photographic laboratory was contrived in the attic of the wooden laboratory building, and there Frederic E. Ives slept, ate, and labored on what was to become the three-color halftone process. The equipment was gradually added to, under the energetic impulsion of Professor William A. Anthony, who came to us in 1872.

Anthony's inventions have already been described. In his teaching, as in the devising of experimental machines, he was an innovator. He promoted the demonstration lecture, still the mainstay of physics courses. He developed especially the work in electricity (unlike Harvard's Lovering, who regarded the prevailing interest in electricity as

A History of Cornell

"only a spurt"). In 1881 Anthony persuaded the trustees to announce a course in electrical engineering—the first in America.

His concept of physics teaching is developed in a letter to the President, of September 1873. He insists on the practical applications of science, and points to the dreadful errors made by builders and industrialists, through ignorance of physical laws. He demands a proper laboratory, wherein the whole class can perform experiments in areas of physical concern: friction and lubricants; strength of materials; the pressure and flow of liquids; elasticity, pressure, and flow of gases; the expansion of bodies by heat, and the convection currents produced by expansion in air and water, with special reference to the warming and ventilation of buildings; the transmission of heat by conduction, radiation, etc.; the heating power of fuels; the condensation of steam in iron pipes; electrical measurements; sound vibrations; mirrors and lenses; the use of the microscope and spectroscope; and photography. Although he pays lip service to theoretical physics, his program seems to have been determined by practical needs, and to be concentrated on applied or engineering physics.

To President White, History and Political Science were the most directly useful subjects in the curriculum. The core of his own faith was the conviction that man and society were slowly evolving toward a better state. The means of man's evolution was his gradual apprehension of that body of truth which exists in the universe. History, properly conceived, is the study which enables man to learn the truth about man. The history of past triumphs and past errors will enable us to avoid present and future errors and to attain new triumphs. Specifically, knowledge of history is our best guarantee against civil uprisings and social disasters; ignorance of history is the prompter of evil laws and of all injustice.

This conviction was early implanted in White's mind. It was the theme of his first magazine article: "Glimpses of Universal History," in the New Englander for August 1857. He cries, with young eloquence:

Contemplation of the bearing of increased liberty on increased virtue, and of struggles, of great good men with great bad men, strengthens a man's heart; study of the sure lines of justice between noble thoughts and noble victories strengthens a man's conscience; contemplation of great lines of purpose running through all that blooms or decays, struggles or suffers in the world-history, connecting all with the great goal which God has set, strengthens a man's soul. This is the higher discipline which gives

162

mental discipline its worth; this repays all discouragement among old books, all buffeting among rugged men.

Yielding to the urgent pressures at the opening, White deferred for a time his project for a great school of history and political science and contented himself with providing a survey of world history. The *Register* for 1869–70 announced a series of lecture courses, arranged in chronological sequence, from ancient history to the constitutional history of the United States. These courses were to be linked with the work in languages; much of the assigned collateral reading would be in French and German.

White undertook a good part of the lecturing himself. He issued to the students in advance printed synopses of the lectures, giving all the essential names and facts. These synopses were interleaved with blank pages. Thus the lecturer was relieved of the wasteful necessity of dictating, and the student of that of recording, the background of fact. The note-taking student tried to capture White's noble thoughts, his dizzy hypotheses, his lyrical outbursts and manly indignation, his little jokes. His was a splendid pedagogical device.

English history was the province of Goldwin Smith, a lecturer no less brilliant, in his way, than the President. Ancient history and, at need, all other kinds of history, including the constitutional sort, fell to Vice-President Russel, professor of south European languages. Russel, the forgotten man of Cornell's history, introduced the undergraduate seminary method in his courses in constitutional history. Eschewing lectures, he assigned topics to groups or individuals. Their written reports were then analyzed and discussed in class. The procedure, adapted from that of German graduate seminars, was applied at Cornell to undergraduate work probably for the first time in America.

From the beginning White recommended the creation of a chair in American history, and he drummed on the theme in his annual reports. We have remarked that in 1871–72 George W. Greene, as nonresident professor, gave a series of lectures on the history of the Revolution. In 1875–76 a course on the history of the United States was offered. However, the subject did not come into its own until the appointment, in 1881, of Moses Coit Tyler, as the first professor of American history in this country.

Political economy, in a rudimentary form, was already familiar in American colleges. The first professorship in the subject was established at Harvard in 1871. White asserted that he was the first educator to propose the creation of a department to deal with the subject; no doubt he is right. The *Register* of 1868–69 proclaims that the School of Political Science "is intended to embrace all the important topics connected with political and social science." But the reality fell short of the intention. The Reverend William D. Wilson, registrar and professor of moral and intellectual philosophy, embraced the whole of political economy in one of the three terms of the college year. Not until the eighties did White succeed in creating regular courses in sociology and economics.

The School of Languages was divided into two parts: ancient and modern languages.

On the subject of ancient languages White had reason to be sensitive. His opposition to the rigid obligatory classical course left in many minds the impression that he was an enemy of classical training. Not at all, he insisted; he valued it for those who sought it eagerly; but he wished to aid the classics by releasing unqualified, uninterested students and by encouraging only those with taste and ability. The desire to learn, he said, will avail the classics far more than did the old compulsions. "Cornell will have the best professors for worthy students." Cornell had also, in the Anthon and Bopp collections, one of the best classical libraries in the country.

The first professor was Albert S. Wheeler, who was brought from Hobart. He was reported to be an admirable scholar and teacher. He was certainly well rounded; an awed student wrote in his diary, "He has been an athlete, a pianist, a boatman, a tutor in Buffalo, a lawyer, a hard drinker, a profligate, a splendid scholar, and is reputed now one of the most respected and beloved professors in Cornell University." [8]

With the work in modern languages White was especially concerned. He remembered with resentment the insufficiency of his instruction at Yale, which he termed "a broad farce." He had noted some betterment at Michigan, but even there classes were on an elementary level. He alleges that at Cornell "the experiment was first really tried of giving importance to these courses in modern languages and literatures, and making them equal in dignity with the courses in ancient languages." [9]

The early teachers of modern languages were by any valuation a superior faculty. All of them, or nearly all of them, had at least been abroad. They were less inclined than we are today to bother about pronunciation, but they were much more punctilious about grammati-

[8] Diary of William H. French '73, 25 Jan. 1871, C.U. Archives.
[9] ADW to W. T. Hewett, 1894 (month and day unspecified).

cal structure. One has the impression that they were determined to prove that French and German grammar could be just as hard and just as disciplinary as the grammar of Greek and Latin.

Some of the early professors' names will already be familiar to indomitable readers of this chronicle: Willard Fiske, who conducted his courses entirely in German; T. F. Crane; Roehrig the polyglot. One should mention also James Morgan Hart, who began in south European languages, shifted to German, and later became head of the Department of English; Waterman Thomas Hewett, who wrote the monumental *Cornell University: A History;* and certainly Hjalmar Hjorth Boyesen, Norwegian man of letters and internationally known Goethe scholar, whose novel *The Mammon of Unrighteousness* (1891) is the first fictional account of Cornell life. Such bravura passages as Boyesen's account of the Founder's Reception, with its gay caricatures of Ezra Cornell, I. P. Roberts, Mrs. Hiram Corson, and others, should be reproduced in some future Cornell anthology.

At the beginning, French, German, Italian, Spanish, Swedish, and Danish were offered—a very unusual linguistic wealth. Portuguese, Icelandic, Chinese, and Persian appeared in 1870. In 1874 the *Register* proffers also Turkish, Japanese, Sanskrit, Hebrew, and other Semitic languages if they may be required. "It is to be hoped that in time sufficient interest in this direction will be developed to warrant the establishment of classes for the Arabic, Syriac, and other cognate languages to the Hebrew, and that Semitic philology in the term's best and widest sense will find a home at the University." The hope was related to the proposal of Joseph Seligman to establish a professorship of Hebrew and Oriental history and literature, of which more anon.

Although Professor Roehrig attracted sixteen students to his class in Arabic in the spring of 1876, the announcements of exotic languages begin to sound less sanguine. "The Hebrew, Chaldee, and Ancient Syriac are taught by Professor Wilson whenever there are classes desiring them," says the *Register* for 1877. In following years the announcement becomes vaguer and vaguer. There is a sudden recrudescence in 1885, with the proposal of several strange tongues, including Malayan. No doubt the offering was the administration's farewell gift to Professor Roehrig, for in the next year it disappears, together with the professor.

On no subject did Andrew D. White lavish more devoted thought than on Literature. As he tells us in his *Autobiography*, he determined that the department should serve to promote the general culture of the students. This concept was still a novelty. Commonly, the classics were supposed to inculcate general culture; but White remembered that at Yale the classics were taught entirely as linguistic exercises, with hardly a reference to their quality as literature. White was also aware of the danger that Cornell might become a narrow technical school: "Highly as I prized the scientific spirit and technical training, I felt that the frame of mind engendered by them should be modified by an acquaintance with the best literature as literature." [10]

In the first *Register*, Literature is divided into three parts: English literature, rhetoric, and oratory. Each of these subjects could be pursued through the four undergraduate years. In English literature the work began with survey courses and continued with critical examination of masterpieces. (There is no reference to American literature.) Rhetoric was, in effect, practice in writing and composition. Oratory began with voice training and ended with public declamation. "Every student is required to declaim in presence of the Professor of Rhetoric."

The early professors of literature, Homer B. Sprague, C. C. Shackford, and others, were capable and devoted teachers. They were, however, soon overshadowed by Hiram Corson, who came in 1870. Corson imposed his own specialties: Anglo-Saxon and the appreciation of poetry by vocal rendering. The modern type of critical exegesis had to wait for a later era.

A minor phenomenon was the work in journalism. The idea of college training in the subject had already been bruited. President (and General) Robert E. Lee of Washington College proposed in 1869 that scholarships be given students with journalism in mind, but no effect came of his proposal. White advocates in his report for 1873 a course for the special training of such students and points to the practical work available in the University Press. Provision for a Certificate in Journalism appears in the *Register* for 1874–75. A two-year course is offered, with practice in the art of printing, in journalism proper, and in phonography (or shorthand) and telegraphy. One such certificate was granted in 1876. However, the course seems to have been abandoned by 1878.

This was the first course in journalism in America and the first degree granted in the subject. Instruction in practical journalism was revived here briefly in the late eighties. Not until 1893 was a viable

[10] *Autobiography of Andrew Dickson White* (New York, 1905), I, 365.

college course established, at the Wharton School of the University of Pennsylvania.[11]

Philosophy, during the early years, was included in the School of Literature. A two-year course was offered, which comprised psychology, logic, moral philosophy, and political science. All the work was in the hands of Dr. W. D. Wilson, the versatile registrar, who found time also to lecture on international law, Hebrew, Chaldee, Syriac, physical geography, climatology, and the philosophy of history, to conduct chapel services, and to write books on psychology, logic, metaphysics, political economy, the theories of knowledge, and even *The Papal Supremacy and the Provincial System Tested by the Holy Scripture and the Canon Law of the Ancient Church.* The students found, however, the courses of this wonderful man dull, and the trustees thought them inadequate. Proper work in philosophy was not undertaken until Dr. Jacob Gould Schurman arrived in 1886.

In the first years, Mathematics and Engineering made a single school. The courses in mathematics—algebra, geometry, including analytics, trigonometry, differential and integral calculus—were at first scanty by modern standards. The work was conducted by Evan W. Evans until his death in 1874. Then the headship was assumed by James E. Oliver, Cornell's famous absent-minded professor. There was, and is, something very engaging about Jimmy Oliver. He was a very fine mathematician, "the best who has ever come under my notice," said his teacher at Harvard, the celebrated Benjamin Peirce. He had also the poetic, mystical imagination of so many great mathematicians. He had even been class poet at Harvard. In a review of his department's ideals, he wrote beautifully:

One great mission of the Department here, as elsewhere, is to show that in healthily developing the geometric and philosophical imagination, in awakening an intelligent interest in the grand systems of worlds amid which our own is placed, as well as a sense of the beauty of purely intellectual relations, in adding definiteness to certain metaphysical concepts, and in that correlation of the abstract with the concrete and with the certain which will help to cure the prevalent distrust of ideals, mathematical studies have peculiar educational and even religious values that could ill be spared.[12]

[11] Albert A. Sutton, *Education for Journalism in the United States* (Evanston, Ill., 1945).

[12] W. T. Hewett, *Cornell University: A History* (New York, 1905), II, 149.

Among Oliver's aides were the stalwart Lucian A. Wait, the unpredictable George W. (Piute) Jones, and William E. Byerly, who was Harvard's first Ph.D. (in 1873).

The work in mathematics was rapidly stiffened. By 1871–72 the *Register* proposes work enough to satisfy a mathematical genius. In that year theoretical astronomy first appears. Practical astronomy had to await the coming of an observatory.

Civil Engineering began modestly. A four-year course leading to the degree of Bachelor of Civil Engineering was outlined, but professional work, in drafting, mechanics, stereotomy, surveying, and construction, was restricted to the last two years. The graduate degree of Civil Engineer was authorized in 1870. The sole professor was William C. Cleveland, an accomplished scholar, botanist, and geologist as well as engineer, and also musician, painter, and sculptor. He is said to have modeled busts of some of his fellow professors. (Where are they now?)

At Cleveland's death in 1873, Estevan Antonio Fuertes, the famous Mogue, took over the work. He introduced engineering instruction in the freshman and sophomore years and expanded the professional training of the later years. Thus by 1877 we find the young engineer occupied with higher geodesy, railroad surveying, metallurgy, stone cutting (no doubt stereotomy), bridge construction, water wheels, and other applications. Fuertes insisted on laboratory work in every course. He established "summer surveys," the students camping by our lakes, mapping the shorelines and hinterland, sounding the waters, and triangulating widths. So accurate were the results that they were accepted by the U.S. Geological Survey and incorporated in its official maps. He introduced an optional five-year course, a noteworthy innovation, forecasting the five-year engineering courses of today. But the innovation made heavier demands than most students were able or willing to accept.

The curriculum included a leavening of cultural subjects, for Fuertes was ever concerned with raising the social and professional standards of the engineer.

From the outset Civil Engineering throve, in spite of or because of its difficulty. Fuertes was recognized as a great engineering educator and engineer, and his products testified to his merits. He assembled a superlative faculty, among them Charles Lee Crandall, Irving Porter Church, Charles David Marx. In 1872, the first year in which enrollments are distinguished, ninety-four students were registered. The numbers dwindled during the hard years at the end of the decade, but by the mid-eighties the course regained all its popularity and prestige.

Mechanic Arts were not regarded at first as engineering, rather, perhaps, as the apotheosis of manual training. The work was imposed on Cornell by the terms of the Morrill Act, which in turn reflected the rise in importance of the skilled mechanic in a new world of industry. Both Ezra Cornell and Andrew D. White recognized the need of providing proper training and equipment, but it appears that the trustees were at first reluctant to pay the costs, enormous in comparison with those of textbook courses like classics.

John L. Morris, professor of practical mechanics and director of the machine shops, was on the spot from the beginning. But since there were no machine shops he helped out by teaching mathematics and physics. President White gave the department its first piece of machinery, a power lathe. Fumbling efforts at improvement were made in 1869. In 1870 came the prayed-for miracle: the offer of Trustee Hiram Sibley to erect a building and help support the work.

The department therefore became, in 1871, the Sibley College of the Mechanic Arts, and the degree of Bachelor of Mechanical Engineering was promised graduates of the four-year course. This is the first recognition that mechanic arts are properly engineering.

In 1873 John E. Sweet was appointed master mechanic and director of the machine shops. He was an original natural mechanic, self-educated like Ezra Cornell and Hiram Sibley. He had exhibited one of the first type-setting machines at the Paris Exposition of 1867. His educational method was to require the students to design and construct needed tools. Thus, to make gauges, they first devised a measuring machine reading to one hundredth of an inch. This was regarded as phenomenal. Sweet left Cornell in 1879, to produce a long-famous straight-line reciprocating engine of his invention. He was one of the founders, and a president, of the American Society of Mechanical Engineers, and a recipient of the very honorific John Fritz Medal. He left his impress on all engineering work in this country.

It took some time to convince a skeptical public that university training in the mechanic arts is useful to the future industrialist and proper for the institution. The enrollment in the department rose from 24 in 1872 to 56 in 1875. It dropped again as low as 29 in 1879, and then climbed to 64 in 1884. The decline was due in part to general hard times in the late seventies, in part perhaps to internal difficulties. A number of students presented an angry memorial in the spring of 1876, accusing Professor Morris of incompetence. He was said to be ignorant of all except common practice, with no desire to improve himself. He was accused of spending most of his time smoking and chatting. The complaints, which ran to twenty-two pages, reveal the students' indignation because they were not held to hard work and to improvement.[13]

No formal executive notice was taken of the petition. Plenty of students, then and later, stated their high regard for Professor Morris. He lived out his career at Cornell, retiring only in 1904.

The School of Military Science existed from the first, in accordance with the terms of the Morrill Act. True, the famous act did not make clear whether instruction in military science should be obligatory or optional; it provided that "the leading object shall be, without excluding other scientific and classical studies and including military tactics, to teach such branches of learning as are related to agriculture and the mechanic arts." The question has never, in fact, been finally clarified.

A federal law of 28 July 1866 authorized the President of the United States to detail an officer of the regular Army to give instruction in military science and tactics to land-grant colleges which should comply with certain conditions. Somewhat later, provision was made for the loan of Army equipment to such colleges and for the appointment of properly qualified graduates to Army commissions.

As to the merits of the military organization of the University, President White could never quite make up his mind. He thought it was probably a good thing to train the young to military smartness, manners, and manliness, and a good thing to prepare Cornellians to lead in repressing civil discord. (It never occurred to him that a Cornellian might be found in the rebel ranks.) At the same time his faith in human reasonableness, his detestation of social and intellectual discipline, his impatient utopianism, made him instinctively an antimilitarist. He was willing to give the military system a good trial, but as it was abrogated bit by bit, he did nothing to reimpose it.

The *Register* for 1869 makes an impressive statement of the opportunities for work in military science, in the fields of military engineering, the art of war, and military law. These are repeated without change

---

[13] The petition is in the ADW Papers, 15 June 1876. Further accusations were made in 1878 and again in 1884 (14 Jan. and 18 June 1884, Trustees' Minutes, C.U. Archives). See also Russel to ADW, 9 Mar. and 11 Apr. 1878. Russel's long analysis of the case, probably made in 1878, is in the first folder for 1880. Henry W. Sage had a high opinion of Morris (Sage to ADW, 21 May 1878).

for many following years. But I find no indication that the instruction was in much demand. The first Cornellians to avail themselves of the opportunity to obtain Army commissions were Frank A. Barton and Ervin L. Phillips of the class of 1891.

Some of the commandants assigned by the War Department were excellent and able men. Major Whittlesey, the first of the list, made a gallant but vain effort to make Cornellians into West Pointers. His successor, Major W. E. Arnold, had time enough on his hands to teach mathematics. There were others popular with the students and with faculty society. But it must have been a discouraging post for an eager, sincere officer. No doubt some of them broke their hearts against the indifference, sloppiness, and buffoonery which soon became the tradition of the Cornell Cadet Corps.

The College of Natural Science, at the first, was composed of the Schools of Botany, Geology, Zoology, and Physical Geography.

The offerings in Botany were more than respectable. Courses were proposed in structural botany, vegetable physiology, systematic botany, and parasitic fungi. Laboratory work was required, as well as field work. Proud reference was made to the Horace Mann Herbarium. This collection, purchased and presented to the University by President White, was made by Horace Mann, Jr., son of the more famous educator. It consists of over 7,500 mounted specimens and is particularly rich in examples from Hawaii. The Herbarium's value has rather increased than diminished with the years. These collections were soon augmented by contributions from the University's Brazil Expedition of 1870.

The work in botany was in the hands of Albert N. Prentiss, formerly of Michigan State College. He was a competent botanist, a specialist in mycology. He encouraged his students to explore the countryside and to record the exceptionally rich and varied flora of the region. These efforts resulted in many discoveries, and in the publication of *The Cayuga Flora* (1886), by Professor William H. Dudley.

Inadequately housed at the beginning, the Department of Botany gained ample quarters (or at least ample for a time) in Sage College. Here Mr. Sage built a group of conservatories. Year by year the work was strengthened until the department became a teaching and research center of considerable fame.

In Geology, Cornell has the advantage of possessing one of the world's great natural laboratories. The work at first proposed was, however, limited and elementary, merely a course of lectures during the winter trimester and some vague laboratory activity. In 1874 the program was reformed. The *Register*'s announcement contains a statement of method which seems well worthy of preservation:

The early training of all geological students consists in the personal, critical examination of specimens, the student being required to find out everything for himself, without the consultation of books. On entering the laboratory, one or more good specimens are placed before him, the difference between *seeing* and *observing* is explained, and he is directed to observe, as carefully as possible, all their characters, and record in drawing and writing, in a suitable book, his observations just as he makes them. . . . Having carefully observed several specimens of more or less nearly related forms, he is then required to compare these with one another, and determine what characters are common to all, or what distinguish each. Only after he has completed his work for himself is he allowed to consult authorities, and, by comparing his own work with that of a master, test the accuracy of his own results.

The first professor of geology, Charles F. Hartt, was a remarkable man, one of those whom James Morgan Hart soberly termed geniuses. He had been geologist with Agassiz's expedition to Brazil in 1865–1866, and Agassiz held a high opinion of his abilities. His interests were wide; he collected botanical as well as geological specimens, learned the Indian languages, studied the native customs. In 1870 he organized a Cornell expedition to Brazil. Three years later he was appointed director of the Geological Survey of Brazil and received a long leave of absence from Cornell. In the course of his work he contracted yellow fever and died.

Brilliant he was, and troublesome to the administration. He was absent most of the time, but punctilious about receiving his salary. The effective organization of the Department of Geology fell rather to his assistants, especially Theodore B. Comstock '70, later President of the University of Arizona, and Orville A. Derby '74, who became chief geographer and geologist of the State of São Paulo, Brazil.

Physical Geography was a separate department until 1871, when it was merged with Geology.

Zoology was from the first one of Cornell's strongest departments. It received a first impulse from the twenty lectures by Louis Agassiz given in the University's opening term, and from the presence of that great, simple, endearing man. He was delighted with Ithaca; he said: "I was never before in a single locality where there is presented so much material in so many branches of Natural History as here in this beautiful valley." Says his biographer: "He came back from Ithaca, the seat of Cornell University, with the most exaggerated views in regard to the future of the new institution, speaking of the backwardness of Harvard, and prophesying that Cornell would soon leave Harvard far behind." [14]

The zeal and vigor of Burt G. Wilder supplemented the inspiration of Agassiz. At first professor of physiology, comparative anatomy, and zoology, he became eventually professor of neurology, vertebrate zoology, and physiology. Ignobly quartered, first in the basement of Morrill Hall, then in the basement of McGraw, his department attracted some of the best students and achieved some of the best scholarly results.

Wilder, with his wide-ranging interests, had made a large collection of insects, and had even given his name to a spider. He presented his trophies to the University, as the foundation of its now remarkable entomological collections. In 1870 fate sent him a surprising student, John Henry Comstock, whom he described as "an inspired anthropomorphic squirrel." Comstock, a poor country boy and a summertime cook on a Great Lakes schooner, had had his life transformed by a Book. The Book was T. W. Harris's *Insects Injurious to Vegetation*. On the flyleaf of his copy is written: "I purchased this book for ten dollars in Buffalo, N.Y., July 2, 1870. I think it was the first entomological work I ever saw. Before seeing it I had never given entomology a serious thought; from the time that I bought it I felt that I should like to make the study of insects my life's work."

Wilder naturally recognized the young freshman's quality and appointed him laboratory assistant. In the following year thirteen students petitioned the Faculty to allow Comstock to give a course of lectures on insects injurious to vegetation. Despite misgivings, the petition was granted. Comstock, who was chimesmaster, turned his lodgings high in McGraw tower into the University Entomological Museum. He taught with unorthodox passion. He made a class exercise out of cutting a bee tree in the woods at night, removing the honey and luring the bees into a box hive. President White and Professor Goldwin Smith joined the expedition. His courses prospered; in 1880 a Department of Economic Entomology, said to be the first in America, was constituted.

With zoology the 1868 offering of instruction ended. The curriculum was well wrought; it served without major change until the nineties. In some ways it fell short of White's ideal. From prudence and econ-

[14] Albert H. Wright, *Agassiz and Cornell* (Ithaca, 1953), pp. 2, 11.

omy, he was obliged to defer the fulfillment of some of his grand ideas —for work in medicine, law, and fine arts, for example, and in music, a subject just making its entrance in American universities (at Harvard it first appeared in 1871). White's intention was to bring a real professor of music from Oxford or Leipzig, but he could find neither the right man nor the money.[15] Haphazard vocal training was given by Professor Piutti of Wells College. No Cornell department of music existed for many a long year.

Another dream was deferred even longer. White envisaged a School of Commerce, for the professional training of future merchants. The first *Register* offered instruction in bookkeeping and commercial mathematics. White wished to elevate the subject into a department.[16] But for some reason the offering disappeared in the 1869 *Register*, not to reappear until courses in accounting were established many years later.

From the first, provision was made for graduate work and for advanced degrees.

The theory of the Master's degree was still inchoate, as it was generally in American universities. Commonly it was awarded to graduates of five years' standing whose conduct was reported good and who would pay a fee of $10. The first Cornell *Register* contented itself with the statement: "The degree of Master of Arts is conferred upon such Bachelors of Arts as may give proof, satisfactory to the Faculty, of literary proficiency." In 1872 the requirements were specified. The candidate had a choice of passing a year in successful resident study, with an acceptable thesis, or of spending three years in literary pursuits, taking an examination, and presenting a thesis.

The degree of Civil Engineer was proposed as a reward for two years of study beyond the first degree.

The first *Register* offered the degree of Doctor of Philosophy to "such Bachelors of Philosophy as may give proof, satisfactory to the Faculty, of literary or general proficiency," or to "such Bachelors of Arts, of Philosophy or of Science as have completed a meritorious investigation in chemistry." The requirements were steadily reinforced. In 1873 a knowledge of Latin and Greek was required and two years of study in residence at Cornell and a thesis based on original investigation.

The looseness of the requirements reflects the state of graduate educa-

[15] Henry W. Sage (to ADW, 21 May 1878) offered $2,000 a year for a professorship of music. But no qualified music scholar was found.
[16] Penciled note by ADW, Faculty Records, 2 Oct. 1868.

tion in America. In 1872 there were fewer than two hundred graduate students in the United States.[17] Every aspirant who could afford to went to Germany, scholarship's home. The American universities, lacking libraries, laboratories, and often competent directors of studies, were well aware of their own deficiencies. Yale granted the first American Ph.D.'s in 1861 (one of them to Eugene Schuyler of Ithaca), but only ten years later did it organize a Graduate School.

Cornell awarded its first graduate degree, that of Civil Engineer, in 1870, to Henry Turner Eddy, B.A., Ph.B. (Yale). Eddy, an assistant professor of mathematics and a glutton for degrees, then went on to become Cornell's first Ph.D. in 1872. In the same year the first Master of Science degree was conferred on David Starr Jordan, who seems to have skipped the Bachelor's degree.

In 1876 Professors Prentiss and Dudley of Botany established the first Cornell Summer School. It was a private enterprise of the two professors; its course of study was botany alone; it was directed toward earnest secondary-school teachers. Its success for a time was only moderate. Informal summer work was likewise conducted in geology and other subjects. Civil Engineering early organized its summer camps for field work in surveying. But not until 1893 did the Cornell Summer School become a coherent part of our educational system.

The essential accessories were gradually developed. The University Library began with an appropriation of $7,500 by the trustees on 26 September 1867. White then persuaded Ezra Cornell to buy the fine Anthon classical collection of 6,000 volumes. White, on his European trip in 1868, bought lavishly from the University funds and from his own. Naturally he was more tempted by bibliophilic rarities than by solid background books for undergraduate use. No matter; the rarities have today become treasures. Goldwin Smith gave the University his valuable private library of 3,400 volumes. There were other important gifts, as the Kelly mathematical collection, the May antislavery collection, the splendid Sparks collection of American history, given by Henry W. Sage. In June 1873 a count showed 34,100 books and 8,000 pamphlets, a number and of a quality matched in few American institutions. From the undergraduates' point of view there was, however, a lack of fundamentals, an excess of scholarly luxuries.

The University Press, the first in America, was established in the University's opening year and recognized officially in the *Register* for 1869. Its purpose was double: to provide opportunities for students

[17] C. F. Thwing, *Education in the United States* (Boston, 1910), p. 123.

to learn and earn, and to provide the University with an economical printshop. The two purposes were hard to reconcile. A few students learned a useful trade, at some cost to the Press's efficiency. The early *Registers* and examinations, the *Cornell Era*, and University miscellanies were printed, under the artistic supervision of Willard Fiske. (His taste was traditional, archaistic, somewhat mincing.) The directors hoped to make of the Press a scholarly printing office, like that of Oxford. It was equipped with foreign-language types and mathematical symbols. It printed, and apparently published in the modern sense, a French reader, some works on American ethnology, and two pamphlets in a scientific series. But in spite of its privileged position, financial troubles beset it by 1876. In 1880 all mention of it disappears from the *Register*, and in 1884 it was officially dead.

Proud as we are of Cornell's priority among university presses, we must own that ours ventured only feebly into the field of book publication. It was a press in the strict and proper sense, as in fact most of the present presses are not.

Organized supervision of student health developed only slowly. At first there was none; sick students were cared for by local doctors or by their room-mates, if by anyone. John Henry Comstock came down with typhoid fever; his life was perhaps saved by Professor Wilder, who put the patient in his study and nursed him devotedly. To be sure, the students were not much worse off than the citizens, for there was no hospital in Ithaca.

The Faculty took notice of the lack, resolving (22 February 1870) that rooms should be reserved for sick students. In June 1877 Dr. Ziba H. Potter, assistant professor of mathematics, was appointed medical examiner, with an annual salary of $250, and with the duty of examining all students applying for exemption from military duties on account of ill health. (One would conclude that the administration was more concerned about malingering than with the preservation of student health.) Miss Jennie McGraw, wealthy daughter of John McGraw, put in her will a bequest of $15,000 to build a student hospital on the campus. From such beginnings did our present clinical and medical service grow.

We have now reviewed the educational organization of the early University. What emerges from this synoptic view?

The modern educator must be struck by the paucity of provision for research, which has become dominant in the universities of today.

The concept of research was still formless in 1868. A university, in the general understanding, was composed only of the teachers and the taught. The idea that teachers and taught together had a common relation to human knowledge was a novelty. It had taken shape in Germany and was transported to America by scholars, like Andrew D. White, with German training. Agassiz, with his Museum of Comparative Zoology at Harvard, promulgated the idea. President Thomas Hill of Harvard proposed research as a university aim in his report of 1864, with no immediate effect. Andrew D. White rather cloudily suggested it in his proposal to Gerrit Smith in 1862. His dream university would be "an asylum for Science, where truth shall be sought for truth's sake." It would be "a nucleus around which liberally-minded men of learning could cluster." But in his Plan of Organization of 1866 and in his Inaugural Address there is hardly a hint of research.

Barring this lack, the early curriculum and organization display the Cornell Idea in operation. Many a speaker and writer acclaimed the Cornell Idea, though they would have been hard put to it to define the term, nor is the task an easy one today.

The Cornell Idea was a compound of two ideas: the Ezra Cornell Idea and the Andrew D. White Idea. The Ezra Cornell Idea was expressed in his famous motto. It was an appeal for education to meet recognized needs and lacks in American life. It insisted on the test by utility, on the practical applications of studies. The Andrew D. White Idea was the motivation by the desire to learn, in place of disciplinary education. It transferred the power of choice from the teacher to the student. It insisted on the individual's rights in full confidence that the free individual, with kindly guidance, will find his way to wisdom and virtue.

Matthew Arnold, condescending to notice, in 1869, our bold new purpose (in the Preface to *Culture and Anarchy*), pricked us with a still-repeated criticism: "The university of Mr. Cornell, a really noble monument of his munificence, yet seems to rest on a misconception of what culture truly is, and to be calculated to produce miners, or engineers, or architects, not sweetness and light." Ezra Cornell no doubt agreed; America's need was for engineers and architects; sweetness and light could come if they would. But Arnold's words must have stung White. Inwardly he agreed. He labored for many years to make sweetness and light a component of the Cornell Idea.

The curricular innovations affected the student's choice of studies and the nature of the studies available for him to choose. The content of the studies remained unchanged. Thus, in spite of all the proclamations of overturn, of radical reconstruction, the educational edifice turned out to be not so different after all from that of the older schools. The body of knowledge in the faculties' possession does not change much. To design a bridge, one must learn mathematics; to destroy plant diseases, one must know botany, entomology, chemistry. By force of powerful fact, the Cornell curriculum looked familiar in its general design, though novel in many of its developments. Its chief virtue lay perhaps in the irreverence with which it was regarded by the young, impatient faculty.

The brave announcements of the new university brought it immediate success. From its very opening, Cornell was one of the largest American colleges. Dissatisfied students in the established schools transferred to it in numbers. The Cornell Idea had a mighty vogue. To the modern historian, Cornell was "the most remarkable phenomenon in higher education during the post-war era." [18]

The influence of the Cornell Idea on other universities was profound. Charles W. Eliot, professor of chemistry in the Massachusetts Institute of Technology, published in the *Atlantic Monthly* in 1869 two articles on the "New Education," filled with demands for university reform. Though his dissatisfactions and his remedies matched essentially those of Andrew D. White, he did not accept the Cornell Idea entire; he insisted, for instance, that an arts college should not be linked with a technical school. Some of his shafts seem to be directed at us: "a University," he says, "cannot be run up, like a cotton mill, in six months." Immediately after the publication of his articles, Eliot was chosen President of Harvard and began substituting the elective system for the fixed curriculum. How far he was inspired by Cornell's example may be disputed; White, of course, thought Eliot a mere unprincipled imitator.

Noah Porter, professor of moral philosophy at Yale, published in 1870 *The American College and the American Public*, defending traditional education and making almost a point-by-point rejoinder to White's Plan of Organization. In the following year Professor Porter became President of Yale, pledged to resist all innovation.

Many other college presidents pondered upon the meaning of Cornell's success. President Barnard of Columbia wrote in 1870: "Columbia cannot grow, or at any rate cannot grow rapidly . . . unless it shall,

[18] Allan Nevins, *The Emergence of Modern America* (New York, 1927), p. 272.

at least to some extent, modify its plan of instruction in a more or less distant imitation of Harvard or of Cornell University." [19]

The Cornell Idea imposed itself to a greater or less extent, more in the west than in the east. The older colleges accepted as much as they desired, absorbed what was beneficial to them, and forgot their benefactor. Cornell itself retained only as much as it could digest. Gradually its novelties ceased to be novel, and the University lost its young intransigence. The Cornell Idea turned bit by bit into the Cornell Tradition. The change was inevitable, though in some ways regrettable.

[19] R. Freeman Butts, *The College Charts Its Course* (New York, 1939), p. 190. See also Daniel Coit Gilman, "Education in America," *North American Review,* Jan. 1876, p. 220.

XI

The Early Years:
Triumphs and Trials

THE infant university was tenderly watched by its trustees. Great though their good will was, their judgments sometimes clashed with those of Andrew D. White, chiefly charged with the care of the nursling. Three of the trustees, self-made men of power, played a particular role in our history.

John McGraw was one of the ten made by the Charter into that body politic and corporate known as Cornell University. He was born in 1815 in the hills ten miles east of Ithaca, in a region still known as Irish Settlement. He clerked in a store in Dryden, married his employer's daughter, and began dealing in timber from the newly cleared countryside. The Lord prospered him. In partnership with Henry W. Sage, he bought and lumbered great tracts of land in New York, Michigan, and Wisconsin. He was comfortably a millionaire, with a sole daughter, Jennie, cultivated and high-minded.

At the opening, Jennie presented the University with its chime of bells, thus expressing a rare public deference to the aesthetic, to the beautiful but useless. John McGraw then offered a building to house the library and museum, with a high tower for his daughter's bells. McGraw Hall was opened in 1872. He died in 1877. He and his daughter are interred in the Memorial Antechapel of Sage Chapel.

Hiram Sibley was also one of the noble ten named in the Charter of the University as trustees. His story, like John McGraw's, is typical of the strenuous times. Beginning as a penniless shoemaker's apprentice, he opened a machine shop at twenty-one, and progressed to banking and real estate in Rochester. In 1850 he got into the telegraph business, met, fought, and finally absorbed Ezra Cornell in the Western Union Telegraph Company, of which he was president for ten years. He was reputed to be Rochester's richest citizen. He was shrewd and tough; he was also broad-minded. His letters reveal a fundamental idealism with a touch of whimsicality and a gift for the pungent phrase, reminding one of Ezra Cornell.

At first he took his responsibilities as trustee lightly. He did not attend a meeting of the Board until 1872. The University of Rochester made claims upon his civic patriotism. There are suggestions, however, that he disliked the sectarian cast of that institution and that he applauded the freedoms proclaimed at Cornell. Andrew D. White took credit for enlisting his interest.[1]

Sibley's aid to the struggling university was magnificent and all-important. He chose as his province the field of mechanic arts. In 1870 he offered a building, which was opened in the following year as Sibley College of the Mechanic Arts. He continued to make gifts for extensions and equipment, and after his death the good work was carried on by his son Hiram W. Sibley.

The dominant trustee, and one of the great figures in Cornell history, was Henry Williams Sage. He used to be called our Second Founder. (The term irritates the purist, who does not see how anything vital can be founded twice.) Born in Middletown, Connecticut, in 1814, he spent his boyhood and youth in Ithaca. At eighteen he entered the employ of his maternal uncles, important Ithaca merchants with far-flung interests. In five years he headed the business. At the same time he passed through a stage of philosophical inquiry, doing much hard reading and reflection, meditating such difficult authors as Kant, Thomas Reid, and Dugald Stewart.[2] With sure instinct he engaged in the lumber trade, in association with John McGraw. Sage knew Ezra Cornell well, of course, and was a director of Cornell's ill-fated New York and Erie telegraph line. Indeed, Cornell bore an old resentment

[1] Carl Becker, *Cornell University: Founders and the Founding* (Ithaca, 1943), p. 178; ADW to W. T. Hewett, 1894.

[2] M. C. Tyler, Diary, 10 Feb. 1886, C.U. Library. For a brilliant analysis of Sage's character and career, see Anita S. Goodstein, *Biography of a Businessman: Henry W. Sage, 1814–1897* (Ithaca, 1962).

against him, due to Sage's effort to strip him of control.[3] Sage's constantly expanding interests caused him to remove to Brooklyn, in 1857. He was a familiar mid-century type—the businessman with a holy conviction that the Business Man is the flower of our civilization. Mark Twain remembered (in his *Autobiography*) Sage's accolade: "What are you an author for? You ought to be a Business Man!" In the eye-gouging business battles of the time Sage usually won, by cleverness and toughness. Old Ithacans still recall with delight the story of his ramming of a New York Central Railroad bridge, in the cause of justice and advantage.[4]

He was a hard man, certainly, as many a professor and administrator was to learn. His impulse was to crash into obstacles; he liked the sound of yielding girders. But he was no mere acquisitive bruiser of the business mellay. He was well and widely read; he displayed a sensitive and even graceful epistolary style. He became a devout liberal Christian, a close friend and unyielding supporter of Henry Ward Beecher, famous pastor of the Plymouth Congregational Church in Brooklyn. Like Ezra Cornell, he masked with a forbidding air his secret sentimentality, especially with regard to the welfare and education of women. He journeyed to Ithaca for the Inauguration. As he listened to White's description of the generous labors of Ezra Cornell, which had brought upon him so much vilification, Sage, with tears in his eyes, turned to John McGraw and said: "John, we are scoundrels to stand doing nothing while those men are killing themselves to establish this university." At the close of the ceremonies—as has already been recorded—Sage promised to White an endowment for educating young women on the same terms as men.

[3] Sage presented a motion of lack of confidence in Cornell, and demanded an assignment of his stock to the trustees (minutes of meeting of N.Y. and Erie directors, 2 May 1850, EC Papers; and EC to J. J. Speed, 3 May 1850).

[4] Sage's lumber tows went down the Hudson to Brooklyn, passing through the railroad drawbridges at Albany and Spuyten Duyvil. Commodore Vanderbilt instructed his draw tenders to give the right of way to New York Central trains and let the tooting river traffic wait. This procedure was contrary to law and a strain on Sage's temper. He fitted a powerful tugboat with an armored bow, a disguised battleship. Taking his stand in the pilothouse, he waited till he saw a long freight train approaching. He churned up to the drawbridge and whistled for it to open. Nothing happened. He then ordered full speed ahead and rammed the bridge head on. The railroad was out of commission for days. The tugboat required extensive repairs, and there was a lawsuit to deal with, but the remembrance of Commodore Vanderbilt's fury well repaid Sage for his costs. So the story goes; but unfortunately I can find no substantiation of it.

He was elected to the Board of Trustees in 1870. The vigor of his opinions, the strength of his will, and the weight of his wealth made him immediately one of the chief determinants of administrative policy and action. In 1875 he was chosen chairman of the Board, and chairman he remained until his death in 1897.

There was need of strength and wisdom, particularly in the realm of finance.

White estimated the resources of the University at its opening to be $1,004,000, and the annual income to be $87,138.40. This income was a little more than that of Yale College, excluding its Medical, Scientific, and Theological Schools.[5] At first blush this seems encouraging, but the point is that Yale's budget was for annual maintenance, whereas Cornell's had to meet all the capital expenses of a new enterprise: the erection of buildings and the provision of equipment, furnishings, books, apparatus. Besides, some of White's innovations, such as the nonresident lectureships, were unduly expensive. The treasurer, George W. Schuyler, soon found the treasury empty and was obliged to advance funds on his personal credit.

The administration looked to the obvious solution: to sell some of the University's holdings in western lands. The trouble was that these lands were held by Mr. Cornell, by his purchases from the state's College Land Scrip Fund and by the setup of the Cornell Endowment Fund. And Mr. Cornell did not want to sell. The current price of such land was a little less than a dollar an acre. In view of the expenses incurred for location and taxes, this was not enough. Cornell preferred to hold the land for the inevitable rise.

His sanguine predictions of future profits were reported in the press and provoked jealous attacks from the University's enemies. The Rochester *Union and Advertiser* (26 October 1869) ferreted out a sinister plot: Mr. Cornell expected to make a personal profit of $24,000,000 from the land; the Cornell Endowment Fund and Cornell University itself were mere subterfuges, created to put over a gigantic "job."

Far from it, indeed! The Endowment Fund was irrevocably committed to University purposes. Mr. Cornell bore the costs of carrying the land until it should be sold, and he had some trouble in finding the money. By October 1870 the University was $100,000 in debt; President White wrote an angry letter of resignation.[6] In December a temporary relief was gained. Messrs. Sage and McGraw agreed to

[5] ADW Papers, 13 Feb. 1867, 17 Sept. 1868, Feb. 1869.
[6] ADW to Alonzo B. Cornell, 25 Oct. 1870.

buy 100,000 acres of white-pine land at $4 per acre, well above the market price.[7] But the timber turned out to be not up to specification, and the contract had to be renegotiated.

On 2 April 1872 White wrote to Cornell, recalling that a year before he had told the Executive Committee that if the land-grant scrip was to be held longer in hope of appreciation he would conclude that he had accomplished his work at Cornell. He had drawn up his resignation, to take effect at the next Commencement. But Mr. Cornell had agreed to sell a portion of the land, if the trustees and the State Comptroller should agree. White had obtained the signatures; the deal would bring Cornell University $125,000, for the increase of the faculty, for the Department of Architecture, for improvements and a sinking fund. White had proposed to build a house in Ithaca, pledging $20,000. He now found the University unable to pay its bills, and Mr. Cornell reluctant to make the sale. If this was true, he would resign immediately. "I could not *live* in Ithaca under such uncertainty and in such suspense."

Mr. Cornell would not sell any considerable tracts and Mr. White did not resign. The financial situation steadily worsened. The treasurer's report showed a debt of $155,000. Bankruptcy loomed. At this point (31 October 1872) Ezra Cornell offered to pay half the debt if friends of the University would contribute the other half. "It seemed impossible," says White in his *Autobiography*. "Our friends had been called upon so constantly and for such considerable sums that it seemed vain to ask them for more. But we brought together at Albany a few of the most devoted, and in fifteen minutes the whole amount was subscribed; four members of the Board of Trustees agreed to give each twenty thousand dollars." The noble four were Sage, McGraw, Sibley, and White himself.

Perhaps this experience taught White a valuable lesson. At about this time he was asked to make a critical review of Columbia University's affairs. He was shocked to discover that the Columbia trustees were laying aside $90,000 a year. He told them they should spend not only the $90,000, but another sum equal to it, and then appeal to the alumni to make up the deficit. He told President Barnard: "We never made a friend at Cornell by doing something for him, but when he does something for us he becomes our friend." [8]

1873 was Panic Year in the United States. Hard times came with the

[7] Samuel D. Halliday, *History of the Federal Land Grant* (Ithaca, 1905), p. 33–34.

[8] Richard T. Ely, *Ground under Our Feet* (New York, 1938), pp. 32–33. White told Ely the story during his ministry at Berlin.

collapse of the overextended railroads. Ezra Cornell was deeply involved. His desire to make Ithaca a metropolis combined with his
speculative instincts and his delight in building to bring him to the
inevitable result. He had been fascinated, as early as 1853, by the idea
of a railroad to Auburn, to cross Fall Creek at the point of the present
Stewart Avenue Bridge.[9] In 1866 he was elected president of the Ithaca
and Towanda Railroad, completed in 1872, now the Lehigh Valley.
Whetted by this experience, he built the Ithaca and Cortland, which
had its first terminus on the campus. He then extended that ill-fated
line over hill and dale to Elmira. (Of this extension the only remnant is
a track from Elmira to Horseheads.) He invested heavily in the Geneva
and Ithaca Rail Road. At least he seems not to have been involved in the
Cayuga Lake line along the east shore of the lake. He put altogether
into his railroad ventures about two million dollars, obtained by the
sale or pledging of his Western Union stock and other sound securities.

White viewed Cornell's actions with foreboding, his railroads with
loathing. He gave Cornell good advice, to devote his time and money
to the University, "that institution by which your name is to stand or
fall." [10] Cornell received the advice with his usual stony calm.

Others were no less alarmed than White, especially Cornell's attorney, Francis Miles Finch. William C. Russel wrote White (12 March
1873) that nothing could change the course of Mr. Cornell's fancy and
that the University administration must save as much as possible if the
Founder should run aground. "We are sailing in a fog with all sails
set and a favoring gale abeam, but whether an iceberg may not be just
ahead we can only tell by our striking it when we get there." White
replied (17 March 1873) that he was "tired to death of trying to maintain a fight against such tremendous odds, and feeling so utterly inse-
cure as to my backing—tired too of this *dependent* position."

Cornell likewise was tired, in poor health, and feeling the weight of
his sixty-six years. He decided that he must transfer all the cares of the
land business to the University. To this end he had a bill introduced
in the State Assembly, providing for a settlement with New York State
of the land-grant matters. The bill authorized him to convey to the
University the title to the lands he had located.

The iceberg dreaded by Russel lay just ahead.

[9] EC to E. Manning, 17 April 1853 (in Letter Book); to Mary Ann Cornell,
5 March 1854. For the story of his railroad ventures, see Philip Dorf, *The Builder*
(New York, 1952), and Hardy Campbell Lee, *A History of the Railroads of
Tompkins County* (Ithaca, 1947).
[10] ADW to EC, 27 April 1874.

In the midst of perfunctory debate in the Assembly, on 12 May 1873, uprose Mr. Jeremiah McGuire of Schuyler County, home of the late People's College. Perhaps with the aim of recapturing the land grant for his district, he assailed, with venomous but plausible words, Mr. Cornell and all his works. Cornell's dealings with the Land Grant Act were undertaken, he said, "with the view, with the intent, and with the purpose of cheating, defrauding, and evading this very Act of Congress. . . . This fund . . . is to be made the subject of speculation and extravagance, and princely fortunes are to be made out of it by somebody." With complete misrepresentation, but with much specificity, he laid bare a plot on Mr. Cornell's part to make a private fortune of $22,000,000 for himself.

The Honorable Jeremiah McGuire was an impressive speaker; and the country had just been shaken by the revelation of genuine plots in high place, such as the Credit Mobilier. The suspicious, the jealous, and the disappointed applauded McGuire's perspicacity.

Ezra Cornell refused to be moved. He said to White: "Don't make yourself unhappy over this. I have always expected that some such attack would come, but my only fear was that it would come after my death, when I would not be here to answer it." He echoed McGuire's demand for an official investigation.

Expressions of sympathy poured in. Hiram Sibley raised his promised endowment of Sibley College by $30,000. Herbert H. Smith '70 sent the University the only thing of value he possessed—an entomological collection of 25,000 specimens.[11]

Governor John A. Dix appointed a distinguished Committee of Investigation, composed of former Governor Horatio Seymour, William A. Wheeler, later Vice-President under Hayes, and John D. Van Buren, a well-known lawyer. The committee was too distinguished. Only Van Buren found time to visit Ithaca. White found him unfit by training and temper to judge of educational matters. He was hostile on principle to all advanced instruction. He proposed that the University give instruction in boat building, to White's covert amusement.

Public hearings were held. Two discharged employees and an ousted ex-professor of agriculture and a ne'er-do-well Ithaca doctor testified against Mr. Cornell. Their evidence was dismissed as baseless supposition and hearsay. On 16 April 1874 the committee reported, vindicating completely Mr. Cornell's handling of the lands and the money.

[11] Smith later removed to Brazil and wrote historical studies of South America. His fine library eventually came to Cornell.

But the committee had been charged also with investigating the state of the University, to determine if it was fulfilling the purposes of the Morrill Act. On this score the committee had some criticisms to make, chiefly with regard to the work in agriculture. Well, with those criticisms President White secretly agreed. The effective organization of the Agricultural Department had so far baffled him.

In October 1874 the formal transfer of the control of the land-grant lands from Ezra Cornell to Cornell University was accomplished. It was high time. Mr. Cornell came down with a severe attack of pneumonia in June. He never completely recovered.

The accounting with the University was a dolorous one. Mr. Cornell had paid out for scrip, location, examinations, taxes, interest, and so forth, $720,000; he had received from sales $146,000. The balance due him was $574,000. This sum was met by the sale of 100,000 acres to Sage and McGraw for $400,000, plus a transfer from the Endowment Fund.

Eighteen seventy-four was a hard year for the administration. The panic of 1873 had shattered the country's economy. The trustees' minutes are filled with items on notes, mortgages, and borrowings. In February the state announced that it would reduce its payments of interest of the Land Scrip Fund in its possession. Everyone was aghast. In March some booksellers sent a sheriff to levy on the Library's books. In September the quarterly payments of the professors' salaries could not be met from the empty treasury.[12]

As President Schurman later summed up the situation:

Never had an institution received such an unpromising endowment. There were those in the Board of Trustees who felt that it was unjustifiable to burden the already struggling University with an investment of this character, which required large annual expenses for taxes and management, and produced no annual income. And the results of the experience in the following years were as discouraging as the outlook had been inauspicious. The taxes on the lands and the cost of administration brought the annual expenses up to $60,000 or $70,000, and one year they were $94,000. Located in 1866 and 1867, the lands had produced an annual crop of expenditures which by 1879 aggregated $874,433.57, against which the total receipts from the sales of land and timber amounted to only $715,537.53. It needed no prophet to see that if this continued for some years longer the lands would be eaten up by taxes and the expenses of administration. Nay, they might even drag the University into bankruptcy; for the re-

[12] Russel to ADW, 16 March 1874; Faculty Records, 30 Sept. 1874.

ceipts from all sales falling short of the cost of maintenance, the endowment of the University had been trenched upon to balance the land account. Mr. Cornell's great scheme for the enrichment of his University appeared to be rapidly working its destruction.[13]

Of course, later on the lands repaid their cost sevenfold, and the stubborn foresight of Cornell and Sage has been abundantly acclaimed. But it is at least arguable that a million dollars during the hard years from 1874 to 1881 would have profited the University more than $4,500,000 in 1897.

Added to the financial woes, with their inevitable effect on faculty and student morale, were rifts and suspicions in high places. White felt something like bitterness toward the Founder. He wrote to Russel (26 December 1873): "To this day I do not know whether Mr. Cornell regards me as a benefit or an injury to the institution. I do not know whether he approves of what I have done. He has sometimes appeared to blame me. He has never thanked me. Now all this I never cared for so long as Mr. Cornell's heart was evidently in the University." But now he cares more for his little railroads than for the University! It could be made the best of its kind in the land. But those one-horse railroads! "Ezra Cornell is too precious a man, too unselfish, to be lost to so great an enterprise, in order to promote enterprises so small!" The only solution, he concludes, is to sell the lands.

White wrote to Cornell (27 April 1874): "You have broken my enthusiasm." He asserts that the trustees also are disheartened and dispirited, fearing that Cornell has lost interest in his own university. That state of mind, he says, has dissuaded many from making intended donations. On 8 October he notes, anent a crucial meeting of the Board of Trustees, that $223,000 has been raised "to carry the University through and cut it clear of Mr. Cornell." These are ominous words.

But all rancor, all mistrust were wiped out by the death of the Founder, on 9 December, 1874. The city and the University were plunged in mourning. The city was suddenly aware that it had lost its greatest citizen, the University that it had lost the cause of its existence.

After a suitable interval, tongues began to wag. The local wiseacres totted up presumed assets and obligations. It was commonly supposed in Ithaca that Ezra Cornell's wealth had gone to the University and that in his hands remained only worthless railroad stocks and evidences of uncollectable debts, such as the bonds of townships issued to tempt

[13] J. G. Schurman, *A Generation of Cornell* (New York, 1898), p. 9.

railroads to their doors. Indeed, there is some question whether Ezra Cornell, at his death, was technically solvent. Immense claims against his estate were presented. Long litigation ensued. Twenty-three years later, the administrator, the Founder's son Franklin C. Cornell, made his final accounting. He showed that a million and a half had been distributed for debts, expenses, and fees and that well over a million remained for the widow and children.[14] Some of the railroads had survived and thriven, honest townships had honored their obligations. Cornell left to his heirs something more than he had once judged to be for their good. Once more he had proved, by patience, to be right.

The financial troubles of the young University pressed heavily upon the faculty. Newspapers and academic gossip had led them to believe that the University was possessed of enormous wealth. They accepted the President's rather hard bargains, which were suffused with great expectations. The professors at the outset received salaries ranging from $1,375 to $2,250. They found the cost of living high and their income insufficient for normal expenses. In February 1869 they submitted a petition asking a general raise. They complained that their salaries were less than the wages of the Cascadilla steward, that the remuneration was unequal, and that they were overworked, with no time for original research or for relaxation; they feared they would degenerate into mere tutors. The President accepted the petition, but to the Board he made no recommendation for the augmentation of salaries.

His failure to act left a residue of ill feeling among the faculty. We overhear many complaints in the following years. White, like every President, had to sense the pressures upon the budget, and yield to the most peremptory, which did not come from the hungry faculty. The trustees generally frowned on salary increases. Trying to get a $200 raise for Willard Fiske, White wrote Russel (27 December 1870): "I foresee difficulty. Mr. Cornell already regards me as having altogether too many bowels of compassion in such matters, and invariably answers with: 'who is to pay the money?' or 'we haven't got the money.'"

Nevertheless, salaries were gradually increased. In 1873 all salaries of $2,000 were raised to $2,250, and $1,800 salaries to $2,000. While this scale did not approach that of Columbia or of some other favored universities (in 1874 Cincinnati established three chairs at $3,500), it was better than the average. In the early eighties the average salary for

[14] Sherman Peer, in Ithaca *Journal*, 16 Jan. 1958; Mulks Scrapbooks, XXIII, C.U. Library.

a full professorship in twenty-four of the larger colleges, including Cornell, was $1,750.[15]

Fringe benefits, such as pension and insurance funds, were unknown. W. C. Cleveland, professor of civil engineering, died suddenly in January 1873, leaving his widow with forty-one dollars. His colleagues raised a subscription for her, though aware that it would probably go to settle claims against the estate. His engineering class gallantly offered to pay for the daughter's education. White promised to continue his salary to the end of the college year out of his own pocket, but he made clear that a professor's untimely death was his own responsibility and created no claim against the University.[16]

Next to the financial troubles, the greatest cause of administrative distress was hostility aroused by Cornell's nonsectarian stand.

Cornell was not the first nonsectarian university, but its bold and perhaps toplofty proclamations brought it most prominently into view. In those days many worthy believers were filled with disquiet. Darwin's *Origin of Species* had appeared in 1859. The doctrine of evolution was taken up by two groups: the scientists and the enemies of revealed religion. Naturally the two were blended in the popular mind. Evolution was taken to be a contradiction of the Bible; even the word carried a hint of Evil in its syllables. Frontier scoffers, nourished on Voltaire and Tom Paine, found in Darwin new and awkward questions for the orthodox. John Fiske gave a series of lectures at Harvard in 1869–70, expounding the evolutionary theory; his course was regarded as evidence of "Harvard's raid on religion."

President White insisted that Cornell, though nonsectarian, was Christian. In his Inaugural Address he had indeed inveighed against the familiar college chapel services—"prayers dogmatic or ceremonial; praise with doggerel hymns, thin music and feeble choir; the great body of students utterly listless or worse." But he had proclaimed: "From yonder chapel shall daily ascend praise and prayer. Day after day it shall recognize in man not only mental and moral but religious want. We will labor to make this a Christian institution—a sectarian

[15] Rossiter Johnson, in *North American Review*, May 1883, p. 493; quoted by Walter P. Rogers, *Andrew D. White and the Modern University* (Ithaca, 1942), p. 147.

[16] ADW Papers, 17 Jan. 1873 *et seq.* A little later, the trustees of the College of the City of New York directed that the salary of a deceased teacher should be continued for six months and paid to his widow. The courts held that the trustees had exceeded their jurisdiction and that the auditor had properly rejected the widow's claim. Abbott, New York *Digest,* VII (1881), 808.

institution may it never be." In his public replies to denominational attacks, he reiterated the Christian basis of the University's structure.

The animosity of the militant churches was not allayed. Cornell's success in attracting students away from small sectarian colleges aroused the denominational magazines. These had an enormous diffusion and power; they were often the only reading matter in simple homes, since they were commonly distributed free to the faithful. The magazines attacked Cornell as the leader and symbol of nonsectarianism, which they equated with atheism. White saw in their unanimity an actual plot. "Their papers, addresses and sermons on our unchristian character are venomous," he wrote to Ezra Cornell on 3 August 1869. But he insisted that he was not at all nervous. "In this thing I feel at home, I shall feel a great deal happier when we can get fairly into the fight. I believe that we can give them a lesson which they will remember. Greeley [of the New York *Tribune*], Godkin of the *Nation*, Tilton [of the *Independent*], Curtis of *Harper's* will all open batteries for us." And indeed they did.

Typical of the charges were those in the *Northern Christian Advocate* in January 1870. At Cornell, it alleged, even atheists may be professors; President White is not a church member; the atmosphere is Broad Churchish; Christian ideas are ignored; the leaders, who call themselves "liberal Christians," are in fact polished skeptics. And, of course, attendance at chapel is not compulsory.

White seldom answered the attacks in his own words, leaving that task to his journalist friends. But in a brochure: "The Cornell University: What it is and What it is not" (1872), he defined the official stand:

The Cornell University is governed by a body of Christian Trustees, conducted by Christian Professors, and is a Christian Institution as the Public School system of this State is Christian. Its inauguration exercises were commenced with simple Christian worship, and not a public exercise of any sort has taken place since that has not been begun with that great comprehensive petition from the Founder of Christianity Himself—the Lord's Prayer.

Every working day since that has begun in the University Chapel in the same manner.

It is not believed, however, that *forcing* young men to attend chapel exercises promotes reverence for Christian graces. . . .

It is hoped and believed that strong young men, thoroughly equipped, will go forth from its halls to do battle for truth and right in the Christian ministry, as in other professions; but its object is not to give an institution for any one denomination exclusively, to train its young clergymen or to provide snug sleeping places for its old ones.

In the same pamphlet White took a satisfying backhander at our rivals:

Any institution under denominational control inevitably tends to make allegiance to its own form of belief a leading qualification. It may become a tolerably good denominational college, like the hundreds already keeping down the standard of American education, but it can become nothing more. . . . The cry of "infidel" is ceasing to scare, the claim of "sound learning" and "safe" instruction is ceasing to allure. . . . As to "sound" learning and "safe" instruction, it has well-nigh killed the great majority of colleges which have boasted it.

In his stand the President had the support of the faculty, most of the trustees, the country's liberal editors, and many bystanders. Senator Morrill of the Morrill Land Grant wrote him (12 August 1873), after an attack on Cornell by President McCosh of Princeton: "There are three or four classical colleges who want to monopolize and direct the liberal education of the country." These colleges are aristocratic and selfish, he continued, "without a particle of sympathy for the noble object of Mr. Cornell."

White's high purposes were ill served by a display of the inevitable student facetiousness. The Cornell Young Men's Heathen Association published a rather laborious pasquinade, satirizing Ezra Cornell's and William C. Russel's liberalism. For instance, it acclaimed "Ezra Cornell, our honored founder, for the good example he sets the community in refusing to attend church, preferring to worship the Almighty Dollar in his closet." The news of a Cornell YMHA was of course broadcast to the press and was taken seriously by many of the righteous.[17]

The situation was further exacerbated by the appointment, in 1874, of Felix Adler as professor of Hebrew and Oriental literature and history. Adler was young, brilliant, and popular with the students, who called him "Young Eagle." His lectures attracted many visitors, especially the gentlewomen of Ithaca. The trouble was that he would not stick to his subject. Clarifying his own code of belief, he delighted in airing strong and startling judgments on reason, faith, and philosophy. Being well versed in the textual criticism of the Hebrew Scriptures, he made assertions about the composition of the Old Testament which

[17] A copy is in an 1873 Scrap Book, C.U. Archives.

filled many a devout bosom with horror and provoked denunciations from pastors whose Hebrew was too scanty to enable them to debate with Adler on his own ground. Russel wrote White, on 15 May 1874, that he feared Adler would upset his kettle. "He described the immaculate conception of Buddha the other day and gave the reason for people favoring such an illusion. i.e., they considered certain acts as sinful which we do not." Four days later he wrote:

It is impossible to say how much of the surface of the fluid in this teapot is covered by the storm which Adler has conjured, but the hissing and sissing and rush of steam and bursting of bubbles are quite animated. The waves of orthodoxy raise their minute crests, and the sullen murmur of the evangelicals is like the noise of many flies. I hear of excitement and of hobnobbing, of lamentations of the righteous and prophecies of the carrying away of the children into captivity on the hill. Not merely the fiend Adler, but the demoniac host of professors generally, with special notice of the Vice-President, fall under the condemnation of the just made perfect.

The cause, he says, is hard to pin down, but "people talk about 'the tendency, the tendency!' " Russel concludes that Adler is very able, but conceited and hard to change, and he irritates those many whom he considers his inferiors. Russel might have added that some enemy used poisoned arrows against Adler, alleging that many students, the cream of the professors, and some eminent citizens were getting "gloriously drunk" on the fine old wines proffered by Adler.

After two years Adler was quietly dropped. His sponsor, the financier Joseph Seligman of New York, who paid his salary, demanded an inquiry. The trustees established the principle that they would accept endowed professorships only if the choice of the incumbent was left to the trustees.

Adler went to New York and founded the famous Society of Ethical Culture.[18]

Cornell's answer to the charge of irreligion was the erection of Sage Chapel. The story goes that Mrs. Henry W. Sage, examining the plans for Sage College one evening in 1872 and noticing a tiny area reserved for a chapel, exclaimed: "Is that the only provision in that great university which is made for chapel services?" And on the following day her husband called on White to offer a proper chapel.

[18] *Alumni News,* 18 May and 8 June 1933; Ithaca *Journal,* 22 April 1874; ADW Papers, *passim;* Trustees' *Proceedings,* 3 May 1877.

Though Mrs. Sage's words may well have been the impelling cause, the lack and need had surely been evident to Mr. Sage long before. His first idea was to appoint a resident chaplain to go with the chapel. This White opposed. He proposed instead a lectureship in Christian ethics and the service of the chapel by visiting preachers. These should be the most eminent divines obtainable, of all faiths, including Catholic and Jewish. Ithaca preachers might also piece out the program. The students should be attracted, not coerced, into attendance. This, White claimed, was the first successful plan for an unsectarian college chapel in the United States.[19]

Sage yielded, contrary to his wont. Professor Babcock of Architecture was commissioned to design the chapel. In its original form it consisted of half the present main auditorium, with a small south wing and a tower topped by a belfry and spire. It accommodated five hundred worshippers. Henry W. Sage's son Dean provided an endowment, originally of $30,000, for the preachership.

Sage Chapel was dedicated on 13 June 1875 with a memorable address by the famous Phillips Brooks, Boston Episcopalian. Since then an endless succession of preachers, including the most eminent, has come and gone. The merits and defects of the system have been much argued. Sustained, as it usually has been, by a strong Christian Association or Religious Work organization, it has provided a century of undergraduates with enlightenment and stimulation.

In the early years the morning congregation was likely to be thin, especially in bad weather, as most of the students, living far down the hill, went to the churches of their own faiths or simply stayed in bed. The afternoon services were commonly well attended, and when a celebrated visitor arrived, jammed. Occasionally the services had to be transferred to the Armory.

One of the most constant and most beloved of the Sage preachers was Robert Collyer, Chicago Unitarian. His connection with Cornell began immediately after the Chicago fire of 1871. Collyer issued a stirring appeal for relief funds; Cornell responded with a mass meeting in which the astonishing sum of $2,250.75 was raised. The students, aware that Collyer had begun life as a blacksmith, imposed a condition: "that the Rev. Robert Collyer shall make for them, with his own hands, and in a proper and workmanlike manner, one small, sufficient, and substantial horseshoe."

The Reverend Robert Collyer had a clerical sense of publicity. Sum-

[19] ADW Papers, 24 Sept. and 26 Sept. 1872; Becker, *Founders*, p. 179.

moning the reporters to a Chicago forge, he donned a leather apron and shaped a small, sufficient, and substantial horseshoe. The story moved America; reproductions of a painting of the saintly smith at his labors soon adorned the walls of countless homes.[20] The precious horseshoe, stamped "Robert Collyer, Maker," is still preserved among the ancient manuscripts and incunabula of Andrew D. White's Library.

Some years later friends of Robert Collyer learned that the north England mill in which he had labored as a child was to be torn down. They bought the factory bell which had daily called him from his bed at dawn and established it in Sibley College. On Collyer's next visit, Director Thurston bade him pull the rope. "The auld bell! The auld bell!" he exclaimed. He dictated the words to be inscribed on the belfry: "By Hammer and Hand all things shall stand" and "The Gift of Robert Collyer to the Smithy." As long as Sibley College served its original purpose the "auld bell" hung in the shops and summoned the students to their duties.

Many an incident of the early days tempts the historian: the students' uproarious but vain effort to vote in the gubernatorial elections of 1870; the Sibley College burglary of 1871; the plagiarism of a Woodford Prize essay; Instructor Simon H. Gage's triumphant entry into Ithaca with a dead camel; a student drowning in Beebe Lake in 1874; Professor Burt G. Wilder's book on sex instruction, which almost provoked the trustees to abolish his professorship. But the recovery of these old excitements must be left to some future antiquarian.

Let us record merely that in 1872 the alumni of Cornell were organized as the Associate Alumni. Such associations already existed in eastern universities. The object of the organization was to promote the interest of the University and to foster mutual regard and attachment to the Alma Mater. The alumni had the privilege of electing a trustee, according to a provision in the Cornell Charter. The institution of the alumni trusteeship had previously existed at Harvard alone. The first Cornell alumni trustee was Samuel D. Halliday '70, elected in 1874. The first June Reunion was held in 1877.

President White confirmed his opposition to the granting of honorary degrees. He had approved of the traditional refusal of the University of Virginia to bestow such degrees and was well aware of the abuses of the system. A committee of three New York State college presidents, including White, pondered upon the subject. Concluding that such

[20] Romeyn Berry, *Behind the Ivy* (Ithaca, 1950), p. 89.

degrees had become almost valueless, the committee recommended that they be awarded only for high achievement in subjects taught by the college faculties. At Cornell White opposed them *in toto*.

In 1876, Centennial Year, America was in the mood to look back upon its past and proudly take stock of its century of achievement.

Cornell was a part of America's achievement. At the Philadelphia Centennial Exposition it had a notable display, chiefly of machines and precision tools made in its shops.[21] Professor Anthony's Gramme machine, or dynamo, ran lathes, sewing machines, and coffee mills. Visitors watched with awe, and then commonly turned the conversation to Cornell's rowing victories at Saratoga. We had just won the varsity and freshman races, and Charles S. Francis '77 had broken the world's intercollegiate record in the single sculls.

Cornell was eight years old. The University was housed in eight buildings in addition to the farm structures. It had a faculty of 44, a student body of 561, including 23 graduate students. Its alumni were increasing in numbers and influence. In spite of all, it had survived the menaces of its early years and had gained stability and recognition, even fame.

Cornell had come of age. It looked forward eagerly to its looming manhood. As Goldwin Smith said, he was used "to a university with its roots in the past, but Cornell's roots in the future appear prodigious."

[21] For a description of the exhibits at the Centennial Exposition, see *Cornell Era,* 15 Sept. 1876.

XII

The Doubtful Years, 1876-1881

THE University being apparently in tolerable shape, President White determined to take a year's leave of absence. The published reason was concern for his health. He was not alone in finding Ithaca winters unkind to a sensitive throat. He was also tired of presidential worries. He longed for a placid stage among the intellectual delights of Europe.

He delayed his departure, however, to receive President Grant in his Ithaca home. The visit, on 27 September 1876, is commemorated by a brass plaque above his hearth. As Romeyn Berry remarked:

We wish there might now be inscribed a postscript to that record, telling the rest of the story as Andrew D. told it so often, and with so much gusto: the terrible time he had searching the pantry and the kitchen closet at 2 A.M. for a nightcap for the General. The butler had gone to bed, after locking up the supplies, and all the President of Cornell could uncover for the President of the United States was a half-empty bottle of inferior cooking brandy. But Andrew D.'s embarrassment was short-lived. Grant took that half bottle of cooking brandy, he said, as promptly, and as unconditionally, as he once took Fort Donelson.[1]

White had a happy stay in England, France, and Italy, so happy that in the spring messages began to arrive from the Italian Lakes that his condition might require another year in Europe. In June the trustees

[1] Romeyn Berry, *Behind the Ivy* (Ithaca: Cornell University Press, 1950), p. 30.

resolved that they heard with delight of the improved and improving health of the President, and that they consented to the extension of his leave "as long as his health or inclination might require." Is there a barb in the choice of the word "inclination"?

The trustees' delight was tempered with concern. Willard Fiske wrote White (2 August 1877) that Henry W. Sage wanted him to come home, if only for thirty days. Sage himself wrote (29 September): "We need the Master's head and hand."

Most of Ithaca agreed. But White had found new obligations. For one thing, he was appointed Honorary Commissioner from the State of New York to the Paris Exposition of 1878. At first, he says in his *Autobiography*, he was inclined to take his duties lightly, but since very few of the American commissioners could speak French he soon found himself deeply involved as a member of the top prize-giving jury. His correspondence reveals that he esteemed his duties at their full value; he wrote a series of irritated letters inquiring about the Legion of Honor due him.[2]

In President White's absence, Vice-President Russel was clothed with the powers of Acting President. Russel had already so served during the frequent presidential absences. His merits were many and great, but his air of sardonic superiority was not fitted to endear him to the faculty, students, and trustees. His view of the faculty is revealed in many letters to White; for example, on 7 January 1874: "The Faculty meeting yesterday exhibited nothing new, only the impracticability of carrying out a system with such a mob." His opinion of his colleagues was all too evident; in fact, he would have regarded tact as a mere euphemism for insincerity. The colleagues reacted in ways that a tactful man would have foreseen. Russel describes (14 March 1875) "the amiable backbiting of others interested only in the general way of demonstrating my odiousness. . . . Prentiss shakes hands with everyone in the room but myself. . . . I accept the fact that literary and scientific men are eminently unreasoning beings, governed by impulse rather than by engrossing interests and that they are always in a state of irritation about their salaries and ready to snap at anyone at any time, and that I am always handy."

White, always faithful to his friends, paid no heed to the rumblings of anti-Russelism. His reception without protest of Russel's scathing criticisms of the faculty suggests that he agreed with them. Perhaps all college presidents would agree on occasion.

[2] 4 Jan. 1877; 11 Jan., 14 March, 5 Nov., 13 Nov. 1878.

Russel's position as Acting President was a difficult one. Times were hard and money extremely tight. Only under the utmost pressure would the trustees authorize salary increases and essential departmental expenditures. Elsewhere salary scales were rising; Cornell's low pay became notorious in the college world.[3] Tuition was raised from $60 to $75 a year. Faculty and students complained of their distresses, but the Acting President was likely to receive their grievances with his unfortunate irony. The suspicion arose that he found a dour satisfaction in the griefs of his colleagues, for whom he had no high regard.

Poor Russel deserves our sympathy. His educational purposes were clear and sound. However, impotent in the absence of his chief, and unable to obtain any enabling funds, he could initiate no changes of policy and practice. He had indeed for a time the grudging approval of Henry W. Sage, who wrote White (30 April 1877): "Russel does as well as he can, and that is tolerably well, in spite of adverse comments." But Russel had less than the full confidence of his trustees, some of whom were nettled by his tactlessness, some by his outspoken religious liberalism. It must have been galling for him to read in the *Era,* on 27 September 1878: "Those who have regard for the prosperity of the University deprecate the non-progressiveness of the institution under the present management." In the circumstances, how could the management be progressive?

After two collegiate years abroad, White returned on 30 September 1878, after classes had begun. (Such tardiness he found inexcusable in professors.) The University soon felt the effects of his energetic direction.

Not, however, for very long. In January 1879 reports came that President Rutherford B. Hayes was considering him for the American Ministry to Berlin. White let it be known that he would regard acceptance as his patriotic duty. He might have gone farther, to say that the Ministry would be the fulfillment of his dearest dreams.

The report filled Ithaca and Cornell with panic. Russel, never one to dodge the telling of home truths, wrote him (17 January 1879): "Some people already think that you are tired of the University and are trying to draw out of it. Your going would confirm this idea." In White's absence, he continued, the University would certainly suffer. Everything would be provisional; the machine would want steadiness; the trustees would lose confidence; and the faculty would be in constant embarrassment. "Everyone expects the Vice-President to assume

[3] M. C. Tyler to ADW, 4 May 1881.

airs, and stands ready to snub him at his first movement." Progress, in short, would be impossible.

A few days later Charles H. Blair '72, Ezra Cornell's son-in-law, wrote White: "I express the general sentiment among the people of Ithaca and a portion, perhaps a large one, of the Faculty, more than my own, when I pray you not to resign your Presidency." He adjured White to limit his stay in Germany, or, if that was impossible, to make Goldwin Smith President. For, he said, it was evident that the University had not advanced during White's absence, the Vice-President being unpopular and a man of scant scholarly repute. Blair concluded his sound advice by asking that, if White must go to Germany, he take the writer along as Secretary of the Legation. White refused to listen to such unpalatable counsel. "My work here can go on well without my presence," he told a friend.[4]

He offered his resignation of the presidency in March 1879. The trustees by unanimous vote declined to accept it.[5] The Executive Committee then granted him a leave of absence and empowered him to choose a replacement. Despite much cautionary advice, he chose Russel. One of White's virtues, or faults, was fidelity to his friends. In this case, White's fidelity wrought the destruction of his friend. White did Russel the kindly but unfortunate service of installing him and his family, pro tem, in the President's House. Russel's ill-wishers wondered audibly if he would ever be dislodged. Rancor and jealousy seethed in the professors' cottages.

White left Ithaca on 16 May 1879 to take up his honorable post. His two years as American Minister to Germany are amply described in his *Autobiography*. He seems to have escaped confrontation with any very serious problems or decisions. His activities were mainly social. Scholarly Andrew D. White and his charming, cultivated wife were admirable representatives of America in the diplomatic world. He was on easy, even friendly terms with everyone from old Emperor William I down. He conceived a great and perhaps naïve admiration for the Crown Prince, later William II, and for Bismarck. It was quite a change from Ithaca.

[4] ADW to Frank Hiscock, 25 March 1879. See also protests against White's departure by Professor W. A. Anthony, 1 April 1879, and Treasurer George W. Schuyler, 9 April 1879.

[5] So he says in a letter to T. M. Cooley, 8 April 1879. No record of a meeting of the Board or of this action appears in the Trustees' *Proceedings*. Perhaps the vote was taken by mail.

Shortly after his arrival in Berlin he received a call from a vigorous young student of philosophy at the University of Berlin, Dr. Jacob Gould Schurman. His record was brilliant; he had lived for eight years entirely on Canadian and British scholarships. He was presented as "a Canadian who feels himself an American." At least, he felt himself qualified for an American professorship.[6]

At home, Russel strove to deal with manifold problems. He tried to smooth ruffled sensibilities, to promote good feeling. "Of course," he wrote on 18 April 1880, "Crane sneers and Fuertes gets mad, but it is their nature to; and I ask Fuertes to dine every Friday, and listen to Crane as patiently and sweetly as if caramels were dropping out of his mouth."

Russel's chief problem was financial. The trustees were more than niggardly with funds. Do not blame the trustees; they had no funds to advance. The western lands continued to drain away the endowment. Two wealthy donors, Ezra Cornell and John McGraw, were dead; Hiram Sibley was miffed about something; Henry W. Sage was more than generous toward his special projects, but his growing dislike of Russel chilled his impulses. And receipts from students dwindled, for the enrollments were falling off alarmingly.

In 1875–76 the total enrollment was 542, in 1876–77, 561. In 1877–78 the number dropped to 529, in 1878–79 to 476. In 1879–80 the enrollment remained fairly steady, at 463, but in the following year, the last of Russel's regency, it dwindled to 399. In 1881–82, when President White returned, it reached its all-time low of 384. Thereafter it began to rise: 407 in 1882–83, 461 in 1883–84, and a triumphant 573 in 1884–85. In the lean years, civil engineering and architecture suffered particularly. In 1879–80 there were only two majors (as they would now be called) in chemistry and physics. However, classics, letters, and the humaner subjects did well, reflecting no doubt the tastes of the women students.

Various reasons were given for the dwindling enrollment: hard times, increased tuition, stiffened entrance exams, coeducation, Cornell's reputation for irreligion. Probably each of these reasons was valid in certain cases. Probably also Cornell was undergoing a transformation of which at the time it was hardly aware. The enthusiasm for technical education, rife in the sixties, died away during the hard times of the seventies, when many a competent builder and engineer could find nothing to do. Cornell had begun as a kind of radical working-class

[6] H. C. Adams to ADW, 3 Aug. 1879; Schurman to ADW, 14 Jan. 1880.

university, with the promise of opportunities for self-help for the penniless. Few of the early students had any money. But by 1880 there were not many working students left, and hardly any could support themselves while doing their scholastic work. The tuition of seventy-five dollars contrasted with the twenty dollars charged at Michigan. We had of course the winners of state scholarships, but they did our treasury no good. We attracted some students by the excellence of certain courses, some by the promise of four agreeable years. We were coming into competition with the old eastern universities on their own terms.

The underlying reason for the diminishing student body was surely the absence of the President for all but seven months of five long years. The lack of an effective head with power to act kept the University at a standstill. The morale of trustees, faculty, and students drooped. Professors at conventions, students on vacation, made gloomy reports; their hearers decided to send their sons or younger brothers elsewhere. No one likes to pledge his love to an Alma Mater with pernicious anemia. Newspapers, sensitive to trouble, diagnosed Cornell's ailments without sympathy.

White read such an article in the New York *Tribune* just before his departure for Germany. He wrote to Willard Fiske (6 May 1879): "It seems to be taken in many quarters as a fact that we are hopelessly running down and that I am leaving the Institution in consequence. This is a cruel blow to receive just at this time. I have never felt any so deeply." The cruel blow did not, however, change any of his plans.

Though enrollments dropped, the stiffening of requirements, and perhaps the hard times themselves, had a wholesome effect on the students. Russel reported to White (30 September and 10 October 1880) that the tone of the University was good, the teaching good, the students enthusiastic. The entering class was above the average of any previous year. He could see no reason for discouragement.

If he had no reason for discouragement, he had at least plenty of subjects of concern, the inevitable problems of the university president or acting president. These may be roughly classified as physical, academic, trustee-connected, and human.

Of the physical problems the first was sanitation. Students sickened and died at an alarming rate. Six undergraduates died in 1876–77 and five in 1877–78, out of a student body of about five hundred. Pro-portionately, that would mean the death of a hundred students annually today. We are inclined to forget, if we ever knew, how familiar was mortality only a few years ago.

Russel suspected that the drinking water, drawn from Fall Creek and unguarded campus springs, was in part responsible. A committee, A. A. Breneman and Caldwell of Chemistry and Law of Veterinary Medicine, was appointed, on 11 June 1880, to survey health conditions. Breneman investigated the sanitary systems of Ithaca and Geneva and reported a menacing lack of drainage and sewerage. His report aroused great local indignation and a demand for his dismissal. White wrote Sage (5 February 1881): "I would see the whole of [the University] tumbled into Cayuga Lake sooner than dismiss this young man because he had aroused prejudice by attempting to call the people to a sense of their duty to themselves, their children, and the University." But Breneman, if not exactly dismissed, was encouraged to seek his fortune elsewhere; and the campus springs continued to supply drinking water.[7]

Sundry small and inexpensive improvements were made on the campus. The electric arc lights of Professor Anthony were installed in the belfry of Sage Chapel in January 1879. (These, as we have already noted, were the first outdoor arc lights serving a public purpose.) The telephone came to us early, a year after its debut at the Centennial Exposition of 1876. Professor Anthony obtained a set of Mr. Bell's apparatus and conversed daily with Instructor George S. Moler over a mile and a half of wire, as easily as if the two were in the same room.[8] Some sort of campus system was in operation in 1879. Russel wrote White, on 20 June: "J. W. Williams has just telephoned me. . . ." The Comstocks had an instrument; in this same year Anthony connected it with a concert hall downtown, and with two receivers the Comstocks listened raptly to the music. This was perhaps the first example of music broadcasting.

A happy incident was that of the Ostrander Elms. White tells the story in the *Autobiography*.

As Mr. Sage and myself were one day looking over matters upon the grounds, there came along, in his rough wagon, a plain farmer from a distant part of the county, a hard-working man of very small means, who had clearly something upon his mind. Presently he said: "I would very much like to do something for the university if I could. I have no money to give;

---

[7] The Faculty called the attention of the Executive Committee, on 14 June 1883, to the importance of a supply of wholesome filtered drinking water (Faculty Records).

[8] Anthony to ADW, 15 Sept. 1877.

but I have thought that possibly some good elm-trees growing on my farm might be of use to you, and if you wish them I will put them in the best condition and bring them to you."

The trees were planted in the spring of 1877, bordering East Avenue, and now for nearly ninety years they have given beauty and grateful shade.

Russel's academic problems were troublesome but mostly minor. In the face of declining income and enrollments he could expect to make no important appointments or even replacements; the best he could do was to hold the staff together and to carry on during the master's absence. He knew, as we all do, that an academic organism must either grow or dwindle; it cannot lead an arrested life. He was forced to watch a gradual dwindling, and to listen noncommittally to student complaints of faculty incompetence and of educational inadequacies.[9]

With some of the complaints the faculty could only agree. The Physics Department, well staffed but shamefully housed and insufficiently equipped, was a disgrace to a university with a special regard for technology. Anthony wrote White (6 June 1880) that Cornell's offerings and requirements were below those of Stevens, M.I.T., and Pennsylvania. "We are twenty years behind the times," he said.

Some dissatisfaction with Civil Engineering was manifest. An article of mysterious origin in the New York *Times*, in May 1881, referred to Director Fuertes as "a dishonest, incompetent Barnum." Fuertes, deeply wounded, resigned. But since the complaints represented only a minority view the trustees refused (14 May 1881) to accept his resignation and expressed their entire confidence in him.

The Department of Mechanic Arts also knew a revolt in 1878, a recrudescence of that of 1876.

Agriculture, fortunately, throve during the hard years. Academically, the scientific bases of agriculture became more clearly defined than before. Young Comstock's pioneer work in economic entomology served well. Isaac P. Roberts, with resistless energy, found his own way toward scientific agriculture, though he says: "For many years I felt that the College of Agriculture existed only by sufferance and that I had no real sympathy or cooperation from the Trustees. I sometimes wonder now why I struggled on—why I did not quit the job; and I can only suppose that it was because the dream of what might be done still lured me on."[10]

[9] *Cornell Era*, 29 April 1881.
[10] *Autobiography of a Farm Boy* (Ithaca, 1946), p. 130.

On the practical side, Roberts built a proper barn in 1880 (on the site of the Agricultural College), collected a fine herd, and made the farm a thing of beauty to visiting agriculturists.

In 1879 Roberts formally established the Cornell University Experiment Station. This followed by only four years the creation of the first Experiment Station in America, at Middletown, Connecticut. The work of the Cornell station was hampered by its lack of any funds at all. Nevertheless, enthusiastic volunteers did enough experimental work in dairying, economic entomology, agricultural chemistry, horticulture, and field crops to publish in 1880 a First Annual Report of 133 pages. The printing cost of $250 was paid by Miss Jennie McGraw.

In general, the historian finds little to record concerning the academic process during these doubtful years. In classrooms and laboratories the daily tasks were performed, sometimes ill and often well. Happily or reluctantly, the young were formed for their future tasks, and here and there a student had in classroom or in study a small revelation, of understanding or of beauty. Florence Kelley '82 remembered with delight Cornell's freedoms and its intellectual seriousness. "No one, so far as I know, read a daily paper, or subscribed for a monthly or a quarterly. Our current gossip was Froude's *Life of Carlyle*." [11] We should not let the news of disaffection and discord dim the fact that the worthy work of education went steadily on.

The trustees, lacking an effective mediator with the faculty, regarded it with uncomprehending distrust. Some professors had indiscreetly allowed their names to be used in manifestoes of free-thinking societies. James E. Oliver had been announced—though without his knowledge or consent—as a cospeaker with the archatheist Robert G. Ingersoll. Such men, said Henry W. Sage (12 September 1880), must be rooted out. On 5 January 1881 the Executive Committee resolved on a purge. Oliver and Jones of Mathematics, Wing and Breneman of Chemistry, Stebbins of French would be "eliminated." And how about abolishing Architecture, and Professor Babcock with his Department of Architecture? T. F. Crane, Sage added, was too weak to be advanced to a professorship.

President White, informed of the proposed decimation, replied from Berlin (5 February 1881) that Oliver was a great mathematician, but let him go. We could part with Jones and Stebbins, but we should keep Wing and Breneman, and we should hold on to Architecture, in the hope of better times.

[11] *Survey Graphic*, 1 Feb. 1927, p. 559.

Fortunately for Russel, he was not called upon to eliminate his colleagues. The purge was left for President White to accomplish, and when it came it was only mildly cathartic.

The routine of undergraduate life was broken by changes and innovations, minuscular in history's perspective, but momentous in their time. Military training, optional from 1876, was again compulsory in 1880. Saturday classes were inaugurated in 1881; they provoked great student indignation and a giant petition for their abolition. Fraternities and clubs lived their satellite lives, many exploding, some settling into permanent orbit. Psi Upsilon came in 1876, Beta Theta Pi in 1879. The first sorority, Kappa Alpha Theta, was organized in 1881. The year 1880–81 was marked by a war between fraternities and independents, with two sets of class officers and two rival class-day programs in June. After a long struggle the Cornell chapter of Phi Beta Kappa was chartered in 1882 and formally organized in the following year.

The *Cornell Sun,* one of the first college daily newspapers, appeared on 16 September 1880, to the fury of the *Era.* It was originally a four-page folder, of about the dimensions of the book you hold in your hand. Its inspiring force proceeded from William B. Hoyt '81, later a prominent lawyer in Buffalo.

The Cascadilla Dramatic Association was organized in 1880. Goldwin Smith bore the expense of making a theatre in Cascadilla Place. *She Stoops to Conquer* was produced, with a cast including faculty and women students. *The Rivals* had an ambitious production in the following year.

The Glee Club sang, the debate clubs debated, the Philidor Chess Club made its pondered moves. The Cornell Congress argued great issues, in imitation of the Congress in Washington. Undergraduate life continued in its accustomed patterns, little heeding the troubles of the administration.

In the world of sport the baseball team played in intercollegiate games without achieving any great triumphs. No football games are recorded. We tried vainly to impose "Cornell football" on others; we were late in adopting the Rugby rules evolved by Harvard and Yale. A Hare and Hounds Club and a Lawn Tennis Club were formed in 1879. In track and field we attempted no intercollegiate meets, but we had local field days from time to time. These incorporated such picturesque contests as three-legged races, sack races, and the hundred yards backward. Though most of the records are not noteworthy,

Robert H. Treman '78 threw a baseball 377 feet 6 inches, breaking the intercollegiate record for the year.[12]

Rowing remained the great sport at Cornell. But after Cornell's resounding victories in 1875 and 1876 Yale withdrew from the Rowing Association of American Colleges. Cornell's outcries of scorn and contumely still faintly resound. The next year Harvard withdrew, and the Association collapsed. The general fear of Cornell made opponents wary and hard to find. Then the lack of Cornell triumphs caused student interest to wane, and with waning interest the crews deteriorated. But in 1880 a resurgent four-oared boat defeated Penn and Columbia on Lake George. This crew, riding a wave of enthusiasm, was sent abroad. It rowed for the Stewards' Cup at Henley, and in a challenge race with Hertford College, Oxford, and in one for the Thames Challenge Cup, and in one with the Vienna Club, on the Danube. In all four races Cornell came in last. In the Vienna race our stroke collapsed. Embittered partisans accused him, on no good evidence, of having sold out to our enemies or to Ithaca gamblers. This first invasion of Europe by our athletes was a pride-humbler.

The undergraduates, male and female, of these years were a serious and worthy group, though perhaps less serious, and in the end less distinguished, than those of the first decade. Some of them remained with Cornell as teachers and administrators. Albert W. Smith '78 became Dean of Engineering, Acting President, and the campus's beloved "Uncle Pete." George Lincoln Burr '81 was our famous professor of medieval history. Many—such as Walter C. Kerr '79, Willard Beahan '78, Ira A. Place '81—rose to importance in industry and engineering. Harriet May Mills '79 became a leading suffragist and worker for hospital reform. A Rockefeller Institute building in New York was recently named in honor of Theobald Smith '81, pioneer of bacteriology, who demonstrated the transmission of infectious diseases through the agency of insects, and thus opened the way to our knowledge of germ-borne diseases. (I said this before, but repetition is an academic virtue.) Herman M. Biggs '82, director of the Rockefeller Institute for Medical Research, is to be credited in some part with the conquest of tuberculosis. Edward M. House '82 was the Gray Eminence of

[12] There is something doubtful about this record. The *Era* (16 Oct. 1879, p. 43) gives the distance as 377' 6", and Robert J. Kane (*Forty Years at Cornell* [Ithaca, n.d.], p. 5) accepts this figure. But W. T. Hewett (*Cornell University: A History* [New York, 1905], III, 348) gives 337' 4". I choose to err on the side of magnanimity.

President Wilson. John A. Dix '83 was Governor of New York State. The women students settled into their destined place in Sage College. Their numbers remained about constant: 67 in 1876–77, 59 in 1880–81, in the proportion of 14.5 per cent to the entire student body.

President White, obedient to his liberal convictions and to European practice, had at first left the women free of restrictions, save such as they themselves might impose. Their behavior was to be ruled only by their innate feminine virtue. Early testimonies, as those of Florence M. Kelley, who entered in 1876, suggest that this freedom was not abused. But Henry W. Sage, authoritarian by temper, and no doubt provoked by "incidents" of which no record remains, was dissatisfied. He drew up a set of rules, mostly concerned with the tight closing of Sage College at 10 P.M. He provided also for the appointment of a Lady Superintendent.[13] The coeds met, and in what Sage characterized contemptuously as "town meetings" accepted the rules, except the proposal of a Lady Superintendent. They insisted, as they have always insisted, that they were quite able to superintend themselves. They appointed their own committee to enforce the rules.

The attitude of faculty and men students toward the women was mixed. The Saturday night dances in Sage were well attended. Willard Fiske, a militant anticoedist, reported to White (27 November 1877) that there was a sad amount of heartburning among the male boarders in Sage, that dancing and flirtation were rife, with the faculty involved, and that he had great difficulty in keeping one of the Psi U freshmen from spending most of his time there. Mrs. Anna Botsford Comstock recalled, with perhaps vindictive feminism, "a slim girl of the class of '79 who succeeded in keeping engaged for an entire year to two Cornellians who were room-mates, without either suspecting her double devotion." [14]

The women claimed and received their due, as in membership on the publications, including the *Sun*. At the sophomore class supper in January 1878 eleven of the thirteen women sophomores attended, alleging that they had paid their class dues and were entitled to all the benefits therefrom. "It is a great step forward," wrote Russel to White, on 27 January 1878. "Everything went off very nicely except that the boys stayed till 4 A.M., claiming that they had to wait for the going

---

[13] Executive Committee Minutes, 20 June 1879, C.U. Archives. The report was accepted by the committee on 6 Sept. 1879.

[14] Anna B. Comstock, in *A Half-Century at Cornell* (Ithaca, 1930), p. 72.

of the ladies before they could have their fun." But the *Era* termed the ladies' invasion "highly improper."

On the other hand, extramural and intramural opposition to co-education gathered consistency. President Noah Porter of Yale made a resounding denunciation of the practice, in October 1877, and a flurry of old-gentlemanly editorials appeared in the metropolitan press.

A code of campus behavior was gradually formulated. Men and women did not recognize their acquaintances of the opposite sex in classrooms or on the campus, and they did not walk together. Opinions differ as to the significance of this public obliviousness. "We were not insulted, only tolerated and ignored," remembers Ellen Coit Brown '82. The cold-shouldering she attributes to "a masculine pose carried out to preserve their self-respect and eminence." But Florence M. Kelley '82 recalls only the happy associations of young men and women, which led to many happy marriages.[15]

And there were some demonstrations, which I suppose an anthropologist would classify among the coming-of-age rites of American culture. The boys turned the hose on the girls' sole retreat on the quadrangle, a soil-closet in Morrill Hall. A primitive panty-raid (the first in history?) occurred on or about 1 June 1878. The Sage laundry was forcibly entered, and articles of underclothing were plucked from the tubs and flown from the steeple of Sage Chapel.[16]

In short (to take the high view) the male and female adolescents were forced to evolve a social structure for which there was little precedent in American culture. Youthful attractions were balanced by hostilities and group rivalries, themselves evidence of pronounced sex-consciousness. Since the men so far outnumbered the women, the men imposed their dominance. Under the eye of authority a *modus vivendi* was reached, a cold war marked by frequent raids, in which often a woman would return, dragging a human captive, to her rejoicing camp.

Student conduct and misconduct demanded, as ever, a large share of the faculty's attention. Most of the matters of official concern fell under familiar captions: smoking, drinking, gambling, mass violence.

Smoking on the campus was banned by faculty action on 10 October 1873. For a year or two defiant students were summoned for violation

[15] Ellen Coit Brown Elliott, "Early Cornell" (MS, C.U. Archives), p. 5; *Survey Graphic*, 1 Feb. 1927, p. 559.
[16] Russel to ADW, 2 June 1878.

of the rules. They pointed to the example set them by more-defiant professors. By 1880 the faculty, in retreat, proposed that smoking be prohibited in halls, public rooms, and around the doors of buildings. Thus began the long invasion by the cigarette, which by the mid-twentieth century conquered even the stronghold of the classroom. At this writing only Sage Chapel stands inviolate.

We hear little about drinking. Alcohol was consumed mostly in the form of beer, purveyed in downtown saloons to which the faculty eye did not penetrate. There was, to be sure, a brief agitation about lager beer in the lunch boxes of certain students in the Chemical Laboratory.

News of gambling in fraternity sancta came to the faculty's attention. In December 1876 some village gamblers were arrested, and one of these declared that there was as much faro playing in the Zeta Psi rooms as in his own. In the following April the Zeta Psi's and the Chi Phi's were summoned to show cause why their clubs should not be disbanded on account of their bad moral influence. Evidently they showed sufficient cause.

Of darker sins there are occasional hints.[17] But sexual misdemeanors were certainly rare, as they were in the social group of nineteenth-century America which was dominated by the Puritan ethic. We find an intriguing item in a letter of Russel's (15 January 1878) concerning an applicant for entrance, the son of a double millionaire in New York, who was arrested for trying to set fire to the Clinton House and the Tompkins House. However, this hotel-hatred is psychiatrist's business, not an example of student mores.

Youthful ebullience occasionally found an outlet in forms sanctioned by tradition. In February 1880 the undergraduates broke up a traveling show in the Wilgus Opera House. The action was a harsh but apparently justified form of theatrical criticism. The battle continued into the street, against the young townies whose critical standards were less elevated. Annually the freshman and sophomore banquets launched hostilities. To such manifestations the authorities were resigned.

On the whole, the years were quiet ones. They were, however, years of decline, in the University's enrollment, prestige, competence, and morale. Its high initial hopes and its crusading educational spirit were not forgotten, but they were overlaid with a mood of indifference, even of discouragement. Cornell could easily have sunk to the status of a small regional institution, unambitious and fairly content.

[17] ADW Papers, 29 April and 21 June 1877, 31 Dec. 1878.

Such a fate was averted by an apparently unimportant event. Henry W. Sage, at sixty-six, decided to retire from active business and to remove from Brooklyn to Ithaca. He built the fine house on State Street which is now the University Infirmary and there took up his residence in 1880. He could now devote most of his attention and energy to Cornell.

His inspection of the state of the University convinced him that three actions were necessary. The President must return to his post. The urgent needs for instruction and equipment must be met and money found to meet them. And Cornell's deplorable reputation for irreligion must be combated.

The first action was facilitated by a resolution of the alumni in June 1880, praying for the President's return. With this in hand, the trustees moved that they earnestly called upon the President "to resume his official and personal relations with the University at the earliest practical day." Sage supported the resolution with a personal letter (15 June 1880), conjuring White to heed the summons. "There is no remedy other than your return. The University must have a President who will be permanently and steadily here. We want assurances of your views and purposes." Francis M. Finch informed White (18 June 1880) that there was a general, and hurtful, impression that the President did not mean to return. "Something strong and courageous must be done or Cornell is dead." A number of the faculty let it be known that they favored the President's resignation.[18]

The annoyance of Mr. White on receiving such messages in his Berlin ministry was extreme. He was enjoying thoroughly his diplomatic eminence. His implication in great affairs, his association with the world's movers and makers, made the troubles of the little lone college by Cayuga seem very insignificant. He must have felt the truth of one of Russel's envenomed shafts (26 December 1879): "You and Fiske, used to talk to nobody smaller than Bismarck and the Empress, may think these uncertainties small things, but I can assure

---

[18] Hiram Corson wrote his son Eugene, on 25 June 1880: "Prof. Russel has worked hard and faithfully, and this indirect condemnation of his management is very unfair. . . . It's crediting President White with too much (if the University has gone down, which I don't admit) to lay it to his absence. He has never troubled himself about the details of the Administration. I think he ought to resign. For if he comes back, he'll do as he always has done—whip off every week or two—and give a broken course of lectures which would be of very little service to the University" (Corson Letter-Books).

you that it is easier to entertain two prime ministers than to make two assistant professors keep time."

White's first response to the trustees' appeal was to send in his resignation. Its acceptance, he told Finch, would be a happy release. He had other things to do, especially historical writing.

Sage, without, apparently, bothering to assemble the Executive Committee, refused to accept the resignation. He wrote White a fine letter of exhortation (13 August 1880). Make Cornell your life work! For mankind's sake! We don't want half of you! "This work is worth the whole of any man, and should have a man who has no higher, no other aspiration!" (But at the same time Sage wrote his son Dean that White, sensitive as a woman, needed gentling.)

White yielded, and promised to return in the following year, 1881.

Sage's second action was to obtain money for the University's renovation. There were three ways to do this: to sell the western lands at current prices, to borrow, or to spend capital from endowment.

Sage boldly decided on the third course. In the summer the Treasurer, George W. Schuyler, consented to advance $50,000 from capital.[19]

Sage then turned to the promotion of land sales. According to the oft-told, the consecrated story, Sage, in opposition to the entire Board, refused to sell lands at the current prices and insisted in holding on for eventual profit.[20] Contemporary records suggest that the matter was more complex. Russel wrote White (24 September 1880) that sales were going well, but "Mr. Sage is impatient, calls these small sales, and wishes to put the whole into the hands of a Detroit man to sell them with a rush." Hiram Sibley was opposed to any such lump sale. At this moment a New York syndicate asked an option to buy the remaining timberlands, 275,000 acres, for $1,250,000, or $4.75 an acre. Sage favored granting the option, for Russel wrote (30 September 1880) that he had voted with Sage, against his own better judgment, in favor.

The option, after a month's extension, was not taken up. The company asked for a second extension. It was evidently at this point that Sage changed his views, while most of the Board were tempted beyond endurance by the prospect of getting rid of the lands. Sage insisted

[19] Russel to ADW, 1 Aug. 1880.
[20] Especially S. D. Halliday, *History of the Federal Land Grant* (Ithaca, 1905), pp. 48–49; and J. G. Schurman, *A Generation at Cornell* (New York, 1898), pp. 18–21.

on raising the price to $1,500,000, which would, and did, discourage the purchasing syndicate.

The brief mirage of golden ease faded before the thirsty university. Sage was plentifully blamed for missing the chance of selling the lands. He then proposed an expedient, which appears to be novel in the history of university finance. The lands were funded and denominated a University investment of $1,000,000. This sum was charged with interest at 5 per cent, and $50,000 annually was withdrawn from the Endowment Fund and credited to the University's income account. The transaction might well seem doubtful to an auditor, as it certainly does to a mere household accountant, for the investment was only an assumption, a hope, while the interest payments were in real money from the endowment. As it turned out, rapidly rising timber prices and profitable sales made the dubious procedure unnecessary after two years.

At least, Sage's course of action was courageous. Even more courageous was the action taken by the Board, under Sage's impulsion. In this dark moment of adversity and despondence, with bankruptcy looming, the Executive Committee resolved, on 18 December 1880, to appropriate $101,075, or so much thereof as might be necessary, for the following purposes:

To erect and equip a building for the Physical Dept.	$50,000
To erect and equip a building to accommodate Veterinary and the Anatomical section of Dr. Wilder's Department	10,000
To erect a greenhouse and other equipment of the Botanical Department	10,000
For Library	20,000
For Civil Engineering and other Departments	10,000
For miscellaneous purposes	1,075
	$101,075

The appropriation was deficit financing, for no statement appears as to the source of the money. But this tangible expression of confidence in Cornell's future did much to redress campus morale.

The third item on Sage's agenda was the combating of Cornell's reputation for irreligion.

In these years the American War of Religion came to its climax. Scientists were converted one by one to the evolutionary doctrine and fell in behind the banners of Darwin, Huxley, and Tyndall, who could be readily identified with Lucifer, Apollyon, and Beelzebub. Robert G. Ingersoll (who was born by Seneca Lake) and other minions of hell lectured to enormous audiences, on such themes as "Some Mistakes of Moses." The forces of orthodoxy rallied, and under the symbol of the Open Bible fell upon their enemies. Of these enemies the chiefest were the colleges and universities, where free thought was likely to fester into infidelity. Of such infections only the college presidents were unaware. A religious journal in 1880 asked the leading college presidents if they permitted the teaching of the doctrine that man is evolved from beasts; the answer, with some qualifications, was "No."

Cornell, the godless university, was the main target of the denominational attacks. In pulpits the country over Cornell was denounced and threatened with God's wrath in the next world and boycotting in this. A Presbyterian divine frankly told Vice-President Russel that Cornell could expect no mercy from the churches until it should impose instruction in the dogmas of historical Christianity. An Ithaca preacher informed the Baptists of New York State that of 476 Cornell students only 76 could be called Christians. He wrote to the *Era* that Andrew D. White's influence is to discredit the authenticity of the Scriptures, that his lectures uphold rationalism, destroy belief in miracles, that he opposes soulsaving, is hostile to the gospel of the grace of God, and that in general he thinks doctrines of slight importance.[21]

The students joyously helped blacken the University's fair name. A group amused themselves, in October 1878, by forming the Young Men's Infidel Association. At one meeting it was moved that God be declared out of order. The motion was defeated, on the ground that God was not a member. The society was of course a joke, but student humor is often baffling to outsiders. The religious press picked up the story and enlarged upon it with delicious horror.[22]

How much of the accusations of the orthodox was true? Some part, certainly. White, Russel, and others were rationalists by conviction,

[21] Russel to ADW, 31 Oct. 1880; *Era*, 18 April 1879. Jennie McGraw, representing an important segment of Ithaca opinion, was disturbed by the moral failings of the University under Russel. She wrote Judge Boardman (8 Sept. 1879): "It *must* have a *head* that shall be felt as an intellectual and moral power. . . . Though I confess to being a miserable sinner myself, I don't propose to help make others so in a wholesale way."

[22] *Era*, 1878–79, *passim*, especially p. 112.

and they would not hide their conviction from inquirers. Russel summed up Cornell's stand with his usual cogency:

We have taken the ground of secular education and we believe that in it are involved several things important to society. Every institution that passes beyond the established lines must be opposed. The consequent injury is the price we pay for liberty to improve society, and we must pay it until society is improved enough to vindicate us.[23]

The liberalism of Russel and others, their appeals to reason, were surely unsettling to some young men who had grown up in the closed circles of evangelical orthodoxy. But others found the religious radicalism very mild. William B. Hoyt (the founder of the *Cornell Sun*) came to Cornell as a freshman in 1877. A sharp-witted youth, he wrote his brother two months later:

Before I came to Cornell I heard much about the *infidelity* and atheism of its professors. I have not seen much of this, but in Vice-President Russel's lectures on Roman History you can detect a little of what is known as *free thinking*. For instance, speaking of the manner in which, the legend says, Romulus and Remus were left in a forest to die, and were found and brought up by a wolf, he said: "You remember in about the same way Moses was taken out of the bulrushes." Many of the professors are believers, and I think the charge of Cornell being an infidel institution is groundless.[24]

Another significant testimony is contained in a letter to the *Era* of 15 November 1878. The writer alleges that "half the ministers that come [to Sage Chapel] represent the loosest element in their own sect, and think 'infidel Cornell' a good place to air the theories that at home they would only dare to hint."

At any rate, "infidel Cornell" was a current phrase, and the world sought an exemplar and culprit, and found him in the person of the Vice-President. Lyman Abbott, editor of the *Christian Union* and a celebrated Congregational divine, visited Cornell in 1881. In his paper he described Russel as a man whose nonreligious convictions were very pronounced, who had given the University a reputation of positive irreligion. The decadence in the number of students, he said, was positive testimony to the evil effects of free inquiry.

This was most unfair to Russel. He was of course a Unitarian, and Unitarians were then regarded by the orthodox as so many Sadducees. He was of a cold, skeptical habit, contemptuous of the excesses of

[23] Russel to ADW, 31 Oct. 1880.
[24] Communicated by W. B. Hoyt's daughter, Mrs. Ansley Sawyer.

evangelical practice. But he was certainly not irreligious. He wrote White (24 February 1881), that he had "for many years begun the day by an effort in prayer to overcome any possible unkind feeling toward anyone." His cast of mind commended him to White, convinced of the perpetual warfare of the hero, Science, against the villain, Theology. But White, more astute than Russel, was careful to bring God into every public pronouncement about the University. Russel, after his dismissal, wrote plaintively to White (6 January 1882): "More than once the opinion was expressed that it was absurd to object to my irreligion, as it was called, and to pass yours over."

Russel's "irreligion" was the cause of a widening rift with Henry W. Sage. One *casus belli* was Henry Ward Beecher. Sage was a parishioner in Brooklyn and a faithful friend of Beecher, who was counted a religious liberal, a modernist of his time. During the scandalrich trial of Beecher for alienating the affections of a friend's wife, Sage proposed to White (4 May and 29 May 1875) that Beecher be invited to the ceremonies at the opening of Sage College, as an expression of Cornell's confidence in him. Beecher did not, apparently, attend. In the following year Sage insisted that Beecher be asked to preach in Sage Chapel. Beecher came, and preached brilliantly, but Russel objected to his lodging in the preacher's suite in Sage College. (Did he fear this wolf in clerical clothing?) During Russel's acting presidency he did not invite Beecher to preach again, despite strong hints from Sage. But Sage later said that he was unaware of Russel's opposition.[25]

Beecher's trial, in which the jury disagreed, associated in the public mind religious liberalism and immorality. Sage felt himself inculpated. He had indeed passed through a free-thinking stage. Russel wrote White (31 October 1880) that Sage "is always in a fever lest somebody should do something to make people think him an infidel. I shall not soon forget his expressing to me his doubts about the evidences of immortality. . . . Brooklyn orthodoxy, or rather Beecher orthodoxy, is very thin but excessively sensitive to reputation." If we accept this statement at its face value, we may conclude that the sacrifice of Russel was an expiatory offering.

At the trustees' meeting in June 1880 Sage took the floor and made a strong speech on the menace to Cornell of its reputation for infidelity. On the following day General Stewart L. Woodford devoted a good

[25] Sage to ADW, 8 and 12 May 1876, 10 and 12 May 1886.

deal of his Commencement address to the same subject, thus spreading the evil he was trying to combat.

To Sage, Russel was the symbol, if not the author, of Cornell's ill repute. He proceeded to the conclusion that Russel must go. Of this conclusion Russel was unconscious. Nor was he aware that he had managed to offend other members of the Executive Committee. He had outraged John McGraw by supporting the Treasurer's request that he pay up his promised donation. Russel explained his action in a characteristic letter to White (23 February 1876): "Duty is duty, and I cannot yield a hair of what I have said. . . . I will not lower myself in my own esteem for any number of such." Further, Russel alienated Judge Douglass Boardman, second only to Sage in influence. In an anguished discussion in the Executive Committee (19 February 1880), Russel inquired how it happened that while our funds were invested at 5¾ per cent we had for several years been paying Boardman 7 per cent on a note held by him. Russel innocently proposed that Boardman's note be liquidated. In the following year (28 March) he discovered that "the man who hates me with a perfect hate is Boardman."

The Executive Committee met in a historic session on 3 January 1881. Russel was absent. It was moved that Russel be asked to resign his vice presidency and his professorship at the end of the college year. And, as has already been reported, the committee moved to "eliminate" four professors and to question the status of others.

Russel wrote White, on the following day, that next to the death of his wife he had never suffered such a shock. He called on Sage for an explanation. Sage gave two reasons: first, disharmony in the faculty and distrust of Russel's leadership; second, Russel's determination to carry out his own policies independently of others. Even granting this, said Russel, how do such reasons disqualify me for teaching French and history? Sage, he wrote, "took the ground that the Trustees, when they believed a person to be injurious to the University, had a right to get rid of him on that mere ground. . . . The true reason is a determination to try and change the reputation of the University in the matter of religion." Since, he continued, the Charter expressly forbids any outward objection to any teacher on the score of religion, Sage "had to give reasons which were no reasons, or take the ground that the Trustees are above reasons."

The trustees took frankly the position that they were above reasons.

The analogy with business was clear in the minds of these businessmen. If a business is going badly, the directors fire the responsible manager and try to get a better one. There was no use talking about an employee's rights. Who had ever heard, in 1881, of a worker's rights to his job?

Russel asked the committee to state the charges against him and called for an investigation. Sage replied blandly that there were no charges and hence there was nothing to investigate.

The principle of absolute control by the trustees was thus clearly stated. Russel saw in its application not only a threat to academic freedom and "tenure" (though he did not use the word), but also an open indication that the Executive Committee was trying to change Cornell from a liberal to an illiberal institution. He suspected a plot on the part of Ithaca clerics and their powerful parishioners to capture Cornell for evangelical Protestantism.

White, from Berlin, made a strong but vain appeal to the trustees to retain Russel in his professorship, if not in the vice presidency.

For some time Russel refused to resign, insisting that he must be discharged, so that the trustees' action and motives would be public. But by 7 March he begins to waver, for fear of his own future. He was sixty-seven years old, penniless, with a large family; he could see no haven other than Cornell. He tried to associate White in his own disaster, certainly an impolitic move: "One of the Trustees puts me alongside of you when he speaks of going out of the way in lectures on history to attack Christianity." (White had a famous lecture on the falsity of modern miracles, which was taken to be by implication an attack on the authenticity of Christ's miracles.) Russel continues:

Outsiders have been talking a long time about a plan of capturing the University for the Church. One of the professors said to me last evening that the Trustees would be as glad to have you go as I. . . . Your intellect and tact will control Sage, and he controls all the others. . . . Oliver accepts my fate as a certain sign of his.

Disturbed, White drafted a letter to Trustee Henry B. Lord. He inquired whether the action in the case of Russel and Oliver was based on a desire to propitiate clerical influence. "I would not for any number of Universities see the right of any Professor abridged to speak the simple truth as history reveals it to him." Some sectarians, he continues, are trying to capture Cornell for evangelicalism. It is impossible to build a university on such a foundation. "If this be the theory on which changes are made in the Faculty, I am just as obnoxious as Mr. Russel." In this mood, he made out a formal resignation of his presidency. He wrote to Sage on 17 March: "I am not the man to carry out the policy which the Trustees think necessary. . . . I have lost something of my old energy and vigor; I am fettered by attachments to old colleagues. . . . I enclose my resignation; and it is final."

It was not final at all. After a little reflection, he decided not to send the resignation or the accompanying letter. Perhaps he was moved in this decision by a letter (16 March) from Willard Fiske, who alone had the right to speak roughly to him.

If you had not insisted upon forcing an utterly distasteful locum tenens upon the University—upon making Trustees, Faculty, and students utterly miserable by placing them in contact with a man whom they dislike and distrust, there would have been little difficulty. . . . The one unfortunate act of your life . . . gradually lessening the prestige of the institution. . . . The presence of R is a deadly blow.

And on 28 March: "You would be crazy to keep R on as Professor."

Russel was at length persuaded to submit his resignation, perhaps by the promise of a year's severance pay—though I find no indication that this was ever paid. In his letter of resignation he recounts the circumstances, observes that no charges are made against him, and that the trustees feel no obligation to give reasons for dismissing professors. The facts of the case will soon be known throughout the educational world, and they will be interpreted as an abandonment of the Founder's ideas and an effort to bring the University into line with popular theology. The reputation of Cornell will be dimmed.

Such institutions are not business enterprises, nor are professors clerks or servants, nor have Trustees any right to look down on them, ignore their claims, or treat them summarily . . . They must be free. No one near being a first-class man will work long under a whip, nor can any professor do a University his best service while he feels in danger of losing his place in spite of success in his department and good conduct. The professors move this University.

Sage describes the document (to White, 12 April) as "by turns arrogant, threatening, and soft and tender as a weeping woman. It about equally excited and repelled sympathy; but it rendered impossible any other course than a prompt acceptance."

The matter was now public. Great excitement, which Sage describes as a mutiny, reigned on the campus. The *Sun* (11 April 1881) admitted

Russel's unpopularity, inevitable in the circumstances, but concluded: "We fail to find the shadow of a reason sufficient to warrant such an action." The *Era* (15 April) protested vigorously against the manner of Russel's ousting. "He has the hearty sympathy of every student for the indignity that was offered him by the Executive Committee in their apparently hasty, arbitrary, and inconsiderate manner of demanding and afterwards accepting his resignation." The *Era* pointed out that the trustees as a body had not been consulted.

The seniors drew up a protest, as did the women of the University. A student mass meeting was held, at which George Lincoln Burr '81 presented a sharp protest to the trustees. The Washington alumni, headed by John Henry Comstock '74 and Leland O. Howard '77, protested. The Cornell alumni on the instructing staff issued a manifesto: "The Executive Committee seems to be governed by the local prejudices of the town; it appears to be willing to sacrifice the true spirit of the University in deference to the views which pervade and govern this community." The manifesto declared that the committee's contention that any member of the faculty may be removed without a stated reason subverts the spirit of freedom set forth in the Charter.

The faculty were torn by conflicting emotions. Many were secretly pleased to see Russel leave, by any agency. Crane wrote James Morgan Hart: "I think the real reason of his removal was to remove him from reach of the President, who for years has been absolutely in his power." [26] But the faculty recognized the threat to their own security. Judge Boardman chilled them by telling Professor Wilder that he or any other professor might be removed any day without any reason being assigned.

Letters from educators, perceiving the menace to academic freedom, poured in. Newspapers commented acridly on the state of affairs in Ithaca. The New York *Times* (8 May) quoted Sage as saying: "We have a right to dismiss every officer, from President to janitor." The *Times* reported that Fiske was about to be made President or Vice-President.

Russel was cheered by ovations and demonstrations in his favor. He seemed suddenly to have become popular. Yet his self-esteem had suffered a cruel blow. The old manner of humorous superiority disappears from his letters, giving place to endless self-questioning and self-justification. This reader of his papers, long his partisan, comes to

[26] 10 April 1881, Hart Papers.

realize that his stern Spartan ruggedness was soft at the core. He was not really very strong, or very wise.

White wrote mollifying letters to the faculty, assuring them that there was no need for alarm about security in their posts, that the spirit of genuine freedom was not endangered. The faculty would not have been mollified if they could have read Sage's letters to White. He said (10 May) that the trustees and faculty should be in harmony. "It is just possible that the only way to make them so will be to ask for the resignation of the whole body—then re-elect only such as we know we can work with." This suggestion had been soberly discussed in the committee. But by 24 May Sage was discouraged. "It has often seemed to me that my work here, based *I know* upon most worthy motives, is to be a waste—the fortune spent here little better than squandered."

White did his best, from far away, to still the tumult. The time element worked in favor of the trustees. By mid-June a good deal of the indignation had dwindled. Through White's efforts Russel obtained the post of acting professor of history at Brown. Many personal sympathies of his colleagues cooled.

At the trustees' meeting in June, Russel asked an examination of the affair by an impartial committee, with publication of its conclusions. The request was accepted and decently interred.

The trustees received at this meeting a remarkable memorial from the New York alumni, which may serve as a summary of the entire case. The University, said the alumni, has been injured by the retention on the faculty of certain incompetent and inefficient instructors, by the replacement of professors of national reputation by men of no standing, and by an undue effort to extend the scope of the University, thus restricting its efficiency and reducing the salary scale. The results have been the decrease in enrollment and the loss of efficient faculty members. The causes are the absence of the President and the dominance of the Executive Committee, which is composed of Ithaca residents, whether competent or incompetent. Such a body must infuse a narrow and provincial spirit into an institution intended to diffuse liberal culture; it is easily affected by local, personal, and social pressures; and it ignores the opinion of the outside public. The memorial proposes that the President be recalled and that management be delegated to a competent committee of the trustees.

The alumni meeting in Ithaca promised for a time to be exciting. A fiery group proposed to nominate Russel for alumni trustee. Nothing came of it. The Ithaca alumni turned out in full force and elected Mynderse Van Cleef '74 of Ithaca. Then everyone went home and busied himself with his own affairs.

The whole imbroglio did Cornell much harm. Moses Coit Tyler summed it up (24 June 1881) by writing that the wide publicity had given people the impression that Cornell was a run-down college under the control of men who treated a worthy old professor basely.

And so, one may agree, they did. Nevertheless, the reader who goes through the endless dispute may well conclude that the Executive Committee's purpose was sound, though its methods were inexcusable. Russel was not equal to the demands of the post he occupied—an extraordinarily difficult post, for it imposed on him responsibility without authority. He did his best, but better than his best was needed. The anger and vindictiveness he showed are evidence enough that if he had been retained as professor he would have been the center of every opposition to the trustees and their authority. Cornell's need was peaceful reconstruction, which the presence of a living martyr would surely have impeded.

The contretemps had at least two good results. It brought back our wandering President, reluctantly, to his post. (He wanted another crowning year as Minister in Berlin. He told M. C. Tyler that his return was the greatest sacrifice he had made for the University.[27] But after making up his mind to return he was recaptured by some of his old fervor.) The Russel affair also defined, in the minds of faculty and trustees, the principle of faculty tenure, though the word was not yet current. The matter was brought into the clear, where it has remained. The trustees gained a technical victory, maintaining their arbitrary right to dismiss a faculty member without assignment of cause. But they would never again venture to exercise that right. The public statements of Russel and his defenders had made the faculty's conception of academic tenure definite and dominant. The grim ghost of W. C. Russel would long haunt the meetings of the Executive Committee.

As for Russel, he brooded forever on his downfall, boring everyone with his justifications and recriminations. He perceived a well-matured plot, in which Willard Fiske was the chief villain. Fiske, with his rich wife's money, planned to oust Russel, and then White, and become president of the University. Or (a variant), Fiske must have informed Sage that his rich wife would give no money to Cornell while Russel

[27] M. C. Tyler, Diary, 23 Sept. 1881.

was at its head. Sage must then have dismissed Russel, to keep his hand in Jennie's pocket; and how well he was rewarded by Fiske's breaking his wife's will, which left her millions to Cornell! [28]

Thus the marble Old Roman turned out to be plaster after all.

[28] Russel to ADW, 10 July 1881, 24 May 1890.

XIII

The Great Will Case

ANDREW D. WHITE arrived in Ithaca from abroad on 16 September 1881, just in time for the opening of classes.

A fortnight later Jennie McGraw Fiske, wife of Willard Fiske, died. The romance of Willard Fiske and Jennie McGraw and the Great Will Case that ensued make the most dramatic story entwined in the history of Cornell.

Jennie McGraw was born on 14 September 1840. She was the only child of our benefactor, John McGraw. When he died, on 4 May 1877, Jennie, still unmarried, inherited most of his large estate. Disregarding the tuberculosis which already afflicted her, a number of suitors sighed for her hand. Among these was Willard Fiske, librarian and professor of north European languages. He wrote to her address a series of love poems, which he did not show her. He later explained that his reluctance to appear a fortune hunter had dissuaded him from confessing his love.

Jennie, wealthy and idle, decided to build a great house. She chose the superb site between University Avenue and Fall Creek now occupied by the Chi Psi house. The University rather reluctantly yielded the land to her. Architect W. H. Miller drew the plans for a great pile of Gothic, with donjon keeps, turrets, and bartizans, cunningly adapted to modern uses. Jennie went to Europe and bought furnishings and works of art, noteworthily (for $4,000) Randolph Rogers's sculpture, "The Pleiad Missing from the Sky," which is now in the Art Institute of Chicago (in the cellar, I suspect).

224

Willard Fiske, for reasons of health, obtained a leave of absence, without pay, in June 1879. (That was before sabbatical leave came to Cornell.) He went first to Iceland, then to London and Berlin. He made no effort to see Jennie, who was then in Italy.

In Berlin, Fiske brought Mr. White, American Minister, inside news of Cornell, and he added his own sharp opinions and judgments. His influence on White was uncanny. For instance, he wrote the President (6 July 1881): "If you will write a letter to T. F. Crane, proposing that he be Chairman of Spanish and Italian and ad interim Chairman of French, I will give the Lepsius to the Library." He enclosed a draft of the letter to be sent Crane, and White copied it out.

White, on his part, lent Fiske money. Shrewd Ithacans, putting two and two together, and knowing well that Fiske had nothing but his professorship, supposed that White and Sage were financing Fiske's courtship in order to bring the McGraw fortune to the University. But if this were so, Fiske certainly delayed long in fulfilling his part of the bargain.

In April 1880 Fiske joined, in Rome, Jennie McGraw, now an invalid with her doom evident. The courtship was brief. One may, if one pleases, let one's imagination play over the episode. Fiske, a bachelor of forty-eight, was, by principle or necessity, a person of apparently exemplary behavior. "He was not a so-called Ladies' man," says his adoring biographer, Horatio S. White. I see him as gentle and caressing in manner, not fiery, not demanding. And Jennie, nearly forty, weak, tired, perpetually coughing, longed for gentle, caressing affection, for a sensitive companion familiar with her own past, with home.

They became engaged in Venice. Fiske wrote White on 18 May 1880 a letter imbued with the sanctity of his love and his undertaking. He added in a postscript that his expenses had been heavy, that White had already advanced him 2,850 marks, and "Please send me 1500 by return mail, for the engagement ring, etc."

When White received the news, he noted in his diary: "Letter from Fiske announcing his engagement. Sent him March: 1500 [marks]; Fred [White's son] gave him at Rome: 1300; I gave him on his leaving Berlin: 950. Total loan to this date: 3750." White sent the 1,500 marks Fiske requested, and more, for on 17 September 1880 Fiske reckons that he has paid off the 5,650 marks owed to the two Whites.

It is all very curious. I think myself that White regarded his advances as friendly service, not as a University speculation. And I think that Fiske honestly loved Jennie McGraw, in his way, that he had hung back from seeing her for fear of making a marriage that would be deemed mercenary, that neither Sage nor White ever suggested subsidizing Fiske's courtship. But I think Fiske's conscious mind had to battle the ungentlemanly visitors from the subconscious. I think that Fiske, Sage, and White were quite capable of helping along the inevitable, as if absent-mindedly. And I think the quoted passage from White's diary reveals a train of associations too horrid for a high-minded President to admit, even to himself.

Not all Ithacans were so high-minded. Hiram Corson wrote his son Eugene, on 25 June 1880, before he had word of the engagement:

Fiske will be absent another year in Europe. He seems to think of nothing but self-indulgence. His self-respect must be very small, or he would not live as he does on other people's money. His expenses were paid by a student when he went to Iceland, and he must be living now on borrowed money. . . . [Fiske is courting Miss McGraw in Venice.] The Whites and the Sages are strongly urging the marriage. . . . She'll discover that he hasn't any other stuff in him than selfishness. A man that treats his mother and father as he does couldn't have any other. His interest in Europe is purely a *sensual* one.

The marriage took place in the American Legation in Berlin on 14 July 1880. Judge Douglass Boardman and the Whites were present. Before the marriage, at the suggestion of Boardman, Fiske signed a renunciation of any rights he might have to his wife's property by Prussian law. He refused even to look at his wife's will.

The couple journeyed southward as autumn came. In November they engaged in Cairo a dahabeah with a crew of seventeen for a trip up the Nile. It was a happy winter, despite Jennie's steadily worsening state. They came to Paris in June and learned from the doctors that she had only a few weeks to live. Her last wish was to die in Ithaca. The Fiskes crossed to New York, and arrived in Ithaca in early September, taking the gentler course by way of Syracuse and the Cayuga Lake steamer. The coachman who met them at the steamboat landing remembered:

Mrs. Fiske was sick, awful sick, and they had her propped up on pillows. I drove them up the hill to Professor Fiske's house, and the Professor sat on the front seat with me. We went right by the mansion that had been built for them to live in. Mrs. Fiske raised up from her pillows, looked at it, and said: "It surpasses all my expectations." That was all.[1]

[1] Ronald John Williams, *Jennie McGraw Fiske* (Ithaca, 1949), p. 65.

She never saw it again. She died on 30 September. Her body was carried to her great house, and thence to the grave. The house, having had a funeral for a housewarming, was accursed. With its craggy towers, its costumed magnificence, it had the look of dominance over time. But it was a mere pretense, a stone shell hiding a wooden frame, to be seasoned and fit for burning.

After the funeral Judge Boardman, executor, asked Fiske for Jennie's will. "Haven't you got it?" said Fiske. A search was made, in vain. Boardman, and White, were in consternation. For according to John McGraw's will, if his daughter should die intestate and without issue, all his property should go to his brother Joseph and his five children. A pretty how-de-do indeed!

At length Jennie's maid mentioned a handbag which had been emptied and thrown on a pile of junk to be removed from Fiske's attic. The handbag was found and examined; it was certainly empty. Again it was tossed on the junk pile. But someone suggested that it might contain a secret pocket. And indeed it did; and the pocket contained the will.

The will was probated without objection. By it Jennie gave to her husband $300,000; to Joseph McGraw and his children $550,000; and, not to mention minor bequests, to Cornell University $200,000 for a library, $50,000 for the development of McGraw Hall, and $40,000 for a student hospital, and, most importantly, her residual estate for unrestricted use. The total value of her estate was variously estimated, but Cornell's share would be at least a million.

The mansion presumably went to the University, as a part of the residual estate. White saw it as his dream home for an Art Gallery. Everyone supposed that Fiske would occupy it, as custodian for the University, though he realized that the income on $300,000 would not suffice to keep the house in proper style. Fiske proposed that the University should take care of the grounds. And, no doubt with a certain swagger, he made a peremptory proposal that the University immediately purchase $25,000 worth of library books and periodicals. This the trustees found inconvenient.

Fiske, Sage, and Boardman, all positive men with no liking for compromise, soon found themselves embroiled in disagreements. Obstacles occurred to prevent Fiske's occupation of the mansion. Boardman was very legalistic about Mrs. Fiske's property. The story went that Fiske asked for his wife's wedding ring and some personal souvenirs, and was told that he would have to buy them in open competition. (I find this story incredible, but evidently Ithaca did not.) On the other hand, Sage was offended by some of Fiske's actions, such as having dinner parties in the room in which Jennie had died, within two months of her death.[2] Fiske felt a marked coolness emanating from Sage and Boardman.

Why the chill? There are suggestions that Fiske's behavior in his European wanderings had not been impeccable.[3] Perhaps Sage and Boardman had wind of something discreditable and vowed that this scoundrel should have none of dear Jennie's money if they could keep it out of his hands.

On 12 May 1882 the state legislature passed a revision of the Cornell University Charter. The revisions were mostly perfunctory, such as the grant to the University of the right to employ three special constables. But a sharp, or suspicious, eye would have noted that Section Five, which in the original permitted the corporation to hold real and personal property to an amount not exceeding three millions of dollars, was now so worded that the limitation disappeared. Fiske's eye was not yet sufficiently sharp and suspicious.

His sense of frustration grew. He was summoned to a final settlement of accounts at a time when, as everyone knew, he would be in Europe. At length (20 June 1883) he resigned his University posts with the intention of residing abroad.

Just before sailing he had a call from an apprentice lawyer in Elmira, who revealed to him for the first time that Cornell was apparently debarred by its original charter from receiving Mrs. Fiske's bequest, that the charter revision was designed (though ex post facto) to remove this disability, that according to state law no decedent having a husband could leave more than half her estate to charity, that Judge Boardman, executor of Jennie's will, had sedulously—and improperly—refrained from informing Fiske of his rights, and that the trustees in the know had surrounded Fiske with a wall of concealment.

Fiske exploded. He later wrote to Judge Boardman (29 May 1890):

The intelligence instantly threw a deluge of the brightest light upon motives and actions which, up to that moment, had continued to be incomprehensible. I saw all the obscure and unpleasant incidents of the previous months— together with such acts as the deed of release signed at your instigation and

[2] M. C. Tyler, Diary, 5 Feb. 1882. The wedding-ring story was in the New York *Herald*, 19 Sept. 1904; copy in ADW Papers.

[3] See a curious letter to Fiske of 10 June 1880, in his papers. This was written just after his engagement.

as the singular bill passed through the legislature—group themselves into what I could not call by any other name than a conspiracy—as unworthy of those who participated in it as it was undeserved by its object. Even if you possess a slighter knowledge of human nature than is usually acquired by members of your profession, you must still, I think, understand that I became, to put it very mildly, furiously indignant, and did not hesitate to affix my signature to the papers which were to initiate the action. . . . I executed an assignment restoring to the institution, in case of my death, any sums which might be given me by the courts. It was a great pity, my dear Judge, and a great blunder, as I now look calmly back on it all, that Mr. Finch, at the very outset, or afterwards yourself, or Mr. Sage, or Mr. White, did not frankly explain the situation to me.[4]

It was indeed a great pity and a great blunder.

Fiske signed the papers initiating a suit to break his wife's will and sailed for Europe in mid-July. A week later the Ithaca Surrogate, Judge Marcus Lyon, ordered Boardman and Cornell University to show cause why the prayer of the petitioner should not be granted and forbade Boardman, as executor of the will, to pay the University any moneys. The McGraw cousins hired their own lawyer and made their separate plea for the breaking of the will.

Boardman and the trustees thought the University's position a strong one. Samuel D. Halliday, trustee, wrote White on 23 July 1883 that Fiske's right was very debatable and that apparently he was shaking the bush for the McGraw heirs to catch the bird. Halliday opined: "We can take any number of millions *in trust* for specific purposes. . . . Fiske's ante-nuptial agreement cuts him off from inheritance."

White immediately took ship for London, to catch Fiske and persuade him to withdraw his suit. It must be said that White's position seems to be hardly on his usual pinnacle of nobility. He knew all about the fatal provision in the Charter, and about its revision, and he had unmistakably failed to mention them to Fiske. He was therefore received in London more than coolly. In any case, negotiation was useless, for Sage ordered White by cable and letter to make no propositions to Fiske.

Ithaca, and the newspaper-reading world of America, resounded with the news of the great Case. White described the press reports as "a mud volcano." Fiske's action was commonly represented as the culmination of a fortune hunter's diabolical and long-matured plot to

---

[4] Quoted by Horatio S. White, *Willard Fiske: Life and Correspondence* (New York, 1925), p. 106.

win millions. Mary White wrote her husband that she was disgusted and angry with Fiske's treachery. "Beautiful as this place is, a perfect Paradise, such things make it such a place of torment that you cannot stay in it." W. C. Russel wrote: "Intellectually Fiske seems to have fallen as much as morally." Senator Justin S. Morrill said that the news made him feel ashamed of human nature.[5]

White was one of the few University people who did not desert Fiske. He recognized that Fiske's motives were not sordid, that he had acted under a good deal of provocation. White's effort, then and thenceforth, was to preserve Fiske's friendship, to soothe his sensibilities, to harp on Jennie's noble aims, to persuade Fiske, in case he should win the suit, to fulfill Jennie's purposes toward Cornell.

Hiram Sibley visited Fiske in his palatial Florentine villa, once the house of Walter Savage Landor, in March 1884. He reported to White:

I am fully convinced that his action was not influenced by avarice or greed for money. . . . I firmly believe that if he should recover all he or his counsel hopes, he would give it all to the University, if by so doing he could secure the object he so much desires and which he claims was the wish of his wife, the dedication of her house as an Art Gallery. He seems to regard our action as especially cruel to the memory of his wife. . . . It is a great misfortune to us and to him that we have not understood each other better.[6]

White continued to write to Fiske, prodding him, as if inadvertently, with psychological stimuli. Thus he noted sadly (26 September 1885) that a student had died of typhoid for lack of the care which he would have had in the hospital envisioned by Mrs. Fiske. Fiske was hardly to be caught by such devices, what the French call *attrape-mouches*.

The Great Will Case soon overpassed its original limits to become a matter of high concern. Such questions as these were at issue: was the Cornell Endowment Fund held in trust by the University (as Cornell claimed), and still subject to the provisions of the Land Grant Act, or was it a personal gift from Ezra Cornell, to which neither state nor federal government had access? If all the sums arising from the land sales were still to be regarded as part of the original land grant, then the University could not use its endowment for buildings or for other purposes not foreseen in the act. And had the State of New York limited or modified the act of Congress by its transfer of the land to Mr. Cornell? The implications interested many an institutional executive and trustee.

[5] Mary White to ADW, 3 Aug. 1883; Russel to ADW, 25 Sept. 1883; Morrill to ADW, 15 Oct. 1883.
[6] Sibley to ADW, 18 March 1854.

Ithaca had never seen such a case in all its history. It produced almost as much business as a small factory. The Surrogate allowed it to grow until its printed record filled six large volumes. On 25 May 1886, after three years of argument, formalized courtroom fury, and meditation, the Surrogate ruled that the will was sound and that Cornell should receive the bequest.

At this point (31 May 1886) White proposed that the triumphant University should make a set of face-saving concessions to Fiske. Sage (20 July) vetoed any such softness. The property in litigation, he said, is all his or all ours. And Fiske is "a selfish, untruthful, dishonest man from his youth up, who never had much character or standing save through you—and you and your hopes and wishes he did not hesitate to *slay* if in his power; and he felt sure of his power!"

Fiske's lawyers appealed to the Supreme Court of New York, which, on 20 August 1887, reversed the Surrogate's judgment, and ruled that Cornell had reached the limit of property prescribed in its charter at the time of Mrs. Fiske's death; hence it could not accept her bequest.

The University's counsel took the case to the New York Court of Appeals (which in New York State has the distinction of being supremer than the Supreme Court). This court ruled on 27 November in favor of Fiske and the McGraws. The University then appealed to the Supreme Court of the United States.

In this year of 1888 Sage offered to build for Cornell a library which would receive the Jennie McGraw endowment if the University should win its suit, and which, if not, would be his own gift. And White filled his diary with bitter recriminations against Sage and Boardman for their "childish, and even criminal, want of ordinary common sense." In his last entry for the year he confessed that their friendship had gone; he never wished to see them again. This anger and animosity is all very sad.

At the end of the year White paid a visit to Fiske in his Florentine villa. He suggested a compromise, which Fiske refused. He was struck by the scholarly splendor of Fiske's life, and by the respect paid him by the great, the learned, the elegant, and the wealthy. Fiske's gains, if ill gotten, were well rewarded.

On 19 May 1890 the United States Supreme Court ruled against Cornell University. The Court reiterated, however, that the Cornell Endowment Fund, the absolute property of the University, could be used for any purpose whatever. This ruling later turned out to be a fortunate one.

The Great Will Case was over. After the costs and the staggering legal fees were paid ($180,000 to Fiske's lawyers, led by Cornell's old enemy, David B. Hill of Elmira, and $100,000 to the McGraws' counsel), about half a million went to Fiske, a million to the McGraws. The mansion was bought by Thomas McGraw for $35,000 ("dog-cheap," said White). The works of art and the furnishings were auctioned off, mostly to the McGraw heirs. The house stood unoccupied until 1896, when it was bought, in an evil hour, by the Chi Psi fraternity. Fiske's lawyer, who had initiated the whole matter, never took another case, but—if old rumor tells the truth—drank himself to death on his fees.

Willard Fiske settled down to book collecting, the entertainment of distinguished guests, and cultured conversation in his villa. He died in 1904, and left nearly his whole estate, including his extraordinary Dante, Petrarch, Rhaeto-Romanic, and Icelandic collections, to the Cornell University Library.

In the meantime, Sage had built and endowed the University Library, at a cost of more than half a million dollars. Thus the Great Will Case ended without causing any great financial loss to the University. Indeed, the Supreme Court's assurance that the Endowment Fund was unencumbered was a financial benefit. The loss to the University was moral—in the hatreds, suspicions, and slanders that resulted. Even yesterday, perhaps even today, the hostilities engendered by the Great Will Case have continued, turning friends to enemies, dividing neighbor from neighbor. There was a trustee who used to shake his fist, from the sidewalk, at a lady riding by in her carriage. . . . And when Willard Fiske was buried beside his wife in the mortuary of Sage Chapel, the surviving Sages severed all connection with Cornell University.

The old anger is cast in enduring bronze. As one enters the undergraduate library, one observes above the marble seat in the porch the inscription:

THE GOOD SHE TRIED TO DO SHALL STAND AS IF 'TWERE DONE

GOD FINISHES THE WORK BY NOBLE SOULS BEGUN.

IN LOVING MEMORY OF JENNIE McGRAW FISKE WHOSE PURPOSE TO

FOUND A GREAT LIBRARY FOR CORNELL UNIVERSITY HAS BEEN DEFEATED

THIS HOUSE IS BUILT AND ENDOWED BY HER FRIEND

HENRY W. SAGE

1891

According to legend an elderly countryman contemplated this tablet and remarked: "Looks as though Hank Sage was bigger than the Almighty, and had a little more capital."

XIV

Reconstruction, 1881-1885

ANDREW D. WHITE'S long vacation in Germany was by no means wasted; it had a considerable effect on his educational as on his other opinions. The deference accorded him in a hierarchical court assured him, in a new voice, of his importance, and of the rightness of his judgments. He sought out and entertained the most famous of Germany's scholars, who, no doubt, approved his account of Cornell's aims and methods, for White's ideal university was German in design and organization, English in architecture and costuming.

With evidence of European approbation, his convictions settled and hardened. The process was aided by Charles W. Eliot's espousal of the elective system at Harvard, for which White assumed most of the credit. The process was further aided by the establishment of educationally radical Johns Hopkins University in 1876. White, consulted about the presidency of Hopkins, proposed (successfully) his old Yale friend Daniel Coit Gilman, with whom he held many ideas in common.

The eighties were booming years in the college world. Enrollments increased rapidly, in part because of general prosperity, in part because educational reform allayed common mistrust of collegiate methods. The colleges and universities were becoming more representative of the people; less did they claim to be refuges of an elite's superior culture.

White's educational views have been more than amply stated. On only three heads may a development in his views be noted.

His experience convinced him that higher education should be supported and controlled by the government. He recognized perfectly well the dangers of such control; he had seen them at Michigan and elsewhere. He did not, however, think the dangers unavoidable. Even in 1874 he had insisted that advanced education must be provided by the state legislatures, with the aid of private donors.[1] The Prussian university system, as he viewed it, was a state-controlled organization with the maximum of advantages and the minimum of disadvantages from the standpoints of teacher, student, public, and the general welfare of learning.[2] During the rest of his Cornell presidency White was to have no reason to confront the subject, but his belief that higher education is properly the state's business had its effect on others, especially Jacob Gould Schurman.

White was convinced, further, of the rightness of his principle of allowing students great freedom in the choice of studies. Essentially this freedom expresses the educator's trust in the individual's capacity to choose what is best for him. Its probable consequence, whether flaw or merit, is that it may sacrifice general education to specialization. But it was warmly welcomed in the America of those years, which perhaps had more need of specialists than of broad humanists. In Germany, White admired the great scholars, monsters of erudition. They were specialists *à outrance*, whose particular area of knowledge was often a luxuriant oasis in a Sahara of ignorance. These scholars had been produced by the free elective system of the German universities; ergo, the free elective system was good.

He was also impressed, more than ever before, by the increasingly important place of research in university life. In his many pronouncements he had paid lip service to the idea of a university's duty to extend the bounds of human knowledge. But he had done very little to facilitate this extension. Cornell's professors were expected to give a full working day to instruction; and few laboratory or library facilities were afforded them for investigations of their own, after hours or in vacation.

The seventies, in Germany, were the great day of the experimental laboratory, in chemistry, physics, in the natural and the applied sciences. Discoveries, occasionally momentous, filled the press. Practi-

[1] New York *Times*, 23 May 1874; *Old and New*, Nov. 1874.
[2] Even fifty years later, Abraham Flexner, in his *Universities: American, English, German*, regarded the German system as the best means of fulfilling proper university purposes.

tioners of the humanities, jealous and alarmed, tried to become experimental scientists too. Phonetics and comparative philology boomed, aesthetics went into the laboratory and archaeology and anthropology into the field, the social studies became sciences, with science's appurtenances, obligations, and privileges. White, deeply impressed, was ready on his return to infuse more of the research spirit into Cornell.[3]

White came back, then, with a program in mind. He must restore harmony between faculty and trustees; he must turn upward the descending curve of enrollments; he must see to the University's financial welfare, which indeed already showed signs of improvement; and he must continue his effort to make Cornell a great university, with provision for research and with expansion, when time should be ripe, into such fields as law and medicine.

On returning to the University in September 1881, White immediately charged the administration with his vital energy. He found himself, however, in constant disagreement with Sage, no mean generator of vital energy himself. As chairman of the Executive Committee, Sage had controlled policy and action during White's absence, and with the ousting of Vice-President Russel he took over, in effect, the presiden-

[3] C. C. Gillespie, in Margaret Clapp, ed., *The Modern University* (Ithaca, 1950), brilliantly summarizes nineteenth-century concepts of research. He points out that to mid-century Englishmen (and Americans) professorial research was primarily a German phenomenon, likely to inculcate heretical views about the Bible. E. B. Pusey fought the expansion of professorial teaching, which was sure to lead to "science, research, rationalism, and infidelity." Cardinal Newman held that the function of a university is the diffusion and expansion of knowledge rather than its advancement. But in 1873 the Devonshire Commission described research as a primary duty of a university. And in the 1870's the services of Cambridge to physics, of Oxford to philosophy, began.

Compare such hesitancies with the assurance of David Starr Jordan '72, in his report as a retiring trustee of Cornell in 1888: "A professor to whom original investigation is unknown should have no place in a university. Men of commonplace or second-hand scholarship are of necessity men of low ideals, however carefully that fact may be disguised. A man of high ideals must be an investigator. He must know and think for himself, and only such as do this can be really great as teachers. The highest function of the real university is that of instruction by investigation, and a man who cannot and does not investigate cannot train investigators. . . . Cornell will not reach her highest possibilities until each of her professors can make the most of himself, until each head of a department comes to feel that it is as much a part of his duty as professor to add to the sum of knowledge in some part of his field as it is to assort and disseminate the knowledge amassed by others" (quoted by W. T. Hewett, *Cornell University: A History* [New York, 1905], I, 286–287).

tial authority. But White had been accustomed to dominating the Executive Committee meetings, and he was irked by Sage's identical habit. (Since the Executive Committee did everything for the trustees, and since Sage did everything for the Executive Committee, the trustees fell into the habit of meeting only annually, in June.)

White found Sage domineering and brutally outspoken. Sage wavered between regard and exasperation toward White. In 1884 he tried, unsuccessfully, to limit the President's powers and duties.[4] He was scornful of White's "theories," a contumelious word which he applied to almost any general principles, such as those on which Cornell was built. Sage suspected that White's loyalty to Cornell was deflected by his desire for a political career; he accused White of attacking him, using first Russel and then Fiske as a shield; or, to sum it up, "White has an insane jealousy lest some man beside himself shall get a reputation as a builder of Cornell."[5] No doubt he was right, and no doubt White could have retorted by turning the same words against Sage. At any rate, it is clear that White found his position less happy than in earlier years.

However, he set himself valiantly to his task. His first concern was with the physical state of the campus.

Franklin Hall, previously provided for, was erected in 1881-1882. Ugly at birth, ugly it remained. President Schurman in his report for 1920 called it "in its exterior an eyesore to the campus and in its interior the darkest and most inconvenient building on the campus." Nor today has time invested it with any hoary beauty. But it has been a faithful, if ungainly, servant. At its opening the basement and first floor were given to Physics. For the first time that department had a real laboratory. It was proclaimed that the equipment for Physics was the finest in the country. Chemistry occupied the second and third floors.

The Memorial Antechapel, or Mortuary Chapel, adjoining Sage Chapel and connected with it, was built in 1883-1884. It now contains memorials to Ezra Cornell, Andrew D. White, Jennie McGraw Fiske, Edmund E. Day, and others of Cornell's pantheon, and their bodies or ashes repose in the crypt beneath. White lavished much care and love on this structure, which was to him the chief architectural jewel of the campus. He believed that students, spending an awe-struck moment amid the Chapel's rich and solemn beauty, would carry away

[4] Sage to James F. Gluck, 16 May 1884.
[5] H. W. Sage to Dean Sage, 28 July 1880, 23 May 1890; ADW, Diary, 8 Nov. 1882, *et passim.*

a lasting moral benefit. Unhappily, few students of today seem to test White's expectation.

The Armory, which served at the same time as gymnasium, dated from 1883. For the first time the community had a meeting place large enough for student convocations, popular lectures, dances, Commencements.

Sibley College was enlarged to the east. Mr. Sage gave some fine greenhouses to Sage College. Projects were drawn for a McGraw library, for a McGraw student hospital, for a chemistry building, for a central heating plant. The lighting of the campus, by electricity from Anthony's dynamo, was extended. The faculty condemned the sanitary arrangements in certain buildings as dangerous to health. The names of North and South University Halls were changed (June 1883) to White Hall and Morrill Hall. The purchase of a typewriter was solemnly authorized by the trustees in 1884.

Physical reconstruction was a fairly straightforward matter. More troublesome was the rebuilding of faculty morale.

Since the spring of 1881, when Russel had been forced to resign with no statement of cause by the trustees, many of the faculty, though willing enough to see Russel go, felt alarm at the manner of his going. Such ominous words as "security," "academic freedom," "grievances" began to be heard.

The first of the faculty grievances was, as always, insufficient salary. The Executive Committee somewhat eased the complaints by raising (29 October 1881) all professors receiving $2,250 to $2,500, by raising a group of assistant professors to $1,200, and by awarding the President $5,000. A year later the standard professorial salary was set at $2,750. This was still lower than the scale in the better institutions.[6]

The professors had to work for their money. Dean Fuertes complained in 1884 that the teachers in Civil Engineering averaged 18.8 teaching hours weekly, exclusive of extra, optional, and laboratory duties. The President investigated and tabulated the teaching load in his report for 1885. Charles L. Crandall, C.E., had 36.5 hours of recitation and 12 of laboratory; Moses Coit Tyler, our bright star in American History, had 10 hours of lectures and 6 of seminaries; Prentiss and Dudley of Botany each had 3 hours of lectures and 35 in laboratory;

---

[6] In 1885 a full professor received at Columbia $5,000–7,500, at Hopkins $5,000, at Harvard $4,000, at Yale $3,500, at Princeton $3,000 and a house, at Virginia $3,000, a house, and six acres of land, at Cornell $2,750, and at Michigan $2,200 (Petition of Faculty, 3 June 1885, in Trustees' Minutes).

Comstock, Entomology, had 3 hours of lectures and 42 in laboratory. The question of faculty salaries and duties was taken up by the alumni and became involved with the larger question of university administration.

In 1882 John D. Warner '72, a New York lawyer, was elected alumni trustee. Warner had been a prominent and troublesome undergraduate; his disputatious taste was to carry him to the House of Representatives. As president of the Alumni Association, he had expounded the view that the trustees should deal with business matters, while the administration should handle educational matters. But in fact, he complained, the local Executive Committee had usurped the duties of the administration. One will recognize that the Board of Trustees gave him a less than cordial welcome to their number.

At an alumni meeting in April 1883 Warner made a number of sharp criticisms of the University. The local trustees were far too powerful, he said, and personal influences too compelling. The faculty salaries were too low, and inefficiency, lobbying, and intrigue resulted. The decline in enrollment he ascribed to the meager salaries. The President was accused of absenting himself and of dabbling in politics; and "he plans new professorships and costly buildings and neither consults the Faculty nor the Trustees, and expects them to pass his measures."

The accusations were extremely newsworthy. Their publication provoked many a letter to many an editor. President White denounced the charges before a convocation of students. Five senior professors wrote a public letter alleging that the drop in enrollments was due only to the raising of entrance requirements and insisting that the students had not deteriorated. The average undergraduate is "more manly, more moral, more studious, and more scholarly than was the undergraduate of fifteen or even ten years ago." Other supporters of the administration employed the *argumentum ad hominem*, describing Warner as a blatant demagogue, or Satan rebuking sin. But though many newspapers denounced the charges as absurd and malignant, the sense that something was wrong at Cornell remained in the minds of the public and of the alumni.

Warner made his report to the Associated Alumni in June 1883. Mincing no words, he pointed to the domination of the University by Sage and his Executive Committee and to the ineffectiveness of the non-Ithacan trustees. He reported that departments were abolished, new ones erected, professors discharged and chairs filled, without the knowledge of the Board. He reiterated that the University's decline was due to the impoverishment of the faculty, to the departure of the best men and their replacement by mediocrities. He accused the President of favoritism, of arbitrary methods, of failure to keep his promises.

Warner went too far for his constituency. The alumni voted their confidence in the President and elected as alumni trustee the proadministration candidate, James F. Gluck '74, over Warner's reform candidate. They recommended at the same time that a professor's salary should be raised to $3,500, as at Yale, even if the action should require the curtailing of building programs.

Alumni concern and criticism had its effect on the administration. The Executive Committee, admitting nothing, nevertheless exhibited a more conciliatory spirit toward the faculty. President White, in his annual report for 1883, propounded the as yet novel principle that the faculty has rights with regard to faculty appointments:

[The trustees should not] create a Department or establish a Professorship without a preliminary study of the matter and a recommendation by the Faculty. And as to individual appointments I think that by far the safest way is for the Faculty to nominate and for the Trustees to appoint—thus leaving the power finally in the Trustees who are responsible for it, but placing the duty of weighing qualifications largely in the Faculty.

White was stating what is roughly our present procedure.

In 1884 Warner issued a long printed review of Cornell affairs. He noted with approval that the administration had dropped its autocratic manner, if not its convictions. He commended warmly certain departments: Agriculture, Architecture, Chemistry, Physics, Physiology, Zoology. On the other hand, Philosophy was deplorable, Mechanic Arts weak, Geology poor, English chaotic. He concluded that the University's chief needs were better professors, increased pay, and insistence on excellence in the work offered, not expansion of offerings.

The administration was stimulated, as well as annoyed, by such criticisms. On 9 May 1884 the trustees adopted a set of standards to be invoked in the consideration of salary advances. The faculty, on its part, petitioned for a general raise (3 June 1885). Its petition pointed out that the University had no retirement or pension provisions; that a professor deserves a decently comfortable life, with means to build his own library, to do his research, to attend learned meetings. It alleged further that the world judges an institution by the salaries paid, and noted our inferior position. It asked that a full professor's salary be set at $3,500.

(On this theme, I notice in the trustees' minutes that on 18 June

1884 Thomas Sheehan, janitor at the gymnasium, who had been paid one dollar per day for 313 days in the year, was raised to thirty-five dollars per month in consideration of his evening work. Thus a janitor's pay was approximately 15 per cent of a professor's pay. Today it is about 35 per cent. One supposes that the janitor is better off, not that the professor is worse off.)

Under the stimulation of protest, the economic status of the faculty improved markedly between 1881 and 1885. Not only were salaries generally raised, the idea of fringe benefits took concrete form. On 9 May 1884 the trustees appointed a committee to examine plans for the retirement of professors incapacitated by age or other cause. Alumni Trustee James F. Gluck drew up a scheme for faculty pensions, in May 1885.

The faculty gained also in power and prestige. White had always insisted that the faculty should exercise large powers, with accompanying responsibility, and that it should help shape University policy. He noted in his report for 1884 that the faculty held frequent meetings to discuss University policy and that these were influential upon the trustees. "It may seem that by this system the President is stripped of power; but I have always found myself easily able to retain all desirable influence under it."

This was clearly an understatement. Moses Coit Tyler, attending his first faculty meeting on 16 September 1881, noted that Mr. White presided with an air of courteous dignity, but he assumed absolute control of the meeting and rode roughshod over the rules of order. At any rate, the faculty had the theoretical right to rule on educational questions, while White was likely to direct the course of the discussions and the character of the conclusions.

Under his pressure the curriculum was somewhat broadened, and more freedom in the election of studies given the students. The general frame of the curriculum, established in 1868, remained unchanged: a series of special, or technical, courses of study, as in Architecture or Engineering, with most of the subjects required; and a series of general courses, in Arts, Literature, Philosophy, Science, Science and Letters, in which the work of the first two years was largely fixed and that of the last two years largely elective. This Cornell system, permitting election among several parallel courses, within which the work of the first two years was mostly prescribed, was less radical than Eliot's elective system at Harvard. On the whole, however, it is the Cornell system of controlled election that has survived and has become standard today.

One of Cornell's disabilities in these years was its lack of fellowships and scholarships, except for the state scholarships provided in the Charter. Now the sales of University lands made possible some expenditures for such purposes. White had a happy thought. In 1872 he and Messrs. Cornell, Sage, McGraw, and Sibley had rescued the University from calamity by advancing $155,000. Although nominally a loan, this sum was regarded by its makers as at best a bad debt, at worst a good deed. In 1884 White established a scholarship fund of $155,000 from University money, terming it a redemption of the original loan. Six annual scholarships of $200, seven named fellowships of $400, were created. During all succeeding years these University scholarships and fellowships have brought inestimable aid to the impecunious scholar.

In 1882–83 an honors course was established, rudimentary in comparison with modern developments. No special courses, no tutorial aid, were involved. The honors student merely wrote a thesis and took a special comprehensive examination.

Research, said the President, was a matter of prime importance. He wrote to Finch (5 February 1881): "The numbers of Cornell's students will be determined largely by its reputation for research as well as for instruction." In pursuit of this aim, the faculty's teaching hours were gradually eased, and library and laboratory facilities increased. The modern concept of contract research was faintly forecast. Professor Anthony recommended inviting the Edison and U.S. Electric Lighting companies to test their machines at Cornell.[7] On the whole, however, research activity was more an aspiration than an achievement.

Thus with some small adjustments the machine of education continued to spin. For whatever cause—financial, personal, spiritual—the fortunes of the University improved. The enrollment, having dropped to its lowest point in 1881–82, the year of White's return, thenceforth rose steadily each year: from 384 to 407 to 461 to 573 in 1884–85.

With the color of the future turning rose, White could again make the large plans he loved. Jennie McGraw Fiske's bequest inspired in him grandiose dreams of the greatest scholarly library in America. He foresaw a gallery of fine arts and of classical archaeology, with a great collection of casts of antique sculpture, in the Fiske-McGraw mansion. The waking from such dreams was drear indeed. A department of mining engineering was proposed from year to year, never coming to

[7] *Trustees' Proceedings*, 24 Jan. 1885.

birth. A College of Pharmacy was authorized in 1884. A group of New York physicians tried in vain to find funds for a Cornell medical college in New York City.

With the opening of the new Armory and Gymnasium in 1883, White realized one of his pet projects: the recognition of physical training as a University subject, on a par with mental training. He brought as director Dr. Edward Hitchcock, Jr., a medical man who taught hygiene, gymnastics, and vocal culture. He was the son of the originator, at Amherst, of organized work in student medicine in America, uniting clinical medicine, health education, physical education, and mental hygiene into a program for student health, which he defined as the development of all bodily powers.

The women had their own gymnasium in Sage College. "There, twice a week, the girls took off their corsets, or were supposed to, put on an ankle-length, full, lined, gray flannel skirt and a blouse waist, and did wand drill sedately round and round the hall. The advanced pupils had dumbbells. I think there were Indian clubs besides." [8]

Against these expansions must be set a contraction. The University Press, established with such high hopes at the Opening, was abolished, as an unnecessary expense. White noted in his report for 1884, a little sadly, that the Press was the last surviving remnant of Mr. Cornell's original plan of affording self-supporting labor.

Certain developments within the departments are to be recorded.

The first professorship of American history in America was established. [9] Extraordinary as it may appear, history in general was very ill served in most colleges. In 1880 there were only eleven professors of history in America. In 1884 Dartmouth had no teacher of history and Princeton only one, who doubled in political science. Cornell's department had always been strong. During White's absence it was served by three visiting professors, still celebrated: Herbert Tuttle, Henry Carter Adams, and Charles Kendall Adams.

The disregard of American history in American universities seemed to White the more remarkable, in that E.-R. de Laboulaye lectured on the subject in the Collège de France. He determined that Cornell should have its professor as soon as circumstances would permit. The man he had in view was Moses Coit Tyler.

---

[8] Ellen Coit Brown Elliott, *It Happened This Way* (Palo Alto, 1940), p. 224.
[9] The University of Pennsylvania may rise to assert that W. B. Reed was professor of American history from 1850 to 1856. But Reed seems to have been a part-time lecturer, without salary, and should be, I think, ruled out.

White and Tyler had known and liked each other at Yale in 1856–57. Returning to their homes for the winter vacation, they were snow-bound for twenty-nine hours between New York and Albany, and had time to explore each other's spirits.[10] Then Tyler had become a Con-gregational minister in Owego, the apostle of a new system of physical, mental, and spiritual training in London, a popular lecturer on litera-ture, and Professor of Belles Lettres at Michigan. White kept in touch with him, and in 1871 offered him a professorship in rhetoric and oratory, which he declined. In September 1880 White proposed to resign his presidency of Cornell and wrote Tyler asking him how he would like to be President. Tyler replied that he would not like it.

In the following spring White, from Berlin, offered Tyler the pro-fessorship of American history. Tyler was in a mood of great dubiety, and also of spiritual uplift, for he was about to take Episcopalian orders. He wrote in his diary: "I earnestly prayed God to give me light upon this grave problem, and my mind became irradiated, and for the first time I seemed to see my way to Cornell made luminous." Thus divinely directed, he telegraphed his acceptance, "in the faith that it is the will of God, and with the earnest prayer for God's blessing on the act." But a fortnight later, what an anguished test of his faith!

I have had an awful shock today. Just as I am fastened to go to Cornell comes an intimation from Pres. Barnard of Columbia that there is a vacancy and a likely chance for me there. I read the letter at Moore's book store. The cold sweat came out on my body, and I almost reeled in my chair. Seven thousand dollars and New York City. Ugh! This is a trial of my faith in Providence! . . . It is very bitter, bitter, to bear this.

His faith successfully passed the test. After another fortnight, he recog-nized that God approved his going to Ithaca. And three years later he wrote: "Very happy. God did the right thing." With divine favor working for Cornell, Tyler lived and died here, and wrote his important books, still honored, still read.

For White the appointment had a special meaning. The President's House is a lonely place at best. However eager for carefree friendli-ness, faculty and President feel an invisible wall between them, a steri-lizing zone wherein casual frank impulses die. And White, rich and well born, was perhaps too consciously superior to have many real friends on the faculty. He wrote Tyler (12 May 1881) that there were "three Professors to whom I have been able at all times to open

[10] ADW to G. L. Burr, 16 Jan. 1901, in Burr Papers.

my heart on any and every question—[Homer B.] Sprague, Russel, and Fiske." With their disappearance, there is "virtually no one on the Faculty with whom I can consult fully and freely as a friend."

Tyler became such a friend and confidant, the companion of many long, free-spoken walks. But it is a good thing White could not read Tyler's diary.

The appointment of Tyler was a part of a general reorganization of the work in history, which was combined with political and social science and general jurisprudence. A four-year course was established, leading to the degree of Bachelor of Philosophy (and including a two-hour course in the Theory of Probabilities and Statistics). One should always be cautious in alleging that anything is the first of anything, but this coherent four-year program in history and social sciences was apparently the first in America.

The work in social sciences was noteworthy for its course in Modern Philanthropy, that is, the study of pauperism, intemperance, crime, insanity, and their correctives. Frank B. Sanborn, the eminent secretary of the Massachusetts Board of Charities, gave the course for the first time in the spring of 1885. The practical work consisted of weekend visits to prisons, reformatories, asylums, and poorhouses. This, the first course of its kind in the country, fitted White's purpose, to train students to shape public opinion and to accept the obligations of social service. This was one of the aims which he hardly achieved in his administration, but which he later saw accomplished by others.

At the urging of the President, Professor Anthony presented in 1883 a scheme for a four-year course in electrical engineering. When the Executive Committee bade fair to defeat the proposal, on financial grounds, White pledged himself to pay from his own pocket any extra costs incurred. The course, under the aegis of Physics, was in operation in 1885, sharing with M.I.T. in primacy. (In the same year we granted the country's first doctorate in electrical engineering.) The course was immediately popular. It brought us also consulting work; in 1886 three dynamo machines were sent to Cornell by manufacturers for testing.

Within the Department of Mechanic Arts—or Sibley College—there was a good deal of stress and strain. Students and alumni issued complaints and manifestoes. The *American Machinist* commented editorially (on 19 May 1883) that a few years before, Cornell's department had been the most popular in the country, but it was so no longer. The fact seems to be that the concept of engineering education was rapidly evolving, with the evolution of American technology, and that

Professors Morris and Sweet still put their faith in practical training in mechanic arts.[11] The trustees appointed a committee, in June 1884, to examine the instruction and organization of Sibley College. A new chief of engineering, with power in his hands, was clearly needed. White picked Robert H. Thurston of Stevens Institute, and the trustees appointed him, on 17 June 1885, professor of mechanical engineering and director of Sibley College of Mechanical Engineering and Mechanic Arts, at a salary of $5,000. Thenceforth all was well with Cornell engineering.

A department, or school, of comparative paleontology was proposed by Professor Henry Shaler Williams of Geology. The school would combine instruction, original research, and exploration. The committee reported favorably (27 February 1884). Paleontology became briefly a separate department, but before long it coalesced once more with Geology.

Weakest, perhaps, of Cornell's departments was Philosophy. The work was in the hands of the Reverend William D. Wilson, the University's handyman, who was registrar, editor of the annual *Register*, and teacher of courses in anything from ancient Chaldee to political economy. He was now old, uncivil, and forgetful, and his illegible handwriting caused endless predicaments in his registrar's functions.[12]

Henry W. Sage had a special fondness for philosophy, which had manifested itself in his youth in an earnest study of philosophical classics. He proposed therefore to establish and endow a department of ethics and philosophy.[13] Several promising young men were suggested, among them John Dewey, recommended by Charles Kendall Adams, and Frank A. Taussig, who became Harvard's famous economist. The appointment went, however, to Jacob Gould Schurman.

Sage's interest in philosophy was naturally related to his religious purpose. He wrote, touchingly, to Elisha B. Andrews (21 June 1889): "No man can know the depth of my love and purpose in trying to lay solid foundations for this institution. . . . I have tried to save it from financial peril—have tried to make it a Christian University resting at

[11] Letter from Walter C. Kerr '79, in Trustees' Minutes, 14 Jan. 1884.

[12] M. C. Tyler noted in his diary (12 Dec. 1881): "[Wilson] is almost universally hated on the Faculty, and I think he is an incumbrance on the University. Moreover, he is charged with lust of petty authority, cunning, and falsehood." And on 10 Jan. 1882: "He seems to me a bad, cunning, envious, malignant, plotting old man."

[13] ADW, Diary, 3 July 1884; Trustees' *Proceedings*, 20 Nov. 1885.

all points upon bases which God himself could approve." He was much in doubt whether God really approved of White's Sage preacherships. Several times he suggested dropping the visiting preachers and installing a permanent chaplain. He had not liked Vice-President Russel's eclecticism, which permitted him even to invite a Paulist Father to preach. The Paulist fortunately refused. (But laymen were admitted to the pulpit—Professor George L. Raymond of the College of New Jersey, on 30 October 1881, with others to follow.)

Student life presented the usual problems to the administration.

Sage was troubled about Sage College. The noble structure could accommodate two hundred occupants, but held in fact only about thirty. The total registration of women dropped to sixty-four in 1881–82, and of these many found cheap lodgings in the village. The Executive Committee therefore proclaimed (29 October 1881) that henceforth all women students, not Ithaca residents, should live in Sage. Many of the women protested, in bitter terms. To the boast of bathrooms in Sage the girls retorted that they were well brought up and had no need of getting into a tub to wash. The ringleader, Ellen Coit Brown, later wrote: "It is true bathtubs were a novelty in 1884 and hardly any of us had ever got into one, but we had been brought up clean and were experts with a washrag, a piece of castile soap, and a basin of warm water." [14]

Sage wondered if, after all, his experiment in coeducation had turned out to be a failure. He wrote to White (29 December 1881) that if such should be the case, he would consent to having the building and its endowment devoted to another purpose. He thought of making it a library and art museum, or a college of engineering (presumably civil) and architecture. [15]

The women students objected on principle to being housed by obligation in dormitories if the men were under no similar requirement. They insisted that they should be as free as their brothers from rule and restriction, and White, with his confidence in innate virtue, agreed. Sage, perhaps more familiar with innate depravity, did not. He favored the Oberlin system of regulation and supervision by lady wardens. He

---

[14] Ellen Coit Brown Elliott, in collection on Sage Memorial, C.U. Archives.
[15] Russel to ADW, 29 Jan. and 22 Feb. 1882; ADW, Diary, 11 Feb. 1882. Mrs. Sage told Tyler (Diary, 29 Jan. 1882) that the ill success of Sage College was a bitter disappointment to her husband. "He put his heart and soul into it, and it has all turned out a failure."

had his way, and in October 1884 Mrs. Agnes M. Derkhiem was appointed Lady Principal, at $1,000 plus room and board. The mother of housemothers, one might call Mrs. Derkhiem.[16]

Sage College and the University as a whole were enlivened by the matriculation in Sibley College, in 1884, of Miss Kate Gleason of Rochester, commonly known as Sibley Kate. She was our first female engineer. Donning overalls, she worked in the shops, at forge and lathe, and held her own with male competition. Afterwards she took her place in the family gear works in Rochester, was the first woman president of a national bank, and achieved other primacies. Some of us remember her well, as a gay and greathearted lady, who adopted an entire French village after the First War. ("What is the industry of your village?" inquired your historian. "Me!" replied Sibley Kate. She would have only the best for her villagers, even obtaining manure from the thoroughbred race horses at the Chantilly Track.) [17]

Student life in general presented some changes and more continuities. A subtle change was taking place among the men. Cornell, long derided as a poor boys' college, was now accused of being a haven for rich men's sons.[18] Certainly the accusation was excessive, but it reflects a change in our social composition, and the effect of circumstances on Ezra Cornell's ideal. These years were the heyday of the "dude." The costume of the dude was a tight jacket with flaring skirts, a stiff, high collar like the gorget of a medieval knight, a tiny bow tie or a billow of heavy silk, lemon-yellow gloves, skin-tight trousers and narrow sharp-pointed shoes, and on occasion a very short tan topcoat, from under which the black tails of the dress coat might bob. The dude was portrayed by cartoonists as commonly sucking the handle of a cane, and speaking a dialect in which the *r*'s were regularly replaced by *w*'s. But thoroughgoing dudes were rare in Cornell's generally unsophisticated milieu.

With increasing social pretensions came a new, and distressing, awareness of Judaism. Jews had always attended Cornell, and had found no prejudice there. John Frankenheimer '73 was nominated for alumni trustee; he wrote Mr. White (8 July 1885) that he had never been

[16] For the controversy, see Trustees' Minutes; Anita S. Goodstein, *Biography of a Businessman: Henry W. Sage, 1814–1897* (Ithaca, 1962); and excellent letters from Ellen Coit Brown, presenting the women's protests, in ADW Papers, 17 July and 1 Aug. 1884.

[17] For some anecdotes of Miss Gleason see *Alumni News*, 19 Jan. 1933.

[18] Letter in New York *Times*, 22 July 1885.

subjected to any of the annoyances and affronts which bigotry and race prejudice called forth at other colleges and that this happy experience was due to the liberalizing influence of Mr. White's teachings. White drew up a penciled list of Jews in Cornell fraternities; he counted seven, including Frankenheimer. But some strange responses were evoked by Frankenheimer's candidacy for a trusteeship. The Syracuse *Standard* said the election would show the Cornell alumni's attitude toward Christianity.[19] He was not, in fact, elected.

In student life athletics during these years played only a small part. Intercollegiate competitions were few, thanks to the faculty's reluctance to grant permission for out-of-town trips. Perhaps it was just as well. Cornell's rivals in the big cities were beginning to feel, and resent, the intrusions of the professional spirit into sports. The trustees took measures (17 June 1885) against the services of professional players in sports and against pool selling, bookmaking, disorderly conduct, and indecent language at games. Although in 1883 Charles E. Courtney of Union Springs was hired to coach the Navy, in the following year Cornell joined with eleven other colleges to condemn professional coaching and the holding of contests away from college campuses. But this early effort at de-emphasis was voted down by the Intercollegiate Athletic Association.

Bicycling on the high perilous wheel began to loom, as a sport and as a traffic problem. The Executive Committee, on 24 April 1883, forbade riding on sidewalks and added that no horses, cows, sheep, fowls, or other animals should be allowed at large on the campus.

Behavior, on the whole, was good. Student effervescence was allowed to escape in class rushes and ritual kidnappings. In an autumnal cane rush the freshmen and sophomores struggled to place the sacred cane in the hands of an upperclassman. The freshmen, if they lost, were forbidden to carry canes till after Thanksgiving.

Halloween made its annual incitement to evildoing. In 1882 the boys destroyed the wooden bridge spanning the gully at the present junction of Central Avenue and Campus Road. Seven students were suspended as a result, and five put on probation. In the Executive Committee, Henry W. Sage blamed White for not intervening to save University property. White wrote resentfully in his diary (8 November): "His view was that I—in feeble health—ought at 2 in the morning to have thrown myself into a mob of nearly 100 men, many disguised and

[19] *A Question for Cornell Alumni*, C.U. Pamphlets, XII. ADW's list of Jews in fraternities is in Executive Committee Minutes, 6 Nov. 1884.

all bent on mischief. His remarks were simply those of a 'good business man,' as utterly blind to the realities of this case as to the beauties of a sonata of Beethoven." However, M. C. Tyler told his diary that at the news of White's distress Sage's eyes filled with tears.

The springtime battles centering upon the class banquets could be ominous. In 1880 the sophs made a vain attempt to drug the freshmen's food. They then tried to extinguish the banquet-hall gas by using an air pump on a bedroom gas jet. But when the festival lights flickered, the embattled frosh sought and found the culprits. (One need hardly remark that this trick could easily have caused asphyxiation, explosion, and conflagration.)

In the following year the sophs kidnapped five freshman officers, although the frosh president fired a revolver at the attackers. The town was roused; the reserve police were called out; the fire-bell rang. In 1884 the sophs, by an elaborate stratagem, deluded the caterer into serving the freshman banquet in Trumansburg, where it was consumed by the sophomores. Through their lifetimes the participants told and retold these mighty jests, strangling with glee. If today the comedy is yellowed with the universal melancholy of the past, it may still provoke a tolerant smile.

Conventional drama was available at the Wilgus Opera House, on the second floor of Rothschild's Department Store. The theatre was brilliantly illuminated by sixty-four gas jets under a central reflector. A brass rail separated the front row from the stage. Fashion decreed that the occupants of the front row should slouch to the horizontal and put their feet up on the rail. On one occasion eight students chalked large letters on their shoe soles during the intermission; and when the curtain rose the actors read the message: THIS SHOW IS ROTTEN.

At about this time Theodore Zinck opened his beer saloon.[20] Zinck was a kindly, even fatherly German, respectable to the marrow. He treated his lager and his bock with reverence, his customers with Prussian high-handedness. He allowed no drunkenness, bawdy songs, or derogatory references to the German Kaiser. His saloon was a school of a certain kind of jovial good manners, and Zinck himself was regarded by generations of Cornellians with an affection accorded no other publican. Such is the power of personality.

The students made themselves a small functioning society, in which play and work had their allotted places. Though crude and rustic in many ways, the University could answer the intellectual and aesthetic,

[20] *Cornell Era*, 1881–82, pp. 158, 184.

as well as the vocational needs of the young. Louis Eilshemius, later famous as a painter, came here in 1882 to study agriculture, at his father's wish, not his own. He tramped the countryside, painted, wrote poetry, studied Arabic. A congenial group, which included C. Wolcott Balestier '85, the novelist, took long walks together, improvised scenes from *Paradise Lost,* and listened to Eilshemius playing Schumann and Chopin.[21]

As alumni made their mark, the esteem of Cornell in what the *Sun* has always called the Great Outside World was steadily rising. The faculty, appeased by raises in pay, grumbled only intermittently. Andrew D. White could look on his work and see that it was good. He could likewise conclude that he might decently confide his tasks to another and seek more congenial courses.

These, he knew, would present themselves. In May 1883 he was offered the New York State Civil Service commissionership by Governor Cleveland. He declined, with bitter regret, because of his Cornell duties. At the Republican National Convention in 1884 he was mentioned for the presidency and for the vice-presidency. He told Tyler that at this convention he was "virtually offered" the secretaryship of state in return for vigorous support of James G. Blaine—which he refused to give. And even if no splendid duty should turn up, he had an old and dear project. He had begun talking and writing of the history of the warfare of science with theology as early as 1875. There was a great book to be written on the subject, a book that he could write, a book that would put the name of White in the scholarly empyrean with the names of Buckle, Lecky, Ranke.

His position as President was no longer a comfortable one. During Ezra Cornell's lifetime, the Founder had commonly deferred to him on all educational matters. After Cornell's death, White had been supreme on the Hill. But now Henry W. Sage wore an air of command and, what is more, an air of dissatisfaction with the President. White could ill brook correction and reproof from anyone and least of all from Sage, whom he secretly scorned as a crude and grasping Philistine.[22]

[21] William Schack, *And He Sat among the Ashes* (New York, 1939), p. 34. Balestier's promise as a novelist was untimely cut short. To him Rudyard Kipling dedicated his *Barrack-Room Ballads,* with words still nobly resonant:

E'en as he trod that day to God so walked he from his birth
In simpleness and gentleness and honour and clean mirth.

[22] Sage's dissatisfaction with White appears most frankly in Moses Coit Tyler's

It was White's habit, when in a quandary, to tabulate the arguments pro and contra. Such a self-scrutiny dates apparently from the spring of 1884. "Shall I resign at the approaching Commencement, calling [Charles Kendall] Adams to take my place?" he asked himself. In favor of such action was his twenty-year service; his ill health; the burden of responsibility, the interruptions, the surprises. "I should be free, to travel, etc., write. (I will have $26,000 per annum.)" And con: various arguments, of which the chief was that he must not seem to resign under the fire of Alumni Trustee Warner.

He postponed the decision for a year. His health took a turn for the worse. His secretary, Ernest W. Huffcut '84, wrote to George Lincoln Burr on 24 October 1884 that he saw "unmistakable signs of growing physical weakness. I hardly see how his health will bear much longer the tremendous strain which is put upon it, despite his growing care for its preservation. Today he was hardly able to read his lectures, and this afternoon he is too ill to see anybody." Dreadful colds and sick headaches followed. Fiske wrote to White in the following May: "I learn from five different sources that another autumn, winter, or spring at Ithaca is pretty certain to put an end to your life."

There could no longer be any question as to pro and con. White presented his resignation to the trustees on 17 June 1885, taking nearly everyone by surprise. He called upon the Board to find a successor.

---

diary. See especially entries for 23 Jan. 1883 and 27 Feb. 1883. Sage "has wholly lost respect for W as a Pres't & declared that under his lead the Univ. never could make headway. He spoke kindly of W personally. . . . He has a high opinion of C K Adams for Pres't. The talk was to me very sad, yet he is right." After a warm scene at an Executive Committee meeting, Sage "now hopes to force an issue with W, and would be glad if it led to the latter's resignation. He also told me of his own greatly reduced estimate of W as a man of intellect & an educator; said W's measure had been taken by the leading educators of the country, and it was not large; and that Gov. Cornell knows W and estimates him as a rather weak man." On 3 May 1883 Sage told Tyler that White was more pained by the attack of the New York alumni than by anything that had happened since the University was founded, but that White is intensely disliked by the large body of students and alumni. On 27 May 1883: "The trouble about White for the Presidency is this—*there's not enough of him.*" On 1 March 1885: "Sage spoke feelingly of A D W's using his present position as a means of making a career for himself in politics."

White, on his part, said much ill of Sage to Tyler. Tyler, remaining a close friend of both, is kinder toward Sage than toward White. "I love that man!" he writes of Sage (14 July 1884). But of White (3 Feb. 1884): "W is the least frank good fellow I know—always with a part of himself hidden by a veil."

Of course he had the successor ready: Charles Kendall Adams, his prize pupil at Michigan, his close friend of many years, his collaborator in a scholarly book. White had had him in mind for the presidency since at least 1879, and sounded him out before presenting his resignation.[23]

The trustees, with only a month for discussion, found Adams's name practically imposed on them. Other suggestions were made: General Francis A. Walker, President of M.I.T.; President James B. Angell of Michigan; James Russell Lowell; and others. But Sage approved of Adams. At the election, on 13 July 1885, Adams received twelve votes, General Walker one, and one vote was blank. The salary was not to exceed $6,000, with $700 for house rent.

Adams accepted, on the right note of prayerful humility.

White's annual report for 1885 is his educational testament for Cornell, his parting message of good counsel.

On internal policy, he listed his recommendations: to strengthen existing departments before creating new ones, but to provide, when the time should be ripe, for veterinary science, mining engineering, pharmacy, law, and medicine; to keep the professorial salaries high, and to make faculty life easy and attractive by such means as housing aid; to provide facilities for research and investigation; never to sacrifice peace and harmony to gain valuable men, for "any sacrifice of individuals is better than to allow discord"; to pay no heed to students' judgments, usually fallacious, of their professors; to interfere in discipline only when liberty becomes license, as in insults to faculty or community, which must be severely dealt with, and as in cases of indecency and misrepresentation in University-sanctioned publications, which must be promptly banned with the dismissal of the guilty editors; to be on the watch for the faculty's favorite misdemeanors, such as the prolongation of vacations and the reduction of classroom exercises. "Any plea for reducing a fair number of hours for classroom instruction on the ground of the necessity of time for research will generally be found baseless." He recommended that the trustees receive the new President's recommendations as those of a specialist and that they recognize their own disabilities, for "the strongest business men in the world would be just the men most likely not to appreciate the most eminent and influential professors modern times have seen—such men as Mommsen, Faraday, Peirce, Dana, Lotze, Hadley."

[23] ADW to Judge Cooley, 8 April 1879; Diary, 27 March 1884; Adams to ADW, 20 June 1885, *et passim.*

He added then a set of recommendations on external policy, most of them noble and uplifting, but not very specific. One notes, however, his advice never to surrender a professor to religious attacks, for all truth is one, and "even error honestly arrived at will do more for religion and for science than truth merely asserted dogmatically." He suggested wisely that in the presentation of envenomed public issues the best plan is to avoid debates, but to engage spokesmen to lecture successively on the two sides. He says finally that the sentiment gathering around a university is part of its success. We must not be hard, dry, and unattractive. We must guard our natural beauty, and we must complement it with architectural, man-made beauty. We shall grow; and we must grow to a plan, with our new constructions part of a harmonious whole.

Looking down from the President's House, White might well have felt deep satisfaction. This campus was the realization of his youthful dream by Seneca's shores, of the dream he had expounded thirty years before to George William Curtis, such a realization as few men can know. The character and spirit of the University, its physical aspect, the innumerable details of its organization, were spun from his own imagination. Of this consummation he was well aware.

His achievement had a larger meaning, which the passage of time has rendered clearer. His work fell in the great days of university building in America, the years from 1865 to 1880. These were the years of Eliot at Harvard, of Barnard at Columbia, of Angell at Michigan, of Gilman at Hopkins. Such men, impelled by their *Zeitgeist*, and not usually very cordial one toward another, transformed the American university, in opposition to the fierce but doomed conservatism of some of the older schools. Of these great reformers White was the first in action, and the first, perhaps, in immediate influence.

In his letter of resignation he points out that the principles on which Cornell was founded, twenty years before, have triumphed. These principles he enumerates, and he summarizes them as "the steady effort to abolish monastic government and pedantic instruction." He was quite right; his principles had triumphed, his battle was won. But the trouble is that he bequeathed to his successor a victory, and not a cause, a program, a course of action.

XV

President Adams, 1885-1892

CHARLES KENDALL ADAMS, second President of Cornell University, was born in Derby, Vermont, in 1835. He worked on his poor father's poor farm, and had only elementary schooling. The family removed to Denmark, Iowa, in 1856. Adams, twenty-one years old, tall, lumbering, dogged, went to the Academy, and sat hunched with the boys, to begin his Latin and preparation for college. By the leniency of the examiners, he was admitted to the University of Michigan in 1857. He worked his way through; during his freshman year he lived mostly on milk and apples. But on principle he managed to buy twelve good books a year. He was captain of the student cadet corps and an organizer of the first Christian Association in an American college. He was slavishly devoted to his teacher, Andrew D. White, who, almost his own age, was everything he would most have wished to be—elegant, cultured, traveled, rich, and already a master of his scholarly field. On his part, White was touched by the gangling young man's adoration and impressed by his rage to learn. Graduating in 1861, Adams stayed on to study history. In the following year White took a leave of absence and left Adams in charge of his courses. He became an effective teacher, respected but not very popular. He married the proprietress of the boardinghouse where he had worked as a student. She was a valiant young widow, supporting two orphan nieces. She also managed to support her husband during a year and a half of foreign study. On his return, he is said to have introduced the German seminar method

CHARLES KENDALL ADAMS, President 1885–1892

to America, whether in 1869 or 1871. In either case, he was certainly anticipated by our William C. Russel in 1868.[1]

His look and manner belied his actual worth. Benjamin Ide Wheeler, his colleague at Cornell, said:

A certain general heaviness of style coupled with apparent slowness of wit, and a considerable uncouthness of manner, classed him as bucolic rather than metropolitan, and earned from irreverent lips the title of "Farmer Adams," which he bore during the earlier years at Cornell. The drowsiness of his facial expression, centering in a peculiar droop of the upper eyelids, combined with his dragging utterance, his heavy manner, and his slow and homely geniality to mark him as presumably an easy victim to the wiles of the wicked and designing, such as dwell in cities. There was, too, a certain mental stubbornness about him which forbade his entering at first meeting with full zest and sympathy into the interests of a stranger. While he listened carefully, he certainly gave the impression of suspending judgment on the new apparition; for it was really to patient judgment, not to immediate intuition, that he trusted. This calm settling back into the seat of the judge gave to him an air of lethargic coldness that concealed the abounding charity of his nature and robbed him of all semblance of magnetism for the first approach.[2]

Adams's letters to White are those of a humble disciple, and White was inclined, I fear, to preen before him and to make use of him. White really loved Adams, his first convert to historical study in his first year of teaching, and in a way his creation, his intellectual son. Paternally, he saw more virtues in Adams than did casual acquaintances, and certainly I do not say he was wrong. When White resumed control of Cornell affairs in 1881, he had Adams, now professor at Michigan, come to Cornell annually, as nonresident professor, to give lecture series on English constitutional history.

White collaborated with Adams on a guide to materials for the study of history and ere long turned over the entire task to his pupil. Adams gained scholarly recognition by his later book, *Democracy and Monarchy in France* (1874), and also gained some scholarly notoriety. It was charged that his account of the philosopher Helvétius corresponded closely, even to phrasing, with the account in Buckle's *History*

---

[1] Charles Forster Smith, *Charles Kendall Adams* (Madison, 1924); C. H. Thurber in *Cornell Era*, March 1901.

[2] *Memorial of Charles Kendall Adams* (Madison, 1903), p. 32; quoted by Smith, *C. K. Adams*, p. 29. Professor Walter F. Willcox, one of the few today who remember Adams, recalls that when he came to Cornell in 1891 as an instructor in philosophy, President Adams's whole welcome was an elaborate caution that the job was only temporary.

of Civilization. Adams replied that both he and Buckle had independently translated from Helvétius's own summary of his contentions and that inevitably they both found similar phrasings. (He might have gone farther, to say that the historian is almost bound to be a plagiarist. He is expected to be scrupulous and exact, to tell only what has been securely reported; how, then, can he be blamed for saying precisely what has been said before?) Adams's reply to his critics is entirely convincing to the modern student, as it was to his fellow historians. But the general public remembered that there was something discreditable in his career. When his nomination to Cornell's presidency was announced, hostile newspapers recalled the small literary scandal with glee. "Should a Plagiarist Professor be Made a College President?" headlined the Brooklyn *Eagle;* and the Syracuse *Standard* referred to him every morning for a week as "that literary thief." [3]

White's resignation of the presidency, presented on 17 June 1885, took most of the trustees by surprise. Their surprise mounted when he proposed that they immediately elect Adams as his successor. White noted in his diary:

Governor [Alonzo B.] Cornell and J. DeW. Warner [alumni trustee] opposed election now on ground of precipitancy and want of notice. Gov. C. at last very bitter. Very bitter feeling produced—catastrophe imminent— but I induced them to adjourn until tomorrow. . . . 18 June: All heads cooler. . . . I urged in interest of peace a compromise on meeting July 13th.

A vigorous cabal among the alumni opposed Adams, asking a man more generally known. The faculty were mostly in favor, being flattered to have a familiar professor chosen, though they would not have settled on Adams as the flower of their own flock.

At the meeting on 13 July the trustees elected Adams President.

---

[3] The accusation of Adams's plagiarism was made in a letter to *The Nation*, 10 June 1875, signed M. G. (rumored to be a Harvard historian). Adams replied, with an excellent and decisive letter, on 17 June. White examines the case at length (*The Presidency of Cornell University: Remarks* . . . [Ithaca, 1885]) and completely vindicates Adams. "Nothing is more natural than that occasionally there should glide into an author's mind or into his text some other author's happy turn of thought or of expression which becomes, as it were, a part of himself." He reveals that some Cornellians opposed to Adams revived and spread to the press the plagiarism story. But he admits Adams's colorlessness: "It is quite likely that . . . those who look for a brilliant display would be at first disappointed. The very quietness, solidity, and depth of his qualities would at first mislead them."

There was a general feeling that the action was a hasty one, forced by the impatience of White and the dominant trustees.[4]

Adams moved to Ithaca and took over the direction of the University. White, not wishing to embarrass his successor, escaped to his dear Abroad.

The formal Inauguration took place on 19 November 1885. Students, faculty, and guests, eight hundred in all, assembled in the Armory. The speakers spoke 26,000 words, which means that the utterances lasted three and a half hours, exclusive of the "Te Deum," the three orchestral renderings, and the choral ode in Latin, chanted by the Glee Club.

President Adams dealt with the Development of Higher Education in America. He gave twenty-five minutes to its development to 1865; then twelve minutes to Andrew D. White, his essential ideas, his concept of a university; then nine minutes to Charles W. Eliot at Harvard; and the rest (thirty minutes) to plans for the New Education. The plans turn out to be not very startling. (Specialization should properly begin at entrance to the University, but since our preparatory schools are so inadequate we must devote the first two years to general education. We must give better training to future teachers, strengthen the classics, establish a law school, and eventually look to schools of medicine and pharmacy.)

The speech seems to the modern reader safe and sound, its overstuffed generalizations unlikely to bruise the tenderest susceptibilities. The modern reader is therefore surprised, and Charles Kendall Adams was astounded, at the rage and heartbreak of Andrew D. White, when he read the text. He wrote in his diary (1 December 1885):

This day came upon me one of 3 great disappointments of my life & in some respects the most cruel—Pres. Adams's inaugural. It has plunged me in a sort of stupor—have I been dreaming 30 years?—ever since I began working for a university—or am I dreaming now? Not the slightest recognition of the Univ. or my work or Gilman's & above all Mr. Cornell's name not mentioned—and this is a man who owed his start in life to me—whom I made President of Cornell Univ against fearful odds—defended him at cost of my health & reputation & the good will of friends—stood by him thro the worst of attacks—and now! He praises unjustly the worst enemy of all my efforts [Charles W. Eliot] & ignores my work utterly—& solely to curry favor with Harvard University & the men who have lashed him of the Harvard Set.

[4] J. F. Gluck to ADW, 16 and 27 July 1885; John Frankenheimer to ADW, 8 July 1885; Eugene Frayer to ADW, 20 Aug. 1885.

There is no other explanation. They are living & active & can do him more harm—I am supposed to be declining in health & can do him no more good. This is the hardest blow I have received. Yesterday my friend as I thought —today what? Yet I was warned by many.

He wrote a sharp letter to Adams, protesting especially against the praise of Eliot. He says that his own speeches and his Report on Organization deeply influenced Harvard. But for them, "Dr. Hill [President of Harvard] would have continued in office and his successor would have been an elderly scholarly man of the old pattern."

His pique was really unreasonable. He had complacently expected a glorification of his own work, which he could then gently, unconvincingly deprecate. Naturally he was disappointed. In fact, in Adams's essay on the Development of Higher Education in America, White has four pages out of 26—about what he merits. On the other hand, Adams might have spared his exhausted hearers on their folding chairs his review of the D. of H. E. in A., and he might have dealt with matters of more intimate concern. And certainly his bare mention of Ezra Cornell revealed a lack of tact alarming in a university president.

After a period of strain and reproach, White became again a good friend of Adams. But always, I think, White had his secret reservations about the disciple who aspired to become a master.

Adams, surveying his new domain, could well feel happy in his eminence. The enrollment of students was 638, the largest in Cornell's history, despite a steady stiffening of requirements. During his presidency the numbers leaped upwards, to reach 1,537 in 1891–92. A raise in tuition from $75 to $100 proved to be no check on growth. It is true that all colleges were rapidly gaining, for reasons which are not entirely clear, but are compounded of prosperity, an "adolescent plateau" in the population, and the academizing of such pursuits as law, engineering, and journalism.

Inspecting the Treasurer's records, Adams had likewise reason for satisfaction. With the profitable sale of western lands, the productive funds grew steadily. Cornell's income climbed from about $300,000 to about $400,000. In 1889 Cornell was regarded as the third American university in wealth and income, after Columbia and Harvard. We could compete with the best, for men and equipment.

With regard to the University's character and needs, Adams made his program. He recognized that White's purposes of 1868 had largely been attained, that Cornell, for all its reputation for radicalism, had little by little become conservative. We no longer needed to protest against the obscurantism and aristocratism of the older universities; they had mostly come round to our point of view. The day for defiance had passed; Cornell could not build its future on protest, for it might find itself protesting against something which had disappeared. Cornell's progress must now depend on excellence within the accepted university frame. It must become more efficient, better ordered, though less idiosyncratic.

"The University was sadly in need of reorganization and refitting," said Benjamin Ide Wheeler.

The seven years of [Adams's] administration were Cornell's *Sturm und Drang* period. Change and unrest characterized it throughout. A college small, provincial, and odd was transforming itself into a university of standard type and standard gauge, and there were as a matter of course some quakings, some throes, and many growing pains. . . . The Cornell which we know today was practically the making of those years.[5]

Adams's first purpose was to keep a balance between general and professional studies, between the humanities and the technologies. The immediate need, he thought, was to elevate the humanities in collegiate regard. James Morgan Hart, returning to Cornell in 1890 to occupy the chair of rhetoric, said that the things that impressed him most, after eighteen years' absence, were the growth of the campus trees and the development of the humanistic side of the University. Naturally, Adams's concern with the humanities inspired accusations of hostility to the sciences. Anna Botsford Comstock says that the scientists of the faculty felt discouraged, and that Anthony of Physics resigned in consequence.[6]

Adams's second purpose was to reorganize the administration, which he found illogical and inefficient. He turned departments, as Agriculture and Civil Engineering, into Colleges or Schools, with responsible deans or directors. Our system of deans, including the Dean of the Faculty, dates from this period.

Another purpose—one never realized—was to eliminate some of the waste of time in collegiate education. He reflected on granting the baccalaureate after two years in college, on turning over freshman and sophomore work, as far as possible, to other colleges of the state, and

[5] *Memorial of C. K. A.;* quoted in Smith, *C. K. Adams*, p. 29.
[6] *The Comstocks of Cornell*, p. 151. B. I. Wheeler (in Smith, *C. K. Adams*, p. 28) more or less bears out Mrs. Comstock. But the New York *Evening Post* in Jan. 1890 criticized Cornell for its disesteem of the humanities. See the *Era*, 17 Jan. 1890.

A History of Cornell

on making the junior and senior years in Cornell frankly preprofessional.[7] Herein he anticipated Robert M. Hutchins and other reformers of the twentieth century.

A dear purpose was the encouragement of faculty research and publication. "The function of a University is to discover truth and to impart it," he said in his report for 1892. He lightened the burdens of many overworked professors, provided equipment and materials for research, and instituted sabbatical leaves. He maintained that research should be endowed and as a step in the right direction secured from the trustees an annual publication grant of $2,000. In his report for 1887 he noted proudly that the faculty had published in a year 122 books, pamphlets, or important articles.

Nevertheless David Starr Jordan, in his alumni trustee's report for 1888, thought the faculty's production scanty, "though a dozen professors have stolen their own time for research." Jordan complained that "such investigation does not seem to have been regarded as a part of their university duties. The neglect of it on the part of any has never been met by a loss in his salary or in his standing in university circles."

Adams's constant effort was to raise the educational level, to stiffen the requirements. The old Optional Course, wherein almost any person could find instruction in almost any study, was in effect abolished.

He looked to the expansion of the University by new schools of law, pharmacy, and medicine, and by important development of Engineering, Agriculture, and Veterinary Medicine. This expansion required a building program, which should be logically conceived and beautifully fulfilled.

All in all, the program was sound and reasonable, if hardly sensational. To put it into effect, Adams needed the adhesion of the Board of Trustees, and particularly of its chairman, Henry W. Sage.

Adams's position was a difficult one, a pretty problem in human relations. Imposed on the Board by Andrew D. White, he was accepted unenthusiastically, as a faithful acolyte, without his master's originality and charm. A good deal of trustee hostility to White had grown up, especially with regard to the Fiske-McGraw Will Case, and this was naturally visited on his representative.[8] Many Board members looked

[7] President's report, 1889; also C. K. Adams, "The Next Step in Education," Forum, Feb. 1891, p. 629.
[8] The hostility to White, blinked by most historians, was compounded of resentment at his long absences, a growing realization that University problems

to Henry W. Sage for guidance. Fortunately Sage liked Adams and approved his practicality. He wrote White (11 February 1886): "Adams exhibits admirable executive ability, with power and disposition to work which I have seldom seen equalled. With this is sound wisdom, prudence, a well balanced judgment, and tact and adaptability to new surroundings." And on 28 May: "He works like a veritable Giant."

However, by the autumn of 1886 the inevitable collisions occurred. Adams regarded the choice of faculty members and the organization of courses as entirely his business, and Sage insisted that these were matters of trustee concern. (The faculty had its own views.) Both men were towers of obstinacy, but Sage had an emotional charge which Adams lacked, and besides, he was in a stronger position. Tyler noted in his diary (26 October 1887) that Adams had taken some steps with regard to the new library without consulting Sage; "hence the old man disciplines him, and lets him know who is Boss here." But a year later (31 October 1888), Sage wrote Tyler that "Adams is a marvel of persistent industry and power to work, in all details of administration. He is wiser and broader than when he came here, has less friction with Faculty and Trustees, has great zeal for the best interests of the

bored him, and mere jealousy of his wealth and brilliance. Sage wrote Erastus Brooks (29 Oct. 1886): "We have had twelve years of practically one-man power in which theories predominated and details were almost wholly neglected, and were rapidly reaping the reward of such management till the Trustees assumed the responsibilities belonging to them and from that moment on our advances in right directions began." Sage tried to keep White off the Board of Trustees in 1887, and yielded only to pressures to preserve the decencies. Tyler recorded in his diary (27 Oct. 1887) that White "was full of pain over his treatment by S. Thinks S has determined to drive him off the campus, and that anything which he expresses favor for is thereby damned in S's eyes and at once opposed by him. W is anxious over the danger of despoiling the beauty of the campus by S's arbitrary decisions as to the location & character of the new buildings—S being satisfied with a factory or saw-mill look." When the Fiske-McGraw suit was finally decided, Sage wrote his son Dean (23 May 1890) that newspaper criticism of himself was directed by "the friends of Fiske inspired and led on by White." He interprets the Fiske troubles as a manifestation of White's rivalry. "Our differences began long ago—when Russel was deposed—the bitter fight then was, with Russel in front, White in the background all the time."

But with Sage's distrust of White was compounded intellectual respect and old, recurring affection. Sage wrote White (2 Aug. 1888): "I pray you let no differences of opinion we may have in our public actions affect our personal relations, or in any way mar the sweet friendship so long existing between us. . . . Let us believe in ourselves, and each in the other." And so on.

University, and all in all is growing to the measure of a sound, wise President." Then, in cautious words, he records his fear that Adams may yield to Other Influences—which can be no other than those of Andrew D. White.

Bit by bit, Sage's liking and esteem for Adams lessened. One cannot take this coolness as a serious criticism of Adams's competence, for Sage quarreled sooner or later with everyone who ventured to disagree with him. Nor should one conclude from the discord that Sage was a purse-proud despot, an ogre delighting in his subordinates' blood. He loved the University dearly, labored for it during twenty-seven years, and gave it well over a million dollars for its urgent needs.[9] The welfare of Cornell became his deepest, most constant concern. He wrote Tyler (24 August 1890) moved and moving words:

I go to the campus twice nearly every day and watch the growth there and try to forecast the future, and see through my imagination what will be there when the men who now try to give form and substance to it have passed away—to see all perhaps from another standpoint which shall make their doings seem small indeed! But, I think, those who are now doing the best they can, sowing, planting, building for others, are not wasting time nor effort, and their imperfect work will help toward the development of grander results than they now dream of.

Adams's relations with the faculty followed the same curve as his relations with the trustees. The faculty, a captious body, greeted him at first with reserve, then came to recognize his honest purpose, his intelligence, his industrious attention to detail.[10] While he was not precisely loved, he was respected. As late as 14 December 1888 Benjamin Ide Wheeler, an excellent observer, wrote Tyler: "Pres. Adams gains in strength, I think, year by year. Both in the Faculty and the Board of Trustees, I think, a respect for his wisdom and his devotion gains ground."

Soon, however, the rifts began to develop. The first was caused by Honorary Degrees.

Andrew D. White had from the first declared against the granting of honorary degrees, a practice sadly abused in the mid-century. Cornell regarded as a proud distinction its refusal to make honorary doctors

---

[9] Sage estimated the total of his gifts to Cornell at $1,177,000 (Sage to H. W. Parker, 17 Dec. 1890; quoted in Anita S. Goodstein, *Biography of a Businessman: Henry W. Sage, 1814–1897* (Ithaca, 1962).

[10] R. H. Thurston to ADW, 26 Oct. and 20 Dec. 1885; Tyler to ADW, 11 Nov. 1885; C. D. S. to ADW, Dec. 1885; Tyler, Diary, *passim*.

of those who could never earn a real doctorate. A faculty committee (12 January 1885) reported against any change in policy. But Adams thought that the time had come when Cornell should honor in the usual manner some of its eminent alumni. He therefore proposed, at the trustees' meeting of 16 June 1886, that Andrew D. White and David Starr Jordan '72, President of Indiana University, be granted honorary LL.D.'s at Commencement on the following day. This was very bad timing. Obviously the nominations were presented as a *fait accompli*, which could not be disavowed without public shame. The trustees, taken by surprise, voted yea, and the awards were made.

The alumni, who had long boasted of Cornell's high moral stand in the matter of honorary degrees, took fire. Petitions were circulated, pamphlets printed. The alumni clubs, less than lukewarm toward Adams at his election, now turned actively hostile. It was widely surmised that Adams was trying to pay off his benefactor and predecessor and create a tradition which would reward him at his own retirement. The trustees resented the agitation and were inclined to blame Adams for putting them in an uncomfortable position. Without taking formal action, they returned to the Cornell principle that all degrees represent achievement under scholastic direction.

A second rift occurred with reference to the appointment of new faculty members.

Andrew D. White had usually assumed without question that the President picked the faculty, subject to the approval of the trustees. But in his report for 1883 he asserted that the faculty should nominate professors—a procedure as new to him as it was to the faculty. The faculty agreed heartily that the faculty alone were competent to judge instructional needs and to choose colleagues of sound achievement and promise. They pointed to the German practice, with the faculty enrolled in a powerful Academic Senate.

Faculty and administration came into conflict when Adams proposed to bring in a young outsider to be Dean of the new President White School of History and Political Science. Thirty-year-old Woodrow Wilson was invited for inspection from Wesleyan, and the later celebrated Herbert Baxter Adams from Johns Hopkins. Moses Coit Tyler, who thought he would be a better dean than any young hobbledehoy, was deeply affronted at the public slight; he became the bitter enemy of the President. He joined with a rebellious cabal of the faculty in an effort to take over the appointive power.

No memory persists of the malcontents' planning, or plotting, if one prefers. The new professor of philosophy, Jacob Gould Schurman, was one of the leaders, perhaps indeed the leader.[11] Schurman was the special protégé of Sage; very possibly he arranged with Sage for the introduction of the following motion, which was passed at the trustees' meeting of 30 October 1889: "In each case of the appointment of a full Professor of the University no election shall be made, except upon the nomination of the candidate by a Committee composed of the President and all the full Professors of the University." The Executive Committee implemented the motion by naming the President and the full professors the University Senate and charging this body to counsel and advise with regard to all nominations to professorships and in general to consider questions of educational policy.

President Adams did not like this measure at all. He did not want to have thirty full professors hemming and hawing over every appointment, perhaps ruining it by delay, jealousy, publicity, and incomprehension of the larger purposes of the institution. He did not want a project for expansion checked by professors concerned chiefly with the welfare of their own departments. Of course, he said, a President must seek advice.

But as soon as the necessity of seeking advice in regard to a nomination becomes official, the persons from whom advice is sought become organs of power, instead of organs of information. Whenever the responsible head of a government listens to advice officially given and then acts independently of it, he will be sure, sooner or later, in one case or another, to give serious offense.[12]

Further, the President was much embarrassed by a system which permitted him to make only provisional offers to prospective appointees. A superior man might resent having his case examined, and perhaps rejected, by all the University's full professors.

The President's point was excellently taken. The University Senate was an unwieldy affair. It represented, however, the faculty's conviction that it must be consulted on educational policy and major appointments. Today that conviction is incorporated in University legislation. The sensitive business of appointments is resolved by the creation of *ad hoc* committees, which examine a candidate's credentials in becoming privacy.

[11] M. C. Tyler, Diary, 22 Nov. 1889, 19 Jan. 1890, *et passim.*
[12] Annual report, 1892, p. 43. See a significant letter from Sage to Hiram Corson, 5 June 1890.

Adams saw in the Board's creation of the Senate "an attempt on the part of one or two members to clip my wings." [13] Some disgruntled members of the faculty, he told White, had worked it up and palmed it off on the Board.

Tyler, who had become a bitter enemy of Adams, paid a significant call on Sage. He wrote in his diary (31 March 1890): "When I told him that the permanence of the Senate would lead logically to the abolition of the University Presidency and the establishment of an annual Rectorship, his face became very bright, and he emphatically assented."

Observers on and off the faculty opined that Sage had withdrawn his favor from President Adams and that Adams, abetted by White, was fighting for survival. Tyler, who had excellent channels of information, describes the Executive Committee meeting of 12 April 1890 as a bitter trial of strength between Adams and Sage, with Adams making an outright attack on the institution of the Senate.

In fact, the Senate occupied most of its brief existence with formulating its own constitution, bylaws, and organization and with the faithful reading of minutes and communications. It accepted all President Adams's nominations except one: the advancement of Spencer Newbury to a full professorship of general, organic, and applied chemistry. The Senate voted him down, on 11 June 1891, by a vote of 17 to 4. Now Spencer Newbury had married Andrew D. White's daughter, and White had just built for the couple a house beside his own campus mansion. I have no way of estimating Newbury's qualifications for the professorship and whether the Senate did well or ill in rejecting him; but I may at least wonder if the case may not justify Adams's forebodings about the Senate's opportunities for the exercise of personal jealousies.

The record of Adams's presidency is one of gathering and increasing troubles. With the highest of motives, he irritated and alienated the faculty. "Poor old pachyderm—befooling himself with the dream of being a Bismarck!" sneered Tyler. He was unpopular with the students, in part because of his disciplinary actions, more, no doubt, because of his slow, chilly, rustic manner. They boycotted his Washington's Birthday address in 1888. Somehow, he did things wrong. He wore habitually a carnelian necktie to show his devotion to Cornell; he showed rather a clumsy undergraduatism which the students recognized derisively as false.

[13] Adams to ADW, 7 Feb. 1890.

He endured a private calamity, in the sudden death of his wife, on 5 July 1889. Her death deprived him of the affectionate counsel he badly needed.

In the following spring (30 April) Tyler noted that Adams "has come out as a rather dandified widower and gay youth, with a jaunty cutaway coat, light trousers, and a cane which he tries to carry in the English manner. The picture . . . is not a little comic: the clumsy frame, the corporeal movements but partially redeemed from rusticity, the habitual ungainliness, all struggling with the effort to seem young, elegant, fashionable." This elegance was, as it later appeared, courtship plumage. In July 1890 he married the wealthy poetess widow of the New York publisher Alfred S. Barnes, the donor of Barnes Hall. But Mrs. Adams did not like Ithaca, no doubt recognizing there the hostility to her new husband.

Even White began to turn against his protégé. Malevolent Tyler informed his diary (20 February 1890) that Adams had been pumping the architect, W. H. Miller, about the presidential mansion. "The old chap would like to get White off the campus, and to be living in the Palace. He is utterly devoid of appreciation for any benefit done him, and would tumble his greatest benefactor over in the gulf to add another advantage to his own greedy selfishness." Unquestionably Tyler, and others, passed on the delicious morsel to White, who conceived the darkest of suspicions.

More important, Henry W. Sage withdrew his favor. As early as 19 January 1890 Tyler recorded that Sage blamed him, most unjustly, for bringing Adams to the campus—"If things do not improve, Adams's head will go off by next June." Sage wrote Schurman on 31 May that in the matter of a faculty appointment Adams had left an impression of deceit, unfairness, and lack of truthfulness. W. C. Russel wrote White (7 August 1890): "I am very much disturbed by accounts which I hear of Adams's loss of influence at Cornell and at Albany." On 20 August Tyler noted: "A. D. W. says Sage and Boardman have formed with others a scheme to get rid of C. K. A. and to put Schurman in his place; and that the latter has entered into the project." And on 30 September he recorded that White had evidently warned Adams that his head was in danger, and that Adams was meek and tractable, "ready to crawl on his belly all the way from his house to Sage's, if necessary."

Make all proper deductions for the mean delight of a spiteful professor; the commentator truly reported the essential facts. Schurman was the rising man, the aureoled Pretender. It was Schurman who now enjoyed all the favor of Sage the Kingmaker.

The reasons are obvious enough. Sage sincerely disapproved of many of Adams's actions and policies; but he was the more inclined to disapprove in that he had come simply to dislike Adams. And Adams was White's surrogate, his appointee, in effect; and the relations of Sage and White in 1890, at the height of the Great Will Case, were more than chill. Sage reproached himself for his own ready yielding to White's choice of his successor. Schurman, however, was Sage's own man. Sage had personally chosen him to be Susan E. Linn Sage Professor of Christian Ethics and Mental Philosophy. The bond between the two was close. Sage saw in Schurman his own young self, ambitious, vital, tireless, competent in the affairs of this and the other world.[14] Like Sage, Schurman had fought his way to success from obscure beginnings by his force of character and intelligence. Perhaps also Sage recognized and approved in Schurman a certain strain of ruthlessness. On his part, Schurman admired Sage and felt for him deep gratitude and an almost filial affection, which could find even embarrassing expression.

Matters came to a head in the spring of 1892. Schurman gave a course of lectures at the University of California. He so impressed the Regents that he was offered the presidency of the rich young institution, at a reported salary of $10,000. He returned to Ithaca to talk things over with Sage (not, one notices, with the President). On 20 April he informed a *Sun* reporter that owing to his affection for the projected Sage School of Philosophy, destined to become the center of philosophical activity in America, he had declined the California offer. One need be no diviner to penetrate what had taken place in his interview with Sage.

According to a no doubt authentic story, Sage drove in his buggy to Adams's house, summoned him from his lunch, informed him in the vestibule that he was deposed from his office, and drove on, having ruined the President's career and his lunch.

On 5 May, Adams informed the world that he had decided to resign the presidency.

On 18 May the trustees met. The resignation of President Adams was accepted, with only one negative vote, that of Andrew D. White.

[14] Goodstein, *Biography of a Businessman.*

Laudatory resolutions were passed. Adams was granted a year's salary and was asked to sit for his portrait—an unusually good one, as it turned out.

Jacob Gould Schurman was then unanimously elected President of Cornell University.

He moved into the President's office on 7 June and wrote this remarkable letter to Sage:

I do not write this letter to ask your support and sympathy and affection: I know I have them. Nor do I write to make any promises: you know I will do my best. But as I took my seat for the first time at the President's desk I felt a sudden inspiration to dedicate myself to the new work by addressing my first letter to you. Beyond this impulse I have nothing to say or ask for. But I pray that God will prosper our work at Cornell University, and that you will long be spared to preside over the Board, you, my friend, my father. Ever cordially and filially yours, J. G. Schurman.

It is a pleasure to record that Charles Kendall Adams was almost immediately offered the presidency of the University of Wisconsin and that, perhaps schooled by his Cornell experiences, he made a complete success of his administration. He died in 1902.

XVI

Cornell under President Adams: The Business of Education

DURING President Adams's seven years at Cornell the appearance of the campus was transformed. Five important buildings were erected, to serve as his monuments: Barnes Hall, Lincoln, Boardman, Morse, and the University Library.

The first was Barnes Hall. In 1886 agitation for a Christian Association building began, the chief agitator being John R. Mott '88, undergraduate leader of the Christian Association and the future world leader of the Y.M.C.A. movement. Students and others pledged $10,000, a creditable sum but far from sufficient. Alfred S. Barnes, New York publisher and a trustee, was touched (in two senses), and offered $45,000 more. Barnes Hall, designed by William H. Miller, was constructed in 1887–1888.

It was an unlucky building, doubtless from the hostility of the foul fiend. During its construction Mr. Barnes died, and also his daughter, and also the superintending architect, the contractor, and the contractor for the gas installation; while Robert Richardson, the sculptor of the stone ornamentation, was stricken with fatal consumption. The evil omens ceased with the opening of the hall in 1889. It was the first college Christian Association building in the country, the model for others at Michigan and elsewhere.

The Quadrangle, today commonly termed the Lower Campus, was

A History of Cornell

as yet no quadrangle. The buildings on the west and north sides were standing, and in the mid-part loomed the ugly wooden barrack housing Civil Engineering and Architecture, temporary in 1868 and still temporary twenty years later. Therein, as Henry N. Ogden '89 remembered, it was often so cold that students and faculty wore overcoats and gloves at work, while watercolors froze during the period in the drafting room.

Adams persuaded the trustees to tear this structure down and to erect a decent substitute to the east, marking the third side of the Quadrangle. Since the funds were to be taken from the University's capital, the trustees were chiefly animated by the desire to build cheaply. They had their way, despite Andrew D. White's vigorous protests. The graceless structure was named Lincoln Hall, for the President who had signed the Morrill Act. It was opened in 1889.

The overcrowding of Franklin, occupied by Physics and Chemistry, demanded relief. The trustees decided, in 1888, to erect a chemistry building directly to the west of Franklin, on a commanding knoll overlooking the lake and valley. White, absent in Europe, uttered anguished cries. This spot, where Ezra Cornell had first looked down on his future home in 1828, where White himself had often gone to dream, was to him holy ground. In his plan it was to be a kind of Inspiration Point, occupied only by a belvedere and monumental tombs of Ezra Cornell and John McGraw. He took the proposal to build a cheap brick building on the site to be a calculated affront to him on the part of Sage and Boardman. "They have spent $2,000,000 in punishing Fiske—why should they not spend $80,000 in punishing me?"[1]

The dull brick building went up nonetheless and was named Morse Hall, in honor of Samuel F. B. Morse, inventor of the telegraph and Ezra Cornell's associate. Morse Hall in fact served its purpose well until its burning in 1916. At this writing, the noble site is a parking space.

Greatest of the constructions under Adams's regency was the University Library.

It will be remembered that Jennie McGraw Fiske's will provided a large sum for the building of a library. For a time Cornell made soaring plans for the greatest university library in America. The darkening Fiske-McGraw Will Case brought the high hopes low. Then in 1888 Henry W. Sage, moved by several impulses, of which surely self-reproach was one, proposed to build the library himself.

The site was chosen, and the architect, William H. Miller. Both

[1] ADW to Adams, 18 Dec. 1888.

270

choices were happy. The Tower, or Campanile (a name that Woodford Patterson '96 struggled through life to impose) became the visible symbol of Cornell. The Library itself was regarded as the finest and the best disposed college library in the country. From the central delivery desk the distance to the farthest point in each direction was 120 feet, and the pages would never have to run up more than four flights of stairs for a single book. The Librarian sat in a glass-enclosed office in the middle, whence he could see everything that went on. (Everyone else could also see the Librarian, if he should faint for lack of oxygen.) The stacks were fireproof; ample seminary rooms were provided, and lecture rooms. Upon some theory which I do not quite understand, no serious toilet facilities were afforded for male readers. The building cost $227,000 and had stack room for 400,000 books. (At the time, we possessed 105,000 volumes.)

Andrew D. White, inspired by the promise of fireproof quarters, presented his historical library of 30,000 volumes, 10,000 pamphlets, and many manuscripts, called the most valuable private historical library collected in the United States. To house it, a special hall was built, a delightful example of Millerian gothic-romanesque-baroque.

Boardman Hall was opened in 1892, to be the home of the new, thriving Law School. Designed also by William H. Miller, it corresponded in style and materials with the Library. It was called the finest law-school building in the country. Noteworthy were the high-vaulting classrooms, which no money or ingenuity could heat on a windy day, the spaciousness of the professorial offices, and the fourteen imposing fireplaces. Their use was forbidden, because of the fire hazard.

Among other constructions was J. H. Comstock's Insectary, probably the first of its kind. Comstock designed and built it in six weeks, to take advantage of an unexpended balance of $2,500 in the Agriculture appropriation. For that sum he had a two-story steam-heated house with adjoining greenhouse.

The University's establishments underwent improvements, perhaps unworthy of the historian's attention, but important to campus dwellers. Electric lights were installed in various buildings and on Ithaca's streets. An electric street railway, one of the first in America, was built from the railroad stations to the Ithaca Hotel in 1887. It was designed and supervised by the indefatigable Professor Anthony. It was motivated from a horrible power plant, which for many years defiled Fall Creek Gorge, just above the present Stewart Avenue

Bridge. Not until 1892 did the cars venture to climb the hill. The line then ran up Eddy Street, crossed Cascadilla on its own bridge (now a footbridge), and ran along East Avenue to the latitude of Andrew D. White's house. There it turned sharp left, and came to its terminus in front of the Library.

Various advances were made in the realms of beauty and hygiene. The trustees ruled that the dumping of the campus's furnace ashes in Fall Creek and Cascadilla gorges must be stopped. A new reservoir was built, commemorated still by Reservoir Avenue. But Director Fuertes of Civil Engineering harped on the theme that the water drawn from Fall Creek was rich in putrescent impurities. He pointed out that the mills near Forest Home dumped dangerous zymotic poisons into the stream and that privies, pig pens, and a slaughter house stood by its banks. The Mogue was always making trouble.

Within the university organism, President Adams reformed the administration in the interest of efficiency. And he gave particular attention to the faculty's welfare and its grievances.

In 1885 a faculty committee asked formally for a rise in the salary scale, with a norm of $3,500 for full professors. It pointed out that a professor needs enough for a decent, secure life, for the collection of a private library, for attendance at professional meetings, for leisure to do research, and for vacations, owing to "the depressing effect of Ithaca climate." A trustee committee responded with the recommendation (18 December 1885) that the older professors should receive $3,000, and in two cases (Anthony and Fuertes) $3,200. The committee considered the old vexed problem of the worthy, faithful, but dull assistant professor. It concluded that honest labor does not entitle a man to be a professor and that promotions should be justified by marked excellence alone. With this judgment President Adams was in hearty accord.

The committee discussed the still novel idea of provisions for retirement. A member, James F. Gluck '74, proposed that $100 or $150 be retained annually from salaries for this purpose.[2] He did not suggest any contribution by the University.

At the President's urging, a system of sabbatical leaves was established, with provision for a leave with pay after six years of professorial service.

Most importantly, the teaching load of the faculty was reduced.

[2] Letter of 18 Dec. 1885, in Executive Committee files; also Trustees' *Proceedings*, 16 June 1886.

The *Register* for 1891–92 reveals that a professor normally taught from nine to twelve hours or the equivalent. Certainly the faculty should have spoken its gratitude for the President's concern for its welfare. But no wise ruler expects gratitude from the People.

(There were limits to the administration's good will. The Executive Committee resolved, on 6 March 1889, that it would be unwise to supply professors with typewriters.)

The most eminent achievement of President Adams's reign was no doubt the establishment of the Cornell Law School.

Andrew D. White had proposed a school of law in his *Report on Organization* of 1866 and had renounced the idea only for financial reasons. In his final report, for 1885, he asserted that the time was at last ripe. President Adams heard and applauded. To make a law school one needed, after all, only a small library and a few professors.

Special committees of the trustees approved the proposal (June and October 1886). They advised a two-year course, with an entrance requirement equivalent to one year of high-school work—whereas four high-school years were demanded for entrance to Arts or Engineering. It is true that such easygoing requirements were normal, that no graduate school of law yet existed in the country; nevertheless many thought that Cornell stooped too low in its effort to attract students. Thanks to alumni protests, the entrance requirement was soon stiffened.

The Law School opened in the fall of 1887 and was quartered in the inconvenient and uncomfortable fourth floor of Morrill Hall. Judge Douglass Boardman was Dean, and Harry B. Hutchins of the Michigan Law School, Francis M. Burdick of Hamilton College, and Charles A. Collin of Elmira were faculty. They were well chosen; Hutchins later was President of the University of Michigan, and Burdick became a prominent professor of the Columbia Law School.

The school prospered and attracted students. It made a specialty of pleading and practice, with an abundance of mock trials. The case system was used from the beginning, though not exclusively. However, Judge Cuthbert Pound '84 said at the dedication of Myron Taylor Hall in 1932 that the original school was in no sense a *university* law school; "it was merely a good place for time-saving organized and systematic study of the law, in lieu of the desultory law-office clerkship or apprenticeship then in vogue."

A true university law school it rapidly became, under the guidance of its excellent staff. In 1891 Adams discovered a rising star—Charles Evans Hughes, who made a deep impress on his students. On his part,

Hughes remembered, long after, that his two years at Cornell were for him the equivalent of a postgraduate course, among men of outstanding talent and students of rare earnestness.[3]

The prosperity of the school brought about the construction of Boardman Hall. The funds therefor emerged from a happy lawsuit brought against the state.[4] Since the passage of the Land Grant Act in 1862 the state had regularly deducted from the revenues under the act the sums paid for premiums and expenses. The Court of Appeals decided that Cornell was entitled to these sums, amounting, in thirty years of accumulation, to over $89,000, enough for a new building. Cornell's agriculturists and engineers argued, as loudly as they dared, that under the Morrill Act they deserved these moneys, but they could not outargue the lawyers.

Within the academic department, President Adams's regime was marked by a general revision of the course of study and by the establishment of special schools of History and Political Science, Philosophy, and Pharmacy.

The Trustee Committee on Salaries and Reorganization of Departments proposed in 1885 that the courses in the Arts division be reduced to three: a Classical Course, leading to the degree of Bachelor of Arts; one with French and German replacing Greek, leading to the Bachelor of Philosophy; and a course without Latin or Greek, leading to the Bachelor of Letters or Bachelor of Science. The committee also made various special recommendations, as that Sanskrit and Oriental Languages be discontinued. (Poor Professor Roehrig had been abandoned by his last student.)

The committee found the Department of History and Political Science ill planned and ill organized and recommended that it be reformed. A special committee examined its case and reported (on 18 January 1887) that the gaps in the teaching of history should be filled and that political science should be strengthened by courses in Political Institutions, in Municipal Institutions, and in International Law. Further, the areas of economics and of social science should be cultivated, with such courses as the History of Industrial, Charitable, and Penal Institutions.

The sailing, one would say, was plain. President Adams determined to make a distinct School of History and Political Science and to recruit a vigorous young outsider for Dean. But every presidential sug-

[3] Hughes to R. D. Fernbach, 30 Sept. 1940.
[4] People *v.* Davenport, 117 N.Y. 549, 23 N.E. 664, 1890.

gestion came to nothing. In the courtly phrasing of the President's report for 1892, "the desire to work in substantial independence seems to have occasioned a dread lest any administrative provisions should interfere with the prerogatives of individual professors." What this means is that the members of the history faculty would permit no change in their affairs. The School of History and Political Science remained incomplete, unorganized, and dissension-torn.

The President did, however, succeed in obtaining some remarkable men in his own favorite subject, political science. Among them were the celebrated economist, Henry Carter Adams; and E. Benjamin Andrews, on his way to the presidency of Brown University and of the University of Nebraska; and J. Laurence Laughlin, who gained his greatest fame at the University of Chicago; and Jeremiah Whipple Jenks, appeaser of international discords; and Edward Alsworth Ross, due to be Stanford's and Wisconsin's pride and trial. And young Assistant Professor Walter F. Willcox offered in 1892 a course in Social Statistics, which he continued to teach for thirty-four years.

The School of History and Political Science never existed as a functioning organism. More successful was the Sage School of Philosophy.

From the University's opening, the Reverend William D. Wilson had been in charge of Philosophy, the Registrar's office, and any miscellaneous subject that happened to be demanded. Most people agreed that he was a dear old white-bearded saint; but he represented the clerical amateurism of earlier times, when godliness redeemed every lack of intellectual rigor. Even as registrar, Dr. Wilson provoked endless complaints. Since his handwriting was almost illegible, and probably set down with pain, he kept the fewest possible records and trusted to his memory, which was failing. The Committee on Organization recommended that he be retired on the generous annual salary of $2,000. This is the first case in which the trustees recognized the principle of pension payments for retired professors.

The way was now open for a genuine philosopher. Henry W. Sage, with his interest in philosophy as the inculcator of Christian morality, took the matter in hand. He endowed a professorship of ethics and philosophy, with $60,000, plus $10,000 for a residence. It was taken for granted that he would choose his own incumbent. He took a liking to Professor George S. Morris of Michigan, largely because he had "a big pair of lungs and pulpit ability." [5] But Morris turned him down, and

[5] M. C. Tyler to ADW, 11 Nov. 1885.

Sage fell back on young Jacob Gould Schurman of Dalhousie College. By such sidelong courses does Fate do its work.

Sage proposed Schurman's name to the trustees in January 1886. He now named his chair the Susan E. Linn Sage Professorship of Christian Ethics and Mental Philosophy, in memory of his wife, killed horribly in a runaway in July 1885. (We should not make mock of the term "mental philosophy"; it contrasted with moral philosophy and natural philosophy, or physics.) Sage stipulated: "I desire to put upon the record for permanent remembrance this statement: that my chief object in founding this professorship is to secure to Cornell University for all coming time the services of a teacher who shall instruct students in mental philosophy and ethics from a definitely Christian standpoint."

Professor Schurman fulfilled this requirement to Sage's great satisfaction. Schurman was a Christian layman, broad-minded, well trained in philosophy. Fears that he might warp the Cornell liberal tradition to a narrow pietism were soon allayed.

For several years Schurman, with the aid of an instructor, gave all the work in philosophy and psychology. He was a brilliant speaker; his courses in metaphysics, ethics, and the philosophy and history of religion became the serious student's favorite electives. Adams wrote to White (22 February 1889) that Schurman's History of Ethics was very successful, "the most remarkable course on the subject ever given in an American university. He almost always seems to be at his best, and every lecture surprises by its thoroughness and brilliance."

Sage was delighted with his protégé and the protégé with his patron. Sage decided to go farther, to establish an entire school of philosophy. In October 1890 he offered $200,000, on condition that the University should find other funds to support the school. In an accompanying letter he stated his views on the nature of philosophical instruction. He complained that Cornell had done little to uplift the moral and religious quality of her students.

Increase of knowledge addressed solely to the intellect does not produce fully rounded men. Quite too often it makes stronger and more dangerous animals, leaving moral quality dormant, and the whole power of cultivated intellect the servant of man's selfish, animal nature. No education can be complete which does not carry forward, with the acquisition of knowledge for his intellectual side and physical wants, a broad and thorough cultivation of his moral and religious side.

The trustees naturally accepted the conditions, and the new school was named the Susan Linn Sage School of Philosophy. Schurman was sent abroad to inspect similar establishments in England and Germany. He recommended a new chair of the History and Philosophy of Religion, a psychological laboratory under competent direction, and the incorporation of pedagogy in the school. Sage suggested the addition of phrenology, but was adroitly dissuaded by Schurman. Campus legend has it that Schurman explained to his patron that "psychology" was merely the new name for "phrenology"; but Schurman was no man for trifling, and Sage no man to be trifled with.

The first appointment was that of Charles Mellen Tyler to the chair of the History and Philosophy of Religion. The circumstances illuminate the university system of the day. Tyler was pastor of the Congregational Church in Ithaca, Henry W. Sage's place of worship. He was a genial, literate, well-liked minister (though there were some who thought him extremely lazy, and so eager to be popular that he agreed with everyone).[6] When in 1881 he received a tempting offer from another church, Sage proposed that he be made professor of ancient history at Cornell. The proposal was somehow averted. Now in 1890 Sage had his way. Schurman, though he had other ideas, was too politic to oppose Sage, and the Reverend Mr. Tyler became professor, and in fact a very popular one, and in fact also the faculty dandy, whose elegances, such as necktie rings, set campus fashions.

In 1891 the school opened, with an impressive entry in the *Register*. The faculty numbered eight; it included Frank Angell, assistant professor of psychology, James Edwin Creighton, instructor in modern philosophy, William A. Hammond, instructor in Greek philosophy, Walter Francis Willcox, instructor in logic. All of these became important men in their fields, though the field of Willcox turned out to be political science and statistics.

"It is the purpose of the Trustees," said the announcement, "to make this School a thoroughly efficient center for the maintenance, diffusion, and increase of philosophical knowledge and activity in America." To this end, a psychological laboratory, one of the first in America, was imported from Germany, and library facilities afforded for philosophical research. Aid for book publication was provided. The *Philosophical Review* was established, its initial number appearing in January 1892. This was the first general philosophical review in the country.

The Sage School of Philosophy put Cornell immediately in the front rank of philosophical teaching. It was a coherent, well-staffed enterprise, with its coverage of various fields, its laboratory, its journal. Its

[6] M. C. Tyler, Diary, 9 March 1883.

opening marks also a stage in the development of Cornell University. Its stated aim was to serve as a center for graduate study and research, and its structure conduced to that aim. Thus a step was taken in the transformation of the idea of a university.

The career of the School of Pharmacy was less glorious. A two-year course, administered by the Department of Chemistry, was offered in 1887. The purpose was to train manufacturing chemists and pharmacists. The entrance requirements were the highest in the country; indeed, they were so high that no candidates passed the examinations. A few students were admitted with conditions. But the course was in competition with commercial schools of low standards, and the trustees refused to authorize a more impressive degree than Graduate in Pharmacy. The professor of pharmacy resigned in dudgeon, and the school was discontinued in 1890. It had had one graduate: Byron Lansing Barber, G. in Ph., 1890.

In the Academic Department (or Arts and Sciences) the studies of the first two years were almost entirely stipulated, those of the last two almost entirely elective. Thus the candidate for the B.A. took in his freshman year Latin, Greek, solid geometry, algebra, trigonometry, English, ancient history, and hygiene. He could escape all contact with the sciences. The candidate for the Bachelor of Science degree took chemistry in his freshman year and physics and botany in his second year. Thereafter the student was free as air, except for the requirement of military science and a senior thesis. Attendance at classes was voluntary, though a student might be excluded from examinations for excessive class absences. Concentration of studies was recommended, but not obligatory. The student was urged, but not required, to gain faculty advice for his choice of upperclass studies. This was the German system, making the student responsible for his own education. Many abused their freedom, of course; but many, who knew what they wanted, satisfied their curiosities better than they could do under the increasing reign of prescription today.

Certain developments within the departments call for comment.

The Department of English included James Morgan Hart, who had taught French, German, and Sanskrit at Cornell's opening, and who now dealt with rhetoric and English philology, balancing with his rigor the aesthetic vocalisms of Hiram Corson. The fledgling William Strunk, Jr., also joined the staff. The department made an excursion into journalism. The class was organized as the city staff of a large newspaper, with the professor, Brainard G. Smith, as editor. The course

278

was dropped in 1889, whether from lack of student interest or from faculty opposition. Many looked on such vocationalism with foreboding. Goldwin Smith thought he was watching, from Toronto, the dying struggles of belles lettres. He wrote M. C. Tyler (8 May 1890): "[H. Rider] Haggard's stories indicate the last attempts of fiction to keep itself alive before it expires. The end of novel-writing has been reached. In fact, there will be no more literature. All now is science."

Unaware of the death of literature, Classics throve, with a heavy registration, increasing from 29 in 1885 to 142 in 1892. The distinguished Benjamin Ide Wheeler, destined to be President of the University of California, came in 1886. In 1891 Alfred Emerson, member of an illustrious Cornell family, was appointed associate professor of classical archaeology, and charged with collecting a Museum of Arts, the basis of the Museum of Casts.

A new department, of the Science and Art of Teaching, was founded in 1886. Such a department was still a rarity in American colleges. (The University of Iowa was the first to create an instructorship in Education, in 1873.) Andrew D. White had vainly proposed the innovation; President Adams made it a reality. With the founding of the Sage School of Philosophy, the department found in it a temporary haven.

According to Fred H. Rhodes, Ph.D. '14, the eminent historian of Chemistry at Cornell, that subject came of age around 1886. "Up to this time it had been able merely to hold its own, being handicapped by an overworked and underpaid staff and inadequate quarters and equipment." William R. Orndorff and Louis M. Dennis came in 1887, Emile M. Chamot in 1891. Dennis organized the first serious course in America in spectroscopic analysis and inaugurated work in colorimetry. The veteran George C. Caldwell developed methods for the analysis of water and foods for the U.S. Department of Agriculture and New York State's Department of Hygiene. The concept of analytical chemistry was transformed from a mere technique to the analysis of particle shape and size. In 1891 the *Register* announced that a course in Chemical Engineering could be laid out for Sibley students. This was our first recognition of chemical engineering as a field.

Physics, always a specialty at Cornell, continued to prosper. The celebrated William A. Anthony, whose interests were primarily practical, indeed resigned in 1887 to practice electrical engineering, but he was succeeded by the no less celebrated Edward Leamington Nichols '73. The department, including George S. Moler '75, Ernest G. Merritt '86, and Frederick Bedell, Ph.D. '92, was an uncommonly strong one, and the laboratory was said to be the best equipped in the country. Under such men the interest of the department turned to fundamental rather than applied physics.

The case of Frederick Bedell has its significance. A Yale undergraduate in the late eighties, he found the instruction there in physics elementary. Reading in a technical journal an article written as a Cornell senior thesis, he decided that, if a student at Cornell could do such fine work, he would go there. Somewhat later (it must have been after 1899) he was privileged to show Presidents Arthur T. Hadley of Yale and Charles W. Eliot of Harvard through our technical and scientific laboratories. He says: "Hadley was aghast, deeply shocked that such work should have a place in college education." [7]

In Botany, Joseph Charles Arthur received in 1886 the first doctorate in science degree conferred in America for a conclusive research on the pathological aspects of a plant disease.

The Sibley College of Mechanical Engineering and Mechanic Arts (having changed its title in 1885) was totally reformed, indeed made anew, by Robert Henry Thurston. A graduate of Brown, he learned creative engineering from his father, a pioneer builder of steam engines. During the Civil War he was a ship's engineer in the Union Navy. He then taught at Annapolis and at Stevens Institute, where he devised in 1871 the first four-year course in Mechanical Engineering, with the first experimental M.E. laboratory. He was an inventor, a prolific writer, and the first president of the American Society of Mechanical Engineers. Andrew D. White persuaded him in 1885 to become the director of Sibley College. A man of wide reading and original expression, he was one of the most eloquent speakers on this or any campus. A wealth of anecdotes, mostly flat in the retelling, clustered about him, like iron filings on a magnet. His course in thermodynamics, in which he assumed the accessory roles of news analyst and philosopher, was commonly known as "Bobbyology." His genial warmth suffused Sibley College, and still glows faintly in the spirits of some few who experienced it. Professor William A. Hammond once said that when Thurston wished you "Good morning" he actually made the morning brighter.

Thurston's success as director was great. In eighteen years the candidates for the M.E. degree increased from 63 to 885, the faculty from 7 to 43. He brought to engineering instruction a new professional spirit, compounded of scientific rigor, idealism, and practicality. He raised the entrance requirements steadily, demanding solid geometry

[7] *Alumni News,* 15 March 1945.

(1887), French or German (1891), trigonometry and higher algebra (1894). He reorganized mechanical engineering, took over electrical engineering from physics, and made of it in 1889 the first Department of Electrical Engineering in America. Its distinguished and inventive head, Harris J. Ryan '87, imbued the work with the engineer's point of view. He built in Ithaca the first American high-voltage transformer. Recognizing that the manual-training features dear to Ezra Cornell must yield to technical preparation, Thurston developed the Mech Lab and shop work, which was always in danger of degenerating into mere artisanship.[8] A four-year course in Industrial Art was established. One of the instructors was Hermon Atkins MacNeil. His "Putting the Shot," done from life, stood long in Sibley College.[9] Thurston's encouragement persuaded MacNeil to turn to sculpture. Therein he gained fame and mastery, of which his campus statue of Ezra Cornell may stand in evidence.

The graduate work in engineering was much enlarged, with special attention to electrical, marine, chemical, mining, and steam engineering, including courses in railway machinery. Means and opportunity for faculty and student research were provided. Thurston envisaged an actual research institute on the campus. He said: "Men who have earned their spurs in the earlier struggles of previous years, and who have acquired a right to liberty to continue their work of solution of the great problems of the unknown, shall give themselves wholly, with all their time, talent, strength and genius, to the work which attracts them." [10]

Among the spur-winning teachers whom Thurston and President Adams brought to Sibley was William F. Durand in Marine Engineering, who, after a dozen years, went to Stanford and ever-increasing fame. And Albert W. Smith '78, the beloved Uncle Pete of later years, in Mechanical Engineering.

Dean Estevan Fuertes of the Department of Civil Engineering, a little jealous of the status of Sibley College, importuned the trustees to make his department a college, and himself director. His request was finally granted in 1890. New faces appeared on the faculty, among

[8] The *Cornell Era* (4 Oct. 1889) recounts the casting of an iron bird in a cage. A mold was made from a live sparrow; after its removal from the sand box it appeared as lively as ever.

[9] *Alumni News*, 9 Jan. 1901. It seems to have disappeared.

[10] William F. Durand, in *Exercises Commemorating the 100th Anniversary of the Birth of R. H. Thurston* (Ithaca, 1940), p. 38.

them Henry S. Jacoby and Henry N. Ogden '89, destined to become old faces in our little world.

The rivalry of C.E. and M.E. was always friendly, and advantageous to both students and staff. Under Thurston and Fuertes the Cornell Engineer became famous throughout the country and indeed the world.

The Department of Agriculture likewise was elevated to collegiate rank. President Adams recommended in 1888 that the college be constituted, with Isaac P. Roberts as director. The trustees so ordained at the June meeting, and the great career of the college, as a College, began.

The rise in status did not allay Agriculture's troubles. The number of students actually decreased, from 58 in 1888–89 to 41 in 1891–92. "We are educating professors of agriculture, not farmers," complained President Adams.[11] The new director labored tirelessly, building a Poultry House with his own hands and with those of James E. Rice '90, whose lifelong labors in Poultry Husbandry are commemorated in Rice Hall. Another lifelong professor, also the eponym of a building, Henry H. Wing '81, supervised the Dairy Department. He raised the product of the University cows to more than three times the average for New York State dairies. Director Roberts sold his products to the faculty; M. C. Tyler complains of his sharp practice, selling milk cheap and charging double for ice.

Three events came to the aid of the tiny College of Agriculture. The first, and greatest, was the coming of Liberty Hyde Bailey in 1888.

The second was the Hatch Act, for which President Adams lobbied actively in Washington. The act was passed by Congress in 1887. It provided for the establishment of agricultural experiment stations in connection with land-grant colleges, with an annual grant of $15,000 for each station.

Cornell had had its own experiment station since 1879. This had done gallant work and had published three reports, though handicapped by a total absence of money. Meanwhile New York State authorized an experiment station in 1880. Cornell sought the appropriation, but was outdone by Geneva. The relations between Cornell and the Geneva Station were for some time friendly, but rivalry later developed into hostility.

To fulfill the requirements of the Hatch Act the work of the College of Agriculture was reorganized. A professor of horticulture was sought

[11] Adams to ADW, 6 April 1886.

282

and found, in the person of Liberty Hyde Bailey. This was the first American professorship of horticulture (as a subject separate from botany and other branches of plant science).

The Cornell Experiment Station promptly justified the government's small expenditures. It studied soil fertility, animal and plant diseases, the development of hardier varieties of peaches, and so on. It inaugurated sugar-beet culture in the state. Comstock's bulletin on scale insects is regarded as an entomological classic. President Adams proudly announced that a bulletin on the pear psylla, by William Stebbins Barnard '71, had saved a million dollars for the growers of a single county.[12] The historian is troubled, to be sure, by President Schurman's proud allegation before a congressional committee in 1904 that Prof. Mark Slingerland '92 invented a spray lethal to the psylla, "and a very distinguished gentleman from Niagara County told me that the discovery was worth a million dollars to that county alone." At any rate, spraying was a Cornell specialty. Bailey experimented with it in 1890, and in 1894 a bulletin on fungicides and insecticides was published by E. G. Lodeman '94. His *Spraying of Plants* (1896) is a classic compendium of the subject, still prized.

The third event that brought advantage to the new College of Agriculture was the passage by Congress of the second Morrill Act, in 1890, in aid of land-grant institutions. Cornell's share, $25,000 annually, was allotted mostly to Agriculture and Mechanical Engineering.

The future of Agriculture at Cornell began to look rosy. Governor Roswell P. Flower of New York State urged the legislature in 1892 to concentrate at Cornell its aid to agricultural education and experimentation, and the legislature responded by appropriating $50,000 for a dairy husbandry building. President Adams, feeling the uprooted farmer's nostalgia for the soil, proposed a two-year course for practical farmers. He organized a Farmers' Institute in 1892 and made to it "A Plea for Scientific Agriculture." (Dean I. P. Roberts had in 1886 summoned a Farmers' Institute to meet at Cornell; this was the first in the state, and the forerunner of the Farm and Home Weeks and of the great Extension Service.) At the end of his term of office, President Adams declared (in his annual report for 1892) that one of the best achievements of his administration was the improvement of relations between the College of Agriculture and the farmer.

[12] First published in the *Proceedings* of the American Association for the Advancement of Science, 1871.

A History of Cornell

In the field of graduate study the increase in enrollment (from 34 in 1885–86 to 164 in 1891–92) moved President and faculty to impose some coherence on graduate work. Previously there had been a time requirement for the degrees, but no fixed prescription for the student's residence, guidance, or examination. In 1886 the M.A. and Ph.D. were newly defined, and the German system of majors and minors, *Hauptfach* and *Nebenfächer*, imposed. The revolutionary proposal was made, but rejected, that graduate students should pay tuition.

In these years the Summer School took recognizable shape. Some professors in Botany had held an informal summer school in 1876; in 1885 J. H. Comstock persuaded twelve students in entomology to engage with him in "the study of living animals under natural conditions instead of preserved specimens and books," and he reported, "To me it was the most satisfactory term's work I ever conducted." [13] The time was ripe for the summer-school idea. Professor Newbury of Chemistry discerned in 1888 an evident demand on the part of teachers for a summer school of science. In 1891 a group of younger professors and instructors organized, on their own, a summer school, with permission to use the University's facilities. The venture was so successful that the trustees authorized (22 November 1892) an official Cornell Summer School, which would grant college credit for work done.

This review of the work done in President Adams's seven years must impress any academic reader. It was a period of organization and especially of reorganization. The Cornell of President White was a very personal university, reflecting White's character, interests, and ideals. When White was bored, or when he took his immense vacations, the University drooped and withered. White could organize magnificently; he was too impatient, and too much bound by old friendships, hostilities, and prejudices, to be a good reorganizer. Cornell's need was for less brilliance and for more dogged labor, directed by an orthodox conception of educational purposes. This need President Adams fulfilled.

An easy measure of an institution's success is its popularity. The enrollment of students at Cornell rose from 573 in White's last year to 1,537 in the final year of President Adams. To be sure, not all of this growth is to be credited to the President. There were external circumstances, such as increasing prosperity, and internal circumstances, such as the improved financial state of the University. But we are ac-

[13] Annual report, 1886, p. 97.

customed to credit or blame a college president for everything that takes place during his time in office. By any reasonable reckoning, the seven-year hegemony of President Adams answered Cornell's urgent need for stabilization, renewal, reorientation. In any institution, the rule of genius needs to be succeeded by the rule of sober talent.

XVII

Cornell under President Adams:
The Teachers and the Taught

IF it is true—and it is true—that the faculty makes a university's greatness, Charles Kendall Adams was the chief artisan of Cornell's middle years. Whether helped or hindered by the University Senate, he chose the new members of the faculty, and chose them well. Many of them spent their lives at Cornell, and by their work and influence made its merit and spread its fame. One has only to scan the record in the previous chapter to recognize the quality of Adams's appointees. Most of the names have faded today, but they linger in books, in the annals of science, in local traditions, and in memories which themselves are old. In the effort, vain indeed, to defend them for another hour against the dark tide, I recall some of these old fames, old friends.

First, Jacob Gould Schurman. He was born in Freetown, Prince Edward Island, on 22 May 1854. His paternal ancestors had dwelt for two centuries near New Rochelle, New York. Tory loyalists, they had removed to the Maritime Provinces of Canada after the American Revolution, and apparently prospered little. The boy worked on his father's farm until he was thirteen, having only the slightest schooling. He remembered afterwards that, being small of stature, he was required to climb into large wool sacks and pack down the wool with his feet as it was thrown in from above. It was inside the stifling wool sack that he decided to become educated. He left the farm to clerk in a store. In three instructive years he saved eighty dollars, with which he entered a grammar school, and there won his first scholarship, to the academy in Charlottetown, P.E.I. Thenceforward he lived on scholarships and grants, which brought him First Class Honours in Mental and Moral Science and two degrees from the University of London, a doctorate of science from Edinburgh, and two years of travel and study in Germany. A man of long views, he called on the Minister, Andrew D. White, in Germany, and suggested that he would be available as professor of philosophy at Cornell. White was impressed by his personality and accomplishments, but made no offer of a job. Schurman became in 1880 professor of English literature in Acadia College, Nova Scotia, then professor of metaphysics in Dalhousie College, Halifax. He married a daughter of George Munro, New York publisher and Dalhousie's principal benefactor.

When, in the early eighties, Henry W. Sage proposed to establish a professorship of philosophy at Cornell, he assumed that he would pick his own professor. He cast about the scholarly world for some time in vain. He began to doubt, he told White, if a good professor of ethics existed. But White brought Schurman to Ithaca, and Sage was immediately won to him. Thus, though Schurman was not elected to the chair of Christian Ethics and Mental Philosophy until January 1886, the credit for his appointment really goes to President White.

Schurman's powerful personality soon made itself felt in the University. He espoused the faculty's causes, in opposition to President Adams, and spoke eloquently in Faculty meetings. "That speech is worthy of a Prime Minister!" declared White on one occasion.[1] He performed his committee duties with apparent delight. He paid his court to Henry W. Sage, demonstrating to him that here at last was a professor who was really practical. An interesting example: he pointed out that his instructor in philosophy and logic, Charles Augustus Strong, was about to marry the daughter of the rich Standard Oil man, John D. Rockefeller. Schurman told Sage that it would be wise to promote Instructor Strong. But Administration objected and kept Strong on as instructor at $1,000 a year; and the golden opportunity was seized by Columbia.[2] Such a display of presidential ineptitude may have given Schurman the idea of taking Adams's place.

[1] M. C. Tyler, Diary, 11 Jan. 1888, 2 Dec. 1890.
[2] H. W. Sage to ADW, 23 Feb. 1888. See the fascinating reminiscences of Mr. Strong and his life as a captive Rockefeller in George Santayana, *The Middle Span* (New York, 1945).

Second in our gallery is Benjamin Ide Wheeler, commonly known as Benny Ide. A graduate of Brown in 1875, he spent four years in Germany and took his Ph.D. *summa cum laude* from Heidelberg. He came to us in 1886 to teach classical philology, Greek, and Sanskrit. A scholar of engaging charm, an enthusiast for sports, especially rowing, a dapper dresser who ordered his clothes from the best New York tailor, he soon gained a vast campus popularity. He was prominent in the University Senate's movement for faculty power.[3] In 1899 he was called to the presidency of the University of California. He stipulated that he should have sole initiative in the appointment and removal of faculty members and in the setting of their salaries. (Thus do proclaimed convictions falter when a man passes from faculty to president, from Tribune of the People to Caesar!) His rule at California was one of rare brilliance, at least until his pronounced pro-Germanism caused trouble during the First War. Your historian heard Benny Ide speak at the Cornell Club of San Francisco in 1915. His words have blown away, but the grace and charm of their substance, phrasing, and utterance remain in memory as a masterpiece of after-dinner speechmaking.

Third, George Lincoln Burr. He worked his way through Cornell as a skilled printer in the University Press and graduated in 1881. His learning as an undergraduate was already phenomenal, and Andrew D. White put him to work correcting his fellow students' papers. White said that he was one of the two geniuses who attended Cornell during his presidency; the other shot himself.[4] Burr became White's secretary, dear friend, and uncomplaining burden-bearer. He rose rapidly to be professor of ancient and medieval history. His enormous erudition humbled his colleagues and terrified his students. He did much of the awesome research for White's *History of the Warfare of Science with Theology*, but refused to have his name appear on the title page. His modesty, and his perfectionism, estopped him forever from writing

---

[3] It is true that the head of his department, William G. Hale, found himself eclipsed, and discovered his subordinate to be grasping, plotting, and ungrateful, and that Moses Coit Tyler regarded Wheeler as "an academic politician, not altogether genuine, a flatterer of the rich and powerful, with intense selfishness and disregard of his obligations to one who had helped him" (Diary, 14 Nov. and 25 Nov. 1890). But Tyler's opinion of his academic colleagues was poisoned by his own spleen.

[4] ADW to Adams, 7 April 1886. The genius who shot himself was Emil Schwerdtfeger '78, whose *History and Development of the English Verb* received a British scholarly prize and was published while he was still an undergraduate. His suicide in 1877 was ascribed to overwork.

the great book that was expected of him. But despite the exiguity of his printed product, his eminence was recognized, and in 1916 he was chosen president of the American Historical Association. He was a great teacher, a true inspirer, whose lectures would often rise to an eloquent chant. And over his ardor for learning, his *libido sciendi,* an elfin humor played. A young man applied for the vacant post of secretary to Mr. White. Burr tested him by dictating the following letter:

Professor Jeremiah Cadwallader, School of Psychology, Baton Rouge, Louisiana. Dear Colleague: I regret that I cannot recall any such postulate as you cite in authentic utterances by Descartes, Goethe, Joinville, Leibniz, Machiavelli, Mazzini, Nietzsche, Robespierre, Rousseau, Schleiermacher, or Schopenhauer. I doubt that any of them dabbled in psycho-analysis or metempsychosis, except perhaps Goethe in his extravaganza, *Die Wahlverwandtschaften.* Sincerely yours. . . .[5]

Up to the end he made his own life, heedless of rule and convention. In retirement he dwelt at the Telluride House, occasionally disappearing for a meditative four-day walk to Rochester or some other destination. An enemy of sloth and sleep, he banished the bed from his rooms and contented himself with an easy chair, in which he could alternately doze and work.

After his death in 1938, Carl Becker wrote of him beautiful words, which I rescue from the twilight of the Faculty Necrology and transport to the crepuscule of these pages:

George Burr—how imperishably the name is written into the history of this university and the life of this community! . . . The short, compact, powerful figure of the man, ceaselessly active, tireless as a dynamo, at any hour of the day to be seen slipping in or out of the Library, hurrying across the campus, hurrying down the hill, and with unabated and triumphant vitality, hurrying up again. The richly stored and alert mind, keen as a Damascus blade, slaying the spurious and the inept with the deftest wit, pouring forth a wealth of relevant and curious lore for the illumination of matters great or small, and, on rare occasions, exploding into detonating wrath when goaded

[5] Edwin Emerson '90, "The Groves of Academe" (MS, C.U. Archives), p. 27. Let me inveigle in here a couple of anecdotes from Roland H. Bainton, *George Lincoln Burr* (Ithaca, 1943), p. 84: Burr commended a daylight lamp which had benefited him. He gave the manufacturers permission to use his commendation in advertising. But when he saw the proof he observed that the advertisers had changed "if it were" to "if it was" and rescinded his permission. Leo Gershoy '19 saw him in the White Library, staring out the great window at a snow storm. Said Gershoy: "Fine day." Burr, abstracted: "Yes." Then he came to himself and shouted after the retreating Gershoy: "Of its kind! Of its kind!"

past endurance by the senselessly stupid, the malicious, or the cruel act. The indefatigable scholar and bibliophile, browsing and brooding in the stacks, with the still concentration of the mystic poring over some rare manuscript, or with loving touch caressing the frayed covers of ancient books. . . . Valiant and intrepid crusader in the cause of human freedom and enlightenment! If there be any intangible possession that distinguishes this university, it is the tradition of freedom united with responsibility—freedom to do what one chooses, responsibility for what it is that one chooses to do. On this memorial occasion it is altogether fitting for us to recall that no one ever did more than George Lincoln Burr to endow Cornell University with this priceless possession.

(Here is the idea which Becker developed, two years later, in his lecture *The Cornell Tradition: Freedom and Responsibility*. The theme has since had a mighty success.)

If we should ever be asked to name the supremely great among Cornell's teachers, fit to be set beside Harvard's James and Santayana, Yale's Willard Gibbs, N.Y.U.'s John William Draper, no doubt Cornell's first candidate would be Liberty Hyde Bailey.

Bailey, the American Triptolemus, was born in Michigan in 1858, the son of a poor farmer.[6] With only the rudiments of formal education, but equipped with nineteen years' close observation of nature, he entered Michigan State Agricultural College. As professor there he was beginning to gain renown when in 1888 President Adams brought him to Cornell as professor of horticulture.

His career thenceforth was quadripartite. As a scientist, first, he soon became the leading American horticulturist, treating his subject as an applied science based on fundamental botany. He inaugurated the teaching of plant science at Cornell. He was an early experimental plant breeder and a great taxonomist, an authority particularly on American sedges and blackberries. In 1945, at the age of eighty-seven, he published a thousand-page monograph on the genus *Rubus*. Once, on a Jamaica vacation, his wife teased him because he did not know the full names of some palms. Piqued, he became a world authority, collected one of the largest palm herbaria, and hunted specimens from the Amazon to the Congo.

He was, secondly, an extraordinary writer and editor, prolific and exact, with a gift for the sharp and telling phrase. We still quote his

---

[6] Triptolemus was given by Demeter a plow, a chariot, and a supply of seeds. He traveled the world giving instruction in agriculture. He was worshipped for many centuries at Eleusis, but not, to my knowledge, in the College of Agriculture.

reply to the lady who asked what to do about dandelions on her lawn. "Learn to love them," said Bailey. (A variant: "How can I get rid of quack grass?" "Die and leave it.") Or again: "Emerson said: 'A weed is a plant out of place.' But it is a question whether a plant is ever out of place except when cultivated." His student, later professor, James E. Rice '90, preserved a couple of gems tossed to the class: "Northern fruits, like northern girls, have red cheeks. . . . Placing fertilizer around the trunk of a tree is like tying a bag of oats to a horse's legs."

Professor George M. Lawrence's incomplete bibliography of Bailey lists over 700 titles, among them 63 books and 5 encyclopedias, of horticulture, agriculture, farm crops, and farm animals. From 1890 to 1940 Bailey edited 117 volumes by 99 authors, on agronomy, economics, botany, pomology, animal husbandry, dairy industry, soils and fertilizers, plant pathology, commercial floriculture, and home economics; and since many of his authors were handier with hoe and hook than with pen, his editorship often meant a total rewriting. He was editor for a time of *American Garden* and of *Country Life in America,* but he dropped the latter, blaming the pressures to turn it into *City Life in the Country.* From 1923 (when he was sixty-five) to 1949 he produced over a hundred scientific papers. He could relieve his spirit with lyrical praise of nature, as in *The Holy Earth* (1915). Some of his many poems were collected in *Wind and Weather* (1916). And one summer at his lakeside home, Bailiwick, he wrote a novel. On a chilly autumn evening he built a good fire and sat down to read the book over. He found the first page bad and tossed it in the fire. The second page followed the first. At the evening's end the entire novel had disappeared in flame. The author had written his work for the pleasure of one sole reader. (Nor was this his only literary infanticide. He burned altogether eight completed manuscripts. The author of a manuscript on a horticultural subject said to him: "I hope you haven't written one on the same topic." Bailey replied: "Yes, I have; it's all complete." The author, woestricken, said: "That's our difficulty. We cannot publish books; you get there first. It's very discouraging." Bailey went home, and, he said; "I burned that book—every leaf of the manuscript and every picture." But, he confessed, after the other man's book appeared, he was sorry.) [7]

Authorship of 68 books, including a four-volume *Cyclopedia of American Agriculture* and a six-volume *Cyclopedia of Horticulture* and a *Manual of Cultivated Plants,* would be more than enough life-

[7] Philip Dorf, *Liberty Hyde Bailey* (Ithaca, 1956), p. 230.

work for most men. Bailey was, besides (and thirdly), a great administrator. In 1903 he became director of the College of Agriculture, which he succeeded in turning into the New York State College of Agriculture. He was a leader also in the establishment of agricultural extension courses. But all this belongs in later pages.

Finally, Bailey was a great teacher. He startled and aroused by questioning premises, by forcing students—and others—to examine the bases of accepted ideas. (An enemy of flower-snobbery, he shocked floriculturists by growing an enormous burdock by the front steps of his house.) Since time was always too short for the things to be done, he liked to enter a classroom talking and to leave it at the hour's end still talking, using the classroom door to make a period. For long he was at home to students every Sunday evening; there he talked and read poetry aloud and talked. The throngs becoming unmanageable, he instituted bimonthly assemblies in Roberts Hall. These were attended by many students who had no interest in agriculture, but much in Bailey.

As a boy, Bailey had made his plan of life: to spend twenty-five years in preparation, twenty-five in earning a livelihood, and twenty-five in doing what he pleased. In 1913, after twenty-five years at Cornell he resolutely retired, at fifty-five, to take his pleasure—in such activities as the pursuit of palm species in the upper Amazon and the Guiana jungles. In 1949, at the age of ninety-one, on his way to hunt palms in tropical Africa, he was caught in a revolving door in a New York bank, fell and broke his hip. Thenceforward he was practically confined to his hortorium. He died on Christmas Day 1954.

Such were four of the many who began their Cornell teaching careers under President Adams. Their influence on the students was stimulating and direct. Many of the faculty dwelt on the campus itself, in pleasant houses now effaced by progress. All lived perforce within walking distance of their classrooms. They accepted the Cornell tradition of intimacy with the students, though with increasing strain as the undergraduate enrollment tripled. A reporter from *Harper's Weekly* (8 June 1889) was reminded of Weimar, during the best years of Goethe's life.

Expansion brought with it strains and problems with which we are all too familiar. Classes swelled faster than the teaching staff, jammed the classrooms and laboratories. Accessory facilities, lodgings, eating places, washrooms, gymnasiums, recreation areas, were painfully inadequate. The only place on the campus where one could eat, except Sage College, was the Sibley Dog. Its origin is recalled by a writer in the *Alumni News* (30 March 1916). "Old John Love . . . drove his dog wagon up by the foundry and began to serve coffee, soup, hot dogs, and desdemonas. The desdemona was a chunk of hamburg steak mixed up with an egg and fried. After a while he took the wheels out from under the dog-wagon and left it there." This planting grew into a shambling green wooden building at the south end of the Triphammer Bridge.

Andrew D. White had always been opposed, on principle, to dormitories for men. Remembering the turbulence in the halls of Hobart and Yale, he insisted that students were best off under the care of high-minded landladies. President Adams took the opposite view. In his first report he pointed out that hitherto classes had been crowded into the morning hours, so that students might return to their homes for lunch, but now the afternoon recitations and the use of the Library in afternoon and evening forced the students to make the long journey from downtown two or three times a day. He therefore called for the construction of dormitories on the plateau west of the campus, where the men's dorms now stand. White reluctantly assented, insisting only that the proposed dorms should lie distant from Sage College and the professors' houses and that they should be oriented north and south, to give sunlight in every room. It was, however, to be many a long year before these plans were fulfilled.

Some of the pressure for student housing was relieved by the building of fraternity lodges. In 1887 a fourth of the men students belonged to fourteen fraternities. Life in their houses cost from $200 to $500 more than lodging-house existence; hence they were restricted to the wealthy.[8] And the wealthy came; and many a voice was raised to complain that Cornell, founded to aid the underprivileged, was becoming the resort of the rich.

To most of the students the Christian Association (hereafter to be termed the C.U.C.A.) was more of a social center and influence than the fraternities. Its common rooms in Barnes Hall filled many of the purposes of a modern student union. John R. Mott '88 claimed that the C.U.C.A. was the largest and best organized college Christian Association in the world. But he admitted that it did not reach enough

[8] R. Spencer, in *Lippincott's Magazine*, June 1887; David Starr Jordan, alumni trustee report, 1888.

A History of Cornell

fraternity men and athletes. He set as its immediate goal the conversion of the five hundred unconverted Cornell students, and as its eventual goal the evangelization of the world within his generation.

This evangelical zeal aroused some forebodings among the liberals and rationalists of the previous generation. Hiram Sibley wrote to Andrew D. White (27 June 1888): "I see or think I see evidence of a growing disposition to drift away from the original intentions of Mr. Cornell in the founding of a purely non-sectarian university. . . . I look to you to protect my investment in Cornell from the common enemy."

Sibley need not, really, have worried. The young skeptics remained free to doubt, to examine and reject or accept proffered doctrines. Those disposed toward piety joined the downtown churches; the lukewarm and the merely curious listened to the eminent divines in Sage Chapel; the unconverted slept.

Student behavior was on the whole admirable, in contrast to some earlier days and to some later ones. The faculty dealt with a few rare cases of drunkenness, "grossly immoral conduct" (nature unspecified), and the employment of beanshooters at a temperance lecture. In general, however, the undergraduates were passing through a virtuous phase. Liquor was barred by class action at the frosh banquet of the class of '89. A student reporter asserted that among the upperclassmen drunkenness was unknown, that one beer saloon and one liquor saloon sufficed for student needs, and that hazing had disappeared.[9] He applauded the students' honesty and their prevailing habit of hard work. Charles Evans Hughes bears him out, remembering: "Cornell was a revelation to me, because of the spirit of work I observed on the campus. There was no eight-hour day among the students. We had to drive them out of the library at night, and had a hard time answering their questions the next morning. For ingenuity and energy I never saw them equalled." [10]

The workaday mood prevailed, though the lot of the self-supporting student worsened, with rising living costs, a tuition raise to $100 or $125 (depending on the course), and a paucity of jobs. Embury A. Hitchcock '90, accounting for every penny, reckoned that his total expenses for four years were $1,290.[11] Some enterprising youths found

[9] R. Spencer, in *Lippincott's Magazine*, June 1887.
[10] New York *Evening Post*, 23 Feb. 1909, quoted by Bainton, *George Lincoln Burr*, p. 15.
[11] *My Fifty Years in Engineering* (New York, 1939).

294

ways of living on the needs of other students. Two young men started in 1886 a Campus Bookstore, ancestor of our Cornell Campus Store. James E. Rice '90 ran a cooperative boardinghouse, as did others. He remembered that the weekly cost per student varied from $1.60 to $1.90. On Easter morning the boarders had eggs ad libitum. Henry Erisman '92, built like a gladiator (and the model for Hermon Mac-Neil's "Putting the Shot"), consumed twenty-four eggs, for a record, though indeed the last four were taken raw. The fellow boarders then walked the winner rapidly to Buttermilk Falls and back, to aid his digestion.[12] Rice gave his life to eggs and chickens, and, poor student though he was, carried on at his own expense the first poultry feeding experiments in America. He later taught the first course in the country on Poultry Husbandry, became the head of the first college department in the subject, and was honored eventually by the Poultry Husbandry building's being named Rice Hall.

Student health was reported to be excellent. Andrew D. White ascribed the state to Professor Wilder's lectures on hygiene and to the new gymnasium and its sound program, especially the "Physical Wreck" class, with forty or fifty members. Professor Edward Hitchcock of Physical Culture asserted that the freshmen, after a winter of hill climbing, had an average lung capacity of 4.22 litres, whereas in other institutions the average for all classes was a pitiable 3.96 litres.[13]

However, provisions for student medical care were inadequate, to put it mildly. The boardinghouses, unsupervised by the University, presented constant danger of infection. Professor James Law of the Veterinary College acted as Health Officer in his spare moments, but no physician had any official concern with student illness. President Adams called in vain for the establishment of a university hospital. He recommended also general vaccination, and a compulsory medical examination for students engaging in competitive sports.

(A curious item, which may be classified either under Health or the History of Pruriency, was the flaming announcement of the *Police Gazette* that its issue of 24 January 1889 would "illustrate the VACCINATION OF THE FEMALE STUDENTS of Cornell University at Ithaca, N.Y.!")

In these years Cornell athletics dropped to their nadir, and began to rise again. Field athletics attracted few spectators. The annual Spring Games were called off in 1889, for lack of interest. They revived,

[12] *Alumni News*, 1 April 1945. (Putting the shot, indeed! Putting the eggs, more likely.)

[13] Annual reports, 1884, 1886, 1889.

A History of Cornell

thanks to some excellent performers, the fleet Waldron P. Belknap '95 and Frank Rane '92, who could do the hundred yards in 10⅕ seconds and the 220 in 23⅕. In 1891 Cornell scored for the first time in the Intercollegiates, E. C. Horton '92 placing third in the 20-yard high hurdles. Cross-country developed, in the form of a Hare and Hounds Club. Lacrosse was first played here in October 1887.

A new era was inaugurated by the incorporation of the Cornell Athletic Association in 1889, with William H. Sage as president and with representation from faculty, alumni, and students. Coincidentally, William H. Sage gave the University nine acres of land at the foot of Fall Creek, now occupied by the Ithaca High School. J. J. Hagerman of Colorado Springs gave $7,000 for a cinder track and buildings, and named the area Percy Field, for his undergraduate athlete son Percy Hagerman '90. Thus the grass-destroying nuisance of sports on the campus was removed; and many generations of Cornellians became used to the long walk down the hill and the long walk back.

Football awoke from its long drowse. It had been confined mostly to interclass contests. Director Thurston wrote to Andrew D. White (13 November 1888): "The football team has been both weak in its play and strong in its tendency to noise and profanity during the games. It looks as if a movement may be made to quash them." But President Adams delighted in watching football and approved of the sport as a means of University publicity.[14] To quicken, not to quash, was his remedy.

Percy Field was inaugurated by a magnificent football game, on 19 October 1889, in which Cornell defeated Rochester by a score of 124 to 0. The inspired Cornell team was reckoned fourth among American colleges.

The crew's reawakening came a little earlier, under the influence of Charles E. Courtney, the Grand Old Man of Cornell rowing.

Courtney was a country boy from Union Springs, at the north end of Cayuga Lake. The Fates marked him from his cradle to be an oarsman, gave him a magnificent physique and a single-hearted devotion to little boats on inland waters. When he was about eighteen, he and

[14] In later years as President of the University of Wisconsin Adams boomed football as an important aid to the institution's drawing power. He retained incompetent football heroes in college after they had been officially dropped by the Faculty. He once changed the date of an extension lecture so that the lecturer could play for Wisconsin against Minnesota (M. E. Curti and V. Carstensen, *The University of Wisconsin* [Madison 1949], I, 572–578).

a friend built a kind of canoe, from a description in a magazine. With this homemade craft he entered a single-scull race on Cayuga and won it against oarsmen in boats weighing half as much as his. He managed to buy a racing shell and entered a contest at Saratoga. He won by a quarter mile, and broke the professional record by a minute. As an amateur he rowed in eighty-eight contests and won them all. He was then persuaded to turn professional ("because I was a fool," he said), rowed in forty-six races, and lost seven.

He coached the Cornell crew briefly in 1883, and two years later was engaged as regular coach. At Cornell he remained, despite many a tempting offer, until his death in 1920.

He was a great coach, perhaps the greatest in athletic history. He taught his crews the Courtney stroke, which became the Cornell stroke.[15] He built and rigged the boats, invented devices such as the seat on rollers, imposed on his men a strict discipline and supervised their private lives. Giving to the cause of rowing his total devotion, he required of his charges that they do the same. Since oarsmanship in an eight-oared craft is fundamentally a moral exercise, Courtney was a stern moralist. Once he overheard a crew man confide to another that he had passed an examination in a somewhat irregular fashion. Courtney pointed to the door, and said: "Young man, go right upstairs, put on your clothes, and get out of this boathouse. A man who will cheat in an examination will quit in a boat race, and I never want to see you down here again."

To the faculty he was not a rival but a fellow educator. He said:

I have found by experience that the best students make the best oarsmen. The students go to Cornell primarily to secure an education, and their athletic sports must be subordinate to that purpose. If I find a man getting behind in his university work, I drop him at once. It is the systematic men who are of the most service in a boat, as everywhere else. There are some students who are without a balance wheel. They will come rushing into the boathouse and throw their coats one way and their hats another. For these men I have no patience. The man who comes to the boathouse the exact minute he has promised to be there, who hangs up his clothes methodically, dons his rowing costume and goes out into the boat quietly and without any "hurrah" about it, is pretty sure to be the man who will do the hardest work in a race, and who can be depended upon not to go to pieces in a pinch. If you

---

[15] For lengthy analyses, see C. V. P. Young, *Courtney and Cornell Rowing* (Ithaca, 1923), and W. T. Hewett, *Cornell University: A History* (New York, 1905), III, 230–238.

get one disturbing element in a boat, one man who is a growler or a grumbler, you will always have trouble to make that crew row fast.[16]

Though an apostle of sober orderliness, Courtney hid within him springs of emotion. A slim flagpole, visible from the campus, stood behind the boathouse. When, in later years, Courtney was upset and threatened to resign, a rigger would haul up the Cornell ensign upside down, and the Graduate Manager would hurry down to soothe the Old Man.

The record of the Cornell crews under Courtney is unique in athletic history. From 1885 through 1892 Cornell rowed in fourteen varsity and three freshman races and won them all. In 1899 the varsity won the Childs Cup in Philadelphia, breaking the world record for one and a half miles. In 1891, at New London, we broke the world record for three miles, with the time of 14:27.5. And in these years we had at Cornell Charles G. Psotta '88, champion single-sculler of the United States. To the later fortunes of the crew we shall return.

Baseball was illustrious by the prowess of Franklin W. Olin '86. He played in the summers on big-league teams, a procedure not then disapproved in the colleges. He made his own bats, slightly square-sided, convex on one side for distance, concave on the other to meet drop curves. Many thought this was a young man who would go far. In a game against the professional Torontos in 1886 he smote from home plate in mid-quadrangle the most terrific hit in history. It landed on the site of the John M. Olin Library, by a symbolism which in Grecian days would have created a myth, and came to rest against Sage Chapel. Frank Sheehan, bat boy and lifelong employee of the Athletic Association, marked the spot on the Sage Chapel wall. In September 1942 Mr. Olin came to Ithaca to inspect the new Olin Hall of Chemical Engineering. President Day, Dean S. C. Hollister, T. I. S. Boak '14, Frank Sheehan, and Mr. Olin paced off the distance and found it to be 180 yards from the presumed home plate.

The concept of Sports for All was making its way on the campus, as in the country, reflecting the increasing ease and leisure in American life and the passing of pioneer conditions. The bicycle proliferated; tennis, at first received with derisive youthful falsetto cries of "Forty love, darling!" began its great career. A Faculty Tennis Club was formed; the Students' Tennis Club had a court on the campus, and Psi Upsilon built its own court. Cornell tennis was dominated by William A. Larned '93, intercollegiate champion in 1890 and 1892, and later

[16] Hewett, *Cornell University*, III, 233.

national champion and a storied name in tennis annals. A roller-skating rink prospered for at least the season of 1885–1886, with intercollegiate games of "polo." But although the idea of intramural sports was now shaped, it did not develop far. No playground was available for those who could not try out for the varsity teams, and between November and April there were no general diversions except skating and bob-sledding.

Indoor student activities throve with the increase in numbers. Many new organizations were formed, by which like could cleave to like. Some were scholarly or parascholarly. A Phi Beta Kappa chapter had been chartered in 1882. The lack of a similar scholarly fraternity in science was felt, and remedied by the formation of Sigma Xi in 1886.[17] The intention of the founders was to make it merely a local club; but scientists from other colleges soon formed other chapters, and the splendid career of Sigma Xi began. The semicentennial of the fraternity was celebrated at Cornell in 1936, with the erection of a commemorative tablet in front of Sibley.

The *Cornell Daily Sun* prospered; the *Crank*, published by the engineering students, began publication in 1887; the *Cornell Review*, founded in 1873 as a literary magazine, changed its name to the *Cornell Magazine* in 1888, led the hard life of all literary magazines, but survived to the next period. The *Era*, caught between the *Sun* and the *Cornell Magazine*, existed precariously as a weekly journal of commentary and opinion. It was put to desperate shifts to allure readers; in June 1888 the President called the Faculty's attention to its impropriety, and at the same time to the indelicacy of the Senior Ball invitations. (The *Era*'s impropriety, on investigation, proves to be a very moral tale of a young man led astray by a ruined woman in Brooklyn; though polluted by absinthe and hashish, he succeeds in escaping her toils.)

---

[17] Frank Van Vleck tells the circumstances of the founding of Sigma Xi in *Science* for 25 June 1936. Van Vleck, a young instructor, ate in a boardinghouse with Charles B. Wing '86 (later professor of engineering at Stanford), George Lincoln Burr '81, and Charles H. Thurber '86 (later Registrar, professor at Chicago, and educational publisher). Burr and Thurber, Phi Beta Kappas, commiserated with Van Vleck and Wing because they, as engineers, were ineligible. Van Vleck and Wing determined to form their own scientific honorary society. Burr then made an appropriate Greek motto with the initials Sigma Xi. Another account (in *Sigma Xi: Half-Century Record and History*, 1936) credits William A. Day '86 and Professor Henry Shaler Williams of Geology with originating the idea.

Drama at Cornell came into its own with the organization of the Masque in October 1890. The club presented as a football benefit *Instructor Pratt* by William C. Langdon '90, in the Wilgus Opera House. This three-act comedy relates the love of an instructor for a beautiful coed, and includes a mock cane rush and a ball at "the Sage." The Masque's encouragement to dramatic art impelled the women to produce several plays, including a dramatization of Tennyson's *The Princess*.

The music makers made their music. Previously the student concerts had suffered from the uncoached individualism of the participants. Several glee clubs lived briefly; that of 1887 has persisted to the present day without a break. In 1889 Hollis Dann, who rose from instructor in penmanship to be director of music in the Ithaca Public Schools, took over the undergraduate music, combined the Glee, Banjo, and Mandolin Clubs, and conducted them on triumphal tours. Though not admitted to the Faculty until 1903, Hollis Dann transformed music at Cornell, and later became a leader in the world of educational music and mass singing. Under his aegis two of Cornell's favorite college songs were written: the "Alumni Song," by Louis Carl Ehle '90, and the "Crew Song," by Robert James Kellogg '91. Dann also inaugurated the visits of serious professional musicians, with a chamber concert and the Damrosch Orchestra in 1891.

Women students, undeterred by the frowns of male traditionalists, increased in numbers, until Sage College could no longer contain them, and the requirement that women live in Sage was relaxed. President Adams reported in 1891 that their scholarship was on the average superior to that of the men and that there were no signs of injury to women's health by education. He reviewed the old vexed question whether the social behavior of the women should be supervised. Yes indeed, he concluded; women are not to have the same freedom as men.

The process of becoming an adult is difficult enough, Heaven knows; and it is more difficult when complicated with the process of becoming a lady. President Adams's concept of a lady was already outmoded at the century's close. In January 1892 the coeds appealed for permission to go coasting; the President wrote the Lady Principal of Sage: "I know that coasting as a juvenile amusement sometimes lapses over into the borders of manhood and womanhood; but it is not a method of entertainment that appeals very strongly to our ideas of gentility or even of propriety in the case of young women at a University."

Reports on the morale and mood of the women students vary. Some coeds bitterly resented the unfairness of the men in barring them even from the editorial boards of publications. Others say that the social opportunities were all that the women desired. There were frequent receptions and dances at Sage, mixed boating parties in summer, straw rides in winter, plenty of informal groups and gatherings. A male student remembered: "It seems to me that the relations between the men students and the coeds were ideal." An investigation made in 1895 revealed the telling statistic that of married Cornell women graduates 55 per cent had espoused Cornell students or instructors.[18]

Some of these young men and young women were destined for high careers. Invidious though it is to choose from many, one may recall Mario García Menocal '88, President of Cuba; Horace White '87, nephew of Andrew D. White, Governor of New York and Supreme Court Justice; John T. Morrison '90, Governor of Idaho; Anna Botsford Comstock '86, scientist, to be acclaimed as one of America's twelve outstanding women; John R. Mott '88, leader of the International Y.M.C.A. and Nobel prizewinner; Henry R. Ickelheimer '88, banker; and S. Stanwood Menken '90, lawyer and political figure.

The period between 1885 and 1892 was one of upturn, reorganization, growth in numbers, in resources, in educational competence, in faculty and student morale. The rebel quality of early Cornell dwindled, though it did not die. The spirit that Andrew D. White fought against was itself dwindling; many of the reforms that he advocated were now accepted as educational commonplaces. (If the rebel loses, he is forgotten; if he wins, his rebellion becomes an imposed orthodoxy; hence the rebel always loses.) [19] The students who came to Cornell included fewer youths from New York State villages, in revolt against their pastors' obscurantism; more came from the big cities, in search of the superior education promised them in a happy and beautiful rural setting.

President Adams wisely prepared and guided the development of the University. The need of Cornell was the strengthening of its understructure and superstructure, and the President responded to that need. Inevitably, every master of institutions makes or remakes them in his own image. President Adams was orthodox, conventional, moderate; his Cornell moved in the direction of orthodoxy, conventionality,

---

[18] Clarence H. Lee '89, "Reminiscences" (MS, C.U. Archives); *A Tribute to Henry W. Sage* (Ithaca, 1895), p. 22.

[19] Epigram.

moderation. President Adams was prudent with ideas, as with money, and a little distrustful of untested novelty, and so was his Cornell. But President Adams, "Farmer Adams," with his sleepy look, his plowboy walk, his earnest thoroughness, was also, I fear, a little dull; and so was his Cornell. When he had done his invaluable work of reorganization, it was time for Cornell to have a more vigorous, inspiring personality at its head. Whatever people said about Jacob Gould Schurman, no one said he was dull.

XVIII

The Nineties: President Schurman
and the State of New York

NOW we come to years that some of us remember, to a world that seems fleetingly familiar. Here are the houses in which we grew up, the chairs and dishes and humble objects that have companioned us through life. Even the appurtenances that have disappeared still live fresh in memory. In dreams we hear the clop-clop of deliverymen's horses, we hear the squealing streetcar take the leafy curve on an autumn day and the angry ping of the warning bell under the motorman's heel. The material background of the nineties may be quaint, it is not strange and foreign, like the homespun civilization of a hundred years ago.

Also familiar is the background of ideas, of culture, in the 1890's. Most of the common fund of ideas was a continuation from previous times, as is our own common fund of ideas. The conservative, or centripetal, forces must be dominant in any culture. Codes of behavior, ethical doctrines and habits, remained unchanged, though many of their sanctions were impugned. Proper young men and women obeyed the rules, went to church, prized purity as the first of virtues. They inherited a romantic view of life from their fathers. Youthful dreams dwelt much on dedication, self-sacrifice, noble immolation to noble causes. The romantic view determined the position of woman, guarding her mystery on an inaccessible pinnacle. Woman, grateful for the adoration, yet recognized that it excluded her from intellectual and economic self-realization.

There was a paradox here, in that tradition favored the flouting of tradition. Men were suspicious of society's norms and forms; they proclaimed the rights of individualism. A man, if not a woman, should be free to be what he pleased, even a billionaire. The mid-century state of mind and set of values had encouraged a youth to seek and find himself, in the wilderness if need be, less readily in the settled cities. American nineteenth-century civilization was still rural rather than urban, and on the lonely farms men were relatively free from social pressures toward conformity. Even in the colleges the development of the personality had been encouraged, to the point of producing outrageous eccentrics.

Against such continuing, centripetal forces in the general mind were operating revulsive, or centrifugal, forces. As the country became organized and urbanized, individualism became a more difficult and socially undesirable goal. Society came to prize competent regularity more than independence. On the college faculties the ripe, genial humanist, knowing more about life than about his subject, was yielding to the efficient specialist.

A centrifugal force was the growth of scientific knowledge, putting its new, troubling questions. Another was radical political and social thought. Alarming doctrines sounded in receptive ears: socialism, populism, single-taxism, free silver. Such doctrines were espoused by angry classes hitherto silent. Their rebellions were large organized movements, not individual refusals. Here again was a paradox, for the rebellions were against freedom and laissez-faire economics and in favor of an ideal conformity and regimentation.

The world, in short, was changing to something that we know.

Cornell too was taking on a recognizable form. The campus ceased to suggest a made-over farm; it became a quadrangle, bounded by the buildings wherein we studied. The scrubby saplings of the earlier days became avenues of handsome trees. Professor W. W. Rowlee of Botany, Superintendent of Grounds from the mid-nineties, followed coherent plans of landscaping and planting. Ivy hid the anfractuosities of the older buildings, gave them that mellow look for which Andrew D. White had longed in vain. On the campus and near by stood splendid fraternity houses, imitating the homes of the arrogant newly rich. The Chi Psi's occupied the Fiske-McGraw mansion, one of the most opulent

Jacob Gould Schurman, President 1892–1920

homes in central New York. No more pretentious fraternity lodges were ever to arise at Cornell, or in fact anywhere.

Wealth and sophistication were invading our little world. Inevitably our microcosm reflected the macrocosm, and reproduced the structure and behavior of competitive society. Cornell still welcomed "the industrial classes" which Ezra Cornell had in mind; it attracted also the well-to-do sons of businessmen, here to prepare for a business career and for a social career as well. The caste division of rich and poor became more marked. Upperclass clubs were formed, frankly in recognition of social superiority. The diversions of "college life" demanded more time, money, and attention of the student. The editor of the *Era* complained (11 February 1893):

Junior Ball week is getting rather overdone. What with the Sophomore Cotillion and the Glee Club concert and the Junior Promenade and numerous private and fraternity parties and the entertainment of guests, for a large number of students the entire week is consumed in pleasure; more than one student cut all his university engagements last week.

"College" took on a new meaning in the public mind. No longer a grim prison where future dominies read Latin and Greek as a mysterious initiation to life, College became a happy Arcadia, where the fortunate few defended themselves from reality in perpetual play. College news, particularly athletic news, commanded ample space in the press. Writers recognized the opportunities for fiction in the college scene. The popular tales of Frank Merriwell of Yale ran through eight hundred installments, not to mention the excellent college stories by Owen Johnson and Charles Flandrau or the *Cornell Stories* by James G. Sanderson '96. The noncollegians of America imitated college customs, dress, slang, and especially the athletic system, which was rapidly being corrupted by commercialism. College life, in short, was bathed in a new glamor, which had nothing to do with the substance of education. In the college fiction of the time the class work is regarded as an incomprehensible infliction, a mumbo jumbo required by simple-minded deities for admission to their elysium. In these years, says Ernest Earnest in his delightful *Academic Procession*, the faculties lost control of the American college, not from the interference of trustees, tyrannical presidents, or alumni, but thanks to the nature of American life. And Henry Seidel Canby of Yale corroborates him: "The Faculty's actual conflict was not with ignorance but with college life and all that it implied; and behind it the ideas and ideals of an American society in which materialism dominated action and governed thought." [1]

Such extremes of collegiatism were a concomitant of the elective system in institutions dominated by the liberal arts college. There the educators trusted naïvely to the intrinsic charm of their subjects to attract students, and naturally very many students chose the courses reputed easiest and often succeeded in completing four years of collegiate residence without any education at all. But the number of congenital idlers at Cornell was relatively small, and the engineers, lawyers, and other professional students established a mood of hard work which abashed and even inspired the dilettantes of the Arts College.

The example of serious dedication was set by President Jacob Gould Schurman.

Schurman was a great college president. Said Alvin S. Johnson, the economist: "He was one of three great university presidents of that time, along with David Starr Jordan and Benjamin Ide Wheeler. They were all disciples of Andrew D. White, and had imbibed White's serene and serious outlook upon the world, his passion for truth and freedom from fear. . . . [Schurman] had command of my admiration and friendship, for life." [2]

He was a man of great physical and mental vigor, strongly built, fond of sports, especially golf and skating. In his tweed Norfolk jacket, he looked, said Romeyn Berry, like a duke off for an afternoon's tramp over the moors. He hated sloth, despised ease. He advised students always to study in a straight-backed hard-bottomed chair. From the first he was determined to do all his presidential duty and more. He regularly visited the sick students in the Infirmary. His wife called promptly on all new married instructors and gave an impressive series of faculty receptions and formal dinners.

"Life was to him essentially neither a comic nor a tragic dilemma, but a challenge to serious endeavor," says Carl Becker.[3] "Never greatly troubled by doubt, he enjoyed in a high degree the will to believe and the conviction that what could be logically defended with adequate knowledge should determine one's conduct and opinion." He was natu-

---

[1] *Academic Procession* (Indianapolis, 1953); H. S. Canby, *Alma Mater* (New York, 1936), p. 108. For a naïve revelation of the snobbery, mean-mindedness, anti-intellectualism, cruelty of class and wealth, and pitiable moral and spiritual valuations of the time, see Owen Wister's once famous best seller, *Philosophy Four* (New York, 1903).

[2] *Pioneer's Progress* (New York, 1952), p. 219.   [3] *Alumni News*, 15 July 1943.

rally an advocate, says W. T. Hewett; his mind assumed instinctively and unconsciously a dialectic attitude.[4] This quality was called combativeness or obstinacy by those who suffered from it; manifested, as it nearly always was, in the best interests of the University, it drew the approbation of trustees, faculty, and students.

He was an excellent speaker, with a vigorous, trenchant platform manner. His habit was to write a speech, read it over several times, send the text to the press, and to deliver the speech from memory, without notes, but with hardly a change from the text. "There is an impressiveness which may not unfitly be called grandeur about his utterances, particularly when, as usual, he speaks upon moral themes," said a reporter.[5] Andrew D. White noted in his diary (3 November 1895) that Schurman's address on Huxley and agnosticism was "remarkably well done. Powerful oratorically and logically and very shrewd in avoiding points which might have led him into trouble." (And very shrewd on your part, Mr. White!) Schurman's annual addresses to students were much applauded as examples of the hearty man-to-man style, and they may still be read with interest. (Nevertheless, when, a freshman, I heard him address our class in October 1910, I thought he was saying the obvious with really unjustified vehemence. But no doubt we needed the obvious, and no doubt I was a very captious freshman.)

There were others who were captious. Recognizing all his intelligence, vigor, industry, and devotion to Cornell's well-being, they saw in him the supreme example of the ambitious *arriviste*, the scholastic go-getter. They pointed to his material success, his change of country, his joining the Baptist Church on his own terms (so that, said Sterrett of Greek, he did not join the church, he made the church join him). The fact is, he possessed what the Italians call *prepotenza*, ruthless self-confidence approaching arrogance and overpassing tactfulness.

I find very illuminating an entry in Moses Coit Tyler's diary for 20 December 1892. Schurman had an appointment with the dentist, Dr. Melotte, at 9:00 A.M. He arrived at eleven. Tyler was in the chair. Said Schurman: "Doctor, are you ready for me now?" Dr. Melotte: "I have a patient now. I think your engagement was for this afternoon, but perhaps I can see you in a few minutes." Schurman: "I can't wait long."

"In a few minutes," continues Tyler, "I resigned the chair to Schur-

[4] *Cornell University: A History* (New York, 1905), I, 200.
[5] Herbert C. Howe in *Frank Leslie's Monthly*, Nov. 1896.

man. He laughed; 'the Doctor thinks my engagement was for this afternoon. It was for two hours ago; but I didn't choose to inform him of that, if he didn't know it.'

"Thus this strong aggressive man pushes his way through the world, and adroitly or by force wins success—never submitting to be on the defensive, and letting other people make the apologies to him even when he is in the wrong. He was built to succeed in the sphere of this world."

No one could point better the lesson of his character, except to add that Schurman's pursuit of success was bound to the success of Cornell University. This "strong aggressive man" by an almost mystical transfer communicated his aggressive strength to his university, and for this gift of himself all Cornellians must be humbly thankful.

Schurman's concept of a university was stated, well in advance of his presidency, in his Founder's Day address of 1888, entitled "A People's University." The qualities of a good university—or of Cornell—should be, he said, first, universality, in contrast to the old exclusiveness; second, the fitting of the curriculum to general needs, with the recognition that industrial pursuits depend on scientific knowledge; and, third, quick adaptation to change. For university ideals are likely to be those of a previous age. "The divorce between the universities and the activities of life is astounding. . . . We are still aristocratic in university matters. We think there are some subjects too common for university instruction. But a People's University, if it is true to the spirit of our age, must hold all subjects equally reputable, and provide instruction in all alike. . . . The analysis of soils is as important as the analysis of literature. . . . A house is as rational as the geometry it embodies. . . . In God's universe there is nothing common or unclean, and whatever is known about it must have a place in the curriculum of a People's University." These qualities of universality, equality, and adaptation, he says, it is the undying fame of Ezra Cornell to have conceived.

Thus Schurman, when a mere professor, gave public notice that he applauded the principles on which Cornell was founded. In his Inaugural Address (11 November 1892) he gave notice that he would push them to new, even alarming, conclusions. He began by retelling the story of the Morrill Act, leading up to an excoriation of the state for not doing its obvious duty in supporting its land-grant college; Cornell is poor and needy, and the state has never given it one cent of its own money! More, the state higgles on the interest due us under the Land Grant Act, paying us considerably less than the 5 per cent the law specifies! Cornell, in its great good will, offered at its beginning to give 128 scholarships free, one for each Assembly district; the state, by a pettifogging device, forced us to increase the number to 512, at a cost to us of more than $150,000 annually. In other states their university is the beneficiary of the state; here the state is the beneficiary of the university! "In the name of equity and expediency, and for the sake of her meritorious sons and daughters whom we educate free of tuition, I ask of the State of New York an annual appropriation to Cornell University of not less than $150,000!" The President then lists some special needs, as for faculty salaries, dormitories, scholarships, and for these he makes appeal to private bounty.

It was a bold statement of policy, a formal announcement that Cornell regarded itself as New York's state university, with just claims for state support. Schurman asked the state peremptorily for money, for a great deal of money.

Six years later Schurman recalled that when he made his sensational demand, he was "met with countenances of surprise and incredulity here and with expressions of dissent and opposition in the world outside." Not one trustee, he says, had the slightest confidence in his program. Charles Evans Hughes remembered at Schurman's Inaugural "the mingled expressions of concern as to the wisdom of his policy, and admiration at his courage—not to say audacity—in announcing it. Rarely has there been vouchsafed to any prophet a clearer vision or a more complete fulfillment of his prophecy. . . . All those who heard marvelled at his dream." [6] Those who expressed concern did so, not because of Schurman's request for great gifts from the state—no one could object to that—but because he dodged the corollary, that the state would certainly demand policy control over the use of its contributions.

(To one person the Inaugural Address caused definite pain. Andrew D. White, Minister to Russia, read the text, and was shocked and shaken to note that Schurman had devoted 250 lines to Ezra Cornell, eight to Henry W. Sage, and only eight to Andrew D. White!)

The Inaugural past, Schurman settled comfortably in the presidential chair (which is hard-seated and hard-backed enough for anyone). His program was, in brief, to enlist financial aid from the state; to en-

[6] J. G. Schurman, *A Generation of Cornell* (New York, 1898), p. 30; C. E. Hughes, in *Addresses at the Dedication of the Buildings of the New York State College of Agriculture* (Ithaca, 1907).

A History of Cornell

courage the growth of the University on a basis of enlightened educational practice; to impose his views on the trustees; and to promote the welfare of the faculty, with whom he felt a professional solidarity.

The times were propitious for an appeal to the state for aid to its farmers. In 1891–1893 there was an agricultural depression, driving many rural dwellers to the cities, where they were likely to become charity cases. The state took official notice of the situation.

To wrest money from a reluctant state Schurman laid careful plans. With Henry W. Sage and former Governor Alonzo B. Cornell he drafted a veterinary college bill, stipulating that when the University should provide a $100,000 agricultural building, the state should establish therein a New York State veterinary college and should contribute annually $50,000 for its support.[7] No doubt the committee, on second thought, decided that it was silly for Cornell to build a $100,000 building; let the state do it. They called on Governor Roswell Pettibone Flower, a north-country farm boy who had made his millions on Wall Street. The Governor was convinced by Schurman's arguments and moved by the nostalgia for the farm which used to hang so heavy in Wall Street. The Governor's address at the opening of the legislature in 1893 included a complete endorsement of Schurman's requests. The Governor urged, in the interests of economy and efficiency, the concentration at Cornell of the state's various agencies for promoting scientific agriculture. He made special reference to the need of aid to forestry and veterinary science. And he sympathized with Schurman's complaints of the cost to the University of the state scholarships.

Plenty of jealous opposition arose to the Governor's proposal. A New York paper editorialized: "The cry of the horse leech is modest and attenuated beside the stupendous greed and the insatiable clamor of this favored institution."[8] But the Governor, the Cornell lobby, and the farmers' organizations carried the day. The legislature voted $50,000 for a dairy husbandry building at Cornell.

This, the state's first direct benefaction to Cornell, was rapidly designed and built, in the main quadrangle. It was later converted into the north wing of Goldwin Smith Hall. The antiquarian may note, carved in the stone by the north entrance, the instruments of Professor S. M. Babcock's famous test for butterfat. And in the French

[7] 26 Sept. 1892, in EC Papers.
[8] New York *Press*, Nov. 1892, in Mulks Scrapbooks, XVII. For all these dealings with the state, see Malcolm Carron, S.J., *The Contract Colleges of Cornell University* (Ithaca, 1958).

310

Department, fifty years ago, it was alleged that on a damp day one could still detect the ghostly odor of cheese.

The legislature visited Cornell for the opening of the building, on 27 January 1894. After the proper words of welcome, Schurman up-braided the legislators cruelly for their stinginess, pointing out that while Michigan and California had bestowed two million apiece upon their agricultural schools, New York had given nothing but a wretched $50,000 building and had bilked us unmercifully on the interest due from the Morrill Land Grant. Apparently that is the way to treat legislators.

Meanwhile Schurman was actively promoting a state college of veterinary medicine. It will be remembered that Ezra Cornell had set great store on the teaching of veterinary medicine, and that the eminent Dr. James Law was a member of the first faculty. Through the years Dr. Law struggled against every discouragement. After a time he gave up awarding veterinary degrees and contented himself with his chair in Agriculture and with service to the state and nation in many posts and on many commissions.

In January 1893 Dr. Law made a sensational speech in Albany on veterinary education. Speaking with "a kind of holy anger at the wrongs done to animals," he pointed to the lamentable laxity of the law; a man could become a licensed veterinary surgeon by merely testifying that he had prescribed for animals for the previous three years. Dr. Law asserted that in Tompkins County sixteen men had registered as veterinary surgeons, none of them with education or proper training.

Their combinations of drugs were as likely to develop poisonous chemical compounds as not, they confounded one disease with another, and blundered along with nostrums and placebos no matter what, so that they might draw their fees for attendance, in short they were licensed to poison, maim, and slay the flocks and herds of the Empire State, and heartily did they avail themselves of the opportunity.[9]

The public at this time became generally aware that tuberculosis may be transmitted in infected milk. (One death in eight in New York State was then due to tuberculosis.) President Schurman and Dr. Law pointed to the obvious conclusion. Governor Flower in his message to the legislature of 1894 recommended the establishment of a veterinary

[9] Veranus A. Moore, "Veterinary Education and Service," *Cornell Veterinarian*, April 1929, p. 204; Simon H. Gage, in *Report of the Conference at the New York State Veterinary College* (Ithaca, 1919).

college at Cornell. The Assembly voted unanimously an appropriation of $150,000 for this purpose, but the Senate cut it down to $50,000. The presumption—justified, as it turned out—was that later legislatures would bring the appropriation to the required sum.

The principle involved was momentous. A state college was to stand on our campus, the gift of the state. But buildings alone do not make a living college. Schurman laid down two corollaries. In the first place, the entire support of the college must come from the state, in annual appropriations. And in the second place, the Cornell Board of Trustees would control its operation, prescribe entrance requirements, fix the course of study, choose the professors, and determine their salaries. Thus, as if casually, Schurman established the formula for the later "contract colleges." The formula, by which the state provides funds and the University provides administration, has worked through more than a half century, very successfully, on the whole.

In 1895–1896 the Veterinary Building, later called James Law Hall, was erected, on the site of the present Industrial and Labor Relations building. An unlovely structure of yellow brick, it seemed spacious and glorious to the veterinarians of the day. The first faculty was headed by Dr. Law. He chose as his aides a group distinguished as scientists and teachers: Veranus Alva Moore '87, Simon Henry Gage '77, Walter L. Williams, Pierre A. Fish '94, and Grant S. Hopkins '89. This faculty made the college immediately a leader in its field, as it has remained.

At this time legislative interest in agricultural education was encouraged by the inauguration at Cornell of short winter courses for farm youths. Costumed and shod sometimes with strange rustic elegance, the "Short-horns" were a picturesque feature of Cornell life. (I remember a pair of green shoes.) Their practical ten-week courses quickly gained much popularity and presented intolerable problems to the harassed staff, who could find no quarters free for instruction, and to the administration, which groaned under the added burden. But the very popularity of the courses pointed to the propriety of the state's assuming the work in agriculture. The Short-horns increased in number until 1912–13, when 597 were enrolled, and then they began to dwindle, until in 1941–42 there were 49. And then there were none. The success of our extension work and the spread of vocational agriculture courses in the high schools had spelled the doom of the Short-horns.

A direct claim upon state aid was made by the development of extension work in agriculture. The idea of a state-promoted agency to bring new technical information to farmers seems to have taken shape with a "Farmers' Institute" at Springfield, Massachusetts, in 1863. Shortly after, Michigan State College began sending out its professors to address local farm groups in the winter. Rutgers organized a formal extension service in 1891. Cornell professors gave a good deal of their time, without compensation, to attendance at Farmers' Institutes, dairy conferences, and the like, and organized a three-day Farmers' Institute at Cornell in February 1886. (This was to become Farmers' Week, Farm and Home Week, and Agricultural Progress Days.) A certain question arose. To put it bluntly, was this what the professors were paid for? Robert H. Treman in his alumni trustee report for 1892 put it more courteously. "Whether this work . . . is properly within the province and scope of the University and whether we are justified in having our professors do this outside work . . . is a serious question."

Circumstance helped to decide the serious question. The rich vineyards of Chautauqua County were attacked by disease. In 1893 Assemblyman S. F. Nixon of Chautauqua asked the Cornell Experiment Station to investigate. "No funds," said the station. Nevertheless, Liberty Hyde Bailey went to look, identified the disease as black rot, and devised a spray which saved the Assemblyman's vineyard. So delighted was he that he introduced in the Assembly in 1894, and carried through, a bill appropriating $8,000 for experimental work in his district. This was the initiation of extension work in New York State. The subsidization settled the question whether Cornell professors might properly engage in it.

Annual grants were thenceforth made, reaching the sum of $35,000 by 1898. The money was spent partly in investigation, partly in diffusion of the results. Thirty-eight bulletins were published by 1896, and many meetings were held for the instruction of farmers.

Now Bailey and his aides set up a coherent program of extension work. In the winter of 1896–1897 fifteen hundred farmers were enrolled in a correspondence course, and the numbers rapidly grew. To the faculty's surprise, the legislature voted in 1896 $8,000 to Cornell "to encourage nature study in the rural schools." Since no one had given a thought to the encouragement of nature study in rural schools, the whole matter was referred to Anna Botsford Comstock. With a committee she questioned rural teachers and found that few of them had any ideas about nature study. Mrs. Comstock said that she would send them instructions. Thus began the series of nature-study leaflets, which had an enormous distribution and were the basis for Mrs. Comstock's *Handbook of Nature-Study*.

A nature-study training course for teachers was organized in the summers. In 1900 began the Farmers' Wives' Reading Course. In that year John Craig was appointed Professor of Extension Teaching in Agriculture, the first such professor in America.

President Schurman gave extension work his hearty approbation, since the state met all the bills. Thus it happens that today Cornell carries on its gigantic work in extension, accepting without question a duty toward the mass of people in the state.

A serious possibility of dissension between state and University arose in 1895. A new state charter increased the Assembly districts from 128 to 150. Since a four-year Cornell scholarship was awarded annually in each district, this measure augmented the scholarships to 600, at an estimated additional annual cost to Cornell of $27,000. As a quid pro quo, Schurman suggested that the state establish at Cornell a school of pedagogy for the training of high-school teachers. But the opposition to this proposal was so sharp that it never got very far. We seem to have accepted the extra scholarship costs, in the hope of other largesse from the state.

Our bonds with the state were closer knit by the creation of the New York State College of Forestry.

The public was becoming aware of conservation of natural resources, of the menace of commercial lumbering to our woodlands, of the need for scientific forestry. But America had no school of collegiate rank to train professional foresters and give serious technical instruction in the subject. Governor Frank S. Black in his message to the legislature in 1898 proposed that a tract of forest be bought and turned over to Cornell for such a purpose. The legislature passed a constitutive law, and the trustees of the University accepted it, on 14 April 1898. Thus America's first College of Forestry was constituted, as an unexpected present by the state to the University.

Schurman chose as Director of the college Dr. Bernhard E. Fernow, Chief of the Division of Forestry of the U.S. Department of Agriculture. German-born, rigorously trained in the Prussian schools of forestry, Fernow was probably the most eminent representative of his profession in America. He was also, apparently, a peremptory Prussian, whose concept of military discipline in education sat ill on some of his subjects. He was assisted by Filibert Roth, likewise of the Division of

Forestry in Washington and a man of high competence and later distinction.

The state bought (for $165,000) a 30,000-acre forest near Saranac Lake in the Adirondacks and presented it to its two-man college. The area had been logged of all its valuable pine and spruce. It was termed a Demonstration Forest. The legislature did not quite know what it expected Cornell to do, except that it was to be scientific; $30,000 was voted for surveying and exploitation of the tract—not enough, said Dr. Fernow. He decided to run the forest as an example of enlightened commercial practice, not as a woodland sanctuary. He would clear-cut the mature hardwoods and regenerate the forest by the artificial planting of conifers. Cornell University therefore contracted with the Brooklyn Cooperage Company to cut the hardwoods, under supervision, and to use them in a wood-alcohol plant and a stave mill, with a five-mile railroad for access. This procedure was regarded as proper silviculture.

Immediately, however, opposition arose, on the part of some wealthy and politically powerful owners of camps in the Saranac Lake area. They failed to understand Fernow's purpose, feared that commercial activity would frighten the game, and wanted to keep modernity from their summer retreats. (A wood-alcohol plant casts a horrid smell to the winds.) The campaign against the college's work became an appeal to all nature lovers. Cornell, it was said, was trying to turn the Adirondacks into barren lands, selling everything down to brush and shrubs, greedily defiling God's—and the people's—playground with alcohol distilleries. Every legislator knows the force of such an appeal. It was in vain for Fernow to reply that he was planting twenty-five trees for each one that was cut down, that he was showing how forestry principles apply in a cut-over forest, and that forestry is a business, not an escape to fairyland. "Forestry is not concerned," he said, "at least directly, with the beauty of trees or with shelter for game, although these aspects may be incidentally looked after." [10] It is concerned, however, with the influence on soil and water conditions. "The forester looks on the forest as a crop, and that involves reaping as well as planting. . . . The lumberman simply reaps nature's product."

The opposition grew louder and angrier. In 1903 Governor B. B. Odell vetoed the item of $10,000 for the support of the College of

[10] *Science*, 17 Jan. 1902.

Forestry in Ithaca, thus effectively destroying it. The trustees then dismissed the faculty. Director Fernow offered to teach for a year without pay. The trustees declined the offer gratefully, but without voting the plaque which it surely deserved. Some of the seventy-three students went to other forestry schools, some shifted to other courses. After long litigation by the Brooklyn Cooperage Company, the Adirondack tract was conveyed to the People of the State of New York and incorporated in the Adirondack Forest Preserve.

The short unhappy career of the New York State College of Forestry at Cornell left us an interesting relic. In 1899 Professor Fernow was a member of the E. W. Harriman expedition to Alaska. In a deserted Tlingit village at Fox Cape the party found a superb totem pole. With much exertion and ingenuity they transported it to the ship and eventually to Cornell. It stood for about twenty years beside the old Armory, and after a period in hiding was in 1933 repaired, repainted, and set up, appropriately and impressively, before the lodge in Cornell's Arnot Forest.

By the coming of the new century President Schurman had taken great strides toward his announced goal. With direct state aid to agriculture, and especially to extension work, with the New York State Veterinary College and the College of Forestry, the claim of Cornell for state support was recognized and accepted. Legislators might grumble at the size of the budgets; they would hardly think of questioning the principle. The fruitful cooperation of Cornell and the state had begun. And more, the procedure of the "contract colleges" was established, by which the state would take care of the costs, and Cornell of the education. The lines were laid on which the state-supported colleges at Cornell, and Cornell itself, would develop.

XIX

The Nineties: Cornell Medical College

THE greatest event in the fin-de-siècle history of Cornell was the establishment of the Medical College.

The University had from the first taught premedical work in the sciences, under the direction of Burt G. Wilder, an M.D. and a former army surgeon. A four-year course in natural science was recommended for the future medic with time and money, and a definite two-year medical preparatory course was offered from 1878 on. But such preparation, a rarity in American education, was generally regarded as a needless luxury. Until 1890 the Medical College of New York University, like many others, imposed no entrance requirements at all.

Typically, a student proceeded from high school to medical college, entering frequently without even the elements of chemistry, physics, and biology. He spent two years listening to lectures in the medical school; and as these were often incomprehensible or unrewarding, he sought out a professional "quiz-master" to prepare him for the exams. The quiz-master, whose livelihood depended on his success, was likely to be an excellent teacher. The student would cleave to him and neglect his professor. Laboratory work commonly consisted of a little chemistry and instruction in the use of the microscope. The "clinical lecture" was a demonstration in a large amphitheatre, without opportunity for the training of the student's hand, eye, and ear. He had no occasion to observe disease outside of his own circle of acquaintances.

With the generalization of the laboratory method in the 1880's and with the increase in medical knowledge, the course was extended in the better schools to three or four years, clinical work was much increased, and the quiz-mastering was brought into the schools' curricula. All this was very expensive. The early schools, "proprietary" since they were owned by their faculties and operated for profit, were forced to seek endowments and support.

In the 1890's the great William Osler at Johns Hopkins, and others, revolutionized American medical education. Osler replaced the didactic lectures by graded courses in the fundamentals, progressing to study and practice at the bedside. The new medicine was essentially a hospital medicine. Its procedures were beyond the reach of a private physician in his office. It demanded of the college a close working relation with an adequate hospital. It demanded also a great increase in staff and in space, with classrooms, demonstration rooms, and laboratories for physiology, bacteriology, and chemistry, as yet hardly known in American medical schools. It produced professional researchers, for a physician found it increasingly difficult to straddle the clinical and laboratory fields.[1]

In Andrew D. White's concept of an ideal university, a medical school had been an essential unit. From the founding of Cornell, its protection and prestige were sought by medical schools existing or proposed. Since such groups usually asked more than they offered, and since they were sometimes committed to eccentric medical doctrines, the proposals came to nothing.

The proposal that came nearest to something was that of the Bellevue Hospital Medical College of New York, a proprietary school. This sought union with Cornell in the winter of 1891–1892. Its secretary, Dr. Austin Flint, engaged in long discussions with President Charles Kendall Adams. The Cornell trustees were, however, adverse.

The Cornell Medical College owes its existence to Colonel Oliver H. Payne. This wealthy son of a Standard Oil founder became interested in medicine through his college friend from Yale, Dr. Lewis A. Stimson, a famous surgeon, and through the ministrations of his physician, Alfred L. Loomis. Dr. Stimson and Dr. Loomis were associated with the University Medical College, a nearly autonomous department of New York University. This college was beset by rising costs. Colonel Payne came to its rescue with a handsome gift, enabling it to hold its own property under the name of the Medical College

[1] Richard Horace Granger, in *The Samaritan* (Cornell Medical College Annual, 1948).

Laboratory. He built also for his friend the Loomis Laboratory, for medical research.

In 1896 the University Medical College and the Loomis Laboratory united with the Bellevue Hospital Medical College to become a branch of New York University. The three institutions agreed to give up their property and their precarious independence in return for the advantages of university organization and fixed salaries. According to the Cornell story, it was agreed in conference that the new college should be administered by a Medical Committee, composed of men selected by the faculties then governing the three component institutions. This committee would have the power of appointment and management. The agreement with Chancellor Henry M. MacCracken of N.Y.U. was oral only; none of its terms were recorded. And Chancellor Mac-Cracken did not remember it as did the faculty representatives, led by Mr. Henry F. Dimock, a Yale classmate of Colonel Payne and Dr. Stimson.

Between N.Y.U. and its new Medical College arose what are known as "unfortunate misunderstandings." The Chancellor transferred the control of the medical faculty from the Medical Committee to the Executive Committee of the University Council, of which only one of the Medical Committee was a member. The Executive Committee assumed the right to appoint the faculty, without consultation; it did not fix salaries, but ruled that compensation should be limited to what each professor might have earned in private practice—an impossible provision. The professors concluded that the Executive Committee was trying to drive the faculty out, leaving N.Y.U. in possession of property obtained under false pretenses.

At the election of the University Council in November 1897 the medical faculty's representative and champion, Mr. Dimock, was defeated. Colonel Payne and others then resigned. The malcontent members of the faculty organized a secession and asked to have their liberty and their ceded property restored. N.Y.U. refused to do so; the representatives of the medical faculties brought suit, and after long dispute won their case in the courts. The last act of the court procedure was the restoration of the Loomis Laboratory to its previous owners by the Court of Appeals decisions of 22 March and 5 April 1904. (The famous Elihu Root represented Cornell, while David B. Hill, Cornell's nemesis in the Fiske-McGraw Will Case, upheld N.Y.U.) The Court based its decisions on the reports of an oral promise from the Chancellor, Henry M. MacCracken, to Henry F. Dimock, representing the medical faculties. This promise, said the Court, was later denied and disavowed, hence voiding the agreement. In short, the Chancellor and Mr. Dimock gave each other the lie direct, and the Court chose to believe Mr. Dimock.[2]

The newly separated faculties, feeling the need of a university connection, considered Yale, Dartmouth, and Princeton, and finally prayed Cornell to accept them. On 14 April 1898 the Cornell trustees established the Cornell University Medical College, elected Dr. William M. Polk Director and Dean, and appointed six professors, including Lewis A. Stimson, H. P. Loomis (son of Alfred L.), and Austin Flint.

Most of the faculty of the University Medical School and four from the Bellevue Hospital Medical College joined the new establishment, accompanied by 215 of their students. The total registration in the opening year was 278, including 26 women. The college, temporarily quartered in the Loomis Laboratory and in adjacent buildings, was formally opened on the fourth of the following October, with appropriate ceremony. Dean Polk stated the conviction of himself and his associates that "clinical demonstration, upon a broad basis of laboratory instruction, is the only way in which to prepare students for the degree of Doctor of Medicine." Further, he announced, the organizers would replace the didactic lecture by recitations from textbooks and the mass clinic of the amphitheatre by hospital and dispensary visits in small groups, under the guidance of trained clinicians.[3]

The angelic Colonel Payne built for the school a home on First Avenue, between 27th and 28th Streets, at a cost of a million dollars, to which he added a half million for equipment. It was opened, with due solemnity, in the autumn of 1900. The exterior was Renaissance, of brick and stone; the interior contained an ample dispensary and everything that physicians and architects could devise in the way of theatres, laboratories, dissecting rooms, and accommodations for such novelties as Roentgen rays. This structure, of unexampled magnificence for its purpose, was for many years Cornell's very particular pride.

Today, like many another Renaissance palazzo, it has fallen into an unhonored age. A variety of tenants occupy its high rooms and, collar-

[2] The story is told from the N.Y.U. point of view in Theodore Francis Jones, *New York University, 1832–1932* (New York, 1933).

[3] One may be amused to recall that one of Andrew D. White's most loudly proclaimed reforms in 1868 was the replacement of recitations from textbooks by inspiring lecturers.

less and even shirtless, lean from its wide windows. Across its front hangs a long banner, "Grace Downs' Model and Airline School."

Coincidentally with the opening of the Medical College in New York, a two-year course was established in Ithaca, paralleling the first two years in the New York school and admitting its successful students to third-year studies in New York. The Medical College in Ithaca, having no Colonel Payne, was supported from University funds. Most of the staff were drawn from existent departments, most of the courses from existent offerings. The requirement was made that all women candidates for the M.D. degree must spend their first two years in the Ithaca school. The establishment was immediately crowded, in cramped quarters on the top floor of White Hall, inconvenient for human anatomy and anatomies. In this sad pass the faithful Dean Sage, son of Henry W. Sage, came to our aid with a gift of $80,000 for the construction of Stimson Hall, in honor of Dr. Lewis A. Stimson. But Stimson Hall belongs in the twentieth century, as does nearly all the history of the Medical College in New York, and to that century we may now defer the record.

XX

The Nineties:
The Educational Machine

THE University grew steadily through the nineties, from 1,390 full-time students in 1890–91 to 2,047 in 1899–1900. Graduate students numbered 84 in 1890–91, rose to 240 in 1894, sank to 174 in 1899–1900. Arts and Sciences rose steadily, from 499 at the beginning of the decade to 755 at its end. Agriculture was still insignificant, advancing only from 52 to 88. Mechanical Engineering and Electrical Engineering combined rose from 435 to 571. Architecture began with 52, mounted to 97 in 1893–94, and fell again to 43. Law rose from 122 to 246 in 1897–98 and dropped to 178. Most of these fluctuations are due to special causes of no very general import.

Growth inflicted its pains and penalties. Schurman said in his report for 1900 that the increasing popularity of the University was the chief source of its perplexities. He spoke of the need for classrooms, laboratories, equipment, teachers, living quarters. The professor of physics was forced to give his lectures twice, and soon it would be thrice. In the Physics building one could hardly move among the machines. (But most of us have lived through one or more periods of rapid growth and could supply plenty of parallels.)

Schurman's conception of a university's structure and operation was stated in a letter concerning the reorganization of Stanford University.[1] He said:

[1] To Horace Davis, 24 Sept. 1903.

The principle for which I have always stood is a complete divorce between the business of the University and the work of instruction, investigation, and discipline. This latter should be vested exclusively in the Faculty. The business belongs as exclusively to the Board of Trustees. . . . When a Board of Trustees goes beyond these functions and undertakes to direct the *educational* work of the University, I consider it guilty of a fatal usurpation.

He continues that the President has no veto on the actions either of the Board or of the Faculty, and it is well that this should be so. The importance of the President arises from two circumstances: he is the only man in the University who is a member of all boards, councils, and organizations; secondly, he nominates all appointments in the University. "I make no nominations without consulting in advance the members of the departments concerned and agreeing with them as to the wisdom of the appointment." When the headship of a department falls vacant, the President consults with the heads of cognate departments. The President should not have the absolute right of appointment and dismissal of professors: "To put a man of the culture and dignity of a professor absolutely at the mercy of one individual is a humiliation and an affront."

With such principles in mind, Schurman did his daily tasks of administration and organization.

Until 1886–87 Cornell was ruled by a single faculty. In that year came the College of Law, with purposes and methods so particular that its professors met separately. From this precedent the professors in other fields argued that they were properly colleges with their own rights and privileges. The trustees therefore reformed the organization, and in 1896 decreed that Cornell University comprehends the Graduate Department, the Academic Department (or Department of Arts and Sciences), the College of Law, the College of Civil Engineering, the Sibley College of Mechanical Engineering and Mechanic Arts, the College of Architecture, and the College of Agriculture. "The New York State Veterinary College is administered by Cornell University, and its work is organically connected with that of the University." Further, the faculties would consist of the University Faculty and of separate faculties for each college and for the Graduate and Academic Departments. Each college should have a director, the Graduate and Academic Departments their deans. (But no Dean of the Graduate School is visible until 1909.) A Dean of the University Faculty should be appointed by the trustees on the nomination of the President and with the concurrence of his faculty. (This dean was Horatio S.

White of German, who had been appointed Dean of the General Faculty by President Adams in 1892.) The matter of discipline was referred to the separate colleges. By and large, this is the system which has continued to our own day.

Certain matters of general university concern may be noted. An honor system in examinations was established in 1892–93, with a Committee on Discipline, composed of the President and ten undergraduates. This marks the first admission of student representatives to the responsibilities of student government. The method of control worked well, for a time at least, and proved to be "a great relief to every professor in the University." A Student Self-Government Council was erected in 1893–94, by which, said the President, the student body was admitted into partnership with the faculty. The old three-term year yielded to a two-semester schedule. A new marking system on a scale of 100 was adopted. The academic costume was prescribed for seniors at Commencement. Some faculty foes of medievalism offered an almost hysterical opposition. (As late as 3 April 1909 the trustees were obliged to rule: "Trustees who do not elect to wear caps and gowns are requested to wear silk hats and frock coats.")

In the Department of Arts and Sciences the entrance requirements were stiffened, and the degrees of Bachelor of Science and Bachelor of Philosophy were dropped. This latter action was of more moment than might at first appear. It meant that all graduates in Arts and Sciences would receive the Bachelor of Arts, the degree traditionally reserved for those sufficiently weighted with Latin and Greek. The classicists of the country attacked us, *vi et armis.* "Few events of recent years in the educational world have called forth more adverse criticism than the action of Cornell respecting the A.B. degree," said the *Journal of Pedagogy* in March 1897. President Melanchthon W. Stryker of Hamilton College, a fortress of the classics, debated the innovation with President Schurman on a public platform. Most Cornellians, at least, agreed that Schurman won the mighty battle of eloquence. His main point was that any possessor of a liberal education should properly be denominated a Bachelor of Arts and that such an education may be gained from other studies than Latin and Greek.

The broad definition of the A.B. degree was naturally related to the elective system, by which a student might take any courses he pleased, in whatever order, provided only that he pass a certain number of hours' work. Cornell was a home of the elective principle. Andrew D. White had proclaimed it even before Eliot of Harvard, permitting students to choose among a series of curricula, and, if these did not satisfy, to take anything they pleased in an Optional Course. Under President Adams this system had continued. By 1896 all specifications were abolished, except drill and hygiene for freshmen. Even the graduation thesis was made optional. The freedom of the Arts student was nearly absolute. Many found their way, by their own efforts and errors, to the kind of education they sought; and many of those who profited by this freedom were ever afterward grateful for it.

Harvard, Cornell, and Stanford stood by the free elective system in its extremest form, and continued to do so through the first decade of the twentieth century. It was a good thing, despite all its abuses, despite the criticisms made then and later. Says a sound historian of education:

The elective system had blown through the American college like a gust of fresh air, and had swept out innumerable features of the old régime that could hardly be justified—its rigidity, its archaic content, its emphasis on discipline and memory rather than inquiry and criticism, its tendency to constrict the lives of faculty members as well as students by limiting their opportunities to deepen themselves in a special field of learning.[2]

Within Arts and Sciences certain departments raise their hands, asking to be heard.

Chemistry, at ease in its new Morse Hall, became a leader in its field. A group of young professors distinguished themselves: William R. Orndorff, Louis M. Dennis, Joseph E. Trevor, Wilder D. Bancroft, Emile M. Chamot '91, George W. Kavanaugh '96. Dennis gave the first extensive and intensive course in America on spectroscopic analysis and gas analysis and did pioneer work in colorimetry. Bancroft and Trevor founded and edited the *Journal of Physical Chemistry*, interpreting their subject as an inquiry why and how chemical reactions occur. Chamot introduced a course in microchemical analysis dealing with particle shape and size, crystallization, fusion, sintering, and phase changes.

Geology throve, under the direction of Ralph S. Tarr (of the Tarr geographies) and with the assistance of a noteworthy group, A. C. Gill, Gilbert D. Harris '86, Heinrich Ries, and others. In 1896 Tarr organized an expedition to Greenland. He accompanied Peary to latitude

[2] Richard Hofstadter and C. de W. Hardy, *Development and Scope of Higher Education in the United States* (New York, 1952), p. 53. Also R. Freeman Butts, *The College Charts Its Course* (New York, 1939).

74°, and with Professor Gill and four students spent the summer studying the ice sheet. They named a glacier at 74° 18′ Cornell Brae, and so it stands on today's maps.

Economics, or Political Economy, or Polecon, had an exceptional group of teachers in the nineties: Frank A. Fetter, Jeremiah Whipple Jenks, active adviser of legislative committees and of foreign governments, Walter F. Willcox, statistician for the census of 1900 and member of the New York State Board of Health. A number of eminent economists had a part of their training here, among them E. W. Kemmerer, Thomas N. Carver, and Thorstein Veblen.

Music began to creep into the curriculum. In 1896–97 two one-hour courses were offered under a Choral Union by staff members of the Ithaca Conservatory of Music. In 1898–99 a chorus was formed, and in the following year Hollis Dann, supervisor of music in the Ithaca Public Schools, was put in charge, though he was not yet admitted to the faculty. The Conservatory took over the music in Sage Chapel, our student singers receiving two hours' credit; and Professor Trevor of Physics organized a University Orchestra. In 1900 a lecture course in the history of music (credit one hour) was offered. Thus gradually Music attained respectability.

The Sage School of Philosophy, under Schurman's active guidance, became one of the country's centers of philosophical thought and training. Some of the teachers, James E. Creighton, William A. Hammond, Frank Thilly, Ernest F. Albee, spent their lives at Cornell; others, such as James Seth and F. C. S. Schiller, gained their greater fame elsewhere. The *Philosophical Review* began its distinguished career in 1892, with Schurman as editor. Education, or Pedagogy, was classed under Philosophy. Schurman established and edited the *School Review*, today a journal of mighty influence.

In 1891 the psychological laboratory was inaugurated, only twelve years after Wundt had opened in Leipzig the first such laboratory. In 1892 arrived Edward Bradford Titchener, pupil of Wundt. He created a particular Cornell brand of psychology, known as structuralism. He detached psychology from philosophy and philosophers, insisting that psychology is a laboratory science. His *Experimental Psychology* in four volumes was called "the most erudite psychological work in the English language." His course in Elementary Psychology became one of the most celebrated courses offered anywhere in anything. Imposing in his Oxford gown, brilliant in speech and in demonstration, he was such a lecturer as few students have ever heard, as few will ever hear.

A masterly portrait of the master by his disciple, Edwin G. Boring '08, must be consigned to the reaches of Excursus II.

Schurman, himself the editor of two professional magazines, always encouraged his faculty to start journals in their fields. The enterprising physicists took him up, founding the *Physical Review* in 1893, under the editorship of Professors Nichols, Merritt, and Bedell. It is strange but apparently true that up to that time no journal wholly devoted to physics was published in the United States.

A new department was founded—that of Semitic Languages and Literatures. The circumstances illustrate the character of Schurman and of his Cornell. Nathaniel Schmidt, eminent and unorthodox scholar at the Colgate Divinity School, was put on trial for heresy in 1895. Schurman, at least a nominal Baptist, protested in ringing words:

Is there room in a Baptist theological seminary for a growing professor who teaches what, according to the best lights of science, scholarship, and reflection, he believes to be the truth? . . . If a theological professor is to teach, not what his investigations show him to be the truth, but what a majority of the denomination who are not called to such investigations hold, or suppose that they hold, to be the truth, the warfare between intelligence and such dogmatism will become so intense that no place will be left for theological seminaries in the modern world. A professor must teach the truth as he sees it; those who hold that a professor must teach what the majority believes would have him stultify himself. It is the old question which Job raised: "Shall a man be partial for God?" [3]

Not content with exhortation, Schurman persuaded Henry W. Sage to establish a chair of Semitic Languages, and obtained—at a bargain rate—Professor Schmidt to fill it. Schmidt's enormous, recondite learning and his startling lectures became a campus wonder. He offered something like forty hours of work weekly, including such subjects as Coptic, Syriac, and Aramaic. He was secure in the knowledge that no one would take them. Some of his books, such as *The Prophet of Nazareth* and his commentary on Job, have well withstood the ravages of time.

A professorship in archaeology and art was established in 1891. The incumbent, Alfred Emerson, was given the task of creating a museum of casts, with funds supplied by Henry W. Sage. This collection, regarded as the best in any American institution, was opened on Sage's eightieth birthday, 31 January 1894. It was quartered in McGraw Hall until it found a lasting home in Goldwin Smith Hall in 1906.

[3] JGS to James Colgate, 8 June 1895.

Within other colleges than Arts, some developments engage the historian's notice.

In Architecture, a new director, Alexander Buel Trowbridge '90, succeeded the veteran Charles Babcock in 1896. Trowbridge had spent two years at the École des Beaux-Arts in Paris. He was assisted by John V. Van Pelt, also a Beaux-Arts man, in fact the first American to receive the degree of Architecte diplômé par le gouvernement. These two sought to impose the Beaux-Arts principle, the insistence on design as an art form. Traditionally in America architecture had been regarded as an adjunct of engineering; the new director insisted that the school belonged in a college of fine arts. He peremptorily demanded a million dollars for the erection of such a school, and the President heartily seconded him. But the quarry, the generous aesthetic multi-millionaire, was not to be found. In fact, he has not yet been found.

Director Trowbridge did his best with the meager funds in hand. He appointed Olaf Brauner to teach drawing and painting and Albert C. Phelps for the history of art and architecture. No doubt at his suggestion, the President called for a department of interior decoration. He proposed further the extension of the architectural course to five years.

The College of Mechanical Engineering, under Director Thurston, prospered amain. Hiram W. Sibley, son of the original donor, built in 1893–1894 East Sibley, on the original plans, and the central block with its dome in 1901. The experimental engineering laboratory did useful work; a Graduate School of Railway Mechanical Engineering was established; a course in chemical engineering was proposed in 1891–92 (but not adopted); the *Sibley Journal of Engineering* began in 1892. The President announced roundly in his report for 1898 that the school was supreme in the United States, with the hardest entrance requirements and courses; our graduates outnumbered those of any other school, and even the European institutions could not match our experimental and research work. In the following year the President noted that 47 per cent of the papers read at A.S.M.E. meetings were by Sibley men. In 1900 he reported that in a survey of engineering schools Cornell was ranked first, both for its scientific and for its practical work. Cornell's standing was attested in 1899, when Andrew Carnegie offered England's University of Birmingham $250,000 to establish a scientific school providing it be modeled on Cornell. Representatives of Birmingham came to visit us and turned in a report almost embarrassingly laudatory.

In the College of Civil Engineering the big news was the construction of the Hydraulic Laboratory beside Triphammer Falls. Director Fuertes had long been pressing for such a facility for the study of water's behavior. The trustees authorized in 1896 the building of the laboratory, with a canal for testing ship models, in combination with the creation of a reservoir to supply abundant water to the campus and power for the electric plant in the gorge. A plan was made by Frank S. Washburn '83, assisted by Elon H. Hooker '96, later to be a celebrated industrialist. The building, completed in 1898, clings to the south wall of the gorge, from top to bottom, beside the falls. Built of the same gray stone as the rock wall, it makes no ugly disharmony; indeed, it adds to the picturesqueness of the cascades, especially when giant streams burst forth from unexpected orifices. (We need not heed the allegation that it is built in twelfth-century Florentine style.)

As a part of the operation, a new dam was built above the fall, ten feet higher than the old one. The stream above the dam had been a tangled muddy growth of trees and brush. This area was now submerged to impound 53,000,000 gallons of water. And thus our Beebe Lake was created, for bathing, boating, skating, and tobogganing.

Gardner S. Williams was appointed professor of experimental hydraulics. He later gained professional renown as head of Civil Engineering at Michigan.

The College of Law came into its own with the formal dedication of Boardman Hall on 14 February 1893. The presentation was then made of the valuable Nathaniel C. Moak law library by the wife and daughter of Judge Douglass Boardman. The school's equipment was said to be second only to that of Harvard. Its reproach, however, was that admission could be gained with about two years of high-school work, and after two years of instruction one could receive the LL.B. The degree, therefore, could represent no more elapsed time than the high-school diploma required for entrance to the Department of Arts and Sciences.

President Schurman insisted in his first report that the entrance requirements must be raised and the course be extended to three or even four years. The alumni were polled and warmly approved such a stiffening and strengthening. Finally in 1897 a third year of instruction was imposed, and in 1898 the entrance requirement was made equivalent to that for the academic course. The result was that the freshman class dropped from 125 in 1897 to 62 in 1898. But the eventual gain was naturally great. Serious students were attracted by the school's reputation and its excellent faculty. The names, and indeed some of the persons, are still remembered: Francis Miles Finch, resident professor from 1896 to 1903; Cuthbert W. Pound '84, State Senator and public servant; Edwin H. Woodruff '88, later Dean; and Ernest W. Huffcut '84, a scholar and teacher of uncommon brilliance.

The Graduate Department became in these years a more coherent structure than before, but the work was still controlled by the several departments. We had had our sprinkling of graduate students since 1871–72, the number never surpassing 50 until 1887–88. Then the enrollments rapidly rose, to 84 in 1890–91, 133 in 1891–92, 170 in 1892–93, and 240 in 1893–94. But in that year two things happened: the country experienced a financial panic, and Cornell imposed tuition fees on graduate students. The enrollment dropped to 145 in 1895–96 and did not surpass the 1893–94 high until 1907–8.

Schurman, the product of graduate years in Britain, France, and Germany, well recognized the importance of graduate work in a university. He could applaud the statement of David Starr Jordan, in his report as alumni trustee in 1888:

The graduate students are the crown of the University, and Cornell cannot afford to neglect them for the sake of any others. . . . One student in quaternions is worth more to the University than a dozen in trigonometry. One student in the Nibelungenlied or in Germanic philology is worth more than a dozen stumbling over the elements in Whitney's grammar, and one trained to carry to an end a scientific investigation is worth more than a dozen learning to analyze flowers, or even to identify the muscles of a cat.

Noteworthy in the Graduate Department was the work done in agriculture. John De Witt Warner, in his alumni trustee's report for 1899, alleged that ours was the only department in the country that offered serious graduate courses and that as a result we had many more graduate students than our rivals.

As the graduate work in Agriculture was linked with the investigations in our Experiment Station, all graduate work was bound up with faculty research. The very idea, the concept, of research as a university function had become axiomatic. Only a half century had passed since President Tappan of Michigan had proclaimed to his incredulous Regents that a university should advance knowledge, not merely preserve it. Hopkins, Harvard, Columbia had picked up and codified the idea. Cornell, by the voice of its President, agreed. "For the future of our civilization, this work is quite as important as teaching," he said in his report for 1900. And he recognized that if a university professor is expected to advance knowledge, he must have quarters, equipment, and release from teaching duties, and that means Money.

One inconspicuous item catches the historian's eye. With the opening of our Hydraulic Laboratory in 1898, the U.S. Deep Waterways Commission detailed an engineer to study the flow of waters over weirs and paid the cost of his investigations. This is the first case in our history of government-sponsored research in engineering. Is it the first case in American educational history?

The military department, lacking all power of enforcing military discipline, suffered during a pacific and pacifistic era. The Cadet Corps was a sloppy outfit, in appearance and morale (although, a little earlier, some cadets were mightily proud of their white helmets badged with a large brass eagle). Only the most innocent freshmen bought new uniforms. The fraternities kept collections of frowsy military wear in their attics for the use of their pledges. An atrocious fit was regarded as collegiate chic. The artillery, clad in red uniforms and wearing sabres, had fieldpieces but no shells and frequently filled their caissons with beer. Mutiny and insubordination were commonplaces. In one sham battle, a detachment, ordered to retreat, retreated all the way home.

Summer schools had for years been held informally on the campus. Professors or groups of professors, especially in the natural sciences, would use the university facilities for summer instruction. The growth of these parasitic schools moved the trustees to establish in 1893 the Cornell Summer School, with a dean and faculty appointed at fixed salaries. Three-fourths of the students were themselves teachers. But more and more, undergraduates entered the courses, to make up failures, to abbreviate their college course, or merely to learn something desirable to know, under the relaxed radiance of an Ithaca summer. There have always been such students, and there still are, thank God.

XXI

The Nineties: Cornellians

and Their Home

ON 7 October 1893, the twenty-fifth anniversary of Cornell's Inauguration, a proper celebration was held. As a stocktaking it was indeed
impressive. The speakers, of whom Chauncey M. Depew, magnate,
legislator, and wit, was the chief, pointed to the puny babyhood, the
sickly adolescence, and the lusty manhood of the University. President
Schurman repeated Ezra Cornell's statement of his aim, to combine
practical with liberal education and to fit the youth of the country to
master all the practical questions of life with success and honor; and
these words Schurman assumed as his own guide.

Some noted that Schurman made no mention of the educational
concepts of Andrew D. White. And Chauncey M. Depew uttered the
name of White only as one of a list of benefactors. The Chancellor
of the State of New York, the Reverend Anson J. Upson, did indeed
give to White a hundred laudatory words, and the other speakers
made courteous reference to him. But to White, in faraway St. Petersburg, the accounts of the celebration, with its neglect of his achievement, strongly suggested a plot to bury his work in oblivion.[1] The
identity of the chief plotter was not clear to him. Was it Schurman? Or
Henry W. Sage?

[1] ADW to Hewett, 1894; G. L. Burr to ADW, 28 Sept. and 9 Oct. 1893, in Burr
Papers.

In fact, was there a campus animus against White? I can see no evidence of a plot. The fact is that by 1893 White's reforms were won, his program accomplished. The elective system, equality in prestige of all subjects, nonsectarianism, coeducation, freedom of behavior for students—all this had become accepted practice, at Cornell and elsewhere. But Ezra Cornell's underlying purpose, his aim to make higher education available to superior youth everywhere, his test of higher education by practical utility, remained a program which the new President could adopt and proclaim.

This program Schurman put vigorously into effect. He sought funds for physical expansion. But as it turned out, the period from 1892 to 1900 was not one of Cornell's building booms. We have spoken of the Veterinary College, of the Hydraulic Laboratory, of East Sibley, of the Dairy Husbandry Building, to be metamorphosed into the north wing of Goldwin Smith. There was not a great deal besides.

Henry W. Sage died on 18 September 1897 and was fittingly interred under the apse of Sage Chapel, beside his wife. Above them rose the brilliant mosaic decorations at which so many undergraduate generations have stared with fascination. Designed by members of the famous artist family of the J. and R. Lamb Company, they were said at the time to be the most extensive series of figure mosaics attempted in this country.

Sage's sons, William H. and Dean, gave his spacious home on State Street to be a University Infirmary, with $100,000 for upkeep. As Henry W. Sage had fulfilled Jennie McGraw's first purpose, to build a great library for Cornell, he now, after death, fulfilled her second, to give a student hospital.

President Schurman dreamed iridescent dreams of a cluster of residential halls, "gems of architecture worthy this exquisite setting, and, towering above them, a stately Alumni Hall consisting of a Club or Common Room, and a Dining Hall (like that at Christ Church, Oxford, let us say), where students from the new residential halls and our present fraternity houses might take their meals in common." [2] Schurman, like Andrew D. White, derived his educational ideals rather from democratic Germany than from aristocratic England, but when it came to architecture, both turned instinctively to the quads and closes of Oxford and Cambridge. With all our practicality, we longed for the pomp, ritual, and ease of England's ancient colleges. We did not realize that such settings are meaningless without the spirit that ani-

[2] *A Generation of Cornell* (New York, 1898), p. 53.

mates them, nor can we today transfer by fiat the gowned decorum of Christ Church Hall to the Domecon Cafeteria.

Andrew D. White made an effort to give our campus the Oxonian look by erecting (in 1896) an entrance gateway at the head of Eddy Street, directly below his old rooms in Cascadilla. The gateway is of alternating courses of sandstone and limestone. It was not much commended, even when new. Charles H. Hull called it frankly hideous, and the world called it "Andy White's chocolate cake."[3] Today it guards a secondary entrance to the campus. A traffic menace, just too narrow to permit two cars to pass, blocking the approaching driver's view of all that lies beyond, it has evoked, through the years, many of the wrong emotions.

More useful, and to many eyes more beautiful, was the stone bridge over Cascadilla, given by William H. Sage in 1896.

If the builders were not active on the campus proper, they were busy in the fraternity world. The rapid growth of the University overcrowded the lodginghouses and stimulated the creation of fraternities and the building of homes, some of them sumptuous, some, for impecunious groups, poor and cheap. At this time the fraternities began installing dining rooms. Chi Phi's house, built in 1891, marked a new achievement in undergraduate elegance. It was outdone when, in 1896, Chi Psi occupied the Fiske-McGraw mansion.

The fraternities were very flammable. Fires were reported with remarkable frequency and sangfroid. The Kappa Alpha lodge, on Central Avenue just north of Cascadilla Bridge, was nearly destroyed on the night of 29 December 1898, during the Christmas vacation. The janitor sent in an alarm at 3:30 A.M. But the firemen were holding their annual banquet, when, in accordance with an old custom, false alarms were turned in from distant boxes, for the amusement of the banqueters. They therefore did not respond until 4:30 A.M., when, one suspects, their efforts were not very intelligently directed.

In 1897 the campus was connected with the northland beyond the gorge by the Triphammer Bridge, built by enterprising land developers headed by Edward G. Wyckoff '89. The streetcar line was extended across it; in May 1900 the cars inaugurated the famous loop, crossing Fall Creek a second time on a new bridge at Stewart Avenue.

In the mid-nineties the Ithaca Traction Company reclaimed a square mile of swampland in the valley to make Renwick Park. It opened in 1894, with a casino, dancing pavilion, ice cream parlor, and bath house.

[3] Hull to Burr, 11 Nov. 1896, in Burr Papers.

Before it becomes Stewart Park and before the name of Renwick is forgotten, let me record that Major James Renwick of New York bought this land in 1790, and that his daughter-in-law, née Jean Jeffrey, was the daughter of a minister in Lochmaben, Scotland, and that Robert Burns wrote for her "The Blue-eyed Lassie" and "When First I Saw Fair Jeanie's Face."

So much for the physical frame. Within our little world the President ruled, with suitable deference to the trustees. The Board numbered, at the decade's beginning, twenty-three. This would seem to be a sufficient number of trustees, but some of the ex officio members never attended, and the alumni expressed a strong desire to have some of the great centers of population represented and also to submerge the "Ithaca influence." Thus in 1895 fifteen more trustees were provided for, five to be elected by the alumni, ten by the Board. One of the alumni's choices was Martha Carey Thomas '77, President of Bryn Mawr, our first woman trustee. The second woman on the Board was Ruth Putnam '78, elected by the alumni in 1899. It cannot be said that the alumni were antifeminist.

In the Cornell scene, Andrew D. White always occupied a place apart. During the nineties he was absent most of the time. In 1892–94 he was Minister to Russia, in 1896–97 a member of the Venezuela Boundary Commission, and from 1897 to 1902 Ambassador to Germany. His adored wife had died tragically in 1887; in apparently perfect health, she was stricken at the breakfast table, and expired in five minutes. In 1890 he married Miss Helen Magill, daughter of the President of Swarthmore College, herself a well-known Greek scholar and the first woman Ph.D. in America (Boston University, 1877).[4]

[4] One minor matter piqued Ithaca's imagination and provoked exaggerated stories. White built his mansion, crowning the campus, in 1871, despite the apprehensions of the trustees, who foresaw that his presence in such an imperial position would be awkward when he would become ex-President; they urged him to build in the town. White would have none of that; but he gave the title of the house to the University, to be a future President's House; and in 1876 the trustees, on motion of Henry W. Sage, leased the house and grounds to him without rental charge for a term of twenty years.

Nineteen years rolled by. White assumed that his lease would be extended, and Sage assumed the contrary—no doubt because he wanted to see President Schurman in the President's House. White wrote in his diary (19 July 1895): "Letter from H. W. Sage taking my letter regarding my continuance in the house I built on the Univ. grounds in a very cold-blooded and business-like way. I understand now as never before Fiske's feeling toward Mr. Sage & his course toward the Univ. I gave the house, my library, more money than I cd afford & all the best

Between President Schurman and his faculty good will generally reigned. They knew him to be a faculty man, sympathetic toward their troubles. He himself noted in his report for 1898 that there was a better *esprit de corps* on the campus and a kindlier feeling between the administration and the University community. His greatest grief, he said, was his inability to promote worthy men and answer departmental needs.

On the ever-vexed question of academic freedom he took a firm stand, insisting that the teacher's duty is to the truth, not to the official or majority view. He spoke splendid words:

If it is asserted that the business of the college or university is to teach that which the average man may believe, or that which is acceptable to the University, or that which the Board of Trustees may assert as the truth, the answer must always be that such a course contravenes the very principle on which the University was founded; and, however true it may be that the majority must always rule in the body politic, the motto of the University must always be: "One man with God's truth is a majority." It has been urged that the teacher represents a corporation, and that if he expresses opinions or beliefs contrary to the belief of the majority of the corporation he betrays his trust. What profanation! The teacher is the representative of no one but the god of truth; he ministers at the temple of learning and scholarship; and it would be sacrilegious or worse for him to give out as true what he knows is false, or to suppress or by compliance conceal what he holds, in order to be more acceptable.[5]

With all his respect for faculty opinion, Schurman developed the administrator's usual distrust of faculty management. "The education of the intellect and the imagination," he said, "with no restraint from the administrator's sense of responsibility for practical consequences, charges a university with an immense fund of critical explosibility." [6]

In practice, Schurman eagerly worked for betterment of the faculty's lot. As a professor, he had been aware of many grievances. For instance, in 1886 C. C. Shackford of English Literature was retired for age with

years of my life to the Univ., and now Mr. S proposes to turn me out of the house as coolly as he wd clear out a tenant who had declined to pay rent, altho the Univ. does not need the house. He even proposes to sell it to the highest bidder during my life-time. It is all very cold-blooded."

The trustees were less intransigent than Sage and in June 1896 voted a life lease to Mr. White.

[5] Quoted by W. T. Hewett, *Cornell University: A History* (New York, 1905), I, 293.

[6] *A Generation of Cornell*, p. 40.

a year's salary. The faculty murmured that old professors were treated like livestock, turned out to pasture when too old for service.[7]

One of Schurman's first actions, therefore, was to propose a retirement and pension plan. He developed the plan in his report for 1895. Admitting that Americans in general look with suspicion on pensions, he thought that professors, perversely, might find them very attractive. His scheme, briefly, was that the University should furnish two-thirds or three-fourths of the retirement funds, that professors should pay into the funds 4 per cent or 5 per cent of their salary annually; and that retirement should be fixed at age sixty-five. The trustees endorsed the principle, but did not see where the money was coming from. No action, indeed, was taken until 1903, when William H. Sage gave $150,-000 to initiate such a fund.

Many Cornell faculty members, famous in their time, not yet quite forgotten, came to us in the nineties. Only a few can be mentioned; and if a reader looks here in vain for the name of a friend or a father, I can only say that I have unwillingly omitted many a sterling teacher from the record.

Here, then, are some random Faculty Notes from those rich years.

Eugene P. Andrews '95, on a graduate fellowship in Athens, gained fame by reconstructing and deciphering the inscription on the Parthenon frieze from the nail holes. He spent his life at Cornell, in Greek Archaeology, with minors in the Savage Club and Track Athletics. His vivid lectures were popular with undergraduates and with visitors who sought intellectual pleasure and not credit. George F. Atkinson '85 was one of our most celebrated professors of botany. Charles E. Bennett, one of the country's leading classicists and author of a famous Latin grammar, came in 1893. Olaf M. Brauner, beloved inspirer of many young artists, taught in the College of Architecture from 1895 on.

Miss Louise S. Brownell, Bryn Mawr A.B. and Ph.D., was named warden of Sage College and lecturer in English literature in 1897. She was our first woman teacher, or at least the first to conduct scheduled classroom courses. Her success was such that in 1899 the Executive Committee proposed her appointment as assistant professor. The proposal was questioned at the full Board meeting in June, and action deferred till the fall meeting. In September Miss Brownell withdrew her name, and in the following spring she resigned her posts. The *Era* (28 April 1900) deplored her departure, saying that she had given an excellent course and had done much to abate campus prejudice. Mean-

[7] Huffcut to Burr, 31 Jan. 1886.

while the President made another effort to appoint a woman professor. Anna Botsford Comstock '85, wife of Professor John Henry Comstock, was named assistant professor of nature study in the Summer School, on 8 November 1898. The trustee opposition to her title was so great that when the summer was over Mrs. Comstock was reappointed as lecturer. She remains on the record, however, as the first female holding professorial rank at Cornell. The matter of a feminine appointment was, in these years, moot, being regarded either as the fulfillment of simple justice or as an Opening Wedge. Miss Ellen B. Canfield came in 1894 to supervise the women's work in physical culture, and here spent her life of gallant service. Dr. Agnes Claypole was named laboratory assistant in embryology in 1898. Miss Martha Van Rensselaer came as an assistant in extension in 1900. The alumni trustee, John D. Warner '72, proposed in 1900 that a woman should be made professor of botany, because of the congeniality of that subject to womanhood. It does look like an opening wedge.

John Henry Comstock of Entomology and Simon H. Gage of Microscopy formed the Comstock Publishing Company in 1893, to market their *Introduction to Entomology* and *The Microscope*. According to all business precedents, such a back-yard publishing company was doomed. On the contrary, it throve mightily, with a valuable specialized list. Mrs. Comstock's *Handbook of Nature-Study*, lately in its twenty-fourth edition, has sold hundreds of thousands of copies. The Comstock Publishing Company, bequeathed to the University in 1931, became a precious component of the Cornell University Press.

T. F. Crane of Romance Languages became the first dean of the Arts College in 1896 and Acting President in 1900–1901, and thus gained undying fame. He had not been a popular professor—he was known as "Vinegar Crane"—but in his higher posts he mellowed and bloomed, and gained the general affection of the campus. Benjamin M. Duggar, one of the foremost botanists and plant physiologists of our time, discoverer of aureomycin, took his Cornell Ph.D. in 1898, and taught here, with some interruptions, in the new century's early years.

One of the pleasantest of faculty reminiscences has to do with the Mogue, Director Estevan Fuertes of Civil Engineering, whose house stood hard by the new Veterinary College of Dr. James Law. As Dean Dexter S. Kimball, an eyewitness, recalled:

One afternoon when there was not much business before the faculty, Estevan arose and, hand in bosom, made a strong denunciation of all veterinary colleges and of Cornell's in particular, claiming that the flies from the college filled his back yard and made life unbearable. He had taken steps to prove his case. He had caught flies in his yard, painted their wings red, released them at the Veterinary College, and again caught them in his yard. His case was clear, and he demanded redress.

James Law, the Scotsman, was a bad man to stir up, which was exactly what Fuertes wished to do. Rising and addressing the chair in his best and most incisive Scottish accent, Law replied: "Well, Mr. President, it seems to me that if the flies forsake the Veterinary College to go to Professor Fuertes's back yard, there must be some very good reason." [8]

Othon G. Guerlac, a young French journalist, accepted a post as instructor in Romance languages in 1900, as a step on his way from Paris to the fabled Klondike. He remained to marry the daughter of Francis Miles Finch and to carry on a Cornell dynasty. David F. Hoy '91, the storied "Davy," was appointed assistant registrar in 1894. By fraternity firesides many a tale was told of his ferocity toward registrants. A student standing in line kept his hat on. "Don't you know enough to take your hat off in an office?" snarled Davy. With a ruler he knocked the boy's hat across the room. Many other tales were told of his secret softheartedness. A girl received a bust notice and went home. Davy was woe-stricken. "Why didn't she come back and cry a little?" he protested.[9] Dexter S. Kimball came in 1898 to be assistant professor of machine design. Everett Ward Olmsted '91, genial linguist and chief inspirer of the Book and Bowl Club, was made assistant professor of Romance languages in 1898. F. C. S. Schiller, later a celebrated British philosopher, was here as a graduate instructor from 1893 to 1897. He failed his orals for the Ph.D. and was bidden to take a make-up. He decided not to bother; he strolled under the window of the room where his committee waited to examine him, and then strolled significantly away. So at least the story ran; and certainly he was not reappointed.

The most striking of the newcomers was Henry Morse Stephens, British historian, appointed in 1894. Gay, friendly, whimsical, he captivated his colleagues and his students. He founded the Thursday Night Club, and the Kipling Club, wherein each member incarnated a Kipling character. His introduction of the Musical Clubs to the Savage Club of London in 1895 led to the formation of the Savage Club of Ithaca. He was a great talker, a great teacher, a great personality. He lived

[8] Dexter S. Kimball, *I Remember* (New York: McGraw-Hill, 1953), p. 62.
[9] *Alumni News*, 11 Dec. 1930, 15 June 1939, Jan. 1955; Romeyn Berry, *Behind the Ivy* (Ithaca, 1950), *passim.*

as a bachelor in Cascadilla, finding his social satisfactions among the students. Few were aware that he had a dipsomaniac wife, supported at considerable cost in institutions in England, and that his hearty geniality was a cover for periods of black despondency. He went from Cornell to the University of California and so impressed himself on its world that the Student Union was named after him.

Jared Van Wagenen '91, polished patriarch of Agriculture, was made Instructor in Butter-Making in 1894. Karl M. Wiegand, one of our celebrated botanists, was appointed assistant in 1895.

The new-founded Leland Stanford Junior University, with David Starr Jordan '72 for President, modeled itself largely on Cornell, and raided us for staff. In 1893–94 thirteen of its professors were Cornellians.[10] The first Jewish preacher in Sage Chapel was Rabbi E. G. Hirsch, in January 1896.[11] When old Professor George C. Caldwell asked for a stenographer for the Chemistry Department, the Executive Committee moved (26 May 1896) that the committee was unwilling to enter upon a policy, directly or indirectly, of furnishing stenographers to heads of departments. Quite the most remarkable item in the Trustees' Minutes is an entry for 10 March 1896:

A letter was presented from Prof. John L. Morris [Professor of Practical Mechanics since 1868] stating that in view of the necessity for retrenchment in the University expenses wherever possible he considered it his duty to ask that his salary be reduced to $2500. Moved and carried that the salary of Professor Morris be fixed at $2500 from and after Aug. 1st 1896.

As for student character and quality, one may generalize only with caution. The old spirit of intellectual eagerness and independence existed still, especially among those who brought eagerness and independence to college. "Here was youth, vitality, and red blood," remembers Emily Dunning Barringer '97:

There was no time for basking in the reputation of generations past; we were making reputations and planting the elms. Here was not an isolated person,

[10] A curious example of a great man's influence, not really any of our business, was reported in the *Stanford Illustrated Review* for April 1941, on the death of Camillo Olivetti. The young Olivetti was assistant in electrical engineering at Stanford in 1893–94. He was so imbued by Jordan's teachings that on returning to Italy he built up the Olivetti typewriter factories, with welfare systems famous the world over. He was less successful in his effort to convert Italy to Jordan's Unitarianism.

[11] For Schurman's advocacy of Jewish preachers—and trustees—see his Letter Books, 23 May 1895.

daring to break with tradition, but a whole community of people making tradition. Here was an institution dedicated to mental freedom; that is Cornell's greatest gift to its sons and daughters. . . . The institution was too young to be stuffy, too vigorous to be formalized, too midwestern to always conform to the dictates of the times.[12]

Emily Dunning Barringer was throughout her long life a tradition-breaker. There were plenty of others who conformed to the dictates of the times. Fin-de-siècle America had made a new conventionality, animated by confidence, complacence, even arrogance. The new wealth made new millionaires, who built their châteaux above their mills and on the correct avenues of their cities, and by their example encouraged a general delight in ostentation and a search for refinement. Social life moved out of the country tavern and into the opulent salon, in the passage displaying a curious mingling of rusticity and sophistication.[13] Dress and decoration reflected the national self-esteem. No student would have appeared in class without his tailored jacket, stand-up collar, and cravat. Hat and gloves were obligatory for lady students. Cornell had its own special styles, cultivated by local purveyors. "Doggy" shoes were in vogue; Pat Wall advertised "the Ugliest Shoe in Town."

Romeyn Berry recalls a significant occurrence in the history of student manners.[14] During a three-hour examination on a hot June day, about 1900, a sweating student asked the professor if he might remove his coat. The professor made a little speech; he too suffered and sympathized, but the answer must be "No." No matter what the temperature, in an examination all must be properly garbed. "Nowadays," said Rym, "that professor would be fortunate if, under comparable conditions, half the class did not arrive stripped to their fountain pens and undershirts."

Vehicular transportation offered an index to social life and its dis-

[12] *Bowery to Bellevue* (New York: Norton, 1950), pp. 50–58. An enchanting book by a brilliant physician.

[13] Sarah Bulkley Rogers '91, writing under the name of Schuyler Shelton, had a story in *Scribner's Magazine* for March 1893, recounting the adventures of a graduate student, professor in a small western college, who comes to Cornell for his Ph.D. She cruelly renders the crudity of his thought, language, dress, and behavior, and was reproved by the *Era* (11 March 1893) for portraying too exactly an actual person. Elsewhere too the new urbanity was often pierced by upthrusts of the old evangelical rigorism. In 1896 the Glee Club of Washington University, St. Louis, was disbanded for singing a song beginning: "If you want a kiss, why take it."

[14] *Alumni News*, 1 Oct. 1952.

tinctions. The president of the streetcar system had a private car, mahogany fitted, with curtained red glass windows. On theatre nights it brought the cream of Ithaca society to and from the Lyceum, arresting all traffic for commoners if the performance was prolonged. The livery stables featured sumptuous equipages; one had a four-horse English shooting brake, which you may see portrayed in Alison Mason Kingsbury's murals in the Gannett Clinic, together with many other piquant representations of Cornell life in the nineties. An enterprising hackman bought a stylish hansom cab, a two-wheeler, with the driver aloft in the rear. But on his first trip up Buffalo Street the driver's weight lifted the horse off his feet, to paw the air like Pegasus. A few of the student gentry had their own horses and buggies. We were briefly host in 1900 to the son of Richard Croker, boss of Tammany Hall, who brought his stables and a $5,000 bulldog to companion him. Claudio Juan Martínez '02, progenitor of many mighty Martínezes, introduced, in early 1898, the first Cornell automobile, a White Steamer. A second arrived before the end of the year. This was presumably the steam-powered Locomobile of Samuel Purdy Howe '02, which Romeyn Berry recalled with admiration and terror. Since there was much debate whether the automobile would ever be developed to the point where it could climb Buffalo Street as far as Stewart Avenue under its own power, Howe staged a triumphant test.

The bonds of the students to the town were closer than they are today. Many fraternities had social relationships with Ithaca families. Clubrooms, offices of activities, all sources of amusement were downtown. The Lyceum Theatre opened in 1892. Many still remember with affection the Lyceum's décor of unembarrassed nudities, its drop curtain representing the Port of Leghorn, its parterre, an Ithaca social club on theatre nights, and even its steep gallery with its hard curving undusted wooden benches. Here played many of the world's great actors, such as Salvini and Modjeska. The audiences manifested their critical judgments actively, unlike those of today, who limply applaud the most lamentable plays when they ought to boo, hiss, and stamp. Long remembered was Charles Hanford's production of *Julius Caesar* in January 1896. On that occasion twenty students, engaged as supes, went wild in the riot scene, using football techniques and tackles. The bearers of Caesar's body rolled it off on the stage, whereat it sat up with a curse. After Mark Antony's funeral oration, a Roman citizen led the mob in "a short yell for Mark Antony!"

Student life ran a considerable gamut, between luxury and squalor. President Schurman feared the undemocratic distinction between rich and poor, and urged dormitories as the best corrective. A survey in 1896–97 showed that 16.8 per cent of the men students paid $1.00 a week or less for their rooms. Most of these were surely very wretched, cold, and bare, though Jared Van Wagenen '91 said that his dollar room was snug and comfortable. Four students spent a dollar a week or less for food; 9.4 per cent paid less than $3.00; and 4.4 per cent, the lavish, paid over $4.50. The average independent bought 21-meal tickets for $3.00 or $3.50 in giant boardinghouses, as the East Hill House or the Brunswick on Huestis Street, now College Avenue. Boarding clubs were popular. An energetic organizer would persuade a householder to cook and serve meals in her house. He would then bring in a hungry band, buy the food for about $2 per mouth per week, and would pay the cook 60 cents weekly for each boarder.

Students too poor to pay anything waited on table or did other low-paid work to eke out their costs. The Student Agencies, organized by Seth M. Higby '97, began in 1894. They engaged in various profitable enterprises, but their success rests on a pile of laundry that would well overtop Mount Everest.

Undergraduate social life could be very busy. There were constant banquets, tied to the classes more than is the case today. The freshman banquet in 1899 was dry, and was said to be a great success. But how about the Law School banquet of 1893? One hundred twenty sat down to a sumptuous feast at 9:30 P.M.; the speaking began at 11:00 P.M.; twelve orators were on the program, which ended at 3:00 A.M. That does not sound dry.

Many clubs, social, preprofessional, regional, or representing common concerns or hobbies, were formed. Most of them faded after a brief bloom. But the senior societies, Sphinx Head and Quill and Dagger, flourished amain, as did some social clubs, such as Nalanda and Mummy. And Pyramid, Gargoyle, and the language clubs, and the Savage Club, with its chartered rights from the Savages of London. And of course the C.U.C.A.

The Musical Clubs made an unfortunate invasion of England in 1895, in conjunction with the equally unfortunate entry of the crews at Henley. Said Professor Eugene P. Andrews: "A rascally professional manager and a misunderstanding as to the English attitude toward a professedly amateur musical organization which charged admission fees resulted in the abrupt termination of the tour after one concert had been given. The members lost their large deposits and much besides." [15]

[15] *Cornell Era*, Jan. 1913.

The Masque, organized in 1890, produced a long series of plays, mostly light comedy. It had not yet found the formula of the all-male college musical comedy. The women's roles were usually taken by young ladies of the campus or the town. The women students formed in 1897 the Sage Dramatic Club.

The *Sun* underwent a Great Schism. The paper had become a profitable enterprise, especially for the business manager. In June 1893 the two '94 board members, John L. Ahern and Samuel Scott Slater, both wanted to be business manager. Since neither would yield, in the autumn two *Cornell Daily Suns*, bloodshot with hate, appeared. President Schurman intervened and summoned the two boards to meet in his library, informing them that they must come to an agreement, like a conclave of cardinals, before they could leave. The arguments continued from 7:30 P.M. to 2:30 A.M., and concluded with an agreement to abide by a majority vote of the student body and the faculty. The Ahern faction won. The fact is of no concern to anyone today, but it is of concern that President Schurman, with impressive tact and patience, enforced the principle that the student body, the Public, has ultimate jurisdiction over even a private organization like the *Sun*.

The *Era*, by the end of the century, begins to look typographically modern, with halftones and illustrations, and without the opening page of poetry and the final page of Exchanges. In 1900 the *Era* amalgamated with the *Cornell Magazine* to become a monthly literary magazine, with long stories, articles, and poems.

The *Widow* began her career in October 1894, following a formula established at Harvard and Princeton. The early lists of editors contain some names celebrated in Cornell annals: Louis Fuertes, Woodford Patterson, Walter C. Teagle, Robert M. Ogden, André Smith, Willard Straight. The tradition exists that the *Widow*, when young, was a great deal wittier than it is today. Of course, no one ever looks at the early issues.

The *Alumni News* appeared in 1899. An undergraduate, Herbert Blanchard Lee '99, conceived of the magazine as a practical possibility and set it going, with Clark S. Northup '93 as its first editor.

This was the heyday of intercollegiate athletics. American prosperity made the contests impressive spectacles, attracting many thousands to sit in new concrete stadiums and ride in observation trains, of converted flatcars, at crew races. The new methods and means of publicity filled the newspapers with sports news, and every factory hand played his favorite among the college teams. The spirit of advertising possessed even college administrations, convinced that athletic success brings larger enrollments, and convinced that larger enrollments must be desirable, since everything in America must get bigger and bigger. At the University of Chicago under President Harper it was said that Rockefeller gifts were celebrated like football victories, and football victories like the Second Coming of Christ. And of course the prizes at stake brought professionalism into the world of amateur athletics.

A strong sentiment adverse to intercollegiate football in any form arose in the Cornell Faculty. Resolutions were passed in 1894, aimed at professional interlopers, at low-scholarship players, and at games on other than college grounds. The Faculty's intent was to keep football a college sport. President Schurman thought the menace was not really very acute. He said in his report for 1895: "Cornell athletics are a mere incident to life and work—a recreation and amusement, not a vocation and business—and in large part are a substitute for required physical training. . . . The taint of athleticism has not infected the spirit of the University." The Athletic Association, founded in 1889, and completely independent of the University administration, seemed to the President a satisfactory method of control; indeed, he scouted trustee or faculty recognition of competitive athletics. But faculty regulation steadily increased.

In fact, our football record of the nineties was not so brilliant as to arouse suspicion that Cornell was sacrificing virtue for victory. The series with Penn began in 1893; they beat us, 50 to 0. Our best record of the decade was made in 1892, when we lost only to Harvard.

Glenn ("Pop") Warner '94 was summoned back to be coach in 1897. As an undergraduate he had played triumphantly in the first game he ever saw. He was probably the most inventive coach in history. He contrived the open unbalanced formation, such as the single-wing back, and the crouch start, the screen pass, the shifting defense. He caused more rule changes than all the other coaches combined.[16]

Pop Warner's most spectacular invention was the hidden-ball play. Allen E. Whiting '98, himself deeply involved, later described its operation. A strong elastic bound the bottom of his jersey; at an opportune moment the quarterback would shove the ball up his back. "Time and again in different games I would go between opponents close enough to almost touch them, and they would stand open-eyed, wondering where the ball was. Generally we would go straight for a touchdown.

[16] Robert J. Kane '34, *Alumni News*, 1 Nov. 1954.

Someone would follow and extract the ball from me after I was over the line and touch it down." This rather ungentlemanly device was evidently first used in the Penn State game in 1897.[17]

On the water, Cornell triumphs continued as a matter of course. From 1892 to 1900 our crews rowed in twenty-nine races and won eighteen. But in July 1895 came our humbling, our mortification. We sent a crew to Henley, with great hopes and at great cost. The first heat was with the Leander club, the champions. Apparently not all the Leanders heard the starting signal. Some dipped their oars, and after a moment's confusion all stopped. The Cornell crew slowed down, but the umpire signaled to them to continue, and they paddled the length of the course, and were awarded the heat. The Cornellians, bewildered, found themselves accused in all the newspapers of unsportsmanlike behavior. Next day, rowing Trinity Hall of Cambridge, a Cornell man caught a crab and lost his oar and the race, thus restoring to England a belief in divine justice.

Charles V. P. Young '99 points to the underlying facts:

It was evident even before the races that Courtney's methods were extremely distasteful to the English rowing public. He kept his charges so close in hand that social intercourse with their jolly and hospitable rivals was grimly tabooed. That boating men at Henley should lead the strenuous and secretive life of professional contestants whose reputation and means of livelihood would be enhanced or destroyed according as they should win or lose was entirely at odds with the spirit of the carnival, and this feeling was changed to positive resentment when Cornell left her formidable rival at the starting post and rowed over the course to a technical and hollow victory.[18]

Courtney ruled his men with a despotism none of them would have suffered for a moment from a faculty member. In early June of 1897 he learned that five of his varsity, tempted beyond endurance, had yielded to the seduction of strawberry shortcake. He dropped them out of hand, summoned substitutes, and won the Poughkeepsie regatta with what was ever afterward known as "the strawberry shortcake crew."

On the track, our athletes merely jogged through the nineties, though I notice some good performances in 1898: C. U. Powell jumped 6 feet 1½ inches straight up; G. A. Larkin jumped 21 feet 9 inches straight ahead; H. H. Bassett ran the 880 in 2:02⅗; Bob Deming and E. A. Kin-

[17] *Alumni News*, 20 Oct. 1932, 19 Nov. and 3 Dec. 1942.
[18] *Courtney and Cornell Rowing* (Ithaca, 1923), p. 44.

zie vaulted 11 feet 3 inches. Everything was to change with the coming of John F. Moakley as coach, in the fall of 1899. He had been thirteen years in athletics and had a good record in long-distance running, but he was best known as a trainer and coach. His first achievement was to bring the cross-country team to victory in the Intercollegiates; thereafter we were to win it with tiresome regularity.

Baseball began its spring southern trips in 1899. The Cornell Fencers' Club was organized in 1894 and had some sensational years. Basketball appeared in 1898–99 and was recognized by the Athletic Council in 1901. Lacrosse had a great popularity in the nineties. The Hockey Association was formed in 1900 and joined successfuly in intercollegiate competition. Tennis continued to thrive, its adepts, like William A. Larned '93, displaying brilliantly colored sashes. The opening of the Ithaca Country Club in 1900 gave golfers their opportunity.

Like their brothers, the coeds learned to play harder than in earlier times. A Sports and Pastimes Association was started in 1896, a boathouse for the women's crew was built on the new Beebe Lake, and within doors basketball raged.

The number of Cornell women increased steadily, from 225 in 1892–93 to 367 in 1899–1900. Socially, their lot was hard, certainly; exactly how hard may be disputed. A sensational article appeared in the New York *Herald* for 24 June 1894, on the ostracism of coeds, especially by the "better" fraternities. The reporter concluded that the girls, mostly good or even brilliant students and very much in earnest, were out of place in fashionable college society; and perhaps the men were compensating for their intellectual inferiority by an assumption of social superiority. (It did not occur to him that perhaps fashionable society was out of place in a college.)

On the other hand, plenty of young women found their college experience a revelation and a delight. Dr. Emily Dunning Barringer recalls:

While the men students as a whole affected to frown somewhat upon the coeds, nevertheless we women managed to have a more than average worthwhile experience. I still thrill to the memory of a young tenor voice soaring over the others as the men of the Glee Club serenaded the girls of Sage College in the winter moonlight; to the memory of the Junior Ball, with my arms filled with American Beauty roses.[19]

[19] *Bowery to Bellevue*, p. 58.

It is well, too, to remember that Cornell's anticoedism was an expression of a national hostility to women's emancipation. The young men were dimly aware that man's dominance in the professions and in the home was threatened. Cornell's lack of gallantry was mild in comparison with the ugly hostility shown to women pioneers in the greater world of affairs. Emily Barringer herself, the first American woman ambulance surgeon, tells shocking tales of the plots and insults of her fellow-physicians in New York.

President Schurman thoroughly approved of coeducation. Commenting on the scurrilous article in the New York *Herald,* he admits some hostility on the part of perhaps 10 per cent of the men. But, he notes, even in the socially pretentious fraternities there was much opposition to the ban on coeds.[20]

During the nineties the women began a conscious campaign for greater recognition, by means of public dramatic club and glee club performances, entry in declamation contests, representation on editorial boards.[21] Their success was only middling. Harriet Connor '94 (later well known as an author) won the Woodford Prize in 1894. Women sat on the *Cornellian* boards in 1897 and 1898. (Ethel McGonigal '93, business manager of the 1893 *Cornellian,* was a man. Poor Ethel McGonigal!) Oreola Williams '97 was literary editor of the *Era* in 1895–96. But such achievements remained exceptional.

With regard to coeducation a remarkable prediction was made by Martha Carey Thomas '77, President of Bryn Mawr College, at the memorial exercises for Henry W. Sage in 1898. She said: "Great and real as is . . . the need for separate colleges for women, separate education for men and women cannot ultimately prevail. It is a mad waste of educational endowments, . . . a madder waste of scholarly power. . . . At the close of the twentieth century it will seem absurd that only men should be taught by men and only women by women."

Student behavior was, in general, good. The President reported in 1899 "irreproachable decorum on the part of the student body as a whole." The old sanguinary interclass and intercollege battles had lost their malignancy. The occasional contestants fought as if burlesquing an old tradition.

On a celebrated occasion, in November 1899, the Law and Sibley students refreshed themselves, as was their wont, by playing touch football on the campus between classes. At the hour, by a sudden inspiration,

[20] JGS Letter Books, 14 Dec. 1894.   [21] *Era,* 1893–94, pp. 246, 284, 304.

the engineers trooped into Francis Miles Finch's lecture on procedure, and the lawyers came in a body to Bobby Thurston's thermodynamics, or Bobbyology. Dean Finch's legal mind immediately sensed some gross irregularity, and he dismissed the class without his blessing. But, according to an eyewitness, Thurston told his class: "I had intended lecturing on thermodynamics, but the class appears so dull and stupid this morning that I will talk about the relation between the engineer and the lawyer." He then spent the hour abusing lawyers and extolling engineers.[22]

There was one deplorable episode in our history which had wide repercussions. The freshman banquet was held in February 1894 in the old Masonic Temple. Some sophomores hid in the room below, pierced the ceiling, and inserted in the hole a rubber tube, connected with a jug of salt, into which they poured sulphuric acid. This combination, I am informed, is likely to produce chlorine gas.[23] They made, however, an error; their infernal device poured its fumes into the kitchen, not into the banqueting hall. A colored cook collapsed and died. It later appeared that she had heart trouble. The freshmen were little inconvenienced. Unaware of the death in the kitchen, the speakers carried on their grisly work until 3:00 A.M.

The furore was immense. The colored people of Ithaca threatened a lynching, but they could not discover whom to lynch. The newspapers of the country, delighted with a Chlorine Gas Banquet, moralized endlessly on lawless youth. President Schurman proclaimed that a crime had been committed and the culprit must pay, but the discovery of the culprit was clearly a matter for the civil authorities, not the faculty. To aid the civil authorities, the faculty voted $500, to enable the coroner to employ a detective. But Coroner and detective were baffled by the total ignorance of the student body. A Grand Jury found itself unable to make an indictment. The case went to the Court of Appeals, and in the end nothing came of it. If the culprit paid, he did so in secret.

In the Grand Jury hearing, a law student, Fred L. Taylor '96, suspected of knowing something about the matter, was asked if he knew where the jugs were bought and to whom they were delivered. He

---

[22] Henry T. Coates '00, letter, C.U. Archives.
[23] Kenneth E. Stuart '97 recalls the event (*Alumni News*, Sept. 1946) and notes that the atmosphere around a cookstove often contains carbon monoxide, and that light and iron are catalysts for the reaction of carbon monoxide to form phosgene, deadliest of lethal gases used in the First War.

would reply only: "I wish to throw myself upon the privilege which the law allows me, and decline to give evidence on the ground that it may tend to incriminate me." The judge found him in contempt, but the judgment was reversed by the Court of Appeals, after a long discussion. The case has become a capital one in the history of the application of the Fifth Amendment.

The students of the nineties included some destined to be known later in the greater world. Among them were Raymond A. Pearson '94, President of Iowa State; Herbert J. Hagerman '94, Governor of New Mexico; Myron C. Taylor '94, business leader and Ambassador; Ernest F. Nichols, D.Sc. '97, President of Dartmouth; Alexander Meiklejohn, Ph.D. '97, President of Amherst; Louis Agassiz Fuertes '97, bird painter; Frank Gannett '98, journalist and publisher; Daniel A. Reed '98, almost lifelong member of the House of Representatives; Walter C. Teagle '99, industrialist; and Cornell's only candidate for the presidency of the United States, Parley P. Christensen '97. For what party? For the Farmer-Labor Party, in 1920.

We come thus to the end of the century, picking our way among the debris of small news items. The greatest news item of the nineties, the Spanish-American War, touched us strangely little. Its meaning— the assumption of world status and responsibility by the United States —was hardly recognized at the time. Cornell played a respectable part in the conflict; 125 graduates and 40 undergraduates enlisted; the majority were officers. One student, Clifton Beckwith Brown '00, was killed at San Juan Hill. A memorial to him stands in the College of Architecture.

The war brought to President Schurman an entry to the world of great affairs. Appointed president of a commission to recommend governmental policy and action in the Philippines, he was absent on this duty from January to September 1899. He found the handling of large diplomatic matters very much to his liking and began to make public pronouncements on all sorts of national issues. During his absence Dean T. F. Crane served as Acting President.

For Cornell the century-end stocktaking yielded satisfaction and self-congratulation. Materially and spiritually we had done well. The strong hand of Jacob Gould Schurman guided and protected us. As the new century opened, peace, equanimity, confidence enveloped the campus. Cornell looked eagerly to its future.

XXII

The New Century: Cornell's Soul and Body

"WHOEVER did not live before 1789 does not know what the pleasure of life can be," said Talleyrand. One may revise his apophthegm by substituting 1914 for 1789. Before 1914 was the happy time of our innocence, when we had perfect confidence in a beneficent deity, or, if one prefers the definition, in a power in the universe, not ourselves, which makes for righteousness. In that happy time we perceived a constant progress toward the good, toward enlightenment, justice, social bliss. Wars were doomed by man's good sense and by the power of high finance. So we said. Man's unconquerable mind, we said, will transform the world, and we shall see Utopia rise on the ugly ruins of error.

So we said, even in Cornell in that happy time, reading Wells, Shaw, Norman Angell, Upton Sinclair. In the debating clubs, Janus and the Owls, reigned pacifism to the death. The Socialist Club, captained by Gus Egloff '12, proclaimed a benign Revolution. It all looked so simple! The only thing we needed was a little good will to set the world aright. We could not have believed what has turned out to be the truth—that a little good will is the one thing the world still lacks.

There was a certain arrogance in our view, and a certain arrogance in Cornell. We were growing rapidly. The full-time enrollment passed 2,000 in 1898–99, 3,000 in 1902–3, 4,000 in 1909–10, and in 1913–14 we

351

reached the fatidic number of 5,015. ("Some of you young people will see five thousand students on this campus," Ezra Cornell used to say to companions, who hid their smiles.) From 1909–10 to 1911–12 Cornell was the second largest American university, reckoning in full-time students; Columbia led Cornell by only sixty bodies in 1909–10. Cornell then dropped to fourth place, and then to eighth in 1913–14. ("Of course we don't want mere bigness," said everyone from the President down, although we had just been extremely proud of mere bigness.) The number of women remained fairly constant, around 400, until 1910–11, and then rapidly increased, reaching 734 in 1915–16. Most of the feminine increase took place in Agriculture, in the new Home Economics curriculum.

Here are the enrollment figures for the convenient years 1898–99 and 1915–16, with those of the autumn of 1961 for comparison:

	1898–99	*1915–16*	*1961*
Graduate	190	383	2,047
Arts and Sciences	631	1,424	2,875
Agriculture	85	1,704	1,814
Mechanical Engineering & Electrical Engineering	501	942	1,083
Civil Engineering	185	450	213
Architecture	48	166	217
Law	164	243	299
Veterinary	23	159	227

Note that in the table above the schools established since 1915–16 are not included: Hotel Administration, Business and Public Administration, Home Economics, Industrial and Labor Relations, and Fine Arts (under Architecture), and Aeronautical, Agricultural, Chemical and Metallurgical Engineering, and Engineering Physics. Also I have had to fiddle with the Engineering figures for 1961, since all the first-year students are in a Basic Studies Division, and I have had to assign a proper proportion to M.E., E.E., and C.E.

Today we hear constant complaints of Cornell's unwieldy size, in comparison with the good old days when all the students knew each other. This complaint provokes three remarks: (1) that since the earliest days all the students have never known each other; (2) that the remembered friendships and loyalties were made in small groups—fraternities, rooming houses, clubs, activities, teams—and that these groups continue, much multiplied; and (3) that the friendships were most commonly formed among those pursuing the same courses in the same college. A glance at the list above reveals that only the Arts College and the Graduate School have inordinately grown; the others remain about the same size as a half-century ago. Most of Cornell's growth since 1915–16 has occurred in the new schools and colleges, which have developed their own spirit and loyalties. And even our Arts College is smaller than those of Harvard and Yale, and about the same size as that of Dartmouth.

Bigness brought an inevitable consequence—the growth of Administration.

Ultimate authority rested in the trustees, and within the Board on the Executive Committee. Within the Executive Committee, the Mighty Trustee, Henry W. Sage, Chairman of the Board and of the Committee, had ruled until his death in 1897. He was succeeded as Chairman of the Board by former Governor Roswell P. Flower, until 1899. Thereafter until 1917 there was no Chairman of the Board. Samuel D. Halliday '70 was Chairman of the Executive Committee from 1898 to 1907. A courtly Ithaca lawyer, he had none of his predecessor's despotic instincts. After a more than two-year interval, he was succeeded by Mynderse Van Cleef '74, Ithaca banker. Thus for eighteen years the Board did without a Chairman, and for two of those years there was no Chairman of the Executive Committee. Into the power vacuum stepped President Jacob Gould Schurman.

To be sure, he protested that he did not desire or willingly accept such power. But he shared the common view that the Executive Committee, composed of the trustees resident in Ithaca, might be inclined to safeguard or even promote their business at the expense of University interests. (Eventually in 1914 the statutes were redrawn, to make the committee more broadly representative.)

Against the power of the business-minded trustees he tried to set the power of the faculty. When a faculty member himself, he had fought for faculty power in the University's operation. At his Inauguration he said to his comrades: "Fellow teachers, I desire to magnify our office." He was the faculty's darling. J. E. Creighton of Philosophy attested the fine *esprit de corps* on the campus.[1] Carl Becker said Schurman was more an umpire than a captain. It was the very freedom of Cornell that lured Becker to join it. When he was being courted, Henry A. Sill of History wrote him:

[1] *Science*, 12 Aug. 1910.

There is no University in the country in which freedom of thought and of speech is more firmly entrenched in tradition and in policy. Everybody is committed to it. The President's established practice of leaving everything to the Faculty, including the *initiation* of educational legislation, has resulted in liberating personal forces, which operate with great spontaneity and in admirable harmony. When the President and Faculty disagree, as happened in the College of Agriculture last year, it is the President who has to yield.[2]

From the faculty point of view, Cornell under Schurman was the land of the free (except for his resolute effort to stamp out smoking).[3] In 1917–18, it has been noted, Cornell was one of ten American institutions that provided for faculty nomination of deans, one of twenty-seven that gave professors the formal right to participate in educational policy, and the only one that allowed for faculty representation on the Board of Trustees.[4]

Cornell's world-shaking eminence as the first college with professors on the Board of Trustees was the outcome of an old conviction of Schurman's, gained in his student years in Great Britain and Germany, and deepened by his experience with the Board. According to the long memory of Walter F. Willcox, Schurman was supported, in the early years of his presidency, by Trustee Henry B. Lord, a scholarly Ithaca banker.[5] In Lord's old age, Schurman missed his support among the business-minded trustees. Hence his proposal for faculty representation.

In Schurman's report of 1910 he insisted that the faculty should control the University's operations. He urged the faculty to present its

[2] Becker Papers; Frederick Bedell writes Becker (17 March 1943), "We were left undisturbed to do as we pleased."

[3] Morse Stephens of History made a practice of depositing his smoldering cigar butts under the President's window. Clark Northup of English, a nonsmoker, on receiving an encyclical forbidding smoking in faculty offices, learned to operate a corncob pipe, under the tutelage of J. Q. Adams.

[4] Richard Hofstadter and W. P. Metzger, *Development of Academic Freedom in the United States* (New York 1955), p. 456.

[5] *Alumni News*, 1 May 1956. Henry B. Lord deserves at least the meed of a footnote. After schooling in a Vermont academy, he clerked in a country store in Ludlowville, became member of the State Assembly in 1865, and guided the bill chartering Cornell University through the Assembly. He was cashier of the First National Bank of Ithaca, was chosen trustee of the University in 1876, and served continuously on the Board for thirty-nine years until his death in 1915 at the age of ninety-four. He had the curiosity and tastes of a scholar. He was well versed in botany and other sciences, read Browning with Corson, mastered Greek in his middle years and took up Arabic when over eighty. He was the type of self-educated scholar in business, more common in his times than in our own.

own ideal of university government to the trustees, and to accept the responsibilities that would go with faculty rule. "The present government of American universities and colleges is altogether anomalous," he wrote in his report for 1912. "The President and Trustees hold the reins of power and exercise supreme control, while the professors are legally in the position of employees of the corporation." This state of affairs is resented by the professors. Of course, he pursued, custom has given them tenure of office, supremacy in educational matters, and the right to freedom of speech. But the professors aspire to the rights of their brothers in England and Germany, where the faculties govern the universities. Well, he continues, the faculties are not likely to become the controlling power here. The laws of New York State forbid a professor to become a trustee of an institution of which he is a member. There is a tendency for power to come more and more into the hands of the President, "by the natural gravitation of human affairs under the influence of the activity of an individual and the inertia of a multitude." However, this natural gravitation should be corrected by a plan of partnership between faculty and trustees. Faculty members should be elected to the Board, and for each college, except the state colleges, a joint conference committee should be established, to consist of the President, two or three trustees, the Dean of the college, and two faculty members elected by the college faculty.

Committees met, petitions were circulated, reports were printed. At length, on 24 April 1916, the trustees voted that the faculty should elect three representatives who would sit at meetings of the Board and of the General Administration Committee (as the Executive Committee was then termed) and should have all the powers of trustees except the vote, which the Charter of the University forbade. The three chosen were Dexter S. Kimball, Walter F. Willcox, and John Henry Comstock. This scheme, which Schurman called the Cornell Idea, was unique in America. It was promptly adopted by Bryn Mawr and Pennsylvania, and had a continuing influence on American university government.

The faculty won prestige and pride, but its spiritual goods were not matched by material gains. The rapid growth of the University brought financial stringency. Tuition fees, raised to $150 a year in 1917, lagged far behind costs, and the productive funds ($9,600,000 in August 1913) were all too scanty to answer our needs.

The faculty was tolerably well off, as faculties go, at the beginning of the century. But the cost of living rose with prosperity, and new household and social needs steadily added to the professorial burdens. The President recorded the salary scale in 1905; assistants, $150 to $500 annually; instructors, $1,000, after a year of probation; assistant professors, $1,500 to $2,000; and professors, $3,000 to $3,500, with a few at $4,000 to $5,000. These salaries, said the President, must be raised.

Things got no better. The accumulated deficit rose regularly, to become $165,000 in 1912–13. The European war immediately caused a jump in the cost of living, but none in the salary scale. Unrest in the various ranks became acute. In the *Alumni News* for 23 March 1916 appeared a letter from an instructor receiving $1,200 after six years of teaching at Cornell and nine years elsewhere. His department called him indispensable, but the University had not $300 to save him and his family from starving. On 25 January 1917 the *Alumni News* calculated that the average professorial salary was $3,300, and for assistant professors $1,770. No instructor received more than $1,200. The cost of living meanwhile had doubled since 1890, and had increased by 40 per cent in the previous two years.

There were some alleviations. William H. Sage set up a pension fund in 1903 with a gift of $150,000, stipulating that it should be put out at compound interest until 1914. Andrew Carnegie established his Teachers' Pension Fund of ten million dollars in 1905, and Cornell immediately qualified for membership in the plan. The payments came as a godsend for seven distinguished retired professors and two widows. But the godsend was not enough. It is never enough.

The administration sought for money by appropriate blandishments of the wealthy. Andrew Carnegie was elected trustee in 1890, and became a faithful attendant at meetings and a generous benefactor. Andrew D. White met Mr. and Mrs. John D. Rockefeller at sea, arranged to sit beside them at table, and sowed seeds. But the trustees boggled at that favorite device of hungry colleges, the Honorary Degree.

We received, to be sure, some handsome gifts. Goldwin Smith left us $680,000 for aid to the humanities, and Willard Fiske half a million, for "the uses and purposes of the Library." But Fiske, in dying (in September 1904), managed to make almost as much trouble as he had in life. The trustees, to allay the memory of the old war, voted that Fiske's body should be interred in the Memorial Antechapel, beside his wife and her father, John McGraw, and Mr. and Mrs. Ezra Cornell. Dean T. F. Crane was despatched to New York to accompany the body to Ithaca. All University exercises were suspended on 26 November, but as this was the Saturday after Thanksgiving and everyone had gone to the Penn game, there was not a great deal to suspend. A solemn ceremony took place, before the very tomb of Henry W. Sage, in the Memorial Apse of Sage Chapel. Four days later William H. Sage and Dean Sage, sons of Henry W. Sage, resigned from the Board and severed all their connections with Cornell.[6] Now that the old passions are cooled, one may see the final irony of the Great Will Case in the companionship in death of the two fierce and unforgiving enemies. It is hoped that they lie quietly.

Fiske's Library Endowment Fund for library uses and purposes yielded over $20,000 a year. The trustees applied it to salaries and up-keep, releasing 20,000 welcome dollars for other purposes. The faculty, having fondly supposed that book-purchase funds would be increased, carped and caviled. Finally in 1912 the trustees ruled that a third of the Fiske income should be used for the purchase of books and periodicals and for binding.

Over these discords and storms, and over many others too small to chronicle, Schurman rode serene. A philosopher by training, he liked the wide view, the large generalization about propaedeutic principles. His annual reports make an excellent history of higher education, as seen from Morrill Hall.

He discusses the problem of growth. In 1910 he insists that our numbers must be restricted. But how? Perhaps by making Cornell a nursery of superior students, an aristocracy of talent, as in fact was already the case in the Graduate School and the Medical School. He proposes that "students shall be selected with as much care as members of the instructing staff." However, he proceeds, this enthronement of superiority will require more teachers, equipment, money. He envisages an eventual proliferation of two-year junior colleges, making the universities homes for upperclass specialization. He was ahead of his time in 1910; he was even ahead of our time.

The distresses of growth could not deter him from proposing new units of the University. He advocated anew the old idea of a Cornell college of commerce. He cherished the project of a school of education, to be supported by the state. He suggested a state school for sanitarians, or sanitary engineers. However, he discouraged the effort of the New York School of Dentistry to join us. In 1907 a suggestion

[6] But their wives continued to do good to Cornell. Mrs. Dean Sage added to the Sage Preachership Fund until 1907, and Mrs. William H. Sage gave a railing and a screen for the Sage Chapel choir loft in 1913.

was made that a Roman Catholic college be established on the campus, but the suggestion did not reach the official ears of the trustees.

Schurman gradually became aware that the American university was being transformed from a teaching institution to a research establishment in which teaching is done. Believing devoutly in the necessity of liberal education, he long opposed the professionalization of the scholar and the schools by research unlimited. In 1898 he criticized a statement by Melvil Dewey, State Regent, that a University should be entirely graduate.[7] Ten years later he said that research should never take precedence over teaching, as he reluctantly allowed Titchener of Psychology to teach only graduate students. Shortly afterward, however, he made his peace with the research-goddess. Though complaining that researchers were inclined to specialize before they gained a suitable general education, he asked for research professorships, for financial support of investigations. Each science department, he said, should be a research center, with an endowment of several millions. And every staff member was expected "to contribute in some way to the advancement of knowledge, and not merely to teach what he has received from others." In short, "the future of the American university is with the graduate school or department of research." For (in 1911) "there seems to be a presentiment that we are on the eve of great discoveries. The discovery of radium and other radio-active substances has not only enlarged the bounds of knowledge but it has given an impetus to speculation and awakened hopes of future discoveries. It has suggested the possibility that the world may have at its disposal hitherto unsuspected sources of energy."

The President had much to say of other problems of the world in general and of Cornell in particular. But before we pass these in review we may make a second perambulation of the campus, to remark the new constructions at the mid-point of Cornell's first century.

From the first Schurman insisted that the growth of the University should proceed according to plan. He persuaded the trustees to buy the land on the western slope, below the original campus, and the farm lands lying to the east. Carrère and Hastings, eminent architects, prepared a plan of development in 1902–1903. Cram, Goodhue, and Ferguson, equally eminent, were appointed consulting architects in 1910–1911. Charles N. Lowrie, stellar landscape architect, made an

[7] JGC to Melvil Dewey, 7 March 1898, cited by Eugene Hotchkiss, "J. G. Schurman and the Cornell Tradition" (Ph.D. dissertation, Cornell University, 1959), p. 189.

elaborate report in 1903. But nothing seemed to do much good. As Woodford Patterson, Secretary of the University, summed it up, our architecture passed through Mansard, Antique-Romantic, Romanesque, and Palladian, to arrive at English Collegiate. And we continue to progress. . . .

At least, the visitor at the century's beginning found the grounds trim and well tended. Professor Willard W. Rowlee of Botany doubled as superintendent of grounds from 1897 to 1911, developing the campus with affectionate care. (Most of his successors have been engineers rather than landscapists.) He planted many exotic trees, with identifying labels (which have now fallen off), established a hawthorn collection east of the present Crescent—our first recognized botanical garden —placed a water garden in front of the Veterinary College, and pied the gorges with azaleas. He preserved and promoted the concept of an arboretum, which was not yet to be.

To make our tour of the campus, we take our start from College Avenue, né Huestis Street, lined by beetling rooming houses, cheap, ugly, and hazardous. At the campus entrance stands Sheldon Court, our luxury private dormitory, a rather countrified version of Harvard's Gold Coast or Yale's Hutch. We cross Cascadilla by William H. Sage's stone bridge, and at the top of the rise contemplate the New Armory, which became the Old Armory, and the shamefully inadequate Gymnasium. Both buildings are desperately overcrowded. The *Era* said, even in March 1901, that the gym was a disgrace to an institution as large as Cornell. Every year the President set up a cry for some donor to come to our aid. But the old Gymnasium, more and more disgraceful, continued to serve until Teagle Hall was opened in 1954.

Continuing north on Central Avenue, we observe to the right a weather kiosk with its busy instruments, and to the left a gaunt structure built by Professor Albert N. Prentiss in the early years, enlarged and converted to the lodging of women students as Sage Cottage, by them abandoned in 1914 and turned over to the newly organized University Club.

Here we cut down the Library Slope to inspect the new Men's Residential Halls.

The President had pled for men's dormitories ever since his accession. He recognized not merely the material need of decent housing, which the lodging-houses failed to supply; he was conscious as well that the rooms we occupy affect us, and may be educational or the reverse. Schurman knew that Cornell could not forever dodge its duty to provide students with homes that would influence their characters. In his 1907 report he made the interesting suggestion that University quarters for men should follow the model of the fraternity lodges, "more fruitful seed-plots of personality than the conventional dormitory." The suggestion was not carried out, no doubt because of the expense. In 1914 a full-fledged campaign for funds was inaugurated, the first "drive" in Cornell history. George F. Baker, celebrated New York banker, gave $350,000 to build the group known as Baker Court, and $100,000 was taken from the Alumni Fund for Founders Hall. The architects, Day and Klauder, adopted a version of English Collegiate Gothic, which has been generally approved. It provides many an artful glimpse and vista, many a beautiful detail arresting to the photographer. The medieval windows do not, of course, admit much light.

The material used was the native bluestone, available by digging down a few feet anywhere. Said Woodford Patterson:

The rock is a shale, broken by frequent transverse faults. The lateral surfaces formed by these fissures are stained in soft tints by the infiltration of water through the crevices of the rock. So here the mason finds at hand a building block having a plane face already weathered. The local bluestone had been used in the University's first buildings, but not so skillfully as in these newer halls. . . . By laying the stone in narrow courses and with random joints they have produced walls of fine texture and soft tone.[8]

From the Residential Halls we climb University Avenue. On the beautiful eminence which Andrew D. White designed for a belvedere stands, or stood until it burned in February 1916, Morse Hall, a nononsense red brick building with an uncanny resemblance to a public school. Behind Morse Hall a steep path leads down to the Suspension Bridge, built by the Cornell Heights Improvement Company in 1900, and ever one of the most picturesque, indeed sensational, features of the Ithaca landscape. In the gorge below we perceive the Power Plant, erected in 1904. Near the north end of the bridge stands a Swiss chalet, the home of the Comstock Publishing Company, due to become the University Press Redivivus. Cornell Heights is now well built up, with electric cars speeding past every five minutes, and with a branch line (the "Great Northern") setting forth from the junction of Thurston and Wyckoff Avenues and venturing as far as Upland Road. In 1905 a short-lived loop was built still farther north, curving back by the lake and arriving at Renwick Park.

We proceed east along the gorge to Prudence Risley, a women's

[8] *Guide to the Campus* (Ithaca, 1920), p. 67.

dormitory erected in 1913. It was given by Mrs. Russell Sage (no relation of Henry W.) and was named for her husband's mother. The building was the last campus structure by architect William H. Miller '70. Its fine halls and parlors contain many artistic gifts from Andrew D. White.

On the north side of Beebe Lake stands the Fuertes Observatory, three times moved from campus locations preempted by rising buildings. On the south side of the lake is the Toboggan Slide, providing a speed-thrill which perhaps today would seem tame. What with the weather's caprices, the varying water level in the lake, and the frequent accidents, the toboggan slide caused the administration winter-long worries. (One boy went down on skates, and, though knocked unconscious, survived.)

Southwest of Triphammer Bridge we see Rand Hall, given by Mrs. Henry Lang in 1912 as a memorial to her father, her uncle, and her brother (Jasper Raymond Rand, Jr. '97). It contains the Sibley machine shop, pattern shop, and electrical laboratories. Between familiar East Sibley and West Sibley rises Sibley Dome, erected in 1902.

South of Lincoln is Goldwin Smith, the Hall of Humanities. Of its spacious lecture rooms, high classrooms, professorial offices, Museum of Casts, and Doric portico we are consumedly proud, though indeed Hiram Corson called it "a Greek temple with bungalow trimmings." It was designed by Carrère and Hastings and built with University funds. The laying of the cornerstone, in 1904, in the presence of Goldwin Smith himself, was a solemn occasion. It was opened in 1906. Before it stands the fine statue of Andrew D. White by Karl Bitter, given by Henry R. Ickelheimer '88 and unveiled in 1915 in the benign presence of its subject.

South again, completing the quadrangle, is Stimson Hall, given by Dean Sage in 1902 to be the home of the Cornell Medical College.

Now crossing East Avenue we contemplate Rockefeller Hall. It was given by the elder John D., after a typically thorough three-day investigation by an expert agent. He offered $150,000, plus $100,000 for maintenance, on condition that the total be matched; and matched it was, by seven well-wishers. At the building's opening in 1906 it was the largest and best-equipped physics laboratory in America. Carrère and Hastings were the architects, but their creation is hardly one of their glories. The interior is uncommonly bleak, because the Physics Department wished to save on décor and spend on equipment.[9]

[9] There is a campus tale that Mr. Rockefeller was so much offended at the

We turn now up the little rise of Reservoir Avenue to admire Bailey Hall, designed by Edward B. Green '78, built by the state, and first used in June 1913. The need for such an auditorium had been urgent. The state, erecting the building for the use of state college students, and incidentally for Farmers' Week gatherings, conferred a boon on the whole University. Bailey contains a magnificent organ, representing in large part a gift by Andrew Carnegie for the eightieth birthday of Andrew D. White.[10]

Beyond Bailey stands the New York State College of Agriculture, created entire since 1906, and rising from the old college farms. First is Roberts Hall, named for our great dean, Isaac P. Roberts. The rapid growth of Agriculture caused the erection of Forestry, Poultry Husbandry, and Animal Husbandry eastward along Tower Road, and Home Economics and Soil Technology, now Comstock and Caldwell, to the north. A new quadrangle was made by the building of Farm Management to the east, on the site of the present Mann Library. Rural Engineering and Landscape Art have small buildings of their own. In the basement of Home Economics is a novel restaurant, operated by the staff, and strangely called a "cafeteria." Beyond Animal Husbandry lie the widespread farms, with their splendid barns, their experimental groves and fields, and even a fish hatchery.

Across from the agricultural buildings, to the south, lies Alumni Field. This was the fruition of an old project, to provide a locus for intramural football and baseball and to give all male undergraduates opportunities for outdoor play within reach of their dwellings. For years committees strove, pled, and prayed. Some important gifts were elicited. The family of Jacob F. Schoellkopf of Niagara Falls contributed largely to the building of the stadium and field, named Schoellkopf Field, and Willard Straight '01 gave Schoellkopf Hall, for the Athletic Association and the football players, in honor of Henry Schoellkopf '02. However, a very large part of the costs was met by small contributions from the alumni. The field was formally opened with a track meet in May 1915.

---

ugliness of Rockefeller Hall that he would have nothing further to do with Cornell. I can find no evidence of the truth of this unlikely story.

[10] The organ suffered a tragicomic mishap around 1935. The air intake was located in the men's washroom. A plumbing disaster filled the washroom with water. The organist, unwarned, sat down at his console and blew a mighty crescendo, which filled the leather organ pouches with water, ruining them.

(The women were mollified by the construction of a playground in Cascadilla glen, directly south of Alumni Field.)

To the west of Alumni Field, on Garden Avenue, stands a group of clinical buildings of the Veterinary College, opened in November 1913. Above all towers the enormous bulk of the Drill Hall. This is a state building, authorized in the 1914 session of the legislature, and later named Barton Hall, in honor of Colonel Frank A. Barton '91, our wartime commandant. No Cornellian needs to be informed about Barton Hall. With its floor bigger than a football field, it was in its time the largest university drill hall in the country.

We have now reviewed the important new constructions between 1900 and the First War. The total must be impressive. A good deal of our development was opportunistic; we took what we could get, even if what we could get was not always just what we wanted. Nevertheless, the whole fell into a scheme, a design. The old or "stone" quadrangle was balanced by the new quadrangle, the Ag Campus. The future development of the state colleges pointed to the east. The playgrounds were reserved, close to classrooms and to living quarters. All the western slope was held for future lodgings for men. On the whole, there is reason for congratulation.

At the same time, here and there the future began to cast its shadows. On 9 May 1911 the trustees enacted the first speed law, setting a limit of ten miles per hour on the campus. And on 19 June 1916 "the matter of providing on the campus parking facilities for autos was referred to the sub-committee on grounds."

XXIII

The New Century:
The Rise of Agriculture

ONE is always tempted to talk of the rise and growth of an institution as if it were a product of the earth's pulse, a tide, a forest. But the fact is that the very existence of the New York State College of Agriculture, and its phenomenal success, and its present character and personality, are directly due to Liberty Hyde Bailey.

Bailey, it may be remembered, came here as professor of horticulture in 1888 and set an example of productive energy that no one else has had the strength and genius to follow. Bailey was a college in himself, teaching, experimenting, lecturing, running a far-flung extension program, publishing eleven books and uncounted articles in five years. "The Holy Earth," title of one of his books, was to him a genuine deity, life in communion with the soil a religion, and agricultural education a religious function. "For myself," he said, "if I have any gifts I mean to use them for the spiritualization of agriculture."

Bailey soon came to the conclusion that at Cornell agriculture had little support from President Adams and the trustees and little prestige among the faculties of traditional studies. "Farmer" still carried on the campus, as in the great world, a derogatory connotation. No agriculture students were asked to join fraternities. Bailey remembered that there was "as much discrimination against Ags as amongst racial groups today." [1]

[1] "Recollections," Bailey Papers.

New Century: Rise of Agriculture

In 1891 the University won a long lawsuit with the state concerning its rights under the original Morrill Land Grant Act. The state was forced to surrender nearly $90,000, as a payment of interest improperly withheld. Bailey and others argued that since the Morrill Act was designed primarily to foster agriculture and the mechanic arts, underprivileged Agriculture was entitled to the sum. But the trustees used it to construct Boardman Hall for the Law School. Bailey regarded this action as an affront to his holy faith.

The accession of President Schurman in 1892 promised better things. Schurman's Inaugural Address contained a peremptory summons to the state to provide a $200,000 building and support for Agriculture. The demand produced in 1893 a mere $50,000 Dairy Building, but after all, Schurman established the precedent that the state should give buildings and money to Cornell Agriculture.

Bailey was making friends up and down the state. As we have told, S. Fred Nixon, vineyardist in the Chautauqua region and State Assemblyman, called in Bailey to diagnose his grape troubles and was so pleased with the result that he put through a bill appropriating $8,000 for horticultural investigation and experiment. The annual appropriation soon rose to $35,000.

The Director of the College of Agriculture, Isaac P. Roberts, had tried to influence the Albany legislators, with little effect. In 1900 or thereabouts he told Bailey to see what he could do. Bailey, in his nineties, talked into the tape recorder of Professor George H. Lawrence; and these words, in his humorous old voice, still emerge:

Well, I told Roberts that if he couldn't get anything started at Albany, certainly I couldn't—a young chap. He said: "You go!" I went. I got off the train at the railway station, started up the hill toward the Capitol, and when I got near the Capitol, around the corner, along came Nixon. I had been in his vineyards many times and knew him well. He didn't say a thing to me except: "Bailey! You can't have it!" I said: "All right. I am going home, but you're going to hear from me."

Bailey turned around, walked to the Albany station, and while sitting in the waiting room (so high and noble in those days) he decided to go to the countrymen, to explain to them the need, to urge them to act, and in short to make a lobby of the embattled farmers.

In Ithaca, he reported to Roberts his ill success and his new purpose. The Director's only words were: "Go to it, boy!" In one following year Bailey traveled 28,000 miles in the state, visiting Granges and

365

farmers' gatherings, and talking forever of the state's need for a great agricultural school.

In 1903 Roberts retired, and Bailey succeeded him as Director of the College of Agriculture. Roberts solemnly crowned Bailey with his old silk hat (bought in 1874 from H. W. Willson, "the Students' Hatter") with the words: "Since you have stepped into the Director's shoes, it is fitting that you should also wear the Director's hat." Still, each new Dean of the College of Agriculture is crowned, in a moving ceremony, with the nearly centenarian top hat.

Bailey promised to President Schurman a ten-year trial of office. Inevitably he called for an immediate reorganization and expansion of the college. It was growing; it needed more teachers, more classrooms and laboratories, more land for experimental purposes. Schurman was not opposed, but he uttered words which make a soft susurrus in every presidential office: "Where is the money coming from?" In this case the answer was clear: from the state, of course.

A bill was introduced in the 1903 legislature calling for an appropriation for the teaching of agriculture at Cornell. It never emerged from the committee's clutch. Worse, Governor Benjamin B. Odell vetoed the appropriation bill for Cornell's state college of forestry, thus ending its life. Clearly Cornell needed something more than right and justice.

Just as the legislative session of 1904 began in Albany, one of those contretemps occurred which drive one to belief in diabolical agencies. At a hearing before the Federal Commission on Agriculture in Washington, the Secretary of Agriculture, James Wilson, attacked Cornell for failure to teach soil physics and took occasion to revive the old canards about our misusing the riches conferred by the Morrill Act. He said of Cornell: "They were better endowed than any institution in the land and should be doing the best work of any institution in the land, yet never did anything." President Schurman demanded a hearing and spoke in Washington with his usual brilliance, refuting the Secretary point by point. He made clear that Cornell received annually from the Morrill endowment and congressional grants $72,500, a fraction of the University's actual expenditures on agriculture and the mechanic arts, and that in these fields Cornell had done a very great deal.

Meanwhile in Albany Senator Ed Stewart of Ithaca introduced a bill drafted by Bailey, establishing the New York State College of Agriculture at Cornell, with an initial appropriation of $250,000 for building. Schurman bombarded the state officials with eloquent letters, while

Bailey spent most of his time in Albany. By the best of haps, the Honorable S. Fred Nixon was now Speaker of the Assembly. Various committees held hearings and received favoring resolutions from every agricultural group in the state.

The opposition was headed by Chancellor James R. Day of Syracuse University, representing six other state institutions. According to Schurman, the Chancellor led a pious army, the Methodists of the state.[2] He was an angry man; his words breathe a rancor too hot to be confined by facts. He charged that Ezra Cornell had so "manipulated" the proceeds of the Morrill Act that more than four-fifths were improperly used. He demanded a share in state bounty equal to that accorded Cornell. And—the usual delaying tactic—he called for a committee to investigate and report. He ended on the clarion phrase: "Either give to all or not to any!"

Bailey broadcast an immediate refutation, but Chancellor Day had his speech published by the Syracuse University Press without change. The Chancellor called for a hearing before the Assembly's Ways and Means Committee. This was granted him; but, since at the hearing the chairman and other legislators were insufficiently attentive to him, the Chancellor broke off in a fury and left the room before he had adduced a single coherent argument. (Bailey later put up in his office a picture of Chancellor Day with the subscription: "Founder of the New York State College of Agriculture at Cornell.") Less thin-skinned than Chancellor Day, Syndic John H. MacCracken of New York University took up the argument and came out with the essential grievance: "We fear that the channel is becoming so worn which leads from the State Treasury to the Cornell University that if any more grants such as these are made it will make such a canyon that everything will flow that way and no stream be diverted to other institutions." (Only the previous day, the Syndic's father, Chancellor Henry M. MacCracken of New York University, had been publicly called a liar, though in stately terms, by the Court of Appeals, in the decision removing important properties from N.Y.U. and awarding them to the Cornell Medical College. Cornell had an ogreish look to N.Y.U.)

Through all the academic vituperation, the united farmers of the state remained unmoved, holding that Cornell, which alone in the

[2] JGS to ADW, 16 and 29 March, 1904; quoted by Eugene Hotchkiss, "J. G. Schurman and the Cornell Tradition" (Ph.D. dissertation, Cornell University, 1959), p. 151. For the story from the Syracuse viewpoint, see W. Freeman Galpin, *Syracuse University: The Growing Years* (Syracuse, 1960).

state had been teaching agriculture, should be encouraged to continue.

The bill rolled smoothly through the Assembly, with Bailey sitting on the dais behind Speaker Nixon. But the Senate was not so compliant; here there were political wheels within wheels, and no friendly Speaker to rule the machine. Bailey, when a nonagenarian, recalled the episode in a typically gusty recorded reminiscence:

In order to get the college bill through the Senate we had to have 26 votes, there being 51 Senators. I had been to see Long Tom McLaren, who led the Democratic forces in Brooklyn, and he was against Tammany Hall. Long Tom told me that he and his people would vote against the Tammany Hall projects. Senator O'Grady was the Democratic leader of Tammany in Albany—all Tammanyites did as O'Grady directed and were opposed to the college bill because he was. I went to call on him to get his views. He said: "Well, Long Tom is going to vote for you, therefore we can't vote for you." I knew that the hearing on the bill was coming before a closed session of the Senate. I was asked by O'Grady to be there, and President Schurman had asked me to let him know when the vote was coming. He wanted to come up and be present, and he thought it would help the vote politically if he were there. Actually I knew it would be just the reverse, because he had expressed political opinions that angered some of the Legislators.

Some three or four nights before that, I heard that Tammany Hall was to have a meeting of the Albany members. It was about eleven that night when I went down to the meeting place and knocked at the door. The doorkeeper opened the door and volumes of tobacco smoke rolled out. I told him who I was and that I didn't want to make a speech—just about two or three sentences. O'Grady was presiding officer and he knew who I was. The doorkeeper came back with the word: "You may come in and speak very briefly." I went in and I said: "Gentlemen, there is a bill for the establishment of a college of agriculture. I just want you to know that I voted for Tilden and Hendrickson [in 1876] and that I went out and took the stump for Hancock and English [in 1880] before some of you voted. I thank you for your consideration."

That same night about 2 A.M. there was a knock on my hotel-room door. "Your bill will pass," is all that I was told. I telegraphed the President and he came up. They didn't let him in, and I went in and sat in the session while the President walked up and down the corridor outside. The time for the vote came. I sat there watching and keeping tally. Whenever a Tammany man was supposed to vote they looked around at O'Grady and he shook his head in the negative. He kept tally too, and gave the nod to two men to vote in favor. We got 28 votes, two more than were needed. That was close work.

Without demur, Governor Odell signed the bill, which provided for a main hall to cost $125,000 and buildings for horticulture, stockjudging, and machinery. Cornell was required to continue paying the customary sums to the new college. And Cornell must convey to the state the lands on which the college would rise. The normal government of the college would rest in the hands of Cornell's Board of Trustees.

The news of the bill's signing reached Ithaca on 9 May 1904. The fire siren blew; bonfires blazed; students filled the streets, firing pistols. Headed by a band and the college's big black bull, they marched to Bailey's home on Sage Place. Three days later there was a formal parade, including a float with white-clad youths and maidens churning butter and another with students from twenty foreign countries. (The Ag College was already very cosmopolitan, especially in the Graduate Department.)

While Roberts Hall was a-building (in three parts, to comply with the act's restriction on expenditure for a single building), Bailey proceeded with a reorganization of his college.

President Schurman wanted Agriculture to be a professional school, like Veterinary or Forestry. Bailey's idea was totally different. "Other institutions aim largely at what is called productive scholarship. The land-grant colleges . . . aim at public service," he told the trustees (21 October 1911). Agricultural education was for him a preparation for life, indeed the best, most rational, most healthful kind of preparation. Even in 1893 he proclaimed that agricultural education was the coming education and that the state must foster it. By an almost mystical concept, the college must be the heart of agriculture, and its lifeblood should flow to every farm home in the state. "The mission of an agricultural college has now extended beyond mere academic lines," he said in his report for 1904. "In the epoch just opening great emphasis is to be laid on the farm home and on the intellectual and spiritual ideals of the family." And in 1906:

The modern agricultural college concerns itself with large public questions of education, trade, transportation, and general betterment, standing for all agencies that will aid in making the farmer a more efficient producer of wealth and a more effective citizen. In shorter words, the agricultural college stands for education for country life. It is not a professional college.

Bailey's dream, in fact, was to develop a new kind of rural civilization, with its directing brain at Cornell.[3]

[3] Malcolm Carron, S.J., *The Contract Colleges of Cornell University* (Ithaca,

In a remarkable address at Farmers' Week, 1909, Bailey set forth what might be called a Magna Carta of the agricultural college movement:

This College of Agriculture represents the State. Its purpose is to aid in developing the resources of the State, in its materials, its affairs, and its people. . . . While the College of Agriculture is concerned directly with increasing the producing power of land, its activities cannot be limited narrowly to this field. It must stand broadly for rural civilization. It must include within its activities such a range of subjects as will enable it to develop *an entire philosophy or scheme of country life.* . . . Agriculture is properly a civilization rather than a congeries of crafts. The colleges of agriculture represent this civilization, in its material, business, and human relations. Therefore they are not class institutions, representing merely trades and occupations. The task before the colleges of agriculture is nothing less than to direct and to aid in developing the entire rural civilization; and this task places them within the realm of statesmanship.[4]

This evangelical faith imbued Roberts Hall with an air of consecration, but understandably it evoked little enthusiasm on the lower campus and among the alumni. Forebodings were increased by news from Albany. The state, realizing belatedly that it was bestowing quite a lot of money without much control of its use, proposed to have the Governor appoint five trustees to Cornell's Board. Schurman was not cordial to the idea, but yielded, as, Bailey recognized, Henry W. Sage would not have done. The bill passed, but Bailey was allowed to handpick the new trustees. Thus the strange character of Cornell as a state-and-private institution was reinforced.

The concession to the state provoked a great outcry in the *Alumni News* and among the alumni clubs. Angry letters poured in, rehearsing all the familiar arguments against state domination. Schurman did a great deal of disavowing, without soothing many critics. The fact is obviously that he wanted state money, since private endowments were not matching the needs of Cornell's growth, and to get state money he would yield a good deal of control.

A part of Bailey's program was to bring the Veterinary College into the College of Agriculture, since, he contended, the union of the two state colleges would be an administrative advance and would increase their political power. Here was a source of plentiful trouble. Director

---

1958), p. 86. This admirable book is an excellent guide through the whole controversy. See also Philip Dorf, *Liberty Hyde Bailey* (Ithaca, 1956).

[4] *The College of Agriculture and the State* (Ithaca, 1909), p. 19.

James Law of Veterinary would have none of it. In principle, he said, veterinary work is allied to the medicine of man, not to soil-tilling; and in practice, he foresaw that Veterinary would become subordinate to Agriculture, and Law to Bailey.

The President had private letters from Law and Bailey printed for the "confidential" use of the trustees (12 February 1908). The trustees, certainly guided by the President, rebuffed Bailey by voting that the relations between the veterinary and agricultural colleges should remain unchanged. When Bailey had a glimpse of the printed document he wrote a very angry letter to the President, calling the publication "a practically official statement of an unrefuted charge of bad faith on my part." [5]

Two mettlesome, dominating spirits were now in open conflict. As it happened, Bailey had often announced his "life plan," conceived in youth, whereby he would spend his first twenty-five years in preparation, his second twenty-five in earning a living, and the rest doing what he wanted to do. According to this schedule March 1908 would mark the end of the second life, the beginning of the third. He proposed his resignation but, at the President's plea, he consented to remain for another year as Director of the college.

In the summer, at the personal request of President Theodore Roosevelt, Bailey served as chairman of a brilliant Commission on Country Life, with the mission of ameliorating farmers' lives. The task was much to Bailey's taste, bringing him national fame and the lifelong friendship of President Roosevelt and other eminences.

On 14 May 1909 Bailey submitted his formal resignation. The trustees, and Schurman, cried out in protest. After an exchange of letters, Bailey consented to a compromise. Instead of resigning, he would take a year's leave of absence at half pay, to investigate agricultural methods and country life conditions.

Before leaving, he wrote to the President (4 June 1909) to clarify his dissatisfactions. He was embarrassed, he confessed, by the common illusion that he could make his own plans and carry them through the legislature, whereas in fact he could work only through the President and the trustees. The Director "is at the head of a State College but is without authority and responsibility to the people." He had already been balked by the trustees when he attempted to obtain additional appropriations. Further, the Executive Committee, after designating funds for specific purposes, would sometimes transfer them to other

[5] 26 March 1908, Bailey Papers.

uses, without warning. He confessed that his defeat on the Veterinary dispute had deeply upset him. He thought, in short, that the Director of the state college should deal directly with the state, not with Cornell's President and trustees.

In October 1909 Bailey dramatically disappeared from the campus. Only one person, John Henry Comstock, knew Bailey's address, and he communicated only in moments of crisis. In fact, Mr. and Mrs. Bailey were in California, preparing for a journey to Hawaii and the Orient.

Bailey's mysterious absence fostered a luxuriant crop of rumors. He is being forced out, said his friends; he will never return. President Schurman called a meeting of the Agriculture and Veterinary faculties, in December, to quash the rumors. He told the meeting that he and the trustees had gone on their knees to Bailey, to beg him to remain. The Agriculture professors were still skeptical. They were delighted that the President seemed so frightened, and "so well aware of the difficulties he has brought on himself," wrote George Lauman of Rural Economy to Bailey. "He is conscious of and afraid of the criticism in the State and especially in Washington," wrote H. H. Wing of Animal Husbandry. "There are rumors to the effect that if matters continue as they are the chances are that President Schurman will have to step aside for you to take his place." And an admirer wrote that the farmers of the state stood ready to move in and "move Dean Bailey one notch higher up."

But this is Revolution! This is the Peasants' Rebellion!

The Agriculture College faculty earnestly petitioned Bailey to return. His best friends wrote him urgent letters, insisting that for the good of the college the rumor that he was being forced out should be denied. So, regretfully, Bailey canceled his trip across the Pacific, showed himself in Ithaca in January 1910, to receive a roaring ovation from the students, and then proceeded to Albany for official conferences. A peace was patched up, and Bailey took the rest of his sabbatical year in Europe.

A year later, in September 1911, Bailey renewed his effort to resign, provoking more of what Andrew D. White called "Bailey trouble." The Agriculture alumni were sure there was some deep villainy afoot. They drew up angry statements, alleging that "the President is aggressive, dominating [which was certainly true], and jealous of the College of Agriculture and the man at its head [which was not unlikely]." The manifesto demanded an accounting of University expenditures for

Agriculture and complained of the local businessmen on the Executive Committee and of the location of the new athletic field. Old Ag men wrote in minatory letters, asserting that "if the tail has outgrown the dog, the tail should do the wagging."

Needled, badgered, and annoyed, Bailey consented to serve as Director for one more year. In 1912–13 he saw the College of Agriculture become the largest on the campus, with 1,263 students to 1,112 in Arts. He saw his creation in most vigorous health, smiled upon publicly by the President, cherished by the generous lawgivers in Albany, beloved by the people of the state. He could retire with confidence and honor. He set the date finally for the conclusion of the Cornell fiscal year, 30 July 1913, thus fulfilling the ten-year term he had promised the President.

Apparently nobody would believe him. Such was the vanity of Cornell professors and administrators that they could not conceive of Bailey's voluntary surrender of the directorship for indulgence in study and scholarship. They felt sure that some hidden reasons existed and that obscure but devilish machinations were at work. Of course they knew Bailey much better than I did, but I feel sure they were wrong. His desire to make scientific discoveries and to write was stronger than his desire to continue the routine of administration. He had no yearning for power and glory; he turned down many a tempting political offer, including the hint of a Cabinet post, including the opportunity to run for Governor on the Progressive ticket in 1912. Further, he was disturbed by the antagonism to the administration that was growing up among the alumni. He wrote: "Without my desiring it this movement seemed to be crystallizing about myself. I felt that I must remove myself from this situation." [6]

Schurman was absent in 1912–13, serving as Minister to Greece and enjoying the Balkan War very much, as a relief from Cornell affairs. He proposed to resign the presidency of Cornell as soon as he could be properly replaced.[7] T. F. Crane, Acting President, did nothing about finding a successor to Bailey, probably hoping against hope that he would change his mind at the last moment. But Bailey, after his final

[6] Bailey to A. R. Mann (presumably 1913), in Bailey Papers. One may still dispute about the motives for Bailey's resignation. William I. Myers '14, long Dean of Agriculture and a close friend of Bailey, thinks that disagreement with Schurman and the trustees was certainly a contributing cause to Bailey's decision, that while Bailey fought Schurman's dictation, he resigned in order not to split the University.

[7] Schurman to Roger B. Williams, 24 May 1913.

day as Director, locked his office door, left the key in the Treasurer's office, and never went back.

On the whole, Bailey had won the battle with the Cornell administration. Although he had not gained complete autonomy for his college, he had established the precedent that a state college Director, or Dean, may do his own lobbying, deal directly with state officials, and, at need, invoke the power of the mobilized farm groups of the state. He had found means for a state college to exist both within and without an endowed University. Any administrator, examining our peculiar structure, would say it could not possibly work. But it has worked for fifty years, and we expect it to work for many more.[8]

And of course Bailey's creation, the New York State College of Agriculture, was itself a mighty force. When Bailey took the reins, Agriculture occupied quarters valued at $60,000; on his retirement, the college buildings were worth a million and a quarter. At the beginning, six full professors, one assistant professor, and two instructors offered 25 courses. At the end, 224 courses were offered by 46 full professors, 26 assistant professors, and 57 instructors. In 1902–3 the college had 114 full-time students; in 1912–13 it had 1,263.

What accounts for this prodigious growth? Bailey, obviously; without Bailey it would not have been. But Bailey was riding a wave. In the second half of the nineteenth century the country had shifted from an agricultural base to an industrial base. The ugliness of the new industrialized world, with its typical failure to fulfill human needs, created a widespread nostalgia for a country life purified by memory and tradition. "Back to the Land!" became a common cry. Books with such titles as *Three Acres and Liberty* and *The Fat of the Land* had an enormous sale in the cities. The farm home was embowered with beauty, to the dweller in drear "railroad flats." The figure of the Farmer was glorified and transformed, from the witless hayseed to a sun-browned muscular philosopher, striding his fields, communing with the holy earth, and spending his long evenings reading the works of Liberty Hyde Bailey.

The country's mood did not last. Our College of Agriculture of course expected to grow indefinitely; it drew up forecasts of needs based on an annual increment of 300 students annually for ten years.

[8] The Evaluation Committee of the Middle States Association of Colleges and Secondary Schools reported, in Nov. 1957: "It is remarkable that such an organization works at all; that it works astonishingly well is even more noteworthy and reflects great credit upon the administration of the University."

In fact the enrollment of full-time students in Ag rose to a high of 1,704 in 1915–16, dropped to 1,068 in 1917–18, rose again to 1,239 in 1924–25, and sank to a low of 676 in 1928–29. The college settled into its place in the University frame, and the overweening ambitions of a few Ag profs faded and died.[9]

The subsidence within the College of Agriculture conduced to harmony with the rest of the campus, which had begun to feel that its denomination as "the Lower Campus" was all too symbolical. A good deal of headshaking, ill-auguring, and omen-pointing had gone on. Professors in the endowed colleges chilled themselves and each other by forecasts of their fate as mere service agents to a rich and mighty College of Earth-Grubbing. But with time such fears were allayed. Henry A. Sill of History wrote Carl Becker (14 January 1917):

There was a time when Arts and Sciences felt afraid and suspicious of Agriculture, but that feeling lingers only among a few mossbacks, and nobody who gets acquainted with the College of Agriculture can feel anything but admiration for its splendid work and for the high scientific spirit that animates the majority of its faculty. The establishment and maintenance of that college by the State has set free for the humanities funds that otherwise would have been needed for the proper development of biological studies.

The students in the other colleges, echoing their professors, regarded the Ag students with some toploftiness. Russell Lord '20 remembers:

An unremitting chorus of derision for the "Cow College" from without strengthened this student group from within and held it compact. . . . Even

[9] And what has happened to Bailey's dream of holy college-educated farmers walking the holy earth? A Symposium on the Role of Agriculture in Future Society, held at the Cornell Experiment Station in Geneva in October 1957, gives it little encouragement. Farm acreage dwindles as fewer workers produce more. Farming is less a country way of life, more a large-scale technical operation. The coming of mass food and field processing means the control of production by great corporations. Professor Richard L. Meier of the University of Michigan foresaw our chief food-production units as shallow aerated pools, breeding algae by photosynthesis and nitrogen fixation. The wet algae will be pipelined to the cities, to be transformed into synthetic bread or sausages or what you will. Said Professor Meier: "Certain dreams, themes, and articles of faith concerning agriculture that are left over from the previous century will doubtless have to be abandoned. The idea of pure, fresh, unmodified foods is likely to be among these. The family farm unit and the rural way of life seem to be another. To be employed in agriculture would mean working for a firm engaged in primary production of foodstuffs, much the same as any other industrial worker, or to operate as an individual with a profitable, seasonal, part-time occupation."

in my years there . . . we Ags had sometimes to stride along, unheeding, with all possible dignity and our ears burning when some raucous Arts students would put their heads together and give "the Cow College Yell." It went thus: "Cornell, I yell, yell, yell, Cornell." Then a long "Moo," a slight pause, and finally three slow claps of the cupped hands: *Flop, Flop, Flop.* . . .[10]

Within the college, under Bailey, a happy activity reigned, in classroom, laboratory, barn and field. Old departments twinned by fission; new departments were born by parthenogenesis (some of them consisting of but a single member); vigorous cross-pollination of ideas was practiced. James G. Needham came in 1907, to give the first college course in Limnology, and to create a department which became world-famous. Agronomy was established under Thomas F. Hunt; and Animal Husbandry, with Henry H. Wing '81; and the first American course in Poultry Husbandry, under James E. Rice '90; and Apiculture; and Ornithology, with Arthur A. Allen '07. (Allen took a Bird Census in 1915, and found some forty kinds nesting on the campus.)

Bailey established in 1913 a new Department of Botany, rivaling the department in the Arts College. The new department had a serious advantage over its elder in that it was amply supported by the state; and ere long it engulfed, ingested, and absorbed the original department. In Botany and in the allied plant sciences were to be found Benjamin M. Duggar, who later discovered aureomycin, Karl M. Wiegand, who became president of the Botanical Society of America, and Lewis Knudson, celebrated for his work on legume bacteria, the effects of x-radiation on chloroplasts, and the physiology of banana ripening. His methods for the germination of orchid seeds led to the creation of practically a new industry. There were other remarkable young men: Lester W. Sharp, Arthur J. Eames, L. H. MacDaniels, and others too.

Herbert H. Whetzel of Botany asked Director Bailey in 1907 to be allowed to devote all his time to plant pathology. "Do you know of any professorship of Plant Pathology in any university?" asked Bailey. "No." "Well, do you think the Trustees will establish a new chair just for you?" "I think they will if *you* ask them." And of course they did.

Thanks to Whetzel's initiative, industrial fellowships were established at Cornell, among the first in America. He proposed to the Niagara Sprayer Company of Middleport, New York, that it support investi-

[10] *American Forests*, Feb. 1960; reproduced in *Alumni News*, 15 March 1960.

gations in the value of lime-sulfur solution as a spray for apple scab. The company responded in 1909 and apparently made its fortune from the results. Thus the system began by which a manufacturer pays a graduate student to study a problem which may result in profit for the manufacturer and a doctorate for the student.[11]

George N. Lauman '97 organized the first American course and department of rural, or agricultural, economics. Thomas F. Hunt's work in farm management was taken over in 1907 by George F. Warren '03, who later became famous as President Franklin D. Roosevelt's monetary adviser. Warren initiated work in marketing, prices, land economics, and rural local government. He made an agricultural survey of Tompkins County which has been termed epoch-making, as the first systematic study of the profits of agriculture and the factors affecting them, such as the size of the farm, production per cow, yields per acre, efficiency of labor per man, and so forth.[12]

Rural Education, a natural outgrowth of Bailey's and Mrs. Comstock's work in nature study, was formally organized as a department in 1914. Agricultural Education and Home Economics Education were incorporated therein. The department emphasized, excessively in some eyes, the differences between rural and urban education.

Bristow Adams appeared in 1914, as professor of extension. His interests, as his influence, soon spread to other fields, as journalism, creative writing, painting. His diverse abilities and his friendly spirit made him one of the most beloved figures on our campus. Many distinguished products of his course in Journalism have testified to the beneficence of his training.

The fame of the college spread throughout the world. A French scientist roundly termed Cornell the most extensive and best-organized

[11] H. H. Whetzel, "The History of Industrial Fellowships in the Department of Plant Pathology," in *Agricultural History*, April 1945. Apparently the University of Kansas beat us by a few months in arranging an industrial fellowship in chemistry.

[12] Frank A. Pearson in *Farm Economics*, Feb. 1957. Warren was a thoroughgoing economist. He would not paint his barns, on the principle: "You paint a roof to preserve it. You paint a house to sell it. You paint the side of a barn to look at it, if you can afford it." When a student asked him why he did not paint his barn, he replied: "The mortgage sticks longer than the paint." Later, when he had undeniably painted his barn, the student remarked that the mortgage must have been paid. Said Warren: "No, I merely painted the barn so I could get more mortgage."

school of applied biological sciences in existence, with special praise for the supreme work in entomology.[13] Foreign students congregated on the Ag Campus, finding there answers to the agricultural problems of their own lands. Chinese students particularly came to Cornell for its precious lessons in tending the good earth. Chinese agriculture was in fact modernized by Hing Kwai Fung '11, according to the eminent statesman S. Alfred Sze '01.[14]

The case of forestry was special. One remembers that Governor Benjamin B. Odell had strangled the infant New York State College of Forestry in 1903 by cutting off appropriations, to the accompaniment of wounding words. Liberty Hyde Bailey was not displeased. (To the indignation of our professors of forestry, he made no opposition to the creation of the New York State College of Forestry at Syracuse in 1912.) Bailey, opposed on principle to vocational training, thought that forestry, like veterinary medicine, should not constitute separate colleges; they belonged under Agriculture. Nevertheless, an efficient farmer should know how to raise trees as a crop. (A third of New York State's area was woodland, largely in the form of farmers' woodlots.) Bailey therefore established in 1910 a Department of Forestry, which, despite his principles, soon became one of the country's foremost agencies for the training of professional foresters. Demand for work in the field was so great that Fernow Hall was erected in 1914 as the home of Forestry. In the same year Professor Frank B. Moody found, fifteen miles southwest of Ithaca, a forest tract excellent for demonstration, experiment, and outdoor laboratory work. The heirs of Mathias H. Arnot of Elmira eventually gave the tract to Cornell as the Arnot Forest. Enlarged by gifts from Jervis Langdon '97 and Frank Gannett '98, it now covers four thousand picturesque acres.[15]

The Forestry students were a close-knit, happy body, bound together by their summer camp fellowship, by the benevolence of their teachers, and by their taste for hearty sylvan frolics. They had even their patron, Saint Murphius. On a forestry trip to Galeton, Pennsylvania, Edwin G. Bishop '14 was delighted to find in a barbershop the embalmed corpse of the town drunk, named Murphy, displayed as an example of the

---

[13] Paul Marchal, *Les Sciences biologiques appliquées à l'agriculture* (Paris, 1916), p. 251. He visited Cornell in May 1913 and was enchanted by "the atmosphere of this ideal city of the arts and sciences."

[14] *Alumni News*, 21 March 1929.

[15] For the history of Cornell forestry see Professor Ralph S. Hosmer's excellent *Forestry at Cornell* (Ithaca, 1950).

barber-surgeon's art. Ted Bishop photographed the unfortunate, and from the photograph Maurice H. Webster '16 painted an elaborately antiqued portrait. For years Saint Murphius was the center of all Forestry Club ceremonies, and messages from the Pearly Gates Tote Road were solemnly read to his disciples.

The College of Agriculture became, and remained, an important center of research. Bailey insisted on it, ordering every staff officer to prepare annually at least one bulletin representing original work. "Teachers of agricultural subjects," he said, "who do not investigate are either dead or superficial, and in either case they are useless." [16]

The Cornell Experiment Station, largely supported by $27,000 a year from the Federal Hatch Act of 1887, was an aid as well as an outlet for research. During seven years Bailey himself wrote more than half the bulletins published by the station. His first, *The Nature-Study Idea* (1903), proclaimed what has been termed the Cornell nature study philosophy.[17] Much essential work was done, resulting in precious discoveries, too ample, and perhaps too special, for listing here. (But let us at least notice the Cortland apple, developed in 1899 by the miscegenation of the McIntosh and the Ben Davis, and now one of the commonest varieties in the state.)

Home Economics was by this time a department in Agriculture. Its story begins in 1899, when Melvil Dewey, State Librarian and multifarious reformer, called a conference on home economics at his Lake Placid Club and suggested its introduction at Cornell. President Schurman cried: "What! Cooks on the Cornell Faculty? Never!" Bailey had however a higher opinion of cooks or a lower opinion of the faculty. He decided as a first step to inaugurate a reading course for farmers' wives and to bring to the campus a woman to run it. The Comstocks suggested Martha Van Rensselaer, School Commissioner of Cattaraugus County, the only woman to hold such a post in the state. In 1900 Home Economics at Cornell began, with Miss Van Rensselaer in a basement room of Morrill Hall traversed with steam and water pipes and containing two chairs and a kitchen table with a drawer for pens and paper.

[16] Staff bulletin, 6 March 1909 (Bailey Papers); Bailey, *The College of Agriculture and the State* (Ithaca, 1909).
[17] E. Laurence Palmer, *The Cornell Nature Study Philosophy* (Cornell Rural School Leaflet, Sept. 1944).

Bailey opened the work with a throbbing letter to the wives of five thousand farmers on his mailing list. Their hearts melted like butter on a griddle. One wrote: "I cannot tell you what it means to me to think that somebody cares. My life is made up of men, men, men, and mud, mud, mud. Send me the bulletins and remember me in your prayers."

In January 1901 appeared Miss Van Rensselaer's first bulletin, *Saving Steps*. This aroused great interest and much publicity. The New York *World* hung a pedometer on a farm wife and found she registered 7⅖ miles per day. "Saving Steps" became a byword; it could almost have made a song.

The series, supported by the state, continued with other such practical messages. Organized as a correspondence course, it eventually enrolled 70,000 wives, many of them grouped in study clubs.

Within the College of Agriculture, by 1903–4 three courses were given relating to home and family life, by Miss Van Rensselaer and Mrs. Comstock. In 1906 Miss Flora Rose was brought in to help. Martha Van Rensselaer and Flora Rose made one of those extraordinary teams which occasionally occur in nature. They worked together all their lives as "coheads" or "codirectors," with never a sign of difference or jealousy. Mrs. Albert W. Smith called it "the only successful double-headed administration in the academic world." [18]

Bailey, after much dubiety, decided in 1907 to make of Home Economics a department, designating Miss Van Rensselaer and Miss Rose "Lecturers." The ladies demanded something more exact and more impressive. Martha Van Rensselaer removed one obstacle by taking her A.B. from Cornell in 1909. After long and acrimonious argument, the faculty voted (18 October 1911) that "while not favoring in general the appointment of women to professorships, it would interpose no objection to their appointment in the Department of Home Economics." The two became thus the first women to be full professors at Cornell. (But, as we have already noted, Mrs. Comstock had been made assistant professor of nature study in the Summer School of 1898.)

The Department of Home Economics flourished, specializing in foods and nutrition, attracting numbers of male students. The codirectors were fortunately excellent cooks and were sometimes called in to help the administration's promotion program. They fed three distinguished visitors, including the director of the Waldorf-Astoria Hotel, creamed codfish, baked potatoes, and johnnycake, to their delight. In March 1909 the Ways and Means Committee of the state legislature came and

[18] Ruby Green Smith, *The People's Colleges* (Ithaca, 1949), p. 78.

was fed in a corridor on the fourth floor of Roberts Hall (to emphasize our need of work room). The scalloped cabbage was particularly successful with a legislator who detested cabbage. In the following January a bill was introduced for an appropriation of $154,000 for a Home Economics building. At the hearing the gallant lawmakers shouted: "I want to vote for the woman who made that salad!" "I want to vote for the woman who taught me to eat cabbage!"

The building, now Comstock Hall, was occupied in 1913. Its cafeteria, a new device and a new word at the time, immediately captured campus gourmets, and spelled the doom of many a Collegetown boardinghouse.

Extension work in Home Economics, like that in Agriculture proper, was closely bound to the college. Martha Van Rensselaer carried on an enormous business outside her college duties, writing bulletins, directing reading courses, corresponding with puzzled or lonely farmers' wives.

The character of agricultural extension work changed gradually. It moved out from the college to establish itself in the counties, to ally itself with a new system of farm and home bureaus, county agents, and home demonstrators, supported by the counties and the federal government as well as by the state. This localized work began in Broome County in 1911, with John H. Barron '06 as the first county agent. The College of Agriculture remained the executive center of the work. Its service was, and is, to provide technical information, to offer lectures and demonstrations, to publish a giant library of bulletins for farmers and homemakers, and to contribute toward the training and support of the county extension agents. Cornell is the state's agent in the supervision of the State Extension Service.

A vigorous thrust to extension work was given by the federal Smith-Lever Act, passed in May 1914. This act provided for cooperative extension work between the U.S. Department of Agriculture and the land-grant colleges. It stipulated that up to $170,000 annually would be furnished on condition that the state would match it, as eventually it did.

All these vast enterprises came under the control of the Director of the College of Agriculture, and were his responsibility. One may well sympathize with the desire of Bailey the scientist to load the whole business on another's back, while he would retire to his private hortorium in Henry W. Sage's old carriage house.

President Schurman, returning from Greece in 1913, took the selection of a new director as a matter of the first importance. He appointed William A. Stocking '98 of Dairy Industry to be Acting Director and began the process known as "scouring the country." By the spring of 1914 he had made his choice: Beverly T. Galloway, well-known research botanist, said to be primarily responsible for the development of applied plant pathology, discoverer, among many things, of a cure for wilting violets. He was at the time assistant to the U.S. Secretary of Agriculture and had been chief of the Bureau of Plant Industry. He was a worthy and competent man; but, unfortunately for any successor to Bailey, he was unimpressive in person and manner, a poor public speaker, and a sufferer from stomach ulcers. Equally unfortunate was Schurman's expectation that he would tame the rearing, tender-mouthed College of Agriculture and break it to harness. Schurman wrote to Charles H. Hull of History:

> Dr. Galloway has a genius for cooperation and I expect soon to see the College of Agriculture back in its normal place in the bosom of the university. Indeed, in nominating him for the directorship, I stated to the Trustees that in my judgment the only alternative to that consummation was complete separation, and I felt the forces had for some time been at work in that direction.[19]

The report that Director Galloway's duty was to replace Agriculture in the bosom of the University commended him not at all to the proud spirits of the college. Nor did the new director's announced program, to study the budgets closely, eliminate waste, check on teaching loads and research results. He found the course offerings given by twenty-six departments overlapping and wasteful. He proposed to reduce their number to eight. But every reform injured someone's interests or habits or hurt someone's feelings. The Faculty of Agriculture opposed, actively or passively, every administrative proposal.

Galloway brought the habits of a Washington bureaucrat to Ithaca. Even his office organization was unfortunate. Bailey had been readily accessible; but Galloway installed in his anteroom a bright undergraduate, who admitted or denied visitors access to the Director with undue hauteur. Professors, rebuffed by a mere student, felt that the world had turned upside down.

[19] 21 May 1914. The extent and bitterness of the New York State farmers' hostility to Schurman appears in an editorial in the *American Agriculturist*, 31 May 1914, warning Galloway not to trust "that misfit state college head," whose "days are numbered."

By 1916 Galloway had had enough. His ulcers no doubt damaged his personal relations, and his personal relations damaged his ulcers. He resigned joyfully, and returned to the U.S. Department of Agriculture. The trustees' resolution on his departure breathes a real regret and a real resentment against the Faculty of Agriculture.

He was succeeded in the directorship, which now was renamed a deanship, by Albert R. Mann, B.S. in Ag. '04, successively secretary to Bailey, registrar, secretary and editor for the College of Agriculture, assistant professor of dairy industry, and professor of rural social organization. His broad experience was reinforced by his being an insider, one of our own people, a member of the club. He was also a man of great warmth, tact, and intelligence. Under his deanship, which lasted until 1931, the College of Agriculture lost its occasionally prickly mood. It cooperated heartily in serving the general welfare of the University. It has taken over, for excellent reasons, much of the scientific work previously administered by the College of Arts and Sciences and countable toward an Arts degree. Its courses in botany, biology, entomology, biochemistry, bacteriology, genetics represent fundamental science at its best. The old quarrels between the colleges have passed into history.

It is always an interesting, though futile, exercise to speculate on what might have been. Alter one trifling factor, and one obtains an enormously different result. It is evident that in the early years of the century the alteration of one factor—the private ambition of Liberty Hyde Bailey—would have totally changed the career of Cornell University. If he had wished to be a great director of large affairs, a University President and perhaps afterwards a mighty man in national politics, the way lay open to him at Cornell. He had behind him the faculty and the students of the College of Agriculture; and he had in the state a following of a hundred thousand farmers, and in Albany the support of legislators deeply sensitive to the farm vote and at the same time his personal admirers. He could readily have led a secession of the New York State College of Agriculture from Cornell University. Or he might even have forced the state college on the University, subordinating Arts and Sciences, Engineering, and the rest to the new, vital, dominant state establishment. President Schurman was ready, even eager, to retire. The President of this transformed University would naturally be Liberty Hyde Bailey.

But no, he preferred science.

XXIV

The New Century:
Cornell Medical College

THE Cornell Medical College in New York, in its fine new building, gained steadily in prestige and professional standing. It was aided and heartened by the decision of the State Court of Appeals in 1904, which restored the Loomis Laboratory to its original donor, Colonel Oliver H. P. Payne. Colonel Payne then transferred it to Cornell, at a valuation of $240,000, to be primarily a research laboratory. The saintly Colonel made up the annual deficit of the college with apparent pleasure.

The college received the highest commendation of the state's inspectors. "It is in almost every particular an ideal institution," they said in 1912. And Abraham Flexner's blasting survey of medical schools, in the same year, gave Cornell almost unqualified praise.

Outstanding in its history for these years are two developments: the raising of standards for admission and instruction, and the securing of hospital facilities.

Though at the century's ingress the college accepted a high-school course for matriculation, it specified physics and inorganic chemistry, thus making its requirement the highest in the state. The flux of applicants, and a national movement for the raising of standards, inspired it to greater rigor. By 1907 two American medical schools, Harvard and Hopkins, required a first degree for entrance, and Western Reserve demanded the completion of the junior undergraduate year. In 1908 Cornell joined this peerless trinity, calling for a first degree, but permitting Cornell students (and some others) to combine their senior undergraduate year with their first year in medicine.

The results were at first calamitous. The previous entering class in the New York school numbered 70; the class entering in 1908 consisted of three members, one of whom soon withdrew. At the Ithaca establishment of the school the class dropped from 35 to 11. The Medical Faculty, to their great credit, refused to take fright and clove to their convictions. They saw the total full-time registration in the Medical College descend from 320 in 1907–8 to 221 in 1908–9, to 201 in 1909–10, to 179 in 1910–11, to a low of 118 in 1911–12, with a graduating class of 11. Then the curve reversed, rising to 216 in 1915–16. In 1920 the flood of 150 applications for entrance caused the setting of a limitation.

The obtention of clinical facilities in hospitals was a long process. A proper school must have entry to wards for observation, with control of clinical instruction. On the other hand, a hospital welcomes association with a medical school, partly for prestige and partly also, no doubt, because the professors and students supply invaluable services without charge. Originally Cornell had access, with other schools, to Bellevue Hospital. The need for closer integration inspired Professor Samuel Alexander, as early as 1902, to work for a union of the college with the famous old New York Hospital, chartered in 1771 by George III.[1] The death of Dr. Alexander in 1910 caused the project to lapse. But in 1912 George F. Baker, a governor of the hospital and chairman of the First National Bank, guaranteed support for the consolidation.[2] He proposed to build a new hospital on 54th Street, between 11th and 12th Avenues. This was the beginning of Mr. Baker's interest in Cornell, which is embodied in Baker Tower, Baker Court, and the Baker Laboratory of Chemistry.

In 1913 an agreement was reached, chiefly through the efforts of Dr. Lewis A. Stimson. The New York Hospital proposed to make half its beds available for instruction of Cornell students, and the college would nominate the medical and surgical staffs of this half of the hospital. For this purpose Mr. Baker pledged two million dollars, and our ever-generous friend, Colonel Payne, pledged four million. Dr. Paul Reznikoff happily terms this arrangement "the engagement of the

[1] New York newspaper, 30 Nov. 1910. Clipping in "Memorabilia," Medical College Library.
[2] News clipping, 15 Nov. 1912, in "Memorabilia."

school and the hospital, which was to result in their marriage in 1927."

At the same time the college was making other extramarital alliances. The Russell Sage Institute of Pathology, center for the study of metabolic disorders, was associated with Cornell in 1912. Here labored Dr. Graham Lusk and such brilliant aides as Eugene F. DuBois and David P. Barr '11, in the fields of nutrition, respiratory diseases, and endocrinology.

In 1914 a close bond was forged with the Memorial Hospital of New York, originally the New York Cancer Hospital. Dr. James Ewing, who served in both institutions, was the chief agent of this union. We received also the important Huntington Fund for the Study of Cancer.

If any large conclusion is to be drawn from this history, it must be that eminence is the work of great teachers, animated by great ideas. The Cornell Medical College had, and has, its full share of great teachers. While we await a proper history of the college, we must mention, however barely, some of its unforgotten names.

The Dean for many years was Dr. William M. Polk, son of Leonidas Polk, the famous "fighting bishop" of the Civil War, and himself a veteran of the Confederate Army. "Magnificently groomed, meticulous as to every last detail of his appearance, he was an imposing figure when he arrived in his carriage behind a spanking team with coachman and footman to attend him." [4] He ruled the college with gentle fury, inquiring into the least details of its management, shouting and pounding about expenses like any worried paterfamilias. But everyone was aware of his anxious rectitude. One of his errors is still remembered, to his honor. He operated, to remove a patient's kidney. But the patient was one of those rarities who are born with a single kidney. He died; and the Dean, far from trying to conceal his tragic mistake, published an account of it, as a warning to others.

Dr. Lewis A. Stimson, professor of surgery, close friend of Colonel Payne, was author of a standard text on fractures and dislocations, and a mathematician, and father of Henry L. Stimson, Secretary of State under President Hoover. He was one of the first to introduce to America knowledge of the bacterial origins of sepsis, and to apply the principles of antiseptic surgery. In those days the rate of mortality for major operations was one in three. For compound fractures the surgeon amputated at once, or fatal infection was sure (hence the profusion of

[3] "Cornell University Medical College," *N.Y. State Journal of Medicine*, 1 Feb. 1957.

[4] Emily Dunning Barringer, *Bowery to Bellevue* (New York, 1950), p. 64.

one-handed or one-legged men, stumping the streets or pitifully begging). In 1876 Stimson dared to treat—and with success—an untended, suppurating compound fracture of the leg with a Lister dressing, instead of amputating.[5]

Dr. James Ewing, professor of pathology, created a department famous in medical history. A brilliant researcher, especially in the field of cancer, he wrote an important book on the subject. New York City's superb cancer hospital, not far from the present New York Hospital-Cornell Medical Center, is named in his honor the James Ewing Hospital.

Dr. Graham Lusk, son of a former dean of the N.Y.U. Medical College, strong-minded, strong-spirited, was one of the first and greatest scientific students of nutrition. Dr. Eugene F. DuBois, his disciple, carried on his work and is still remembered with affection. Dr. DuBois constructed a pioneer calorimeter, which is preserved in the Smithsonian Institution.

Dr. Charles R. Stockard (later professor of anatomy) worked with Ewing in pathology and performed important research in embryology and genetics. He had an animal farm near Peekskill, peopled with strange anomalies that allured reporters as well as scientists. (The Island of Dr. Moreau, indeed.)

Another of Ewing's disciples was Dr. Frederick Gudernatsch, who came to New York from Germany on a visit in 1907, and who still remains there, the beloved survivor of the early years.[6] In an important experiment he showed the modification of the tadpole's development under endocrine influence. Awarded an honorary doctorate by his Alma Mater, the University of Giessen, he was hailed as "the Dean of Endocrinology."

Distressing as it is to choose only a few from so many worthy, one must at least mention Dr. Rudolph Witthaus of the original faculty, professor of chemistry, physics, and toxicology; and Robert Hatcher of pharmacology; and Lewis A. Conner, who came as professor of clinical medicine in 1900 and exercised his beneficent influence on the college throughout his long life; and Stanley Benedict of biochemistry; and particularly Walter L. Niles, who became Dean in 1919,

[5] George A. Boyd, "Lewis Atterbury Stimson M.D." (MS, Medical College Library). Mr. Boyd gives a fascinating picture of surgery's state at the century's end.
[6] See his delightful reminiscences, "Out of the Early Cornell Years" (mimeographed, 1958).

succeeding Dr. Polk, and who was a most capable and popular administrator. In 1913 came Dr. G. N. Papanicolaou, whose work in exfoliative cytology has made possible the early detection of cancer. Nor can we omit Miss Jessie Andresen, the Secretary, who, in the recollection of several elders, "ran the school."

The students of the early years were obviously a very superior group, thanks to the strict requirements for entrance and the notorious difficulty of the course. Many of them have risen to eminence as teachers, researchers, specialists, and practitioners. We cannot in decency choose among them for this record. But let us at least note that from its beginning Cornell was one of the few medical colleges that welcomed women students. The lionhearted Emily Dunning Barringer, M.D. '01, was the first woman to obtain, against all odds, an appointment as ambulance surgeon, and later as house surgeon and house physician. Her fascinating *Bowery to Bellevue* tells of her adventures in the villainous slums of New York, against the banded opposition of the male doctors. Mary M. Crawford, M.D. '07, became the head of a surgical and medical staff at the Williamsburg Hospital in New York. Like Dr. Barringer, she had trained by rowing on the women's crew at Ithaca, under Courtney. She was followed at the Williamsburg Hospital by Emily Bruyn, M.D. '10. In the graduating class of 1911 the two highest honors went to women students. The winner, Helen Dudley, married her classmate, Harry G. Bull, and became a professor in the College of Home Economics.

An item in the history of race relations: Roscoe C. Giles, A.B. '11, M.D '15, being required to care for six maternity cases to obtain his degree, registered at the Manhattan Maternity Hospital. When the directors discovered that he was colored, they requested him to withdraw. I have not discovered how the case turned out, but at any rate he received his degree.

According to the arrangements made in 1898, the first two years of the four-year medical course could be taken either in Ithaca or New York. At the end of the second year the Ithaca contingent transferred to New York without formality.

For the college in Ithaca, Dean Sage, son of Henry W. Sage, built Stimson Hall, designed by W. H. Miller, and named for Dr. Lewis A. Stimson, who was so largely responsible for the existence of the Cornell Medical College. Stimson Hall, opened in 1903, was regarded as the best building for medical instruction in the country.

But the Ithaca division did not thrive. Its enrollment dwindled to nine in 1909–10, and in the spring the trustees reduced the course to a single year, which could be combined with the senior year in Arts. Why did the school not prosper? Its students did well in the New York division; it had some excellent teachers, Abram T. Kerr '95, Benjamin F. Kingsbury '94, Luzerne Coville '87. (It employed in 1903–4 a woman assistant, Effie Alberta Read '03; "her instruction has been as acceptable to the men as to the women students," said President Schurman with apparent surprise.) However, the instruction in anatomy presented many problems; and of course there was no opportunity for clinical work. And the Ithaca section, meagerly supported from the general funds of the University, made a sorry comparison with the richly endowed New York section. Indeed, the Ithaca section was doomed by the possibility that it could be transferred to New York, thus releasing general University funds for other crying, screaming needs. But this transfer belongs in a later chapter.

XXV

The New Century:
The Other Colleges

IN these early years of the century the structure of the University was altered only by the creation of the New York State College of Agriculture and by the disappearance of the College of Forestry. Plenty of proposals for expansion were made. Director John Van Pelt of the College of Architecture had very impressive plans drawn for a college of fine arts, to cost $4,500,000, a noble enterprise. Everything was provided for except the four and a half million. President Schurman's favorite project was a school of education, to be fathered by Cornell and mothered by the state. Andrew D. White's old conception of a school of commerce was picked up again by a faculty committee in 1915, and again let fall. There were other bright ideas.

In general, however, the University refrained from growth by fission. We had troubles enough from the rapidity of our natural increase. Administrators as well as observers called for a halt in expansion, or even for a reversal of the trend. Dean Ernest Merritt of the Graduate School pointed out in 1910 his school's disabilities, such as the increasing proportion of instructors to professors, and asked: "May it not be that we can do more for the cause of education by directing our efforts toward making Cornell the best university in the country, rather than the largest?" Others ruminated on the view enunciated long since by both Andrew D. White and Charles Kendall Adams, that the true line of cleavage in higher education comes at the end of the sophomore year; and that most of the small colleges should become junior colleges; and that a university course should properly begin with the present junior year; and that the technical and professional schools should require two college years for entrance. The public took a hand, criticizing the theory of a gentleman's education and the abuse of the elective system, demanding discipline and rigor.

In fact, we were moving toward rigor and discipline, though with no giant strides. Entrance requirements were stiffened in several schools. The semiannual bust lists were of a severity unmatched today; occasionally 10 per cent of a class would be eliminated. A contemporary observer noted that many technical alumni were developing a caste or guild spirit; they wanted admission to their trade made as difficult as possible, "to keep the muckers out." [1]

The general educational facilities of the University varied from excellent to disgraceful.

A dozen years after its construction, the Library was reported in 1904 to be overcrowded, with 286,000 volumes. Then came the Willard Fiske Dante, Petrarch, and Icelandic Collections. And then the Fiske bequest of a half million, making the Library the best-endowed department of the University. But, as we have noted, the trustees applied the Fiske money to salaries and upkeep, thus releasing unrestricted funds for other purposes. When, in 1910–11, accessions dropped to 9,500 items from an annual average of 12,000, the campus outcry was so great that in 1912 a third of the Fiske fund was devoted to book purchases.[2]

Music began to receive a late and timid official recognition. In 1903 Hollis Dann became instructor in music, and full professor in 1907. He announced that his purpose was to promote interest, knowledge, and appreciation of music, not technical training for the few. Many enrolled in his two courses in vocal music. Mendelssohn's *Elijah* was sung in Sage Chapel in 1904, and annually thereafter an oratorio, or Music Festival, was presented. In the fall of 1904 David Bispham and the Cornell Glee Club gave, in Sibley Dome, the first concert under departmental auspices.

[1] Edwin E. Slosson, *Great American Universities* (New York, 1910), p. 331.
[2] "I understand that [Trustees Ira A.] Place and Senator [Frederick C.] Stevens were very emphatic indeed in their disapproval of the way that fund has been managed. Stevens said to me himself at President Schurman's house that he considered it 'disgraceful dishonesty' " (C. H. Hull to G. L. Burr, 20 May 1912, in Hull Papers).

Physical culture, like music, was long kept waiting at the doors of the official curriculum. C. V. P. ("Tar") Young '99, famous athlete, who had played on the varsity baseball and football teams for four years, was made professor of physical culture in 1904. His predecessor, Dr. Edward Hitchcock, was a physician; Tar Young came to his position by way of the ministry. For him exercise was less a medicine than a moral duty; and in fact he inspired a new enthusiasm in his department. He insisted that gym work should have the same academic standing and reward as other university work, and that opportunity to engage in athletic sports should be open to all male undergraduates.

The question of student health had long given the administration concern. The small Department of Hygiene had during most of our history restricted itself to giving physical examinations and excuses from university work. In 1911 Dr. Samuel A. Munford was appointed Medical Examiner, charged with supplying such care as would be usual in families—the lancing of boils, the application of emergency dressings, the tending of the corns which abounded in those days of tight, pointed shoes. Here was an implied admission that the University had some medical responsibility toward its students. Indeed, as Dr. Norman S. Moore and Dr. C. Douglas Darling have pointed out, the concept of medical care of students was changing.[3] It had rested on the conviction that a healthy body, a healthy mind, and a healthy soul were indivisible. But experience taught that muscular and spiritual development are not necessarily related. The inculcation of health began to draw apart from physical education.

The military establishment was fortunate in the detail to Cornell in 1904 of Frank A. Barton, M.E. '91, who had become a captain in the U.S. Cavalry. On his reassignment elsewhere in 1908, President Schurman bestowed on him a special encomium for his reinvigoration of the work at Cornell, and for his investing it with "a sentiment of regard and popularity such as it had never before enjoyed." Such reinvigoration came perhaps at a useful time. Andrew D. White noted in his diary for 5 December 1906: "Interview with Secretary of War Taft to prevent abolition of Military dept. at Cornell, and was, I think, successful."

With the rise in the importance of research, the Graduate Department gained in standing, and in 1909 was constituted a school, with its own dean. All agreed that we suffered a serious need for research professorships. Everyone quoted a remark of the famous physicist, Lord

[3] *Student Health and the Changing Order* (Ithaca, 1951), p. 6.

Kelvin, when he visited Cornell in 1904: "Our great universities should have in some of their chairs a leisure class of thinkers and investigators." Who would not long to be endowed as a member of a leisure class of thinkers and investigators? But who would provide such endowments?

Within the Academic Department, renamed the College of Arts and Sciences in 1903, the elective system was a constant subject of controversy. The President reported in 1902 that, while most student choices of studies were wisely made, many were ill considered, to say the least. He raised the question whether a faculty committee should inspect all student schedules. The Arts Faculty itself, well aware of the abuses of the elective system, or lack of system, favored obligatory guidance. The Briggs Report at Harvard in 1904 showed that the average Harvard student spent twelve hours weekly in class and thirteen hours in preparation. But this was an average; the earnest enthusiasts who spent fifty or sixty hours a week in study were balanced by idlers who accorded only a few rare hours a week to their formal education.

Our Committee on Educational Policy reported in June 1905 that Cornell gave its Arts students more freedom than did any of fourteen universities queried. A year later the Faculty adopted a system which, though much altered in detail, remains today the essential requirement of the college. This curricular system comprised two parts. The first part was intended to ensure Distribution, that is, the student's acquaintance with four areas of knowledge. He was required to take six credit hours in English and history, six in languages, six in philosophy and mathematics, six in science. The second part of the system ensured Concentration. At the beginning of the junior year the student chose one of twelve groups for his major study, and was required to complete twenty hours of work therein, under the direction of an adviser. These requirements, specifying only forty-four out of 120 required credit hours, certainly do not seem very onerous; one would think that every Arts and Sciences student would fulfill them without even intending to. However, the importance of the legislation lies in its marking the end of Free Election, and the beginning of Relative Freedom under Guidance. One may be tempted to see in this action a reflection of a similar shift in our national and social life.

The problems of the Arts College seem as fresh today, and as unresolved, as they did to those who reported them, proposing solutions, in the early nineteen-hundreds. There was the problem of the autonomy of departments versus the unifying action of the Dean. And the problem of vocationalism versus fundamentalism. In 1907–8 the faculty favored vocationalism, offering specific curricula preparatory to teaching, organized philanthropy, the civil service, and business management. There was the problem of the bored, apathetic student, the unintellectual, in short; should we labor with him or eject him? And there was the old problem whether we should divide the College of Arts and Sciences into a College of Arts and a College of Sciences.

Leaving such problems unsettled, we glance at some departmental particulars.

In Classics, Charles Love Durham was appointed professor of Latin in 1901. He came to Cornell as a fellow in 1896, and here took his Ph.D. "Bull" Durham, as he was inevitably called, made a deep impress on the campus. With his boyish geniality, his sonorous southern eloquence, his Horatian elegance, he was the undergraduates' delight during his active years. On his retirement he became the administration's ambassador to the alumni.[4]

In English, Martin Wright Sampson came in 1908 and was made chairman in 1909. An impassioned lover of beautiful thought and beautiful writing, he directed the work in English toward the appreciation of literature and toward the encouragement of original writing. A course in short-story writing, given from 1904–05 on, was certainly one of the first creative-writing courses in American colleges. The Manuscript Club, which met at Sampson's house every Saturday night, was the inspiration of a whole generation of Cornell authors. He gave readings regularly in Sibley in the evening dusk; a surprising number of overalled engineers attended them, and still remember them with emotion. He was staunchly supported in his department by William Strunk, Jr., whose *little* book, *Elements of Style*, has lived a new abundant life, thanks to his devoted pupil, E. B. White '21.

Lane Cooper came as instructor in 1902. His force of character and his utter devotion to the great literature of the past brought him a long succession of disciples, who in their turn have preached his message from many a professorial pulpit.

Psychology, under Titchener, broke loose from Philosophy in 1912 to become a Department. Titchener, an autocrat (to put it mildly),

[4] One anecdote among so many: after a club meeting downtown, two boys drove Bull home in the midnight. They became lost in the sinuosities of Cayuga Heights. They stopped at a roadside dwelling and rang the doorbell. Lights snapped on; an alarmed lady appeared in a wrapper. Said Bull, at his courtliest: "Madam, could you inform me of the location of the residence of Professor Durham?" "But you are Professor Durham!" "Madam, you are evading the question."

admitted no kind of psychology but his own to his curriculum. The Department of Education was forced to give its own courses in educational and developmental psychology, mental tests, and so forth.

History was fortunate in possessing a group of powerful scholars, unforgettable to those who sat thrice weekly in their courses. There was Charles H. Hull '86, omniscient, whimsical, with his five-minute sentences that always came out, and with a rare gift for the telling phrase. (Ed Woodruff, Dean of Law, remarked to him, of something or other: "His success depends on his environment." "What do you mean by *environment?* Do you mean his undershirt, or do you mean the starry firmament?") There was Ralph Catterall, a master in the blending of high thought and low comedy; and Henry Augustus ("Gussie") Sill, so warm and kindly, who carried on a perpetual comic war with Catterall; and of course there was George Lincoln Burr.[5]

The Department of History, and a good part of the faculty and the student body, were stirred by the case of Hendrik Willem van Loon '05. Van Loon, a gigantic, brilliant, unorthodox Netherlander, and one of the most amusing men that ever lived, took his Ph.D. from Munich, wrote some good—but popular—historical works, and served abroad as correspondent for the Associated Press. Retreating from the war, he was appointed lecturer in European history in 1915. He was an extraordinarily vivid lecturer, illustrating his evocations of the past with rapid sketches on large sheets of brown paper, which he would immediately tear off and trample underfoot. His audiences were enthralled, but not some of his colleagues, who heard tales of monstrous historical errors, and who saw their own classes dwindle in direct proportion to the increase of Van Loon's. They alleged that Van Loon's system instilled in the students little knowledge, and that little incorrect. Van Loon, piqued, gave his class a surprise prelim; and indeed it appeared that the class had learned very few facts indeed.

It was the old conflict of inspiration, though inaccurate, with scholarship, though dull. Van Loon had on his side Hull, Burr, Andrew D. White, and the entire student body. Against him were most of the remaining faculty of history. Schurman, with apparent reluctance, cast

[5] In 1903 President Schurman, about to address the freshman class on How to Study, asked advice from some staff members. Burr replied in words which should somehow be preserved as a statement of an aim of historical study: "I want my boys and girls to be broadened and deepened, mellowed and sweetened, by living the life of other men and other days, by living the larger life of cities and of people, by living themselves through all their past into their own present" (Schurman Papers).

the die against Van Loon. Much anger and reproach ensued among the students and alumni. The decision seemed a pity at the time, and seems so still. Cornell should be large enough to contain a man with Van Loon's rare virtues and common faults.

At any rate, Cornell's History Department did not suffer. Van Loon's field was entrusted (in 1917) to Carl Becker, who was to become one of America's greatest historiographers.

Becker was also one of the greatest men who have served on the Cornell faculty. Since his death in 1945 his reputation has steadily grown, as his books have been reprinted and his views discussed. His constant, central concern was the nature of historical truth. Profoundly skeptical, he could not accept the ready affirmations of many confident historians. He came to the conclusion that a re-creation of the past is only relatively true; but, though the absolute is unattainable, we must forever search for it, discarding the less true in favor of the more true. "The value of history is . . . not scientific but moral: by liberalizing the mind, by deepening the sympathies, by fortifying the will, it enables us to control, not society, but ourselves. . . . It prepares us to live more humanely in the present and to meet rather than to foretell the future." [6]

He was a shy, stolid man in his ordinary dealings. Though a brilliant stimulator of ideas in his informal seminars, he was a disappointment to undergraduates in his lecture course. *Time* published a sketch of him in 1934, asserting that he trembled in face of a class, and that he lectured in a voice too weak to fill the room. He replied: "I do not 'tremble.' On the contrary, nothing is more restful for me or, I should imagine, for the students either, than my lectures in modern history which are given at 3 P.M., a proper hour I have always thought for the siesta. If I cannot be heard beyond the front rows, so much the better, since no one wishes to be disturbed when taking a nap." [7]

Becker was essentially a writer, and he has left us some very sensible words on the art of writing. No more artful, scrupulous, witty prose than his has ever been penned on this campus.

The work in chemistry at Cornell was always regarded as superior, and in some aspects outstanding. Until 1901 Cornell and Wisconsin had the only professorships of physical chemistry, the specialty of Wilder

---

[6] Charlotte Watkins Smith, *Carl Becker: On History and the Climate of Opinion* (Ithaca, 1956), p. 117.

[7] Phil L. Snyder, ed., *Detachment and the Writing of History: Essays and Letters of Carl L. Becker* (Ithaca, 1958), p. 161.

Bancroft and J. E. Trevor. In 1904–5 a division of microchemical analysis was created in the department, and in the same year a division of sanitary chemistry and toxicology. In 1910–11 Bancroft offered a pioneer course in colloid chemistry.

Some perfunctory work was done in industrial chemistry, as had been done since our beginning. According to Fred H. Rhodes, historian of chemistry at Cornell, it lacked encouragement, since industry did not give recognition to trained men. The manufacture of chemical products was regarded as an art, not a science, and was based on rule-of-thumb procedures, with secret formulas and methods. The war, with its cutting off of chemical imports from Germany, changed all that. After Morse Hall burned in 1916, Fred Rhodes took over industrial chemistry in the general shake-up. He says himself: "Dr. Rhodes was peculiarly and doubly qualified to give the new course; he had done some work for the Anaconda Copper Co. on metallurgical problems and he had a book on industrial chemistry." Before long he turned his courses into Chemical Engineering.

The courses in chemistry were very extensive, and also very demanding. Students specializing in chemistry wished to spend all their time on chemistry and allied subjects and found the new distribution requirements in the Arts College irksome. The faculty of chemistry asked a great deal of its major students and in fact imposed its own required course. At the same time a good many professors in Arts, reading the catalogue, complained that much of the work in chemistry was technological rather than basically scientific; it should not be counted, said they, toward a degree of Bachelor of Arts. Schurman proposed to settle the dispute by establishing a College of Chemistry. He looked about for an endowment, but none was discernible. The Arts College settled therefore in 1910–11 on the establishment within the college of a fixed chemistry curriculum leading to the degree of B.Chem.

Physics continued to be an eminent department, at ease in its new Rockefeller Hall. It was animated by a splendid spirit of inventiveness, which was communicated to well-endowed students. Hannibal C. Ford '03, while still an undergraduate, built the first cathode ray oscillator used in America for the determination of wave form and power. (Later, as the animator of the Ford Instrument Company, he made many inventions; he has been called the founder of the science of naval gunfire control.)

From the Geology Department the most striking news of these years dealt with field trips. These had always been a local specialty. Professor

Gilbert D. Harris used his naphtha launch; Professor Ralph S. Tarr conveyed parties as far as Watkins Glen, a two-day trip, in surreys and tallyhos. Around 1910 the automobile truck, a kind of converted farm wagon with solid tires, became sturdy enough to transport the geologists, standing massed together, tossing over the deep-rutted roads. Then Mr. Dean, Ithaca entrepreneur, bought a lot of discarded church pews and bolted them to truck beds, and thus the Charter Bus Service began.

The Law School became more exacting in its entrance requirements and in its standards for graduation. In 1907 an optional four-year course, including a year of Arts work, was offered. In 1911 a year of college work was required for admission. In 1917 the school demanded two years in college as a qualification for entrance. Thus Cornell put itself abreast of the better current practice. The *Cornell Law Quarterly* began its distinguished career in 1915. Frank Irvine '80 was appointed to the faculty in 1901, and Charles K. Burdick, son of the Francis M. Burdick of the original Law faculty, in 1914.

The College of Architecture enjoyed a period of vigorous bloom. Its enrollment rose from 43 in 1899–1900 to 168 in 1916–17. It escaped in 1906 from intolerably crowded quarters in Lincoln Hall to the upper reaches of White and Franklin, which soon became intolerably crowded. Clarence A. Martin '88, becoming Director in 1904, found it his first duty to decide whether architecture should be taught as a science or as an art. There was no question in the mind of Pa Martin. Though he had begun his career as a carpenter, and was said to be very brilliant on such themes as winding back stairs, he chose Art. The architect, he insisted, must have a background of artistic appreciation and understanding. "There must be developed at Cornell a true art sentiment such as has yet had no material manifestation in the community at large," he wrote in his report for 1905. His purpose was seconded by Professors Olaf Brauner and George R. Chamberlain, who organized loan exhibitions in a temporarily converted Goldwin Smith classroom. (Childe Hassam lent fourteen pictures for the first show.)

An optional five-year course was established in 1914–15. A course in City Planning was offered in 1916–17, certainly one of the first in the country. But Landscape Design was forced from Architecture to Agriculture by the overcrowding in White Hall.

The Director's wife, Gertrude Shorb Martin '99, made an excellent statement of the Cornell policy in architecture.[8] In earlier days, she says, the first two years of the four-year course were given to general culture, the last two to technical training. But two years are not enough to make a passable draftsman, much less an Architect. Hence Cornell required that culture be obtained before matriculation; it set the highest entrance requirements in the country outside of Columbia's Graduate School of Architecture. Much of Cornell's curriculum resembled that of an art school, with nine hours weekly of freehand drawing and sketching in the first two years, plus six hours in water color. In the junior year, clay modeling, rendering, and so forth. In the senior year, life class. The student averaged about eight hours of such work throughout his course. Design, the core of the curriculum, began in the sophomore year.

Those were the great days of Beaux-Arts competitions, of *charrettes* and *esquisses en loge.* The students made dream pictures of glorious cloud-capped palaces, with little concern for construction and plumbing and none for expense. The Beaux-Arts attitude had its effect in early twentieth-century building, with its stone pomposities and whimsicalities, its festoons and astragals, its state capitols, monumental post offices, and palatial Newport cottages. A later generation of architects has mocked the Beaux-Arts style and acclaimed its own, stripped to skeleton purity. But if the history of taste teaches anything, it is that we should wait a hundred years before making positive statements about Beauty.

The students began to win important awards in national competitions. Edward G. Lawson '13 was the first Cornellian to receive the Prix de Rome in Landscape Architecture, offered by the American Academy in Rome. Then Raymond M. Kennedy '15 took the Prix de Rome in Architecture.

The engineering colleges stood at the height of their national reputation. Schurman noted in his report for 1901 that no Cornell engineering graduate was out of work, except by choice. Ten years later a surveyor of the college scene said: "A degree in engineering from Cornell is as good as gold." [9]

But Sibley College sustained a calamity in the sudden death of Director Robert H. Thurston in 1903, and Civil Engineering another in the passing of Director E. A. Fuertes in the same year. Eugene E. Haskell

[8] *Architectural Record,* July 1907.
[9] Slosson, *Great American Universities,* p. 326.

'79 succeeded Fuertes; Albert W. Smith '78 took the place of Thurston. Director Smith, "Uncle Pete" to many generations of Cornellians, was a man of broad interests and culture. He published at least one volume of poems and a half-dozen prose works, including lives of Ezra Cornell and John E. Sweet, and other Cornelliana.

Director Smith cleared away some superfluous departments, Naval Architecture, Marine Engineering, and Railway Mechanical Engineering. Mining Engineering, which had tempted administrators since our foundation, was briefly taught before disappearing for good. The Director's stated principle was that students would do best by spending their time on the fundamentals underlying all engineering. He did however permit the creation of the country's first Department of Industrial Engineering in 1904 (later Administrative Engineering), under Dexter S. Kimball, who had been on the staff since 1898 (with a three-year gap). He also reorganized the shopwork, abandoning the purpose of developing dexterity or handicraftsmanship as an end, and aiming to illustrate modern methods of manufacturing. A course in aerial engineering was offered in 1910–11; it included the physics of the atmosphere, aerodynamics, and the practical applications for the airplane builder. We had also courses in wireless telegraphy and telephony.

Uncle Pete, himself a humanist, insisted that the engineer should be a man of cultivation, at home in the various worlds of aesthetic and intellectual enterprise. Since the four-year curriculum in engineering left no moment for liberal education, he proposed that the course be lengthened to five years. Such optional courses were established in 1909–10. For a long time they did not attract many students.

Some well-known servants of Sibley and Cornell joined the faculty in these years. There was Herman Diederichs '97, and William Nichols Barnard '97, and Vladimir Karapetoff, the picturesque and ever original scientist, musician, and reformer. (He ran for Mayor of Ithaca on the Socialist ticket, with the slogan: "Make Ithaca a seaport!")

In these prewar years both Mechanical and Civil Engineering attained their largest enrollments in our history. In Sibley the peak was attained in 1909–10, with 1,186 students. The number fell off to 902 in 1913–14, and rose again to 955 in 1916–17. In Civil Engineering the highest enrollment was 569 in 1908–9. Thenceforth the numbers dropped steadily to 409 in 1916–17.

Why? The downcurve was not taken as a reproach to the new administrations of the colleges; it was part of a national trend. The *Bulletin of the Society for the Promotion of Engineering Education* in November 1913 plotted a curve for fifty-five engineering schools, showing that over-all enrollments rose up to 1909, then fell off markedly. The causes assigned for the decrease were the raising of standards, the new popularity of agricultural and commercial courses, and the widespread belief that the engineering profession was overcrowded.

This was true enough; but clearly all was not well with Engineering. We were a little inclined to rest on our laurels. Our quarters and equipment were already antiquated. We lost more well-known engineers from our faculty than we gained. We had to sustain a new fierce competition from western rivals, lavishly supported by prideful legislatures. And our static salaries did no good to our morale.

The Summer School boomed. No longer a set of informal enterprises of faculty groups, it became an important unit in the educational system. There were background reasons for the change: the increasing professionalization of education; the relative leisure of a prosperous period, which gave to many more idle time than they wanted, and sent them to Chautauquas and summer institutes; and the widespread custom of learning something by taking a course, not by private study and experiment. There were more specific reasons: the stiffening of high-school curricula, sending many teachers back to school, and the establishment of the four-quarter system at the University of Chicago, which set a principle of continuous college work.

At any rate, the Summer School grew steadily, to reach an enrollment of 1,846 in 1915–16. It became self-supporting for the first time in 1912–13. It included special summer schools in Agriculture and in Architecture. It gave intensive courses in elementary languages; it offered delightful field trips; life in the Summer School came to be much relished, both by earnest teachers from the great hot cities, and by students who were abbreviating their college course, or who had had scholastic misfortunes, and who idled in drowsy, nearly empty fraternity houses, and spent happy sunny Sundays on the lake in canoes, and happy dusks in Renwick Park, or in the twinkling streets of Ithaca, where the cool smell of beer was wafted out from under swinging doors.

XXVI

The New Century: Prewar Cornellians

WE came to college wearing our new suit from the home-town clothier, kollege kut, with long loose high-shouldered coat and high-water trousers. Clocked silk socks winked above sharp-prowed patent leather shoes, even with buttoned cloth tops. Our head was upheld by a tall stiff collar (Clifton, Field Club, or Devon), meeting in front and barely masking our knitted four-in-hand, with bright horizontal stripes and bearing a roguish stickpin at the correct angle. On our head we wore a flat-topped felt hat with a gay hatband. (Extremists turned up the brim in front to meet the crown, thus revealing the face in all its luster.)

We were met at the station by compets from the Student Agencies, bearing a red *S* on their white felt hats.[1] By them we were convoyed to the rooming-house district on East Hill, shown into immaculate student rooms, invited by courtly landladies to admire the steam radiator, the morris chair, the bath on every floor. We attended Get-Wise meetings and football rallies, signed blindly for the publications and an athletic

[1] The Student Agencies became a valuable property, annually sold by Board to Board. In 1910 the Student Agencies was incorporated. It was and is a serious business, with an annual volume of $250,000, and also a college honor, complete with competitions and hats. Its business training has well served a long line of Cornellians.

season ticket, bought a frosh cap. We were told strange tales by solemn sophomores, as for instance that we would get better service from Davy Hoy by tipping him a quarter.

We soon learned, had we not known it before, that a caste system existed at Cornell. At the top soared a half dozen of the best fraternities, though no one could define wherein their superiority lay. Below these were several grades of fraternities, ranging down to scrimy; and still lower groveled certain professional and religious rooming clubs. Under all these elect lived in a vast plebeian mass the Independents, the outsiders, the pills, the poops, the drips. They composed about two-thirds of the male student body. They were the rustic, the repellent, the unsociable, the overearnest in study. They were also the poor, who worked for their education. They were the nonconformists, at whom the fraternities took fright. And they were often the superior, who refused the subjections and the juvenilities of the fraternities. Many of the men of whom Cornell is proudest, to whom it is most grateful, were in their time pills, poops, and drips.

Some of the fraternities seemed more than luxurious to outsiders. They were modeled on the gentlemen's clubs of the great cities, then rich and arrogant, now mostly beloved anachronisms, if not merely memories. Chi Psi, in the Fiske-McGraw mansion, outdid them all; but the Alpha Delta Phi lodge with its separate temple set a new note in 1903, and Delta Phi occupied Llenroc, Ezra Cornell's splendid home, in 1911. The allurements of luxury to idle wealthy youth disturbed the President. "Rich parents send their sons to college as in summer they send them to the seashore or the mountains," he said in his 1907 report. The fact seemed to him surprising.

Foreign students arrived in increasing numbers, most of them to be classed among the Independents. Six Hindus entered the College of Agriculture in 1905, the first of a considerable annual migration. Half of the Boxer Indemnity, imposed on China after the Boxer Rebellion of 1900, was used to send Chinese students to the United States. (This precedent later inspired Senator Fulbright's system of scholarships.) From the first, Cornell was one of the colleges most favored by the Chinese. (There was an historic event in the summer of 1915. Some Chinese students went canoeing on the lake. A squall came up; a girl student was soaked. The party landed, built a fire, and dried out her clothes. Hoong C. Zen '16 celebrated the adventure in a poem; Hu Shih '14 criticized its traditional poetic diction. A controversy started which grew and spread until it became a literary revolution in China, with Hu Shih, professor of philosophy at the University of Peking, at its head. To put it briefly, he imposed on China the use of the vernacular as a literary language, and thus bridged the chasm between the scholars and the mass.)

Some racial discrimination existed. A southern student withdrew in 1900 because there were two colored men in his class. In 1911 two colored coeds applied for rooms in Sage, and 269 women undergraduates petitioned that they be excluded. President Schurman would hear nothing of this. He said: "All university doors must remain open to all students, irrespective of color or creed or social standing or pecuniary condition. The last colored woman student who resided in Sage College writes me that she was politely and considerately treated by the other women students, and that these years of residence in Sage College were the happiest in her life." [2]

Anti-Semitism, barely perceptible in the early days, became more pronounced, as a mass movement from Polish ghettoes and the Ukraine disturbed the social structure of our cities. The fraternities ceased, generally, to enroll Jewish members, and Jewish fraternities appeared. The first was Zeta Beta Tau, in 1907. Jewish students complained of discrimination on the publications and in other activities. They were probably justified; but of course, one never knows when one is discriminated against as a group member and when as an individual. As individuals we are all discriminated against, all the time; that is the corollary of freedom.

The Independents led a restricted, often dreary life. They had no escape from their lodging-houses, except the rather prim public rooms of the C.U.C.A., no club except the downtown billiard parlors. They had indeed some social intercourse in the boardinghouses, mostly College Avenue half-basements. According to Romeyn Berry's investigations in local cultural anthropology, these were the Alma Maters of fraternities.

I suspect that more than half of our fraternities were born of student boardinghouses, without knowing it. It was a matter of unconscious social evolution. The congenial table of one year became the private alcove of the next. When gaps appeared about the board, the survivors took thought to fill them with pleasant persons of their own selection. The table gave itself a name and something like a self-perpetuating organization followed. From there on, it was just a series of logical steps to a rented house and a charter from some Greek letter fraternity. Doubtless, the official history now starts

[2] *Alumni News,* 12 April 1911.

with the rented house and the organization of the local club, ignoring the student boardinghouse that unwittingly spawned the Cornell chapter of Sigma Delta Whoop.[3]

The boardinghouses were usually cheap and rarely very good. Professor Walter F. Willcox made a statistical investigation in 1911–12 and found that the student's average board bill was $4.53, his room rent $2.82. But even in the poorest boardinghouses, where one was nourished for $3.00 a week, white-jacketed student waiters transported the food from kitchen to table, and one was assured of chicken fricassee and ice cream on Sunday. Undergraduate mores were altered by the advent of the cafeteria, first announced as a feature of the coming Home Economics Building, in April 1911. By 1916 the cafeteria almost displaced the boardinghouse. Romeyn Berry did not like the change. He found the cafeteria unsociable, the tray bearer inclined to teeter off into a social void in the manner of a dog with a bone.

Though the center of student life was moving up the hill, with clusters of shops on Eddy Street and College Avenue, downtown was still familiar to undergraduates. The merchants, like Louis Bement of the Toggery Shop, befriended the students, and not entirely from mercenary motives. Pinochle Wells gained fame as a secondhand clothes dealer and as a private banker. Certain bars and cafés, the Dutch, the Senate, offered a warm welcome to all but freshmen, who could console themselves in the Alhambra, Meany's, the Stag, or the Office. (Romeyn Berry adds Puss Hammond's and Joe Brost's, but these I cannot substantiate.)

The Lyceum Theatre became aware of competition from the cinematograph. The early films were shown in vacant stores, converted by the installation of wooden chairs and the hiring of a piano and a piano player. No provision was made for ventilation. Five cents was charged for admission to the Happy Hour, the Billiken, the Manhattan, the Lyric. In 1911 the Star (lately the Ithaca College gymnasium) was built on Seneca Street, showing five acts of vaudeville as well as a feature picture. The Crescent followed; and the theatre gained the adjective "legitimate," and not long after its legitimation it fell into its long agony.

The first Ithaca movies were made by Lyman H. Howe, producer of full-length documentary films. On 14 October 1911 he took shots of students leaving the Armory after the President's address. In the summer of 1913 Theodore W. Wharton and Francis X. Bushman made a

[3] *Behind the Ivy* (Ithaca: Cornell University Press, 1950), p. 40.

two-reeler, mostly in Fall Creek gorge, entitled *The Hermit of Lonely Gulch*. The youthful Louis Sumner Fuertes '27 played the important role of Little Ned. Other stirring dramas were enacted in following years. There was a fight to the death on the Suspension Bridge; an automobile with two lifelike occupants went over the brink of Taughannock; a streetcar plunged from the Stewart Avenue Bridge to the gorge below; a wooden submarine disgorged its German crew off Stewart Park; and a frightful marine disaster occurred off the Remington Salt Works. Pearl White (of *The Perils of Pauline*), Beverly Bayne, Irene Castle walked our streets like ordinary mortals, and many students and Ithacans played in background roles, for the fun of it. (The Actors' Equity was yet unthought-of.) [4]

Adventurous, mechanical-minded students began to buy motor cars or motorcycles, and with them to explore the countryside. There was also a vogue for walking in jolly bands into the southern hills, or over the successive western ridges to Watkins. One could still find in the country cultural pockets where old customs, old speech, lingered, where distances were reckoned in rods and furlongs and prices in York shillings. William Wigley '07, in the engineers' summer camp, was one of a group that asked a farmer for a drink. He brought them a pitcher of metheglin, the Welsh honey brew, which magicked them strangely.[5] Lynn B. Mitchell, Ph.D. '06, was inspired to walk with a party to Watkins one moonlit night. He recalls (in a private letter): "You will hardly believe it, but when we were about half way to the Glen, we passed through a small town [Mecklenburg] about 3 A.M., and a watchman was going about, carrying a lantern and shouting: 'Three o'clock and all's well!' "

Cayuga Lake allured many, in the warm days of spring and early fall. Canoes were rentable from Johnson's Livery. But these were peri-

[4] Louis Wolheim '06, fearsome broken-nosed athlete and for a time instructor in mathematics, here began a distinguished career of stage villainy. Many still remember his Sergeant Quirt in *What Price Glory*. S. E. Hunkin '17 contributed an interesting bit of dramatic-literary history to the *Alumni News* of January 1954. In 1914, he said, Wolheim was cigar clerk in the Ithaca Hotel, where Lionel Barrymore lodged. Barrymore liked Wolheim, and was struck by his theatrical possibilities. Calling on Eugene O'Neill in New York, Barrymore found him asleep with his usual hangover. While waiting for him to rouse, Barrymore read a stray manuscript, entitled *The Hairy Ape*. O'Neill wanted to tear it up, as no gorilla was available to play the role of the stoker. Barrymore offered to supply one, sent for Wolheim, drilled him through the rehearsals, and obtained one of O'Neill's first great successes.

[5] Wigley, Diaries (MS, C.U. Archives), p. 122.

lous craft; five students were drowned in 1913. Cold winters, as in 1903, permitted skate sailing on the lake. In February 1912 Cayuga froze over from end to end. Floyd R. Newman '12, George I. Dale '10, and three other Bandhus skated the forty miles to Cayuga, at the north end, a brave but dangerous deed. Only two days later two emulators were drowned.

Student behavior was at first generally commended. University discipline, originally administered by the faculty as a whole and later by the separate colleges, gradually got out of hand as our numbers increased. A University Committee on Student Conduct was formed in 1902. Shortly afterward a Student Self-Governing Council was set up; it did not seem to work very well. In 1911 a Philadelphia policeman and ex-cavalryman, Theodore H. Twesten, was appointed Proctor. Immense, genial, radiant with good will, he was warmly received by the students, and was in great demand at fraternity gatherings as an analyst of Custer's Last Stand. The Student Council as we know it today was formed in 1915.

Misdemeanors and altercations occurred, of course. For a time (October 1911) there was a vogue for whirling the speedy revolving doors of the new Post Office. One student was shot as from a sling fifteen feet into the Post Office, and was arrested. A mild correction administered to freshmen by their elders was to hold them up to kiss the statue of Purity given by the W.C.T.U. and crowning the drinking fountain opposite the police station. ("Purity" was later banished and eventually sold for scrap; herein we may perceive a certain symbolism.) In 1916 the custom flourished of debagging offending freshmen, even in the heart of the business district. And there was the theatre riot of February 1911, when the students broke up a performance of *Three Weeks* at the Lyceum by throwing coins, potatoes, and eggs at the actors. Having manifested a critical judgment which was generally sustained, the demonstrators marched to the Happy Hour Theatre, where they were held off by the police. Several were arrested and sentenced to a week in jail. To one of them, Ralph Perkins '14, Andrew D. White sent a copy of *Les Misérables*, with the message that a week's tranquillity should be welcome for the sake of rereading the book. Surely Mr. White chuckled at his own choice of the adventures of an escaped jailbird.[6]

Drinking was not generally a serious problem. For most students it was confined to the ritual celebration of athletic victories, of which,

[6] Personal letter from Arthur S. Wells '14.

indeed, there were a good many. Those years marked the apogee of the prohibition movement, which treated drinking as a personal sin, as well as a social plague. Even the class banquets, at which old tradition decreed that the participants should become "piffed," turned dry. The President announced that drunkenness would be punished by immediate dismissal.

Class feeling, and hostility, dwindled, with the increasing heterogeneity of the institution. The class rush had traditionally taken place at the University's opening; the sophs defended Cascadilla Bridge against the frosh trying to enter the campus. The classes voted to abolish this dangerous frolic in 1908. Organized mud-rushes took its place for a few years; then these too died, as the students grew contemptuous of "collech" behavior. More honored were indigenous ceremonials, like that of the Architects' St. Patrick's Day snake, a hundred feet long, pursuing a frog and himself pursued by St. Patrick. The snake perambulated the campus and was immolated on the Library Slope.

Spring Day originated in 1901. The festival of 1905 had sensational repercussions. It was announced, with a fairly straight face, as a bullfight, a *corrida de toros*, with imported *toreros*. The parading fighters were in fact genuine Mexican students, wearing genuine costumes. The bull, however, was a fantastic structure built on a baby carriage and propelled by a student. This bull was solemnly fought and killed according to all the ancient rites. By the fault of an unscrupulous Ithaca reporter, the most hair-raising tales appeared in the metropolitan press. It was said that the bulls were specially developed by the College of Agriculture, that President Schurman closed the University so that everyone might enjoy the horrid spectacle, that a matador was unhorsed and three bulls killed, while women screamed and fainted. Indignant letters poured in from animal lovers of the entire country.

Social events, such as Junior Week and Senior Week, were decorous indeed, by modern standards. Drinking was firmly banned; a suspicion of alcohol on the breath called for expulsion from the floor. Romeyn Berry remembers the junior proms in the Old Armory,

with George Coleman's orchestra playing the waltzes in a balcony temporarily erected over the North sally port and Patsy Conway's Band doing the two-steps from another balcony over the door that leads down to the locker room and the swimming pool. Mr. Alberger served supper in the gymnasium, which had been cleansed for the occasion but not completely deodorized. He gave the dowagers hot chicken patties one year and hot oyster patties the next, accompanied by potato croquettes, little sandwiches, ice cream, and cake, for sixty-five cents. Old Prom chairmen will recall how indignant they were when in 1905 Mr. Alberger raised the price to seventy cents on account of the high cost of living.[7]

Such occasional gayeties as Spring Day and Junior Week did not fairly represent the workaday mood of normal undergraduate life. The purely social, or Hat Clubs, which had no other purpose than to confer on their members the right to wear a peculiar hat, were frowned upon by the student editors and leaders. In 1913 the senior societies and a number of fraternities took action against them. Most of them succumbed to public disapproval, but Mummy and Nalanda survived by the simple expedient of changing their names to Beth L'Amed and Majura.

Something brazenly termed an intellectual revival was noted on the campus. To anyone familiar with British or continental universities it was mild indeed, but in comparison with earlier times student concern with philosophical and social speculation, with writing, music, art, and unprofessional studies was certainly increasing. Such concern was strongest among the Independents, for the fraternities, with their social distractions and their massed competition for college honors, were generally unpropitious to the meditative mood.

Cornell has never posed as a nursemaid of literary genius. She has nurtured young authors as it were absent-mindedly, while teaching her brood to deal with the world's tangible realities. Still, the list is striking of those who have gained distinction in the trade of words. One who contemplates this list, which had best be consigned to Excursus III, will observe that many of the authors congregate around certain years, or nodes. We had an outburst of authors around 1904, around 1914, around 1921, around 1951. Mutual stimulation is necessary to the young writer, to transform his coagulated emotions into prose and verse. (Literary history is largely a history of groups.) Such a stimulation was provided for a time by Professor Martin Sampson's Manuscript Club, which gave the literary aspirants a precious chance to write, to be heard, and to be sharply criticized. The new courses in Creative Writing, inaugurated about 1947, have already borne their published fruit.

Many clubs of the early century manifested intellectual pretensions. The Cosmopolitan Club, formed in 1904 to provide cultural and social opportunities for foreign students, opened its rather forbidding house in 1911, and there assembled, in 1913, a convention of *Corda Fratres*,

---

[7] *Behind the Ivy*, p. 242.

which, inspired by Cornell, had become the Cosmopolitan Clubs of the World.

Mr. Lucien L. Nunn, who made his first fortune in the Telluride mine in Colorado, brought to us the Telluride Association. (He apparently picked a site and built the Telluride house without authorization, so that Telluride is technically tenant-at-sufferance of the University.) The sumptuous building was opened in 1910, to demonstrate Mr. Nunn's educational doctrines, then surely unique in America. The association would select a group of young men of exceptional promise and give them release from all material concern, a background of culture, the responsibility for managing their own household, and the stimulation of dwelling with resident faculty members and eminent visitors. President Schurman, in his report for 1909, offered the Telluride plan as a model for future university residential halls.[8]

Other clubs with intellectual aspirations appeared: Book and Bowl, the Civic Club, the Graduate Club, the Socialist Club, the Art Association, the Sunday Night Club, and several debate clubs.

Many congregations clung to the University's departments, e.g., the English Club, the Philosophical Club, and the various foreign-language clubs. Some of these distinguished themselves by producing plays. The English Club put on *Twelfth Night* and other Shakespearean dramas. A French dramatic club, Les Cabotins, produced two farces in Barnes Hall in 1903, and in the following year took over the Lyceum for a full-length comedy, *Le Monde où l'on s'ennuie*. For several years thereafter a French classic was annually performed in the Lyceum, scoring a financial as well as an artistic success. One marvels that paying audiences for such enterprises could then be found.

The Deutscher Verein took fire, and put on *Alt Heidelberg*, with music, first in Ithaca and then in the German Theatre, New York, in 1908. This was so well received that the Deutscher Verein obtained from the New York theatre the scenery, costumes, and equipment, valued at $10,000, for Schiller's *Wilhelm Tell*. It was performed in the Lyceum in December 1910, and a brilliant production it was, as your historian remembers after fifty years. After this unsurpassable feat the German Department seems to have fallen back exhausted, or perhaps rebellious, for during the long preparation for the performance the department members as well as the actors could attend to nothing else.

[8] *Alumni News*, 1 Dec. 1932. See an interesting statement of Mr. Nunn's convictions and principles by Elmer M. Johnson '22, Chancellor of Telluride, in the *Alumni News*, 13 March 1946.

The drama in English likewise throve. At the century's incoming the Masque was uncertain as to the direction it should take. In 1901 it produced *The Taming of the Shrew*, enlisting the aid of four coeds. In 1904 it staged its first comic opera, *Anno 1992*. The spectacle of heavy-footed bass-voiced "chorines" proved so irresistible that the Masque clung to its formula until, and after, transvestite comedy lost its salt. Oldsters still recall with gusto *Popocaterpillar, The Misfit Man, The President of Oolong*, and other facetiae, the texts of which are now buried in kindly oblivion. The Savage Club also, whose specialty was the "stunts" so dear to the early century, began giving public performances in 1903. The stuntster par excellence was Jake Fassett '12, who gained fame on the professional stage as Jay Fassett.

The concentration of the Masque on the broader forms of comedy opened the way to the adepts of serious drama. The Cornell Dramatic Club was organized in 1909, through the efforts of James A. Winans, chairman of Public Speaking, and his assistant, Smiley Blanton (who took his Cornell M.D. in 1914 and became a famous psychiatrist and writer). Ibsen's *An Enemy of the People* was the Club's first production; then annually it put on at the Lyceum a full-length play, by Ibsen, Gogol, Henry Arthur Jones, Pinero.[9]

Alexander M. Drummond of Public Speaking became Director in 1912. He manifested such exceptional ability that his fame spread far beyond our walls, as a producer, as playwright and play-carpenter, and as a trainer of budding actors. He fitted up Goldwin Smith B as a theatre, in 1917—a sorry makeshift, but the club was glad to have any home of its own.

Music meanwhile flourished, under the direction of the new department. The times were propitious. The opera (with Caruso, Schumann-Heink, Mary Garden, Geraldine Farrar, and the rest) imposed itself on the national consciousness, symphony orchestras drew popular support, the pianola and the phonograph brought music into numberless homes, and the serious study of music became respectable. Hollis Dann elevated, though not dangerously, the quality of the music sung by the Glee Club, and George L. Coleman '95 organized a University Orchestra in 1904.

We cannot here review the activities of the multitudinous clubs, which served to promote special interests and make friends of the like-

[9] For the origins of the Dramatic Club see Barnard W. Hewitt '28 in *A Half-Century at Cornell* (Ithaca, 1930), and an important letter from Will Rose '11 in the *Alumni News,* Jan. 1957; also 16 Nov. 1933.

minded. Two, however, arouse a pallid curiosity in the searcher among old records. The first is the Agassiz Club, composed of fanatic naturalists. At their annual banquet in June 1910, held appropriately by a brookside, they dined on fried lampreys caught in the Inlet and cooked at a campfire, and watercress sandwiches, prepared on the spot, and dandelion coffee, and greens and birch bark. The second club was the Cornell Aero Club, formed in 1909, which offered (without credit) a course in the theory, construction, and manipulation of gliders. They did their gliding behind the College of Agriculture. In November 1911 Charles H. Wetzel '13 broke the intercollegiate glider record for altitude and distance. Drawn by an automobile speeding at 30 miles an hour, he rose 40 feet from the ground and flew 500 feet.

(And by the way, Charles M. Manly '98 can be called, by a technicality, the first airplane pilot. He assisted Dr. Samuel P. Langley in building his "aerodrome" and piloted it at its trials in 1903. The machine was launched by a catapult, and plunged immediately into the Potomac River. Manly was awarded a medal posthumously by the Smithsonian Institution. And by the way within by the way, Edmund W. Roberts '95, who wrote his senior thesis on aeronautics, worked on Hiram Maxim's four-ton steam-powered biplane, which, he says, in the summer of 1894 flew 200 feet before crashing. Roberts later developed the Roberts Motor Company in Sandusky, a leading early maker of airplane motors.)

Among the publications, the *Cornell Countryman* began its distinguished career in 1903, the *Cornell Veterinarian* in 1911, the *Cornell Law Quarterly* in 1915.

The *Sun* developed into a serious and responsible business enterprise. It was incorporated in 1905, establishing thus its status as an independent business, related to the university only by the membership of its editors in the student body. In 1909 it became actually a morning newspaper, justifying its title. It was printed after midnight and distributed in the dawn. Its readership increasing with the expanding university, it was enlarged to eight pages, and it arranged for a service of "Telegraphic News of the Morning" from the New York *World*. This led in 1912 to a franchise from the Associated Press. The *Sun* prized its independence, its freedom of opinion and right to make uncensored criticisms. The Editor's occasional impulse to abuse this independence has commonly been checked by the Business Manager's terror of financial calamities, and particularly of damage suits. The financial responsibilities, and rewards, were great. Stanton Griffis '10 recalls that in his senior year as Editor he made $3,000, in cash and trade. That was the salary of a full professor, and would be equivalent to at least $10,000 today.

The *Era* was by no mean so affluent. The *Sun* had driven it from its original function as a news weekly and bulletin; the *Alumni News* took over its role as a dispenser of alumni notes; the *Widow* usurped the field of light comedy. The *Era* tried to be a literary magazine, but found the costs high and the field barren. In 1910 it took the muck-raking magazines, *McClure's, Hampton's, Collier's,* as its models, and tried to horrify the campus with photographs of ominous cracks in the Armory wall, and of thumb-printed pats of butter allegedly served in College Avenue boardinghouses. At such revelations the public twitched only lethargically.

"Sensation" became the journalists' watchword, their monotonous editorial rule. In November 1913 the *Widow* published a Temptation Number. This is a curious document in the history of journalistic and social convention. The cover shows a vaguely Polynesian female, overdressed by modern beach standards, patting on the chin one of those crabbed, ungainly, white-bearded creatures which represented, to the *Widow*, the Professor. The original drawing of this and other innocuous comicalities drew large crowds when displayed in a State Street window. The W.C.T.U. and the Federation of Women's Clubs termed the issue "highly subversive to the public morals." A survey of the text reveals several jests which braved the current proprieties of print. Extreme examples are:

"Let there be light," piped the sacrilegious mut, as he spied the maid in the X-ray gown.

He: I'll bet you are chicken. Aren't you now? She: Yes, I'm chicken all right, but I'm not scratching for you.

> Mary's skirt was trim and tight,
> But she slit it right in half,
> So all the people on the street
> Could see the "fatted calf."

For these offenses against morality and good taste, the *Widow's* Editor was suspended, and the Art Editor put on probation. The Editor took his punishment lightly. He immediately found a good newspaper job on the sole ground of his sensational suspension.

Athletic enthusiasm—or overemphasis, or madness, if you prefer—rose to its apogee. The celebrations of victory, the lamentations for defeat, reached an intensity never since equaled. It was an accepted axiom that the undergraduate's first duty was to Support the Teams. He was expected to spend his afternoons critically observing practice, his Saturdays attending games, and many of his evenings at rallies and pep talks. Sports reporting became one of the chief industries of the journalistic world. Various results ensued: the athletic Hero received an adulation approaching deification, which unsettled many a Hero for life; betting on games became habitual, alarming moralists and social philosophers; the temptations of glory and profit in amateur athletics led to many improprieties, to put it mildly. At Cornell we escaped many of the familiar reproaches. The disguised professional player did not come here, because he could not get in or stay in. Our isolation, before the day of the universal automobile, kept the attendance at sports events small, gate receipts low, and temptation to ill-doing slight.

However, what disturbed President Schurman and other observers was the tendency of athletics to concentrate on the few. Every advantage was given to candidates for the teams, while the average undergraduate, content to be a critical spectator, had little encouragement or opportunity for exercise. It was for such students that the alumni gave the fifty-acre Alumni Field, in the hope that every student would join in some sort of healthful play. To promote this end, the professor of physical education, C. V. P. Young, organized a grandiose program of intramural athletics. The President reported proudly in 1911 that about three thousand students, three-fourths of the males, were taking regular exercise. (But all Sunday sports were long prohibited.)

The Cornell crews under Courtney carried on their monotonous record of supremacy. In 1901 at Poughkeepsie they set a world's record for the four-mile: 18 minutes 53⅕ seconds. This stood apparently until 1928. There was another remarkable crew in 1905; at Poughkeepsie it finished a quarter-mile ahead of its nearest pursuer. From May 1909 on, the several crews, varsity, junior varsity, four-oar, freshmen, won every intercollegiate contest, eighteen of them, until June 1911, when by some oversight the freshmen lost to Columbia. We then won six more, until in May 1913 the spell was broken. Courtney's over-all record of success was certainly unapproached in all history. In his years at Cornell his crews won ninety-eight victories in 146 races, including fourteen out of twenty-four Intercollegiate Rowing Association varsity contests. His boys made seven clean sweeps in intercollegiate regattas.

Such was the power, which it is not too much to call genius, of a great coach. But Courtney was no fanatic, who lived for victory alone. Speaking to an alumni gathering in early 1914, he uttered a blast against the overworking of college athletes, against big business in the graduate manager's office, against overscheduling of contests, against the pressure to persuade athletes to neglect their education, and against other excesses.[10] His words must have surprised his hearers. He sounded much less like a coach than like a faculty critic of coaches.

In 1915, on the train to the Poughkeepsie races, Courtney was thrown against a berth and sustained a head injury. He made light of it, refusing to see a doctor. But after the race (which Cornell won) it was recognized that his injury was serious and lasting. He continued to coach, but without the old-time vigor. He died in 1920, at the age of seventy.

The assistant coach, for a time, was John L. Collyer '17. As he has told your historian, he conceived the project of taking over Cascadilla School and becoming in time its honored headmaster, and of course crew coach. But circumstances, which included war, were unfavorable. He became instead president of the B. F. Goodrich Company and was for years Chairman of Cornell's Board of Trustees, tasks which indicate that he would have made an excellent headmaster.

Cornell football had seldom been of championship quality. The reasons are not far to seek. Administration and faculty would rarely make any concessions to athletes; athletic scholarships, if they existed at all, did so under disguises so effective that they might as well not have existed; laboratories lasted late into the afternoon, and then the candidates had to walk or run a mile down Gun Hill to Percy Field, where the autumnal dark was already descending. (Effective floodlights had not yet come.) Yet in spite of all we began to turn out some excellent teams. In 1901 we lost only to Princeton, 6 to 8. William J. Warner '03 of that team was chosen all-American guard, and Henry ("Heinie") Schoellkopf '02 was an outstanding player. (Heinie was a beloved gentle giant; once, it seems, he dove 70 feet into a gorge pool to rescue a drowning dog.) In 1913 Cornell defeated Penn, for the second time in twenty years, with a score of 21 to 0. The celebration, in Ithaca and Philadelphia, was something like the Bolshevik Revolution. Our best season was in 1915, our first on Schoellkopf Field, when we won nine,

[10] *Alumni News,* 5 Feb. 1914.

lost and tied none, to be named national champions. No touchdown was made through our lines in eighteen games in 1914 and 1915. Those were the years of Charles Barrett, Murray Shelton, Paul Eckley, Gib Cool, Fritz Shiverick, Fred Gillies.

In track, the effects of Jack Moakley's coaching appeared. In 1901 we triumphed at the Intercollegiate Games held at the Pan-American Exposition in Buffalo. Warren E. Schutt '05 won the Intercollegiate cross-country in 1904. But he went to Oxford as Cornell's first Rhodes Scholar and was lost to us. Some good performances are reported, by Edward Cairns '05, Joseph N. Pew '08, Anton Vonnegut '05, and others. In 1905 we won for the first time the Intercollegiate track and field meet; the championship had previously been passed around among Harvard, Yale, and Penn. We won the meet again in 1906 and in 1908. In the Olympic Games for 1908 Eddie Cook '09 tied for first in the pole vault at 12 feet 2 inches, and Harry F. Porter '05 won the high jump with 6 feet 3 inches. Both were new Olympic records. John Carpenter '08 won the 400 meters, but an unwarranted cry of "Foul!" along the course brought an order for the race to be run over, and this all the American contestants refused to do. One evening in 1909 Lee J. Talbot '11 threw the hammer over the Percy Field fence; this would have been an intercollegiate record if it had been measurable. Next year he broke the record officially, with a toss of 173 feet 6 inches.

The 1911 team was a very great one. The four-mile relay team (Herb Putnam, Tell Berna, John Paul Jones and either Ed Hunger or Leon Finch) made two successive world's records. We won the 1911 Intercollegiates with a team called the greatest collection of athletes ever assembled for a college meet. John Paul Jones broke the world's amateur record for the mile with 4:15⅖, and twenty minutes later set a new American record for the half-mile of 1:54⅘. In 1912 Tell Berna broke the American record for the two-mile (which stood till 1929); and in 1913 Jones made a world's record in the mile of 4:14⅖, which was unbroken for many years. At the Olympics in 1912 Alma Richards '17 (not yet a Cornellian) won the high jump, Jones was fourth in the 1,500 meters, Tell Berna ran on the winning 3,000-meter relay team, and Herb Putnam and two or three other Cornellians competed.

In 1914 we took the Intercollegiate track championship for the fifth time, thus gaining permanent possession of the first ICAAAA trophy. Dave Caldwell '14 beat Olympic champion Ted Meredith of Penn in the half-mile, and set a record of 1:53⅖, and C. L. Speiden won the mile. In 1915 Frank Foss '17 vaulted 12 feet 10 inches; and Alma Richards high-jumped 6 feet 5 inches for a collegiate record. (Notice that both these figures surpass the Olympic records for 1908.) Again we won the Intercollegiates, and again in 1916, when Linus Windnagle '17 won the mile in 4:15, and when Cornellians, led by Daniel F. Potter '16, finished first, second, third, and fourth in the two-mile.

All this was very fine. At the same time many of the track men were doubling on the cross-country teams, which now became a Cornell specialty. From 1899, when the cross-country Intercollegiates began, until 1921, we were the winners in seventeen out of twenty-one contests. In 1914 we had a dual race with Harvard and made an actually perfect score. The first seven finishers counted; the first eight across the line were Cornellians.

This almost absurd record of success was due mostly to the coaching of Jack Moakley. It was abetted, however, by conditions: by the daily hill-climbing journeys of the undergraduates and by the general vogue for cross-country walks and runs. (Even your historian, a grotesque of an athlete, used to run the three-mile course on burnished autumn days, not for fame, certainly, and not for gym credit alone, for pleasure too.)

The minor sports (minor in public acclaim, not in merit and effort) flourished amain in these years. Lacrosse, begun at Cornell in 1885, floated on waves of enthusiasm and in troughs of indifference. The teams of 1902, 1903, and 1910 are applauded by historians of athletics, modern Pindars; in 1902 and 1903 we won the Inter-University League championship. The Cornell Fencers' Club was formed in 1894 and engaged in many a spirited duello. Ice hockey came to Cornell in 1896. Professor Johnny Parson of Engineering, fascinated by the game, built and maintained a rink on Beebe Lake through popular subscription; his name was long preserved by the Johnny Parson Club on the shore of the lake. The team of 1907–8 was undefeated, and in 1911 we won eleven games and the collegiate championship. (But this primacy was obtained on city rinks, owing to Beebe Lake's habit of melting before a scheduled contest.) Tennis, long established, but handicapped by Ithaca weather, produced one top-ranking player, Francis T. Hunter '16. In wrestling, the power of an inspired coach was manifest in the record of Walter O'Connell, who came in 1908 (and who took a law degree in 1911). His teams won the intercollegiate championships in 1910 and in every year from 1912 to 1917. And the end was not yet. Basketball appeared here as an informal exercise in 1898; in 1901 the Intercollegiate League was formed by Yale, Harvard, Princeton, and

Cornell. (This, says Bob Kane, was the first intercollegiate athletic league and the origin of that indefinable entity, the Ivy League.) Soon after, the game attained popularity, as the indoor sport par excellence. Soccer was introduced to the campus in 1900 by students who had learned to love it abroad. With the influx of foreign students and with the popularity of the game among intramural groups, who found it an easy game to play badly, it gained a considerable local popularity. The first match with an outside team occurred in 1905, and in 1908 Cornell was admitted to the Intercollegiate League. A cricket team was formed in 1903, and a professional coach hired. The team had a brilliant season in 1906, and then interest seems to have waned, for about fifty years.

Before we leave athletics we must record two Great Days. On 27 May 1905 Cornell won the Intercollegiate track championship for the first time, and the varsity crew race with Harvard; and the junior varsity beat Penn and Yale on the Schuylkill; and the baseball team defeated Manhattan; and the tennisers outdid two Syracuse clubs. But this Great Day was far surpassed on 27 May 1911, when Cornell won the Intercollegiates (with J. P. Jones making the world's amateur record in the mile); and all three crew races, the varsity and the freshmen beating Harvard on Cayuga and the JV's winning the American Henley at Philadelphia; and the varsity baseball, by defeating Yale in the fourteenth; and the freshman baseball, downing Dartmouth. A bonfire was built at the junction of Buffalo and Aurora Streets, and a procession wended its way to the President's House, where Governor John A. Dix '82 made a speech. On that tremendous night many a student had his first taste of champagne.

Now we leave athletics.

In these prewar years the coeds, increasing rapidly in numbers and aggressiveness, began to emerge from the purdah in which they had so long been confined. In the great world the status of women was altering; no longer were they restricted to marriage, teaching, or nursing. They were factory hands, shopgirls, stenographers, and social workers, editors, librarians, publicists. These were the days of Women's Rights and the suffragettes. (In Sage in 1904 there were fifteen members of the National Equal Suffrage League.) In short, a social war was in progress, in which the Cornell conflict made only a minor engagement.

At the century's beginning the women were still conscious of their isolation on the campus, and were in general not much distressed by it. Women kept themselves to themselves, not only here but on other coeducational campuses, as they did in conventional life. Everywhere men sought the Smoking Room, women the Ladies' Lounge. At Cornell the women governed themselves by the Women's Self-Government Association, the WSGA, under the mild supervision of the Warden of Sage, who turned into the Adviser of Women in 1909, and into the Dean of Women, with full professorial rank, in 1916. They had their own amusements, produced their own stunts and plays, conducted their own sports. (To their basketball tournaments no men were admitted, for propriety's sake.) In Sage and Prudence Risley (1913) they were much better lodged than the average male student. Many young women, scornful of competition for male favor, found this free conventual life much to their taste. If they were not asked to the Junior Prom, they did not repine; they gave an Anti-Junior Prom.

Even so, their lot was not a pleasant one, and the historian may well commend their courage and constancy under frequent humiliation by boorish males; and he may think the male boorishness the most unpleasant manifestation in Cornell history. President Schurman took official cognizance of the anticoedism. He said in his 1906 report: "Women have occasionally complained of a certain frigidity in the atmosphere which is created by and which envelopes the undergraduate community." An acute observer, Edwin E. Slosson, whose wife (May Preston) was a Cornell Ph.D., averred that anticoedism was due rather to caste and guild spirit, to social and professional exclusiveness, than to antifeminist ideas or instincts. His words are charged with sympathy and indignation:

We have the spectacle of young men sitting on the porch of a luxurious fraternity house and criticizing certain passing "coeds" with an acridity almost feminine, expressing disgust because their clothes do not fit them and their hands are not neatly manicured. The criticism, although unjustifiable, might not be unfounded. It might happen that the girl under scrutiny had not shown artistic genius or even creditable craftsmanship in the dress she had made herself, and that her hands were the worse for wear, for she, unlike her aristocratic critic, had slaved and saved for years to get an opportunity for the education which he obtains without sacrifice, and of which he would, if he had his way, rob her.

The class of young men who object to the presence of the young women is, however, small at Cornell; smaller than in the other eastern universities, though larger than in the western. But as they are leaders in the fraternities, which here, as everywhere, dominate the society life of the university, they make themselves unpleasantly conspicuous at times.[11]

Happily, continues Mr. Slosson, the Cornell girls are by no means ostracized. About two hundred male callers are counted at Sage on a Sunday afternoon, about one per inmate. "On the whole," he concludes, "I think the women get as much masculine attention as is good for them."

A no less acute observer than Mr. Slosson, Gertrude Shorb Martin, Ph.D. 'oo, Adviser of Women, analyzed in her report for 1912 the

attitude of a part of the University toward the work and office of the Adviser of Women—namely, an unwillingness to admit that the institution is really and permanently committed to the policy of coeducation; a feeling that the presence of women somehow renders it inferior to the other great eastern universities; a hope that by some arrangement the stigma of coeducation may be removed and the institution may be admitted without question to that august sisterhood; a determination to keep it meanwhile, in curriculum and atmosphere, as distinctly a man's institution as possible.

Two years later, however, Mrs. Martin noted that the old traditional opposition to coeducation was rapidly breaking down. And the downbreaking brought its problems, for while the WSGA regulated the social life of the girls, nobody exercised any control over the men.

Little by little, women invaded the men's domain. In 1908 Elizabeth Ellsworth Cook '08 made the debate team chosen to argue with Columbia. Columbia protested, on the ground that a woman contestant might sway the judges unduly. Our manager rejected the protest, giving assurance that the judges chosen would be of sober temperament, proof against allurement. All too proof, as it turned out; for Elizabeth Cook debated, but Columbia won. She then took the Woodford Prize in Oratory, as Harriet Chedie Connor had done in 1894. In 1915–16 two sororities, Kappa Alpha Theta and Delta Gamma, found houses of their own, where the members could live together and entertain their male acquaintances with humbling formality. In short, there were many signs of the breaking down of the old prejudices, but the actual emancipation of women at Cornell had to await the social dissolvents of the war.

In the history of these early years of the century, two major disasters afflicted Cornell.

[11] E. E. Slosson, *Great American Universities* (New York, 1910), p. 331.

The first was the typhoid epidemic of 1903.

Ithaca was not a very hygienic or a very healthy city. It had no general sewage system. The University had its own water supply from Fall Creek, which fed Sage College, the professors' cottages, and a few fraternities. The Ithaca Water Works, a private corporation, brought water from Buttermilk and Six Mile Creeks to a part of the town. But many householders, including lodging-house keepers, got along with wells and cisterns. Dr. Mervin T. Sudler, who came here as instructor in anatomy in 1902, learned that the town water supply was viewed with dark distrust, and that Professor Chamot of Chemistry made regular analyses, which regularly revealed high pollution in the water. Dr. Sudler was told that outbreaks of "Ithaca fever" or "Six Mile Creek colitis" occurred every autumn, and were to be regarded as acts of God. Dr. Luzerne Coville reported that 10 to 15 per cent of the entering class were usually troubled with "freshman diarrhea," due to the water.

In November 1902 the Water Works imported sixty laborers to build a dam in Six Mile Creek. After the typhoid declared itself, the citizens naturally blamed it on these invading foreigners, but in fact it could just as well have come from any streamside privy erected by a Mayflower descendant.

Eight cases of typhoid were reported on 15 January 1903. The numbers rapidly increased during a month of horror. The University fought valiantly beside the city's medical men to stem the plague. The Sage Infirmary, designed to hold twenty patients, contained sixty. Another building was leased, and Stimson Hall was turned into a hospital. Emergency corps of nurses were imported from other cities. A third of the students left town, many for good. "For weeks the campus was fanned hourly by the wings of Death, as the bells in the tower were forbidden to ring and no man smiled or looked upon his neighbor," remembered Romeyn Berry '04. President Schurman dropped every other duty to organize the defenses, and to visit daily every sick student.

By mid-February the peak was passed, and by the end of March the epidemic was over. The Ithaca Board of Health counted 681 cases up to that time, with 51 deaths. Of these cases, 131 were students, of whom 13 died. In addition, many stricken students went home or to friends' houses. Their number was estimated at 160, and of them 16 died. But no cases were declared among those who used only the University water supply.

With returning health came manifold rumors and recriminations. Many insisted that the sick and dying had not received proper care, and blamed the Administration.[12] Many maliciously pointed out that some members of the Executive Committee were at the same time important stockholders in the Ithaca Water Works. The conclusion—which defies all common sense—was readily drawn that the epidemic resulted from the local magnates' disregard of public health in their pursuit of private profit. The University itself was accused of being a stockholder in the Water Works. President Schurman protested angrily that it was not a stockholder, just a bondholder, and what of it anyway?

In mid-March, as the epidemic was waning, arrived a touching letter from Trustee Andrew Carnegie. He had himself suffered from typhoid fever. Well aware how costs of illness could eat up precious reserves set aside for education, he asked the privilege of defraying the expenses of all ill-provided student victims of the disease. Surely there was never a kindlier act in the records of large-scale philanthropy. Carnegie asked, further, permission to build a filtration plant on the campus for the University's water supply. This permission was granted. Carnegie's gifts on both scores amounted to $131,000. At the same time, the University's extraordinary expenses and its loss of tuition revenue plunged it deep into a deficit from which it was many years in recovering.

The city of Ithaca, under a threat from Schurman that unless there was a proper supply of pure water in the city's mains in September the University would close for a year, bought the Water Works from the private owners and installed an efficient water system, which has since evoked no complaint on the score of health.

The second major disaster of these years was the Chi Psi fire.

The Chi Psi's, one recalls, had bought the Fiske-McGraw mansion, heedless of the ill luck that traditionally dogged it. Part of the ill luck was that Architect W. H. Miller had provided an elevator shaft, but no elevator. The bottom of the elevator well was used as a broom and rag closet. Presumably oily rags took fire by spontaneous combustion.

It was the early morning of Friday, 7 December 1906. A forty-mile wind was blowing off the lake, and the temperature stood at four above zero. At 3:45 A.M. a somewhat incoherent alarm of fire was telephoned

[12] Dr. Luzerne Coville, lecturer in surgery, resigned his post in anger on 19 March 1903. He wrote a long, detailed condemnation of the administration's actions and the conduct of the hospitals (Coville Papers). For a summary of the whole epidemic, see the article by a visiting expert, George A. Soper, in the *Journal of the New England Water Works Association*, 1905, and the report of the Ithaca Board of Health, 1904, with a budget of frightful exhibits of country life in America.

in. The fire horses did their best up icy University Avenue, but the fire was not immediately located, and when it was found, the water pressure was low. Meanwhile, within the house, the flames had shot up the elevator shaft and then fanned out laterally and downward. Most of the twenty-six boys in the house awoke to find themselves enveloped in flame, and escaped by makeshift ropes or by jumping into blankets. But two were caught in the flaming house, and two others died of burns. And three firemen were killed by a falling wall.

The Chi Psi fire and the typhoid epidemic are the sort of calamities that bulk large in a history. There were also plenty of small private calamities, which do not enter a history, being part only of our own little biographies. And there were plenty of small private joys, which remain entirely our own business.

These were good years for Cornell, years of growth under strong leadership. Many of our men and women of fame and power, many who have richly benefited Cornell by their counsel and material aid, were students here during the early years of the century. So abundant are these eminent Cornellians that one must not mention any names at all.

These were years in which the alumni became more than ever conscious of their role, their privilege. The Cornellian Council was organized in 1910, with a full-time secretary, to organize fund raising. This organization promptly became effective, and by 1916 was receiving gifts of $50,000 a year for the general needs of the University. The Federation of Cornell Women's Clubs was formed in 1914; it established a Federation Scholarship Endowment, which has grown to a capital of nearly $100,000. The Cornell Club of New York took quarters in the Royalton, on West 43d Street. More and more the alumni came together, bound by common interests as well as old friendships. To be a Cornellian came to have a specific though undefinable meaning, at the very least the sharing in a community of memory. Thomas S. Jones '04, one of the few poets we have produced, put it beautifully in his address "To a Hill Town":

> This to you across the swift years that gather,
> This to give for ways that were filled with gladness,
> Ways hill-girt and under the spring's first sunrise—
> Paths that were golden.
>
> Here they lie in memory's early keeping,
> Wind-swept hills dim-misted with purple vapor—

One lone hill and three lonely pine-trees tossing
Black on the sky-line.

For these most—yet dusk on the lake's still edges,
Dusk and moonlight sweeping a wash of silver,
Chime of bells and softly an organ's throbbing—
Music and moonlight.

And for these, long gone from the hills of morning,
Song and laughter, voices that faintly echo;
All to you, who made as a dream of beauty
Youth's little springtime! [13]

[13] From Thomas S. Jones, *Shadow of a Perfect Rose* (New York: Farrar and
Rinehart, 1937). By permission.

XXVII

The First War

ONE who, a half century after, explores the campus records and journals of 1914, 1915, and 1916 must be struck by collegiate disregard of the war. President Wilson had enjoined neutrality upon us, and President Schurman repeated his injunction, refusing even to let partisan lecturers speak. The war was there in the news, of course; a faraway drama, Europe's ignoble affront to pacifistic idealism. Individuals, mostly those who had some family tie with one country or another, protested, wrote letters to the paper. Professors Othon Guerlac of Romance Languages and Georges Mauxion of Architecture were summoned to the French colors in September 1914. A few students slipped off to Canada or some far homeland to enlist.

But by and large Cornell dismissed the war, and Cornell was a miniature of America. A legend has grown up that the sinking of the "Lusitania," on 7 May 1915, roused the country to warlike fury. Well, distinct in one man's memory resides the echo of many voices, saying of the victims: "They were warned, weren't they? If they were so crazy, or so greedy, as to go abroad on a munitions ship in war time, there is no reason why we should die to avenge them." Only a few firebrands, mostly well over military age, advocated our entry into the war. The *Sun* mentioned the "Lusitania" editorially merely to reprove a student who was circulating a petition against warmongers, chauvinists, and jingoes. The editors and letter writers were chiefly exercised about senior blazers, the convocation hour, the holding of the Arts

Association banquet in dry Prudence Risley, and student apathy with regard to the crew.

Too much partisanship was looked at askance. Professor George L. Hamilton of Romance Languages, dunned by a German bookseller, wrote him an abusive, nay obscene letter, describing what he would do to the bookseller before paying his bill. The bookseller sent the letter to our German Department, which mimeographed and distributed it, as a breach of neutrality and as a *casus belli* with the Department of Romance Languages. The trustees took cognizance of the matter, and Professor Hamilton was gently censured by a Faculty Committee of Seven.

A sensitive observer might have noted premonitory gusts before the storm. The Cornell Cadet Corps, hitherto applauded by few, began to command student interest, and to fit itself to the new kind of war, and thus Cornell was commended by the War Department as one of the country's rare "Distinguished Colleges." Rifle practice crepitated on a new range, close-order drill and ceremonies were minimized in favor of extended order and field practice. In 1915 a Signal Corps unit was set up, with wireless telegraph, heliograph, and a motorcycle squad. We gained an Engineer Corps of fifty men, and a sanitary detachment. The old gray cadet uniforms, which reminded ancients of the ragged Confederate Army surrendering at Appomattox, were replaced by olive-drab army service uniforms. These were regarded with such favor that many students wore them all day. Freshmen understandably preferred the army cap to the frosh cap.

In 1914 the state authorized the building of the Drill Hall, for as much as $350,000. The building became, just when it was most needed, the training school for future soldiers. It was in its time one of the largest armories in the country, and perhaps it still is.

War is a summons to youth. The deeds of the Escadrille Lafayette, of the American Ambulance Field Service, stirred generous spirits. In February 1916 Edward I. Tinkham, senior in Forestry and a varsity track man, heeded the call and went to France as an ambulance driver. Early in 1917 he returned to Cornell, wearing his Croix de Guerre, and recruited thirty-five students for a Cornell ambulance unit. By the time it arrived in France, the United States had declared war, and the unit was set to driving ammunition trucks up to the battle line. The Cornellians appeared on the Aisne front on 24 May 1917, and were the first group of combatants to carry the American flag in action. Tinkham later transferred to Naval Aviation and flew in Italy. He died in the Military Hospital at Ravenna, of spinal meningitis.

After the election of Woodrow Wilson in November 1916, to the cry of "He kept us out of war!" and to the tune of "I didn't raise my boy to be a soldier," the President and the country too decided to enter the war after all. This is no place to examine the astounding revulsion of the national mood. Let it suffice that public opinion was inflamed by Germany's resumption of unrestricted submarine warfare and by the publication of an intercepted message from Germany which promised Texas, Arizona, and California to Mexico and Japan if they would enter the looming war against us. We were ready for the declaration, on 6 April 1917, that a state of war existed, and we threw ourselves into the struggle with characteristic enthusiasm and, of course, effectiveness.

The faculty immediately voted leaves of absence to all men in the service, and degrees to disappearing seniors. In April and May, when student blood is most effervescent, two thousand undergraduates and many of the younger teachers joined up. Many went to the Officers' Training Camps. Some of the fraternities were left half empty. Spring Day was abolished, and most of the intercollegiate sports, and all the reunions except that of the Class of 1877. As the campus quivered to the tread of soldiery, classroom morale sank to a new nadir. Few could concentrate on the eternal verities, which seemed very dull, even to their professional devotees, in comparison to the eternal emotions. The College of Agriculture assumed the leadership of the New York farmers, initiated a campaign for food economy, fostered war gardens, took an agricultural census of the state which revealed many a shortage. The Department of Home Economics led the movement for household thrift, demonstrated home canning, war bread, sugarless recipes, and waged war upon waste. Martha Van Rensselaer was called to Washington to direct the Home Conservation Division of the Food Administration.

A unit of the Reserve Officers' Training Corps had been established here in 1916. Most of the able-bodied male undergraduates were enrolled in it, and some devoted to it their full time. To the University's good fortune, Colonel Frank A. Barton '91 was assigned as Commandant, in July 1917. He had filled the same post from 1904 to 1908.

The work of the R.O.T.C. was seriously presented, and was taken seriously by its members. In the muddy middle of the roads marched the columns, the army boots stamping the rhythm, the sergeants barking "Hep," the campus dogs also barking in their own rhythm and bounding with delight. The quadrangle was the scene of incessant reviews, with pup tents rising and promptly struck, with rifles neatly stacked, with packs ever rolled, unrolled, and rerolled. On Schoellkopf Field cadets in pairs practiced the bayonet duel. Using French 75's the artillery shot live ammunition over Cayuga Lake. All this was a far cry from the close-order drill and manual of arms of earlier years.

The University opened in September 1917 with 3,859 students, against 5,264 in the previous year. Deflation turned out to be as troublesome as inflation. But the University's financial problems were somewhat alleviated by the establishment of the School of Military Aeronautics and other enterprises supported by the government. Also, the number of women students increased. And the faculty helped out by leaving in large numbers for war duties.

Student activities struggled on, though limping. The fraternities suspended rushing rules, sometimes combined dining rooms. There white bread was banished, sugar and fried foods restricted; Tuesday was meatless, Thursday wheatless. The *Sun* retrenched, producing a smaller paper in smaller offices. In its extremity, it inaugurated a Women's Page, with the name of Harriet A. Parsons '19 on the masthead. Albert F. Hinrichs '20 got out the first issue of the *Era* singlehanded, or nearly. Though many clubs became dormant, and even extinct, the Dramatic Club and the Women's Dramatic Club were active.

On the faculty passions ran high. The Professor of Latin tried to have the Professor of German expelled from the Town and Gown Club, on the ground that any reader of the *New Yorker Staats-Zeitung* was a traitor. Dark stories were privately whispered about certain pacifists and German sympathizers, tales of concrete tennis courts designed to serve as gun emplacements, tales of bomb manufacture in faculty cellars. Some color was given to these accusations by the exploits of Erich Holt, Ph.D. '14 and instructor in German. He deposited in the United States Senate a suitcase, which exploded. He then went to Long Island, and called on J. P. Morgan, Jr., chief organizer of munitions shipments to Britain. Forcing his way into the house, he shot Morgan in groin and hip, but the dauntless financier fell upon him, the British Ambassador (Cecil Spring-Rice) wrested away his revolvers, and the butler, named Physick, administered the *coup de grâce* with a lump of cannel coal. Holt was carried to the Mineola jail, where he committed suicide by throwing himself head downward eighteen feet to the concrete floor. It was then discovered that Holt had begun his graduate studies at Harvard, under the name of Erich Muenter. When his wife died suddenly of arsenic poisoning, Muenter removed to Mexico, to emerge later under the name of Holt. He had a new and phenomenal scholastic career, doing four undergraduate years in one in the Fort Worth Polytechnic Institute before coming to Cornell to take his Ph.D.

Patriotism rose to a frenzy. Professor Nathaniel Schmidt of Semitics, Swedish by birth and a pacifist by conviction, was harried by the populace, particularly because he refused to buy Liberty bonds. His house was besmeared by night, and he was insulted and threatened. But the faculty and trustees would lend no ear to demands for his dismissal. When David Starr Jordan '72, one of Cornell's two Honorary LL.D.'s, called for peace without victory, the Class of '73 demanded that all his honorary degrees be rescinded, on the ground that he was "soiled, smutted, besmattered, bedaubed, stained and stinking with un-Americanism." The demand was passed from committee to committee until the war ended.

The winter of 1917–1918 was bitter cold. Beebe Lake froze over by Thanksgiving. The average temperature for December was 20 degrees; on 30 December, —22 degrees was recorded, a new record. Some 1,400 plumbing casualties were reported in Ithaca. January was the coldest in history, with an average temperature of 14.4 degrees. Beebe Lake was frozen so solid that the University power plant ran short of water. Cayuga Lake was frozen north to Sheldrake, and motorists amused themselves by driving on its surface. Sentries protecting the sleeping soldiery had to be relieved every half hour. The grim war weather lingered on. The R.O.T.C. inspection on 12 and 13 April was held in a foot of snow, turning to trampled slush and mud.

President Schurman spent the summer of 1918 in France, haranguing the troops on war purposes, under the auspices of the Y.M.C.A. One who remembers as one of the chief war atrocities the summons on balmy French summer evenings to assemble in Y.M.C.A. huts to hear an exhortation on war aims may hope that Schurman's lectures were better than most. Indeed, they surely were. One thing is certain, that the President thoroughly enjoyed himself.

In the summer of 1918 (with Dexter S. Kimball of Engineering as Acting President) the University's life and character were radically altered under the pressure of events. Congress extended the Selective

Service Law, on 31 August, to include youths from eighteen to twenty. The War Department then organized the Students' Army Training Corps for the preparation of future officers, and contracted with Cornell and many other colleges to receive inducted soldiers who would satisfy the scholastic entrance requirements and to give them special academic and military training. The War Department paid the University for its soldier-students' tuition, board, and lodging. The twenty-year-olds would have a three-month course, the nineteen-year-olds a six-month course, and the eighteen-year-olds would have nine months of study. Cornell's quota was 1,700 men.

This arrangement was obviously a godsend to the University, floundering in wartime troubles. It was also an interesting rudiment of the system later in vogue in totalitarian countries, whereby regimented youth is trained for the state's purposes and at the state's expense under a semimilitary system. Perhaps the arrangement was even a forecast of things yet to come.

Thus Cornell became in 1918 a military school. Most of its men were in uniform. The official figures for 1 December show 1,696 in the S.A.T.C., and 848 civilian men and 800 women in the Ithaca colleges, including 166 graduates.

The S.A.T.C. courses were in part military, in the hands of army personnel, and in part the regular university courses useful for future officers: mathematics, languages, science, engineering, and so forth. The academic year was divided into four three-month terms, the first to comprise October, November and December, 1918.

The student soldiers were quartered in the fraternities, which, as fraternities, disappeared. With furniture removed, as many as seventy-five cots could be crowded into a house. The Domecon and Cascadilla cafeterias became Messes, the Telluride House the Officers' Club. There were no undergraduate social clubs, no intercollegiate athletics, no publications, except the indomitable *Widow*. The lodging-house keepers and the restaurateurs were engulfed in despond.

In addition to the S.A.T.C., other military schools occupied our quarters and classrooms. The School of Military Aeronautics continued, and schools for radio engineers and aerial photographers were established. We sheltered a Navy training unit of 310 men, a Marine unit of 170 men. An Army Trade School was set up in Sibley, for successive delegations of 320 men each. They learned automobile repairing, blacksmithing, carpentering, tinsmithing, benchwork in wood, electrical work, farriery. The Medical College in New York became the headquarters of a School for Military Roentgenologists.

In October, with the S.A.T.C., came the Spanish influenza; 900 cases were cared for by the University and about 1,300 in the city. Thirty-seven deaths among the students and soldiers were recorded and about the same number among Ithacans. With many physicians absent at the wars or themselves stricken, the care of the sick devolved upon the well, however ignorant of their task. The women students of the Medical College in Ithaca served as nurses, the men as hospital orderlies. Instruction was almost suspended in their school. The sole instructor in anatomy, Henry K. Davis '12, died; his place was taken by Leo P. Larkin '18, instructor in physics (and now Ithaca's leading radiologist).

Amid the flu's terrors and war's alarms, an important socioeconomic date passed almost unnoticed. As a result of a vote by local option, Ithaca went dry on 1 October 1918. The saloonkeepers had in fact long been resigned to this step toward civic virtue. The serious mood of the war, the popularity of the movies, the cessation of student activities, and the abandonment of Percy Field all operated to keep the students away from beer's redolence. The coming of national prohibition in January 1920 demonstrated that America was to be delivered forever from the drink demon.

As the defeat of Germany became evident and its surrender inevitable, the university community was saddened by the death of Andrew D. White, on his eighty-sixth birthday, 4 November 1918. His last years were melancholy. Four of his six children, three of his five grandchildren, were already dead, two of them by suicide. The confident world in which he had lived, which he had helped to build, had turned into something unaccountably evil. His faith in the ennobling influence of reason enlightened by history was shaken to the roots. Bitterly he brooded on Germany, his "second mother country," where his life had been "a blessed dream." Perhaps he recognized that as Ambassador to Germany, as friend of Bismarck and Emperor William, he had totally failed to penetrate the character and purpose of the country and its leaders. In the early days of the war his idealism was shocked by the invasion of Belgium, the air-bombing of Liége, the shelling of Rheims cathedral, and the contempt of the Germans for the rights of nations, which he thought he had secured at the Hague Peace Conference. Surely his end came as a release from a world which had disappointed him.

431

A History of Cornell

Andrew D. White was the living symbol of Cornell University through more than a half century. His character and ideals are implicit in its very structure. They are explicit in scores of personal relics scattered here and there about the campus. He can still speak to those who are attentive, in carven words as in ghostly murmurs. Behind the old Library stands a stone seat, placed there by Andrew D. White and his second wife in 1892. The inscription reads:

TO THOSE WHO SHALL SIT HERE REJOICING,

TO THOSE WHO SHALL SIT HERE MOURNING,

SYMPATHY AND GREETING;

SO HAVE WE DONE IN OUR TIME.

1892

A. D. W.—H. M. W.

His funeral fell on 7 November, the day of the "false armistice." The City Council, eager to avoid an unseemly mingling of celebration and mourning, refused to have the joyous fire whistles blown until the armistice report should be confirmed. Thus the true armistice, 11 November, came in Ithaca as a climax and not an anticlimax. The whistles were then bidden to blow, chimes chimed, church bells rang, and aviators from the Thomas-Morse plant and a flying circus of army aviators swooped, with, luckily, no casualties.

Then came the reorganization. The Army schools were promptly dissolved. The S.A.T.C. was disbanded before the end of December. It had enrolled 1,790 men altogether for the three services. Most of them, demobilized, remained as civilian students.

Faculty and administration made plans to reconvert the institution to a civilian status. A full college year was announced, to begin on 30 December, to end in August. Returning soldiers would be admitted at any time. An emergency athletic program was set up. The *Sun* resumed publication; the fraternities cleaned up; the lodging-houses reopened; and little by little normalcy was restored.

The part Cornell men played in the war was magnificent; 8,851 Cornellians were in uniform, 5,376 in active service. Of these, 4,598 were commissioned officers, over 2 per cent of all the officers in the Army, Navy, and Marine Corps. (The remarkable proportion of officers is a testimony to the work, however fumbling and hampered, of the prewar military department.) Cornell accumulated 526 decorations and citations, including a Congressional Medal of Honor to Alan Louis Eggers '19. We had four Aces in the U.S. Flying Corps: Jesse

Orrin Creech '20, John O. W. Donaldson '21, James Armand Meissner '18, and Leslie Jacob Rummell '16.

Two hundred sixteen Cornell men died in service.

Three Cornell women physicians, Caroline Sanford Finley, M.D. '01, Anna Irene von Sholly, M.D. '02, and Mary M. Crawford, M.D. '07, surgeons in overseas hospitals, were made Lieutenants in the French Army, and were the first American women to attain army rank (and the Croix de Guerre as well).

The effects of the war on the University were both intangible and tangible.

The intangible effect was to plunge the University, and the country, in a bath of seriousness, doubt, questioning. I am reminded of ancient paintings of the Fountain of Youth, in which we see the old, tottering or transported in wheelbarrows, journeying to the fountain; and on the other side of the picture they emerge from the fountain, young, brisk, and galliard. But the fountain of 1918 was a Fountain of Age, which we entered young and quitted old, bent, and solemn-visaged. With the war ended America's innocence, and also ended the Cornellians' sense of living in an enchanted palace, secure against "the outside world."

With the war came, tangibly, a new habit of discipline, and an acceptance of it. The casual freedoms of student life were steadily infringed, regulated, channeled. The Military Department had become a fixed part of Cornell life; it never again sank to its prewar levels. The R.O.T.C. was reorganized in 1919, providing a direct path toward a Reserve Officer's commission. In the college year of 1919 an impressive artillery unit was set up, with eighty-eight horses and eight guns, two of them of 155-mm. caliber. Major Ralph Hospital was in command.

The war left its mark on social structures and habits. Sunday golf, Sunday movies, permitted during the war to divert the soldier-heroes, remained for the pleasure of the ununiformed. The nuclei of student life moved up the hill from the valley, as stores, a post office, doctors and dentists, fixed themselves on the campus or its periphery. The bars were closed; Bevo and other near-beers made a brave but futile effort to live on the sentimental memories of beer in bottles. However, it was reported—alarming harbinger—in January 1919 that officials had seized hundreds of gallons of hard cider.

Cleavage between hill dwellers and townies became more marked. The Hill prided itself on its broad-mindedness, its humanity above all nations and nationalisms. Fritz Kreisler, the Austrian violinist (who had played in Bailey Hall in October 1917, before an enthusiastic capacity audience), was again invited for a concert on 11 December 1919. But downtown a fervid patriotism reigned. The American Legion had condemned in national convention the appearance of any German or Austrian performer. Ithaca's Mayor called on all patriotic citizens to stay away from the concert. Nevertheless Bailey Hall was packed, the front seats being conspicuously occupied by the football team. In mid-concert about eighty hoodlums, as the *Sun* termed them, cut the lighting circuit and tried to invade the hall. The students rose and fought. A large band returning from a basketball game took the invaders in the rear. Kreisler, unperturbed, played on in the din of the Battle of Bailey Hall. President Schurman took his stand beside the performer. A volunteer leaped on the stage with a flashlight for the accompanist. The invaders were magnificently repelled, to the strains of Viotti's Concerto in A minor. No tumult since Nero's time has had such a fine violin accompaniment.

Thirteen years later—so time does its work—Kreisler again played in Bailey Hall, and the American Legion invited him to dinner. (He told the Legion: "I predict that Hitler will establish a firm government and lasting peace in Germany, and that we will have a great rebirth of prosperity.")

The President in his reports for 1918 and 1919 drew some of the war's lessons for the country and for Cornell. The war had made clear the importance of science as a factor in national progress. "Without applied science the war would have found us helpless. . . . But there can be no applied science unless there is science to apply." Basic science is therefore essential. The importance of research does not rest upon its applications alone. What Cornell needs, what the country needs, is endowment for research in pure science, restricted to that end, for most of the great fundamental discoveries of science have been made in the universities. "The function of the university as a center of research is so closely connected with its effectiveness as an educational center that it is scarcely possible to separate the two."

What we need no less, he pursued, is advanced study leading to the enforcement of the country's spiritual life. We have seen "how even a learned nation may relapse into barbarism when it loses its ability to appreciate the great ideals of liberty, justice, and fraternity." Our humanistic studies must be developed and broadened.

Specifically, the President made proposals for bettering administration and instruction. In the Arts College a department of music was urgently needed. Area studies should be introduced; the language, literature, history, philosophy, politics, social and economic institutions of a country should be treated together. We must make experts! (But it was long before these words were heeded.)

Further, said the President, the two engineering colleges should be united, to eliminate duplication in administration and instruction. Two colleges are a superfluity, "and therefore, like every unnecessary organ, a disadvantage to the system." Cornell was falling behind the richly endowed Massachusetts Institute of Technology and the vigorous schools in the state universities, such as Minnesota and Illinois, better equipped than Cornell and paying higher salaries. We must obtain an endowment of four or five million for salaries in Engineering, and find money to support research, for "no technical college can be great, in fact it is doubtful if good teaching can long exist, if it is not closely connected in some way with independent scientific achievement." Finally, we must erect five new buildings for Engineering, at a cost of a million and a half. These would replace ugly Lincoln and uglier Franklin.

Architecture, he pointed out, has become a whole field of activities, including building, decorating, mural painting, sculpture. Architecture must have a building of its own, wherein a college of fine arts could be accommodated.

He proposed again a college of business administration, first mooted by Andrew D. White at the University's founding. This school should offer a two-year graduate course, leading to a Master's degree. All we would need for this purpose was a million dollars. And with a million and a half we could establish a college of education. Another project, which would come much cheaper, would be the re-establishment of the Cornell University Press.

The President, underestimating the forces of conservatism, foresaw great changes in university life as a consequence of the war's lessons. In his report for 1918 he said that military training should be given to all men students and should be combined with athletics. Such training should occupy not less than one hour of the student's time daily. Intercollegiate athletic contests would disappear. "The completed system of military and athletic training should take the place of the unhealthy intercollegiate athleticism which has usurped so large a place in the life of our colleges."

In the same report he dealt with other collegiate flaws. The fraternities, he said, have become socially noxious, undermining the students' will to work and study and turning their loyalty to the fraternity, not the Alma Mater. "The fraternity must be baptized with the spirit of the University. The University stands for truth and knowledge; so must the fraternity. . . . The University demands hard study; so must the fraternity. And until the fraternity recognizes this fact its relation to the University will be ill adjusted. . . . How to make the fraternities centers of intellectual life and activity? That is the great problem." To solve it, he looked at the history of Oxford and Cambridge. There the colleges developed from lodging houses, by the introduction of coaches or tutors. Similarly, tutors should be introduced into the fraternities, and a tutorial system would naturally spring up. Indeed, he noted, such an organization had existed at the Telluride Association from its beginning.

Such was President Schurman's review of the state of the University and his projection of its future. A happy event, our Semi-Centennial, provided an occasion for both backward and forward looking.

The original intention was to celebrate the fiftieth anniversary of the Inaugural in October 1918, with a pageant, military evolutions, parades of learned delegates in scholastic motley, illuminations, the unveiling of a statue of Ezra Cornell, and speeches innumerable—but with no award of honorary degrees. However, War intervened. After the Armistice the trustees decided to hold the deferred Semi-Centennial in June 1919. It would be a family affair, with reunions of all classes, and without delegates from other institutions. Observances would be of "a constructive character."

The "constructive character," at first obscure, was soon clarified. Some collegiate genius had already recognized that a celebration, with its massed publicity, provides an emotional focus, stimulating the charity of alumni and well-wishers. Thus every important anniversary has since been blended with an appeal for funds. It was decided that the Semi-Centennial Celebration should lead into the Semi-Centennial Endowment Campaign.

The celebration opened on Friday, 20 June 1919, on Schoellkopf Field, with a salute of fifty guns by the Field Artillery section of the R.O.T.C. Addresses were made to five thousand hearers by President Schurman, Governor Alfred E. Smith, Frank Hiscock '75, chairman of the Board of Trustees and Chief Judge of the New York State Court of Appeals, and by Charles Evans Hughes, former Governor of the state. (How many orators, in our puling times, could speak without a public address system on Schoellkopf Field?) In the afternoon, conferences of teachers and alumni of the several colleges and major departments took place. A University Dinner was served in the Drill Hall to four thousand guests, something of a miracle. A giant birthday cake with fifty candles was paraded about the hall by the class secretaries, solemnly cut by President Schurman, and ritually distributed in a mighty communion. After dinner representatives of the classes, of the faculty, and of the students spoke.[1] The President announced that an anonymous donor had offered a million and a half dollars for a new laboratory of chemistry.

Saturday was the alumni's day. A series of addresses had been prepared for the evening session on Schoellkopf. But no one wanted to listen to speeches. The crowd simply sang until dark. The volume was so great, the evening so still, that people on West Hill, two miles away, sat listening entranced. (Such quiet evenings come no more; there is ever the motor-mutter, overhead and round about.)

On Sunday the statue of Ezra Cornell was unveiled by Mary Cornell, the Founder's daughter. The statue was the work of Hermon Atkins MacNeil. His Ezra Cornell, spirited and faithful (save for the hat and the walking stick) has survived so far all the vicissitudes of taste. (MacNeil was instructor in industrial art at Cornell from 1886 to 1889, and here first began modeling.)

President Schurman summed up the celebration in his report for 1919. It was "a great and inspiring family gathering. . . . And while amusement and even frolic were not wanting, there was a pervasive dignity, a serious pride in the University, and a solicitous sense of responsibility for it, not only appropriate to a gathering of educated persons, but highly encouraging for the future of the institution."

In the celebration the coarse subject of money was barely mentioned. It was, however, deep in the preoccupations of the administration, and as deep, or deeper, in those of the faculty. A committee was already at work; it estimated our minimum needs at five million dollars for general purposes and, most urgently, another five million for the raising of salaries.

The state of the faculty was parlous indeed. The U.S. Bureau of Education estimated that living costs had risen 70 per cent between July 1914 and July 1919. Industrial wages had mounted, while pro-

[1] Major General George Bell '95 made a remarkable prophecy. "Unless we take steps to prepare for the future, we may, within the next twenty years, still have to pay the price [of unpreparedness], for there is no race suicide in Germany, and ten years from now the Boche will be stronger than ever in man power and in hatred." It was exactly twenty years until the Second War.

fessorial salaries remained stationary. Edwin W. Kemmerer, Ph.D. '03, made an exhaustive study at Princeton, showing that, with 1900 as a base, retail prices of food rose 80 per cent by 1916, while Princeton salaries increased 13 per cent. Between 1916 and 1919 food prices rose a further 52 per cent, and salaries less than 2 per cent. If Princeton salaries had kept pace with the cost of living, the professor would be receiving from $8,500 to $9,000.

The situation of the Cornell faculty was as bad as that at Princeton, or worse. Salaries were practically unchanged since 1900. At the war's end, the average for professors was $3,285, for assistant professors $1,751, for instructors $1,029. In 1919 increases averaging $400 for the professorial ranks were arranged, by the device of raising tuition from $150 to $200. "In this direction," said the President, "it is impossible to go farther." He said that the present staff would probably remain, by choice or through necessity, but they would find few successors, for a young man would hardly accept enforced celibacy or destitution for wife and children. The various deans' reports belabor the point, eloquently or plaintively. The straits of the men in Agriculture were acute. The Law School faced the disappearance of its faculty.

With such moving facts in hand, the Semi-Centennial Endowment Campaign set to work, with J. Du Pratt White '90 as chairman. As the technique of campaigns was as yet hardly formulated, the committee naïvely proposed a vigorous drive, to last from 20 October to 1 November 1919, whereafter the campaigners would return to their own businesses.

The undergraduates joined cheerily in the movement. Between the halves of the Williams game, on 11 October, a group paraded on the field, bearing such placards as "Feed the Profs"; "A Prof Teaches on his Stomach"; "$125,000 Will Feed a Prof and his Family for a Million Years." Those professors who could afford to attend the game laughed, but yellowly, as the French say. They felt that their old dignity and prestige were gone, that they had become objects of pity and derision to their students.

The campaign went slowly and badly. Its closing date was repeatedly postponed. In January the announcement came that only a little over two million had been pledged. The workers recognized that money raising is an arduous task, requiring endless time, labor, devotion of its agents. Through the whole of 1920 the campaign continued, with an attempt to allure the general public. Enormous advertisements appeared

438

in newspapers and magazines, with the slogan: "Producer of Producers —She *Must* Go On!" While sensitive spirits cringed, the total of pledged contributions slowly mounted. Finally, in January 1921, the results were published: $6,243,617 for the Endowment Fund, plus the previously announced $1,500,000 for the laboratory of chemistry, plus the August Heckscher Research Fund of $500,000, plus $500,000 for the Medical College, plus other restricted gifts of $708,733—making the grand and welcome total of $9,452,650.[2]

As a result of the campaign and of a second rise in tuition to $250 in 1921, salaries were raised to an average of $4,100 for professors, $2,630 for assistant professors, and $1,429 for instructors. The Heckscher Research Fund gave blessed aid; and in general faculty morale was restored. The financial stability of the University seemed for the moment assured. The enrollment in 1919-20, 5,765 full-time students, including 1,136 women, was the largest in history. Cornell could face the postwar years with reasonable confidence.

Within the educational structure certain wartime developments are to be recorded.

A Department of Hygiene and Preventive Medicine was established in 1919, with Dr. Haven Emerson in charge. All first- and second-year students were required to attend lectures on hygiene. Thus a dear conviction of Andrew D. White, imposed by him in 1868, was reiterated. Dr. Emerson was convinced that the University should provide clinical care for the students. But his purpose was baffled by entrenched interests, perhaps also by the costs involved.

In Chemistry, the Du Pont de Nemours Company granted, in 1918, a fellowship to encourage advanced study. This seems to have been the first general endowment made by industry.

A Biological Field Station was set up on twenty acres of swamp and marsh land at the southeast corner of Cayuga Lake.

Following President Schurman's recommendation, the College of Civil Engineering and Sibley College of Mechanical Engineering were combined in 1919, to make the College of Engineering, with a common

[2] An interesting item: Professor John H. Tanner of Mathematics and his wife gave $50,000, to accumulate until 2020, when, according to mathematics, it would amount to $6,500,000, and would then serve as the endowment of an institute of pure and applied mathematics. But in 1949, after the death of Mrs. Tanner, the fund amounted to only $60,000; the trustees devoted the income to the current support of the Department of Mathematics.

freshman year. Professor Dexter S. Kimball, who had signalized himself in many ways, and especially in industrial engineering, was appointed Dean of the new college.

Architecture once more angrily demanded a building of its own. In Agriculture, the straits of the faculty were relieved by an annual appropriation by the state of $195,000. A building program was authorized, and the Game Farm established. Within the college the rise of agricultural economics, with its professorships of farm finance, transportation, marketing, struck the observer. Evidently, with the growth of cities, agriculture was becoming less a self-sufficient home industry and more a business. Home Economics, a department since 1907, became in 1919 a school within the College of Agriculture. In 1920 the trustees asked the legislature to make it the State College of Home Economics. The bill died in the Senate committee.

A windfall to the College of Agriculture was the passage in Congress of the Smith-Hughes Bill in 1917. The bill appropriated to the states federal funds to prepare teachers of agriculture, home economics, trades, and industries. New York's share came to $100,000, which the state matched. Cornell was designated as the agent to train teachers of agriculture and home economics. But its Department of Rural Education was broad enough to attract many students from the Arts College.

The supervision of Farmers' Institutes was turned over by the state from the Department of Farms and Markets to the College of Agriculture. Extension work boomed; in one year five million printed items were distributed. Close relations with the Geneva Experiment Station were joined, with the exchange of professors and with provisions for credit for advanced work in either institution.

The Veterinary College found itself in difficulties, through no fault of its own. The number of licensed veterinarians in the state dropped from 1,200 in 1909 to 736 in 1917, thanks to an economic depression among cattle raisers with a surplus of animals, to the replacement of horses by automobiles in cities, and to the ability of motorized veterinarians to do four times as much work as in the days when they were buggy-borne. The enrollment in the college dropped from a maximum of 159 in 1915–16 to a low of 79 in 1921–22.

The Medical College in New York went through something of a crisis. In one year died Colonel O. H. P. Payne, the benefactor, Dr. William M. Polk, the first dean, and Dr. Lewis A. Stimson, professor of surgery and perhaps the college's chief animator. People felt that an epoch had closed. The college found itself hampered by its insufficiency of full-time professors and by the inadequacy of its hospital facilities. The college needed to be integrally united with a hospital for its research, especially in pathology and clinical subjects. It needed to control the wards and outpatient departments, with ample laboratory accommodations. For the moment nothing was done. But better times were at hand, to be inaugurated by the appointment of Dr. Walter L. Niles '02 as Dean, in 1919.

With the University's affairs in this, on the whole, prosperous state, President Schurman felt justified in tendering his resignation. He was sixty-six years old; he had ruled Cornell for twenty-eight years; he felt that his work here was done. His vigor was undiminished, as was his ambition. He had new and vaulting plans.

He announced his resignation at Commencement, 1920. In his report for that year he made his valedictory. He stated as his long-time educational purpose the combination of "the idealism of ancient Athens with the industrialism of modern America." The menace to the fulfillment of his purpose was the mere growth and overcrowding of the institution. The universities, he said, should be reserved for the diligent and the keen to learn; it was hard to arouse in many a real interest in the intellectual life. "Student activities are first of all studious activities." Our conditions of entrance are at fault, with too many of the intellectually torpid admitted. Our need is "to make a more rigorous selection of candidates, to lay stress on an active intellectual life, to insist on strenuous work, and to prescribe searching examinations, followed by the elimination of all who fail to reach the required standard."

After a period of repose Schurman was appointed, in 1921, Minister to China, by President Harding. His later brilliant career in diplomacy, concluding with the ambassadorship to Germany, lies outside the scope of this history.

His service to Cornell was inestimable. When he assumed office, it was a courageous, high-spirited, but somewhat radical, somewhat eccentric institution. It was a personal university, reflecting the scholarly humanistic ideals of Andrew D. White, complicated by the quirks and dislikes of Henry W. Sage. Many of its guiding principles were negative; it was "against"—against old-fashioned required curricula and the recitation system, against the hierarchy of studies, against clerical domination, against theological and social obscurantism, against imposed discipline, against social distinctions based on wealth. Many of the enemies that Cornell was against had quietly disappeared.

Schurman was both positive and orthodox. His long effort was to make the University complete in its structure, competent in its operation. With his purpose to combine the idealism of ancient Athens with the industrialism of modern America no one was likely to quarrel. Unlike Andrew D. White, he was not agitated by perpetual projects for reform. He was a happy man, well satisfied with the world as it was, the world which had so well rewarded his own abilities. He had no desire to make it over. The Cornell which he formed in his own image was a happy, vigorous place, at peace with itself and adjusted to the world, devoted to serving ancient idealism and modern industrialism with all its might.

His success was the success of Cornell. During his regime the enrollment increased from 1,538 to 5,765, the physical domain from 200 to 1,465 acres. He boasted at the Semi-Centennial Celebration that of the 20,000 Cornell degrees he had conferred more than 17,500. The Veterinary College, the College of Agriculture, the Medical College, the College of Forestry were his creations. In his time Cornell became one of the great universities of America, indeed, of the world.

XXVIII

Interregnum I, 1920-1921

WHILE the trustees sought a worthy successor to President Schurman, Albert W. Smith '78, Director of Sibley College, was appointed Acting President, in the spring of 1920. The Acting President, universally addressed as Uncle Pete, was a tall, benign man, with the singularly sweet expression of one who has resolutely thought only high thoughts and believed only the best about his fellow men, including students. He had rowed at Saratoga on the triumphant freshman crew of 1875 and on the triumphant varsity of 1876. Save for terms in industry and at Stanford, he had given his life to Cornell. A man of letters, familiar with all the Faculties, he was most acceptable in every area of the University.

In his position, he could hardly make serious changes or inaugurate policies. His task was to keep the machine running until the new master should arrive. Nevertheless, his year in office is marked by some developments of note.

In the physical world, he planned a new central heating plant for the University, chilled as it expanded. It arose, after his time, near the East Ithaca railroad station, and cost $700,000. It was said to be the most extensive college heating system in existence.

Barnes Hall, home of the C.U.C.A., was badly battered by its war service. A. Buel Trowbridge Jr. '20, president of the association, led a vigorous campaign for funds, raising $22,000. Therewith the building was remodeled, and in its basement a Coffee House was installed. This filled a most urgent need for a meeting place of men students and faculty. Lane Cooper of English, James F. Mason of French, and others had their own consecrated tables, and there held regular court, as in a French literary café. (Professor Mason's Ten O'Clock Club proclaimed that it was organized with a shingle purpose.) Many still regard the source of their intellectual life as welling up in the basement of Barnes Hall.

Not much occurred in the academic area. The amalgamation of the engineering colleges, prepared under President Schurman, became fully operative in June 1921.

Agricultural Chemistry was transferred from Agriculture to Arts, and Landscape Architecture from Ag to Architecture.

The limitation of numbers proposed by President Schurman was put into effect. The Faculties voted to check further increase in Arts and Engineering, and to limit registration in Architecture to 200, in Law to 300, in the Ithaca branch of the Medical College to 40. The total enrollment, they said, should not exceed 6,000.

Alumni relations were greatly strengthened by the appointment in 1920 of Foster M. Coffin '12 as alumni representative. He was an officer of the University, and was expressly debarred from the solicitation of funds.

The elders were troubled and taken aback by a new spirit among the students. Half the men had served in the armed forces. Many had been under fire; more had seen the realities of death, fear, hardship, cruelty, hate. To them the return to the campus was a return to a juvenile and rather absurd world. The receding war left, even among the young who had not seen it, a feeling that the easy inherited sureties could not be trusted, that the proud world was sick, and the heroic remedy of war had left it sicker than before. The famous "postwar disillusionment" was slow in developing and was not yet acute. Nevertheless a new mood was perceptible. In his annual report for 1921 Dean Frank Thilly of the Arts College remarked on "a somewhat 'demoralized' element in the student body. . . . Although our own University does not seem to have received into its membership as large a proportion of this post-war group as some other institutions, we did have a sufficient number to give us a problem." Uncle Pete had a famous lecture on Loyalty, a lyrical apostrophe to traditional virtues. I think that at about this time he put it away, in fear of overt sneers.

Violations of the National Prohibition Act were first reported in the *Alumni News* in January 1921. Spring Day in that year was a public brawl. The Faculty demanded that its sponsors show cause why it should continue to exist. Romeyn Berry commented in the *Alumni News* (9 June):

This community has awakened to the realization that the young person of the present day no longer follows mid-Victorian standards of deportment. It has become aware that the combined elements of totally undisciplined stags, jazz music, synthetic spirits, girls, and powerless chaperones form an unstable compound. It has discovered that the gin man is almost as regular and faithful as the milk man.

The campus was violently agitated by the Morelli Case. A freshman, Fred Morelli, an individualist, refused to wear the little gray frosh cap, not at all out of principle, says Elmer M. Johnson '22, but because he simply didn't like the thing. The *Sun* discovered his offense in April 1921 and wrote editorially: "It is up to public opinion to make it quite evident to the offender that he cannot continue in his ways, and there are plenty of means that can be resorted to in case it comes to a showdown." This sounds very much like incitement to riot.

Morelli, defying public opinion, appeared again on the campus without a frosh cap. He was set upon by about two hundred students, haled from Rockefeller Hall to the quadrangle, and chained to a tree. He was then borne in triumph to Beebe Lake and deposited in its waters. The *Sun* gloated: "He was made the object of merited ridicule and contempt. . . . Cornell showed a very healthy reaction." But during the night an occasional publication called *The Critic* produced a special issue on pink paper, protesting against conformity's violence.

The indomitable rebel once more showed himself on the campus without his cap. Uncle Pete intervened against a gathering mob, saved the boy, but told him, apparently, that he should obey the students' rules or go home, lest he meet serious injury. Morelli took the advice, and next day disappeared with a leave of absence.

If the administration and the students thought this a proper solution, many of the faculty did not. George Lincoln Burr interrupted his lecture on Martin Luther to make a passionate attack on "lynch law on the campus." He wrote in the *Telluride News Letter* (1 June 1921):

I have not been all these years a student of the history of liberty without observing how in any community a habit of resort to violence soon represses all departures from the prevalent orthodoxy or without learning that revolutions are quite as much due to the conservatives who use force for repression as to the radicals who use force for revolt. There is no safety valve so precious to civil order as legitimate freedom of thought and speech.

The next Faculty meeting was stormy. Burr, Charles H. Hull of History, Simon H. Gage of Zoology, and other eminent professors offered their resignations if mob action should be condoned. But the faculty voted that no student rules might be enforced by corporal violence, and that Morelli should be welcomed back. The resignations were not presented. A year later Morelli returned, and took his degree in 1926 without further publicity.

It would be pleasant to record that Morelli became a consecrated defender of the rights of the oppressed. But it appears that he was simply a rebel. He rebelled against the Eighteenth Amendment and the Volstead Act by dealing profitably in forbidden liquors while in college. He later operated an ill-famed night club in Utica and was known to the police as an outstanding gambler. Still following the dictates of his daimon, he rebelled against the rules of his trade association, and one evening he was murdered by persons unknown outside his place of business. Some men have the vocation of martyrdom.

But let us turn to the legitimate conflicts of the world of sport.

The face of Cornell athletics was changed by the appointment in 1919 of Romeyn Berry, A.B. '04, LL.B. '06, as graduate manager. "Rym," as he was affectionately known to generations, was totally a Cornellian. His family memories went back to his grandfather, John Stanton Gould, trustee of the University and lecturer in Agriculture in our earliest years. As a student Rym had been involved in every activity. He had played freshman football, edited the *Widow*, written the first Masque show. A wit with that rarity, an individual, recognizable humorous style, he contributed his *Sport Stuff* and *Now in My Time* to the *Alumni News* until his death in 1957. His commentaries in book form still gladden and instruct. Picturesque in impeccable tails, white tie, and topper at track meets, or in outrageous tweeds and knickers—and finally in overalls—in his daily doings, he bestrode at least one of our little worlds like a colossus.

Berry's task as graduate manager was no easy one. He had to reconstruct Cornell athletics after their long abeyance during the war, and he had to reconcile two opposing forces. On the one hand, a student majority and the impassioned alumni demanded victory at any cost. On the other hand, the administration, the faculty, and even many of the students were perturbed by prewar athletic overemphasis, with its many evils. They saw in the wartime eclipse an opportunity to reconstitute intercollegiate athletics in a more reasonable form, with contests only among peers and without professionalism and improper proselytizing. As Rym Berry came to adhere more and more to the second school of thought, his troubles correspondingly increased.

His term in office was unhappily initiated with the death in 1920 of Charles E. Courtney, the Old Man. Substitute crew coaches were sought, but of course no comparable genius could be found, since none existed.

Football was revived in 1919, under John H. ("Speedy") Rush. The game with Union on 16 October 1920 was noteworthy in that, apparently for the first time, a football match was reported from one city to another by radio. An R.O.T.C. operator at the field communicated the plays by wireless telephony to Professor W. C. Ballard in Franklin Hall, and he relayed them by wireless telegraphy to Schenectady.

In track, Cornell won the Intercollegiates for the fifth successive year in 1919. Ivan Dresser '19 won the two-mile in the record time of 9:22.2. In the following year Walker Smith '20 made an American record in the 70-yard hurdles, and Jack Watt '20 broke the world record for the 440-yard hurdles, in 54⅕ seconds. Frank Foss '17 made a world record for the pole vault (with 13 feet 3⁹⁄₁₆ inches) at the American Athletic Union meet. The combined track teams of Cornell and Princeton tied Oxford and Cambridge in 1921. Jack Moakley was the head track coach of the Americans in the 1920 Olympics. Cornell's trainer, Frank Sheehan, went along. Frank Foss won the pole vault with a world record of 13 feet 5 inches and C. D. Ackerly '20 took the featherweight wrestling championship.

In 1920 came Nick Bawlf as coach of lacrosse, and later of hockey and soccer. Here he remained until his death in 1947.

In the sedentary world, most of the prewar clubs, publications, and activities revived. The Dramatic Club inaugurated "The Country Theatre" at the New York State Fair in 1919, to set an example to rural theatre groups. Some six thousand visitors saw its one-act plays, and in the following year the number of spectators was doubled. Some new organizations appeared on the campus. The Delicate Brown dinners of Sigma Delta Chi began, with the intent of roasting the guests, in the manner of the Gridiron Club of Washington.

To those who returned to the campus after years of absence the status of women students seemed to have much improved. "Dancing and sentimentality have replaced prize fights, sucker fishing, cock, dog, or booze fights," said the *Alumni News* on 9 December 1920, crediting the war and the Eighteenth Amendment with the change. But some of the fraternities set their faces firmly against recognition of women students, and they were abetted by the *Sun*. The coeds' conquest of social acceptance was won not without opposition, indeed not without a little war.

The precipitating cause of the war was the invitation to women students to join the parade before the Dartmouth game in 1920. They were unwisely put at the head of the procession, just behind the band, and they were not well received. A rumor arose that the women were demanding the right to try out for athletic managerships. Some of the fraternities threatened to boycott the *Cornellian* unless women were omitted. On Thanksgiving Day the Penn game returns were reported in Bailey Hall; a group of female supporters of the team were hissed, as were screen pictures of Sage College. The Acting President then wrote a letter to the *Sun*, to the effect that those who disagreed with the Founder's policy should leave the University.

The antifeminist campaign waxed hot. A self-appointed committee of nine prominent students condemned women en bloc, calling for segregation, reduction in the number of coeds, and their ultimate elimination. The *Sun* agreed heartily. The story was of course picked up by the press of the country. However, the senior societies rejected the report and censured the committee. The women and their friends effectively boycotted a Musical Clubs concert, the manager of which was said to be chiefly responsible for the report of the Committee of Nine. The Independents, overwhelmingly pro-coed, demanded a larger share in the student governing bodies.

And then the uproar and fury simply died away. On 17 February 1921 the Ithaca *Journal-News* reported that just as many Cornell women had been invited by just as many Cornell men to attend the Junior Week festivities as in previous years. The women won, of course. Prejudice lingered on in a few of the die-hard fraternities, but by the end of the twenties it was imperceptible to casual observers.

There were plenty of small indications of women's rise, which was visible in the great as well as the little world. The Women's Glee Club, an outgrowth of wartime community singing in the dorms, led by Mrs. Eric Dudley, was organized in 1920 and gave concerts in unison with the men's clubs. The Women's Dramatic Club, after staging a fine performance of *She Stoops to Conquer* at the Lyceum in February 1918, gradually lost its health, as girls with histrionic abilities joined the Cornell Dramatic Club. In 1919 Delta Gamma bought its own house (the old William H. Sage house on Seneca Street), while ten other sororities lived in rented houses. The Medical College in New York admitted women to the first year of study, as well as to the later years. And the *Alumni News* announced (on 3 March 1921): "Trousers for coeds were furnished by a recent sale of army goods. Olive-drab riding breeches are proving popular as parts of winter sports costumes for skiing and tobogganing."

A couple of other fragments from the basket of miscellanies: the great hardware store, Treman, King, & Co., burned down on 4 May 1921, with a loss of $350,000. And Romeyn Berry noted in the *Alumni News* for 14 April 1921 that certain students had discovered that by walking wearily by the roadside they could induce motorists to stop and convey them to far cities. He had no name for this practice.

And on 30 June 1921 it was announced that Dr. Livingston Farrand, chairman of the American Red Cross, would be the new President of Cornell University.

XXIX

President Farrand – The Campus

LIVINGSTON FARRAND was born in 1867, in Newark, New Jersey, of an old, patrician American family. He graduated from Princeton in 1888, and then took the degree of M.D. at the College of Physicians and Surgeons in New York. However, said one of his companions, he studied medicine to know it, not to pursue it.[1] After two years of study abroad, he became instructor in psychology at Columbia, and later adjunct professor. Interested in primitive psychology, he joined expeditions to northwestern America with Franz Boas and others, and was appointed professor of anthropology at Columbia in 1903. His concern with public health questions brought him the post of executive secretary of the National Association for the Study and Prevention of Tuberculosis in 1905. For this enterprise he produced a plan of operation which became a model for later public health movements. Between 1905 and 1914, under his impulsion, antituberculosis associations rose in number from 32 to 1,200, dispensaries from 24 to 400, and 250 open-air schools were established.

In 1914 he was appointed President of the University of Colorado. He is said to have revivified the university, to have founded its medical school, and to have revealed his diplomatic abilities by settling bitter labor disputes in the state.

In 1917, as director of the Anti-Tuberculosis Commission sent to

[1] Dr. James Ewing, of the C.U. Medical College, in *In Memoriam Livingston Farrand* (New York Academy of Medicine, 1940).

450

LIVINGSTON FARRAND, President 1921–1937

France by the International Health Division of the Rockefeller Foundation, he applied his tested methods, with health education, clinics, social service, hospitalization, sanatoria. His success was so marked that after the war he was appointed chairman of the Central Committee of the American Red Cross. While serving in this important post he was persuaded to become President of Cornell.

He married in 1901 Margaret K. Carleton of New York. Known to the entire campus by the affectionate cognomen of "Daisy," this great and vivid person imposed upon the community her robust vigor, humor, and charm. Her Sunday afternoon "at homes" were open to any student; the College of Architecture, in which she enrolled as a student, had her special affection. A bold horsewoman, an indefatigable gardener, she promoted Horse Shows and founded the Garden Club of Ithaca. The five Farrand children, at various stages of growth, enlivened and delighted the University.

Livingston Farrand was one of the most likable, nay lovable, men this campus has known. His person, his eyes, his voice radiated warmth and good will. No one could receive a professorial request with such understanding sympathy; no one could turn it down with such adroitness, so that the suitor felt somehow that he had won his point. No one was more deft in healing breaches, in allaying quarrels. Faculty, students, and alumni came soon to feel that they had a friend in the President's House.

He was a very extraordinary public speaker. Standing dapper and at ease on the platform, his hands clutching his coat lapels, he spoke without notes, informally but with spontaneous elegance of diction, as if his words sprang involuntarily from his heart. He was always brief, and always apt. He liked to be the last speaker, so that his fancy could play lambently over what the others had said. Each listener had the sense of receiving personally a message of importance; the only trouble was that he had later some trouble in remembering just what it was.

The Inauguration took place on 20 October 1921, a day of drizzling rain. The academic procession, with cough drops hidden in togas, marched to Bailey Hall. Chief Justice Frank Hiscock '75, chairman of the Board, made an address. The Acting President, Albert W. Smith, presented the seal and charter to the new President. Dean William A. Hammond spoke for the Faculty, Foster M. Coffin '12 for the alumni, Presidents Lowell of Harvard, Burton of Michigan, Wilbur of Stanford for the scholarly world. The faculty listened eagerly for the

President's announcement of his educational principles and program. But he spoke rather of the European crisis, with special regard for the plight of Poland.

As Dr. Farrand surveyed his new domain, so may we. Let us first glance at the city which nourishes the University and which is nourished by it. Ithaca's center remained relatively static. Some banks and office buildings thrust upward as high as seven stories, but without altering the dominantly Civil War aspect of State Street. With the generalization of the automobile, rows of neat little houses crept out along the highways. Traffic lights were installed downtown in 1926, and the citizens were educated in the symbolism of red, green, and yellow. But a yodeling chimney sweep still paraded the streets, wearing a top hat. The Flats were tidied, with a municipal golf course, and a municipal airport across the Inlet. Only the Fuertes Memorial Bird Sanctuary remained wild, to welcome uncivilized birds.

The internal combustion engine brought about a revolution in transportation. The streetcars, which had ground to and fro since 1888, yielded to buses in 1935. The Ithaca-Auburn Short Line was sold for junk in 1924. The Lackawanna renounced its sleeping-car service in 1933; the early morning train (called the Hound because of its mournful wails) switchbacked no more down South Hill.

Ithaca weather was constant in change. There was a record snowfall on 29 January 1925, 25.5 inches in a day, with a temperature of −22 degrees. In compensation, the winter of 1931–1932 was so warm that ice hardly formed on Beebe, and the lake was never opened for skating. But the winter of 1933–1934 was very cold. The temperature dropped to a new official low record of −24 degrees. During Junior Week it twice fell below −15 degrees, and hardly ever rose above zero. Cayuga Lake was frozen from end to end, for the first and only time since 1912. Half the honey bees of the state were killed. The following August was the coldest on record, with a low of 38 degrees. In July 1935 came the Flood, inundating the lower parts of the city. Seven hundred refugees were housed in the Drill Hall for four nights; eleven lives were lost in Tompkins County. And in March 1936 we had a memorable three-day sleet storm. Above the level of Stewart Avenue all the trees and wires were enameled with sparkling ice. Many power and communication lines came down; the roads were impassable; Ithaca was isolated for two days. The damage to the campus trees, as to the state's orchards, was pitiable. They bent double, sighed, and broke in two.

452

Everywhere lay fallen branches entangled with wires, crushing the careful shrubberies of the landscapers.

The undergraduate sneered, as he has always sneered, at "Ithaca weather," being convinced that when skies are gray over Ithaca they are bright over his distant home town. Is the ill fame of Ithaca weather justified by official records? I am afraid it is. One calculation shows that while Ithaca's annual rainfall is about 33 inches and that in New York city 42 inches, Ithaca has 147 rainy days to New York's 125. A cloudy belt extends south from Lake Ontario along the Appalachian ridge. Only the Pacific northwest, a bit of northern Vermont, and the city of Binghamton can boast more cloudy days.[2]

The wild natural beauty of our surroundings was preserved, thanks to an increasing appreciation of the bounty granted us. Robert H. Treman '78 bought Enfield Glen and Buttermilk Glen and gave them to the state, to be forever parklands. He gave lower Six Mile Creek to the city for a public playground, cleared away ugly houses at the foot of Cascadilla Gorge, and gave the space to the city. The remains of dismal mills below Ithaca Falls were demolished, and proposals to utilize the water power of Fall Creek were sternly rejected. Colonel Henry W. Sackett '75, a trustee, born in Enfield and raised in Ithaca, was inspired by Mr. Treman's example. He gave over $200,000 to preserve the beauty of the gorges, for the building of access paths, for reforesting and opening vistas. Beebe Lake was dredged, and the Athletic Association developed and supervised a swimming pool at its upper end.

An Arboretum, or outdoor botanic garden, had long been the dream of the plant scientists. Cornell's situation, where the plants of northern latitudes meet those of the south, local variations in soil and altitude, supply a fortunate setting. Professor A. N. Prentiss proposed an arboretum to the trustees on 3 May 1877. Andrew D. White warmly recommended it in his report for 1883. Professor W. W. Rowlee urged it anew in a report to the trustees in 1908. In 1914 a handbook of the College of Agriculture, by Albert R. Mann, mentioned plans for a botanic-garden planting around Alumni Field. At last in 1935 work

[2] *Alumni News,* 17 Nov. 1932, 29 April 1937. Has the climate of Ithaca changed in the last century? Apparently not, to judge from records kept here in 1828–1848, and published by the state in 1855. The temperature range, and the extremes, match our own. Occasionally would come a warm winter. In 1842–1843 the ground never froze; plowing went on all winter, except for a single week (*Alumni News,* 4 Feb. 1932).

was actually begun. With the labor of the depression-born Civilian Conservation Corps an area east of the College of Agriculture, along Fall Creek, was cleared, roads and walls were built, and planting performed.[3]

Important additions to Cornell's wild lands, Nature's laboratories, were made in outlying districts. The Lloyd Library and Museum of Cincinnati gave 620 acres of upland marshes, including Ringwood swamp and tracts near Slaterville and McLean, with the provision that they be left forever in the feral state. John P. Young '97 made a practice of buying marginal farms, sold for tax arrears, and giving them to the University for botanical study. The Arnot Forest, covering eventually over four thousand acres of high hills and tangled valleys, fifteen miles to the southwest, came to Cornell by formal gift in 1927. The Schwarz Foresters' Lodge was built there, with the Indian totem pole in front. The CCC boys were lodged there during the dark days, and there they labored nobly in elementary forestry. Curious woodland rites were enacted. When a new draft arrived, the oldcomers roused the newcomers at 3:00 A.M., gave each a candle, and made them kneel in a circle around the totem pole and solemnly bump their foreheads on the ground. This must have pleased the spirits of the Tlingits.

To supervise the development on the campus proper an Architectural Advisory Board was created in 1923. This board sponsored a series of plans and projects for future developments, and wielded from time to time a courageous veto.[4]

The appearance of the campus was transformed by great building activity. The first structure was the Baker Laboratory of Chemistry. After Morse Hall's burning in 1916, the Department of Chemistry had camped miserably in its ruins and in other haphazard refuges. In 1919 President Schurman had announced the anonymous gift of a million and a half dollars for a new laboratory. Chairman Louis M. Dennis of Chemistry drew visionary plans of an ideal laboratory, to be the largest, best organized, and best equipped in the country. None of Cornell's buildings resulted from a closer cooperation between the planners and the architect (who was Arthur N. Gibb '90 of Ithaca).

The cornerstone of the building was laid on the very afternoon of Farrand's Inauguration, as the climax of the proceedings. The new President revealed the donor to be George F. Baker, New York banker.

[3] Ralph S. Hosmer, *The Cornell Plantations* (Ithaca, 1947).
[4] Kermit C. Parsons, "History of Campus Planning at Cornell" (MS, 1952, C.U. Archives).

454

Not a college man, he had first taken an interest in the Cornell Medical College, and was then led by J. Du Pratt White to regard the whole university with favor. It was he who built the group of men's residential halls known as Baker Court. The President revealed the name of the donor and his presence at the President's right hand. After much laudation Mr. Baker was summoned by universal acclaim to speak. His speech was the following: "I am glad that my offering is welcome, and I hope it will be useful." Two years later, on 22 December 1923, the laboratory was dedicated and opened for service.

The ruins of Morse Hall were turned into an Art Gallery. Under the zealous (and uncompensated) direction of William H. Schuchardt '95 a remarkable series of traveling exhibitions came to Ithaca during the mid-twenties.

Willard Straight Hall is a memorial to Willard Dickerman Straight '01. As an undergraduate he was one of the dominant campus figures, impressing both students and faculty by his character and personal charm. On leaving college he obtained, through Benny Ide Wheeler, a post in the Chinese Customs Service. He rose rapidly to become an American consul and was for a time in charge of the State Department's Far Eastern affairs. As a representative of American bankers, he negotiated matters of international importance. He married Miss Dorothy Payne Whitney, daughter of the financier William C. Whitney and sister of Payne Whitney, benefactor of the Medical College. A major during the war, Willard Straight died of pneumonia in Paris on 1 December 1918, only three weeks after the armistice. His will directed his wife to do "such thing or things for Cornell University as she may think most fitting and useful to make the same a more human place."

Mrs. Straight laid up this rather painful injunction in her mind. She was moved to action by a visitor who turned out to be momentous in her life. Leonard K. Elmhirst '21, elected president of the Cornell Cosmopolitan Club, discovered that his society had amassed $80,000 in debts. With uncommon initiative, he went to New York to raise money. He called on Mrs. Straight, who was moved by Elmhirst's picture of the barrenness of Cornell undergraduate life. She saved the Cosmopolitan Club, conceived the idea of Willard Straight Hall, and married the emissary.

As Willard Straight himself had recognized, Cornell was not in fact a very human place, simply because, outside the fraternities, no provision was made for the amenities of existence, even for friendly intercourse. In consultation with President Farrand, Mrs. Straight proposed to provide these amenities by building a great student union. The plans were drawn by the celebrated William Adams Delano and were presented to the trustees in June 1922. The plans, and the scale of the proposal, were breath-taking. The building was to be, and is, of native stone in the collegiate Gothic style, possessing that Oxford dignity of which Andrew D. White had vainly dreamed. It contains vast halls for general meetings, banquets, the dance; and a library, formal dining rooms and a cafeteria, game rooms, guest bedrooms and a dormitory, offices for campus activities, and the finest campus theatre in the country at the time. The décor, the equipment, the furnishings, were of the best, putting to shame most gentlemen's clubs. Ezra Winter of New York filled the lobby with murals, symbolizing the career of Willard Straight, and J. Monroe Hewlett adorned the theatre's walls with characters from Shakespeare and the Greeks. The wood carving, the stonecutting, the ornamental iron work, were of a craftsmanship that can hardly be reproduced today. Mrs. Straight believed that beautiful surroundings conduce to the making of admirable characters.

Though we did not realize it at the time, Willard Straight Hall marked the end of an era, in architecture, in taste, and in our reckoning of human values.

The detailed plans were long in making, the great building long in erection. It was opened, without exercises, on 18 November 1925. Mrs. Straight (who was now Mrs. Elmhirst) was the first to dine in the hall, the first to occupy the guest rooms. Foster M. Coffin '12 was appointed director, but the administration was, and still is, in the hands of undergraduate committees. The beautiful theatre was inaugurated on 26 November, with a brilliant production of *The Contrast* by Royall Tyler, the first social comedy written and produced in America. Franchot Tone '27 starred, ably supported by Judson W. Genung '27, Virginia Van Vranken '27, and Frances P. Eagan '26.

The opening of Willard Straight Hall caused some rearrangements on the campus. The faculty's University Club, which had no magnificence at all, was hard hit. The Coffee House in the basement of Barnes Hall surrendered, and the Co-op moved in to take its place, after thirty years in the basement of Morrill.

After Willard Straight came the splendid Balch Halls, dormitories for women, given by Allen C. Balch '89 and his wife, the former Janet Jacks, graduate student from 1886 to 1888. At a cost of about $1,700,000, four connecting units were built by Frederick L. Ackerman '01 and sumptuously decorated and furnished under the direction of Mrs. Ackerman. The buildings were dedicated and gratefully occupied on 23 September 1929. There are still not wanting those who shake their heads sadly, remarking that it is a pity that girls should be educated in surroundings more luxurious than they will ever match in their own homes. But no complaints have been received from women graduates who have been thus exposed to disillusionment.

Thus the women were for the moment provided with proper quarters. The administration's purpose was to house all its men students likewise with decency. It proposed to extend the dormitories greatly, and to find sites for fraternities also on the western slope below the campus.

As soon as the war was over, agitation for a War Memorial had begun. Committees met and decided that Cornell's greatest need was an extension of the men's dormitories. Baker Court and Founders Hall already stood, pleasing to the eye and pleasant to the occupants. Day and Klauder, the original architects, sketched a fine development to the south of Founders Hall, with a pair of towers, a cloister or colonnade, a Memorial Chapel, all in Gothic stone. A committee of the Cornellian Council, under the compelling leadership of Robert E. Treman '09, set actively to work. In June 1927 it reported over $300,000 in hand. Construction was begun on the group, which eventually included Boldt Tower and Hall, Mennen Hall, Lyon Hall, and McFaddin Hall, as well as the War Memorial proper.

On 23 May 1931 the Memorial was dedicated, with a brilliant and moving ceremony. President Hoover spoke by telephone, his words amplified to the throng on the Library Slope. Hoover recalled with much felicity the Tinkham Unit, which first carried the American flag to the front. At the same time, in Ravenna, Italy, an American Consul placed a wreath on the grave of Edward I. Tinkham '16.

There was just one awkwardness. The names of all the Cornellians who died in the war are cut in stone tablets in the cloisters. Some campus liberals discovered an omission: the name of Hans Wagner '12, who died in battle, but on the wrong side. It was necessary to station a guard at the Memorial to prevent a midnight cutting of his name. The committee adroitly took the insurgents in the rear by offering to match all contributions and to erect a memorial to Hans Wagner in his German home town. The liberals being more liberal with protest than with cash, the fund never amounted to much. In 1934 the $300 collected was allocated to the expenses of Dr. Kurt Lewin, acting professor of education, a refugee from Hitler's Germany. The trustees approved, though perhaps the shade of Hans Wagner did not.

The Law School building was given by Myron Taylor '94, chairman of the Board of the U. S. Steel Corporation, government servant in matters of world moment, Ambassador to the Vatican. The building displaced the houses of the Psi Upsilon and Sigma Phi fraternities; these were aided to build homes south of the new men's dormitories. Myron Taylor Hall is a spacious, imposing, beautiful structure, with ample classrooms, social rooms, a Moot Court Room, a great library, and even a squash court. Its majestic tower contains apartments for distinguished guests or professors, with a dizzy view of lake and valley. The building was dedicated on 15 October 1932.

The plant of the state colleges grew from year to year. A south wing (Moore Hall) was added to the main Veterinary College building. Far out on the Ag campus, a new dairy building, Stocking Hall, was dedicated in October 1923. The enormous Plant Science Building, opened in 1931, at a cost to the state of $1,400,000, gave us, for the time at least, the best facilities in the country for study in its field. Warren Hall, for Agricultural Economics, Farm Management, and Rural Social Organization, opened in May 1932. The state followed its worthy custom of naming the college buildings after eminent past professors (Roberts, Bailey, Stone, Comstock, Caldwell, Fernow, Rice); in this case the professor honored, George F. Warren, was still active.

The College of Home Economics was at last suitably housed, with the opening of Martha Van Rensselaer in the autumn of 1933. The building was incomparably the best for its purpose then in existence. It contains an auditorium and an amphitheatre, library, lounges, art gallery, a drafting room for Household Art, laboratories for Textiles and Clothing, etc., a Nursery School penetrated with corridors wherefrom spectators, invisible *voyeurs,* may watch through one-way glass the unsuspecting children, and a Practice Home or set of elegant apartments in which students go through the experiences of running a household, complete with live Practice Babies. And a cafeteria and a tearoom. At a rough computation, the Ag Caf has at this writing served 7,500,000 meals.

Much other construction went on, minor in the large cosmic view, but major to those concerned and benefited. The Central Heating Plant was erected, and a new water supply system, drawn from Fall Creek above Varna. The Johnny Parson Club by Beebe Lake, primarily

458

for skaters, opened in December 1922. It was named in honor of Professor John T. Parson '99 of Civil Engineering, a vigorous proponent of skating. The attractive house was built and managed by the Athletic Association. Romeyn Berry strove to give its restaurant elegance in atmosphere and distinction in cuisine, with a club dinner for a staggering $1.50, and with an imposing maître d'hôtel in tails. Mr. Berry, as often, was ahead of his time. Ere long the Johnny Parson Club's chief business was in franks and hamburgs.

The Athletic Association built also a toboggan house, using waste stone from the new Balch Halls and War Memorial. The C.U.C.A. constructed in Twin Glens, three miles to the northward, a cabin which many remember with sentiment. The equestrian set, led by Mrs. Farrand and abetted by the Army detachment, raised funds for a Riding Hall, out near the Heating Plant, by Dwyer's Dam. It was finally built in 1934.

In 1927 the Westinghouse Electric and General Electric companies presented us with a radio transmitter and broadcasting station. (A tiny transmitter had already been operating in Franklin Hall, mainly for demonstration purposes.) Cornell's new station began broadcasting in August 1929. Lofty plans were made to keep the University on the air. Pick-up lines would be placed in the lecture-rooms of eloquent professors; higher education would resound through the length and breadth of Tompkins County. The University Hour, from 5:00 to 6:00 P.M., would typify Cornell life and activities. Each department would have its day; Fridays, for instance, would be devoted to law and hygiene. But the valiant effort immediately failed. Broadcasting was found to be strangely expensive, and even the most eloquent professors strangely unwilling to prepare scripts for nothing. There was some question, indeed, whether the University as a whole has any obligation toward non-fees-paying listeners. The only successful part of the enterprise was the Agricultural Hour, prepared by the Department of Extension with a professional staff. In October 1932 the Cornell station merged with WESG, Elmira, a commercial station, retaining only the Agricultural Hour.

One more item falls under the head of Buildings and Grounds. In 1926 Major Louis L. Seaman '72, acting on his own initiative, persuaded the British Government to give Cornell a colossal World War British tank, the "America," to be a perpetual souvenir of the world's final war. By a triumph of engineering, the monster was established on the lawn south of the Drill Hall. It was the bête noire of Woodford Patterson, Secretary of the University. One summer, a few years later, it disappeared. Repeated questioning of Mr. Patterson failed to elicit an explanation of how and where it had gone. "Just a student prank," is all he would reply.

XXX

President Farrand's Regime: Organization and Administration

CORNELL'S vigor and success have been largely due to the labors of its trustees, anonymous to most students, frequently contemned by the faculty. With apologies to the many deserving, we single out a few who, by long exercise of their wisdom, left their impress on the institution that others have inherited. Mynderse Van Cleef '74 of Ithaca, trustee from 1881 to 1891 and from 1895 to 1935, was chairman of the all-important Committee on General Administration from 1914 until his death in 1935. Frank H. Hiscock '75, Syracuse lawyer, eventually Chief Judge of the New York State Court of Appeals, was trustee from 1889 to 1894 and from 1901 to his death in 1946; his fifty years on the Board match those of Van Cleef. He was Chairman of the Board from 1917 to 1939, throughout the presidency of Livingston Farrand. Robert H. Treman '78 of Ithaca was as much a part of Cornell as the Library Tower. He was elected alumni trustee in 1891 and remained on the Board until his death in 1937. His was the longest continuous membership. He sat on all the powerful committees, and succeeded his lifelong friend Van Cleef as chairman of the Committee on General Administration. Delighting in the natural beauty of the countryside, generous in gifts of wild lands to the people, he was a high-minded and high-spirited man, whose motives were not always appreciated by faculty and alumni. Justin Du Pratt White '90, New York lawyer, was on the Board from 1913 to 1939. As the very laborious and punctilious chairman of the Committee on Buildings and Grounds from 1922 to 1939 he was largely responsible for the physical development of the University. He succeeded Hiscock as Chairman of the Board in January 1939, but his service was ended by his death the following July. Bancroft Gherardi '93, chief engineer of American Tel and Tel, trustee from 1928 to 1941, followed Treman as chairman of the Committee on General Administration in 1937, and so served until his death in 1941.

The curious composition of the Board (ex officio, appointive, elective by the alumni, self-perpetuating by the Board itself, and hereditary) remained unchanged throughout the period. In 1923 the women alumni campaigned for an enlargement of the Board by three women, but the proposal came to nothing. In fact, Martha Carey Thomas '77 had been elected in 1895 and Ruth Putnam '78 in 1899, and Mrs. Harriet T. Moody '76 served from 1912 to 1922. Dr. Mary Crawford '04 joined the Board in 1927, and ever since it has had at least one woman member.

The faculty, though proud to have had their representatives on the Board and on the important committees since 1916, were distressed because their delegates had no vote. Requests for full voting privileges were made in Faculty meetings from 1920 through 1923; a committee of the Board responded that the time was not yet ripe. The agitation resumed in 1933. In the following year the Board replied that it was satisfied with Faculty participation and would in principle welcome the representatives as full-fledged members. It pointed out, however, that the change would require an alteration of the University Charter, and the moment was not propitious for bothering the legislature. The Board proposed to await a favorable occasion. The matter was then laid in abeyance for seventeen years.

A notable addition to the University's structure came by the state legislature's act of 1923, placing the Experiment Station at Geneva under the control of the College of Agriculture. The trustees responded to increasing administrative needs by forming in 1925 a State College Council, with trustee, administration, and faculty members. This replaced previous separate councils.

In 1931 the post of Provost was created. President Farrand, overburdened with the routine of administration, needed an executive officer with power to decide matters of secondary importance, but above the competence of a secretary. Albert R. Mann '04 was chosen for the post. He had served.as Dean Bailey's secretary, as professor, registrar, secretary and editor in the College of Agriculture, as Director of the Experiment Station, as Dean of the state colleges, and had taken time off to be Federal Food Administrator for New York State during the First War.

Evident needs caused the administration to expand in many ways. In 1927 Louis C. Boochever '12 was appointed to issue Public Information to the world. A Motor Vehicle Bureau was created in 1931. In the face of much resentment, all student owners of cars were commanded to register, and all faculty parkers as well. A Bureau of Educational Service to place teachers appeared in 1932. Depression evoked in 1933 a Placement Bureau, which, under the direction of Herbert H. Williams '25, found permanent positions for seniors and alumni and summer jobs for students. The Department of Purchases, which has become a colossal business, was set up in 1921 and reorganized in 1935.

With the restrictions on entrance in Arts and Engineering, the problem of admissions became acute. Faculty committees judged applicants on their examination marks, and also on such intangibles as character, personality, and potential capacity for leadership. By 1927 there were over two thousand applications for five hundred places in Arts. The faculty committees were forced to surrender. In 1928 a Bureau of Admissions was established, with Eugene F. Bradford, Registrar, as Director.

Various ancillary enterprises bore the name of Cornell. Such was Cornell-in-China. It began with an effort by the Chinese Students' Club, in 1921, to raise $3,000 for famine relief. It was taken over and vigorously promoted by the Cornell United Religious Work (which had replaced the Cornell University Christian Association). It developed into a "Plant Improvement Project," sponsored by the University of Nanking, Cornell, and the International Education Board. For six years, from 1925 to 1931, Cornell professors (Charles H. Riggs, Harry H. Love, Clyde H. Myers, R. G. Wiggans) were sent to Nanking, where they directed a widespread plant-breeding program.

In the case of wheat, over 50% increase in yield was possible with some of the new varieties. In rice, a gain of nearly 80% over the standard was possible, and in sorghum nearly 50%. There was also set up a comprehensive plan of seed multiplication and distribution. . . . Of all the accomplishments, the one that has had the most lasting significance was the training of the group of specialists. . . . As we look back on this program today, there

463

seem to be many reasons why it should serve as an example for contract aid in agriculture and in other fields wherever technical aid is being offered.[1]

Cornell University Press, America's first, had fallen into a long coma in 1884. In 1930 the trustees passed statutes providing for its reawakening, and in the following year the Cornellian Council recommended as a stimulant an annual appropriation of $5,000 from the Alumni Fund. In April 1931 John Henry Comstock died, bequeathing to the University the thriving Comstock Publishing Company, with its books on nature study, and also the Comstock home and offices on Roberts Place. The trustees then appropriated the recommended $5,000 a year for five years, and the Cornell University Press was again in being, with Woodford Patterson, Secretary of the University, as manager and University Publisher. The Press took over the Cornell series in philosophy, classics, and English, and the library publications, some sixty titles in all, and began to seek new scholarly manuscripts.

Certain administrative failures, actual or relative, are to be recorded. The proposed sponsorship of a Graduate School of Tropical Agriculture in Puerto Rico fell through (in 1928) for lack of a million dollars. And one of President Farrand's dearest projects, a coordinated plan of scientific research (in 1928–1929) came to nothing. Farrand wished to establish a research center in the area between biology and the physical sciences, especially in physiology, biochemistry, and biophysics, blended with the agricultural sciences of plant physiology, cytology, plant pathology, genetics, soil sciences, and so forth. He sought $9,000,000 for the center. The General Education Board in 1929 offered $1,500,000 as a starter, if the University could match it within a year. But 1930 followed 1929, and 1931 followed 1930, and the woes of depression years dissipated the President's dream.

A little later the administration was allured by another shimmering hope. Dr. D. K. Tressler of the Geneva Experiment Station and our Professor Faith Fenton of Food and Nutrition developed the perfect foods for a hungry world. They were called Milkorno, Milkwheato, and Milkoato. They were compounded of whole ground meal, dried skim milk, and salt; they were rich in minerals, proteins, and vitamins; they were termed "a cereal pemmican"; and they cost practically nothing. In February 1933 Governor Herbert H. Lehman and Mrs. Franklin D. Roosevelt were served a Milkorno lunch (tomato juice, Milkorno,

---

[1] Sanford S. Atwood, "Cornell and Technical Cooperation," talk at Conference for Agricultural Services in Foreign Areas, Washington, D.C., 7 Feb. 1955.

scrapple, cabbage salad, baked apple, cookies) at a cost of six cents a plate. The guests smacked their lips for the photographers. In 1933 over twenty million pounds of the three Milkos were distributed by the Federal Relief Administration. The enterprise, with its giant free-sampling operation, bade fair to make Cornell the greatest (and richest) food producer in the world, while ruining the makers of patent cereals. But there is a danger in oversampling, as was the case with bully beef in the First War and spam in the Second. Where are Milkorno, Milk-wheato, and Milkoato today? They have blown away like last year's cornflakes, perhaps because they were merchandised on merit and cheapness alone, perhaps because they were associated forever with depression, relief, distress, perhaps because people did not like them much.

The administration received constant aid, spiritual and financial, from the alumni, conscious of their role in the greater university. The Cornell Alumni Corporation replaced the Associate Alumni in 1923. Many of the local clubs undertook to seek out promising high-school students (with, certainly, special interest in noteworthy line-plungers and forward passers). They organized the first Cornell Day in 1934, bringing some six hundred fifty prospective Cornellians to the campus. The alumni established a placement bureau for victims of the depression. And chiefly they contributed nobly, both in money and in precious time, to the annual Alumni Fund, which passed $140,000 in 1937.

Cornell received also some important gifts. John McMullen of Norwalk, Connecticut, in 1921 left the residue of his estate for the education of young men as engineers. This splendid bequest has steadily grown, until now the principal amounts to over $4,500,000 for engineering scholarships. In 1923 Hiram J. Messenger '80 left $74,000 to provide lectures on the evolution of civilization. The Messenger Lectures have become one of the celebrated series of the country, and have brought to the campus a long procession of world eminences. Of these the first three were James H. Breasted, Egyptologist, Robert A. Millikan, physicist, and H. J. C. Grierson, literary critic. In 1933 Henry H. Westinghouse '75 left half a million to the University for the advancement of the science of engineering. There were other valuable and valued gifts, too many for listing here.

But finances were a perpetual distress. In 1924 the budget for the endowed colleges in Ithaca topped $2,000,000 for the first time. The accumulated deficit steadily grew; in 1924 it reached $435,000. With

465

the depression many of our investments defaulted on their payments. The rate of return of our portfolio dropped from well over 5 per cent to a bare 4 per cent. At the low market of 30 June 1932 our holdings were reckoned at 60.56 per cent of their book value. By 1933 the accumulated debit balance stood at $689,000. At President Farrand's retirement in 1937 it dropped slightly, to $625,000, but it was still a vexatious bequest to his successor.

The stringency was slightly alleviated by tuition increases in 1923 and 1927, bringing the annual fee to $400 in Arts, Engineering, and Architecture. But during the depression no such increases were possible.

The President succeeded in partially healing one open wound in the financial body. Cornell awarded annually six hundred tuition scholarships within the state, for which it received no compensation. In 1932 Farrand made a new agreement with the state, by which each scholarship holder would receive only an annual remission of $200 on his tuition.

Hard times forced painful economies everywhere. Budgets were sharply cut; promotions and raises were rare. "We are both undermanned and severely handicapped for lack of new equipment," wrote the President in 1933. In that year came the inevitable salary cut. A 10 per cent reduction for all personnel in the endowed colleges was imposed. The state colleges took a 6 per cent cut on all salaries over $1,000, and a 20 per cent reduction in departmental allotments for instructors and assistants.

On the whole the faculty was philosophical about it. We had heard of diminutions of 40 per cent in other institutions of higher learning. The cost of living had somewhat receded, while we had enjoyed a lag of nearly four years since the coming of depression. And at least, unlike many of our previously opulent classmates in business, we had jobs. (We sourly enjoyed their visits; after a preliminary exhibition of weight throwing, they would suggest that they might be persuaded to accept a fitting position in the administration. Or how about a professorship in applied economics? Or even, at worst, an instructorship in English, which they used to be good in?)

President Farrand had from the first urgently advocated a pension plan for faculty and administrators, since the Sage Pension Fund had become totally inadequate with the growth of the University. An elaborate plan was presented in 1931, but the trustees were too hard pressed to accept it entire. They did however inaugurate a group life insurance scheme, with a top limit of $10,000, for those dying in service. Not until 1937 was a genuine pension system, the Contributory Retirement Income Plan, put into effect. Less generous and comprehensive than those in some other eastern universities, it was nevertheless a beginning, and a godsend to the elder faculty members. It cost the administration about $50,000 annually.

The administration was for a time alarmed by a lawsuit, fraught with implications. A girl student in a laboratory course in elementary chemistry lost an eye and suffered disfigurement when a test tube exploded. She brought suit in 1919 for $100,000 and was awarded damages of $25,000 at the first trial. A dangerous precedent was thus set for all educational institutions, which would have to protect themselves with liability insurance, at enormous cost. The case was carried to the State Court of Appeals, which ruled in 1925 that Cornell, as an eleemosynary institution, was not liable for damages. (But in 1919 a girl student sued for damages in an accident to a College of Agriculture car, and won. The Court ruled that the college was not an agent of the state, and was responsible. Another interesting case was that of Miss W, who in 1926 sued Professor Arthur J. Eames of Botany for slander, alleging that he had made derogatory remarks about her mental capacity. The jury ruled: "No cause for action." Where would we all be if it had ruled otherwise?)

In summary, the period from 1921 to 1937 was one of general material progress, sadly interrupted by the depression. The enrollment remained fairly constant, rising only from 5,681 in 1921–22 to 6,341 in 1936–37, after a dip during the depression years. The endowment was nearly doubled, the value of buildings, grounds, and equipment nearly trebled. The administrative organization became more logical and efficient. The all-important plans for faculty insurance and pensions were put into effect. The union of the Medical College with the New York Hospital—of which we shall soon speak—was brought about. But on the whole no fundamental changes, in organization or education, occurred.

XXXI

Cornell under President Farrand: Education

STUDENTS sat in their classrooms and stood in laboratories from 8:00 A.M. till late afternoon, receiving their stipulated education, and thereafter they sought their own, in competitive sports, in student activities, in the passivities of the Library, in a myriad midnight bull sessions. In many a course, in many a department, the educative process was soundly performed, without producing one of those novel forthputtings or upsetting reversals which make present news and past history. In this record we can do no more than report some of the novelties and reversals which for a moment brought a college, a course, a teacher, into the news.

The honor system in examinations had been established, with great acclaim, in 1892–93. Though regarded as a giant step forward, it soon after began to take little steps backward. In 1901 President Schurman reported that the system was dwindling in effectiveness, that the situation was chaotic, and that students and faculty wanted proctoring back. The honor system vanished. In 1921, in obedience to some collegiate law of perpetual oscillation, the campus voted overwhelmingly for the honor system, as a giant step forward. It was reinstated; but it soon appeared that students were reluctant to report frauds by their mates. In 1927 an investigation showed that the students favored proctoring, since they would rather leave supervision to the faculty than be squealers. (This is a kind of honor system too.) The University Faculty dodged the issue by transferring jurisdiction over examinations

468

to each separate Faculty. By 1931 the honor system existed only in Law and Agriculture. As these words are written the students are clamoring for the installation of an honor system. It is promised that this will be a giant step forward.

The campus was long agitated by the question whether military drill should be compulsory or optional. In 1926 a petition to make drill optional was submitted by 1,783 students. The Faculty rejected it, on the ground that students should have some exercise, which the gymnasium was inadequate to provide. This answer was regarded by many as an evasion of the fundamental question.

In 1931, in full Depression, the mood of students, and of elders, was more rebellious. A Student Peace Committee was formed, under the leadership of Albert E. Arent '32. This committee proved to its own satisfaction that the University was under no legal necessity to make drill compulsory. It was unmoved by the consideration that the state supported the Drill Hall and that the military establishment furnished us with a band, stable, polo team, rifle team, and an indoor running track, and an arena for basketball, indoor tennis, and wrestling.

The Faculty, in a memorable meeting, voted 81 to 38 to recommend optional drill. The trustees pondered the matter for two years. They declined to judge of the academic propriety of compulsory drill. They found the legal obligation unclear, but observed that a continuation of the current practice would at least raise no question of the University's compliance with the law. The Board was disturbed by possible financial complications. The Drill Hall was given by the state to enable the University "adequately to discharge its obligations to give instruction in military science," and if these obligations should not be adequately discharged, the University would be held to repay the state the duly appraised value of the building—something in the millions. The trustees were moved further by considerations of public policy. In the feverish state of mind then current, the abolition of compulsory drill at Cornell might be accorded great significance, harmful to the University and to the country. The Board concluded that for the moment no change should be made.

The Faculty received the decision with regret, and hoped that considerations of public policy would not long delay the substitution of elective drill for compulsory.

The students were less submissive. Basic training has never been really popular, in any army. Few students willingly interrupt their afternoons to walk to the Drill Hall through rain or snow, to be barked at by undergraduates practicing the sergeant's bark. Activist units of campus protest found the sluggish student body an ideal *corpus vile* on which to work, with the announced goal, Peace, the holiest of watchwords.

An Optional Drill Corps was promptly formed, conducting a spectacular campaign. In a student poll in November 1933, 1,532 voted for optional drill, against 481 for compulsory. Protests against all militarism were made by groups with such noble names as the Student Council against War, but with small effect. Returning prosperity stilled the mood of rebellion for rebellion's sake; ominous news from Europe and Asia spread the feeling that a little military training might not be a bad thing. Peace was attained upon the campus, as it receded in the Great Outside World.

President Farrand, with his concern for public health, found the medical and health services of the University inadequate. He appointed Dr. Dean F. Smiley '16 University Health Officer in 1920, to be in charge of the work in hygiene and preventive medicine. Dr. Smiley and his nine physicians spent two-thirds of their time detecting defects and faulty habits, one-third in personal health instruction. Some 25,000 voluntary calls were made by students yearly. However, the administration could not or would not take the crucial step of assuming full responsibility for the care of students in sickness.

Dr. Norman S. Moore describes the state of affairs (in the President's report for 1950):

Before 1940, no responsibility for true clinical care was shouldered by the University. Giving medical advice was as far as staff physicians could go. When a student became ill, he was shunted off for treatment to a second unrelated community physician. No suggestion as to the qualifications of a particular community physician could be given the sick, and thus more vulnerable, student. No working relationship between town and gown medicine existed. Clinical facilities at the University had not been developed. The quarters for medical advising were noisy rooms adjacent to the gymnasium. The offices were inadequate and obsolete in equipment. The doctors on the medical staff were isolated from the practice of their chosen profession. At the Infirmary, convention had demanded an adequate modern hospital, but medical practice was not controlled within it—in fact, there were no specific qualifications for men who worked there. Bed, board, nursing care, and modest laboratory and X-ray services were provided under the authority of a nurse administrator.

Dr. Smiley revealed, in 1926, some interesting facts. Male students averaged five visits to the University doctors annually, female students three visits. Colds were the commonest complaint, then pinkeye. Men had many injuries, abrasions, wounds; women very few. Nearly half the freshmen men were undernourished, more than half the women. (But what is "undernourished"?) Physical defects were evenly distributed between urban and rural dwellers.

Dr. Smiley gave us in 1932 further troubling statistics. Undergraduate health habits grow steadily worse through the college course. In the class of 1932, 5.5 per cent of the freshmen and 16.9 per cent of the seniors had insufficient sleep; 8.9 per cent of the freshmen and 20.4 per cent of the seniors took insufficient exercise (what is "sufficient"?); 5.1 per cent used tobacco to excess (more than half a pack a day) when freshmen, 20.4 per cent when seniors. But the graduates were the worst of all. In addition, the graduates were unduly prone to mental disorders.

The Graduate School grew mightily through the twenties, reaching an enrollment of 1,139 in 1932. The depression, reducing available assistantships and closing the door to many prospective teachers, hit the Graduate School hard. The enrollment dropped to 753 in 1934–35. Thereafter it climbed to 935 in 1936–37. The decrease in numbers was on the whole a relief. An influx of graduate students makes serious inroads on a teacher's time, crowds seminaries and laboratories, reduces precious personal relationships. The day was at hand when admission to the Graduate School had to be restricted.

The Arts College presented Farrand with one of his first problems, inherited from the previous regime. A Trustee Committee on Plan of Organization found the situation of the College of Arts and Sciences anomalous. Until 1903 it had been merely the Academic Department, under the direct control of the President. It was then made a college, to match the other campus colleges. But although it offered four times as many student hours of instruction as its nearest rival, it resisted organization. The Dean was hardly more than *primus inter pares*. The departments felt few common bonds; they tended to deal directly with the President, hardly noticing the Dean, and President Schurman continued to settle their difficulties, as he had always done.

On 1 February 1921 the trustee committee voted that the Arts College should be administered on the same basis as the other colleges, and that the President should have no more primary responsibility for the details of administration in Arts than elsewhere. Clearly this vote

471

comported the appointment of an administrative dean with power. An Arts Faculty Committee reported its fears of a Dean with power, responsible to the administration and not to the Faculty. The committee insisted that the autonomy of the departments be preserved; it sought "educational, not administrative efficiency."

The case was argued for two years, while the Arts College was run by its capable Secretary, Archie M. Palmer '18, and a couple of clerks. The President used all his diplomacy, insisting that he would keep "adequate contact" with the departments and would control the budget, policy, and major appointments. A harmonious conclusion was reached, which included a formula for making Deans. (The President, after accepting suggestions from the Faculty, makes his nomination and presents it to the Faculty. He need not be bound by the Faculty's response, but he would not conceivably outface the Faculty's disapproval. He then nominates his candidate to the Board, with a statement of the Faculty's opinion.)

Professor Robert M. Ogden '01 of Education was thus chosen Dean in 1923. He entered on his term of duty with high hopes. He had views on the reform of the curriculum, which would guarantee an educated product by means of a series of six survey courses, followed by specialization in six more courses. Thus the student would take only three courses at a time.[1] But his proposals found little favor in the Faculty.

Since Dean Ogden accepted that the office of Dean should be executive rather than administrative, his incumbency was one of harmony and good feeling, without much disturbance of departmental rights and habits. Certain consolidations took place. The Department of Classics was formed in 1924 of Greek, Latin, and Archaeology. The Department of Animal Biology was constituted in 1925 from the former Departments of Anatomy, Biology, Entomology, Embryology, Physiology and Biochemistry, and Zoology. In 1936 the faculty of History, which had been composed of almost as many departments as professors, was made into one department. A Department of the Comparative Study of Literature was created, which was really a Department of Lane Cooper, enabling him to do what he pleased, without harassing or being harassed by the Department of English.

The teaching of education was reorganized. Several efforts had been made in previous times to establish a school of pedagogy, without

[1] R. M. Ogden, "A Curriculum for the College of Arts," *Educational Review*, April 1923.

any success. Courses were given by the Department of Education in Arts and the Department of Rural Education in Agriculture, with a good deal of overlapping. In 1926 the trustees created a University Division of Education, which did not however unite the two departments. A Graduate School of Education was set up in 1931, with power to administer the professional degrees.

Dean Ogden's chief private joy was in music and the pictorial arts. He sought to elevate their status within his college. Otto Kinkeldey, chief of the music division of the New York Public Library and an eminent musicologist, was brought here in 1923; in 1930 he was appointed to the first American chair of Musicology. Paul J. Weaver, a vigorous organizer and impresario, came in 1929. Music became an authorized major study; the staff was much enlarged, with the appointment of a scintillating group of men in applied music, Gilbert Ross, Andrew C. Haigh, Harold D. Smith, George L. Coleman '95. The offerings proliferated, covering the theoretical, historical, and practical fields.

The Sage Chapel vesper service programs show the evolution of taste. The sentimental musical pietism of the prewar mainstays, Mendelssohn, Gounod, Horatio Parker, Barnby, Stainer, yields to Palestrina, Victoria, and other sixteenth-century composers. Paul Weaver conducted an all-Bach program in 1930, and in following years oratorios by Saint-Saëns, Haydn, Beethoven, and Brahms.

Beginning in 1934 the Arts College offered a major program in Fine Arts, in cooperation with the College of Architecture. The program combined elements of music, literature, dramatics, and aesthetics.

The Department of Speech and Drama, under James A. Winans and Alexander M. Drummond, gained wide renown. Both came from Hamilton College, home of high eloquence under President Stryker. The department developed a rhetorical doctrine, known as the Cornell Idiom. This was "more concerned with rhetorical theory than with the criticism of speakers. . . . Its standards are classical, applied venturesomely and imaginatively; it is deeply rooted in literature; . . . it is perhaps more sensitive to literature than to history and other branches of the social studies; . . . it has not concerned itself much with audience studies or similar investigations." [2]

[2] Review by Loren Reid of *The Rhetorical Idiom: Essays . . . Presented to Herbert August Wichelns* (Ithaca, 1958), in *Quarterly Journal of Speech*, Oct. 1958.

Drama blossomed under Professor Drummond. His productions in the beautiful Willard Straight Theatre were regarded as supreme in the world of academic drama. "The Boss," as he was affectionately known, was a sensitive, compelling director, eager to try out novelties in playwriting and staging. The Rockefeller Foundation made him a grant in 1936, to be used in part for a survey of rural drama in the state, "with a view to determining its cultural implications and possibilities."

In psychology, Cornell became a center for the study of Gestalt psychology. Dean Ogden introduced it to this country, and translated Kurt Koffka's *Growth of the Mind* in 1924. He brought the author to the campus as visiting professor in the same year. Ogden's *Psychology and Education* (1926) was the pioneer American publication in Gestalt psychology.

In connection with psychology, the Physiological Field Station, now the Behavior Farm Laboratory, was begun by Sutherland Simpson of Physiology in 1922 and carried on by Howard S. Liddell, Ph.D. '23. Significant, and picturesque, experiments in the conditioned reflex have ever since been carried on there, with sheep being chivied through mazes, pigs harried into nervous breakdowns, fainting goats terrified by human ogres.

The vestigial Arts course in Botany was abandoned in 1922, and all the work in the plant sciences concentrated in Agriculture.

In Architecture, the course was lengthened to five years, to provide more general and cultural study. The degree of Bachelor of Fine Arts was authorized in 1920. The course did not thrive numerically; by 1937 only twenty-five such degrees had been awarded. However, the presence on the campus of teachers of creative art stimulated art appreciation and aided the work in Architecture and in Arts.

During the depression, with the practical stagnation of private building, architects were among the worst sufferers, and architectural schools suffered sympathetically. From a high of 196 in 1928–29 our enrollment dropped to 131 in 1936–37. But we steadfastly refused to reduce requirements, and at length we were rewarded.

City planning, first taught in 1916, developed in 1934–35 into courses sponsored by Architecture and Engineering, with the aid of a grant from the Carnegie Corporation. The distinguished Gilmore D. Clarke '13 was brought from New York to be professor. The courses were an immediate success; they turned into one of the strongest and most useful areas of work in the college.

Architecture was one of the schools of which we had most reason to be proud. Its success is manifest in the success of its graduates and in the monuments they have erected in our own and other lands. They have received many an honor, many an award. In landscape architecture their achievement was phenomenal. By 1937 Cornell placed ten winners in the fifteen competitions for the Prix de Rome fellowship, which grants three years' residence in Rome.

Dexter S. Kimball, who had come to Cornell to teach machine design in 1898, became Dean of the new consolidated College of Engineering in 1921. (He was a great wit and storyteller. Only one of the dear anecdotes: he passed, in front of Goldwin Smith, a group of students adjuring a dog to Lie Down. The dog smiled, uncomprehending. "Gentlemen," said the Dean, "the trouble is that that is an Engineering dog." He commanded sharply: "Lay down!" and the dog laid down.)

During Kimball's regime, the College of Engineering expanded its offerings to keep pace with new developments. Chemical Engineering, which had been advocated by Thurston as early as 1901, loomed larger, under the stimulation of our wartime discovery of our dependence on German industrial chemistry. The holder of a B.Chem. degree from the College of Arts and Sciences, or from another, might attain the degree of Chemical Engineer by a graduate year in Engineering. The first such degrees were awarded in 1933.

New courses in Administrative Engineering were established, out of awareness that many engineers end in administration, for which they have not been specifically prepared. The Society for the Promotion of Engineering Education favored the training of future administrators as well as future technicians. Accordingly, the new courses included such arts subjects as economics, accounting, business management, labor relations, finance, applied psychology, and public speaking. The first Bachelors of Science in Administrative Engineering were graduated in 1934.

A course in Aerial Engineering had been taught as long ago as 1910–11. In 1936 a Department of Automotive and Aeronautic Engineering was created, with George B. Upton '04 as its head.

In the same year extramural courses in engineering were set up in nearby cities.

But despite all efforts for progress, the popularity of engineering declined. The enrollments, which had reached a high of 1,755 in 1909–10, fell off year by year to touch a low of 812 in 1935–36. The decline was variously interpreted. Perhaps our entrance requirements were too high, our courses too demanding. The falling-off in engineering enrollments was general, possibly because of the rise of schools of business administration, the new glamor subject. The depression threw many engineers out of work, and the big companies ceased to send their scouts to the campuses to sign up likely graduates.

The fact had to be faced that Cornell was losing, even in competition with other engineering schools. The reasons were partly physical, partly moral. The quarters in Sibley and Lincoln were cramped and unsuitable; in 1937 Cornell was reported to be the worst housed and equipped among twenty-five top schools of the country. The equipment was of an interest all too exclusively historic. Most of it was acquired before 1900; little was bought between 1919 and 1937. Virtually no research was done, except that which the new Director of Civil Engineering, Solomon Cady Hollister, started in the Hydraulic Laboratory. Faculty morale was as low as its salaries, which ran considerably below those in Arts and other colleges. In 1936–37 professors averaged $4,210 a year, assistant professors $2,686, instructors $1,781. Only those who had outside consulting jobs could attend their professional meetings, for the college had no travel funds. Thus Cornell's teachers were cut off from contact with new developments in the engineering world.

The situation was no secret. President Farrand admitted in 1933 that our equipment was inadequate and, in the face of engineering progress, obsolete. Some of the alumni were more forthright, asserting that the new facilities at Illinois, Wisconsin, and Purdue made ours look pitiable. Charles Weiss '13 wrote to the *Alumni News* (24 September 1936): "All the progress in Cornell engineering may be summarized in the rearrangement of a few courses, and the obtaining of Dean Hollister. In electrical engineering, a field dominated by Cornellians, Cornell was not even a 'distinguished school' in a recent study of one of the great Foundations." He pointed to N.Y.U.'s aeronautical engineering (an opportunity which Cornell had turned down, by the way), to Purdue's work in housing construction, television, and railway research, to M.I.T.'s over-all leadership. He concluded that it was time to do something for engineering, and with him plenty of alumni agreed.

Dean Kimball retired in 1936, yielding his post to Herman Diederichs '97. "Deed," as he was invariably known, had arrived in the United States from Germany at fourteen, unable to speak English. On graduating four years later from the high school at Dolgeville, New York, he walked fifteen miles to Herkimer to take the state scholarship examinations, which naturally he won. Though waiting on table for his board at college, he found time to be a mighty shot-putter. He kept always his interest in athletics and was long the president of the Athletic Association. He had little opportunity to demonstrate his capacity in the deanship. He died in 1937, and was succeeded by Director S. C. Hollister of Civil Engineering. Like everyone else, Dean Hollister recognized the parlous state of Cornell engineering; unlike everyone else, he proposed to do something about it. But this story belongs to the presidency of Dr. Day.

The Law School, which changed its name from the College of Law in 1925, became in that year a graduate school, with only the qualification that seniors in Cornell's Arts College and in certain others could combine their final year with their first year in Law. The great event in the Law School's history was of course the building of Myron Taylor Hall in 1929–1932. Mr. Taylor's ideal was not so much to train competent practitioners as leaders in industry, finance, and diplomacy. He hoped to make Cornell a center for international law, preparing young men for foreign service. He emphasized the importance of the study of foreign languages, especially French, Italian, and Spanish.[3]

The College of Agriculture was uplifted by the words of the state's Governor, Nathan L. Miller, at President Farrand's Inauguration: "I undertake to say that the vast improvement in agriculture in this State has been due to the work of Cornell University more than to any other single cause. . . . If there is to be any change [in state policy] it will have to be along the line of greater liberality." The college was further heartened by the passage in Congress of the Purnell Act, in 1925, giving increased support to experiment stations and subsidizing research in agriculture and home economics, for "the development and improvement of the rural home and rural life." The college was given by the state a farm near Riverhead, Long Island, for experimental work in vegetables, and five tracts in the Hudson valley for the study of orchard tillage, fertilization, and varietal adaptation.

Perhaps the most important event in the history of the college during these years was the state's decision, in 1923, to put the State Agricultural Experiment Station in Geneva under the administration of Cornell's Board of Trustees. In fact, the two institutions had worked together in general harmony for forty years, with frequent conferences to advance common enterprises and to reduce duplication. In 1920 a form of affiliation had been established, without resort to law. Amalgamation was clearly advantageous to both parties. The Geneva Experiment Sta-

[3] *Alumni News,* 3 Jan. 1929.

tion, with its scientific staff of fifty-five, its brilliant record of investigation and discovery, and its farms, orchards, and vineyards, could well serve the college in Ithaca, and at the same time it could use the machinery of the Extension Service, including the county agent system. A few years after the consolidation, in 1932, the acting director, Cornelius Betten, observed that the emphasis in the work of the Experiment Station was changing. Instead of helping farmers to produce good crops economically, it was more concerned with converting farm products into new improved forms, to resist disease, to stimulate consumption, and to promote the utilization of by-products. He noted the cooperation of the station with the Birdseye Laboratories in problems of quick freezing.

Finally in 1940 the teachers on the Geneva staff were made members of the Faculty of the College of Agriculture.

Despite these advances, the legislature proved for a time strangely reluctant to provide for the day-to-day needs of the state colleges in Ithaca. Dean Albert R. Mann of Agriculture berated the state, in 1927 and 1928, for its parsimony. The time had been, he said, when the college was well treated, but now foresight and generosity were not so apparent. The college has slipped backward, he asserted. The salary scale, seriously inferior to that in the endowed colleges, was not adjusted to the cost of living, increases were denied, promotions rare. The overcrowding in inadequate buildings was intolerable. Plant Pathology, for instance, was doing its inestimable work in cramped, gloomy warrens underneath Bailey Hall.

Various causes conspired to bring agriculture low in the twenties. The romantic view of farm life faded, leaving a good many disillusioned amateur farmers. While the cities boomed, the average of farm incomes remained low. The abandoned farm became a familiar sight in the hill country. Correspondingly, enrollment in the College of Agriculture dropped, from a high of 1,704 in 1915–16 to a low of 676 in 1928–29, and of these registrants less than half proceeded to a degree. In these circumstances, Dean Mann's pleas for increased support fell on deaf Albany ears.

The legislature's penurious mood changed in the late twenties. Franklin D. Roosevelt became Governor in 1928 and called on the college for advice in planning his programs. Depression increased enrollment in the free-tuition colleges, and inspired many to regard food-raising as a better way of life than economic warfare. Registrations turned upward, to reach a triumphant 1,359 in 1936–37 (208 of these were, to be sure, in a special two-year course). Overcrowding was eased; with the opening of the Plant Science Building in 1931 many of the essential sciences were suitably, even magnificently, lodged. Salaries were raised, and staff members were admitted in 1930 to the State Employees' Retirement System, which afforded provisions generous for the period. At the same time, they benefited from the University's group life insurance.

Dean Mann moved from the deanship to the provostship in 1932. Director Isaac P. Roberts's top hat, which had been solemnly presented to Liberty Hyde Bailey as the symbol of authority, was no less solemnly placed on the head of Carl E. Ladd '12. Dean Ladd served until his death in 1943. His incumbency was marked by many instructional advances within the departments, many achievements in research, many personal triumphs among the professors. An adequate review lies beyond the scope of this history.

We must notice, however, the fate of Forestry. The distinguished work done in the department was recognized and furthered by the gift in 1927 of $130,000 by the Charles Lathrop Pack Foundation to endow a professorship for research in forest soils. But only five years later a state inquiry, while commending the work done at Cornell, recommended that to avoid duplication of effort the state's aid to professional forestry should be concentrated at the State College of Forestry at Syracuse. Therefore the undergraduate work in professional forestry at Cornell was discontinued, and the department devoted itself to graduate work and research. In 1937 the department was further limited to courses meeting the needs of undergraduates in Agriculture or in Wild Life Conservation and Management. It remained also active in extension work.

All this is very sad. The first College of Forestry in the country thus dwindled away. So many high hopes were dashed! So many eminent graduates in Forestry were left without a collegiate home!

The work in plant sciences received a precious aid in the gift by Liberty Hyde Bailey, in 1935, of his private hortorium, a term of his own invention to characterize his collection of about 150,000 mounted specimens, especially of cultivated plants. Bailey gave also the two buildings which housed the collection, across Sage Place from the Infirmary, keeping, as Curator, life tenancy. He had been publishing since 1920 the lessons drawn from his hortorium, in the form of *Gentes herbarum*. After his death the hortorium, having overflowed its original quarters, was transferred to the top floor of the Albert R. Mann

Library, where it exists as an administrative unit of the College of Agriculture.

Some agricultural notes of these years: Farmers' Week, metamorphosed into Farm and Home Week, became the climax of the college year, attracting as many as 16,000 visitors. We received in 1930 a collection of 22,000 moths and butterflies, made as a hobby by Addison J. Ellsworth, a printer. In 1925 died a famous campus figure, Glista Ernestine, a Holstein-Friesian born in our barns, who broke almost every record in the cow world; in her lifetime she produced enough milk to fill three railroad tank-cars, and also mothered thirteen calves. A full life. In 1933 the Department of Animal Husbandry had a herd of 245 animals of every breed; they were well lodged, with insectocutors, or electrified screens to trap and kill flies. The bulls, if inclined to sloth, were hitched to an electric exerciser; their nose rings were attached to a revolving power-driven arm, which led them around and around. The bulls fought bullfully, but always lost. Herbert H. Whetzel of Plant Pathology was quoted as saying that plants are subject to nasty colds, and that a certain fungus, when so suffering, sneezes its head off.

Albert R. Brand, a retired stockbroker with a passionate interest in birds, settled here about 1930 with the complimentary title of Research Associate in Ornithology. He devised an apparatus for recording bird songs. His sound-recording truck, after exhausting the musical possibilities of the local wild, made long journeys for fresh material. On returning from an expedition in 1935, Paul P. Kellogg '29 reported some of his adventures. He had caught the song of a water ousel in a dashing stream, getting the diaphragm only two inches from the bird's mouth. A Carolina wren insisted on building a nest in the truck while singing for the record. In Colorado the mike was carefully lowered from the rim of a canyon to the nest of a golden eagle; and the eagle did his best to swallow the mike. And in Florida a mockingbird recognized the recorded song of a rival being tested, and dashed at the window to drive it away. Said Mr. Brand in 1931: "The new type of bird library will be composed of talkie records." Mr. Brand died in 1940, leaving by bequest a Foundation to carry on his work.

Home Economics, which had crept into the Extension Service in 1900 and had become a department in Agriculture in 1907 and a school in 1919, attained its ambition to be a college, by legislative enactment in 1925. It was the first state-chartered College of Home Economics in the country. The inseparable Martha Van Rensselaer and Flora Rose were named codirectors. Codirector Van Rensselaer handled resident teaching and research, Codirector Rose extension and general administration. "It was an interesting experience," remembers Dean Howard B. Meek of Hotel Administration, "to see Flora Rose come up with a new idea, sell it to Miss Van, and then by force of personality enlist for it the enthusiasm of the staff." [4] Their college prospered so much that it was soon necessary to limit enrollment. At length, in 1930, the legislature appropriated a million dollars for the construction of a new building, which became Martha Van Rensselaer Hall.

The pioneering boldness of the college made it many friends in high place. Mrs. Franklin D. Roosevelt took an interest in it, at least as early as 1925. She was a regular visitor and speaker at Farm and Home Week. In fact, in March 1933 Mrs. Roosevelt, beginning her house-keeping in the White House, served a depression lunch recommended at Farm and Home Week: hot stuffed eggs with tomato sauce, mashed potatoes, prune pudding, bread, and coffee, at a cost of 7½ cents a plate. The President ate it all, and then signed the bill legalizing 3.2 per cent beer.

Still, those were not wanting who shook their heads sadly or angrily, asserting that Home Economics has no place in a university. It depends, I suppose, on one's view of what a university was, is, and should be. There is not much point now in appealing to the classical trivium and quadrivium. If a university's work must depend upon fundamental science and abstract thought, half of our present offerings must go by the board. If the criterion is preparation for life, anything is admissible, for life can be anything. The College of Home Economics, sensitive to criticism, sought to justify itself by imposing fundamental science courses and by stiffening its curriculum to match in difficulty that of the Arts College.

Codirector Rose made an apologia for home economics in her report for 1930. Food, health, child training, clothing, are important in our world, she said, if anything is important. Home economics serves general education, by producing healthy, free human beings, competent in their environment. It serves also vocational education, for, with the general deferment of marriage, women must have a means of self-support, and they must also be trained to make a right use of their leisure. The community needs women's work and trained abilities. And women need "to follow into the community the activities lost

[4] *Alumni News*, 15 May 1950.

to them in the home, and thereby to free both home and community from the burden of supporting women in idleness."

In 1921 the American Hotel Association, desirous of profiting by the advances in technology, proposed to father an adequate course in hotel management. The hotelmen were well acquainted with the work of the College of Home Economics and chose it to mother the project. No doubt, says Dean Meek, their personal confidence in Miss Van Rensselaer and Miss Rose was an important factor in their choice.[5] With financial assistance from Ellsworth M. Statler of the Statler Hotels, Dr. Meek, a Yale Ph.D. and instructor in mathematics, who had given a noncredit course at Boston University for students looking for hotel summer jobs, was brought here in 1922 to establish the first hotel course of college grade in the world. The initial enrollment in his course was only twenty-four. But the work, appealing to an evident need, expanded rapidly and soon strained the available resources, for it received financial support neither from the University nor from the state. It was however fondly fostered by hotelmen everywhere, and especially by Mr. Statler, and, after his death, by his heirs and trustees. It attracted much professional attention by its annual hotel-for-a-day, the Hotel Ezra Cornell, the first of which was staged in Prudence Risley in 1926. (The celebration was called to campus attention by an admirable device—a Waiters' Derby, in which jacketed waiters, bearing aloft a bowl of soup on a tray, raced from the Library to Willard Straight. Spilled soup meant disqualification. The Waiters' Derby immediately became a hallowed Cornell tradition.) At this first hotel-for-a-day Mr. Statler, called on to say a few words, made a famous speech, which I quote in toto: "Meek can have anything he wants."

The Hotel School's record of success was remarkable. It never knew a depression. In July 1932 all the year's graduates were placed in jobs. A survey in 1935 showed that of 232 alumni 98 per cent were employed, most of them in hotel work.

On 26 May 1932 died the mighty Martha Van Rensselaer, chief maker of the College of Home Economics, one of the greatest American women of her time. (Indeed, in 1923 the National League of Women Voters chose her as one of the twelve greatest living American women.) Two weeks after her death the cornerstone of Martha Van Rensselaer Hall was laid.

The Veterinary College, after a period of trial immediately follow-

[5] "Origins of the Hotel Administration Course," in *Alumni News*, 15 May 1950.

ing the First War, reflecting the general despondency among veterinarians in a horseless world, found that the need for trained veterinarians did not abate. Cornell's graduates were always in demand. The small-animal business boomed, as people began to seek proper medical care for their pets. And more and more veterinarians became leaders in live-stock sanitation and in the scientific study and prevention of animal diseases. The Veterinary College responded to the changing state of affairs. Its enrollment rose to a maximum of 214 in 1931–32. Thereafter one year of college work was required for entrance to its four-year course, with the result that registration dropped off somewhat, to the great relief of the overworked staff.

The Summer Schools, in Arts, Agriculture, Law, and (from 1935) Home Economics and Hotel Administration, attracted the maximum of 2,440 students in 1931. Then the depression struck home, and the enrollment dropped to 1,464 in 1933. The figure afterwards gradually rose, to 1,996 in the summer of 1937.

It is fitting to conclude this review of education under President Farrand with a look at the Library. In 1930, on the retirement of Willard Austen as Librarian, Dr. Otto Kinkeldey, who had been professor of music from 1923 to 1927, was brought back from the New York Public Library to replace him (and to fill the chair of Musicology). His reports are an incessant reiteration of woe. The burden of his complaint is intolerable crowding in the stacks and reading rooms, insufficient work space, inadequate and underpaid staff, and parsimonious purchase funds.

Some small relief came in 1936, with the construction of a nine-story stack between the south and west wings. This accommodation for 200,000 books brought a brief respite to the storage problem. It settled none of the others. In 1924 the Library, with 710,000 books, stood fourth among American university libraries. But it was ninth in the amount spent for books, and twelfth in the amount spent for library service. The accessions in 1927–28 were only 10,807, fewer than in a typical year of the eighties or nineties. In 1929–30 the Library bought only 5,627 books; it dropped from fourth to fifth place in its holdings, to nineteenth in expenditures for books. The downward trend continued; in 1933–34 it purchased only 3,484 items. In 1936–37 the number rose to a mere 4,739.

The resentment in the faculty was acute. A sharp report was made by a Committee on the Library in 1930, directed at the trustees' long-established custom of using only one-third of the Willard Fiske funds for book purchases, and two-thirds for library administration. This, said the committee, was an evasion of Mr. Fiske's purpose. It urged that all administrative expenses be charged to the general resources of the University.

To be sure, the collections were enlarged by many gifts, some of them of first importance. The Wason collection on Far Eastern subjects, bequeathed by Charles W. Wason '76, with an endowment, grew steadily. The Benno Loewy collection, rich in law, literature, philosophy, occultism, Masonic history, came to Cornell. Victor Emanuel '19 gave the Wordsworth collection made by Cynthia Morgan St. John of Ithaca, and thanks to Mr. Emanuel this collection has been increased until now it is supreme in the world. There were other important gifts; but how can we record the good works of all our well-wishers, or the faithful labors of all our University's servants?

XXXII

Cornell under President Farrand:
Campus Life

THE faculty was happy during this era of good feeling, under the benevolent gaze of the President, and the generally benevolent gaze of the Deans. Placidly, on the whole, it watched the postwar disillusionment, and flaming youth, and depression, and the New Deal, and the ominous rise of the dictators.

For observatory it had only the old University Club on Central Avenue, built by Professor Prentiss in the 1870's and much made over, always for the worse. Its grim smoking room with its creaking wicker chairs served as our forum, our news exchange and editorial office, the control room of our imitation ivory tower.

Here we weighed and judged, often sardonically, the news of the day. We followed with admiration the career of former President Schurman, Minister to China from 1921 to 1925, Ambassador to Germany from 1925 to 1930. On his retirement from diplomacy, at the age of seventy-six, he spoke in Bailey Hall with a fire and vigor beyond the capacity of most youngsters. We heard with delight reports from the lecture room of the distinguished Alfred Zimmern, theorist of government, here in 1922–23. His wife sat in the front row, knitting; and, as the *Alumni News* put it in courtly style, "she interpolates additional light on the topic about which her husband lectures, her services being purely voluntary." We were proud of James B. Sumner of Biological Chemistry, who isolated and crystallized the enzyme urease in 1926, and who later received the Nobel Prize for his achievement. We applauded the coming as Commandant of Colonel Joe Beacham '97, who inspired with his magnificent zest the military department, heralded by his famous one-hundred-piece band. We heard from Howard Liddell of Psychology the distresses of his pig Achilles, driven to a nervous breakdown between his desire for an apple and his fear of an electric shock. We acclaimed Laurence H. MacDaniels of Floriculture, whose eleven-foot hollyhock was the second tallest in Tompkins County. We snickered at the story of Julian Bretz of History. He was awakened by a telephone call at 3 A.M. Said an irate lady: "Your dog has been barking continuously, and neither Mr. X nor I have been able to get a wink of sleep." Bretz replied mildly: "I am sure the dog won't bother you any more." The next night at 3 A.M. he telephoned the lady, to say: "I just wanted to tell you that I never had a dog."

Saddest of the subjects for comment was the increasing necrology. Burt Green Wilder, last of the original Faculty, died in 1925. In 1927 Louis Agassiz Fuertes, the great bird painter, was killed by a train. The Fuertes Bird Sanctuary in Stewart Park is dedicated to his memory. In Fernow Hall is the Fuertes Memorial Room, with his mounted specimens, books, and some of his paintings. In 1928 Professor John G. Pertsch '09 of Electrical Engineering died, overcome while rescuing a young woman from drowning in Cayuga Lake. In the same year died Teefy Crane. Though not formally a member of the original Faculty, he had been drafted for service in the University's opening year. Anna Botsford Comstock '85, pioneer of nature study, died in 1930, and so did Martin Sampson of English, one of the most notable figures in our academic history. He was a great teacher, with an original mind. Only the year before his death he made an experiment in the union of poetry and music, reading Keats while Vladimir Karapetoff played the cello and Harold Smith the piano. Of Sampson a former student recalled that in the lecture room "he appeared to be in a state of exaltation—as one who had just spoken with the gods and was about to repeat their message. Students believed and worshipped." [1] A plaque by his old friend Christian Midjo of Fine Arts, representing him in a characteristic pose, was placed in his favorite classroom in Goldwin Smith. Davy Hoy '93, the fabled Registrar, died in the same year. He was a byword for ferocity, affectionately cherished in recollection and passed on as an exemplary scarebabe for freshmen, who would

[1] *Alumni News*, Sept. 1933.

tremble so that they could scarcely sign their names when their turn came in the Registrar's office. But his ferocity hid a lamblike soul. Many, like this writer, first entered his lair with quaking knees and lips muttering defiance, and were disarmed by his kindly consideration. And finally let us lay a posy on the grave of Alexis Babine '92, son of a Volga fisherman, who arrived in Ithaca in 1888 with fifteen dollars and a slight knowledge of Elizabethan English. As a cataloguer for Russian books was needed, he worked in the Library till 1910, and then returned to Russia to publish his *History of the United States.* He became an Imperial School Inspector, survived the Revolution, escaped, and resumed his old post in the Library in 1922. Five years later he went to the Library of Congress as head of the Slavic Division.

To observe student life, we must proceed from the University Club up Central Avenue to Willard Straight. The great building immediately fulfilled the most sanguine hopes of the donor. Students basked in its elegance, dined in its formal dining rooms, fed in its cafeteria, danced, worked, read, and dozed under the eye of its capable manager, Foster M. Coffin '12. They were also barbered by the genial and ingenious Jerry Fiddler, Sp.Agr. '07–'08, whimsical commentator on world affairs, who featured his Chiaroscuro Haircut, who insulated his new house with student hair.

The student parade moved ever onward, with new faces replacing the old, but bearing a marked resemblance. We continued to attract foreign students. Ten young men were sent to us by the U.S.S.R. in 1931, most of them studying engineering. One wonders what has happened to them. In 1935 came George Couvaras, Cornell's first matriculate from Ithaca, Greece. In 1930 the Chinese Students' Club won the prized '97 All-Round Athletic Championship trophy.

No statistics exist to show the proportion of the earnest, the valiant, the happy and unhappy, the crooked-minded, the secretly doomed. We had always our obscure heroes, apparently convinced that an education is worth every sacrifice and deprivation. We are told of a man who arrived in Ithaca in 1921 with $2.16 in pocket. He lived for two days on a lunch packed by his mother; he then got a job in a restaurant and worked there until his graduation in Forestry. I hope the experience was worth the pains. An *Alumni News* inquiry in 1928 showed that 50 per cent of the men and 35 per cent of the women were partially self-supporting. Most of them waited on table at thirty-five to fifty cents an hour.

It was generally held that more academic work was required of students than in the past. Courses were certainly made harder with the coming of more necessary knowledge, and more afternoon hours were utilized. Some evidence that Cornellians could work hard without sacrificing the admired well-roundedness is afforded by the selection as Rhodes Scholars of Russell H. Peters '20, William D. P. Carey '23, George R. Pfann '24, and Eugene W. Goodwillie '27.

Not everyone was pleased by the new seriousness. Romeyn Berry wrote, in the *Alumni News* for 4 February 1926:

It's fine for undergraduates to be hard working and well behaved, but I wish this crowd wasn't so terribly middle aged. They wear rubbers and apparently have no emotions. Nothing makes them mad except their inability to find a desired book in the Library. They gargle their throats and take life seriously. They are good because it is too much trouble to be bad.

This was a minority report from the prewar era. But certainly the college spirit of Good Old Siwash, of Stover at Yale, was fading away. Said a writer in the *Alumni News* (23 April 1931):

No more do the better students chant their Alma Mater in a happy trance; they sing from the side of the mouth, with the air of cynical priests of old Egypt; these mummeries are all very well for the masses. No more do torch-bearers by the thousand escort departing teams with pomp; no more do inebriates walk the streets disguised as babes and sucking candy sticks; and cows are found no more in belfries.

The class spirit, with its tumultuous rivalries, suffered especially from the new sophistication. The sanguinary autumnal class rush became a pushball contest, and even that was abandoned in 1923. The spring mud rush, regarded askance by the fastidious, was abolished three years later, together with organized cheering at baseball games and track meets. In a bareheaded period, many freshmen refused to wear frosh caps, and went unpunished. Class elections caused only a ripple. The junior smoker, which used to jam Bailey Hall, became in 1928 a formal dinner at three dollars a plate.

But Maytime could still stir the old enzymes. In 1928 the sophomores seized members of the freshman banquet committee. After a series of captures and escapes, the sophs held the door of Willard Straight against the frosh arriving for their banquet. But the frosh took the sophs in the rear and drove them forth with a fire hose. Again in 1933 there was a battle at the sophomore smoker in Willard Straight. The freshmen threw eggs and other organic matter at the defenders of the portal and drove them in. The victors remained outside, "shout-

ing, singing, thumping their chests, stripping sophs to the skin, throw-
ing captured garments into the trees." They then marched through
Collegetown, with atavistic gestures and outcries. Well, said Frank
Sullivan '14 in the New York *World*, "give me an unruly student body,
and I will give you a healthy, active Faculty and some of my old
Victrola records."

Mightily proud of their postwar disillusionment, the more vocal of
the students delighted in questioning all the accepted verities. The *Sun*,
usually far in advance of student opinion, to be sure, treated holy
things with mockery. "Loyalty" became a comic word; the sneer and
jeer replaced the cheer. Even the fraternity was not exempt from public
criticism. Many campus intellectuals seceded, to set up apartment life
with their own kind. The *Sun* suggested in January 1928 that the
fraternities cut loose from their national affiliations. Why pay $50,000
annually to national offices? "Affiliations after college amount to naught.
The frat is forgotten and the chapter remembered only as a convenient
lodging and boarding house over occasional weekends." Some elders
regarded such judgments as evidence that the undergraduate was growing up, while others thought they portended the coming of Antichrist.

In December 1926 "Five Bewildered Freshmen" wrote to the *Sun*,
asking what education was all about anyway. Plenty of people wrote
in to tell them, and a delightful controversy ensued. Noteworthily,
Carl Becker answered that in fact we are all bewildered.

Professors could reorganize the College of Arts if they knew what a College of Arts should be. They could give students a "general education" if
they knew what a general education was, or would be good for if one had
it. Professors are not generally to blame because the world has lost all certainty about these things. . . . I would like an orientation course for freshmen. I would like one for seniors. I would like one for professors and
trustees. I would like one for President Farrand. . . . Only, who is to give
it? And what is it to consist of? . . . The Five Bewildered Freshmen have
got more out of their course than they know. It has made them ask a question—What is it all about? That is a pertinent question. I have been asking
it for thirty-five years, and I am still as bewildered as they are.

Such texts help us to make an image of postwar disillusionment at
Cornell. It existed, certainly, though it did not represent the normal
mood of the majority. We had always had our share of cynics with
regard to religion, politics, imposed dogmas, conventional morality.
Now the cynics increased in numbers and in the scope of their criticisms, which brought some of them to total nihilism. The intellectual

fashion was to outdo everybody in condemnation of everything. I remember one young despairer who argued that the only solution for the world's ills was mass suicide.

The cynic mood was promoted by two national phenomena: prohibition and the depression, with their accompaniments of lawbreaking and radical rebelliousness.

Drinking has always been a problem among students, free for the first time to experiment with delights hitherto forbidden. One remembers Bismarck's dictum on European universitarians: "One-third drink themselves to death, one-third study themselves to death, and the other third govern Europe." At Cornell, however, the drink problem was a minor one, at least until the beginning of the century. Then the beer taps were opened; but they flowed only downtown, and mostly on Saturday nights, as a ceremonial observance of athletic victory.

Prohibition came in with 1919. For a brief space it was faithfully observed, as most people, familiar with alcohol's maleficence, thought enforced abstinence a good thing. Soon, however, the mood changed. The elders set the example, infringing the law to satisfy old cravings or out of mere bravado. Noisome brews bubbled in many a professorial cellar. Jolly journeys were made to the wine country westward, where gallon jugs were passed out of vineyardists' back doors.[2] Furtive speakeasies sprang up, where one ran the delightful risk of the revenooers' raid and the less delightful risk of wood-alcohol poisoning. Acquaintance with a speakeasy lookout conferred status. In the fraternities the no-liquor rule, hitherto respected, went the way of the law of the United States. Previously drinking and dancing had been rigorously separated; now they were blent, and even the girls had their nips from the boys' hip flasks.

For some time the forces of order and decency struggled. In December 1921 the Student Council, presided over by Daniel B. Strickler '22, demanded the enforcement of antiliquor rules in fraternities, the abolition of uncontrolled fraternity dances, and the persuasion of visiting alumni to keep sober and abate their generosity. But matters got steadily worse, in Cornell as in the great world without. Anyone who lived through that period can recall all too many instances, comic or

---

[2] Your historian remembers as characteristic of this strange period a visit to a local pundit. He brought forth a nauseous fluid of his own fabrication. Shuddering, your historian forced down a draught, and exclaimed: "How do you make this?" "Very simple. Just put malt and yeast in water and let them work." "Don't you put in any hops?" "Nah. Hops just make it taste better."

tragic, of drunken brawls and misbehavior, of alcohol-begotten accidents, of the beginnings of disastrous addictions.

At the same time, one must not picture the fifteen-year period of prohibition as one long gin-soak. Most of the students came here for an education, toward which, they found, sobriety conduced. Most of them much preferred a chocolate malted to juniper-flavored alcohol, and for most of them one experience of a prohibition hangover was plenty. During the depression years most of them found the illicit brews far too expensive for their purses. Some elders could see an educational advantage in the undergraduates' freedom to see the evil and choose the good. "Strength and decision of character are tested only by temptation, and, until the peculiar temptations of college life have been met, one may not easily decide who will stand and who will fall," said Cuthbert W. Pound '87 and John L. Senior '01, in their alumni trustee report for 1928. (One might conclude that if no temptation was available, it would be the University's duty to provide it.)

Repeal came in 1933, without much affecting either drinkers or abstainers. Said the *Alumni News* (14 December): "Almost immediately drinks became smaller, poorer, more expensive and harder to get. Cocktails ran from 40 to 50 cents each, and a hardy alumnus twenty years out of college could have poured four of them in his eye without blinking." Early in 1934, after some controversy, beer was authorized in Willard Straight. It seems not to have been abused, since it is still there.

Sumptuary note: in February 1923, for the first time, the Co-op put tobacco on sale.

The second phenomenon affecting college life was the depression.

The depression, officially inaugurated by Black Friday on the stock market, 29 October 1929, was not immediately felt in our seclusion. But as businesses contracted and failed, as parents found themselves jobless, as remittances dwindled, hardship came to the campus. Within a year our loan funds were severely taxed. Graduating seniors had great trouble in finding employers, the architects and Bachelors of Arts being worst put to it. In October 1932 it was reported that student jobs providing board and room were all taken by juniors and seniors, and that five hundred working students could find no work to do. One student was a professional dancer, nay rather a gigolo. Others worked as meatcutters, plumbers, painters, decorators. One was a tailor, one did embroidery, one gave religious talks. Four Russians formed a vocal quartet. Two boys lived in a tent by Six Mile Creek.

491

The fraternities became economy-minded. House parties and dances were curtailed, and the Junior Week assessment was commonly abrogated. Initiation fees were slashed. The jobs as waiters went to the brothers. To met the lowered income, the scale of living was reduced until sometimes one could live as cheaply in a chapter house as in a dormitory.

A Student Emergency Loan Fund was established in 1932. It was aided from various sources, including a Depression Ball, to which entrance could be had by barter. Clothing, desk lamps, slide rules, surgical instruments, and even a Bible were accepted. One dancer got in for twenty-five cents and a dozen original drawings, including "A Design for a Simple Tombstone."

Many ingenious devices for survival were found. The Handy Andy Association lived in a semicooperative rooming house and did household work in organized bands. Two hundred men formed a dining association, meeting in the Cosmopolitan Club and obtaining fourteen meals a week for $2.50, later reduced, with a University subsidy, to $2.00.

The *Alumni News* printed (2 February 1933) a remarkable theme submitted in an English course, telling how a nearly penniless student might survive. He had a top-floor room on College Avenue for $2.50 per week. He insisted on making his own bed and cleaning his room, ostensibly from consideration for his landlady's rheumatism, in fact to hide the use of an electric grill. He bought a quart of milk a day. Breakfast: cereal and half the milk. Lunch in a cafeteria, twenty-five cents. Supper: a five-cent can of beans or soup and the rest of the milk. Add bread, and a carrot a day (three cents a pound) for vitamin content. This makes a daily expense for food of forty-four cents. On Sunday a walk in the country, to pick up vitamins under a vitamin tree. Total cost, board and room, $5.58 per week.

In 1933, with the New Deal, matters began to improve. The class of 1932, only 15 per cent of whom had jobs on graduation, found full employment, though perhaps not in work of their choice. The National Youth Administration gave federal aid to students, in return for new-found jobs, such as cataloguing departmental records, and outdoor work, as cleaning up and path building in the gorges. In 1935-36 the N.Y.A. subsidized students to the extent of nearly $100,000. Although no one remarked upon it at the time, or perhaps since, it was a resurrection of Ezra Cornell's Voluntary Labor Corps.

Inevitably the depression promoted political radicalism. Some students inherited socialist or communist faith. Others, natural malcontents, accepted the easy conclusion that the depression proved the failure of capitalism and that the absence of depressions in Soviet Russia proved the superiority of its system. The Cornell Liberal Club was organized by a group of students and faculty in 1929. It opposed the condemnation of Sacco and Vanzetti, the brutal treatment of striking miners, the ban on working foreign students, and compulsory military training at Cornell. It demanded the abolition of war as an instrument of national policy. Itself apparently infiltrated by communists, it was in turn infiltrated, in March 1933, by fifty visitors, led by Thomas Maxcy '33, editor of the *Widow*. Each paid his initiation fee of fifty cents, thus wiping out the club's deficit. As the new members bade fair to put an end to liberalism, the president illiberally adjourned the meeting without permitting a vote. A week later five hundred alleged liberals appeared at a meeting in Willard Straight. In a mighty hurly-burly Albert E. Arent '34, a moderate, was elected president and soon guided the club back to its previous obscurity.

Several advanced organizations, including the American Student Union and the Young Communist League, met unmolested. In November 1936 State Senator John J. McNaboe, chairman of a committee investigating subversive activities, discovered the two clubs openly listed in the Freshman Desk Book, issued by the C.U.R.W. He therefore told the press: "Cornell is a center of revolutionary communistic activity."

President Farrand took the revelation calmly. He said:

I do not find myself perturbed . . . My information is that there are twenty-five or thirty students with communistic leanings or convictions, which, in a student body of more than six thousand, does not strike me as creating in any way a serious or unwholesome situation. I am more disturbed by the thought that an elected representative of the people of New York State could make this indirect attack on the whole spirit of free inquiry, of free discussion, and of free assemblage, which is the inherent right of every university worthy of the name. I trust that Cornell will always maintain its traditional liberal attitude on this fundamental American principle.

And, at a testimonial dinner to him in New York, he added: "I don't mind saying that I find that small group stimulating." [3]

[3] *Alumni News*, 3 Dec. 1936; *Sun*, 4 Dec. 1936. President Farrand is frequently quoted as saying: "If we had no Communists at Cornell, I would feel it my duty to import a few." Perhaps indeed he said this, but I do not find it reported at the time.

The matter ended, as such matters do in colleges, with a "Communist Rally," at which enormously bewhiskered speakers with peculiar Russian accents demanded the progressive abolition of prelims, final exams, courses, and morality.

Despite depression, students were increasingly motorized. A census in 1922 revealed 200 cars, 117 of them Fords. In 1929 it was noted that some fraternities boasted one car per member, though many of the vehicles possessed no brakes, lights, or insurance. The Motor Vehicle Bureau was established in 1930, to control driving and parking. In the following year, in depression's depths, 1,063 student cars were registered, and it was estimated that 500 car owners had refrained from paying the registration fee. Anti-student-car feeling on the faculty ran high. Many favored, as they still do, the prohibition of student ownership of automobiles. Eloquent diatribes, recounting personal misadventures, were made in Faculty meetings. But efforts to abolish student driving in the automobile age were baffled by the expense and difficulty of enforcement, and by a general unwillingness to impose a law which would be immediately flouted.

Organized student activities flourished, depression or no depression.

The Spring Day celebration, abrogated during the First War, was revived in 1922. However, it suffered the fate of most revivals. It became perfunctory, an exhibition of very primitive humors, which one prefers not to recall. In 1926 the special publications for the day, judged indecent, were withdrawn as far as possible from public sale and eleven editors put on parole. A snowstorm on Spring Day 1931 delivered the *coup de grâce*.

However, Spring Day was dear to many. In 1933 a committee decided to rescue and renovate it. The committee had a brilliant idea—an aquatic carnival on Beebe Lake, with boat races, canoe tilting, and as a climax a duck race, the Donald Duck Derby. The idea captured campus imaginations. Fraternities and sororities trained their entries: Pearl S. Duck, the Duck of York, Epsom the Old Salt, Pancreatic Duck, Delta Delta Delta's Duck Duck Duck, and even a captured mallard, Moby Duck. News from the training camps filled the *Sun*. On the great day fifty-three ducks, each wearing his club colors, were released at the starting pistol, which paralyzed many of the contestants. The wild mallard rose from the water, crossed the finish line far ahead of the pack, and headed for Canada. Mrs. Livingston Farrand, the judge, disqualified him on the ground that the Derby was not an aviation meet, and awarded the prize to a rank outsider, Ducky Strike, entered by the Syracuse chapter of Psi Upsilon.

Student organizations lived their various lives. The Cornell University Christian Association, under the impulsion of its director, Richard H. Edwards, took a momentous step in 1929, transforming itself into the Cornell United Religious Work and admitting Roman Catholics and Jews. Father T. J. Cronin and Rabbi Isadore B. Hoffman established offices in Barnes Hall. Four years later the Friends and the Unitarians joined the C.U.R.W. The men's and women's religious work was coordinated in 1934. The implications of these transformations are many and obvious. Cornell, if not the first, was among the first to seek unity rather than rivalry among the faiths, and to represent in actual deed that above all religions is religion. Though it was no easy task to convince some dogmatic believers of their deeper brotherhood, and though there must have been many a stress and strain within Barnes Hall, the union has proved a triumphant success. It has served rather to strengthen than to debilitate the work of the various faiths.

On Good Friday of 1937 a Roman Catholic service was celebrated for the first time in Sage Chapel. To be sure, Catholic priests had often previously preached at the regular services.

Among the publications, the *Alumni News* was reorganized in 1927 by its Editor, R. Warren ("Tubby") Sailor '07. It took over the Cayuga Press and moved into its own building on East Green Street. The basement was and is the home of the Savage Club.

The *Sun* beamed on, though sometimes obscured by financial clouds, and though sometimes editorial sunspots provoked electrical storms among the faculty. In 1930, to celebrate its fiftieth anniversary, it produced *A Half-Century at Cornell*, containing the recollections and commentaries of two-score eminent Cornellians. To this precious compendium your historian is deeply indebted.

In the same year the two editors of the *Sun*'s humorous column, the Berry Patch, attained national fame. Lester A. Blumner '30 was deeply impressed by Martin Sampson's anecdote of a Parisian hoax. (A newspaper editor invited the members of the Chamber of Deputies to the unveiling of a monument to Hégésippe Simon, author of the immortal words: "When the sun rises, the clouds disperse." Those who came to the party were cruelly ridiculed, and eight Deputies were forced to resign.) Blumner and his mate, Edward T. Horn '29, conceived a similar hoax, to amuse the annual Berry Patch party. On the letterhead of the Hugo Norris Frye Sesquicentennial Committee they wrote to a number of Republican eminences, asking messages in honor of the little-known patriot, Hugo N. Frye, whose slogans, such as "Freedom in the land of the free," led to the formation of the Republican party. Many of the eminences, including Vice-President Charles Curtis and Secretary of Labor James J. Davis, fell into the trap and sent congratulatory telegrams. The contrivers of the escapade insisted that they had no intention to make these public. But a reporter for the New York *World*, tipped off, came to the dinner and scored a mighty scoop. Senator Pat Harrison (Miss., Dem.) read the dispatch aloud on the floor of the Senate. Vice-President Curtis joined in the laughter as he rapped for order. But no one resigned.

It was a good joke, certainly. Nevertheless, critical amateurs of hoaxes pointed out that there was nothing in the come-on letter, except the double meaning of Hugo N. Frye, to arouse suspicion even in the suspicious. Said Jerry Fiddler, the philosophic barber of Willard Straight: "It's as if I should go to Cleveland and tell everybody my name was Henry, and then come back and say: 'Jeez, those Cleveland people are dumb! They think my name is Henry!'" [4]

The grand old *Cornell Era* made a last gallant effort in 1924. It became a literary quarterly, under the leadership of Richard S. Hill '24. It published one enormous (and very fine) issue, and then expired. The day of the literary magazine was about over, as many editors in the greater world found to their cost.

The *Era* left as a posthumous child the *Cornell Graphic*, which attempted to profit by the vogue for picture magazines. But the costs of graphic reproduction could not be covered by the limited circulation, and the *Graphic* gave up in 1926.

There were other ventures in the field of literary and para-literary journalism: the *Literary Review* in 1922, the *Columns* in 1926, *Areopagus* ("A Journal of Opinion") in 1936. As initial enthusiasms ebbed, as editors found themselves caught between waning readership and mounting costs, these too disappeared. Only the *Widow* went on forever. The phenomenon of the college comic is curious indeed. The old

---

[4] Ithaca has always been a great place for hoaxes. Back in 1844 William Linn invented a long citation which he ascribed to Roorbach's *Tour through the Western and Southern States in 1836*, reporting the passage of 43 manacled and shackled slaves bearing the brand of James K. Polk, candidate for President. The accusation nearly brought about Polk's defeat, and the word *roorback*, or fictitious report for political purposes, entered the language.

humorous magazines, like *Puck, Judge, Life,* have long since vanished. There is no avowedly humorous American magazine on the newstands today (for the *New Yorker* is not primarily humorous, and I can make little of *Mad*). Yet the college comics bloom forever, to illustrate the time lag which characterizes youth.

The drama in these years altered its character. The Lyceum Theatre, sweet in many memories, ended its career ignobly in 1924, staging a series of prize fights. The Masque was said to be sick, its comic-opera formula outworn. Its last production was *Lady Luck* in Junior Week, 1926. It was reported even by Junior Week revelers to be frightful. The Masque then decided to surrender to the new age. The dramatic critic of the *Alumni News* wrote:

The timbers of the old Lyceum will shiver no more as the Masque girls land together on the left foot. No more will the handsome hero stagger as the smooth-shaven heroine falls into his arms and both together kiss the air. The comely stripling doffs his dresses and yields his place to the feminine actress, as he did in Greece, and in the medieval mysteries, and in the time of Shakespeare. Dramatic history is repeating itself. But a fat lot the Masquers care about history.

The Masque died gloriously, bequeathing its assets of some $5,500 to the University for the encouragement of student dramatics, specifically in aid of playwriting, experimental productions, or a special library.

The Dramatic Club meanwhile rose steadily in achievement and prestige. Its staging of classics, vanguard novelties, and popular successes made it one of the country's notable little theatres. Its first Shakespeare was the *Midsummer Night's Dream* in 1927, admirably played by Franchot Tone '27, Robert T. Henkle '27, Zenia Powell '27 in the leading roles. In the same year it gave the first public performance in America of Pirandello's *Right You Are (If You Think So)*. In 1927 its *Doctor Knock*, by Jules Romains, was the first staging of the play in the United States. In 1928 began a series of annual revues, witty and smartly produced. It turned to Gilbert and Sullivan in 1933. In cooperation with the Department of Music, the Glee Clubs, and the Instrumental Clubs, a magnificent *Mikado* was staged in Bailey Hall, with a chorus of sixty-four, and with Bruce Boyce '33, Robert S. Hopper '34, Dorothy Sarnoff '35, Margaret L. Schramm '35, and Archie G. Durham '35 starring. This was followed by *H. M. S. Pinafore* in 1935, and by others in the Savoyard canon.

The Dramatic Club touched the lives of many. In an average year four hundred students helped in staging a dozen full-length plays and as many one-acters before a total audience of fifteen thousand. Director Alexander M. Drummond's purpose was primarily educational, to enable all interested students to share in the creative art of the theatre. Though he did not aim to develop undergraduate stars, the club helped form eminent professional actors, playwrights, and producers, among them Jay Fassett '12, Samuel Karrakis '19, Geoffrey R. Wardwell '22, Marie Powers '24, Franchot Tone '27, Sidney Kingsley '28, Daniel Duryea '28, William Prince '34, Richard Stark '34, Dorothy Sarnoff '35, Arthur Laurents '37. More, the club has produced a striking number of directors of college theatres throughout the country.

We must renounce any effort to record the history of the innumerable student clubs, professional or preprofessional, honorary, executive, social, literary, religious, polemical, recreative, musical, subversive, and miscellaneous. We shall make but a single note: that in 1936 Sigma Xi, the honorary society in science, celebrated the semicentennial of its founding at Cornell, with four of the nine original organizers present.

From now on we need no longer give much attention to the life of women students. The old anticoedism disappeared, except in a few embattled fraternities. Women's life coalesced more and more with the life of the male, often permanently; 38 per cent of the married women graduates of 1919, 1920, and 1921 married Cornell men.[5] The coeds joined the undergraduate clubs, made the boards of the publications, competed in the activities. (But they were never admitted to a cheer-leading competition.) They steadily overtopped the men in scholastic averages. They were, after all, a select group, most of whom came to college with a serious purpose.[6]

Only in athletics were the women forced to renounce competition with the male. Women's teams never became much implicated in inter-

[5] W. A. Anderson, *Marriages and Families of University Graduates* (Ithaca, 1950), p. 17.

[6] The *Sun*, thanking God we are not as others are, reported in December 1926 that 99 coeds at Ohio University replied to a questionnaire asking why they had come to college: 26 came to enlarge their circle of acquaintances and friends; 22 to have a good time; 15 to escape the home town in winter; 12 were "tired of boarding school"; 8 to "get collegiate"; 5 to belong to a sorority; 4 to learn the Charleston and 3 to teach it; 2 to have a last fling before marrying; 1 to escape work; and 1 to guard her "prospective." But one may regard this sociological item with suspicion.

collegiate sports. However, there were exceptions. Fencing enjoyed a vogue under the guidance of Coach François Darrieulat. Kathryn M. McGuire '29 became the intercollegiate champion in 1928. Muriel Evelyn Guggolz '26 carried on after graduation and was a member of the Olympic fencing team in 1932. Our rifle squad in 1928 was of champion quality, winning 25 out of 26 matches. We had even a women's polo team in 1935.

In 1923 Cornell women, and Cornell men too, had a moment of great pride. The National League of Women Voters named the twelve living American women who "have contributed most in their respective fields for the betterment of the world." Three of these were Cornell alumnae: Martha Carey Thomas '77, President of Bryn Mawr; Anna Botsford Comstock '85, pioneer in nature study; and Martha Van Rensselaer '09 of our College of Home Economics.

Some miscellanies from these years, ere they escape down History's drain: In December 1921 the Women's Cosmopolitan Club announced a lecture on "Dreams and the Calculus, or the Freudian Theories with Later Developments," by Dr. Herman Vosberg of Budapest. Dr. Vosberg was none other than Charles M. Stotz '21, with a luxuriant beard and no less luxuriant German accent. His was a proper hoax, with assertions and accompanying charts sufficiently absurd to arouse suspicion in the astute, sufficiently fair-seeming to gull the unwary. It was reported that he gulled certain highly placed unwary, who should have been astute. In August 1923 Arthur C. Milliken '24 dove from the top of the Hydraulic Laboratory 100 feet to the pool below. He was uninjured, but the impact of the water burst the straps of his bathing suit and stripped him clean. In 1926 George R. Conklin '27 plunged in his car 150 feet into Fall Creek. He recovered. Rosalie Cohen '29, blind soprano and pianist, rejoiced the campus in her time, and devoted herself afterwards to teaching music to the blind. King of campus dogs was Napoleon, a dribble-jowled wheezing bulldog of great dignity. His legal home was the Skull house. His habit was to hail streetcars for transport to his destination. Taken to the Penn game in 1929, he got lost in Philadelphia, but somehow made his way to New York. An old grad recognized him on the street and put him on the Lehigh train in the Penn Station. At Ithaca he left the baggage car, hailed a streetcar, and rode up to the Skull house.

In June 1929 Carl Weagant '29, the football manager, set sail from Ithaca in his 46-foot auxiliary sloop, or ketch, with three companions, Dudley N. Schoales '29, the football captain, Joseph M. Rummler '29, and H. M. Devereaux, a friend. They threaded the inland waterways and set forth on the Atlantic. Seven days out, Weagant informed his crew that they were bound for Ithaca, Greece. They stopped in Rome and called on the vacationing Farrands. Arriving in Ithaca, Greece, they were riotously welcomed. They laid a stone from Ithaca, New York, inscribed "Cornell Forever" on the summit of the island's highest mountain. (It may puzzle future archaeologists.) Returning with a marble slab from old Ithaca, they followed Columbus's course to San Salvador. The craft arrived in Bayside, Long Island, in June 1930, having covered 13,000 miles. Captain Weagant was given the Blue Water Medal of the Cruising Club of America. (We have not yet got around to planting the marble slab on a Cornell summit.)

Cornell was enlivened, from 1922 to 1927, by the presence of Hugh Troy. He was a campus child (they used to be known as "campus tigers"), son of Hugh C. Troy '95, professor of dairy industry. He absorbed in early youth the Ithaca delight in the bewildering jest, a subspecies of the practical joke. His uncle, Pat Wall ("The Ugliest Shoe in Town"), amused himself by including a live garter snake in a shoe box delivered to Mrs. Robert E. Treman, the famous Irene Castle, celebrated as a friend of animal life. Hugh adored, with all the campus youngsters, Louis Fuertes, who loved to startle and bemuse, who planted a roadside admonition: JESUS SAVES, in front of the Ithaca Savings Bank, and a composite homemade bird on a tree in Stewart Park, to the confusion of Arthur Allen's early-morning bird walkers. Perhaps a determinant in Hugh's career was an experience at the age of ten or twelve. He and his coeval, Dexter Kimball Junior, were sitting one noonday on the front porch of Dean Dexter Kimball's house, on Central Avenue, where now stands the Gannett Clinic. The Dean proposed to demonstrate the power of the written word. He lettered a neat sign: LOOK BEHIND THIS TREE, and tacked it on the great elm beside the sidewalk. Says Hugh: "Dexter Jr., his father and I then sat back on the screened porch and watched approximately 2,000 students on their way for lunch walk around the tree. It seemed to give the Dean great pleasure, and I was very much impressed."

Some of Hugh's whimsicalities are told in H. Allen Smith's *The Compleat Practical Joker* (New York, 1953). For example, he borrowed a professor's rubbers and on them painted a pair of bare feet, which he covered with a layer of lampblack. The next time the professor wore them in the rain, the lampblack washed off, and the campus regarded his feet to its amazement and his bewilderment.

Then there was the great rhinoceros invasion. Louis Fuertes had in his studio a wastebasket fashioned from a rhinoceros's foot. Hugh borrowed it, weighted it suitably, attached ropes to both sides, and one snowy night he and his accomplices marched across the campus, raising and lowering the wastebasket to make a set of rhinoceros tracks in the snow. The tracks led to half-frozen Beebe Lake and out to the edge of the ice. Next day a knowledgeable professor of zoology identified the tracks as those of a rhinoceros. Since Beebe Lake was then the source of the University water supply, a good proportion of campus dwellers, including Hugh's own father, gave up drinking tap water.

So, at least, says H. Allen Smith, with the approbation of Hugh Troy. But the conscientious historian must record that no one in Ithaca remembers hearing the tale till long afterward. However, Louis Fuertes certainly did have a rhinoceros-foot wastebasket.

Hugh Troy has now become a mythical figure, like Paul Bunyan, to undergraduates. He is credited with fantastic exploits, such as stealing the hands of the Library clock.

Long after Hugh's departure appeared (in November 1936) a set of footprints on the campus, giving one to believe that the statues of Ezra Cornell and Andrew D. White had left their pedestals in the midnight, had held a colloquy, and had returned to their stations. The footprints immediately became a Tradition, forever piously renewed.

Finally an extraordinary historical contribution by Ted Shawn, who brought his six men dancers here for a performance in November 1933. He applauded the government sponsorship of dancing in Germany: "They are obtaining from their rhythmic expression in group patterns a general feeling of unity and mass action which will be useful in the case of a national emergency."

Thus generation succeeded generation at Cornell, growing in wisdom and in stature, and emerging to confront the greater tests of the greater world. Into this greater world we cannot pursue them, nor answer the old question: "What happens to Cornell alumni?" However, a researcher into the fate of the classes of 1919, 1920, and 1921 found that in 1950 over half the men were professional or semiprofessional workers, 30 per cent business executives, 9 per cent in clerical or sales jobs, 5 per cent farmers or farm managers, and 1 per cent factory operatives, firemen, or policemen; 85 per cent of all graduates were married, and they had 1.64 children apiece.[7]

[7] Anderson, *Marriages and Families.*

XXXIII

Cornell under President Farrand: Athletics

AS we have already recorded, Romeyn Berry '04 became graduate manager of athletics in 1919. His sixteen years in office fall into three stages: Triumph; Decline; and Fall.

As the veriest infant knows, collegiate fame and disgrace depend upon football. Rym Berry's period of triumph began with the engagement of Gilmour Dobie as football coach in 1920. In 1921 Dobie produced the first of his great teams. It won all its games, beating Penn 41 to 0, with Eddie Kaw '23 scoring five touchdowns. (Eddie Kaw was a mudhorse, with an uncouth style, striding farther with one foot than the other. He used the ball for interference, smiting opposing tacklers with it.) Brilliant work was done by George Lechler '22, George Pfann '24, Floyd Ramsey '24, Leonard Hanson '24, Frank L. Sundstrom '24. (George Pfann's underslung center of gravity made him impossible to overturn. "He crept, crawled, and ran on all fours with tacklers draped about him.") [1]

In 1922 Cornell won everything (Kaw, Ramsey, Pfann, and Charles E. Cassidy '25 starred); 1923 was another triumphant year. But in October 1924, after 26 straight victories, we lost to Williams, 7 to 14. For a time our record was respectable but no longer peerless. In 1925 we lost to Dartmouth and Penn, in 1926 to Columbia, while we tied

[1] *Alumni News*, 3 Feb. 1927.

Penn. Then the team became merely middling, though we had good seasons from 1929 to 1931. Captain Samuel Wakeman '30 made the All-American second team. Bart Viviano '33 starred in 1931, the best football year since 1923.

During the football heyday the physical plant was enlarged to accommodate the crowds. The Athletic Association replaced the east stands at Schoellkopf Field by the great concrete Crescent, seating 21,500, topped by the stoa of thirty-nine private boxes. It was opened for the St. Bonaventure contest in September 1924. A big game was a noble spectacle, with all the waving pennants and raccoon coats and bright finery, with Colonel Joe Beacham's ten-square band quick-stepping in their red tunics, white Sam Browne belts, and scarlet capes with white linings, and with the sun sinking to rest beyond the western hills.

But the invisible worm was at work within the football fabric, the termite at the base of the Crescent. The undermining of Cornell's football might proceeded from several sources.

A first source was our refusal to engage in improper athletic recruiting. The alumni, satisfied with nothing less than perpetual victory, grew captious, and insisted that we should outproselyte the proselytizers. Rym Berry was amazed at the letters he received. He gives an example in the *Alumni News* for 10 April 1924: "This boy Smith at Humper Academy is one of the greatest pitchers that ever lived and is also a sweet basketball player. A lot of other colleges are after him strong, but as far as I can find out no one has made any effort to interest him in Cornell. Why don't you birds wake up and get busy?" Rym replied: "The one and only way for old grads to recruit for Cornell teams is to beget little athletes and send 'em up here."

Mr. Berry would have nothing to do with athletic proselytizing. He was heartened, as were many others, by the report of a Carnegie Foundation inquiry into college athletics, published in 1929. It found Cornell one of only four great universities beyond reproach athletically. (The others were Yale, Chicago, and Illinois.) Cornell, with ten others, was warmly praised for its intramural sports program.

This report caused a national sensation. The *Sun* greeted it with the words: "Cornell yesterday derived more favorable publicity from her much-criticized 'football for students' policy than could be gained by walloping Penn five years straight. That 'football situation at Cornell,' curiously enough, today comes nearer to being of the best, not the worst, in the nation."

A second obstacle to football success was the faculty. Many of them were jealous of football overemphasis and would make not the slightest concession to football heroes, in bud or in bloom. The Committee on Admissions gave little consideration to athletic prowess. Probation rules were strictly enforced. Some teachers delighted in assigning football celebrities to afternoon labs and shops. Said Gil Dobie at the Penn-game rally in 1928: "The faculty is the cause of the poor football teams at Cornell, not the players or the coaches."

Certainly a third obstacle was Dobie himself. He was a hard task-master, a driver, given to wounding sarcasms. His habitual pessimism, which brought him the sobriquet of "Gloomy Gil," was a depressant to his men as to his public. His policies were most unpopular: exclusion of student and alumni spectators from practice, with even the Field House windows boarded up to keep out spies, the playing of "set-ups" in the early season, an open date in midautumn, and the scheduling of the important games far away. He had a poor sense of public relations. Nevertheless, Dobie had, and has, his vigorous partisans, especially among the players of his triumphant years.

The chief obstacle to football supremacy was the student body in this Age of Disillusion. In 1930 a committee of the Cornell Alumni Corporation examined the case. Robert E. Treman '09 reported on the student attitude. He noted the indifferentism and the increased individualism in the college world. Attendance at games had dwindled, as many students dared, on Saturdays, to play golf or a scratch game of their own. Organized cheering was almost a thing of the past. Rallies were ill attended, and few would rise to greet a team returning at six in the morning. The same tendency was observable elsewhere. Said the committee: "Two years ago the Harvard *Crimson* decided that students were not much interested in athletic news, and the Harvard Athletic Association was obliged to publish its own paper. . . . Last fall Yale undergraduates boycotted a pep rally as fictitious, boyish, and outworn." In general, youth refused to march in formation and cheer at the word of command.

The committee made many recommendations for the strengthening of athletics, but urged the continuance in office of the graduate manager and the coaches.

Most of the criticism would have been stilled by a few seasons of victory. But the curve turned ever downward. The football record of 1932 was fair; we were beaten only by Columbia and Penn. José Martínez-Zorrilla '33 made the All-American team, and Bart Viviano '33 and Abraham George '33 played brilliantly.

Then came the crisis. The Athletic Council, appalled by deficits, decided in January 1933 to discontinue all varsity games except basketball and some wrestling matches and to cut the salaries of staff and coaches. Our situation in these depression days was in fact a general one. Michigan had asked the cancellation of a dual track meet; only two colleges were found willing to row at Poughkeepsie. Some alleviation of the blight followed. We had track meets with our neighbors, Syracuse and Colgate. The crews rowed Syracuse, traveling by truck and eschewing hotels. In the autumn football returned; the season was mediocre. That of 1934 was terrible. We lost six games and won only two, against St. Lawrence and Dartmouth.

What with depression, students stayed home on Saturday afternoons and listened to as much of the games as they could bear on the radio. Appeals to support the teams were received with derision. Gloomy Gil's exculpations became ever more gloomy and angry. Rym Berry, harried by financial distresses, answered back to his critics in no diplomatic style. His wit often made him injudicious, as in his published verses in the *Alumni News:*

> Of all the pests who homeward roll
> From Crescent, Stadium, or Bowl,
> The one who always makes me sad
> Is the inebriated grad.
> You'd hardly think he'd be so proud
> To snap his luncheon in the crowd.

Although the undergraduates had failed to support the teams, they were angered to see the eclipse of Cornell's athletic greatness. A monster petition to the trustees in April 1934, asked a reform of the athletic organization. The trustees responded by appointing an official Committee on Athletic Control, with Director Herman Diederichs of Mechanical Engineering as chairman and Comptroller Charles D. Bostwick '92 and Professor Donald English of Economics as members.

The committee recognized that our athletic organization was antiquated. It was an outgrowth of the student club for recreation alone. In theory athletics were a private enterprise of the private Athletic Association. The faculty intervened in its affairs only by authorizing schedules and ruling on the eligibility of players. The University's Department of Physical Education, controlling intramural sports, was unrelated to the intercollegiate sports organization, and often hostile to it. The financial problems of the Athletic Association were serious.

During its boom years it had invested $250,000, mostly borrowed, in its plant; now it was running a feverish deficit.

In May 1935 the decisive step was taken. The trustees decided to take over intercollegiate athletics. They authorized the appointment of a Director of Athletics and Physical Education as a University official with a seat on the University Faculty. He would administer intercollegiate sports, intramural games, and physical education for men and women. An Athletic Policy Board of five members, faculty-trustee-alumni, would be appointed, with special committees for the various sports. A recreation fee of four dollars per term would be levied on all undergraduates.

Thus the undergraduates lost their theoretical control of their own sports. They did not seem to mind. The alumni gained a larger voice in athletic policy. The University took over the debts and the substantial assets (valued at $450,000) of the Athletic Association, assuming at the same time financial responsibility in a menacing period.

The first act of the Athletic Policy Board was to appoint as Director of Athletics and Physical Education James Lynah '05, who had had an outstanding administrative record as manager of plants for the Du Pont de Nemours Company and as director of purchasing for General Motors. Romeyn Berry was put in charge of intercollegiate athletics for a terminal year. Charles V. P. ("Tar") Young remained in his post of professor of physcial education; Howard B. Ortner '19 supervised intramural sports. The coaches were given a final year to prove themselves.

They did not prove themselves very well. Dobie's team tied Columbia but lost everything else, being trounced even by St. Lawrence and Western Reserve. We had not known such total defeat since 1887. Rym Berry retired in 1936 to his rural retreat of Stoneposts, in what he loved to call the Swamp College School District, within easy reach of Ithaca. His valedictory was a paean of rejoicing. He was delighted to be quit of "the grim duties of the football season—the responsibility for doing something (but not much) about the eight obstreperous inebriates in Section H Row 52, the three nauseated adolescents in Section D Row 45, and the extremely dead-looking alumnus laid out under the Crescent."

Rym thenceforth devoted himself happily to literature. He was indeed essentially a literary man, only by circumstance a graduate manager of athletics. He had done excellent work, building up the physical plant of the association, developing the recreational facilities of the campus, and by the charm of his personality improving athletic relations with other colleges. And he had kept Cornell athletics antiseptically pure. Nevertheless, he had taken over the faculty point of view and its set of educational values, and he treated the alumni bodies with a good deal less than sympathy. And of course he did not win football games.

Dobie resigned in February 1936, after sixteen years at Cornell. He was succeeded by Carl Snavely, a coach for twenty years, lately at North Carolina. His record was excellent, his standards high, his personality genial. His first team did respectably. Jerome H. ("Brud") Holland '39 received honorable mention for the All-American team.

Lynah's policy was to knit closer bonds with the large older universities of the east, to form, in brief, a real Ivy League. Much student sentiment supported this aim. On 3 December 1936 an identical editorial appeared on the front pages of the student newspapers of Cornell, Columbia, Dartmouth, Harvard, Pennsylvania, Princeton, and Yale. It called for the formation of a league, to reassert the amateur principle, to abjure the current athletic sordidness and cynicism, to save, in short, athletic idealism. But the time was not ripe for such an organization.

Lynah took a firm stand for amateurism. He forbade the coaches and players to visit prep schools and high schools, except those of which they were graduates. This action was part of a united effort to "eliminate the degrading effects on our intercollegiate athletics of the evils of gossip, recruiting, and subsidization." Said Lynah (in the *Alumni News* for 11 March 1937):

It is not the function of a coach to recruit matriculants. . . . I want the coaches to be men of such character, personality, and capability as teachers that through their work with students, as evidenced by the manner in which the members of our teams conduct themselves in contests and elsewhere, boys of the desired types will be encouraged to come to Cornell and participate in our sports.

Were we, in fact, quite as pure as we claimed? It is hard to know. In the nature of things, most secrets remain secrets, and if an alumnus gives a high-school star a present and the star comes to Cornell, no one is likely to find out. A noticeable number of holders of regional scholarships have played football at Cornell. And yet, all of them were regular matriculants, and most of them made excellent scholastic records. Athletic prowess should not be exactly a bar to entrance. One can only conclude that subsidization, if it exists, is rare, furtive, and certainly ineffective, for Cornell has never since the early twenties been a national football champion.

The death of Courtney put an end to Cornell's supremacy on the water. John Hoyle, Cornell's great boat builder, coached through four seasons. Charles A. Lueder '02, who had rowed on some of Cornell's greatest crews, was appointed coach in 1924. In his first test, against three antagonists at Cambridge in 1925, Cornell came in last in all three races. This was not to be borne. Lueder was replaced by James Wray, a professional sculler and head coach at Harvard from 1906 to 1915. Thus the effort to carry on the Courtney tradition was abandoned. Wray's record at Cornell was good enough to satisfy any college which had never had a Courtney. His 1930 crews were very fine. They swept Cayuga Lake against Harvard and Syracuse, and won the varsity and junior varsity at Poughkeepsie. This was our first varsity championship in fifteen years. Wray retired in the general revolution of 1936 and was replaced by Harrison ("Stork") Sanford, former coach at the University of Washington.

Incidentally, in 1927 the crew was launched on the Inlet on 11 February, the earliest date recorded. Unfortunately, by mid-March it was necessary to blast a way through the ice. In 1930 we were on the open lake on 26 February.

The last observation train by Cayuga Lake ran in 1936.

Jack Moakley's trackmen alone never seemed to know a depression. In 1922 the cross-country team was almost superhuman. It won every competition, and in the Intercollegiates six Cornellians finished in the first nine. Robert E. Brown '22, Norman P. Brown '22, and Charles C. Carter '22 came in one two three. Henry A. Russell '26 was one of Cornell's great runners. He broke the world record for the 75-yard dash and equaled the records for the 70-yard dash, the hundred yards (in 9.7 seconds), and the 220 (in 20.8 seconds). In 1928 we won the indoor track championship, with Norwood G. Wright '29 making a new intercollegiate record in the 35-pound weight throw. In 1930 we tied with Penn for the indoor championship. Next year Everett Colyer '31 broke the intercollegiate record for the pole vault, soaring 13 feet and 8¼ inches. Stalwart John F. Anderson '29 broke the Olympic record for the discus throw in 1932. In the hard year 1933 the track team paid its own expenses to the Intercollegiates in Boston, and did respectably. (In that summer thirteen trackmen became rickshaw boys at the Chicago World's Fair. In the Collegiate Open Rickshaw Race, Joe Mangan '33 and Bill Davis '31 triumphed. One pulled while the other rode; then, by rule, they changed places at mid-course.) In 1935 we placed second in the indoor Intercollegiates, and in the outdoor meet James H. Hucker '37 broke the record for the 200-meter low hurdles, and Charles R. Scott '36 high-jumped six feet three. In 1936 we won the outdoor Intercollegiates for the first time since 1919. Herbert H. Cornell '38 took the 3,000-meter race, and Walter D. Wood '36 was first in the discus throw and second in the shot put. And finally, in 1937 we were third in the Intercollegiates. Ham Hucker broke the record for the 220-yard low hurdles, and Howard W. ("Wreck") Welch won the two-mile in fast time.

Meanwhile an annual contest, instigated largely by Romeyn Berry, in 1921, aroused patriotic as well as collegiate fervor. Cornell and Princeton united for a track meet with Oxford and Cambridge. The Englishmen won steadily until 1929, when at last we triumphed, with Orson C. Beaman '29 setting a record of 9:33.8 in the two-mile. In 1930 we won again. In the 1933 contest Joe Mangan '34 set an American record of 9:15.4 for the two-mile, and Bob Kane made a meet and Cornell record of 48.5 for the 440-yard run.

In basketball we won the championship of the Eastern Intercollegiate League in 1924, under the direction of Howard B. Ortner '19.

Soccer rose in popularity and in achievement, thanks largely to students who had been trained abroad. In 1921 Chao Chi Kwong '22, star right half, was the first Chinese to win the varsity "C." In 1934 our undefeated team was champion of the Middle Atlantic League. In the following year we tied for league leadership, with brilliant playing by Walter C. Chewning '36 and Adolph Coors '37.

In wrestling, Coach Walter O'Connell carried on his record of success. His teams won the intercollegiate championships in 1922, 1923, 1926, and 1930. Among his fifty-four winners of individual championships we can mention only the mighty Glenn D. Stafford '30 and John D. Anderson '29.

Tennis had some good years and some bright stars. Stephen E. Hamilton '35 during four years was never defeated. In 1935 Lloyd A. Doughty '37 ungallantly beat Miss Anderson of Penn State, the only woman to play in the Intercollegiates.

Fencing was revived in 1922, and François Darrieulat was brought here as coach. His 1927 *équipe*, led by Fernando Chardon '28 and Earl

M. Good '28, won in the central division of the Intercollegiate Fencing League, and took the Iron Man Trophy, with a clean sweep in the foils.

Our rifle teams in 1934 and 1935 were extraordinary. In a postal match our sharpshooters scored 1,424 out of a possible 1,500, the highest recorded in intercollegiate competition, and in a shoulder-to-shoulder match we broke the record, with a score of 1,408. Jonathan P. Blount '36 led, with a score of 291 out of a possible 300.

Polo galloped into our ken in 1928, when four undergraduates formed the Cayuga Heights Polo Club. They bought their own ponies and scheduled their own matches, without numerals, letters, shingles, or membership in senior societies. In 1930 Cayuga Heights reached the semifinals of the National Class C championships. Cayuga Heights then coalesced with Cornell, with the active benevolence of the R.O.T.C. and Mrs. Livingston Farrand. In 1931 a composite team defeated the officers at West Point. And in 1937 our sterling players gave the Army its first defeat in thirty-four games played. But, sadly, Army resurged to beat us in the Intercollegiates.

Thus the varsity teams, major and minor, underwent their trials and gained their occasional triumphs. In their shadow, unregarded by history, flourished the intramurals, under the supervision of Professor Tar Young of Physical Education and (from 1936) of Nicky Bawlf, soccer and hockey coach. The play spirit reigned. Fraternities, clubs, informal groupings of all sorts, struggled, however inexpertly, in a dozen sports. One could no longer assert that college sports were for the few, while the many sat semisupine in the stands. The complaint was rather that the student body was exercising itself instead of sitting semisupine in the stands. In 1927 the coaches were incensed to discover that many freshmen were signing up for club and intramural teams, and all too few for freshman football, track, and crew.

In 1927–28, 3,945 students were engaged in intramural activity in soccer, touch football, basketball, tennis, hockey, softball, and other sports. In basketball, despite the insufficient gymnasium facilities, there were 600 players in 12 leagues, divided into 59 clubs. (The soccer intramurals in 1928 were won by the Cosmopolitan Club over the Chinese Club. What price Nordic supremacy?) After a succession of dismal rainy winters, skiing came into its own, with the Ski Club providing buses to the Caroline hills. In May 1937 the *Alumni News* reported the existence of 24 golf teams, 34 four-oared crews, 79 softball teams, and handball and horseshoe-pitching leagues. Athletic rivalry implicated even religion. Rym Berry recorded in January 1937: "The Hillels outsmarted the Baptists [in basketball] and won (as you might expect) by a score of 30 to 9. The Methodists beat up the Catholics 15–14, thereby evening things up for the Revocation of the Edict of Nantes."

A new athletic menace arose. In 1933 Cornell's champion touch football team played the champions of Colgate, with considerable cheering sections on both sides. The complaint was voiced, from time to time, that too many club members went up to Alumni Field merely to encourage their teams, and stood on the sidelines, inert, chewing peanuts, even proffering bets, instead of participating in healthy outdoor sports. But, so far as your historian can discover, there was no movement for intramural subintramurals.

Here and there one still hears from deplorers and menacemongers the accusation of athletic overemphasis in American colleges. Well, at Cornell it disappeared about thirty years ago.

XXXIV

The Medical College—Retirement
of President Farrand

THE nineteen-twenties were a period of great advance in medical knowledge, practice, and educational standards. In this advance the Cornell Medical College fully shared. Its reputation as one of the country's foremost, and most difficult, medical schools brought to it a flood of applicants. In 1920 it was necessary to limit classes to sixty in each year. In 1927 the entering class was set at sixty-five, with twenty assigned to the Ithaca school and forty-five to New York.

The influence of President Farrand was beneficent. Himself a Doctor of Medicine, he understood the special problems of medical education. He favored instruction in small groups, a policy which has been one of the distinctions of the Medical College. His special interest in public health and preventive medicine encouraged Cornell's noteworthy development in that field. In the all-important matter of faculty appointments and promotions he exercised his informed judgment.

Cornell's eminence was due chiefly to its eminent professors. Dr. James Ewing, classmate of President Farrand at the College of Physicians and Surgeons, continued his pioneering work in cancer. Dr. Graham Lusk, always a powerful influence upon the students, added to his fame by his studies of metabolism. Dr. Eugene F. DuBois performed important work in nutrition, as did Dr. Charles R. Stockard in anatomy, embryology and genetics. Dr. G. N. Papanicolaou's fame among cytologists and endocrinologists steadily increased. There were many others, among them Robert A. Hatcher in pharmacology, William J. Elser in bacteriology and immunology, Charles L. Gibson in surgery, George G. Ward in obstetrics, Oscar M. Schloss in pediatrics, George H. Kirby in psychiatry.

These few, chosen perhaps unfairly from among so many, upheld Cornell's distinction in the medical world. That distinction was gained by men, not money. Mutual stimulation encouraged a spirit of research, closely linked to clinical needs and practice. Our basic research was always fortunately blended with applied research.

In 1921 the college established a novel clinic for middle-income patients, too poor to pay the fees for superior care, too proud to attend charity clinics. In the words of Dr. Paul Reznikoff:

In keeping with the tradition of the school to experiment in medical education and patient care, the clinic of Cornell University Medical College was reorganized in 1921. Dr. Lewis Conner, Professor of Medicine, was dissatisfied with the perfunctory services rendered to clinic patients, especially since the students received their first introduction to clinical medicine in the clinic. Therefore a clinic was established where patients were given definite appointments for moderate fees, the doctors were paid for their services, their work was supervised by senior physicians, and examinations of patients were performed as carefully as in the best private physicians' offices. This gave the students an opportunity to see good ambulatory medicine practiced. The Cornell Clinic, housed in the Medical School, was made possible by a grant from the Dispensary Development Committee of the United Hospital Fund. Considerable credit for the success of the educational features of this pioneer project was due to the untiring efforts of Dr. Connie Guion.[1]

The Pay Clinic was an immediate, indeed an overwhelming, success. In its first year it treated more than 22,000 persons at an average cost of $2.03, but at an average charge to the patient of $1.57. The magazine *Survey* (for June 1925) reviewed its operations and found that it received 100,000 visits annually. The typical patient was a member of a family of two or three with an income of $2,400. He received diagnosis and care at a fifth of a specialist's rates, or two-fifths of the charges of general practitioners. The really poor were guided to free dispensaries, the unduly well-to-do to private practitioners. The clinic, at first viewed with alarm, gained the general support of practicing

[1] "Cornell University Medical College," in *N.Y. State Journal of Medicine*, 1 Feb. 1957.

physicians. It continued in successful operation for ten years, until it was merged in the new Medical Center.

By the mid-twenties the Medical College outran its resources and outgrew its building—so magnificent a quarter-century before. The college's chief drawback was the lack of a unified approach to a clinical teaching program, which means that it needed a fuller, more intimate association with a hospital.

It will be remembered that the Medical College had been casting covetous eyes on the New York Hospital as early as 1902 and that in 1913 a working arrangement was made by which the College controlled half the beds of the hospital. The Cornell staff, particularly Dean Walter L. Niles and Professors Ewing and Conner, dreamed of a closer union. They found their agent in Payne Whitney.

Payne Whitney was the nephew and heir of Colonel Oliver H. Payne, the creator of the Cornell Medical College. His sister was Mrs. Willard Straight, now Mrs. Leonard Elmhirst. He inherited his adored uncle's enthusiasm, and his concern for medical education. During the twenties he joined in informal discussions with President Farrand, Edward W. Sheldon, president of the New York Hospital, and various men of power, wealth, and good will. Looking forward, he bought for his project the squalid blocks along the East River between 68th and 70th Streets. In imagination he could see his Temple of Healing rise splendidly from the redeemed disease-ridden slum.

He saw it only in imagination. With all the plans completed and the promises recorded, he died on 25 May 1927. By his will he left $18,600,000 to the New York Hospital, $6,200,000 for a psychiatric clinic, and $2,300,000 to endow the Cornell Medical College. (At the final accounting, the gift to the college was reckoned at $3,285,605.)

Less than a month after Payne Whitney's death, on 14 June 1927, the agreement for union of the hospital and the college was signed.

Great foundations and public-spirited men of wealth recognized their opportunity for good works. The General Education Board gave $7,500,000 for the Medical College buildings, and later $6,000,000 for the Women's Clinic, which replaced the old Lying-In Hospital. J. Pierpont Morgan, Jr., gave two million to the Women's Clinic, as did the Laura Spelman Rockefeller Fund, and George F. Baker Senior and Junior each gave a million. The New York Hospital absorbed the Manhattan Maternity Hospital and Dispensary and the New York Nursery and Child's Hospital (whose endowments were used for the Children's Clinic). The total resources of the New York Hospital–Senior Cornell Medical Center at its beginning were $60,600,000.

The direction of the center was put in the hands of a Joint Administrative Board of seven. The hospital chose three: Edward W. Sheldon, its president, a rich and powerful lawyer; William Woodward, banker and horseman; and Frank L. Polk, a busy lawyer, son of the Cornell Medical College's first Dean. Cornell was represented by President Farrand, J. Du Pratt White, and Dean Walter L. Niles. The six chose a seventh, J. Pierpont Morgan.

In March 1927 the Board appointed the Director of the center, Dr. G. Canby Robinson. A Hopkins man, he had on graduation in 1903 served as assistant to Dr. Martin B. Tinker (later an Ithaca surgeon) in Clifton Springs. He then taught anatomy briefly in the Ithaca division of the Cornell Medical College. He had a distinguished career in Washington University, St. Louis, and built and directed the Medical College and Hospital of Vanderbilt University, in Nashville, Tennessee. He seemed an excellent choice, by experience and character. An outsider, he was bound by none of the loyalties so likely to be disastrous in an amalgamation.

Dr. Robinson assumed his full-time duties in September 1928. His initial tasks were two: to plan and build the plant, and to assemble the staff.

Architectural studies had been begun even in 1924 by Henry R. Shepley of Boston. The builders chosen were Marc Eidlitz ('81) and Son, who had just constructed the Columbia-Presbyterian Medical Center. It was stipulated that each department of the college and hospital should be self-contained, but should be correlated with allied departments; that facilities for research, for staff, and for a small body of students should be provided; and that each unit should be planned for the optimum number of patients. Provision was made for a thousand beds and for five hundred nurses in their residence. The cost was estimated at thirty million; and in fact the final charges were within the estimate.

The architect was inspired by the Palace of the Popes in Avignon, with its rugged mass, its Gothic grandeur, its tall pointed windows. The center is indeed one of the most beautiful of the city's enormous buildings, and well merits the award made to the architect of the Architectural League's gold medal. Dr. Henry E. Sigerist, medicine's great historian, was moved by its symbolism:

At the center of medicine is the sick human being, the sole reason for its existence. The center of the building contains the hospital, with the two departments of medicine and surgery, which rise toward heaven like a prayer for healing. . . . The specialist clinics branch out as separate wings. . . .

Greek science and Christian charity are the ground on which our western medicine is rooted. . . . In this building the snake of Aesculapius twines, not around a staff, but a cross.[2]

Essential in Dr. Robinson's plan was the training of nurses. The New York Hospital School of Nursing, established in 1877, stood very high in its field. A splendid Nurses' Residence was built as part of the Medical Center complex. Proposals were made for a Cornell School of Nursing, to combine arts and sciences with nursing practice and to confer a bachelor's degree. However, the necessary endowment was not yet obtainable. Miss Anna D. Wolf, appointed Director of Nursing, organized the hospital school with energy, skill, and understanding. The bonds with Cornell were tightened. In 1932 an agreement was made by which students who should finish the three-year course in nursing could receive as much as two years' credit toward Cornell's B.S. in Home Economics.

Dr. Robinson planned that each division of the hospital would be headed by a chief of service, who would be also the professor and head of his department in the Medical College. These men would be full-time appointees, at proper salaries, and would be debarred from engaging in private practice for fees. There would be five university clinics, adequate for patient care, teaching, and research. These would have the air of a private doctor's office, as the hospital rooms would resemble those in comfortable private homes.

The staff lived in a dream of a medical heaven. But remember the date—the fateful year 1929. Black Friday came, and then the black years—or no, the years in the red. Day by day the reckoning of the center's resources was reduced. Finally it was forced to liquidate, at great loss, about fifteen millions of its investments. Economies were sought, and programs cut. Suspicions, carpings, resentments bloomed in the soil of insecurity.

The chief cause of discord was the delicate matter of staff appointments. Dr. Robinson wished to assemble in his Temple of Medicine the most distinguished medical teachers and practitioners in the country. He had little direct acquaintance with the Cornell Medical College; naturally he turned to those prominent physicians whom he knew, who were, again naturally, mostly graduates of Johns Hopkins. In his view, long service on the Cornell Faculty did not constitute a claim for continuance. Almost the contrary, in fact; in his role as new broom, he wished to sweep out the accumulated traditions and practices of

[2] H. E. Sigerist, *American Medicine* (New York, 1934), pp. 142–143.

the college. In particular, he objected to the faculty's privilege of carrying on private practice and doing research outside the college. He insisted that his major appointees should give full time to their college duties. Today such a principle would seem well justified, but in 1930 it offended many. He dismissed some of the oldest and most honored members of the faculty. Much resentment was aroused among the alumni and some staff members who survived the cut. Even today the old resentment has not been entirely dissipated.

The great hospital opened on 1 September 1932. A month later instruction began in the college quarters. The size and magnificence of the Center filled the occupants with pride and rejoicing. The services provided more daily meals than the largest New York hotel; the power plant could light the city of Bridgeport; the purchasing department supplied everything conceivable, white mice, forty-two types of hypodermic needles, human milk.

For all the pride and rejoicing, the morale was not good. Dr. Robinson speaks of the unrest and tension, after a year's operation.[3] Edward W. Sheldon, chairman of the Joint Administrative Board, died in 1934 and was succeeded by Wilson M. Powell, attorney for the New York Hospital. Dr. Robinson complained, in his reminiscent *Adventures in Medical Education:*

Mr. Powell investigated and planned without consulting me. . . . He also conferred directly with the heads of the clinical departments regarding the administration of their clinics. Such activities were probably justified by the serious financial problems the hospital was facing, but they served to weaken my position as Director, not only with the hospital staff but also with the heads of departments in the Medical College. Salary cuts had to be made, and departmental budgets had to be reduced—measures which generated a sense of insecurity new to men holding academic posts. Deterioration of the high spirit of earlier days set in. Early in 1934 it was decided that the hospital would have to cut drastically its support of the departments of medicine, surgery, and pediatrics, and that it would not be able to share equally with the college in supporting these departments after the year beginning July 1. This created a serious condition for the Medical College, as it meant either that these departments would be badly disorganized or that all departmental budgets of the college would have to be reduced in order to help support these clinical departments. I brought this situation to the attention of Alan Gregg of the Rockefeller Foundation, and through his good offices and understanding the foundation made a grant of $100,000 to Cornell.

[3] G. Canby Robinson, *Adventures in Medical Education* (Cambridge, Mass.: Harvard University Press, 1957), p. 221.

This temporary relief of the financial state did not change the emotional state of some members of the executive faculty, who began to create a situation in which my position as director soon became untenable. Mr. Powell seemed to concur in the position taken by these members of the Faculty, while President Farrand was sympathetic and friendly to me throughout this difficult time. Farrand was, however, also sympathetic to those who opposed me and did not take a strong position in the controversy, partly because of his desire not to disturb the relations of the medical college and hospital. Arrangements were made by Powell and Farrand, acting for the Joint Administrative Board, for my retirement on 1 October 1934.

. . . Under the strain of disappointment and dispute, some of the more aggressive leaders of the faculty became particularly concerned with the attainment of selfish objectives and seemed to disregard the good of the Medical School as a whole. Their state of mind and feelings were, I thought, unfavorable for the creation of an environment in which medical students should develop, and I regretted leaving when signs of a demoralized spirit were apparent.

In justice to Dr. Robinson, his ex parte statement has been given in his own words. No rebuttal by the discontented faculty has been published, nor shall we attempt one here. Perhaps it is just as well that the old recriminations should fade from the pages of history.

After his retirement, the post of Director was not filled for thirteen years. The Dean of the Medical College and the Executive Director of the hospital reported independently to the Joint Administrative Board. Thus, in Dr. Robinson's opinion, the close tie between the medical school and the hospital was weakened.

Dr. William S. Ladd, Associate Dean since 1931, was advanced to the deanship in 1936. Under him the college flourished. About a thousand applications were received annually; of these, in a typical year, fifty-six were accepted for entrance at New York, twenty-four for Ithaca. The financial situation improved; a Health Center was erected on 69th Street, with a grant from the Rockefeller Foundation; important research was carried on in the laboratories.

One of the last acts of President Farrand's administration was the discontinuance of the Ithaca Division of the Medical College, to take effect in June 1938. Though it had done splendid work in its forty years of existence, giving instruction to 1,515 students of medicine, many of them destined for brilliant careers, though it was excellently staffed and adequately equipped, it provided a duplication which was at length judged unreasonable. No doubt the trustees were more than willing to transfer its upkeep to the endowment of the Medical College in New York, and to gain much-needed space in Stimson Hall for the work in zoology and biology.

We may conclude this review with a brief statement of the medical student's course of training in the mid-thirties.[4] His first two years were spent almost entirely in classrooms and laboratories. In anatomy he became familiar with every muscle, nerve, and tissue in the human body. In physiology he turned from human architecture to human engineering. He studied pathology, or the effects of all kinds of diseases on the organs. In biochemistry he learned to duplicate the processes of that chemical factory, the human body. In bacteriology he identified and pursued our minute enemies.

His junior and senior years were passed largely in clinical training in the hospital wards. He then spent a year or two as hospital intern. If he chose to become a surgeon, six years of training after graduation were required. By that time he had made, on an average, 22,780 visits, had attended a thousand medical consultations, had assisted at four thousand operations, and had performed two thousand operations under supervision. Comparable advanced training was given in such fields as medicine, obstetrics, children's diseases. At last the young man or woman, no longer quite so young, was fitted to be a New York Hospital–Cornell M.D.

President Farrand, reviewing his record in 1937, said: "The problems of the Trustees and the Administration [in 1921] were not those of reorganization but of development. This meant that the chief considerations were financial. . . . Up to the year 1929 steady progress was made. Since that time drastic retrenchment has been imperative."

With the financial and material considerations he dealt effectively. He carried to completion the men's dormitories, Baker Laboratory, the Veterinary Laboratory, the heating plant. He arranged for the construction of Willard Straight Hall, Balch Halls, Myron Taylor Hall, and, on the Ag Campus, the Dairy Building, Plant Science, Ag Economics, and Martha Van Rensselaer. During his years the endowment of the Ithaca colleges rose, despite depression, from $12,200,000 to $19,800,000, while the endowment of the Medical College increased from $5,000,000 to $11,200,000. The value of the buildings and grounds was lifted from $10,200,000 to $26,400,000. The condition of the faculty was bettered, with increases in salary (up to 1929), with the provision of group life insurance, with the Contributory Retirement

[4] *So Near the Gods* (New York Hospital, 1938), p. 25.

Income Plan of 1937. The College of Home Economics was created, and its Department of Hotel Administration. The State Experiment Station at Geneva was placed under control of the University. The Cornell University Press was revived, the Arboretum constituted, a Placement Bureau established. New departments and curricula were formed, in Music, Fine Arts, Drama, Regional Planning, Chemical Engineering, Administrative Engineering. Entrance requirements were raised in the Law School and the Veterinary College. The University assumed responsibility for physical education and for athletics. A selective admissions system was set up. And, most importantly, the Medical College merged with the New York Hospital and the Lying-In Hospital to become the great Medical Center.

So summarized, President Farrand's record is an impressive one. But in justice to his successor one must note certain qualifications. One seeks in vain, in Farrand's recorded words, any statement of positive educational conviction or purpose. In sixteen years of tumultuous change in the greater world, President Farrand hardly touched our educational structure. An anthropologist, he did not move to introduce the teaching of anthropology until his final year. A famous exponent of public health, he let the service of student health lag behind the norm in other institutions. In general, he let the colleges run themselves. Some of them ran themselves very well; and some, lacking vigorous leadership, ran themselves gently downhill, comfortably doing over just what they had done before.

Here, perhaps, is the crux of the matter. A Faculty always insists that it can manage its own affairs better than can any central administration. Provost Albert R. Mann lauded President Farrand for his abstentions: "He was sensitive to the respective domains of the academic and the administrative organizations, and constantly alert to protect the academic from intrusion by the administrative." [5] There is another point of view: that the administration, in touch with the needs of the changing world, should impose its larger purposes, however unwelcome they may be, on units chiefly concerned for their own well-being.

(This is an ancient and continuing quarrel, which it is not our business to resolve. Cornell was founded on Andrew D. White's conviction that a university must serve the greater organism of which it is a part; it cannot serve only itself. There must be some extrinsic

[5] *In Memoriam Livingston Farrand* (New York Academy of Medicine, 1940), p. 26.

measure of value, which applies to a university as well as to other human institutions. Faculties, by their nature, are conservative, resistant to change. When we describe an Educated Man, we describe ourselves, and we demand that others follow the courses that have made Us. A curriculum is likely to represent a balance of inner, not outer forces. Professor Richard Robinson, Ph.D. '30, of Philosophy, remembers that he proposed to a curriculum committee in the Arts College a compulsory course in philosophy, for the evident benefit of all students. The proposal failed; and a committee member said to him: "I am sorry that we couldn't do that for the Philosophy Department.")

By his very reluctance to make changes President Farrand endeared himself to the campus. He sought our welfare, defended us from outside attacks, irradiated the community with his sunny spirit. Provost Mann speaks of his courage, kindliness, resourcefulness, tact, equity, and integrity. The nouns are well weighed, and they are exact. Livingston Farrand was a gentleman, in the old outmoded sense.

President Farrand's achievement was to communicate his own mood and temper to the University through sixteen difficult years. The Cornell of Andrew D. White partook of his indomitable idealism; the Cornell of Jacob Gould Schurman shared his superb, almost ruthless energy; the Cornell of Livingston Farrand became somehow more kindly, more human. His friendliness, his good will, his quick smile, animated all his campus. It was only natural that his good will should be returned to him. Innumerable Cornellians whom he could hardly have known felt for him a personal affection. Unique in the University's history was the tribute paid him at his retirement in 1937, when thousands of Cornellians gathered in New York to honor him, only to feel, at his leave-taking, an emotion that expressed itself unashamedly in tears.

He had little time to enjoy his retirement. He died on 8 November 1939.

XXXV

Cornell under President Day: Prewar

ON 7 November 1936, well in advance of President Farrand's retirement, the trustees elected Edmund Ezra Day to be the fifth President of Cornell.

Day was born in Manchester, New Hampshire, on 7 December 1883. His forebears came from northern New Hampshire. He attended the public schools of Worcester, Massachusetts, entered Dartmouth, and made an excellent undergraduate record. He was a varsity debater, manager of the track team, a member of Theta Delta Chi and Phi Beta Kappa. He received a Rufus Choate scholarship and thus acquired the nickname of "Rufus," which clung to him all his life. He received the B.S. in 1905, the M.A. in 1906. He then entered the Harvard Graduate School, gained the Ph.D. in economics in 1909, became professor of economics and chairman of the department at Harvard. During the First War he served as statistician for the U.S. Shipping Board and the War Industries Board.

In 1923 he left Harvard for the University of Michigan. There he was professor of economics, organizer and first dean of the School of Business Administration, and Dean of the University. His abilities attracted the attention of the great foundations, and in 1929 he left Michigan to become director for the social sciences with the Rockefeller Foundation. He carried on concurrently the duties of director

EDMUND EZRA DAY, President 1937–1949

of general education with the General Education Board. He was the author of *Index of Physical Production* (1920), *Statistical Analysis* (1925), and co-author of *The Growth of Manufactures* (1928).

He married (in 1912) Emily Sophia Emerson, daughter of Dean Charles F. Emerson of Dartmouth.

He was a man of power and dominance, keen in his judgment of men and things, serious of purpose, zealous for social betterment, utterly devoted to his task, and, as it turned out, utterly devoted to Cornell.

He was also impatient, sometimes tactless in dealing with opposition, inclined to rely rather on statistical evidence than on intuition. He lacked the grace of President Farrand in attaining his ends. Some professors of the humanities complained that he never really understood the aims of humane education, recalcitrant to statistical analysis. This was a misconception, to which President Day deliberately lent himself. Convinced that the menace to successful teaching is complacency, satisfaction with routine, he liked to shock, unsettle, disturb. He enjoyed playing dumb. He liked to affront a professor of, for instance, English, with the demand: "What are you trying to do? What are the educational outcomes of the study of literature? Why not drop it from the curriculum?" The Professor of English usually found, after his bewilderment or anger had died, that the necessity of defining his aims was very wholesome. He did not always realize that Dr. Day knew the answers before he asked the questions.

He assumed office on 1 July 1937 and was formally inaugurated on 8 October. At the ceremony addresses were made by Presidents Ernest M. Hopkins, James B. Conant, and Alexander G. Ruthven of Dartmouth, Harvard, and Michigan, the three colleges where Dr. Day had taught.

The new President's Inaugural Address began with a considerable quotation from Andrew D. White's *Autobiography*, detailing the Foundation Ideas, the Formative Ideas, and the Governmental Ideas on which Cornell was established. These he approved and applauded, thus linking Cornell's past with its future. He continued that our students should be led to seek out all sorts of ideas, that they should learn how knowledge is gained and wisdom won, that they should be trained to critical thinking and introduced to imaginative and creative thought, that they should come to know what is really meant by the intellectual life. He pointed to certain barriers to the attainment of the intellectual life, for example, the disjointed accumulation of formal courses, the purely informational character of much instruction, the cult of campus indifference, the lack of social consequence in liberal arts education. "A sense of social obligation should be induced," he said. "The time has passed when it can be assumed that social well-being will flow automatically from self-interested individual enterprise. If democratic institutions are to be preserved and individual liberty remain our proud possession, the citizen must recognize his obligation to make his life add to the common weal."

He promised that he would hold his new policies in abeyance until he should have full opportunity to confer with faculty, students, alumni, and other advisers. True to his promise, he spent most of his first year observing and learning, and visiting fifty alumni clubs in thirty-seven communities.

These were times of disquiet and alarm. Hitler swallowed Austria and Czechoslovakia; Mussolini attempted to digest Ethiopia; there was war in China, Manchukuo, and Spain. The terror of another war occupied every mind until it came, in September 1939; and then every mind was filled with fear of war's outcomes and fear of American involvement. The old securities, or what was left of them, were badly shaken. Fear of the future implied distrust of the past, which had brought about the present. President Day, in his first annual report, noted the widespread confusion among educators, as in the political, social, and economic worlds. He found a general skepticism about the efficacy of long-established educational procedures and the validity of long-respected educational objectives.

He found at least the temper of the times favorable to change and reform. And in his review of the University's affairs he recognized that change and reform were necessary in several fields. The physical plant had lamentable lacks; the administration needed overhauling; many instructional units demanded strengthening; and certain new areas of instruction should be opened. He listed in this report our most urgent needs: a library; a new plant for the College of Engineering; indoor sports buildings for men and women; and money for salaries and research.

To encourage the generosity of Cornellians and others the President set up a new fund-raising committee. He appointed, as a major full-time officer, H. Wallace Peters '14, with the duty of seeking gifts, and with the title of Provost.

The Board of Trustees suffered the resignation, in 1938, of Frank H. Hiscock as Chairman, after twenty-two years in office. He was succeeded, for less than a year, by J. Du Pratt White, who died in 1939. His successor was Howard E. Babcock, commonly addressed as "Ed." A graduate of Syracuse University, he studied agriculture in the Cornell Summer School of 1911. This experience, he said, was the turning point of his life. He then taught school; and after further training became professor of marketing at Cornell. The Grange League Federation, a disintegrating farmers' cooperative, appealed to him to save it. He made of it eventually the largest farmers' cooperative in the world. As president of the State Grange, he became an ex officio member of Cornell's Board of Trustees in 1930. From 1940 to 1947 he was Chairman of the Board. His influence on the Board was sometimes deplored in professorial offices in Goldwin Smith. It was presumed that he would make of the University an adjunct of the G.L.F. and that he would exalt the College of Agriculture above its sisters. There seems to be no basis for these alarms. It is true that the state colleges throve during his chairmanship; but the College of Arts and Sciences likewise throve. I find no proof that Ed Babcock, a man of culture and cultivation, misprized or disesteemed the work in the humanities.

Dr. Day's first year in office was marked by a considerable overturn in the educational administration of the University. The impressive list of his new appointments includes George F. Rogalsky, Comptroller; S. C. Hollister, Dean of the College of Engineering; William N. Barnard, Director of Mechanical Engineering; Paul M. Lincoln, Acting Director of Electrical Engineering; Gilmore D. Clarke, Dean of the College of Architecture; and Percival J. Parrott, Director of the Agricultural Experiment Station.

Naturally the most harassing concern of any president is finance. Thanks to many splendid gifts, from individuals and from the foundations, the President managed to show a small operating surplus annually until the war smote us. (In 1938 the Treasurer sold the last parcel of western lands left in Ezra Cornell's great endowment enterprise—160 acres for $350.)

Enrollments rose steadily, annually breaking the previous record, to reach 7,315 in 1940–41. The common judgment was that we had gone about as far as we could go. Many plans were laid to accommodate the increasing number of Cornellians. The trustees decided, in 1940, to relocate the College of Engineering at the south end of the campus. The removal was initiated by the magnificent gift of $685,000 by Franklin W. Olin '86, to construct a Chemical and Metallurgical Engineering building as a memorial to his son, Franklin W. Olin, Jr., '12.

Some minor constructions appeared on the campus's periphery: a U.S. Plant, Soil, and Nutrition Laboratory, at East Ithaca; a Service Building near the heating plant; and a high-voltage laboratory for Electrical Engineering, near the East Ithaca station. (Its facilities for research were unique in the east. It contained a 60-cycle 3-phase current at 433,000 volts, or a single-phase current at 750,000 volts. It had a 3-million-volt surge capacity. This is apparently remarkable.)

Sage Chapel was enlarged and a new organ installed. The Arboretum became the Cornell Plantations. With the precious aid of the Civilian Conservation Corps, roads and paths were built along Fall Creek and masses of trees and shrubs were planted, as much for education and investigation as for beauty. President Day, no mean golfer, pushed the construction of a University Golf Course, encouraging students to practice "carry-over" sports, lifetime diversions. Charles K. Bassett '14 relieved a quarter-century irritation by giving two new bells, D-sharp and F-sharp, for the Chimes. And there were some deletions to be set against these additions. The horse barns burned on a bitter night in January 1938, symbolizing the end of an era. The toboggan slide, after providing twenty-one injuries, seven of them fractured vertebrae, in the winter of 1939–40, was quietly abandoned. Anyway, there were plenty of new ways to satisfy youth's lust for speed and danger.

President Day had proposed in his Inaugural to begin his term by making a critical examination of Cornell's educational system. His own convictions were gradually revealed. He foresaw that the general school-leaving age would continue to rise, and that American universities would have to furnish a "general education" for the general student, to prepare him for democratic life. The state, he recognized, would play an ever greater role in providing higher education. And, he insisted, "education, in its upper reaches, must be substantially vocational in purpose and content." [1] The scorn of some academics for vocationalism, he said, is misdirected.

He examined the research situation and found it spotty. In many fields admirable work was done; in others there was little activity. He noted an upswing in the agricultural sciences and education, a decline in languages and literatures. He set up a Trustee-Faculty Committee on Research, with Dean Floyd K. Richtmyer of the Graduate School as chairman, and soon noted an amelioration.

The President's plans and purposes were disturbed by the threat

[1] *Oncoming Changes in the Organization of American Public Education* (Ithaca: Committee on Teacher Education, n.d.; about 1940).

of war and of our engagement in it. Many emergency committees were organized, to deal with war shortages, to lay courses through an uncharted future. Special programs were offered in such subjects as nutrition, housing, conservation. Agricultural Extension, under Director L. R. Simons, was oriented toward Defense, pouring out advice on seed and labor shortages, on the use of electricity and other labor-saving devices, on increasing food production. With the coming of Selective Service, the R.O.T.C. became popular. It dropped infantry training, concentrating on field artillery, signals, and ordnance. Agitation against compulsory R.O.T.C. died away. In 1941, 138 seniors were commissioned Second Lieutenants, and 47 were made Ensigns in the Navy. Many students learned to fly, under the Civilian Pilot Training program. The Law School accelerated its course, to save a year. Eminent professors disappeared, to reappear in Washington. Engineering defense courses were given in cities from Buffalo to Binghamton. Secret research began in laboratories; the word "classified" took on a new meaning.

In these prewar years three new schools were established: Chemical Engineering, Nutrition, and Education.

Courses in Chemical Engineering had already been given by Fred H. Rhodes and C. C. Winding, under the dual control of the Arts Department of Chemistry and of the College of Engineering; it was the stepchild of both, according to Professor Rhodes. In 1938 it became a new school, under Engineering, and an integrated five-year course was offered. The success of the five-year course encouraged Dean Hollister of Engineering to propose a similar requirement throughout his schools. With the building of Olin Hall, Chemical Engineering received the finest accommodation of any such school in America. Rhodes, Herbert Fisk Johnson Professor of Industrial Chemistry, was made its Director. But the history of the school may best be deferred to a later chapter.

The School of Nutrition was the particular pet of Trustee Howard E. Babcock. Nutrition, animal and human, was of course one of the chief subjects of research in Agriculture, Veterinary, and Home Economics. Man must always be concerned with the relation of nutrition to the productive life of himself and his animals, to the onset of senility, to longevity. Professor Clive McCay's sensational experiments with rats and dogs showed that the life span may be deliberately controlled by diet.

In 1939 a Federal Nutrition Research Laboratory was established on the campus edge, to study problems related to soils, plants, and animals. Two years later, with the warm cooperation of the Federal Laboratory, the University founded a School of Nutrition, under the direction of Leonard A. Maynard, Ph.D. '15. In its first year thirty-five graduate students were enrolled. Undergraduates in Arts, Agriculture, or Home Economics could prepare for entrance, and receive eventually the degree of M.S. in Food or M.S. in Nutrition. The work leads to positions in industry, health agencies, and teaching.

Education had long been taught both in Arts and Agriculture, with a good deal of overlapping. In 1926 a Division of Education was organized, which became in 1931 the Graduate School of Education, its faculty still holding seats in the undergraduate colleges. Now in 1940 came an autonomous School of Education, with its own faculty and its own budget. The new school reorganized its program and featured a five-year course for future secondary-school teachers, another for teachers of art, and a curriculum in guidance. A graduate course in industrial education, with preparation in economics, sociology, and technology, attracted prospective teachers in the technical fields.

President Day planned two new schools, in development of his own chief areas of interest: a School of Business and Public Administration, and a School of Industrial and Labor Relations. But the preparations for these schools were interrupted by the war.

Within the established units of the University the effects of the President's concern were felt.

Dean Robert M. Ogden of the College of Arts and Sciences complained to the trustees (23 March 1940) that the popularity of his college was slipping. He assigned no cause; but one suspects that having resigned himself to being a Dean Without Power, he blamed his strong-minded Faculty. The President told the Executive Committee that the University was trying to increase both the quality and the quantity of the enrollment in Arts, since he thought it essential that a University have a strong student group pursuing a liberal education.

When a Faculty becomes aware that something is going wrong, it draws up a new curriculum. The new curriculum in Arts and Sciences was chiefly noteworthy for its substitution of proficiency tests for certain course requirements, in English, foreign languages, history, and mathematics, and for stipulation that work in a major field should comport work in related subjects.

The President's direct influence was felt in the creation of a Department of Sociology and Anthropology, under the chairmanship of Leonard S. Cottrell.

Dean Ogden called for a development of general and comparative linguistics, in his report for 1939. "The study of language has been too highly departmentalized," he said. His recommendation did not bear immediate fruit. But we obtained a grant from the Rockefeller Foundation for work in Slavic language and literature. A new department was formed, with Ernest J. Simmons as professor, in 1941. It featured intensive twelve-week courses, under the supervision of the American Council of Learned Societies.

The extraordinarily rich Wason Collection of materials for East Asian studies was turned to account by the appointment, in 1938, of Knight Biggerstaff to teach Chinese history. His courses were soon supplemented by cognate work in anthropology and in Chinese and Japanese art.

The Rockefeller Foundation made a handsome gift for a statewide program in music and drama, in which the Departments of Music, Speech and Drama, Rural Sociology, and Rural Education collaborated.

The Music Department adopted the scheme, familiar elsewhere, of appointing an eminent creative musician or performer to be in residence, with some light teaching duties and with freedom to pursue his own career from an Ithaca base. The great gay pianist Egon Petri was here from 1940 to 1945; and Roy Harris the composer in 1941–42; and the Walden String Quartet made its headquarters with us in 1946. (Its performers were made part-time assistant professors.)

A new Department of Zoology was formed, coincident with the discontinuance of the Ithaca Division of the Medical College. The department took over Stimson Hall from the Medical College, as well as the remainder of its staff. It amalgamated the previous Arts Department of Zoology with members from Entomology, Animal Husbandry, and Veterinary Physiology. Frederick B. Hutt of Animal Genetics was the first chairman.

Interesting news releases kept emerging from the Department of Physics. Lloyd P. Smith, Ph.D. '30, produced an atomic gun. Hans Bethe proved that carbon is the source of the sun's heat, that the nucleus of the atom "burns," and that the forces holding the nucleus of the atom together are transmitted by mesons.

The College of Architecture established a five-year course in Fine Arts, leading to the degree of B.F.A., and, with another year, to the M.F.A. John A. Hartell '24 was in charge. The work in Regional Planning grew. A Master of Regional Planning would not be architect alone; he would have knowledge of engineering, economics, government, law. The college proudly announced in 1938 that Stuart M.

Merz '38 was our eleventh winner, in sixteen starts, of the Prix de Rome in Landscape Architecture, and in the following year Frederick W. Edmondson '37 made the twelfth. In 1939 a team of four students won the annual competition of the Alumni of the American Academy in Rome, against a field of over a hundred teams.

The state colleges continued to thrive. It was necessary to restrict entrance to the College of Agriculture, with a policy favoring country boys planning to return to agricultural work, discouraging city boys seeking primarily free tuition for what was termed a cut-rate Arts course. We were amused to learn that the Sandy Creek Grange #127 demanded the dismissal of Professor James E. Boyle of Agricultural Economics because he had expressed certain economic views with which Sandy Creek Grange #127 disagreed. We quaked to read that Liberty Hyde Bailey, at seventy-nine, was caught in a storm off the Bahamas in an eighteen-foot open skiff, with no food and little water, for five days and four nights, and was raked with gunfire in making a landing in the midst of a local uprising. "But," he said, "I got what I went after." What he went after was of course specimens of rare palms.

In his report for 1939 Dean Carl E. Ladd of Agriculture recalled that twenty-five years had elapsed since the passage of the Smith-Lever Act in aid of rural adult education. He took the occasion to summarize, during those years, the achievement of the Extension Department. He noted the development of rural leadership, the reforestation and conservation programs, the improvement in schools, farm-to-market roads, rural electrification, protection from fire and flood, and civic participation:

Twenty-five years ago it still was not uncommon to hear disparaging remarks about "book learning," and for the "professor" to be subjected to some rough hazing designed to expose imagined impracticality and unsoundness. Today a large majority of farm men and women bring their problems to the colleges as a matter of course and with an embarrassing degree of faith in the infallibility of the institution to solve these problems correctly.

Director Flora Rose of the College of Home Economics retired in 1940. Mary F. Henry was acting director for a year, and then came Sarah Gibson Blanding, professor of political science and dean of women at the University of Kentucky. She soon became one of the most popular and respected figures in the community. She found the college in good shape; indeed, the demand for Home Economics graduates was so great that it could by no means be filled.

Nor were there any complaints of the Veterinary College. It could admit only one of every ten applicants. Its cramped quarters prevented it from expanding its instruction, clinical work, and research. In 1941 Dean William A. Hagan reviewed the research activities of the previous five years. These included the improvement of mastitis control in dairy cattle; the determination of the results of calfhood vaccination for Bang's disease; the resolution of problems connected with the blood test for Bang's disease; the differentiation between acetonemia and other apparently similar disorders of dairy cows; the method of spread and control of Johne's disease; the proof of the spirochetal nature of Stuttgart disease of dogs; the clarification of chronic coccidiosis of chickens; and the recognition of the infectious nature of certain common tumors of chickens. These studies, he said, are of immediate practical value. "The work on the physiology of digestion, on the study of acid-fast bacteria, and on brain tumors has, so far as I know, yielded no immediate returns except for a better knowledge of these matters. 'Pure' science today may be 'applied' science tomorrow."

The President took note of the ominous situation of the University Library. Since the First War, Cornell's position relative to other university libraries had steadily receded. Everything about the Library was inadequate—the storage, working, and reading space, the insufficient, underpaid staff, the care of rare books, the services to undergraduate readers and to researchers. The Librarian, Otto Kinkeldey, speaks of "the growing feeling of despair on the campus at the apparent retrogression in library development." Annual grants of $5,000 for book-buying were now made from the President's Surplus Fund, and the general appropriations were increased. A new Library Council was constituted, and in 1941 the Cornell University Library Associates was formed, to furnish some of those precious rarities beyond the reach of normal purchase funds. The retrogression in the Library was checked, even though noteworthy progress had still to be delayed.

In the Medical College, the President reported harmony, "an increasing cordiality in the relations between the College and the Hospital." The Joint Administrative Board was revitalized in 1937–38, under the chairmanship of Henry G. Barbey. A Department of Military Medicine was re-established in 1937, and became a popular elective. Seven '41 men were Commissioned First Lieutenants in the Medical

Corps Reserve. A Department of Psychiatry, previously under the New York Hospital, was set up on the same basis as the other departments. The college collaborated closely in the cancer work of the Memorial Hospital, in its fine new building across the street from the college. Active pourparlers were in progress looking to the adoption of the New York Hospital School of Nursing by Cornell. (The hospital, not being empowered to grant degrees, found its school handicapped in competition with nursing schools in universities.) Many important gifts were received, especially from the Rockefeller Foundation, which endowed the work in public health and preventive medicine and gave $75,000 for research in biochemistry under Professor Vincent du Vigneaud.

More and more, the University intervened in student affairs. Such intervention was not in fact generally unwelcome. The mere size of the University made organization and direction useful to students, most of whom had been so familiar with guidance and control in their preparatory schools that they accepted them as a matter of course.

The President told the trustees that he had been repeatedly warned against instituting a dean of men at Cornell. However, he was convinced that the University must assume more responsibility for the welfare of men students. He therefore created in 1939 the post of Counselor of Students.

Dr. Day was convinced that we were not doing our duty about student health. "The University will assume full responsibility for the medical care of sick students," he promised. In 1940 the services were reorganized and much extended. Dr. Norman S. Moore '23, son of the celebrated Dean Veranus A. Moore of the Veterinary College, was appointed Physician-in-Chief and Clinical Director, and three resident physicians were added to the staff. The old McMahon house, on the site of the present Gannett Clinic, was remodeled as a clinic. All entering students received a rapid physical examination, to catch illnesses in the bud. Thereafter they returned whenever they didn't feel too good. Special clinics for skin conditions, mental hygiene, and athletic injuries were set up. The athletic clinic reported at the end of its first year 57 severe cases, comprising 10 concussions of the brain, 14 dislocations, 33 fractures. The mental hygiene clinic recorded six suicide attempts, of which two were successful. (But the successful suicides had not consulted the clinic.) The University physicians began visiting sick students in their rooms. The Infirmary, with its staff physicians on twenty-four-hour duty, received 58 per cent more patients than in the previous year, an indication of increased student acceptance. In short, the University was now doing its full duty toward its charges.

Student health bears its inevitable relation to student exercise. Exercise makes the student body glow with health, except when interrupted by concussions of the brain, dislocations, and fractures. A new council, composed of trustees, faculty, and student members, watched over physical education and athletics. This council reported in 1939 the rise in importance of intramural sports, especially of such individual diversions as skiing, bowling, handball, squash, and badminton. The council noted that many graduates regretted that while in college they had not learned the fundamentals of golf, tennis, and such. The University, it contended, must provide such training, and it must think of faculty recreation also. Intercollegiate athletics may well keep their existing proportions, and may be carried on as long as they are supported by student interest. But we shall not try to expand our income by football overdevelopment and the like.

Intramurals flourished. In the spring of 1939 two thousand men took part in the organized spring games, with three hundred teams in eight sports. Sigma Nu's four-oared crew won among thirty-two contestants. Alpha Chi Rho was the panathletic champion. Touch football, curiously, was the most dangerous sport, causing twenty-six injuries in 1937. Tar Young Hill, a dozen miles to the eastward, was very popular, with its various slopes and jumps, its 1,000-foot ski tow, its shelter and open fireplaces. Much frequented in winter was Mount Pleasant Lodge, off the Turkey Hill Road, a headquarters for overnight and weekend outing parties. Marguerite I. Wilder '41 and Edward J. Moore '39 were crowned by the Ag-Domecon Association as champions of potato racing on roller skates.

The intramurals did not, however, usurp the place of proper intercollegiate sports. The athletic frenzies of the century's first quarter had certainly much abated. Cornellians could seldom dream of national and world championships, but they battled fiercely to prove themselves a little better than their natural peers. Cornell adhered to the "Three Presidents' Agreement" of 1937, by which the Presidents of Harvard, Yale, and Princeton laid down sensible rules for athletic eligibility. The athletic enterprise, under the able management of James Lynah, showed an annual profit. Lynah left in 1940, to be coordinator of specifications for the National Defense Commission. He was succeeded by Robert J. Kane '34, no less able; he kept athletics in the black even through the war years.

A series of fine football teams helped, of course. In 1937 we did well, and Jerome H. ("Brud") Holland '39 was named to the All-American, as were A. Sidney Roth '39 and William McKeever in 1938. The 1939 team, coached by Carl Snavely, was definitely great. It was undefeated and untied; it beat Penn 26 to 0, before 69,000 spectators. (Ah, where are those throngs of ticket-purchasers today?) Nicholas Drahos '41 was crowned All-American tackle, and many others were highly commended by the critics.

The 1940 team was also brilliant. It beat Army 45 to 0, the worst defeat in the history of Army football. But our hopes of an Ivy League championship were grotesquely undone. In the crucial Dartmouth game the score stood, up to the last moment, Dartmouth 3, Cornell 0. Cornell fought its way to the edge of Dartmouth's goal line. With six seconds remaining, Walter Scholl '41 threw a pass to William J. Murphy '41 for a touchdown. Score, Cornell 7, Dartmouth 3.

But, as Bob Kane, who was then assistant director of athletics, remembers, the Dartmouth manager's chart showed that we had scored on a fifth down. "A tempest started in the Dartmouth dressing room, which reached Jim Lynah and me at the Hanover Inn about 45 minutes after the game. We decided to look at the films on Monday before making a statement. There was no doubt after running and rerunning the films that the officials had erred." The press was informed and Dartmouth was declared the winner, three days after the game had ended. (It was rumored that much distress occurred in the betting world.)

The players were not happy. "They figured that they had been victimized many times before by officials' errors and no one had been generous enough to correct the mistakes," says Bob Kane. But today, I suppose, no one really cares very much whether or not we beat Dartmouth in 1940. We do care that Cornell sportsmanship was nobly vindicated, that we were willing to yield our victory for the sake of honor. Cornell's Fifth Down takes its place with the great renunciations of history, rivalling that of Cyrano de Bergerac.

The crews, coached by "Stork" Sanford, had their good years. In 1940 we were second at Poughkeepsie, less than a length behind Washington. But the old days of sweeping the river were over (until 1955).

534

The track team's record was more than respectable. In 1938 Cornell and Princeton defeated Oxford and Cambridge, five Cornellians taking firsts. William W. McKeever '39 made a Cornell record of 57 feet 3⅛ inches in the 35-pound weight throw. We won the heptagonals in 1939, James B. Pender '39 winning six races (including heats, of course) and taking two individual titles. Howard W. ("Wreck") Welch '38 finished first in the 1937 ICAAAA cross-country. We took the cross-country heptagonals in 1940, John L. Ayer '41 coming in first.

We had a succession of superlative baseball teams. In 1939 we tied for first in the Eastern Intercollege Baseball League, in the following year we led without a rival, and in 1941 we were second.

There were plenty of other Cornell triumphs. The indoor polo team in 1937–38 was almost irresistible, winning sixteen and losing one. In 1938 the rifle team outshot eighteen other college teams, and won the Hearst trophy. In the following winter the skiiers gained the New York State Ski Association title, leaping and slaloming in the Caroline hills. In 1941 we had the eastern intercollegiate tennis title, Kennedy Randall Jr. '41 and William E. Gifford '41 taking the doubles championship. In the autumn we led the Middle Atlantic Soccer League, with William H. Starr '44 shining brightest.

Student affairs in general presented little worthy of remark, perhaps because time has not yet gilded them with legend. Foreign students came to Cornell in increasing numbers, as their own countries were invaded or darkened by war's shadows. In 1937–38 twenty-one countries were represented; fifty-three graduate students from China were counted. Many of these suffered obscurely, half-starved in dismal lodgings. And not the foreign students alone. A survey in 1937 showed that some students prepared their own food for as little as $1.50 a week. Fortunately the National Youth Administration relieved the direst distresses. In 1940–41 it gave work to 673 students and paid them a total of $73,000. The number of working students increased from 34 per cent in 1937 to 41 per cent in 1940–41; 274 of them earned all their expenses. In 1942, 2,612 working students were recorded; they earned a total of $304,000.

But of course these were the minority. Most students came to college with enough money for their reasonable expenses. They were increasingly motor-borne; in 1940, 1,300 student cars were registered. The fraternities followed their immemorial cycle. Driscoll Brothers did an annual business of $300 in paddles (not canoe paddles). The question of liquor was much vexed. The Interfraternity Council ruled that none might be sold in the house, but there was no reason why it should not be checked in lockers.

Student behavior was rated on the whole excellent. There were occasional disorders, mostly in the period from 20 April to 21 May, under the zodiacal influence of Taurus the Bull. Class warfare feebly resurged. In 1938 the soph smoker, the frosh banquet, and an "approved rush" were canceled, as a punishment for turbulence. In the following year a frosh-soph flag rush occurred. All was well controlled, gentlemanly, perfunctory, dull.

The rebellious impulse found some expression in political action. We had a series of leftist clubs with high-sounding names. They were small and inconspicuous, occupied mostly with mimeographing smudgy ultimatums. Whether or not they were actually communist, they followed the communist line. In December 1939 the Cornell Civil Liberties Union (of thirteen members) invited Earl Browder, then under indictment for subversive conspiracy, to give a public lecture. The authorities forbade his appearance, on the grounds of legal impropriety. They permitted, however, a speech by Robert Minor, an almost equally celebrated communist. He drew an audience of 350 persons, without, apparently, making any converts. The *Sun*'s editor, John C. Jaqua '40, counterattacked by forming the Young Capitalist League.

In the following spring came the Dilling Affair. Kirkpatrick W. Dilling '42, son of Elizabeth Dilling, celebrated erythrophobe and author of *The Red Network*, was brought before the Student Conduct Committee and put on parole for blowing dormitory fuses, filling a ceiling light with water, and burning a sulfur candle in the washroom. His father charged that the committee's action was motivated by its approval of communism. His mother came to Ithaca, made her own investigation, and published a long and furious article in the *Areopagus* (May 1940), which prolonged the life of that magazine for several months. She saw Reds in every classroom and found most of the staff, from President Day down, tainted with communism.

A salmagundi of circumstances: A wing of the Zeta Beta Tau house burned in May 1939. The women joined the men for senior singing in that year for the first time. Marne Obernauer '41 won a bet of $8.00 by swallowing a live goldfish. He was outdone by Edwin Maisel '39, who swallowed four in the lobby of the Hotel Astor in New York. In June 1940, during a Physics Department picnic at Taughannock,

Henry S. Birnbaum, grad, and Mrs. Marshall G. Holloway, technologist in the Medical Office, drowned while rescuing two women swimming at the foot of the falls; the currents were so strong that the bodies were recovered only two days later. In 1940 the campus went for Willkie, 8 to 1; as Cornell goes, so goes the nation, in reverse. Phyllis F. Dittman '43 won the chimesmaster competition in 1941, and Jean Hofstadter '44 in the following year. In the 1941 Summer School slacks and shorts were banned in Willard Straight. Treman, King's store closed in 1939, after ninety-five years in the same location. A thirty-pound bobcat was shot in the Danby hills, a timber wolf carcass was found in a trap, and bears were seen in Newfield, Trumansburg, and Caroline. Deer, beaver, possums, pheasants, ruffed grouse, trout resumed their old life in our woodlands. Raccoons became a householders' pest.

The alumni organization was reformed. It had consisted of four autonomous bodies, with separate offices, of seven alumni organizations of the various colleges, and of a hundred independent alumni clubs. The Cornell Alumni Association brought them all together in 1939 in a coherent unit, responsible to the new organization, not to the Board of Trustees. The association's duties were to unite all activities, supervise the local clubs, purchase and publish the *Alumni News*, direct secondary-school contacts and club scholarships, sell Cornellian merchandise, organize placement activities, and stimulate trustee nominations. Elbert P. Tuttle '18 was the chairman of the association; the first alumni secretary was Emmet J. Murphy '22.

Thus we come to the crucial date of 7 December 1941.

XXXVI

Cornell under President Day: War

IN the midafternoon of Sunday, 7 December 1941, campus dwellers, placidly tuned to the New York Philharmonic, were startled from their easy chairs by the announcement that the Japanese were bombing Pearl Harbor. "A hoax!" was the usual cry. "A student prank!" But as the news poured forth the most skeptical were forced to conclude that this was a prank of world-wide dimensions.

Shocks seldom benumb and more seldom provoke to immediate counteraction. A group of students, fulfilling a social duty, called on your historian in the late afternoon. "This is the most momentous date in your lives!" said the historian. The students looked blank, aghast. The realization crept over them that war might interfere with their transportation home for the Christmas holidays.

While declarations of war crackled, the University's National Defense Council met, on Monday, 8 December. It announced: "This is no time for hasty decisions," and pointed out that the emergency had not essentially changed (both very questionable statements). It urged the students to remain in college awaiting their summons, and not to rush off to enlist.

In fact, very few students had any idea of springing to arms, nor could they have done so had they wished. The Selective Service Act was in full operation; the generations of the early forties, unlike those of the First War, were trained to the idea of obligatory military service, at the orders of central authority. They would fight, of course, in fulfillment of a duty, mostly disagreeable. But they had no illusions of glory, and they refused to attend patriotic rallies and pep talks, and they would sing no songs to the effect that the home fires must be kept burning, that their troubles should be packed up in old kit bags, or that they would not come back till it was over over there. This was a drab, dirty, businesslike war, which produced no popular song except a German sentimental ballad.

The students' calmness contrasted, indeed, with their elders' frenetic upheavals. President Day noted with surprise that emotional disturbances among students were far fewer than might have been anticipated. Youth, lacking means of comparison, accepts a current abnormality as its normal, and refuses to worry because things are as they obviously are.

President Day wrote of the war in a manner that no college president of 1917 could have ventured or even conceived. "War," he said, "is by its very nature a direct nullification of the basic purposes of higher education." Total war is in disaccord with all human and rational living. But our long-range services must yield to the complete mobilization of national resources. "For the duration of the conflict . . . there can be little or no education as usual."

After the Christmas vacation the new war program was announced. Vacations would be omitted and courses accelerated. The Medical and Veterinary Colleges would have compulsory year-round programs; other colleges would conduct optional semester-length summer terms. Summer schools would be summerlong. A physical fitness program, including mass calisthenics, would be required of all male students. Athletics would continue. New war-oriented courses would begin in various fields, such as mathematics.

At first, confusion, aided by conflicting directives from Washington, reigned. Most male students had appeared before their local draft boards and were on the campus awaiting call, as members of the Army Enlisted Reserve. It was assumed at first that student reservists would be allowed to take their degrees before being summoned. But in September 1942 came the order that members of the Enlisted Reserve would be called to active service at the end of the term in which they should reach selective service age; and in November that age was lowered to eighteen.

On 5 December 1942 the Army and Navy stopped all voluntary enlistments. A week later the Army A-12 and Navy V-12 programs were announced. Students would be inducted, uniformed, and sent to college for prescribed training offered by contracts between the services and the educational institutions. In the Army plan men did thirteen weeks of basic training in camps, and were then assigned to the institutions. In the Navy plan, the men were sent to the campuses for their first training. Thus at the end of the first term of 1942–43 two groups were present: the Army selectees, who expected to be called at any moment to do their basic training; and the Navy and Marine reservists, eligible for the V-12 program, who expected to continue as civilian students until June, when they would be inducted into the V-12 program.

On 27 January 1943, during final exams, the Army announced the call of the Enlisted Reserve to active service "at the end of the first academic period completed after 31 December," in other words, immediately. However, the Army could not digest the men so fast, and students were encouraged to continue their college work until summoned. Most of them were called up in March, except for majors in engineering, chemistry, biochemistry, mathematics, meteorology, physics, psychology, and veterinary medicine, and except also for premedical and preveterinary students.

Thus order was brought. The services assumed the task of selection of students and their support, and the institutions were paid for providing instruction and housing.

The first contingent of 600 Army men arrived in June 1943, and 1,642 Navy V-12's, including 300 Marines, came soon after.

A new directive, of 15 February 1944, canceled deferment in many fields, and restricted it to a few in chemistry, physics, and engineering.

A steadily dwindling number of civilian men, mostly under draft age, remained on the campus, following the old curricula; and the number of women students increased, rushing into voids.

At the end of the war, President Day reckoned that we had had in our programs for enlisted service men 3,578 from the Army and 13,577 from the Navy.[1] 4,500 civilian undergraduates had left without completing their studies.

The Army programs on the Ithaca campus were grouped under the general head of the Army Specialized Training Program, or ASTP, and were administered by Colonel E. R. Van Deusen, Professor of Military Science. The general purpose of the program was to provide

[1] Captain R. B. Bretland, Commandant of the Naval ROTC, corrects this to the figure of 14,896 Naval personnel in training at Cornell between 1 July 1943 and 1 March 1946. Of these 9,848 were in the V-12 program.

specialized educational and technical training beyond the scope of the Army's normal facilities. The ASTP was composed of the following groups:

The Basic Reserves consisted of enlisted men who were under eighteen when they arrived at the University. They were uniformed and under military control. They received food, quarters, medical care, and tuition from the government, but no pay. They took basic courses at college level in such subjects as mathematics, physics, chemistry, English, geography, and history. They were called to active service at the end of the term when they became eighteen.

The Preprofessionals were enlisted men on active duty detailed to prepare for entrance to medical college.

The Area and Language Students pursued special work in Russian, German, Italian, Czech, and Chinese. Of this we shall have more to say presently.

The U.S. Military Academy Preparatory Students looked to entrance to West Point.

Veterinary Students were enlisted men on active duty detailed to study veterinary medicine.

Personnel Psychologists and Basic Engineers were two groups that did not last long.

In addition, civilian undergraduates continued to drill in the old R.O.T.C., which now became the ROTC (for a minor benefit of the war was to banish a billion periods).

The naval invasion of the campus began in the spring of 1941, before our entrance into the war, with the detailing of fifty ensigns to study Diesel engines in the College of Engineering. The Navy then built and equipped a Diesel laboratory on Sage Green, the first wartime eyesore. A full-fledged Navy program began in July 1942, under the command of Captain B. W. Chippendale. The men were lodged in the dormitories, in mobilized rooming houses, in dispossessed fraternities, and in Sage College, from which women students were dislodged (naturally). A Navy Mess Hall sprang up on West Avenue, south of the dorms. (The Army men were fed from Willard Straight Cafeteria; the terrace was roofed and enclosed to receive them.)

The Navy offered several programs, to wit: V-1, for freshmen and sophomores, preparatory to training for a commission. This program attracted few, and was soon dropped. And V-5, for future Flying Cadets. Naval Aviation took over the Civilian Pilot Training Program, which had existed since 1939. And V-7; its members would receive on graduation a brief training leading to commissions as ensigns. This was submerged, in 1943, in V-12, which gave a comprehensive training for selected apprentice seamen and marine privates in one of three curricula: Basic, Engineering, and Premedical. These trainees were of college age and were taught in large part in regular college classes.

Extramurally, the College of Engineering, with the sponsorship of the U.S. Office of Education, conducted an Engineering, Science, and Management War Training Program, or ESMWT, in eleven centers of war industry. More than 30,000 persons were enrolled eventually in its courses.

The College of Engineering also set up a one-year program for the industrial training of women, under the auspices of the Curtiss-Wright Corporation. The University tried to tempt its women students with courses in nursing, social work, industrial supervision, and secretarial skills, with very little success. Nor did many of our coeds join the WAACS and WAVES.

Of course, everything was frightfully crowded, even with the diminution in numbers of our male civilian students. A blessed measure of relief was brought by the opening of Olin Hall of Chemical Engineering, in October 1942.

Olin Hall, made possible by a noble gift from Franklin W. Olin '86, was the first building of the present Engineering Campus. Though designed by the famous firm of Shreve, Lamb, and Harmon, it roused many aesthetic criticisms from the partisans of Gothic. Dean Hollister of Engineering and Director Rhodes of Chemical Engineering were opposed to Gothic, which might suit a Department of Alchemy but not Chemical Engineering. (The *Alumni News* recalled that every new building had had its detractors, that Sibley Dome was labeled "The Breast of the Campus," Rockefeller "Public Grammar School No. 16," and Baker Lab "a U.S. Post Office Conferred by a Republican Administration.") The principle of Olin Hall's design is the interchangeability of space to meet changing needs. The only nontransformable areas are the lecture rooms and the laboratory for unit operations. In place of large common laboratories wherein set experiments are performed under supervision, many small labs for two to four students are provided.

In the emergency, much of the new building was turned over to the Navy for its administration and classes.

War's burdens weighed on all, but most heavily on the President, responsible for every serious decision, and indeed for many of the initiations which would lead to decisions. He was much relieved by the appointment (in October 1943) of George H. Sabine '03, professor of philosophy, as Vice President in charge of academic affairs.

The problems of staffing were acute. Large numbers of the faculty sprang to arms, or to the OWI, the OSS, the FCA, the OSRD, and to other agencies of which the initials have probably already become incomprehensible. One quails at the thought of cataloguing the gallant faculty's martial services, often in very interesting sectors. The Medical College was particularly hard hit by military summonses.

Those who stayed home were weighed down with a vacationless calendar, heavy teaching schedules, and large classes in technical courses, and with discouragingly small classes in the eternal verities. Eminent authorities in the classics or philosophy found themselves teaching trigonometry to sailors. Aristotle, for the moment, yielded to Bowditch.

A special concern of the administration was student health and fitness. A new Department of Clinical and Preventive Medicine was formed in July 1943, under the chairmanship of Dr. Norman S. Moore, who, as Physician-in-Chief, had reorganized our clinical services. The department incorporated the previous Department of Hygiene and the control of the Clinic and the Infirmary. Formal courses in hygiene were abandoned, except for Mental Hygiene. The Clinic was expanded, with a dental office, a cold clinic, and the service of a nutrition counselor. All entrants received a quick medical examination, to catch developing cases. Total medical and surgical care and liberal hospitalization provisions thus became available to all students.

The Department of Physical Education and Athletics was headed by Robert J. Kane '34, after the resignation of James Lynah to enter war service. Lynah had in eight years retired debts of $246,000 and had rebuilt the physical plant. Now, under wartime urgency, physical training was made compulsory for all men, military and civilian. A commando course was erected on Kite Hill, above the Crescent. It included a swinging log, an eight-foot water jump, a six-barred gate fifteen feet high, parallel bars over water, an overhead ladder from which one swung or hung, a pole to climb, and a rabbit warren of wooden arches through which to squirm. Coach Georges Cointe's cry "You can do eet, fat boy!" became a campus catchword.

Most of the athletic teams continued, reinforced by military enrollees. The footballers accomplished nothing worthy of remark. Coach Carl Snavely resigned at the end of 1944, to return to North Carolina.

In 1943 the baseball team tied Penn for the league championship. The swimming team, though handicapped by its tiny pool, had undefeated seasons in 1944 and 1945, and the lacrosse team did brilliantly. The basketballers lost the 1945 league championship to Penn by two points in an overtime game, and the track team scored second in the heptagonals and third in the ICAAAA meet. Grace Acel '44 was the champion of the Women's Intercollegiate Fencing Association in 1942, and Helen I. Barnhard '43, winning the New York State tennis tournament, became the fourth-ranking woman tennis player in the country.

Very surprisingly, the athletic establishment ended the operations of 1944–45 with a surplus of $40,000.

Within the colleges, courses were oriented toward war needs. Commercial and economic geography turned into geopolitics. The Department of Psychology busied itself with a seminary in military psychology and in such operations as testing plane pilots by salivary techniques. Three departments united to give a course in Nationalism, and weekly lectures were delivered on the impact of the war on America.

In the Arts College, the most striking novelty was the initiation of area studies, with the aid of the Rockefeller Foundation, in the summer of 1943. A course in Contemporary Russian Civilization, demanding the students' full time, was established. Soviet history, government, social institutions, economics, and culture were studied. Distinguished experts came to lecture. Some of the teachers were sympathetic to the Soviet regime; others were hostile. Said President Day: "The program was an effort to implement a fundamental faith that knowledge is a better bet than ignorance, however deep-seated may be the elements of controversy."

The success of the course led to the organization, in the fall of 1943, of an intensive course in the Russian language, with the cooperation of the ASTP. Selected students from the military devoted all their waking hours to the acquisition of colloquial Russian.

The inevitable happened, as, by definition, the inevitable must. The New York *World-Telegram* blazoned to the world the news: CORNELL GOES BOLSHEVIST. A reporter alleged that in the area and language courses some aspects of Soviet life were favorably presented, and added the accusation that Cornell proposed to give a lecture series on civil liberties.

President Day replied spiritedly.[2] He pointed out that "we put guns

[2] President's report 1943–44; *Saturday Review*, 4 March 1944.

544

and grenades into the hands of young soldiers without any fear that they will use them against their homes." He said that area work had to be taught by those who had seen and studied Soviet Russia, and that no instructors were found to be unduly or uncritically favorable to it, and that anyway indoctrination was forbidden. As for the scheduled lectures on civil liberties, two would be given by eminent faculty members, one by a scholar in political science now employed on a newspaper, one by the chairman of the Federal Communications Commission, and one by the Attorney General of the United States. The purpose of the series was to illuminate our traditional concepts in the light of social change.

In the imbroglio, "the Trustees and Faculty showed unyielding courage," said the President. Their sense of being under fire, he continued, created a feeling of unity and independence. The early Cornellians, he said, would have approved; we did not back down in the face of criticism. All this is true. But while the New York *World-Telegram* soon found new menaces with which to terrify the home-going subway reader, in many timorous minds the impression remained that Cornell and its President were plotting to sovietize America.

The success of intensive Russian-language teaching led naturally to similar intensive work, under Army auspices, in German, Italian, Czech, and Chinese. Professor Cornelis W. de Kiewiet of History was in charge. Himself a linguist fluent in Dutch, Afrikaans, German, and French, he found the Army's oral approach to language learning so effective that he proposed that the University retain it after the war.

The revitalized College of Engineering profited by the war-born interest in industrial production. In June 1944, as the invading allies were landing on the Normandy beaches, the trustees boldly approved a five-year requirement for all engineering courses, for the first time in America.

All departments of the College of Agriculture were put on a war basis. The college seized the opportunity to abolish the winter short courses, which had been failing for some years, as the Extension Service filled their place. Only forty-nine "Short-horns" attended in 1942. Times had changed since Bailey's heyday.

The resources of the college were turned to the increase of food production, distribution, and marketing. The scientists sought substitutes for all sorts of scarcities, such as poultry rations, fungicides, insecticides, formaldehyde (used to check onion smut), tin containers, rubber. They hunted new sources for bioflavin, which is found in dried milk. (All American dried milk went to the armed forces.) They studied weather, farm prices, farm labor supply and its distribution, machinery, transport, and food packaging. They continued their important work in land classification, to remove submarginal land from vain competition, and to protect naïve buyers. The work in artificial breeding attracted wondering visitors from the whole country and from abroad.

The Extension Service issued a stream of bulletins, on means of increasing production. It distributed thirty instructive films, such as "Picking Pointers for Apple Pickers" (which would make a nice song). It established victory garden programs and held repair clinics for farm machinery. It organized 17,000 local Minutemen and the 4-H Clubs in a Food for Freedom campaign. It brought into being 1,500,000 garden plots, aggregating 200,000 acres, and producing a yield equal or superior to the state's commercial vegetable crop. And it took practically full responsibility for handling the state's farm labor program, seeking, distributing, housing, and feeding migratory labor, including 5,000 prisoners of war, 6,000 Bahamians and Jamaicans, several hundred Newfoundlanders, and 140,000 vacationists.

The College of Home Economics found itself swamped by the demand for dietitians and clothing specialists. Graduates of the Department of Hotel Administration were sought, to run base facilities at airfields, to supervise munition workers' housing and feeding, to officer the Quartermaster Corps and the Naval Supply Corps. Manufacturers clamored for the results of Home Economics research, as in kitchen design through work analysis, as in the study of changes of posture and other physiological responses in relation to changes in elevation of the ironing board, as in the capacity of narrow shelving for the kitchen storage of packaged supplies. Other research answered special needs, as the "Study of the Design of a Pinless Diaper Acceptable to Mothers in a Leper Colony in South China."

Home Economics extension workers, with the slogan "Serve, Save, and Sacrifice, for Victory," cooperated with the agricultural extension group. They organized the 4-H Club girls on military lines: Mother's Helper, Housekeeper, Salvage and Trash Collector, Family Fire Warden, Kitchen Captain, Clothing Corporal. The Extension Service proudly counted in 1943–44 81,073,798 glass jars of food put up in homes, and 23,080,059 containers of fruit butter, jams, jellies, and marmalade.

The School of Nutrition worked with Home Economics and Agriculture on various nutritional problems. Professor Clive McCay and Marion Pfund showed that brewer's yeast remedies vitamin B_1 deficiency, and started a national yeast-feast. Dr. Norman S. Moore and Leonard A. Maynard experimented on a group of conscientious objectors to find the effect of a high-protein diet on resistance to cold. The objectors, docile for once, were confined for over two hundred days in a laboratory with controlled temperatures varying from zero to 60 degrees. The conclusion: temperature differences have only a slight effect on metabolism.

The School of Education confronted a shortage of secondary-school teachers in the state and a shortage of undergraduates preparing for a teaching career. It prepared a curriculum for nursery-school teachers, in cooperation with Home Economics. Professor E. Laurence Palmer gave a very popular course on Outdoor Living, in preparation for the end of settled civilization.

The Law School suffered grievously from the war. Its enrollment dropped to 49 in 1943–44. To be sure, this shrinkage was a national phenomenon.

Two of President Day's fondest projects—a School of Business and Public Administration and a School of Industrial and Labor Relations —had to be deferred to the war's end. Likewise deferred were the plans for a Statler Inn, which the Statler Foundation proposed to build on the shore of Beebe Lake for the Department of Hotel Administration.

In spite of war, the trustees created, in December 1942, the Collection of Regional History, with the aid of the Rockefeller Foundation. Whitney R. Cross, curator, began assembling documents from the University Library, from various departments, and from donors throughout the state.

In New York, the Medical College had heavy war burdens, but Dr. Joseph C. Hinsey, appointed Dean in July 1942, bore them valiantly on his broad shoulders. An Army Student Training Program was installed. Most of the students were in uniform; they received pay, quarters, food, textbooks, instruments. Many were called to active service as Army or Navy officers; others were placed on inactive service on graduation, to serve their internships. The courses were accelerated, with detrimental effects. Especially in surgery the students suffered, being allowed only twenty-seven months of advanced training, including their internships. Forty-five per cent of the staff were lost to military service or war work. The faithful who remained were barely able to cope with their extra duties. The faculty complained that the General Staff would not recognize the future civilian need for qualified physicians.

The college sponsored the Army's General Hospital No. 9. It was staffed by fifty-five doctors, forty-seven of them members of the Cornell Medical College organization. Lieutenant Colonel Ralph F. Bowers, associate professor of clinical surgery, was chief of the surgical service, and Lieutenant Colonel Bruce Webster, assistant professor of clinical medicine, head of the medical service. The hospital was called to active duty on 15 July 1942. After languishing for a year in Boston Harbor, it was sent to Brisbane, Australia, and thence (18 October 1943) to Goodenough Island, off southeast New Guinea. Since only native huts stood in the area, the medics had to build their own buildings, develop their water supply, and install their own plumbing. Soon scrub typhus, or Japanese river fever, broke out, and a typhoon struck, destroying most of the buildings and depositing twenty-four inches of rain in an eighteen-hour period. After a year on unhappily named Goodenough, the hospital was transferred to Biak Island, off northwest New Guinea, closer to operations. At one time 2,500 patients crowded wards built for a maximum of 1,500. At the end of the war General Hospital No. 9 received the Meritorious Service plaque for superior performance of duty.[3]

In New York, the harried faculty found time to do important war research. Thirty-four major projects were assigned to the college; for example: nerve regeneration; nerve testing at surgical operations; the amplification 100 million times of the female mosquito's mating call, which can attract males from afar to a waiting doom; work on mustard gas, antimalarial agents, and the chemical structure of penicillin; the rate of healing, under various imposed conditions, of standardized burns on the forearms of volunteers; the effects of kidney secretion on blood pressure in surgical shock; the dangers of prolonged bed rest, with loss of calcium and body proteins; the screening of selectees for emotional instability; and airplane crash injuries. This is interesting. Hugh de Haven, after a year in the Medical College in Ithaca in 1914–15, became a war pilot. He crashed, and, to his surprise, lived. He then spent years studying the cases of persons who had survived long falls by landing on structures that yielded a few inches, such as freshly turned earth or automobile tops. At one point he tested a new sponge

---

[3] Stewart G. Wolf, Jr., "The Completed Saga of the Ninth General Hospital," *Cornell University Medical College Quarterly*, Jan. 1946.

rubber by dropping fresh eggs on it from the eleventh floor of the Medical Center. The eggs bounced, unbroken, thirty-five feet in air. He tried to catch them on the bounce, and usually met disaster. He concluded that the human body could, under the right conditions, survive terrific impacts. He associated the patterns of injury with cockpit structure and found that 80 per cent of serious injuries are caused by the impact of the skull on the instrument panel. Professor W. A. Geohagan then invented a self-locking harness, which was adopted by the Army and the Navy.

The most far-reaching achievement of the researchers was surely that of Dr. Vincent du Vigneaud of Biochemistry. His discovery of the chemical architectutre of biotin was called one of the greatest triumphs of modern chemistry. Biotin was in 1942 so rare that the world's supply was about one-tenth of an ounce. Dr. du Vigneaud identified it with nature's powerful, life-giving vitamin H, and he determined the arrangement and the quantities of carbon, hydrogen, oxygen, nitrogen, and sulfur atoms in the biotin molecule. Shortly after the war, Dr. du Vigneaud and his team synthesized penicillin, and made a synthetic pituitary compound, important in the checking of dwarfism.

On 1 July 1942, almost unnoticed by most Cornellians, a thirteenth school was added to the instructional units of Cornell, with the creation of the Cornell University–New York Hospital School of Nursing. The School of Nursing had operated for sixty-five years as a function of the New York Hospital. One of the oldest and most esteemed in the country, it aspired to a university connection, with the right to confer a degree. According to the agreement made, the new school would require for entrance two years of college work acceptable to Cornell. Its graduates would receive the degree of B.S. in Nursing from Cornell and a Diploma of Nursing from the New York Hospital. The hospital would bear all the costs, then amounting to about $200,000 a year. Miss Bessie A. Parker, the first acting dean, reported that in September 1943 twelve baccalaureate degrees were granted for the first time.

On the Ithaca campus student life was supervised by the new student counselors, Donald H. Moyer and Thelma L. Brummett. Miss Brummett replaced the Dean of Women. The counselors reported that student conduct was on the whole excellent. A large proportion of the men were under military discipline; the others were imbued with wartime seriousness. The Student Council found even that the faculty lagged in its duty, being infected with too much of a "business-as-usual" spirit. The council organized a Cornell for Victory Committee, which advanced all sorts of programs for saving, prohibiting, and doing, with the agency of many Victory Wardens. The students accepted without demur the Faculty's prohibition of student-owned automobiles; there was no gas anyhow. A ban on overnight house parties was imposed, but as this proved to be unenforceable, it was rescinded. The fraternities suffered a decimation in membership and had great difficulties with food rationing. Many of them gratefully accepted the commandeering of their houses to lodge the Army and Navy men. The lot of the working student was somewhat bettered, as student labor, or any labor at all, was in great demand.

The "activities" suffered, what with difficulties of travel, shortages of supplies such as paper, and especially shortage of leisure. The *Sun* suspended in November 1943 and was replaced by a weekly *Cornell Bulletin*, directed by the administration and staffed largely by women. (Guinevere G. Griest '44 was the first female editor-in-chief.) The *Widow* also gave up, but in March 1944 it revived, with Marion Fear '44 (Mrs. A. Richard Heidt) as editor. Women also headed the *Cornellian* and the *Countryman*, and chaired the Willard Straight board of managers, the Cornell for Victory Committee, the Campus Chest. Even the Waiters' Derby became a Waitresses' Derby. (Joan E. Blaikie '45 won handsomely, spilling not a drop on her uplifted tray.)

At the same time and in spite of all war's ravages, certain beginnings are to be noted. In June 1945 the Departments of Fine Arts, Music, and Speech and Drama, with the dance section of Physical Education, put on the first Festival of Contemporary Arts. The festival included concerts, a play by the Dramatic Club, a dance recital, and shows of painting and sculpture. At about the same time the Octagon Club was formed, to stage musical reviews.

Some random relics of these war years: The Kappa Alpha Professorship, endowed by the fraternity, was established in 1945; such a fraternity professorship is certainly rare in American colleges, and may be unique. Morris Bishop '14 of Romance Literature was the first to occupy the chair. Victor Reynolds was appointed University Publisher, succeeding Stanley Schaefer '28 at the Press, in October 1943. The Lackawanna Railroad gave up its passenger service to Owego in March 1942. Scrap drives cleaned out University cellars and disposed of, among other things, all the official records of Charles Kendall Adams's presidency. A drive unearthed, in a fraternity cellar, two giant clock hands of copper; these were said to be the original hands of the Library clock, stolen, hidden at Hobart College, and kept for two years under the waters of Cayuga Lake. January 1945 was very cold, with a mean temperature of 14.8 degrees. More than eighty inches of snow fell in December and January. Faculty wives still shiver as they recall that winter, with a paucity of snow shovelers, with fuel rationing, food rationing, gas rationing, with impassable streets and no grocery deliveries, and with the husbands far away, enjoying the war in Paris or the South Pacific.

The alumni gave up their reunions for the duration, substituting, in 1942, a "reunion by Radio," with a nationwide broadcast from WHCU. In the following year we had a "Bonded Reunion"; reuners were asked to devote their presumed travel costs and other expenses to the purchase of war bonds. Through all the upheavals the alumni demonstrated their loyalty to Cornell, even giving to the Alumni Fund in 1945 a record $211,700.

No reckoning of the services of the alumni in the war has been made, since those services were so great, so varied, so universal. Something like 16,000 Cornellians were in service, and at least twenty were generals. Cornellians were everywhere, from arctic wastes to tropic jungles—even in Germany, where Eric B. Erickson '21 wormed his way into Himmler's confidence, and under the pretext of supplying oil from Sweden indicated every important German oil-producing plant to Allied bombers.[4] A Cornellian broke the Japanese cipher; others helped contrive the first atomic bomb; many others led the vast mobilization of industry and served the government in high place. We can but conclude that the total war involved every adult, and that an effort to extricate Cornell's contribution from the mass is very nearly impossible, and probably not worth the doing.

On V-J Day, 2 September 1945, the war was over. President Day had time to take a quick look backward, before taking a long look forward.

The civilian enrollment in the University in 1944–45 was 4,783, considerably down from 7,315 in the last prewar year of 1940–41. Financially we had fared tolerably well, though in 1944–45 we had an operating deficit of $64,700. Important gifts had come in: $467,000 from the Candace C. Stimson estate for the Medical College; $285,000

---

[4] Alexander Klein, *The Counterfeit Traitor* (New York, 1958).

from the Statler Foundation; $494,000 from the estate of Horace White '87, nephew of Andrew D. White; $200,000 from the Grange League Federation for a nutrition building. And the annual Alumni Fund, yearly setting new high marks, provided inestimable aid for current general expenses.

The military guests had been accommodated with the help of repulsive temporary wooden barracks. Only emergency repairs had been permitted for the permanent buildings. Everything was sadly in need of renovation, refurbishing, paint.

In the proper educational business of the University the only changes had been those provoked by war needs. In some cases, as in the teaching of languages, the novelties held much promise. But most of the changes had been in the direction of acceleration, hurry, and the attenuation of the fundamental for the enhancement of the practical.

President Day's first duty was to find room for the expected flood of postwar students. He calculated that we could house, at most, 8,000 students, though many of them improperly. We could find classroom space for about 7,300.

The President presented his building program in his report for 1945. While the war was still on, ground was broken for a women's dormitory, later hight Clara Dickson Hall, in honor of Andrew D. White's mother. It was expected eventually to pay for itself. (This in itself was a considerable novelty. Previous administrations had conceived a dormitory as a grandiose structure given by a well-wisher. President Day regarded it as a self-liquidating business enterprise.) Work likewise began on an administration building at the corner of East Avenue and Tower Road. This was an urgent need. Administration had been crowded into the lower levels of Morrill Hall and into various nooks and crannies about the campus. Scheduled for early construction were Statler Hall, to be a Faculty Club and small hotel as well as the home of the Department of Hotel Administration; a field house, to be known as the Jack Moakley House; a metallurgical and materials testing laboratory; a new biochemistry and nutrition laboratory; an agricultural library, an agricultural engineering building, and an addition to the Veterinary College; and a food science and technical building at Geneva. And the President uttered his hope that he might soon announce a great new indoor sports building for men.

The President had long been concerned about Ithaca's physical isolation, as Ezra Cornell had been concerned, years before. The airport in the valley was inadequate and was bounded against expansion by city, lake, and hills. The only place for an airport was the level farmland to the north of the University. But suburban colonists were planting their ranch houses along the roads, and prices were due to rise. The city of Ithaca was eagerly interested, but no mayor could survive a proposal to buy a second airport, outside the city, with tax-payers' money. The only organism free to act was the University. On 9 September 1944, at the very peak of war, the trustees authorized the Treasurer to seek options. Within three months options on 1,146 acres were obtained, at an agreed price of $202,000.

The President's educational purposes and plans were soon to be displayed in practice.

It is hard enough, heaven knows, to bear the troubles, disruptions, and makeshifts of war. It is much harder, in the midst of these troubles, to foresee the afterwar and make preparations for it. One must wonder now at President Day's unending activity and at the earnest thought with which he prepared the time to come.

XXXVII

Cornell under President Day:
Postwar Administration

"WE have a moral obligation to provide educational opportunity for the maximum number of well-qualified applicants who can be handled without impairment of the quality of Cornell training," said President Day in his 1947 report. He returned frequently to the theme of Cornell's moral obligation, brushing aside the arguments of those who wished to fix the University at its prewar size. Our first moral duty, he said, is toward the returning veterans whose education has been interrupted; our second toward the superior youths of the state; our third toward the children of old Cornellians; and our fourth toward the country at large, for Cornell, a national and indeed international institution, must preserve its catholic character.

The administration's difficulties were vast. In the shadow of universal uncertainties, it could not draw up a secure budget. It had to commit itself to expenditures and hope to find funds to cover them. Applications for entrance tripled; operating costs soared; scarcity of labor and materials hampered every effort to lodge and care for the incoming students and teachers.

In 1945–46 Cornell enrolled in Ithaca and New York 7,465 civilian students, and about 800 Navy V-12 men. The registration in Engineering jumped from 661 to 1,556, in Law from 53 to 229, in Medicine from 68 to 327, and Agriculture and Hotel Administration more than doubled. The pressures may be gauged by the single fact that in March 1946 there were 56 vacancies for nonveterans in the Arts College, and 1,500 applications.

In the fall term of 1946 came the flood, a total enrollment of 10,560, against a prewar registration which had climbed gradually to about 7,000. New records were set in most of the colleges, including Arts (2,522, up from 2,075), Engineering (2,667, a fourfold increase in two years), Architecture, Industrial and Labor Relations, Hotel, Law, and the Graduate School (up to 1,217). A new record was set in 1947–48 with a total enrollment of 10,830. Of these 10,302 were in the Ithaca colleges. The Graduate School now numbered 1,391.

Thenceforth the enrollment dropped off slightly, though it did not fall below 10,000. The Battle of the Bulge, as the President said, was won. But he gave no hope of a return to the comfortable prewar size. "We face not a peak, but the edge of a plateau," he said in his 1947 report:

This is not a matter of independent choice; it is a matter of public obligation. . . . This demand for education is based not so much on mere personal desire for the honor of a degree as on an expanding need for men and women with semi-professional or professional training and with a sufficient background of knowledge to make an intelligent approach to social and economic problems. Since colleges and universities are granted tax exemption and are committed by intent and tradition to operate in the interests of the people, they have an obligation to help meet this need. Cornell, besides being a land-grant institution drawing substantial support from both State and Federal Governments, has the special responsibility of a great endowed university— educational leadership. It is our inescapable duty to offer education to all the men and women we can accommodate without lowering our standards of instruction.

The administration labored nobly to fulfill its obligations. The government's policy was to bring the soldiers home as fast as transport permitted; and to all it offered, by the famous G.I. Bill of Rights, the privilege of continuing their education for years at public expense, provided they could find a place in an accredited institution. This was probably the greatest educational handout in history. Cornell received 17,000 applications in the first months of 1945, while the war was yet unfinished. Herbert H. Williams '25 and his devoted staff in the Admissions Office worked days, nights, and Sundays. Two assistants spent their full time opening mail. And not veterans only pounded at our doors. "We could fill the entire contingent of women in the Arts College with the daughters of Cornellians," said the President.

Provost Arthur S. Adams was charged with housing, feeding, and equipping the thousands of newcomers, in a small community officially designated as a critical housing area. He obtained wooden barracks from vacated military bases and set them up in new settlements for married students, one on Tower Road (where the Veterinary College now stands) and one in Vetsburg, across the railroad tracks in East Ithaca. He leased the Glen Springs Hotel in Watkins and organized a bus service for the twenty-six-mile journey. He and his staff lived in a frenzy of worried activity—where, in those days of shortage, to get stoves, refrigerators, beds, chairs, doorknobs, can openers?

The Treasurer, George F. ("Count") Rogalsky took vigorous part in the search for housing, telephoning numberless bureaus and agencies in Washington. There is a story that eventually he was told by a bureaucrat to consult the ultimate authority on the matter, a fellow in Ithaca named Rogalsky.

Together with the new students came some two hundred new faculty members to teach them. The teachers and their families had to be housed. One of the Provost's expedients was to build a new faculty settlement on South Hill. By 1 August 1945 the land was acquired and contracts let. One month later fifteen houses were finished, and the others came in at the rate of one per day, to make fifty-two homes. The enterprise turned out to be a financial disaster. Houses built in a month by unskilled labor began to show senile degeneration in another month. But it would be indecent to judge the operation from the point of view of investment policy. The important thing is that the faculty, as well as the students, were somehow housed.

Additional temporary construction went on in 1945–46. A new set of structures sprang up on what is now Pleasant Grove Road, beyond the Observatory and across from the golf course. And in October, two days before college opened, five of these two-story barracks, for three hundred men, burned to the ground. Those who had been assigned to the smoking ruins had to be received. Much doubling up ensued, with three men in rooms barely adequate for two. The eating problem was acute. But of course both soldiers and civilians were used to standing in line.

The peak of veteran enrollment came in 1946–47, with 6,227 on the books, or 77 per cent of all men students. The veterans brought with them a new problem: some 1,300 wives and a thousand babies. The President noted in 1948 that "the wife is neither student nor townswoman. . . . She affiliates herself with other 'Vets' wives' in a world of their own." While visitors to the barrack settlements thought them a horrid prefigurement of mass existence, most of the young brides found their communal life a happy one. They operated in the Tower Road agglomeration, nicknamed "Fertile Valley," a cooperative grocery, a nursery school, a news bulletin, a radio program, a charm school, and a unit of the League of Women Voters. They organized medical talks on prenatal care. They held even Baby Shows in Willard Straight, to the consternation of returning alumni in search of the Cornell of their youth.

The College of Home Economics, with its restricted enrollment, had particular veteran problems. Dean Sarah G. Blanding noted in 1946 that women veterans twenty years out of high school were applying for entrance, after gaining an interest, during their military service, in dietetics or institution management. The college was besieged by veterans' wives, anxious to increase homemaking skills, and all of them trying to get their children into the college nursery school.

The scholastic and extramural conduct of the veterans was universally approved. They were credited with elevating the general tone of undergraduate manners and conversation. "We have never had a more diligent, intelligent, and generally satisfactory body of students," said the President. The expected neurotic problems did not appear. A study showed that single veterans received slightly better grades than the average undergraduate, that married veterans did markedly better, and that married veterans with children did best of all. Veterans won most of the college honors, headed the publications, held all the offices in the Interfraternity Council, were the bulwark of the athletic teams. They were of course vocationally motivated (to use an ugly but accurate phrase). Their motivation dealt one more blow to the old conception of college life as four carefree years of cultural escape.

The physical problems of instruction were somewhat relieved by the throwing up of temporary wooden buildings: two for Physics behind Rockefeller, two for Engineering and one for Home Economics on the Forest Home Road, two for Industrial and Labor Relations on Sage Green, one for Aeronautical Engineering at the new airport. Space was found chiefly by fuller utilization of plant, as the boys say.

Classrooms were occupied from 8:00 A.M. to 4:30 P.M. and from 7:00 to
10:00 P.M., with the provision that all student schedules must allow a
free hour for lunch.

All this organization required a large increase in administration, to
the accompaniment of faculty forebodings. (The faculty recalled forever the happy days when faculty committees settled nearly everything, when a part-time dean and two clerks ran the Arts College, when
the students were allowed to do whatever they pleased, provided they
didn't make too much noise about it.)

The trustees gave the President their full support. Howard E. Babcock resigned the chairmanship of the Board in 1947, for reasons of
health. He was succeeded by Neal Dow Becker '05. In the following
year Arthur H. Dean '19 accepted the exacting duties of chairman of
the Executive Committee.

Arthur S. Adams, who came to Cornell in 1940 as Assistant Dean of
Engineering, returned from war work in 1946 to be Provost. He was
a sort of junior executive, handling such knotty problems as the housing
program, as the affairs of the Aeronautical Laboratory in Buffalo. He
resigned, in January 1948, to become President of the University of
New Hampshire, and was replaced by Dean Cornelis de Kiewiet of
Arts, whose mission was to supervise academic and educational matters,
especially as they related to government agencies and foundations.

The business side of the University grew apace. Take for example
the Purchasing Department. It was organized on a small scale in 1921
by George S. Frank '11. By 1947 it had a staff of eighty, engaged in
supplying both endowed and state colleges with everything from paper
clips to a 25-ton locomotive crane for the heating plant. It did an
annual business of some three million dollars, including the supply of
150 tons of mimeo paper and of pregnant guinea pigs scheduled to
deliver at a certain hour of a certain day. "When the phone rings, you
don't know whether it's someone wanting formaldehyde delivered to
Point Barrow, Alaska, or wanting a dead cat," said George Frank.

Or take the Office of Admissions. Within times that some of us can
remember, it was merely Davy Hoy, the Registrar, who would answer
preregistration inquiries with insulting postcards, beginning "would
say." In 1946 Admissions was separated from the Registrar's office, and
put in charge of Herbert H. Williams '25, with fifteen full-time
workers, including a night staff.

Or take the counseling and supervision of students. The counselors,
Frank C. Baldwin '22 and Lucille Allen, became Dean of Men and

Dean of Women in 1948. With their assistants, they had about 6,500 interviews with students yearly, kept an eye on the publications and club activities, handled term-time employment and student loans. A counselor to foreign students, Donald C. Kerr '12, did very necessary work. Some forty student counselors were given free rooms in dormitories, chiefly to guide freshmen. This gentle oversight was generally welcomed by students who needed and wanted friendly counsel.

Again, take the development of Clinical and Preventive Medicine. The Clinic received about 50,000 visits a year and sent over a thousand of the visitors to the Infirmary. The treatment was personalized as far as possible; the diagnostician followed the patient through to his discharge, and the patient returned afterward at need to consult his own familiar doctor. Various specialty clinics carried on: Orthopedic and Athletic, Skin, Dental, Mental Hygiene, Allergy, Endocrine, Nutrition, Colds, Eye Refraction, and Physiotherapy. Fascinating to the non-physician was the work in mental hygiene. It was long viewed with fear and distrust. But in the postwar mood psychic disturbance became almost fashionable. Students would ask to be excused from class in order to run over and see a psychiatrist. In 1948, 200 mental hygiene patients were reported, 70 of them veterans; 25 were so emotionally troubled that they were given leaves of absence. But the general policy was laid down that if an emotionally ill student can do academic work without threatening himself or others he should be allowed to remain.

When the student neared the end of his career, he consulted the Placement Service, under John L. Munschauer '40. Gone were the dark days when the Placement Service hunted vainly for jobs for despairing graduates. For a time the Placement Service was swamped with requests from employers for both men and women. In some fields there were more employers' representatives on the campus than there were candidates. By 1949 a change was noted. The big companies were less eager for young administrators, more desirous of salesmen. Women needed secretarial skills to get business jobs. Munschauer reported:

The class of 1949 wanted security which "Big Business" seemed to offer— it offered pension plans, health plans, savings plans, vacation plans, free lunches and no heavy lifting. . . . We had to help [the students] develop ingenuity in finding a job (a lost art). Security-minded students were forced to take jobs where they will have to gamble on luck and ability.

All this expansion of the accessory services was very expensive and voracious of office space. The financial situation was complicated by the rapid rise of inescapable costs. The coal bill, for instance, jumped $75,000 in one year. The manual workers demanded a forty-hour week, with time and a half for overtime. (The faculty was in no position to demand anything.) The budget rose steadily, to reach in 1949–50 $28,000,000, including all the auxiliary enterprises and including $9,000,000 of sponsored research. The deficit rose as steadily. By 1948 the University was about a million dollars in the red. Tuition charges were increased to $600 in most colleges, and room rentals in the dormitories and food prices in the restaurants mounted.

Undeterred by financial alarms, the President proceeded with his building program. The new women's dormitory, Clara Dickson, received lodgers in 1947; the Administration Building (later Day Hall) and the home of the School of Nutrition were opened in the same year. This was named Savage Hall, in honor of Elmer S. Savage, Ph.D. '11, long professor of animal husbandry.

One of the boldest presidential actions in the history of Cornell was the building of the Laboratory of Nuclear Studies. Cornell had, as it happened, a group of supreme nuclear scientists on its staff, including Hans Bethe, Robert F. Bacher, Richard P. Feynman, Philip Morrison, and Lloyd P. Smith. But after the epochal development of atomic studies during the war, they found nothing at Cornell to work with. "The problem," said President Day, "is not to control nuclear forces but to control nuclear physicists. They are in tremendous demand, and at a frightful premium." He was faced with two alternatives: either to lose the scientists to other institutions and to discontinue serious Cornell research in this most fundamental field of physics, or, risking financial disaster, to build and equip a home for nuclear research.

He chose the latter course. He later told Professor Maurice Neufeld of Industrial and Labor Relations that this was the most desperate chance he had ever taken, that he was ready to resign if the Board did not support him. (Indeed, he met severe criticism in the Board meeting of 1 November 1946.) He obligated the University, in its extremities, to advance $1,100,000. By adroit action, he obtained as a gift from the Navy a synchrotron, valued at $500,000. And eventually a high-mettled trustee, Floyd R. Newman '12, gave a million dollars and got our President off what is vulgarly known as the hook.

Meanwhile the state of New York, ever benevolent, made appropriations for an agricultural and home economics library and buildings for Agricultural Engineering, Entomology, and the Veterinary College. The most sharply criticized of the administration's actions in the physical realm was the purchase of lands for an airport. The President had boldly embarked on this course during the war. He found himself then entangled with the local airline, Robinson Aviation. Whenever one of its planes touched the ground it was met by a bailiff; they were in safety only in the skies. In the first six months of 1947 the airport operated at a loss of $103,000. The University's involvement ran to about $300,000. The President insisted that this was a long-range undertaking, like nuclear studies, and should be supported, for the money invested would surely be recovered some day. But the trustees declined (13 June 1949) to put another penny in it.

Today, with railroad passenger service to Ithaca ended and with the transfer of the airport to Tompkins County, we must applaud the President's courageous foresight. And as we observe the present development and future promise of the Industrial Research Park, we may conclude that the purchase of these empty lands for $300,000 was one of the most fortunate investments in our history, ranking not far below Ezra Cornell's assumption of the western pinelands. At the time, few of the faculty reached any such conclusion. To most of them the purchase of an airport was a monstrous manifestation of presidential caprice. Could not Dr. Day take the sleeper to New York, like anyone else? The President had to defend himself in a hostile Faculty meeting, nor did his defense persuade many that he was not wasting our precious funds on a flying chimera.

For the faculty was in an ugly mood and in a precarious state. The cost of living was rapidly rising, and the salaries were nearly stationary. The lower teaching ranks suffered especially. The Cornell chapter of the American Association of University Professors asked a study of the economic situation, regular increments of salary, and budget conferences with the trustees. The trustees responded (26 April 1947) by authorizing lump-sum bonuses for academic staff members receiving less than $5,000 a year. (The state employees were already receiving cost-of-living bonuses.)

In April 1948 the Faculty Committee on the Economic Status of the Faculty, headed by George P. Adams of Economics, reported the disquiet of the staff members. They were looking toward other institutions and toward industry; they sought supplementary income by outside work. They could not give their full energy, strength, and intellect to the University. The committee requested a universal 10 per cent increase and a $6,000 minimum for full professors, to make a total salary rise of $318,000 annually.

The dilemma of the administration, faced already with a monumental deficit, is obvious. Obvious also is the solution—a compromise. An across-the-board bonus of $500 was authorized, with the added provision of $30,000 for merit adjustments.

Living costs continued to rise; "inflation" became a household word, familiar even at nursery-school levels. In 1949 we came to crisis. At the spring meeting of the trustees Frederick G. Marcham of History, Faculty Representative on the Board, expressed the general alarm and displeasure. The proposed budget showed a deficit of $800,000, while salary raises were insufficient and while the faculty were bidden to retrench in every way.

The trustees took Draconian action. They ordered the administration to balance the budget, by any and every means. Arthur H. Dean, chairman of the Executive Committee, said that for the first time in his experience he could see hope of solving the University's financial difficulties.

His hope was based largely on the Greater Cornell campaign, launched in 1948 to raise $12,500,000. A group of devoted Cornellians gave to it their labor and their enthusiasm. A committee directed it, with Harold T. Edwards '10 chairman, Francis H. Scheetz '16 vice-chairman, and Asa S. Knowles, Vice President for University Development, executive director. Its duties were to make recommendations on Cornell policies and affairs, to mobilize the alumni, to coordinate fund raising, and so forth. This committee organized the Greater Cornell Fund campaign, with John L. Collyer '17 as chairman and Nicholas H. Noyes '06 as vice-chairman. Professional generosity-floggers were hired, who helped in the formation of numberless local committees and the provision of beautiful booklets and of free dinners with inspirational speeches. But we had no slogans, for these, apparently, have lost their magic.

The Special Gifts Committee, captained by John P. Syme '26, reported splendid success. Myron C. Taylor '94 gave $1,500,000 for an interfaith center, to incorporate a War Memorial and to bear the name of his wife, Anabel Taylor; and, as already noted, Floyd R. Newman '12 gave a flat million for the laboratory of nuclear studies, thenceforth the Newman Laboratory; Walter C. Teagle '00 and his wife gave $1,500,000 for a men's sports building; and an anonymous donor gave a million without restriction. (This was apparently the Phillips Foundation, the creation of Ellis L. Phillips '95.) More than ten thousand others gave handsomely, within their means or beyond. But the total of gifts, by June 1949, came to only eight million. It was necessary to carry on the good work. Finally in 1951 the campaign reported reaching its goal, with subscriptions of $12,758,000.

Cornell's financial difficulties provoked in many minds the question whether the endowed university could long endure in a society which seemed bent on eliminating large accumulations of private wealth. The question was complicated by the establishment of the State University of New York. President Day was a member of the Temporary Commission on the Need for a State University, created by the legislature in 1946. Some thought that this might end with Cornell's becoming outright a state university, and some thought that this might be a good thing—better governmental control than creeping destitution. (One will recall that this, for a time at least, was President Schurman's conviction.)

But President Day was jealous of Cornell's identity and independence. In his report for 1948 he put the question boldly: can we continue as a private institution? Noting the drift toward government in all our affairs, he would not have Cornell join therein: "We must retain private initiative and management in certain important fields, and certainly some of it in higher education." He had confidence that Cornell would surmount its troubles, that it would resist "the subtle corrosion of our social institutions," that Cornell would remain Cornell. Once more, Dr. Day was right.

The State University of New York was formally established in 1948. The State College of Ceramics at Alfred and Cornell's College of Agriculture, College of Home Economics, Veterinary College, and School of Industrial and Labor Relations are defined as "contract or statutory colleges" and as constituent parts of the new State University. There is a rather bewildering distinction between their status and that of the State College of Forestry at Syracuse University, which is a "state-operated" unit of the State University. Our four colleges are merely "state-supported," and all formal statements so refer to them, no longer terming them "state colleges." Control, power, and authority over them are vested in the Cornell Board of Trustees by the State University of New York, which replaces the State Department of Education with its Board of Regents. Cornell must bear its own responsibilities. The courts so determined in 1953, with regard to some allegedly infected turkeys which an alleged Morris F. Effron alleged that he bought from the alleged College of Agriculture. He sought redress from the State University. The courts held that Cornell University is not a governmental agency and is liable for its own torts.[1] In practice, the shift of ultimate supervision from the State Department of Education to the State University has not made much difference.

[1] For an excellent analysis of this whole question, see Malcolm Carron, S.J., *The Contract Colleges of Cornell University* (Ithaca, 1958), pp. 151–165.

XXXVIII

Cornell under President Day:
Postwar Education and Research

THE postwar period was a time of new beginnings, a time also for the resumption of businesses interrupted by the war.

The faculty had on its mind the crucial matter of tenure and its corollary of duties.

Tenure, or the right of a professor to occupy his chair without dislodgment by the executive, became a holy word. The concept goes back no doubt to medieval practice, whereby a professor was The One Who Professed a Subject. He could secede from the *universitas* and go to another city, taking his chair with him. Though all his students, and even the university, should disappear, he would remain The Professor.

This concept had no currency in the early days of Cornell. Henry W. Sage and the trustees regarded professors and even presidents as their employees, and discharged them with hardly more consideration than they would show to a refractory janitor. It was Jacob Gould Schurman who established in faculty consciousness the European idea of a professor's dignity and rights. But the idea was implicit, unformulated. The first mention of "tenure" in the University Faculty's records appears on 14 December 1938.

In the thirties the question of tenure began to agitate seriously the American professorate. The American Association of University Professors recommended that all appointments should be made permanent after six years. Our administration was alarmed, seeing in such proposals the cementation in their posts of the incompetent and the half-competent. Recognizing a tendency to regard old assistant professors as in possession of tenure, it reestablished in 1939 the long-abrogated rank of associate professor, carrying permanent tenure, whereas the assistant professor would specifically not possess tenure.

The Faculty, aware of the need for definition, appointed a Committee on Tenure and Efficiency, under the chairmanship of Edwin A. Burtt of Philosophy. The committee submitted an extensive printed report in March 1942. It recommended securing the rights of professors and associate professors to their chairs and drastically limiting the terms of assistant professors and instructors. The trustees deferred the matter till the war's end, and finally in January 1948 enacted legislation guaranteeing tenure to the higher ranks, and limiting the assistant professor to two three-year terms, the instructor to one five-year term.

These stipulations, still in effect, have now become ancient custom, and have brought peace and presumably justice in a region where anger and dissatisfaction are commonly rife.

The faculty was for a time agitated, or titillated, by accusations of communist sympathies. Of course a few of its number were always ready to sign any resolute forward-looking manifesto, and frequently these manifestoes turned out to be the product of red-front inspiration. The Progressive party of Henry Wallace had its adherents. But no ticket-holding Communist party members, no thoroughgoing fellow travelers, turned up in the professorial ranks. The University Faculty affirmed, in April 1949, its policy of permitting open discussion of controversial issues. And President Day agreed. He informed the trustees, in the same month, that he would willingly permit communists to lecture, in order to give students the chance to hear all points of view. As an example, he told how the Marxist Discussion Group had brought an advocate of Soviet genetics to the campus; and "a competent group of animal and plant majors matched wits with him after his lecture and were able to win out very substantially." This, he thought, was the right procedure.

But, the President insisted, there was no place on the Faculty for a communist. The matter presented itself to him as a simple syllogism. Major premise: a Faculty should be composed of "free, honest, competent, inquiring minds, undertaking to find and disseminate the truth." Minor premise: a member of the Communist party must subject his freedom and honesty to party authority. Conclusion: a communist has renounced his intellectual obligation and is debarred from the Cornell Faculty.

Confident that free discussion would support the democratic-capitalist system, the University arranged, in the spring of 1949, an important series of lectures defining the American tradition. This was needed, said the President, "to protect the right line against infiltration, not by communism, but by those who, under the cloak of attacking communism, proceed to attack something quite different."

The communist drama turned to comedy, as such dramas do on American campuses. On May Day 1949 the chimes rang out at 6:50 A.M. with a clangor of the "Internationale" and other left-wing hymns. Red kites flew from the Library Tower. The subversive concert was planned to last an hour, but the Campus Patrol, fearing that Moscow's agents had arrived, brought it to an untimely end.

When the war was out of the way, the President was able to take up again two long-shelved projects: the School of Industrial and Labor Relations and the School of Business and Public Administration.

The School of Industrial and Labor Relations (universally known as ILR) was conceived by Irving M. Ives, majority leader in the New York State Assembly. As Speaker of the Assembly in 1936 he was an ex officio trustee of Cornell, but he attended no Board meetings. As chairman of a State Committee on Industrial and Labor Conditions, he was impressed by the paucity of university courses in personnel problems, general and technical. He thought that employers and workers should settle their mutual problems by discussion, that wise discussion supposes long previous study, and that the state should afford opportunity for such study in its own school. His committee therefore recommended in 1942 that the state establish such a school at Cornell. The recommendation had the eager approbation of President Day, a lifelong advocate of such socioeconomic studies. But the President had to convince a rather dubious Board of Trustees, to allay fears of sponsoring a center of trade-union propaganda and fears of making enemies among industrialists and farmers. The President succeeded in persuading the trustees, though he did not assuage all their misgivings. (Faculty members often apprehend the illiberalism of state control of higher education. Here is a case in which the state was more "liberal" than the trustees of an endowed institution.)

Despite vigorous counteroffers from Syracuse and Union Universitics, the bill establishing the ILR at Cornell was passed, and signed on 15 May 1944 by Governor Dewey. As we were then at the very peak of war, nothing could immediately be done. A Temporary Board discussed general plans with the Planning and Development Committee and settled the very scabrous question of the manner of state control. It was decided that the Cornell charter should be amended to include five new trustees: the state Industrial Commissioner and the state Commissioner of Commerce, ex officio, and three others to be elected by the Board from the field of New York State labor. Some trustees objected, fearing that the labor representatives "would be for organized labor, first, last, and all the time, instead of solicitous for Cornell." In fact, these fears have proved groundless. Some of labor's representatives have been among our most faithful attendants at Board meetings, and some of them—noteworthily Louis P. Hollander of the C.I.O.—have taken an active part in debate and action on the general welfare of the University.

The school opened on 1 November 1945 in temporary quarters on Sage Green. Irving M. Ives was the first Dean, but his rise to the U.S. Senate forced him soon to resign. He was succeeded by Martin P. Catherwood, Ph.D. '30, professor of public administration. Eleven graduates and 107 undergraduates enrolled. A foundation course was required, with studies of collective bargaining, social security, personnel management, the labor movement, and labor legislation. A technical background was provided, with work in the organization of corporations, psychology in industry, human and property rights, government regulation; also accessory work in sociology, economics, English, public speaking, accounting, statistics, etc. The plan was to train the students for jobs as research specialists, analysts, economists, mediators, statisticians, field workers, and government agents. In fact what has occurred, according to a survey in 1958, is that 65 per cent of the employed graduates are doing personnel and labor relations work with corporations, 8 per cent are working for government, 24 per cent are in education, professional work, and related fields, and only 3 per cent are employed by labor unions.

The staff embarked on a grandiose extension program, holding workers' educational conferences, institutes, community courses in many communities, even giving a course in Spanish for Puerto Rican members of labor unions. Some five thousand students were enrolled in the extension courses in 1948–49. The faculty's summers were occupied with seminars in personnel management and with workshops

568

and short courses for labor, business, and government groups (such as plant training directors, social security administrators, and hospital administrators). Any spare time was given to research, recorded in books and in the weighty *Industrial and Labor Relations Review.*

The state, a proud mother, proposed to establish its darling in a fine new home. The Buildings and Grounds Committee picked a site on Campus Road, encroaching somewhat on Hoy baseball field. The state drew up plans, which cost over $80,000. But when the announcement was made, early in 1948, anguished outcries arose. C. V. P. Young, professor of physical education, emeritus, acted as tribune of the people, insisting that Hoy Field was given by the alumni to be used in perpetuity for athletic purposes. "The invasion of Hoy Field" became a battle cry. The Association of Class Secretaries and fifty-three undergraduate organizations made formal protests. The President, perhaps instructed by ILR's recommendations for dealing with grievance committees, yielded to the clamor.

The state was chilled by the ill reception of its bounty. For a dozen years thereafter the ILR lived uncomfortably in its distressing wooden barracks. But eventually all turned out for the best. In 1960 a new ILR building, Ives Hall, began to rise at the junction of Tower Road and East Avenue, replacing the old Veterinary College. And in the intervening years most of the site originally chosen (except Hoy Field) was occupied by Phillips Hall of Electrical Engineering. Backward-lookers reflected that this area was necessary for the expansion of the College of Engineering, and that its occupation by ILR would have blocked the logical development of the present Engineering Campus.

The second school established as the war ended was the School of Business and Public Administration. This project was particularly dear to the President, who had organized and deaned the School of Business Administration at Michigan.

The idea was no new one at Cornell. Andrew D. White had proposed in his Plan of Organization of 1866 a Department of Commerce and Trade, of which no example then existed in an American university. At the Faculty meeting of 2 October 1868, just before the University opened, White suggested the creation of a professorship of bookkeeping. A penciled note by White in the Faculty Records adds: "This was in view of the establishment of a higher sort of commercial college as a Department of the University." If he had had his way, he would have given Cornell priority over the Wharton School of the University of Pennsylvania, founded in 1881. Cornell's first *Register* announces courses in bookkeeping, accounting, and commercial mathematics, but it does not appear that the subjects were actually taught. White caressed the idea until his death. On 10 March 1899 he wrote to Governor Roswell P. Flower, suggesting a state college of commerce at Cornell. And in 1906 he tried to get congressional approval for a scheme drafted by Professor Jeremiah W. Jenks for federal support for departments of commerce and business education in state universities.

Other voices were raised. In 1900 M. Carey Thomas '77 proposed, in her alumni trustee report, a state school of commerce at Cornell, such as the Board of Trade advocated for Columbia, such as already existed at Penn, California, and Chicago. In 1914 a Faculty Committee on a Commercial Course was formed, with Allyn A. Young of Economics as chairman. The committee recommended, in 1916, the creation of a college of business administration and public affairs. The trustees asked that the school be extended to include "preparation for public service." The committee deemed that business is a profession, like law or medicine, to be served by the universities. The school would be of "semi-graduate" standing, admitting students after three years of undergraduate work, and giving them two years of vocational training, leading to the M.A. In all essentials, this is the plan of the school of today. But what with war, what with one thing and another, nothing came of it.

President Day, on his accession, again bruited the matter. He was authorized by the trustees (19 October 1938) to look into the possibilities. Finally in 1942 the trustees authorized such a school. And another war intervened. At war's end, the President reactivated it, and appointed Paul M. O'Leary of Economics as Dean. The school was at the time, and perhaps still is, the only one in the country which united preparation for business and for public administration. And it is one of only nine graduate schools of business.

The school began operation in September 1946, as an unwelcome interloper in Goldwin Smith, with forty-one students and a Faculty of seven. In 1947 it moved to more commodious quarters in McGraw Hall. By 1948–49 the enrollment rose to 120.

The established schools and colleges pursued their several courses and performed their various duties, usually with effectiveness. We cannot follow their labors in a thousand classrooms, labs, and workshops; we can remark only upon certain adventures and misadventures which brought them briefly into the public eye and into the deliberations of administration.

The Graduate School grew rapidly, too rapidly for its own good. The enrollment rose from a low of 596 in 1942–43 to 1,505 in 1948–49. The University's organization was strained; its scholarship and fellowship provisions, always insufficient, became ludicrously inadequate for the demands upon them. A stipend which would keep a graduate student alive in 1935 meant starvation in 1945. In the early years of the century the graduate student expected to pay his own way for the first year, and then hoped for a fellowship or assistantship; he took the vows of poverty, chastity, and obedience, and kept at least one of them. But in the forties the graduate student expected support for himself and for his wife and children, and he expected the University to supply living quarters. The University did its best, but it could not meet the new demands.

The influx of grads burdened many departments. There are too many graduates per teacher, said Dean Charles W. Jones in his 1949 report:

No professor can with full success serve on more than a dozen special committees or direct the work of more than six doctoral majors or have more than two doctoral theses coming to completion at the same time. Yet in one field we have three professors with fifteen or more doctoral majors each, and elsewhere one professor serves on 60 committees while two others serve on more than 40.

Obviously these professors, even with a minimum of conscientiousness, could do no work of their own. The Dean was also disturbed by "a growing class of applicants who think graduate education is to be purchased like social security, and for much the same reason."

Despite our complaints, we were proud of our production of young scholars. The National Research Council reported that from 1936 to 1946 Cornell granted more Ph.D.'s in the thirty-eight most important scientific fields than any other American institution, being first in agriculture, horticulture, and entomology; second in geology; third in engineering, anatomy, and biochemistry; fourth in botany and genetics; fifth in physiology; sixth in physics; eighth in psychology; and ninth in chemistry.

In the Arts College, Professor C. W. de Kiewiet of History succeeded Robert M. Ogden as Dean in 1945. The new dean had served during the war as director of Cornell's outstanding Army courses in area studies and foreign languages. (Remember?) These he carried on in our civilian metamorphosis. The Department of Chinese Studies, created in 1944–45, was broadened to become Far Eastern Studies. The department's purpose was to impart a knowledge of whole cultures, with the aid of social anthropology. Such knowledge, said the Dean, is a form of national power.

Fundamental to this powerful knowledge is a thorough acquaintance with the current languages. The Dean, deeply impressed by the success of the Army's oral approach to language teaching, made a bold innovation. With a $125,000 grant from the Rockefeller Foundation, he established in 1946 a Division of Modern Languages, which took over all the language teaching from the several departments of language and literature of the several countries. The division was headed by J Milton Cowan, who had chiefly devised the methods used in the Army's language schools, and was staffed with linguists and specialists in language education. Except in the advanced courses in linguistics, most of the actual teaching was done by native speakers in daily drill sections limited at first to ten students per section. Much use was made of recording devices, by which the student, alone in a little booth, practiced idiom and pronunciation.

The system has been a marked success. The students like it, because even a qualified conversational facility in a foreign language is a positive pleasure. Most of the initial fears that the system would lead only to a phrase-book facility without developing reading ability have died away. Products of the system have done at least as well and often better in reading tests than have those inducted entirely by the reading approach. It is now possible for the departments of foreign literature to give their courses in the foreign language with confidence that the students will understand the teachers.

Dean de Kiewiet planned as a correlative to the Division of Modern Languages a Division of Literature, which would unite under a general director the work in English, Speech and Drama, Classics, Romance Literature, German Literature, Chinese, and Slavic Studies. He wished to imbue the division with a sense of literature as a universal phenomenon, readily leaping national and linguistic boundaries. Himself a product of the culture of three continents, he was, and is, a foe of localism in learning. He conceived a course in Classicism, for instance, or Romanticism, as one requiring the student to read in at least three languages. The proposal, heartily supported by some, found many foes. These thought it a violent and impractical upset of established practice, and they particularly feared a new administrative ruler, between the

Dean and the department heads. In the end a nominal Division of Literature was created, hardly more than a catalogue entry for general courses contributed by the various departments.

Within the Department of English, the teaching of creative writing gained a new importance. A group of enthusiastic young teachers taught many crowded classes, published volumes of student work, encouraged undergraduate literary periodicals, and established *Epoch* in 1947. This vanguard magazine has received national recognition, and has survived to this day all the perils of publication.

The current mood encouraged the union of departments into divisions. A Division of Psychology was created in 1947. It brought together the Departments of Psychology, Child Development and Family Relationships, and Rural Education, as well as the psychologists in Sociology and Anthropology, Hotel Administration, and ILR. It was a correlating, not an executive organization.

An interesting new venture was the American Studies Program, begun in 1947. Seven departments, under the leadership of Henry A. Myers of English, cooperated in giving basic courses, designed to display to the student our civilization as a whole. This was a happy revival of Cornell's early advocacy of studies in American history and culture.

The College of Engineering, under the direction of Dean S. C. Hollister, experienced a renaissance. Its enrollment rose from a low of 812 in 1935–36 to a high of 2,667 in 1946–47, and then dropped off slightly. The overcrowding, in many temporary and many antiquated buildings, was terrible. But the construction of Olin Hall brought some relief, and notable gifts gave promise for the future.

The Dean hunted funds for a new engineering college. The Cornell Society of Engineers helped, as did many faithful friends of the college, including J. Du Pratt White '90, Bancroft Gherardi '93, Maxwell M. Upson '99, Ezra B. Whitman '01. The persuading of well-wishers to the stage of ultimate donation is a long process. One may learn from Dean Hollister's experience that it takes twenty years of unremitting labor to transform a vision into a reality.

The most important educational development in Engineering was the establishment of a required five-year course throughout the college (authorized in 1944). Cornell was the first to impose such a requirement, "a major departure from the traditional concept of engineering education," as Hollister says. The curriculum included an infusion of courses in Arts, especially in English, public speaking, history, psychology, and economics. It was designed to prepare the engineer to play an effective, even dominant, role in human affairs and to answer the frequent criticism of his lack of social awareness.

To meet the demands of changing technology, new schools and services were inaugurated. The Graduate School of Aeronautical Engineering, authorized in 1945, opened in 1946 as a division of the College of Engineering. Though its students have never been numerous, they have done valuable work, and have had the great advantage of association with the Aeronautical Laboratory in Buffalo.

A Department of Engineering Physics began its career in 1945, as a unit of Engineering. Bridging the gap between basic sciences and fundamental engineering, it combines mathematics, applied physics, and engineering principles to prepare for careers in research and its applications. The course has the popular reputation of being the hardest on the hill, and its students are regarded as intellectual supermen.

The School of Chemical Engineering, established in 1938, became in 1947 the School of Chemical and Metallurgical Engineering. The Director, and the historian of Cornell chemistry, Fred H. ("Dusty") Rhodes recalls that instruction in metallurgy at Cornell is nothing new.[1] Assaying was taught from 1868 to 1916. The 1875–76 curriculum for the B.Sc. in Chemistry required metallurgy and assaying. In 1881–82 one term of metallurgy and mineralogy was obligatory for chemists. The course was dropped in 1896, when Wilder D. Bancroft inaugurated a course in electrochemistry. Metallurgical work expanded, including crystallography and materials of construction. From 1880 on foundry work was required of all M.E.'s. In the twenties Herman Diederichs taught courses in materials, and George B. Upton applied metallography. Meanwhile other schools were developing their work in metallurgy, and the big steel companies established research laboratories. The demand for metallurgical engineers increased, as new metals with special properties were needed.

Cornell's School of Metallurgical Engineering stressed physical rather than process metallurgy. It featured unit operations—that is, processes were broken down into individual operations common to most or many processes.

---

[1] This would be as good a place as any to record that at a recent celebration of Engineers' Day, a faculty member stood by a microscope, inviting the public to look at a slide of steel structure. Dusty coached an eight-year-old girl, who stepped up, begging and whining for a look. When the kindly professor permitted her to peer through the microscope, she chirped: "Oh, see the graphitic precipitation of carbon in the grain boundaries!"

Mechanical Engineering received a handsome gift from the Navy in the form of the Diesel Engine Laboratory, with engineering equipment worth more than two millions.

The war's end, marking the world's shift from destruction to rebuilding, brought a horde to the doors of the College of Architecture. By 1947 the ratio of applications to places was 17 to 1, and in a following year there were 700 applicants for 62 vacancies. Dean Gilmore D. Clarke noted that the term "Landscape Architecture" was becoming a misnomer; the subject was really turning into Land Planning, with the new emphasis on large-scale public and semipublic works, such as throughways and housing developments. Vincent C. Cerasi '35 and Brooks E. Wigginton '39 won our thirteenth and fourteenth Rome Prizes in Landscape Architecture, out of nineteen possible, and Henry V. Jova '49 took the Rome Prize in Architecture in his senior year.

In the Law School, even the spacious quarters of Myron Taylor Hall were overcrowded. The enrollment reached an all-time high of 437 in the fall of 1950. The school became cosmopolitan; in 1948–49 78 per cent of its students received their prelegal training at other schools than Cornell. The Legal Aptitude Test helped to sort out applicants. A special program in international affairs was established in 1948, with work in comparative law, international economics, politics, and administration.

The College of Agriculture established its Department of Biochemistry, the modern version of agricultural chemistry, and also the important new Department of Conservation. The subject was no new one at Cornell. J. G. Needham's work in limnology, from 1906 on, and G. C. Embody's in fish culture and fishery biology were properly conservation. The State Department of Conservation built an experimental fish hatchery on Judd Falls Road in 1929. Since 1917 Arthur A. Allen conducted work in wildlife conservation and game farming. Finally in 1948 the pertinent studies in zoology and forestry were united in a new department, which supervised the fish hatchery and the Arnot Forest, added courses in such fields as marine fisheries, and carried on an important extension program. The work in Conservation was popular; in 1950 sixty undergraduates and thirty graduates were enrolled.

Dean Sarah Blanding of Home Economics left us in 1946 to become President of Vassar. She was succeeded by Dr. Elizabeth Lee Vincent, head of the Department of Psychology in the Merrill Palmer School in Detroit, and lecturer in medicine at Wayne University.

The Veterinary College was distressed by its popularity. The upsurge of interest in the scientific study of animal life and disease overwhelmed the country's ten veterinary colleges. By 1947 we had 750 applications for entrance, or fifteen for every place. Since our first duty was to New York State boys, out-of-state applicants had one chance in forty of admission. The same situation prevailed elsewhere; a boy who lived in a state without a veterinary school had practically no chance of entering the field. The need led to the creation of a number of new schools, and the pressure upon Cornell gradually eased.

The College took advantage of its popularity to raise, in 1948, its entrance requirement from one year of college work to two. The course became more exacting, with emphasis on nutrition, roentgenology, medical botany, genetics, food hygiene, virus diseases. Didactic methods were largely abandoned, and the final year was given almost wholly to clinical teaching by the case method.

The Army ROTC was reactivated after the war, with units in Field Artillery, Ordnance, Quartermaster, and Signal Corps. Four terms of Military Science were again required of all able-bodied students. To the grief of many, the Army decided that the martial career of the horse was at length ended. It presented thirty-two horses and equipment to the University, which ruled that equitation would continue, at the cost of the equestrians.

A Naval ROTC was established in 1948, to include Regulars, clothed, fed, and paid by the Navy in expectation of becoming Ensigns in the regular Navy on graduation, and Contract Students, with lighter obligations and smaller compensation, who would enter the Naval Reserve.

In the Library, the glimmer of a new day dawned. In 1946 Dr. Stephen A. McCarthy was brought from Columbia to be Director. He had Dr. Day's assurance that the Library would be renovated, with a liberality hitherto unknown. He brought in a largely new staff, appropriated the old seminary rooms for working space, and inspired a new hopeful spirit among the workers and users. The purchase funds in 1948 jumped to $101,500. Typical was the experience of Howard B. Adelmann of Zoology. Coveting a rarity in a London bookseller's catalogue, he went cringing to Acquisitions, expecting the usual response: "No funds." But the new head of Acquisitions, Dr. Felix Reichmann, agreed that the book was important and telephoned the London bookseller to hold it. Howard Adelmann was dizzied for weeks.

A much-needed unification of libraries took place. Jurisdiction and budgetary responsibilities for the separate libraries of Business, Chemistry, Engineering, Physics, and Regional History were transferred to the University Library. The Library of Congress classification replaced the old system invented by Librarian George W. Harris around 1880. This meant of course two card catalogues and two systems of shelving, with the separation of books on a single subject between perhaps the eighth floor and the crypt. The recataloguing of the million books under the Harris classification has gone steadily on.

The storage system began. Books presumably in small demand were interred in various basements. One could of course conjure a book out of a basement if one knew exactly what the book was; but if one remembered only that it was a red book about so big on medieval thaumaturgy one was lost. Anyway, the important book is not the one that you find in a bibliography, but the one that falls out on your foot while you are looking for something else. Well, we did not complain, or not very convincedly. There was simply no more room in the main Library. No one has succeeded in getting a quart into a pint pot.

The Library received many precious gifts, of which the most sensational was a holograph copy of Lincoln's Gettysburg Address, presented by Mrs. Nicholas H. Noyes in honor of her husband, of the class of 1906. Let us note also the Gandhi Memorial Library, established by C. K. Nair, a graduate student, and his friends of the Hindustani Association.

In New York, the Medical College went through some hard years, due to its popularity and its poverty. In 1948, 3,200 qualified applicants fought for 80 places. The defeated uttered cries of "discrimination," which had become a bad word instead of a good one. In 1946 the City Council of New York, on the complaint of the American Jewish Congress, took action against the city's medical colleges, but Cornell was absolved of racism.

The college's financial situation was hard indeed. Its endowment, once so ample, could not meet the costs of inflation days. True, the University included a goal of $2,500,000 for the Medical College in the Greater Cornell Fund campaign; but in the end only $130,000 earmarked for the college was received. Many began to look longingly to the federal government for support for the ailing private medical colleges of the country. But somehow the college managed to carry on until better times arrived.

The college's loose association with the New York Hospital gave rise to many awkwardnesses. In 1947 the controlling authorities decided to put the whole center under a responsible officer, appointed jointly by the University and the Hospital, to be Director of the two and

President of the Joint Administrative Board. Dr. Stanhope Bayne-Jones, Dean of the Yale Medical School, was thus appointed Director.

Even without money, the college branched out in new directions. In cooperation with the New York City Department of Health, it opened in 1947 the Kips Bay–Yorkville Cancer Prevention-Detection Center, directed by Dr. Emerson Day, son of our President. The clinic soon demonstrated its value. In its first twenty months it examined fifteen hundred patients, discovered twelve cancers, and found significant conditions in 25 per cent of the examinees.

A new Institute of Child Development brought together faculty members from Pediatrics, Psychiatry, and Public Health and Preventive Medicine, to study the physical and emotional development of the child. At the other end of life's scale, much research was done in the new field of gerontology.

The Vincent Astor Clinic began operation in 1949. This was designed to give a thorough diagnostic service for patients able to pay for their own examinations.

These were active years in research, sponsored and private. The historian is defeated in his duty by the very amplitude of the work done in technical subjects, as physiology and pharmacology. At least comprehensible to the unmedical were such projects as the study of the emotional factors in disease, headed by Dr. Harold G. Wolff, or such as the study of the causes of chronic alcoholism. The work in aviation safety continued, in cooperation with the Aeronautical Laboratory; it resulted in a bioengineering manual for designers of high-speed aircraft. We have mentioned the work of Dr. du Vigneaud in biochemistry.

The School of Nursing suffered briefly from a postwar eclipse of enthusiasm for nursing. It refused however to lower its standards and its requirement of two years of college work for entrance, and was rewarded by an upturn in enrollment in 1949. Its standing was recognized; the National Organization for Public Health Nursing named it one of five out of the country's twelve hundred nursing schools whose graduates would be automatically qualified as public health staff nurses. (The others would have to study an extra year.)

The war made research respectable in the general view. What had been the peculiar passion of unworldly professors became a necessity in international and industrial warfare, and its practitioners the darlings even of the vast *profanum vulgus*.

Research demanded ever more of the faculty's time, more space and equipment, more administrative supervision. Before the war, our research expenditures amounted to about two million dollars a year; in 1947–48, they totaled (including contract research) twelve million. Three-fourths of the enabling funds came from the government, the rest from corporations, trade associations, foundations, individuals, and Cornell budgets. The University made certain stipulations: that work on the campus be not secret, and that it be of a fundamental character. (However, much of the work done in the state colleges and perhaps elsewhere is certainly applied research.) [2]

To supervise Cornell research, to seek out—and to reject—sponsors, we gained in 1948 a new vice president, Theodore P. Wright. A scholarly engineer, he came to us from the government post of Civil Aeronautics Administrator and soon became one of the most influential and respected figures on our campus. He found himself in charge of nearly a thousand research enterprises and of funds running into many millions. Of course, money expenditures are a poor measure of research values. One can readily picture a mathematical physicist penetrating to a fundamental formula for matter's behavior at a cost of ten cents for chalk; and one can picture a gigantic enterprise which spends millions to discover what everybody already knew. Nevertheless, money does somewhat measure the expected value of the results sought, and it testifies likewise to the world's esteem of Cornell research.

It is clearly impossible to make even the most inadequate review of the work done in our laboratories and library cells. Only some of the most outstanding research groupings can here be touched upon.

The Newman Laboratory of Nuclear Studies was dedicated in October 1948. Its director, succeeding Robert F. Bacher, was Robert R. Wilson, former chief of experimental physics at Los Alamos. He had a staff of fifty-nine (not including a certain Bruno Pontecorvo, appointed Research Associate in January 1948; instead of making an appearance in Ithaca, he ran off to Russia, where, it is reported, he is busy devising

[2] One recalls the principles enunciated by President James R. Killian, Jr., of M.I.T.: "1. The primary purposes of an educational institution are to educate men and women and to increase knowledge, and are not to compete with industry in industrial or development research. 2. Sponsored industrial research should be closely related to the normal program and recognized objectives of the institution. 3. Imposition of restrictions on publication of research results, either for secrecy or patent reasons, can become incompatible with the basic concept of an educational institution as a source and distributor of knowledge" (*Proceedings of the Association of Land-Grant Colleges* [Washington, 1948], p. 190).

means of demolishing us). Within the building, from the synchrotron in the basement to the cosmic ray laboratory on the roof, new knowledge is pursued and often overtaken.

Beside the Newman Laboratory stands Savage Hall, the School of Nutrition. It will be remembered (or will it not?) that the school was organized in 1941, under the impulsion of Trustee Howard E. Babcock. A gift of $200,000 from the Grange League Federation made the building possible. Said Neal Dow Becker, Chairman of the Board: "It is the only building on any campus anywhere financed by farmers." It was dedicated on 10 October 1947, with an allocution by Governor Thomas E. Dewey. Under Director Leonard A. Maynard a busy program of research was carried on, with state aid and with subventions from firms and foundations, on such subjects as food freezing, teeth injuries from acid beverages, calcifications from diet, the isolation of three unknown B-vitamins, etc. A nutrition survey was carried on in Groton; 850 persons in 225 families were relentlessly examined, to provide the most complete survey of family nutrition in existence.

The most sensational research development, and the most significant, was the acquisition of the Cornell Aeronautical Laboratory.

The Curtiss-Wright Corporation, famous builders of airplanes, had a research laboratory in Buffalo, built at a cost of $1,500,000, with the largest altitude chamber in the world, with a giant wind tunnel, uncompleted, which had cost $2,500,000. C. C. Furnas, former professor at Yale, was its director, supervising a staff of five hundred. Curtiss-Wright, moving Pacificwards in 1945, proposed to divest itself of what promised to be a postwar burden. Dean S. C. Hollister of Engineering got wind of the matter and recognized its possibilities for Cornell. He suggested that Curtiss-Wright should give the plant to Cornell, and that Cornell should operate it as a general research laboratory for the various aviation companies and for the government and as an incomparable workshop for the new School of Aeronautical Engineering. He examined the books, and concluded that while the laboratory was operating momentarily in the red, its fundamental health was sound. But if Curtiss-Wright should pull out, the laboratory would need immediately some $750,000 of working capital. At a historic dinner in New York the Dean, abetted chiefly by J. Carlton Ward '14 of Fairchild Aviation, persuaded eight airplane manufacturers to advance the working capital.

President Day presented the proposal to the Executive Committee on 15 December 1945. An immediate decision was necessary, for the time limit was the last day of December. There was no time to appoint investigative committees or to refer the matter to the full Board, wherein, in fact, cautious counsels might have prevailed. The Executive Committee accepted the heavy responsibility of ratifying the proposal. On 31 December 1945 the Aeronautical Laboratory became the property of Cornell University.

This was a solemn moment in Cornell's history. The University assumed the direction of a great research institution far from its own campus. It took the chance of financial troubles which might conceivably overwhelm the University. And it accepted implicitly a bold new principle: that research divorced from education is part of the proper business of a university. (Perhaps the initiation of this concept in America was the establishment of the Argonne Laboratory by the University of Chicago during the war.)

The announcement of the new acquisition filled the Ithaca faculty with more alarm than satisfaction. Some found the action a typical example of administrative irresponsibility and foolhardiness, some envisaged the laboratory as an ailing monster bent on devouring faculty salaries, some objected merely out of habit. If the acquirement of the laboratory had been put to a Faculty vote, it would certainly have been rejected.

Some anxious moments followed. The first months of 1946 brought the terrifying news that the laboratory was losing $30,000 a month. But after a period of stress and strain, it found its financial feet. Contracts came in, chiefly from the government, to the tune of three and a half millions a year. The Cornell Aeronautical Laboratory is not, and by its consititution cannot be, profit-making; but it is soundly self-supporting.

The nature of the work done was in large part secret, in large part incomprehensible. But certain announcements piqued lay curiosity. The laboratory developed the strongest plastic known, much stronger and lighter than aluminum. It worked on air safety and crash injuries, in cooperation with the Medical College. It invented for the Air Force's arctic installations a hemispherical inflatable house of rubberized glass fiber. The house, supported by air pressure, withstands a 100-mile wind and supports a three-ton load of snow or ice. When deflated, it makes a 1,600-pound bag the size of two office desks.

The national need, the world need, of research led into other extramural activity. The Associated Universities, Inc., with government funds, established a great center at Brookhaven, Long Island, to do fundamental research, mostly in the nuclear field. Cornell was naturally one of the Associated Universities. Many of the faculty, in Nuclear Studies, Chemistry, Electrical and Mechanical Engineering, were detached for service in Brookhaven for periods up to eighteen months.

In Geneva the Agricultural Experiment Station continued its amelioration of the fruits of the soil. A Department of Food Science and Technology was added in 1944. One or two examples only of the station's multitudinous activity: the Cortland apple, Ithaca's child, became the third most widely planted variety in the state. The station has introduced forty-four new varieties; the apple lover who visits the station in autumn has a revelation of the apple's possibilities which almost excuses the fall of Eve. Thanks largely to the station's work, the state's grape crop has increased more rapidly in value than has any other fruit crop. While acreage has declined, the yield per acre has risen since 1935 from 1.4 tons to over three tons. And the station has been a leader in the propagation of size-controlling fruit tree rootstocks.

In Ithaca the research spirit permeated more and more the University's collective character. A Bureau of Educational Research and Service was set up in the School of Education, assuming many tasks under the head of Testing. On the fringe of the University labored the Paleontological Research Institute developed by Professor Gilbert D. Harris '86. A Social Science Research Center was formed in 1949, to facilitate individual and group research and provide an organization to deal with foundations and government agencies. It was soon successful in obtaining over half a million dollars to study such subjects as civil liberties, social and political problems of western Europe, real capital formation in the Far East, etc.

In the humanities proper, research activities were not spectacular. Foundations rarely come to the aid of literary critics and speculative philosophers. In fact, the humane scholar has not much need of crews of fact gatherers and questionnaire tossers. What he chiefly needs is time to sit and read, to sit and think, to sit and write. Such tranquil time is the hardest thing to obtain in the ambience of university activity. But in spite of all, the staffs in the humanities, of the Department of English in particular, produced a steady flow of books and articles, usually valuable in their field, sometimes even important in the wider world.

Some of the more picturesque examples of research in these years: Karl M. Dallenbach of Psychology studied the perceptions of the blind;

he found that 15 per cent of the blind persons tested could perceive and avoid obstacles by an inward radar, enabling them to hear vibrations at a pitch of over 10,000 vibrations per second. How then can we teach this faculty to the other 85 per cent? Charles L. Seeger '42, fascinated as an undergraduate by stories of "celestial static," became professor of electrical engineering and undertook the building of an eight-ton radio telescope. This receives sounds from the planets, radio waves from the sun and stars. "It listens to the music of the spheres," said an awed reporter. Work in artificial insemination was carried on in a new building on Judd Falls Road. Milkdale Aristocrat Rag Apple died in 1948 after fathering more than fifteen thousand calves, living and posthumous. Well done, good and faithful servant. Home Economics issued a series of treatises on the palatability of chocolate cakes, and found that kitchen sinks in general and ironing boards in particular are placed too low.

A graphic illustration of Cornell's contribution to the world of knowledge was afforded by a banquet in the Waldorf-Astoria on 17 February 1947 to honor five Cornellian winners of Nobel Prizes. These were John R. Mott '88, religious leader; Isidor I. Rabi '19, nuclear physicist; Pearl S. Buck, A.M. '25, author; Professor James B. Sumner, first crystallizer of the enzyme urease; and Professor Peter J. W. Debye, world-famous chemist. One likes to imagine that the ghostly hands of Andrew D. White joined in the applause.

XXXIX

Cornell under President Day: The Postwar Student

IN the early postwar years campus sociologists detected a fresh attack of the New Seriousness, which has been alarming alumni for at least forty years. Emerson Hinchliff '14 noted in the *Alumni News* for March 1947 that managership competitions were lagging, that it was hard to get crowds out for rallies, that organized cheering was weak. He blamed the situation on the sophistication of the returned veterans. At the same time he found manners in general better and thought the fraternities displayed more savoir-faire in dealing with guests.

Well, the old historian is very dubious about the New Seriousness. Alumni memories are notoriously fallible, retaining the smallest detail of the postvictory riot of 19—, and rejecting the long earnest labors involved in the composition of a Mech Lab report or a term paper in Economics. Some students have always worked hard and some have idled; the proportions have changed somewhat under external influences, but on the whole not very much. Reporters, however, always like bold, outright statements, qualifying as news. One could sell an article to the Sunday New York *Times Magazine* on the New Seriousness, whereas an article on the Old Immutability would certainly be rejected. In the recollection of your historian, student seriousness parallels the curve of unemployment in the United States; it varies directly with parents' hardship and with the necessity of taking a good degree in order to get a good job.

The inflationary period after the war was hard on parents, and many students were serious by necessity. At least half the women earned part of their expenses. The counselors of students found in 1948 that the women they placed earned $126,700, the men $303,000. At the same time the nonsorority women, who furnished most of the female gainful workers, had the highest average grades, while the fraternity men were the lowest group scholastically.

The foreign students especially were in serious plight. In 1948–49 Cornell had 352 of them, from 53 countries. Many were refugees from hostile lands; many more came from countries whose currency could not be transformed into dollars. The Chinese were in particularly dire straits. Some fraternities and sororities helped out by inviting foreign students to be nonpaying guests. The Counselor of Foreign Students arranged lifesaving loans. But many young foreign intellectuals lived lives of obscure penury.

An interesting and useful enterprise was Watermargin, a cooperative club dedicated to fighting racial and religious prejudice. It had and still has its own house in the cluster of fraternities off upper University Avenue. The name had its origin in a Chinese classic, translated by Pearl Buck with the title "All Men Are Brothers." It tells the story of the fugitives who gathered at the water's margin to fight the injustice of the Ming dynasty.

Among the numberless clubs were some which filled timorous elders with alarm. The Labor Youth League, with eight members, espoused militant Marxism and probably advocated the overthrow of American institutions by force, while other groups were devoted merely to the annoyance of American institutions. The Marxist Discussion Group, frankly communist, was not an action group. American Youth for Democracy, with twelve acknowledged members, was trumpet-tongued on all controversial issues, and was proud of its inclusion in Attorney General Tom C. Clark's list of subversive organizations. The Young Progressive Citizens of America carried on the FDR-Henry Wallace tradition; the Students for Democratic Action were anti-Wallace but pro-Roosevelt; the Student League for Industrial Democracy, with thirty members, was prosocialist but anti-Stalinist. The Cornell Civil Liberties Committee, the United World Federalists, the NAACP, gave opportunity for protests at any desired temperature. All these organizations were on the whole prolabor, pro-Palestine-partition, antidiscrimination, anti-universal military training, anti-Republican. But their total membership was small and contained much duplication.

The *Sun* resumed in 1946, replacing the wartime *Bulletin*, and of course the *Widow* was sempiternal. The *Era* reappeared briefly as a pictorial, patterned on *Life*. The *Cornell Review* made its bow, with the intention, soon defeated, alas, of becoming a quarterly.

The Department of Physical Education and Athletics resumed a full schedule of intramural and extramural sports after the war. With rising costs, it soon fell into financial troubles. Director Robert J. Kane reported in 1948 "an astounding gross income of $430,300, more than dissipated by an even more astounding expense figure of $431,300." Still, he managed to keep the prices of tickets constant, while absorbing a 20 per cent tax. In the following year Kane recorded a deficit of $11,300, plus an accrued debt of $72,400. Other colleges were said to be in similar straits. Obviously it would be necessary to raise athletic fees and ticket prices, or the University would have to meet the deficits.

The old days of sports for profit were ended in the large eastern universities. The presidents of the eight so-called Ivy League colleges made an agreement to reduce athletic excesses, inevitably entailing a reduction in gate receipts. Stadia and Bowls took on the mournful air of the Coliseum in Rome. Committees on eligibility and admissions made recruiting difficult and athletic scholarships suspect. Postseason and sectional championship tourneys were forbidden. The National Collegiate Athletic Association published a rigorous "Sanity Code" in 1948, enforcing the principles of amateurism. James Lynah '05 was head of the responsible panel, and John T. McGovern '00 and Charles M. Sarratt '11, Vice-Chancellor of Vanderbilt University, were co-members.

George K. ("Lefty") James became football coach in 1947 and promptly proved his worth. His 1948 team led the Ivy League for the first time since 1939, and lost only to Army. (But the championship left it merely nineteenth in the nation.) Among the stars were Bob Dean '49, Joe Quinn '49, Jack Rogers '49, Hillary Chollet '50, Pete Dorset '50 and Jeff Fleischmann '51.

No one should be surprised to learn that Cornell footballers were and are superior men. Professor Frederick G. Marcham of History studied the records of the twenty-four football letter men of 1947 and found their academic standings well above the norm of the student body. A reporter for the New York *World-Telegram* investigated the championship team of 1939 and discovered that all were doing well in the world; there were no "gridiron bums" among them.

The crew, coached by "Stork" Sanford, won the intercollegiate eight-way regatta at Seattle in June 1946. The 150-pounders were champions in 1949.

In track Cornell had its share of champions. Paul Robeson, Jr., '48 leaped and John L. Haughwout '44 vaulted high in air. In 1949 the mile relay set a Cornell record of 3:14.9; Walter S. Ashbaugh '51 and Robert G. Hunt '50 broke some Penn meet records; the team was second in the heptagonals; and Cornell with some aid from Princeton defeated Oxford-Cambridge by 9 to 4. Charles H. Moore, Jr. '51 won the national collegiate title in the quarter-mile, in a record-breaking 47 seconds flat.

In 1949 Jack Moakley retired, after fifty phenomenal years as track coach. He continued as adviser, with Louis C. Montgomery as his responsible successor. In June 1947 died genial Nicky Bawlf, after twenty-seven years as varsity soccer, hockey, and lacrosse coach and director of intramurals.

Soccer led its league in 1948 and 1949, with Joaquín Molinet '49 as its shining star. There were some astounding tennis players in these years, with Richard Savitt '50 and his fraternity brother in Pi Lambda Phi, Leonard L. Steiner '51, gaining national recognition. In 1948 Cornell was champion of the Eastern Intercollegiate Tennis Association for the first time, and repeated in 1949, making twenty-one straight wins in league play. The golfers, led by Arthur H. Bishop, Jr. '49, were Ivy League winners in 1946. The rifle team, champions of the northeastern area, won the Hearst Trophy in 1946. The polo team was eastern intercollegiate champion in 1949, and Dorothy S. Van Winkle '49 was crowned, in 1946, national equitation champion at the Horse Show in Madison Square Garden. The skiers took the state championship in 1948. Five Outing Club members were the first (in February 1949) to climb Dix Mountain, in the Adirondacks, in winter.

Surely I have overlooked other mighty achievements.

Meanwhile the mass of students played their body-building games, fiercely though inexpertly, in the old gymnasium, the Drill Hall, and on the playing fields. In 1946–47 it was recorded that 5,716 men competed in 893 scheduled contests in nine sports. New tournaments were established in skiing, wrestling, table tennis, billiards; 52 fraternity basketball teams and 64 independent teams were in competition. Softball was the most popular sport.

Some random scrapings from these years: Cornell's radio station WHCU won an award for outstanding community service. In a flash flood on 15 August 1947 three and a half inches of rain fell in forty minutes, and a student was killed by lightning. The last passenger train to Auburn ran in August 1948. A bird census revealed 179 varieties of birds in the Cayuga Lake basin. And Heinz K. Meng '46 seized a live duck hawk in flight. He did so by burying himself in sand, covering his head with grass, and holding a pigeon on his chest. The duck hawk dove, Meng uprose and took the bird prisoner. Mrs. Mary Sheldon Lyon died at the age of eighty-five, leaving her half share in Sheldon Court to Father Divine, Negro cult leader. The campus, though disapproving high-mindedly of discrimination in the deep South, did not welcome a Heaven to College Avenue. Evan J. Morris, owner of the Triangle Bookstore, resolved the matter by buying the building. The signers of the bill of sale included Blessed Thomas, Wonderful Experience, Sincere Determination, Great Love, Sweetness Love, Radical Love, and Mr. St. Peter. Miss Sebela Wehe, locally famous dramatic soprano, presented her two-hundredth concert in Military Hall in December 1946. Her shirt-cardboard placards, laboriously written by hand in the Post Office, announced: "She has sang over the Long Distant Telephone to King George, Queen Elizabeth, Marshal Stalin, Gen. MacArthur Tokyo, Gen. Eisenhower, President Truman and Mrs. Truman, who invited her to the White House as a guest. . . . Come early and avoid the rush! The early bird gets the worm." Miss Wehe, "the supreme entertainer with the golden voice," was a feature of several Spring Day performances, doing a fan dance. But, as she herself insisted, "Even in my fan dance, I have always been well dressed."

We come now to the end of Edmund Ezra Day's presidency. At the trustees' meeting on 13 June 1949 he presented his resignation. Two years before he had sustained a coronary difficulty, which we may interpret as a slight stroke. He had disregarded the warning and had remained in office to promote the fund-raising campaign, traveling 23,000 miles and speaking to alumni gatherings everywhere. Now, at the age of sixty-six, he felt that the University's affairs were so stabilized that he might heed his doctor's commands and retire.

The trustees accepted his resignation with reluctant understanding, and created for him the post of Chancellor. It was understood that he would give his energies to the major over-all aspects of University development, to the higher levels of fund raising, to the cultivation of the University's relations with the state, and that he would continue to serve as the chief executive officer of the Medical College and the

School of Nursing. Committees would undertake the search for a new President.

Any reader of this record must be aware of the enormous services of President Day in his twelve years at Cornell. His strong hand at the helm guided us among the reefs of war and through the troubled waters of the postwar period. He reformed the administration, from the committee organization of the trustees down through the whole structure. The college councils and the administrative boards were reorganized, the academic divisions grouped in new coherences. The Greater Cornell Fund was carried through to success, while the annual Alumni Fund of unrestricted money rose from $86,700 to $407,600. The Schools of Chemical and Metallurgical Engineering, Business and Public Administration, Industrial and Labor Relations, Nutrition, Aeronautical Engineering, and Nursing and the Laboratory of Nuclear Studies became part of the University. The enrollment rose from 6,341 to 10,034.

The physical development through these difficult years was phenomenal. Moore Veterinary Laboratory, Olin Hall of Chemical and Metallurgical Engineering, Savage Hall of Nutrition, Newman Laboratory of Nuclear Studies, the Clara Dickson dormitories for women, the Administration Building (so appropriately renamed Day Hall), the U.S. Plant, Soil, and Nutrition Laboratory, and the faculty housing development were constructed, and the Aeronautical Laboratory in Buffalo was acquired, and the airport and its surrounding lands were added to our domain. Under construction or in preparation at Day's retirement were Statler Hall, Anabel Taylor Hall for religion, Teagle Hall for men's sports, a new heating plant, and state-given buildings for Animal Husbandry, Agricultural Engineering, Agronomy, Industrial and Labor Relations, the Veterinary College, and the Agriculture and Home Economics library. Preliminary arrangements were made for the Engineering Materials Processing Laboratory and for an Electrical Engineering building.

His spiritual contribution is harder to assess. He was by character an innovator, a creator. He was less respectful to tradition than eager to begin something new, a school, a line of investigation, an idea. His eagerness provoked him to great daring. He was willing to take million-dollar chances, as in the creation of the Laboratory of Nuclear Studies, and sometimes his daring led him and others into dire hazards and difficult passes.

His training as a social scientist reinforced the cast of his mind. He was inclined to apply to every question the test of social utility, social service. He had not much sympathy, or even understanding, for the purely aesthetic. The old humane ideal of self-cultivation seemed to him a selfish dilettantism, almost indecent in the comradely world. Making his own life useful, he was determined that his university should be useful above all. Herein he resembled that other Ezra, our Founder, "Old Man Useful."

In his final report, President Day took occasion to review his educational beliefs, in words which may still be profitably conned and pondered.

In 1868, there were still formidable barriers against new subjects in the curriculum, the admission of students from less privileged classes, and the completely untrammeled pursuit of truth. Those barriers have for the most part been removed. . . .

As I would define the frontier of those earlier days as having to do with the freedoms of higher education, I would view the frontier of this day as having to do with the responsibilities of higher education given freedom. We now have freedom. What do we make of it? . . .

There are . . . areas in which a real frontier still exists for American higher education. I will cite three.

In the field of technology . . . there is a present frontier with respect to the relationships of technical applied knowledge to the basic sciences. To what extent should engineers know their physics, and chemistry, and mathematics? . . . Should we ask of our lawyers in training that they know something about the social sciences, that they know something about psychology? . . . Should we expect theologians to know more about human nature, psychology, possibly domestic relations, maybe psychiatry, or social work and sociology? . . .

Another part of the present frontier in higher education relates to the understanding of social consequence in the practice of the skilled arts by those who are turned out of these institutions. To what extent may we assume that the doctors and the lawyers and the engineers know enough about the social impact of the practice of their professional arts? . . . Here we have another present frontier for higher education, that of identifying and implementing the social responsibilities of our great professions. . . .

In the third place, this frontier of higher education . . . has to do with the responsibility of higher education for the protection of our American way of life. . . . We must all give continuing thought to specific ways and means of defense against the attacks which are being made on our freedoms. . . . Colleges and universities must do more than exemplify American ways. They must help the American people to see more clearly and live more fully the ideals of American democracy. We must, all of us, have a quickened awareness of injustice and. how it is to be righted. We must be more concerned with good will and peace among men. We must resist more than we do violations of the law and all resort to force. We must be concerned with the promotion of beauty as an essential element of wise living. We must try to get more virtue, individual and collective, in our day-to-day living. We must develop more of the love of truth, and the disinterested pursuit of truth wherever it leads. We must be more concerned with the protection of these essential freedoms upon which all of these other values are so dependent.

Edmund Ezra Day was one of the great Presidents of Cornell University. He renovated and revivified it; he pointed its way into the future. He identified himself with it totally; he became Cornell. At the trustees' meeting on 13 June 1949, when he presented his resignation, he cast aside for a moment his usual reticence to declare, in memorable words: "The ideals and traditions of the University come very close to coinciding with my religion in life."

XL

Interregnum II, 1949-1951

WHILE the search for a new President began, the administration of the University was put in the hands of Provost Cornelis W. de Kiewiet, ex-professor, ex-dean.

His was no merely formal incumbency; he construed an Acting President to be one who acts. Not only did he continue policy, he made it, in consonance with the large general views of a historian.

Some of his convictions, illuminating his executive actions, are embedded in the minutes of the Board of Trustees. There is a European strand in our University, he told the trustees on 20 October 1950, a tradition of academic exclusiveness. Another strand is enwound in the Morrill Act, the concept that "the life of an academic institution should be directed to the problems of the outside anxious world." This is the strand he would strengthen. Some interpret the University as a zone of neutrality, he said on 21 October 1949, but no American university has the right to be a zone of neutrality; we must not remove ourselves from the national scene. Our great need, he said, was unity of purpose and action. Cornell grew up as a confederacy of academic principalities. As long as Cornell remained small, these could meet together and make decisions. Now, however, we have lost the means of working together for the common good. "Decisions are made in one school or department that have no relation to decisions made in others." We need more consolidation and integration; and as to the ultimate purposes of education, the trustees are rightly charged with the duty of fitting education to society. "The wisdom gained through experience in a world where decisions must be translated into actions and realities provides members of the Board with an opportunity to contribute to Cornell in a way which it is very difficult for members of the academic community to do."

Such utterances jangled in the ears of many, convinced that educators should have sole authority over education, and that trustees should confine themselves to providing money and buildings. More and more, in faculty conciliabules, the opinion was proffered that the Acting President, our ex-colleague, was a *faux frère*, that he had gone over heart and soul to Administration. Moreover, the Acting President had a certain peremptoriness of manner which made his most helpful actions seem sometimes suspect to the very beneficiaries. The result was that Dr. de Kiewiet enjoyed a considerable unpopularity on the campus, which was both unjustified and unjust.

His unpopularity was intensified by the formal command laid upon the Acting President by the trustees to balance the budget.

Our financial situation was ominous indeed. The accumulated deficit rose at the end of 1948–49 to a terrifying $936,000. The endowment was much less than sufficient, and it was diminished by the application, during the previous decade, of six millions of free funds to buildings and equipment. The budget for 1949–50 showed an estimated deficit of $828,582. It was clear that President Day's policy of plunging in and then shouting for rescue would no longer do. The Acting President was ordered to remove $828,582 from a budget of $7,998,289.

Dr. de Kiewiet succeeded, by vigorous effort, in raising 300,000 unforeseen dollars. He called on every dean and department head to cut down on the original budget, without reducing salaries, but permitting increases only in extreme cases. Every sort of project was abrogated, new developments postponed, orders for equipment, supply, and maintenance cancelled. Vacancies for research assistants, instructors, and other nontenure jobs remained unfilled. Retiring professors were not replaced. "Faculty cooperation was outstanding," said Dr. de Kiewiet officially. "Their understanding of the needs of the University, of the great benefits that would accrue by operating on a balanced budget, was a constant solace to those of us who had to hold the line." All this is true, of course; we did recognize Cornell's necessity. But a good deal of strong language was heard before we decided to become a constant solace.

At the year's end of 1949–50 the operations showed a deficit of only

$69,100. At that time some salaries were raised. A minimum salary of $4,000 (little enough, God knows), was attained for assistant professors. The group life insurance provisions were increased by as much as 50 per cent.

It was a mighty achievement. On the very day that Howard E. Babcock, former Chairman of the Board, was stricken, on 12 July 1950, he told Trustee Victor Emanuel '19 that "for the first time he had confidence in the financial integrity of this University." [1]

In 1950–51 the budget was in balance at the beginning, and at the end the books showed a surplus of $150,000, thanks to an increase in income, savings, and transfers, and an improved efficiency in operations. The faculty salaries were brought up to the minima set several years before.[2] Substantial merit increases were granted. The faculty gained full Social Security coverage, with the University paying its share. The faculty's morale rose in direct proportion to its income.

The Greater Cornell campaign ended its efforts with a formal success on the last day of December 1950; $12,500,000 had been sought, and $12,758,000 was subscribed. There were a number of magnificent large gifts, and many small ones, some of which, representing actual deprivations, were magnificent too. But we were disappointed in the number of useful medium-sized gifts, and disappointed too that many of the subscriptions were never paid. We were astonished also at the expense of fund-raising: over $1,100,000. Instructive indeed were the responses to the appeal for contributions toward special goals. We had asked three million for faculty salaries, and we received subscriptions of $761,000. To the Medical College goal of three million only $130,000 was contributed. To the athletic plant a mere $19,000 was given toward a goal of $250,000. But fortunately nearly four millions for unrestricted use came in. With this aid the University's accumulated deficit was almost wiped out, and allocations of $1,161,000 went to faculty salaries, $409,000 to the Medical College, $1,244,000 to engineering development, $737,000 to the humanities, and so on.

The Greater Cornell Committee, which had served so long and so well under the direction of John L. Collyer '17, turned into the permanent Cornell University Council, to coordinate all the fund-raising activities of the University, with Francis H. Scheetz '16 as chairman of

[1] Trustees' Minutes, 20 Oct. 1950.

[2] The averages in the endowed colleges were: instructors, $3,566; assistant professors, $4,528; associate professors, $5,594; professors, $7,631. The salaries in the state-supported colleges averaged higher.

its administrative board. It has continued to serve the University long and well.

The Acting President took counsel with his so-called Cabinet, consisting of three Vice Presidents (for Research, Theodore P. Wright; for University Development, Asa S. Knowles, succeeded in January 1951 by Willard I. Emerson '19; and for Business, George F. Rogalsky '07 (followed in May 1950 by John E. Burton); of the Treasurer, Lewis H. Durland '30; and of the Dean of the University Faculty, Carleton C. Murdock '10. Dr. de Kiewiet also attended the weekly Deans' luncheons and innumerable Faculty and committee meetings.

For a short time Dr. de Kiewiet was counseled by Chancellor Day. But the Chancellor, already threatened by a coronary attack, soon received a second warning from his high Superior.

The circumstances were dramatic. Dr. Day loved football and watched the games with a passion he rarely revealed elsewhere. At the Columbia game, on 29 October 1949, he was companioned by Robert J. Kane, Director of Athletics, who later told the story. Pete Dorset threw a long pass to Henry Cassel. "The President moved into his box to get a better look. As he did so, he dropped down hard to the seat under him, his head falling to his chest, his body slumping ominously to one side." Kane cried out to Dr. Norman Moore, who by happy chance was near by. Dr. Moore worked rapidly and restarted the pulse, which had ceased for thirty seconds. Dr. Day's eyes opened and his color returned. Dr. Moore suggested that he go home.

As he arose from his chair, he carefully arranged his tie, adjusted his hat at a rakish angle, called out: "Well, gentlemen, let's go." I reached for his arm. "Here, here, young fellow, I need no help," he said, pushing my hand away. "I'll walk under my own power." With his head in the air, a smile on his face, and some bantering remarks to friends on the way, he actually strutted out of the stadium. As he rounded the corner near Barton Hall there was a tremendous clamor from the football field. "What was that?" asked the President. "Stop by that police car and find out what happened." "Cornell scored again on an intercepted pass," shouted the cop. "Well, I feel better. I guess we'll win now." As we alighted from my car at his home, with a sly glance at Dr. Moore, he said: "Dr. Moore tells me that was my last football game, Bob. I'm glad it was a good one. Many thanks for the ride." [3]

It was his last game indeed. His resignation of the chancellorship was announced on 8 January 1950. A number of his friends on the Board of Trustees subscribed the cost of a new house on Cayuga Heights for

[3] *Alumni News*, 15 April 1951.

him and his family, and informed him of the gift on Christmas Eve. The trustees conferred on him the title of President Emeritus.

For a year he led a reasonably prudent life, though refusing to be a recluse. On 22 March 1951 he attended the ninetieth birthday dinner given to Professor Walter F. Willcox. The following morning, early, he set off in his car, with his daughter, to look for a lost dog. Suddenly, at the wheel, he was dead.

His ashes were placed in the Memorial Chapel of Sage Chapel, with the remains of Ezra Cornell and Andrew D. White.

While a committee sought his successor, Acting President de Kiewiet accepted a call to become President of the University of Rochester, and almost on the same day came the announcement that Vice President Knowles would be President of the University of Toledo. Dr. de Kiewiet's resignation as Acting President took effect on 27 January 1951. The trustees on the same day named as the sixth President of Cornell Deane Waldo Malott, President of the University of Kansas. He would take office on 1 July 1951. Until then Theodore P. Wright, Vice President for Research, would serve as Acting President. In the circumstances, the new Acting President could hardly do other than carry on previous policies and deal with routine matters and with emergencies.

Cornell's advance under the two Acting Presidents is impressive. Customarily, a President receives praise or blame for everything that happens under his régime, whether or not he has been responsible for the occurrences. Customarily also, the praise and blame are awarded him for the outcome, praiseworthy or blameworthy, of policies established long before his time. Even with recognition of the flaws in this convention, one must regard the two-year presidential interregnum as a period of notable achievement.

Dr. de Kiewiet brought order into our finances, at great cost to his personal popularity, and turned a giant deficit into a surplus.

The building program initiated under President Day was pressed vigorously forward. Statler Hall was dedicated on 5 May 1950. One remembers that Hotel Administration began as a Department in Home Economics in 1922 and grew steadily in stature and in the world's esteem, under the direction of Professor Howard B. Meek. The Statler Foundation, pleased with its fosterling, offered before the war to build for it a modest million-dollar building, with an Inn, on the edge of Beebe Lake. After the war, the plans became more pretentious, the Statler Foundation's generosity more lavish. Statler Hall finally arose on East Avenue, at a cost of more than $2,500,000. Four of the remaining faculty cottages were doomed, but the plans were so drawn as to preserve a fine oak tree.[4] The building includes, in addition to ample classroom and laboratory space, a thirty-six-room hotel and a Faculty Club of Statlerian magnificence. (The University contributed $200,000 for the faculty's happiness.) When the glistening building was dedicated, Hotel Administration ceased to be a Department in Home Economics, and was henceforth denominated a School, with Professor Meek as its Director.

On the Ag Campus the great library, named for the former Dean and Provost Albert R. Mann '04, was nearly ready.

On Snyder Hill, above the sheep and pig barns, rose the Veterinary Virus Research Institute, at the cost of the state. But the state, earnestly concerned with the diseases of profitable cattle, felt little obligation toward the citizens' pets. The Veterinary College therefore proposed to establish by private subscription a research laboratory for canine diseases, in conjunction with the Virus Research laboratory. The two laboratories would attack in concert the virus and rickettsial diseases of animals. Dog owners, veterinarians, and companies involved in supplying canine needs contributed a handsome $260,000. The Cornell Research Laboratory for Diseases of Dogs, unique in the world, was completed in January 1951.

The Veterinary College was at last promised release from its cramped and unsuitable quarters. The State University of New York prepared plans for a vast new establishment far out on Tower Road.

Ground was broken for the Materials Processing Laboratory, nucleus of the new Engineering group at the south end of the campus. Work was begun on Anabel Taylor Hall, the interfaith center, given by Myron Taylor '94. The plans for Moakley House, to be a recreational center and a lodging for visiting teams, were advanced. The desperately needed men's dormitories came a little nearer. The Buildings and Grounds Committee recommended (19 September 1950) that we wait no longer for donors of Gothic magnificence, but that we build structures that would pay their way. Said the Chairman, John S. Parke '23: "Engineering rather than architectural construction is advisable."

Research blended with big business, indeed it became big business.

---

[4] The last of the remaining cottages of the early days was the James Law house, built about 1873. It used to stand north of President White's house on East Avenue. It was removed to the east side of the Circle in 1905, to make way for Rockefeller Hall. It disappeared in 1962, to make way for the Materials Science Center.

The Vice President for Research, Theodore P. Wright, worked on certain announced principles. Cornell's first aim, he said, should be teaching, its second research, its third public service. On the Ithaca campus we should concentrate on fundamental, nonsecret research which would be profitable to our teachers and our teaching. Applied or secret research for governmental or commercial sponsors should properly be done in the Aeronautical Laboratory in Buffalo, in the institutes attached to the Medical College, in the Experiment Stations in Ithaca and Geneva, and in proper areas of the state-supported colleges.

Under these provisions, Cornell's contributions to the world's fund of knowledge steadily grew. In 1950–51 $11,500,000 was received for sponsored research. Of this sum roughly two million went to the endowed colleges, four million to the state-supported colleges, $1,250,000 to the Medical College, $4,500,000 to the Aeronautical Laboratory. Three-fourths of this mighty sum came from government agencies.

The research activities brought about new groupings in cooperative projects. A Housing Research Center, drawing from Home Economics, Agriculture, Architecture, and Engineering, tested methods and materials, and studied the influence of human behavior on shelter requirements. The Bureau of Educational Research and Service developed into the University Testing and Service Bureau. The Guggenheim Foundation established an Aviation Safety Center with $180,000; its precious work was done at Ithaca, Buffalo, and at the Medical College in New York. A Center for Integrated Aerial Photography Studies appeared, with implications for geology and engineering as well as for aviation.

Thrilling reports came from many laboratories. The synchrotron of Nuclear Studies operated around the clock, yielding information about the meson and about high-energy processes. Cornell made a specialty of cosmic rays, with the aid of a 35-ton cloud chamber magnet, which permitted study of particles with energies above ten billion electron volts. (It was built with funds from Naval research.) Agents went to the Arctic to examine the aurora borealis and radio wave propagation from the ionosphere, and they constructed an observatory for radio astronomy in New Mexico. Astronomers built the largest portable telescope in the world, with a 25-inch reflector. Electrical Engineering developed electronic equipment for the Medical College's study of thrombosis. And so on almost ad infinitum. The Veterinary College's work was never done, for new diseases appeared as fast as the old ones were controlled. A cattle disease was found in cats, suggesting that cats may transfer it from herd to herd. A highly contagious disease of ducks destroyed nearly a million birds before the virus was isolated and an effective serum developed. The character of the work in Agriculture shifted with the change in the state's agricultural economy. In earlier days its watchword had been increased production, the effort to make two blades of grass grow where one grew before. But with the war's end came overproduction and the abandonment and consolidation of farms. The concern of the college and its Extension Service turned more and more to marketing and business management, to quality production, to making one blade of better grass grow where two grew before. The Experiment Stations in Ithaca and Geneva made many a notable discovery. Home Economics made significant studies of reaching, bending, stooping, and twisting, revealing that reaching to a height of 56 inches above the floor requires twice as much oxygen as reaching to a height of 46 inches, whereas reaching to a height of 72 inches requires four times as much oxygen, and bending to 3 inches above the floor nineteen times as much.

Meanwhile research was proceeding in many a quiet study and laboratory, unsponsored and unpublicized, impelled only by an inquisitive person's desire to find out the answer to something. The production in Music, English, Modern Languages, and Zoology especially caught the observer's attention.

And from dawn to dark, in many a hundred classrooms, the teachers did their proper business of teaching.

Two important new professorships were announced. Friends of the lamented Howard E. Babcock, chairman of the Board, raised $300,000 for a professorship of Nutrition. Herrell De Graff '37 was the first incumbent of the chair. And Mrs. John L. Senior fittingly commemorated her husband, of the class of 1901, organizer of the first Spring Day, first graduate manager of athletics, proprietor and bulwark of the *Alumni News*, by endowing a professorship which would signalize American values and lead to a greater understanding of the heritages, traditions, and freedoms of American society.

The Southeast Asia Program was initiated in 1950–51, with a grant of $325,000 from the Rockefeller Foundation. It was an area study, directed by Lauriston Sharp of Anthropology, supported by specialists from various departments. Other important subsidies followed, from the government and from several foundations. With their aid Cornell became the American center for study in this field, with instruction in Ithaca and with stations in Indonesia, Thailand, and elsewhere.

The School of Industrial and Labor Relations throve. Its periodical, the *Industrial and Labor Relations Review,* its book series, *Cornell Studies in Industrial and Labor Relations,* established its authority. The staff were swamped by demands for their services, to conduct community courses, educational programs, conferences, institutes. ILR graduates found ready employment and justified all the bold previsions of the school's founders.

In Agriculture, the undergraduate enrollment of 1,776 in 1949–50 was the highest in the college's history.

In our military world, we added, in July 1950, an Air Force ROTC to the Army and Navy establishments. The work in Naval Science became an academic department of suitable standing, while the properly military training was relegated to the summer cruises.

The Summer School declined, after the postwar boom. Undergraduates returned to the normal four-year pattern of schooling; and the education-hungry veterans, supported by the GI Bill, faded away. The Summer School turned more and more to brief workshops, institutes, one-week and two-week special courses.

The Library received some splendid gifts, among them the Frank Hull collection of Braziliana, giving by Herbert F. Johnson '22, and the Napoleonic library of Claude G. Leland. Mr. and Mrs. Nicholas H. Noyes added rarities from American history to their previous gifts. The Cornell University Archives were created, with Mrs. Edith M. Fox '32 as curator, to preserve and seek out the records, official and intimate, of this institution. And one little item by the way: Mrs. Clyde H. Myers, widow of the professor of plant breeding, studied bookbinding under the highest masters in England, France, and Italy and returned to devote herself, without compensation, to the delicate repair of the Library's precious ancient books.

The Music Department outdid itself with its performance of the *St. Matthew Passion* in 1950. To the stellar group of performers and scholars in the department was added the famous British singer, Keith Falkner.

The students during this interregnum were deeply conscious of the Great Outside World. No longer could they cast care aside on entering the dreaming courts of college. These were years of inflation and rapidly rising costs, including tuition fees. Pocket money dwindled with the parents' reserves. Students worked during vacations as a matter of course; if they went to summer resorts, it was to wait on table. Many foreign students were hard hit by the devaluation of sterling. The Korean War came in 1950 and with it a tightening of draft deferments. A government order announced that only those in the top 50 per cent of college classes would be deferred. The result was a frantic eagerness on the part of all men students to be in the top 50 per cent, a statistical impossibility. Cheating on examinations increased, as did nervous troubles; morale drooped.

The University extended its supervision of undergraduate life, partly in accordance with the general social assumptions of the time, partly in response to the students' own desires. A Guidance Center, erected in 1948, proved very popular. The Deans of Men and Women in 1950–51 recorded 1,642 registered social events and 1,062 informal parties and dances. (When old-timers snorted that they had never registered anything with anybody in the good old days, new-timers retorted that when you have 2,704 parties some few of them had better be supervised.)

Nowadays when you want to explore a common state of mind you make a Survey and obtain a lot of statistics. Our Social Science Research Center issued a Report on the Cornell Student Body in June 1951. Its researchers found that more students were critical of their own efforts than of their courses and teachers: 64 per cent of the respondents thought they did not study enough; 18 per cent found their courses badly presented or useless. Engineering and Architecture students had the highest opinion of their courses and teachers. In Arts 56 per cent, in Architecture only 28 per cent, thought that few or none of their teachers took a personal interest in their students. Of all students 44 per cent found their basic education satisfactory, 52 per cent were satisfied with their vocational training. In Hotel Administration 69 per cent approved their vocational training; in Arts only 42 per cent. The response to questions on free enterprise versus government planning was interesting. In ILR 43 per cent favored government planning outright, in Engineering only 11 per cent; 41 per cent of the Hotel students replying favored big business without restriction, but a mere 8 per cent of the Home Economics girls wanted it.

Such statistics represented the students in their serious mood. The reverse existed, of course, in milieux inaccessible to questionnairers. A nearly tragic occurrence in December 1949 revealed a social underworld hardly suspected by most campus dwellers. At the initiation of a social club a student drank a quart of martinis in an hour and a half. He was carried to the Infirmary and remained unconscious for fifteen hours, while physicians labored upon him. His life was saved, but it was apparently a very near thing indeed. The Faculty Committee on Student Conduct banned two social clubs, but the problem of student drinking was not solved, nor has it ever been, nor perhaps will it ever be.

In the world of sports, the Athletic Department managed to show small surpluses, thanks largely to fine football teams. In 1949 Cornell was Ivy League champion for the second year in succession. Hillary Chollet '50 was called the outstanding player in the league, and Richard G. Clark '50, Lynn P. Dorset '50, Walter G. Bruska '50, John G. Pierik '51, and William T. Kirk '52 were particularly commended. Lynn ("Pete") Dorset, the 155-pound five-foot-eight quarterback, was the spiritual heart of the team. No wonder! He came to us with the Distinguished Flying Cross, the Air Medal with three clusters, the Silver Star for exceptional gallantry, the Presidential Unit citation with one cluster, the ETO ribbon with four battle stars, and two Purple Hearts. He had three times parachuted into enemy territory and had escaped via the underground to free country. In the great Penn game of 1949, the half-time score was Penn 21, Cornell 7. In the first half Pete Dorset broke his nose. He did not even take time out; and in the second half he drove Cornell to victory with a score of 29 to 21. Coach Lefty James called it "the greatest second half 1 have ever seen."

The track teams were among the best in Cornell history. Charles H. Moore '51 held the AAU title in the 400-meter hurdles. In the Cornell-Princeton meet with Oxford-Cambridge in London, 1950, the team took six firsts, with Robert C. Mealey '51 making a Cornell record of 1:52.4 in the half mile. It then soundly beat a picked Irish team in Dublin. At the Penn relays in 1951 we had four firsts, a second, and a third. The mile relay was won in a record 3:13.1 by Moore, Mealey, Meredith C. Gourdine '52, and James M. Lingel '53. Richard N. Brown '51 set a Cornell shotput record of 50 feet 6½ inches. We won the heptagonals for the first time in twelve years, with Gourdine breaking the record for the 220 low hurdles in 23.6 seconds. And then in June we won the ICAAAA championship for the first time since 1936. Gourdine took the 220 low hurdles and the broad jump, with a record 25 feet 9¾ inches, although he had six stitches in his heel from a spike wound. Walter S. Ashbaugh '51 won the high hurdles, and Mealey the half mile.

We had our best basketball season since 1924 in 1950–51, winning twenty and losing five, though we were only second in the Ivy League.

Frank Bettucci '53 was intercollegiate 147-pound wrestling champion. Baseball did well; soccer retained the Ivy Championship in 1949. And in 1950 the great tennis player Dick Savitt fought his fraternity brother Leonard Steiner for the eastern intercollegiate championship, and won. Then the two combined to win the doubles championship.

During the Interregnum, the Medical College followed its own course without much supervision from the Acting Presidents, who hardly had time to acquaint themselves with the college's special concerns. But during Dr. Day's brief chancellorship, he and Arthur H. Dean, chairman of the Executive Committee, arranged an important partnership with the Sloan-Kettering Institute for Cancer Research, which adjoins the New York Hospital–Cornell Medical Center. For educational purposes, the Sloan-Kettering Institute became a division of the college. Cornell's trustees appointed the faculty and staff. Graduate students in cancer research would receive their degrees from Cornell. The college was already in close cooperation with the Memorial Hospital for Cancer and Allied Diseases, across the street from the Center. In 1950 New York City built, a block away, the James Ewing Hospital for cancer patients, naming it for our pioneer professor. The facilities for cancer study offered by this group of institutions are probably unique.

Social and cultural anthropology entered the Medical College, with courses in the application of social studies to problems of medical and nursing practice. An interesting clinic was established for the diagnosis and treatment of patients in stressful life situations. Said Dean Joseph C. Hinsey: "Disease is being considered more in terms of the host's adaptive processes to the assaults of environment rather than damage done by the hostile forces themselves. . . . Processes of disease may be initiated by stresses arising from personal adjustment to life situations as truly as from the stresses of burns, injuries, or parasitic invaders."

With the far-flung research activities and with the teaching process in these (and indeed in other) years we are incompetent to deal. Their recording must await the labors of an accredited medical historian.

The Interregnum ended with the accession of President Malott on 1 July 1951. It must be evident that the period was not one of mere perfunctory caretaking. The financial health of the University was restored; its organization was tightened and its material resources increased. The faculty, with its morale in at least passable state, was held together against the temptations of rivals. With the promise of men's dormitories, of the Teagle sports building, of the interfaith center, proper care of the students' bodies and souls, as well as their minds, was at length assumed by the University. The two years from 1949 to 1951 were years of advance and not of decline.

XLI

Cornell under President Malott

THE historian dealing with times well past speaks with classroom in-fallibility—for he knows how things came out. But when he attempts to treat of current matters his confidence fades. This presidential ven-ture—is it courageous or foolhardy? This turn taken—is it toward prosperity or disaster? For old questions and problems he is equipped with what teachers call an Answer Book. But for these new-posed prob-lems there is no Answer Book.

What makes history, what indeed is important? The life of a uni-versity consists of daily events infinite in number and possible meaning. An hour in a classroom could be described in a year-long dissertation. What events shall we choose for preservation? For all we know, the most important event may be the spilling of a solution in a laboratory, an ill-considered joke in a trustee meeting, a virus infection in a dean's body. The reporter picks from the roaring flux those incidents that fit a familiar value system; the historian copies down those of the reporter's words that fit his own system or fancy. Soon a pattern emerges, preserving the things that we wish to be preserved. Memories come to adorn the pattern, with the decorations that memory has cherished, and with the enrichments of later reflective judgments. Thus history is made, a legend agreed upon, said Voltaire. But in the midst of legend's making, the historian finds himself distressed and unsure.

For this and for other excellent reasons, your historian will hence-forth renounce his privilege of weighing and judging, and will provide merely a brief, bald record of supreme events, to be filled out by the reader who has lived among them, or by the future historian blessed by the knowledge of how things came out.

Deane Waldo Malott was elected sixth president of Cornell University by the trustees on 27 January 1951. He was born in Abilene, Kansas, on 10 July 1898. His father was the dominant banker of the town. He received the A.B. from the University of Kansas in 1921, the M.B.A. from the Harvard Business School in 1923. He remained at Harvard as Assistant Dean of the Business School until 1929, was for four years Vice President of the Hawaiian Pineapple Company, and then returned to Harvard as Associate Professor in the Business School. In 1939 he was called to the presidency of the University of Kansas. He is the author of *Problems in Agricultural Marketing* and coauthor of four books on business and finance. He married, in 1925, Eleanor Sisson Thrum of Hawaii. The couple have three children.

It is natural that the President, with his long training in business administration, found Cornell's organization loose and even incoherent. This was a reasonable and logical view, and not his alone. It seemed to him obvious that the responsible officers of the institution should report directly to him, as the responsible delegate of his Board of Trustees. In accordance with his design, new organisms of the University, such as the Andrew Dickson White Museum of Art and the Laboratory of Ornithology, were created under his control, and others, such as the Cornell United Religious Work, were brought under the central jurisdiction. Responsibility for student affairs passed from the Faculty to the President, by trustee action, but the President delegated his powers to the existing Faculty committees, renouncing his right of veto on committee actions.

"A university is not a business," insists President Malott. "We are not efficient and never will be." And yet we must be businesslike, for we are dealing with immense sums of money. The operating budget for 1962–63 was $100,045,419. This is big business by any reckoning. The endowment, with a market value of $152,000,000 in June 1961, pays for only 6 per cent of the staggering educational expenses.

To meet the costs tuition charges and fees have been repeatedly raised. But only by charity can an endowed university live. The generosity of Cornell alumni and of others in recent years makes a lustrous record of beneficence. They gave over $110,000,000 during the decade

DEANE WALDO MALOTT, President 1951–

ending in June 1961. Of the multitudinous benefactions for Cornell's continuance we may here mention none, while acclaiming all.

The physical appearance of the campus has been transformed under President Malott. The Engineering group took form, according to plan. Below the Law School, Myron Taylor Hall, looms a dormitory for law students, given by Mr. Taylor. Beside Myron Taylor stands, so fittingly, Anabel Taylor Hall, the interfaith center, named for Myron Taylor's wife. (This building marks the last of Gothic in Cornell architecture.) Just to the north is the Gannett Medical Clinic, given by the Gannett Foundation in honor of Frank E. Gannett '98. The south end of the main quadrangle is occupied by the magnificent Olin Library for research, made possible by a gift from John M. Olin '13, supplemented by many other notable contributions. Behind Rockefeller Hall is rising the Materials Science Center, subsidized by the federal government. Statler Hall has expanded to the south, with a giant addition offered by the Statler Foundation.

Building by the state-supported colleges has matched that on the lower campus. On the site of the old Veterinary College rises the massive home of the School of Industrial and Labor Relations. The agricultural quadrangle is walled on the east by the Albert R. Mann Library for the Colleges of Agriculture and Home Economics, opened in 1952. Farther out on the Ag Campus stand the sumptuous Animal Husbandry building, named for Professor Frank B. Morrison, and the Agricultural Engineering building, named in honor of Professors Howard W. Riley '01 and Byron B. Robb '11. Farther still to the eastward is the spacious Veterinary College, nineteen buildings on twenty acres, opened for service in 1958. No finer plant for the study of veterinary medicine exists anywhere.

On Alumni Field stands beautiful Teagle Hall, the men's sports building. At hand is the vast skating rink, Lynah Hall, and also the Grumman Squash Courts. The student body is further served by the golf course, expanded to eighteen holes, with Jack Moakley House, containing a dormitory for visiting teams. Down by the Inlet stands the Collyer Boat House for the crews; and the Helen Newman women's sports building ascends beside Beebe Lake.

One of President Malott's first concerns was the provision of housing for men students. Six freshman dormitories were built near the existing dormitories on West Avenue. Now a new housing development has gone up to the north of Beebe Lake. It includes an apartment building for men, a galaxy of little houses for married students, and a women's dormitory, Mary H. Donlon Hall.

Many lesser structures must pass unnoticed, such as Noyes Lodge, Von Cramm Hall, the Big Red Barn, the Heller House.

Adventuring to the northward, we find the Laboratory of Ornithology in Sapsucker Woods, and, beyond, the Laboratory of Radiation Biology. About the airport lies Cornell's Industrial Research Park, a portent for the future. And in Geneva a Food Research Building, said to be the finest in existence, was dedicated by Governor Nelson A. Rockefeller in 1960.

Thus the physical frame of the University has been transmuted during President Malott's term of office. The new buildings in Ithaca, completed and actively undertaken, are valued at $100 million. The transmutation has not been greeted with universal delight. But with all sympathy for the critics, one must point out that the construction program was not prompted by a mere rage for building, like that of Emperor Nero, Cheops, or Louis XIV. The overcrowding came first, with the Second War; the building followed, as a necessary effort to ease the overcrowding. The administration has been trying to meet evident necessities; most of them, we hope, have now been met. Barring a new increase in enrollment, the physical expansion of the campus should be near its close.

Much of the new building houses the immense research business of the University. The sponsored research rose, in money terms, to the dizzy sum of $39,400,000 in 1960–61. The money comes from the government and from foundations, corporations, individuals, trade associations, and university appropriations.

Research became the occupation of groups and teams. We are far from the days when Pierre and Marie Curie could discover radium in their back-yard laboratory. Now research crews work on machines each costing enough to run the early Cornell for decades. The old departmental and even collegiate limits fade, as the projects cross the old comfortable boundaries. Nor are they confined to campus laboratories; they fly at will about the earth, from darkest Africa to the whitest Arctic. Only one example: the U.S. Department of Defense's Ionospheric Research Facility in Puerto Rico, under Cornell's supervision. Its radarscope, designed by Cornell engineers, is the world's largest. It will be able to pick up an object a cubic yard in size twenty thousand miles from the earth.

(Absorption with research, at Cornell and elsewhere, has provoked some qualms. Lonely voices question if the ends always justify the gigantic means. When everything is regarded as equally worth knowing, when every teacher must have his research projects for the sake of mere academic respectability, when he thinks rather of dressing up a project to allure a foundation than of the intrinsic value of its outcome, one wonders if the research race may not become a rat race, to the cost of the teaching function.)

In our still major business of teaching, one notes, as in research, a tendency to overpass or disregard the traditional collegiate limits. An example is the Senior Professorship of American Institutions, which lies outside the familiar frame. But with all the developments without and within the colleges we shall forbear to deal.

The faculty's state has markedly improved. In the decade ending in 1963 the median of professorial salaries rose by 73 per cent for full professors, 77 per cent for associate professors, and 67 per cent for assistant professors, with a notable increase in insurance and other fringe benefits. Four faculty trustees, with full voting powers, sit on the Board of Trustees.

Students became, in the fifties, a little more earnest and mature than in the past, a little more amenable to direction and counseling, a little more conscious of the world beyond the college, a little sloppier in appearance and dress. Their earnestness was imposed by events beyond their control. It became harder to get into Cornell, and competition in the secondary school for high grades became a stern necessity, early comprehended and accepted. High grades in college were essential for admission to professional and graduate schools, and an increasing proportion of our undergraduates looked to continuance of their studies beyond the first degree.

Today the student plans his college career with the aid of an Assistant Dean; for advice he goes to undergraduate counselors and trained graduate residents in his dormitory, and to a corps of guidance specialists in the office of the Dean of Students; and if he is low in spirit he runs to the Mental Health Clinic. Some elders hold that the students are overguided. The elders do not always recognize that students have been accustomed to guidance services in their high schools, and that they expect professional advice in college, and that for $1,425 a year they are entitled to such service. Nor do the elders always recognize that professional counselors have taken over a function which was once performed informally by the faculty. Professors used to live on the campus, and instructors in Collegetown rooming houses;

now they are scattered from Dryden to Trumansburg, from Groton to Candor. Further, the teachers had more time for student association in those easygoing days than now, when the necessity for publication harries them until their retirement—and even after.

Despite the increase in supervision, Cornell students are not treated as a subject class. They have gained, indeed, more control over their own affairs. The Men's Judiciary Board, composed of undergraduates, has initial jurisdiction over cases of student misconduct. The Executive Board of Student Government, elected by the students, with only non-voting advisers from the faculty and administration, has effective power over most student affairs. Students sit on four faculty committees and have voting rights on two of them.

One might think that the New Maturity would comport an elderly formality in the exterior. One would be wrong again. The ritual daily shave has lapsed, to encourage the growth of ragged beards. The dirty sweatshirt remains the common classroom badge of the male; he studies in the Library with bare feet on the desk. Few possess a tuxedo, and the tail coat is extinct. The girls, to be sure, do not descend to the jeans and free-flapping men's shirts common in the late forties.

Cornell's athletic history in the fifties was notable in three ways: in its ultimate attainment of proper facilities, in its cleaving to the Ivy League, and in its deficits. But in spite of the costs, we have the largest athletic program in the country, with twenty-one varsity and eighteen freshman sports. And in the shadow of the intercollegiate sports, over three thousand men and a thousand women are annually registered in the innumerable intramural sports contests.

While renouncing any effort to follow the fortunes of the teams, this history must record our football championship of the Ivy League in 1953. And the Navy's great year, 1957. We took practically everything, with a varsity crew of whom none had rowed before entrance, only one of whom had ever seen a crew race. We went to England and won the Grand Challenge Cup, defeating the Russian champions in the semifinals (breaking the Henley record) and Yale in the finals. The boys then went to Lucerne and defeated Italy's champions. The track team had also its great days, winning indoor and outdoor heptagonals, and sending its stars—Charles H. Moore '51, Meredith C. Gourdine '52, Walter S. Ashbaugh '51, Albert W. Hall '56, Irving ("Bo") Roberson '58—to win or place in Olympic championships. And brilliant records were made in wrestling, basketball, tennis, fencing, polo, and skiing.

In New York the Medical College made its own history. The vast complex of which it is a part was reorganized in 1953 and titled officially the New York Hospital–Cornell Medical Center. The Graduate School of Medical Sciences was established in 1951–52, to administer the program in the Medical College and in the Sloan-Kettering Division for Cancer Research. An affiliation was made in 1953–54 with the Hospital of Special Surgery. The physical frame expanded, with the Connie M. Guion outpatient wing, with the Samuel J. Wood Building (for research and for the Library), and especially with the F. W. Olin Student Residence. In its castle of medicine the college conducts innumerable research endeavors, supported by grants and gifts momentous in number, ideals, and results. The most sensational of the researchers' achievements was the synthesis of oxytocin by Dr. Vincent du Vigneaud of Biochemistry. For this feat Dr. du Vigneaud received the Nobel Prize in 1955.[1]

The first eleven years of President Malott's administration have been years of extraordinary achievement. Never in our history have we had such a period of building. The expense has been met by state appropriations and by gifts in sums hitherto undreamed of. The budget increased by 120 per cent, to over a hundred million dollars. Research came to rival teaching as the business of the University.

The administrative structure of the University has been profoundly altered, rationalized, and strengthened. To some, who regard all administration as a usurpation of faculty rights, this is a cause of grief; but it is hard to conceive how the far-flung and fantastically diverse affairs of the University can be handled with less administration.

In the strictly educational business of the University the President has intervened little. We know, however, that he is deeply concerned about the improvement, the personalizing, of teaching. He deplores mass procedures, and the lack of reward for the good or even brilliant teacher who is not fecund of learned articles. Some steps have been taken in this regard.

The material state of the faculty has markedly improved. Never since the 1890's has the faculty been so well at ease. And the President has stoutly defended the rights of teachers to tenure, security, freedom of expression, freedom of conscience, freedom to teach.

[1] For a vivid account of the daily activities of the Medical Center see Milton L. Zisowitz, *One Patient at a Time* (New York, 1961).

The state of the students has likewise been bettered. The deplorable absence of proper housing has been corrected or will be corrected. Responsible care is extended to student souls, minds, and bodies. The opportunities for religious development, for the preservation of health, for physical and social recreation, are such as have never before existed at Cornell.

One seeks, in the light of history, a general characterization of the decade just past. It seems to your historian that the presidency of Deane Malott may come to be termed the Era of Well-Being.

XLII

Postlude

WHEN I began this interminable record, I put to myself a number of questions. I wrote: "How and why has Cornell, young as such institutions go, become one of the best-known American universities, indeed, in some parts of the world, the best-known? How and why has Cornell attained, to put it baldly, greatness, whereas—not to name any names—the University of Binghamton and the University of Watkins Glen have not? In the greatest century of change in the world's history, how has Cornell changed? And what are its constants in a sea of variables?"

To some of my questions I made a provisional answer. Greatness is the product of great ideas, conceived by great men, with the favor of circumstances. Great ideas may not prevail, but surely small ideas, small purposes, can lead only to small results. Now that my long task is nearly done, it seems to me that I have found out just what I knew at the beginning. (That sometimes happens in greater Researches.) I see no reason why my provisional answer should not be made definitive.

Ezra Cornell and Andrew D. White dealt with great ideas. Ezra Cornell's purpose to found an institution where any person might find instruction in any study was a conception of extraordinary scope and daring. Andrew D. White's purpose was no less than the overturn and rebuilding of the entire system of higher education in America, in the light of human and of national needs.

These great ideas were on the whole accepted and absorbed in

American education by the end of the last century. Then came Jacob Gould Schurman, with his concept of service to the state, to be fulfilled without loss of the University's traditional independence. In his own words, he sought to combine the idealism of ancient Athens with the industrialism of modern America. This purpose was renewed and extended by Edmund Ezra Day, with his conviction of the social obligation of the University, an obligation not merely to serve but to guide society. For Dr. Day, the duty of the University was to impose its old wisdom and its ever-new discoveries upon the world, "to help the American people to see more clearly and live more fully the ideals of American democracy."

These are great ideas indeed. However overlaid by momentary preoccupations, they animate us still, they represent our purpose and our desire.

As one looks back over Cornell's century-long history, one recognizes certain changes and certain constants.

The most momentous change is the rise of research as a University purpose. Barely conceived at Cornell's beginning, it has become coequal with instruction in our world. An accessory phenomenon is the increase in the Graduate School to comprise a fifth of the student body. The tendency of research has been to isolate itself in institutes and laboratories, often far from the campus. Though the future is not the historian's business, he may well wonder if this tendency will continue, if the active researcher will find time to teach classes, if the teacher will have time and competence to engage in the all-demanding, highly specialized procedures of the researcher. He may wonder if the Cornell Aeronautical Laboratory may not adumbrate the shape of things to come.

Another change is the increase of the professional spirit. A familiar type in college memories is the dear old kindly prof, doddering about the campus, quoting Horace, clutching a student's lapel as he told some ancient jest. He has gone, with the student's lapel. We have no time to dodder, and little time to bestow on students when classes are over. We know a great deal more about our subjects than did most of the faculty of the early heroic days, but we cannot quote Horace. Our courses are more exacting and better organized than they used to be, our equipment incomparably better, our teaching methods more efficient, but the student has less opportunity for education by mere association.

The problem of Time looms larger. Professional training, in whatever field, demands more years of study than in the past; and the emerging student faces the demands of military service. Education asks all his time, until he is well into his twenties; it leaves him little to stand and stare, to pursue his own troubled courses, to follow unique curiosities. Youth, the creative period, is bound over to controlled learning. The self-educated genius, a Priestley, a Mendel, an Edison, has become almost an impossibility in our time.

We have seen an increase in conformity, or perhaps of mass-regulation. I would not push this too far, for there are still plenty of nonconformists, and we have always had our regulations, which the astute have always been able to evade. Nevertheless, fifty years ago the individual student was given freer play than he is today. He had then more right to choose his studies; he was relatively free of supervision; he had more direction of his own life. What he made of his life was his own affair; if he made a hash of it, the University felt no responsibility. Now his work, his leisure, and his life are organized according to the wise rules of his superiors. But mass-regulation is not a peculiarly Cornell phenomenon. We have simply been changing with the greater world.

Again, we have changed in an increasing cosmopolitanism. Students and our faculty come from the entire nation, from every part of the world. One of Cornell's proper boasts is that it is a cosmopolitan, urbane university in a rural setting.

These are some of the changes in our history. What are some of the constants?

Constant is the natural beauty of our home. How inspired was Ezra Cornell to choose his ragged hilltop farm for his University! A hundred thousand Cornellians keep close in memory their gorge-gashed campus, looking afar over lake and valley.

Constant also throughout Cornell's history has been its blend of idealism and practicality, of the spirit of Andrew D. White and the spirit of Ezra Cornell. This is illustrated by the stated principle of Jacob Gould Schurman, by the evangelical mood of the early College of Agriculture under Bailey, and by the research purposes of the present day. Standing as we do between the tradition-serving liberal arts colleges of the east and the western universities of the people, we seek to blend the idealism of the first with the practicality of the second.

Constant also has been the blending of the humane purpose of education with the ideal of public service. The humane purpose, naturally strongest in the Arts College, pervades also the other colleges. Contrariwise, the dedication of the state-supported colleges to public service reacts upon the students and faculties of the other schools. In its union of endowed and state-supported colleges Cornell is of course unique. This uniqueness it prizes and proclaims.

There is another constant, harder to grasp and define. It lies in the union of memories, of the spirits who have dwelt upon this hill in the century past. There is an old doctrine of the Treasury of the Saints, according to which the surplus virtues of the saintly may be drawn upon by the unsaintly. I like to think that this doctrine points to a large reality. Past lives, past thoughts and emotions, are not utterly lost; they linger faintly in our own thoughts, our own emotions. There are old ghosts about us. They reappear in dreams and sudden recollections; they help to make us all Cornellians; they are the spirit of Cornell.

Professor Charles Love Durham, Bull Durham, used to quote with gusto a passage from Cicero (*De Oratore* 1. 44. 196): "Ithacam illam in asperrimis saxulis tamquam nidulum adfixam sapientissimus vir immortalitati anteponeret." That wisest of men, Ulysses, would trade immortality itself for a glimpse of his Ithaca perched like an eagle's nest upon her rocky cliffs. Ulysses, that wisest of men, bespoke the proper spirit of the Cornellian.

Excursus I

President White in His Library

MRS. ELLEN COIT BROWN ELLIOTT '82 wrote when over ninety her recollections of President White in his private library in 1882–1884. Her letter is in the Cornell Archives.

When I began to do catalogue cards in President White's private library, which was in September, 1882, there was lying in the grass under the tall narrow glass door on the west wall of the room a large hewn block of stone obviously left by the builders. But Mr. White's house was brick not stone, so I suppose this block was brought from Morrill or McGraw and planted there to serve for a step up to the glass door. Mr. [George Lincoln] Burr brought me in there on my first day. Mr. Burr, only recently graduated, had been confidential secretary for some time; this was his invariable entry and it became mine.

If the secretary had been any other than Mr. Burr we would doubtless have come in by the door opening from the entrance hall of the house and proceeded decorously up through the somewhat dim and dusky north end of the library, with books both sides of us shelved from floor to ceiling. This was the appropriate introduction to the Library; the room itself and the books were the heart, I am sure, of President White's personal, instinctive life.

Between this bookish end of the room and the bright southern part there was a small domestic item, a door which led into the family sitting room and—if I may digress—I was once conducted by the Chief with the courteous manners any gentleman would use to any lady to and through this door and requested to remain in absentia until called for. This was because some men had come to the Library to speak with him on business and as it was the only time I was thus disposed of, men on business must have been rare occurrences in Mr. White's private library. Mr. White must have had callers in his library, now and then. He was a man of affairs, as every one knows, with many associates and connections; and he was a man to collect and cherish friends, his heart was large and warm and sensitive to human life—I saw him once at a public assembly held in his honor turn away on the rostrum to hide his emotion, near tears at the climax of the tribute.—The incursions of other people did not seem important to anybody including, perhaps, Mr. White. By now I should say nobody ever came there to talk to him if I did not know from mere common sense that it must have been otherwise. But the library seems to have been his only office, and he may have conducted business during his occasional absences for a day or a week.

The Library's south end was bright and open with great windows looking out into the dooryard. My post was at the east window and I very often stopped to gaze a moment across the garden space towards the Outcalt house [1] and perhaps glimpse a little grandchild—the President called him "sorrel-top" and rubbed his crop of ruddy hair affectionately, when, rarely, his mother came in with him to the Library. I had a small desk, of an odd sort, and wrote catalogue cards. I had ink, a pile of blank cards and a pen, all provided along with the low chair adapted to my height, by the ingenious and thoughtful secretary. The pen had a collar around its top to protect my fingers from ink, the secretary having noticed me getting ink on my fingers with the ordinary one. Mr. Burr instructed me all about how to catalogue and criticized—but kindly—my cards because my printing was not like the copperplate of Kephart [2] who catalogued at the University. He brought me the books from their shelves and dumped them around me on the floor. They were apt to be from Mr. White's collections gathered in his travels, especially the Reformation—Luther's Sermons and such, black-letter, bound in heavy white pigskin; and for the French Revolution old precious documents, for instance copies of "Le Cri du Peuple." As to Mr. Burr's place and status, he sat in an oldfashioned rushbottomed arm-chair which projected its right arm into a miniature table for writing. This was his own obstinate choice, and the President allowed it, with a little amusement. However, the chair was usually empty, for the secretary hated to write—or even to sit. His temperament was executive and his variety of ability superb. He was always in movement, flitting—and I use the term accurately—here and there as rapidly as a bird in a tree. He was out and away for an hour and presently tripped in, softly, with his hands full of papers, assuredly of importance. These he would bear (oh so quietly!) to the President's table, stand there waiting, deference in his mien, until the President should look up from his

---

[1] Occupied by ADW's daughter Clara and her husband, Professor Spencer B. Newbury.

[2] Horace S. Kephart, grad. '81–'84, librarian and writer.

writing to attend to him. Then would be his rapid low-voiced explanations, the President listening gravely and only occasionally asking a question or making a brief comment in a deeper voice nicely modulated.

Mr. Burr's attitude toward Mr. White, notwithstanding their intimate relations, was always perfect—I had almost said profoundly perfect—for it was indeed the expression from the depths of his nature, a recognition of Mr. White as a great man, an understanding of what made him great, a considered admiration for his culture and his accomplishments, and, beside, his humble yet proud acceptance of the friendship, confidence and appreciation of a man so far—he would think—above him. The secretary did not tell me all this, probably did not know it himself; I only guessed it from the sight of him standing there by the President's chair, so quietly waiting, his papers in his hands, respect and devotion clothing him like a garment.

The Library was always quiet. I should say, if I were not afraid of being thought fanciful, that there was always unheard music there. Necessary conversations seemed mere murmurous islands not affecting silence. The typewriter had been invented and brought to the President's notice but he paid no attention, considering it only a negligible contraption and went on doing his own script, or occasionally dictating. A telephone was put up on the wall. Mr. White seemed to think it funny, a plaything; nobody used it and it hung there forgotten.

The day's beginning, some time after we had arrived and begun work, was when the President came in from the hall and walked up the room, not a business man—absorbed, preoccupied, distant—but easily, naturally, a gentleman at home coming into his study of a morning with pleasant thoughts in his mind. He said a courteous good morning to me as he passed my chair; once he came holding a rose in his hand and when he passed laid it on my desk.

The president's table, made into a desk by an imposing rank of pigeonholes set up at the back, was of heavy oak, large, carved at the edge; it must have been brought home from his travels. His chair was a simple straight-backed chair with carving at the back and a leather seat. At the table's right was Mr. White's substitute for a scrap-basket: a great copper jar such as you find in Aladdin's cave, and it was wrought with silver (I think) and possibly (I think) set with diamonds and emeralds. It was, Mr. Burr said—Mr. Burr knew everything—a wine-cooler. And, notwithstanding that, Mr. White used it nonchalantly to throw his scraps in.

Those great windows at the south end gave the room light and took us out doors away from the dim fragrance of the tall and sombre bookshelves that surrounded us at work. The President's window, the biggest, brought the grassy yard and the great low-bowered trees into the Library, and the squirrels that ran up and down the tree-trunks were our playmates; the secretary tamed one and it lived in his pocket and threw out nut shells on the floor.

Excursus 1

This one died, deplorably drowned in Mr. Burr's bedroom water pitcher.

Mr. White sat at his table quietly writing; I did not know what, it did not matter. His face was thoughtful, not disturbed or anxious; neither was it businesslike, still less the look of a man of importance. Sometimes he would get up and turn and stand looking out of his window, watching the squirrels frolic in the grass. Sometimes he would chuckle at them with a sort of an inner tone to his mellow voice. But he stood there and looked out and he was thinking.

I began this on a personal note and so it must conclude. It is hard after seventy years to relive the past and know what influenced and even, in a way, determined one's mind and provided the spirit with standards. I suppose Mr. White's lectures on European history in my undergraduate days began it. He opened to my astonished gaze the great gates of human life as it flowed richly down the centuries. I realized the Reformation, the French Revolution; I knew Luther and Melanchthon and Comenius, persons full of breath and life. The great cathedrals rose and glowed with life and beauty. He described a sculptured Gothic church porch, and some small delicate carving in a way that fixed a picture in the mind, and thirty years afterward I went to Europe myself, sought out that porch and that carving and looked at them with his eyes.

But there was about him a more subtle and personal influence. This I find it impossible to describe; psychology might elucidate but I do not move with ease in the psychological labyrinth. Other approaches seem too vague, too tenuous. At any rate Mr. White cannot be analyzed, not by me seventy years after.

As he sits there beyond the fabulous wine-cooler at his table, his thoughtful eyes upon his writing, and beside him the great clear window that lets in the green trees and the grass and squirrels racing—as I look way back at him there, it is this: that I knew him as a man, an aristocrat, with culture upon him like a rich and fluent garment. And there was in him exceptional ability fused into warm, vital imagination and action. He was a scholar, he loved books and knew them with discrimination, yet he was no recluse but gave himself and the riches of his nature to the practical activities of the life where he found himself. It was all this, and the integrity of his spirit, that gave him his place. The one word that will express it all is, perhaps, quality.

Los Angeles, April 1, 1954

Excursus II

Boring on Titchener

EDWIN G. BORING '08, professor of psychology, emeritus, at Harvard, wrote me (20 January 1960) a wonderful letter about Professor E. B. Titchener, whose faithful assistant he was until 1918. Here are some excerpts:

I first heard Titchener lecture in the top of Morrill Hall in the fall of 1905, when I as a sophomore engineer asked permission to elect psychology, much to the disgust of Professor Diederichs, who said to his colleague at registration in Sibley: "Hell, here's a damned engineer wants to take psychology!" Titchener, lecturing in his Oxford Master's gown, which gave him, as he said, the right to be dogmatic, was fascinating. I remember almost nothing of what he said, except that I know he was fascinating and that after the first prelim he lectured on the one gift that everyone has without working, i.e., the English language. His magnetism was transmissible, though, for my roommates twice every week wanted to know the content of his lecture in order that they might be fascinated at second hand.

Goldwin Smith C was built to Titchener's specifications, so it was said. The slope of the room was said to have been determined by Titchener, and the color of the walls was said to be neutral gray, the center of the color pyramid. (All this is nonsense, but I tell you what was said.) There had to be a demonstrational laboratory; that was required ever since psychology went scientific with Wundt in the 1870's. So a demonstrational laboratory there was, with tables on which apparatus was set up to be wheeled out and fitted into the desk. Titchener had his little office at the side toward the hall, which he occupied for three hours twice a week in the first term and never otherwise. The lectures, Tuesday and Thursday at eleven, were events. Titchener began the night before. He told us that no one should ever have an engagement the evening before a lecture! In the morning he prepared further, came over on the trolley from Cornell Heights, got off and was in this little office. For some years I was demonstrational assistant, a job that brought me close to Titchener but had its fearful aspect lest I should set up something that did not work. He would see the demonstration and I would put it out. Perhaps we would be talked to, perhaps not. The staff would all gather in the demonstrational lab, because they all attended. Really they were expected to attend, but the pressure came out of the Ortgeist and was not explicit. As the hour approached, I brushed the cigar ashes off Titchener's blue serge suit (always blue serge with a white lawn tie), helped him into his Oxford Master's gown, and then departed with the rest of the staff through the barn doors that opened out for demonstrational purposes, to sit in the side seats at the front of the hall. At the right moment Titchener appeared in gown and gave a perfect lecture. No sentence was ever unfinished. The choice of language was exquisite. He handled apparatus with the skill of a loving mother handling a baby. I thought he was a great apparatus man, but I think this was part of the show. And then after the lecture Titchener would talk for an hour as we all sat around and listened and asked questions, sometimes about professional gossip, sometimes about psychology proper. We attended in order to hear whether "the truth" had changed since last year, and there might be further discussion about whether "truth" had changed. . . .

Titchener had organized a little Society of Experimental Psychologists of his own. (It still exists as an honor society limited to 50 active members.) No one ever could go unless Titchener approved it, no matter who was being host that year. . . .

Münsterberg had died on the platform at Radcliffe in December 1916 and Titchener had been asked by Lowell to succeed him [at Harvard]. Titchener said he would not come to Harvard unless they would appoint me as Assistant Professor. He needed someone to dominate, and he saw no one there whom he could dominate. So all this was very exciting, and presently Titchener insisted, as a test of Harvard's sincerity, that it should run a two-inch compressed-air pipe from the attic down to the lecture room. President Lowell seemed to think that this was a trivial requirement to attach to a Harvard professorship, and the whole thing fell through. We never knew which turned which down. . . .

There used in those days to be a great deal of talk about honor and insult in the Laboratories. I have never heard those phrases used since I was with Titchener. We don't seem to have honor any more, or to insult people. But Titchener knew all about them and all of his young disciples were sensitized to them. The Briton believes in a code and sticks to it, and woe betide those who do not. So let me tell you the story of [Harry P.] Weld and tennis, and then the Hollingworth story.

Titchener in the summer played tennis across Thurston Avenue every clear day with three other people. When the three had been selected, they had no escape. They had to play. One day Weld, our Assistant Professor, a lovely, charming man with all the generosity and grace that you could ask in anyone, was receiving from Titchener. Titchener's partner called "Out!" I think I have this right, that the server's partner is the one who calls *out* under the British rules. Weld shouted: "No! It was in! Look! It hit right here!"—pointing to the streak. Weld was not again welcome at the Titchener house for over a year. He had broken a code.

Then there is the Hollingworth story. Titchener published the first half of his textbook in 1909, including in it the two-level theory of attention. Enough sheets were printed for the full edition the next year when the second half was done. You could not change the first half, but in the meantime a third level of attention seemed to have been discovered in Titchener's own laboratory, and Titchener added the correction on the blank half-page at the end of a chapter in the second half. Conscientious young Hollingworth at Columbia reviewed the book and suggested that Titchener had put results obtained in his own laboratory, but contrary to his own theory, in a place where no one would find them. This was an insult, and caused the word *Hollingworth* to be always prefixed by the words *that skunk* when uttered by Titchener. Scientific meetings had to be planned so that not both Titchener and Hollingworth would be there. At least this is the way we youngsters saw it all, and that lasted for over ten years, from about 1913 to about 1924. Then Hollingworth turned up in Ithaca, was shown the laboratory in Morrill Hall by [Karl M.] Dallenbach, and then Dallenbach phoned Titchener to ask if Hollingworth might call on him. Titchener hesitated and said Yes. They went over, and Titchener opened the door, stood there, and then said: "Well, Hollingworth! Who would ever suppose that *I* would be shaking hands with *you?*" And then they shook hands, and Hollingworth became a guest with all the courtesy and deference that any true Briton gives to his guest once he is across the threshold.

What a man that was!

Excursus III

Cornell Authors

WHAT is an author? Clearly not anyone who has written a book, for who has not? An Author, let us say, is a professional or semiprofessional writer in the field of imaginative literature: poetry, fiction, or drama. I am willing to admit a few borderline cases, like Romeyn Berry, a frustrated poet. The following list, certainly incomplete, may qualify as Cornell Authors:

Julius Chambers '70; William Oscar Bates '75; Forbes Heermans '78; C. Wolcott Balestier '85; Hobart C. Chatfield-Taylor '86; Philip Payne '88; Rennold Wolf '92; Harriet Connor Brown '94; Anna McClure Sholl '95; Stephen E. Rose '98; Lewis J. Palen '00; Elsie Singmaster '02; Jane Abbott '03; James French Dorrance '03; Romeyn Berry '04; Thomas S. Jones, Jr., '04; George Jean Nathan '04; Jessie Fauset '05; Warren E. Schutt '05; Hendrik Willem van Loon '05; Frank B. Elser '06; Kenneth Roberts '08; Dana Burnet '11; Charles H. Divine '11; Stuart N. Lake '11; Marjorie Barstow Greenbie '12; Georgia E. Harkness '12; Morris Bishop '14; Austin G. Parker '14; Hu Shih '14; Frank Sullivan '14; William Hazlett Upson '14; Signe Toksvig '16; Dunbar M. Hinrichs '17; Louis Bromfield '18; S. Karrakis '18; Russell Lord '18; Charles G. Muller '18; Henry W. Roden '18; Henry F. Pringle '19; Laura Zametkin Hobson '21; E. B. White '21; Laura Riding '22; Robert C. Washburn '22; Paul Green, Grad. '22–'23; Maribelle Cormack '23; George Harmon Coxe, Jr., '23; Harlow Wilson Estes '24; Hoffman R. Hays '25; Pearl Buck, M.A. '25; Hugh C. Troy, Jr., '26; Edward R.

624

Eastman '26; Elspeth Grant Huxley, Sp. '27–'28; Sidney Kingsley '28; Philip H. Freund '29; Miriam Levant ("Merriam Modell") '29; James D. Proctor '29; Alec R. Hilliard '30; Stanley Burnshaw, M.A. '33; Arthur Laurents '37; Kurt Vonnegut '44; William Mulvihill '45; Donald Plantz '45; Bernard H. Friedman '48; Robert V. Williams '48; Ann Aikman '49; Clifford Irving '51; Charles Thompson '51; Clay Putnam '52; Robert Gutwillig '53; Thomas Pynchon '59.

And while I am about it, let me list some published works of fiction in which the Cornell campus, more or less transformed by art, serves as a locale, in whole or in part: H. H. Boyesen, *The Mammon of Unrighteousness*, 1891; James G. Sanderson, *Cornell Stories*, 1898; Anna McClure Sholl, *The Law of Life*, 1903; Anna Botsford Comstock, *Confessions to a Heathen Idol*, 1906; Grace Miller White, *Tess of the Storm Country*, 1909; Evelyn Schaeffer, *Isabel Stirling*, 1920; Elsie Singmaster, *Ellen Levis*, 1921; Austin Parker, *Here's to the Gods*, 1923; Eric Linklater, *Juan in America*, 1931; Florence Elise Hyde, *The Unfinished Symphony*, 1934; Clarissa Cushman, *I Wanted to Murder*, 1940; W. Bolingbroke Johnson, *The Widening Stain*, 1942; Sherman Peer, *Sabbatic Leave*, 1946; Stephen E. Rose, *Our Father, Right or Wrong*, 1948; Vera Brittain, *Born 1925*, 1948; Kurt Vonnegut, *Player Piano*, 1952; Elfrieda Hochbaum (Pope), *The Stain*, 1954; Clifford Irving, *On a Darkling Plain*, 1956; Vladimir Nabokov, *Pnin*, 1957; Charles Thompson, *Halfway Down the Stairs*, 1957; Robert Gutwillig, *After Long Silence*, 1958; Elizabeth Fenwick, *The Long Way Down*, 1959; Vin Packer, *The Girl on the Best Seller List*, 1960.

And while I am still about it, here are some artists, professional and amateur, who have made an impression on the world of art: Chester Loomis '72; Louis Eilshemius '84; Louis A. Fuertes '97; André Smith '02; Arthur G. Dove '03; Richard E. Bishop '09; Randall Davey '09; Truman E. Fassett '09; Marcel K. Sessler '13; Charles Baskerville '19; Charles L. Goeller '24; John A. Hartell '25; Kenneth Washburn '26; James W. Grimes '27; Erling B. Brauner '29; Dorothy Hoyt '31; George M. Sutton, Ph.D. '32; Elfriede M. Abbe '40; Jason L. Seley '40; Allen C. Atwell '47; John R. Richards '49; Victor Colby, M.F.A. '50; Jack L. Squier, M.F.A. '52; William H. Sola '54; Gabriel Laderman '57; Charles A. Ginnever, M.F.A. '59; and Alfred J. Pounders, M.F.A. '59. And of course many have made of painting and allied arts an avocation, with meritorious results.

Key to Map

1. Mary Donlon Hall
2. Clara Dickson Hall
3. Balch Halls
4. Risley Hall
5. Pleasant Grove Apartments
6. Hasbrouck Apartments
7. Fuertes Observatory
8. Helen Newman Hall
9. Noyes Lodge
10. Hydraulic Laboratory
11. Rand Hall
12. Sibley Hall
13. Sculpture Building
14. Franklin Hall
15. White Hall
16. McGraw Hall
17. Morrill Hall
18. Undergraduate Library
19. John M. Olin Library
20. Stimson Hall
21. Goldwin Smith Hall
22. Lincoln Hall
23. Baker Laboratory
24. Rockefeller Hall
25. Andrew D. White Museum
26. Big Red Barn
27. Bailey Hall
28. Savage Hall
29. Newman Laboratory
30. Van Rensselaer Hall
31. Comstock Hall
32. Caldwell Hall
33. Warren Hall
34. Mann Library
35. Plant Science Building
36. Roberts Hall
37. Stone Hall
38. Fernow Hall
39. Poultry Research Building
40. Rice Hall
41. Stocking Hall
42. Wing Hall and Judging Pavilion
43. Riley-Robb Hall
44. Morrison Hall
45. Veterinary College Buildings
46. U.S. Nutrition Laboratory
47. Greenhouses
48. Lynah Hall
49. Teagle Hall
50. Barton Hall
51. Industrial and Labor Relations Buildings
52. Statler Hall and Alice Statler Auditorium
53. Day Hall
54. Sage Chapel
55. Sage Hall
56. Barnes Hall
57. Olin Hall
58. Willard Straight Hall
59. Gannett Medical Clinic
60. Anabel Taylor Hall
61. Myron Taylor Hall
62. Hollister Hall
63. Carpenter Hall
64. Kimball-Thurston Halls
65. Nuclear Reactor Laboratory
66. Grumman Hall
67. Upson Hall
68. Phillips Hall
69. Grumman Squash Courts
70. Bacon Cage and Hoy Field
71. Schoellkopf Hall and Field
72. Riding Hall
73. Heating Plant and Service Facilities
74. Graphic Arts Services
75. Baker Dormitories
76. University Halls
77. Sheldon Court
78. Cascadilla Hall
79. Food storage and Laundry

Ithaca Campus, Cornell University, Fall 1962

Acknowledgments and Bibliographical Note

I AM grateful indeed to President Malott and the Board of Trustees, who granted me a year's leave of absence to work on this book. And to the ever-helpful officials of the Cornell University Library, and to the learned and cordial staff of the Cornell University Archives. And to Dean-emeritus William I. Myers and Dean-emeritus S. C. Hollister and Director Robert J. Kane, who have critically read the pages, respectively, on agriculture, on engineering, and on athletics. I am particularly grateful to the many old grads who have written me long, rich, and evocative letters. These will be deposited in the Archives. And I have been notably aided by the literary judgment as well as the critical scrupulosity of the staff of the Cornell University Press.

Permission has been granted by the publishers to use the following copyrighted material: two passages from *Bowery to Bellevue*, by Emily Dunning Barringer, W. W. Norton & Company, 1950; "To a Hill Town," by Thomas S. Jones, in his *Shadow of a Perfect Rose*, Farrar and Rinehart, 1937; a passage from *I Remember*, by Dexter S. Kimball, copyright 1953, McGraw-Hill Book Company; a quotation from Paul Reznikoff in the *N.Y. State Journal of Medicine* for 1 February 1957; and a passage from *Adventures in Medical Education* by G. Canby Robinson, Harvard University Press, 1957.

Acknowledgments and Bibliographical Note

References to authorities will be found in the notes. Letters and papers from which passages are quoted will be found, unless a contrary indication is made, in the Cornell University Archives.

Anyone wishing to pursue a course in Cornell history should read at least the following:

Andrew D. White. *Autobiography of Andrew Dickson White.* New York, 1904.

Andrew D. White. *Diaries of Andrew D. White.* Ed. by R. M. Ogden. Ithaca, 1959.

W. T. Hewett. *Cornell University: A History.* New York, 1905.

Carl Becker. *Cornell University: Founders and the Founding.* Ithaca, 1943.

Philip Dorf. *The Builder: A Biography of Ezra Cornell.* New York, 1952.

Philip Dorf. *Liberty Hyde Bailey: An Informal Biography.* Ithaca, 1956.

Romeyn Berry. *Behind the Ivy.* Ithaca, 1950.

Anna B. Comstock. *The Comstocks of Cornell.* Ed. by Glenn W. Herrick and Ruby G. Smith. Ithaca, 1953.

Albert H. Wright. *Pre-Cornell and Early Cornell.* Ithaca, 1953–1960.

Notice that in accordance with the usage of the Alumni Records Office class numerals generally indicate the four-year class in which the individual matriculated. Some alumni, however, have chosen to become members of other classes.

Index

Index

Gourdine, Meredith C., 602, 610
Government, *see* Political science
Government control of education, 234, 308, 309, 314-316, 323, 526, 563, 564
Graduate School of Medical Sciences, 611
Graduate work and Graduate School, 174, 175, 278, 281, 284, 323, 330, 352, 353, 357, 392, 393, 471, 473, 571, 614
Grange League Federation, 525, 552, 580
Granger, Richard H., 318 n.
Grant, James B., 123
Grant, U. S., 197
Greater Cornell Fund, 562, 563, 577, 594, 595
Greek, *see* Classics
Greeley, Horace, 54, 55, 64, 69, 191
Green, Edward B., 362
Green, Paul, 624
Greenbie, Marjorie Barstow, 624
Greene, George W., 104, 105, 163
Grierson, H. J. C., 465
Griest, Guinevere G., 550
Griffis, Stanton, 412
Grimes, James W., 625
Grumman Squash Courts, 607
Gudernatsch, Frederick, 387
Guerlac, Othon G., 339, 425
Guggenheim Foundation, 598
Guggolz, Muriel E., 499
Guion, Connie, 513, 611
Gutwillig, Robert, 625
Gymnasia, 94, 237, 242, 359, 562, 589, 607

Hadley, Arthur T., 280
Hadley, James, 33
Hagan, William A., 531
Hagerman, Herbert J., 350
Hagerman, J. J. 296
Hagerman, Percy, 296
Haigh, Andrew C., 473
Hale, Benjamin, 52 n.
Hale, Edward E., 82
Hale, William G., 288 n.
Hall, Albert W., 610
Hall, G. Stanley, 37 n., 101 n.
Hall, James, 83
Halliday, Samuel D., 61 n., 140 n., 184 n., 195, 212 n., 229, 353
Hamilton, George L., 426
Hamilton, Stephen E., 509
Hamilton College, 324, 473
Hammond, William A., 277, 280, 326, 451
Hanson, Leonard, 502
Hardy, C. de W., 325 n.
Harkness, Georgia E., 624

Harris, George W., 140 n., 577
Harris, Gilbert D., 325, 398, 582
Harris, Roy, 529
Harris, T. W., 173
Hart, James M., 23, 106, 109, 113, 129, 165, 172, 220, 259, 278
Hartell, John A., 529, 625
Hartt, Charles F., 86, 172
Harvard University, 36, 37, 42, 51, 71, 75, 143 n., 163, 168, 173, 177-179, 207, 233, 237 n., 240, 245, 257, 258, 325, 384, 393, 522, 606
Haskell, Eugene E., 399
Hassam, Childe, 398
Hatch Act, 282, 379
Hatcher, Robert, 387, 513
Haughwout, John L., 587
Hayes, Rutherford B., 199
Hays, Hoffman R., 624
Hazing, 132
Health, student, 133, 178, 202, 203, 295, 392, 421, 422, 431, 439, 470, 471, 532, 533, 543, 559
Heating plant, 237, 443, 459, 589
Hebrew, teaching of, *see* Semitics
Heckscher, August, Research Fund, 439
Hedge, Frederick, 132 n.
Heermans, Forbes, 624
Heidt, Marion Fear, 550
Helen Newman Hall, 607
Heller House, 39, 609
Hemstreet, Ralph, 118
Hendrix, Joseph C., 100 n., 123
Henkle, Robert T., 497
Henley, races at, 207, 346, 610
Henry, Mary F., 530
Hewett, W. T., 94 n., 110 n., 116 n., 126 n., 165, 167 n., 181 n., 207 n., 235 n., 297 n., 307, 332 n., 336 n., 628
Hewitt, Barnard W., 411 n.
Hewlett, J. Monroe, 456
Higby, Seth M., 343
Higgins, Malvina, 145
Hill, David B., 67, 232, 319
Hill, Richard S., 496
Hill, Thomas, 71, 143 n., 177, 258
Hilliard, Alec R., 625
Hinchliff, Emerson, 584
Hindu students, 403
Hinrichs, Albert F., 428
Hinrichs, Dunbar M., 624
Hinsey, Joseph C., 547, 603
Hirsch, E. G., 340
Hiscock, Frank, 200 n., 436, 451, 461, 462, 524
History, teaching of, 104, 105, 154, 155, 162, 163, 242-244, 263, 274, 275, 395, 396, 472
Hitchcock, Edward, Jr., 242, 295, 392